AF059903

PEAK DISTRICT GRIT

By members of the BMC Guidebook Committee

WIRED GUIDES

PEAK DISTRICT GRIT

By Ian Carr, Niall Grimes and a team of volunteers.

The Guidebook Team: Paul Evans, Becky Hammond, Graeme Hammond, Lynn Robinson, Richard Wheeldon

Designed and typeset by BMC/Niall Grimes, based on Wired templates

Copyright © 2020 British Mountaineering Council
Published by: British Mountaineering Council
ISBN 978-0-903908-44-3

Maps reproduced by permission of Ordnance Survey on behalf of HMSO.
© Crown copyright. All rights reserved.

All rights reserved. No part of this work covered by the copyright herein may be reproduced or used in any form or by any means – graphic, electronic, or mechanised, including photocopying, recording, taping, or information storage and retrieval systems – without the written permission of the publisher.

The information in this guide is derived from a number of sources. While every effort is made to check its accuracy please do not presume that any of the material in this book is accurate. Neither the publisher nor anyone involved in the production of this book can be held responsible for omissions, mistakes, nor held liable for any personal or third party injuries or damage, howsoever caused, arising from its use.

 Printed in the UK by Cambrian Printers Ltd on responsibly-sourced paper.

Photo on this page: A climber on The Right Unconquerable, HVS 5a, Stanage (page 309).
David Simmonite

Cover photo: Graham Hoey on L'Horla, E1 5b, Curbar Edge (page 160).
David Simmonite

PHONE: 0161 445 6111   EMAIL: office@thebmc.co.uk   WEB: www.thebmc.co.uk

BMC Participation Statement

The BMC recognises that climbing and mountaineering are activities with a danger of personal injury or death.

Participants in these activities should be aware of and accept these risks and be responsible for their own actions and involvement.

CONTENTS

INTRODUCTION — 6
- This Book — 6
- Acknowledgements — 8
- We Are Wired — 10
- Peak District Grit — 14
- Choose Your Crag — 20
- Graded List — 28
- Visitor Info — 36

STAFFORDSHIRE GRIT — 40
- The Roaches — 44
  - Lower Tier — 46
  - Upper Tier — 58
  - The Skyline — 70
  - The Five Clouds — 80
- Hen Cloud — 84
- Ramshaw Rocks — 96

SOUTHERN GRITSTONE — 106
- Cratcliffe Tor — 110
- Robin Hood's Stride — 116
- Black Rocks — 118

THE FROGGATT AREA — 126
- Froggatt Edge — 130
- Curbar Edge — 146
- Gardom's Edge — 164
- Birchen Edge — 178
- Chatsworth Edge — 190

EASTERN QUARRIES — 194
- Lawrencefield — 198
- Millstone Edge — 206
- Yarncliffe Quarry — 222

THE BURBAGE VALLEY — 224
- Burbage North — 228
- Burbage South — 240
- Higgar Tor — 252

STANAGE EDGE — 256
- Stanage North — 260
- High Neb — 270
- Count's Area — 284
- Stanage Plantation — 290
- Stanage Popular — 310
- Apparent North — 358

THE NORTHERN EDGES — 362
- Bamford Edge — 366
- Dovestone Tor — 378
- Rivelin Edge — 382
- Agden Rocher — 394
- Wharncliffe — 398

THE CHEW VALLEY — 412
- Alderman Rocks — 417
- Standing Stones — 418
- Ravenstones — 424
- Dovestones Edge — 428
- Rob's Rocks — 434
- Wimberry Rocks — 436
- Running Hill Pits — 444

KINDER & BLEAKLOW — 450
- Tintwistle Knarr — 454
- Laddow Rocks — 456
- Shining Clough — 458
- Hobson Moor — 464
- New Mills Torrs — 468
- Windgather — 472
- Castle Naze — 478
- Kinder Downfall — 484
  - Upper Western — 485
  - Kinder Buttress — 485
  - The Downfall — 486
- Kinder South — 490
  - Upper Edale Rocks — 490
  - The Pagoda — 491
  - Crowden Clough Face — 492
  - Upper Tor — 494
  - Nether Tor — 497
- Kinder North — 500
  - Misty Buttress — 502
  - Big Brother Buttress — 504
  - Jester Buttress — 505

OUTRO — 506
- Where Next? — 506
- Index — 510

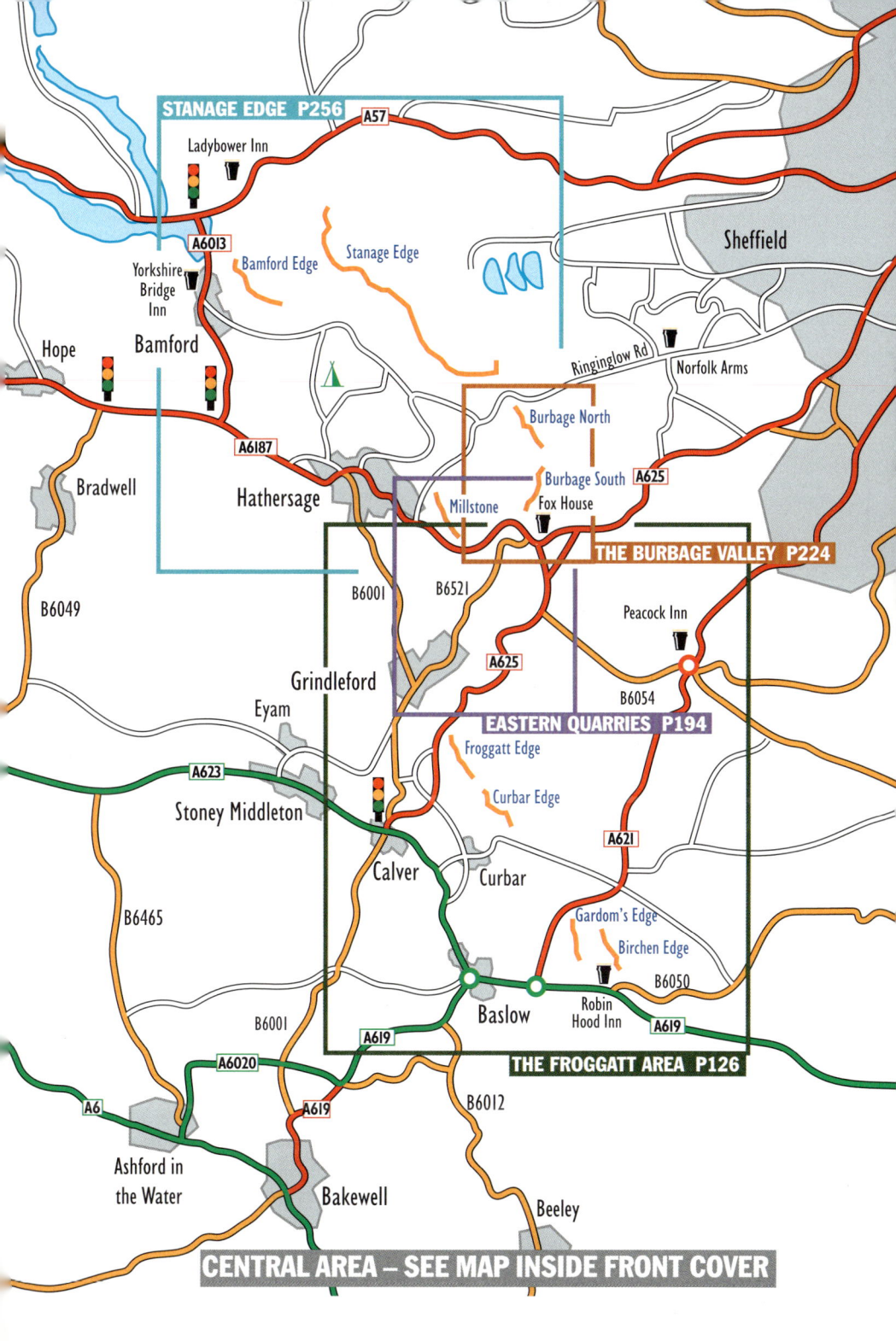

THIS BOOK

I have to confess that I'm a Peak Gritstone addict. You can tell one by the deep scars on the back of their hands. I'm no exception.

I'm lucky to live in Saddleworth, surrounded by the Chew. Even luckier, to have been introduced to climbing by an inspirational teacher during Wednesday evening Outdoor Pursuits.

By the time I was 16, doing an Engineering Apprenticeship, I'd made friends at Den Lane Quarry. You could say that these early years were the start of my Gritstone Apprenticeship, forming relationships that have lasted 40 years. Chris Hardy lived close by, between us we cobbled together some form of climbing rack. The Troll Factory 'seconds' box in Uppermill, and help from Tony Howard added useful bits of aluminium, webbing belts and a twisty rope. I had access to milling and drilling machines, making a Sticht-plate and drilling holes in my recently acquired large Hexes. We'd walk to Dovestones Edge, and climb the classics, in a pair of worn out walking boots.

On college days, I'd go to Paul (Tut) Braithwaite's climbing shop in Oldham, from where I got my first pair of EB climbing boots. Suddenly we were climbing Hard VS. John Smith and his van were on the scene. He introduced us to the Eastern and Western Peak. John was (and still is) merciless with his banter; only serving to sharpen us up. As the youngest, I took the brunt of it.

Pretty soon after, I'd passed my driving test and had access to my Mum's Mini. Armed with my first guidebook, Paul Nunn's "Rock Climbing in the Peak District", I grew to love the drive over the Snake, and the better weather of the east.

By the time I was 20, we were climbing the hardest grit routes of the day. We gave them no respect, just got on them. I can remember doing Curbar's *Profit of Doom* one evening, and being so chuffed that I had to tell 'Tut' in the shop the day after. We were all lucky to survive unscathed, apart from the usual gravel rash and jamming flappers. Barracked and pushed on, you often climbed way above your comfort zone. There were some big falls, but never any sympathy.

That was forty years ago, and my love for Peak District Gritstone is the same now as it was then. There is nothing better, on a cold winters day than, to wrap-up warm and cruise around the Stanage classics. That's the thing about gritstone, it doesn't have to be hard to be good, it just has to be grit!

It's therefore a privilege to have created this latest BMC guidebook with the Wired Cooperative. A super team effort, editing five BMC guidebooks into one. The current team and previous authors are acknowledged later, but deserve a great big thank you!

We have over 2750 of the best routes on the best crags to showcase 'God's Own Rock'. The objective was to provide balance across the grades, concentrated within the mid grades. To include essential classics across the spectrum from Mod to E10. As with the BMC's definitive guidebooks, photo-topos have been blended with colour coded route numbers, grades, descriptions and first ascent details, to provide the climber with an easy to use format. There are also over 135 full colour action photographs. These both highlight the routes and capture the ambience of the crags.

Whilst writing this, we learned of Joe Brown's passing. It is only fitting that we recognise his legendary contribution to Peak District gritstone.

He was inspiration to me; The Hard Years; leaving an outstanding list of grit routes to his name. From the bold and delicate *The Great Slab* on Froggatt; to the Stanage classics of *The Right Unconquerable*, and *Terrazza Crack*; to the Curbar testpieces of *Elder Crack*, and *The Right Eliminate*; the Higgar Tor thuggery of *The Rasp*; the Staffordshire essentials of *Saul's Crack*, *Matinee*, *Delstree*, *Hen Cloud Eliminate*; and not forgetting the moorland classics of *The Trident*, *The Hanging Crack*, and *Freddie's Finale*. A three star roll-call if there ever was one.

There are so many...

Ian Carr

April 2020

Ian Carr at home on Wimberry, contemplating the crux moves of the gritstone classic, Route 1, HS 4b (page 443). ● Paul Evans

ACKNOWLEDGEMENTS

Editor and design
Niall Grimes has been the BMC's guidebook coordinator and series editor throughout the creation and publication of the current 6th Series of gritstone and limestone guidebooks to the Peak District. Niall has stamped his unique creative mark throughout this period.

Selection and scripts
Ian Carr provided the crag and route selection, together with the edited scripts, the start point being the current BMC definitive guidebooks. Graeme Hammond used his extensive local knowledge of the edges in providing editing support and advice. The original script authors from the current definitive guidebooks are detailed below.

Staffordshire Grit
The Roaches Lower Tier Andi Turner
The Roaches Upper Tier Chris 'Gus' Hudgins
The Skyline Chris 'Gus' Hudgins
The Five Clouds Andi Turner
Hen Cloud Niall Grimes
Ramshaw Rocks Richard Patterson

Southern Gritstone
Cratcliffe Tor Adam Long
Robin Hood's Stride Simon Wilson
Black Rocks Niall Grimes

The Froggatt Area
Froggatt Edge Ben Heason
Curbar Edge Pete Robins
Gardom's Edge John Cameteras
Birchen Edge Steve Clark & Lynn Robinson
Chatsworth Edge Simon Wilson

Eastern Quarries
Lawrencefield Simon Jacques
Millstone Edge Niall Grimes
Yarncliffe Quarry Simon Jacques

The Burbage Valley
Burbage North David Musgrove
Burbage South & Quarries Niall Grimes
Higgar Tor David Law & Simon Jacques

Stanage Edge
Niall Grimes, David Simmonite, Ian Smith

North Eastern Edges
Bamford Edge David Simmonite
Dovestone Tor Martin Kocsis & David Simmonite
Rivelin Edge David Simmonite & Percy Bishton
Agden Rocher Paul Harrison
Wharncliffe Frank Horsman & David Simmonite

The Chew Valley
Aldernan Rocks Con Carey & Ian Carr
Standing Stones Ian Carr & Craig Hannah
Ravenstones Martin Kocsis
Dovestones Edge Ian Carr
Rob's Rocks David Simmonite
Wimberry Rocks Ian Carr
Running Hill Pits Duncan Irving, Goi Ashmore & Ian Carr

Kinder & Bleaklow
Tintwistle Knarr Martin Kocsis
Laddow Rocks Rick Gibbon
Shining Clough Jez Portman
Hobson Moor Andy Stewart
New Mills Torrs Duncan Irving
Windgather Martin Kocsis
Castle Naze Martin Kocsis
Kinder Downfall Ben Tetler & Martin Kocsis
Kinder South Neil McAdie, Iain Johnson
Kinder North Keith Ashton & Martin Kocsis

Editors
All these guides were created under the chairmanship of Ian Carr, and were edited by the following:

The Roaches: Dave Garnett & Niall Grimes
Burbage, Millstone and Beyond: Niall Grimes, David Simmonite
Froggatt to Black Rocks: Lynn Robinson, Steve Clark & Niall Grimes
Over The Moors: Martin Kocsis, Ian Carr & Niall Grimes
Stanage: Niall Grimes

Introduction | 9

Photography
This guide contains over 130 action photos, chosen to convey the very essence of Peak District gritstone climbing. Photos were selected by Niall Grimes and Paul Evans. The crag and landscape photographs were taken by Niall Grimes, with the exception of the Chew Valley, that were taken by Ian Carr.

Photographers
Andy Birtwistle, Ian Carr, Mike Cheque, Steve Clegg, Mike Delderfield, Paul Evans, Neil Foster, Niall Grimes, Dan Hamer, Becky Hammond, Craig Hannah, Mike Hutton, Charlotte King, Martin Kocsis, Dan Lane, Alex Messenger, Jon Moulding, Pete O'Donovan, Ian Parnell, Mark Rankine, Jon Read, Clare Reading, David Simmonite, Andi Smith, Chris Tan, James Thornton, Pete Wilson, Paul Winder, Jon Winter.

Checking and proofreading
In addition to the guidebook team, the following provided support during the final stages of production - Andy Birtwistle, Andy Boorman, Steve Clark, Steve Clegg, Gary Gibson, Paul Harrison, Simon Jacques, Dan Lane.

Commercial and Wired coordination
Richard Wheeldon provided commercial support, advertising and marketing advice, together with being a key interface with the Wired Group.

BMC Guidebook Committee
Ian Carr (Chair), Paul Evans, Niall Grimes, Graeme Hammond, Dave Turnbull, Lynn Robinson, Richard Wheeldon.

ROCKFAX Guides, UKClimbing Database & logbooks
Since 2001, Alan James and Chris Craggs have produced their popular ROCKFAX selected guidebooks to Eastern and Western Gritstone. These books are acknowledged as game-changers in terms of style, presentation and ease of use when compared with guides that had been produced prior to the digital age. The UKC / ROCKFAX database and logbook allows climbers to record their ascents and comment upon grade, condition, style, etc. This online user-defined content is a useful reference source, as it is continually updated by active climbers.

WE ARE WIRED

In terms of guidebooks, Britain is one of the richest countries in the world. Since the word Go, activists and clubs combined to record the efforts of the day, meticulously noting the pioneering ascents of explorers so that those who came after could follow in their footsteps and marvel at their achievements. This all began back in 1909 in Snowdonia when JM Archer Thomson & AW Andrews wrote the first complete guidebook to the mountain crag of Lliwedd.

For over a century the clubs have maintained this incredible record of first ascents. These have been chronicled and revised to give climbers the most up-to-date and accurate account of climbing in Britain. These organisations have undertaken the gargantuan task of publishing definitive guidebooks to put this knowledge into the hands of climbers. This work has depended on volunteers, climbers who are committed to contributing something invaluable to the rest of us, putting something back into the world they love.

Wired is a new concept that brings these clubs together. Under this banner, the voluntary guidebook producers share their collective knowledge, skill and enthusiasm to take the information they have spent so long creating and use it in new and creative ways.

www.wired-guides.com

> Wired Guides are published by a co-operative of UK definitive guidebook publishers including: the British Mountaineering Council, The Climbers' Club, the Fell & Rock Climbing Club of the English Lake District, the Northumberland Mountaineering Club, the Scottish Mountaineering Club, and the Yorkshire Mountaineering Club. Wired guidebooks aim to document the whole of the UK describing the very best – world-class – rock climbing these beautiful green islands have to offer.

The **Wired Guides** collaborators:

The **Fell & Rock Climbing Club** of the English Lake District publishes definitive guidebooks documenting the Lake District National Park and Cumbria.
www.frcc.co.uk

BMC The **BMC** produces definitive guides to the gritstone and limestone crags of the Peak District and Lancashire. With gritstone guides to Stanage, Burbage, Millstone and Beyond, Froggatt, Over The Moors, The Roaches and Lancashire as well as Peak Limestone, it maintains the definitive record in this great area.
www.thebmc.co.uk

The **Climbers' Club** published the world's first ever guidebook in 1909 and is today still one of the world's largest definitive guidebook publishers with guidebooks covering Snowdonia, Pembroke, the South West and South of England. The club has eight huts in: Scotland, the Lake District, the Peak District, Cornwall, Pembroke, and Snowdonia. Club membership is open to all experienced climbers.
www.climbers-club.co.uk

The **Northumberland Mountaineering Club** documents climbing and bouldering in Northumberland.
www.thenmc.org.uk

The **Scottish Mountaineering Club**, founded in 1889, has recorded new routes in its annual journal since 1890. It now publishes a range of climbers' guidebooks covering the whole of Scotland, as well as scramblers' and hillwalkers' guides. All profit from SMC guidebooks goes to the Scottish Mountaineering Trust, a registered charity providing grants to support the Scottish mountains and the communities who enjoy them.
www.smc.org.uk

The **Yorkshire Mountaineering Club** publishes definitive guidebooks documenting Yorkshire's gritstone and limestone.
www.theymc.org.uk

Dominic Oughton concentrates hard to protect his own mortality on the final arête of Pollux, E1 5b (page 396). High above the oak trees of Agden Rocher. 📷 Paul Evans

THE BMC

The British Mountaineering Council (BMC) is the representative body for climbers, hillwalkers and mountaineers in England and Wales. It exists to promote their interests and to protect their freedom. Since its formation in 1944 it has worked, negotiated and acted in the many different aspects of outdoor life to ensure that the rights and freedoms that we share can continue in a responsible and sustainable way.

It has many core programmes that cover a broad spectrum of activities, which include: negotiating and securing access to hillwalking and climbing areas; promoting cliff and mountain conservation for the benefit of users and the environment alike; representing the interests of climbers, hillwalkers and mountaineers in the broader political world; promoting and advising on good practice in the worlds of training, equipment and facilities; promoting British climbing and British climbers throughout the world through international meets and the support of everything from bouldering competitions to Himalayan expeditions; supporting specialist programmes and events centred around youth, safety and excellence; organising and promoting events in the world of competitions; providing expert advice on all aspects of climbing wall use, design and management; support and advice to climbing, hillwalking and mountaineering clubs; providing the definitive record of climbs through its guidebook programme; giving up-to-date information on all aspects of work programmes; providing insurance cover for all members.

If you are not a member and would like to support the work that the BMC does on your behalf, then contact us on the addresses below. If you would like to volunteer to help in one of the many projects the BMC are active in please visit the website and see what the BMC is involved in at the moment, then get in touch. For these, or any other inquiries, contact us at:

EMAIL: office@thebmc.co.uk WEB: www.thebmc.co.uk TELEPHONE: 0161 445 6111

THE BMC PEAK AREA

The BMC Peak Area is pleased to support the BMC Guidebook Committee as it presses forward with its successful programme of high-quality guidebooks to rock climbing in the Peak. Our team of regional access volunteers continue to do sterling work throughout the area. Without them, Peak District guidebook volumes might be considerably slimmer.

The Peak Area is one of ten BMC areas in England and Wales and is right at the heart of the British climbing community. We are lucky to have a very active local area. Turnout at the area meetings is consistently high and the standard of discussion and debate reflects the passion members feel about their area. By getting involved with your local area, you can influence local and national issues and support the work of the BMC.

The Peak Area meets five times a year. The debate is always lively, but friendly. Every meeting sees new faces, which is essential if we are to keep evolving and meeting the needs of what is one of the biggest concentrations of climbers anywhere in the world. Meeting information is hosted on the BMC Local Areas site – http://community.thebmc.co.uk/peak

In addition to the meetings we organise litter picks, crag clean-up sessions, and the odd social. If you've got an interest in climbing in your local area, we encourage you to come along to a meeting and find your level of involvement.

To keep members informed about what's happening in the area, we publish a newsletter a few days before each meeting, and the area has its own Facebook page – www.facebook.com/bmcpeakarea

THE BMC AND GUIDEBOOKS

The BMC first became involved in publishing Peak District guidebooks in 1972 and has had a continued involvement ever since. Over those years, and even before, there have been trials and tribulations, dramas and controversies, much hair pulled out and much of what hair remains gone grey. However, what cannot be denied is that there have now been nearly 50 years of tremendous definitive guidebooks to one of the world's best climbing areas. The roll call of volunteers who are responsible for this series of guides is too long to list, but they are heroes one and all.

Chris Hindley on Froggatt's bold Three Pebble Slab, E1 5a (page 137), the scene of many wobblers. Be careful out there! David Simmonite

PEAK DISTRICT GRIT

Many people will need no introduction to the Peak District. It is, after all, the busiest National Park in Britain. Nearly half of the population of England live within 80km of its boundary and there is a growing interest from overseas visitors, especially from parts of Europe and the USA.

The small but intense hilly region lying at the southern end of the Pennine range was Britain's first National Park. The choice reflects its proximity to the industrial regions of Greater Manchester, South Yorkshire and The Potteries as well as the West Midlands. The bulk of its area, however, lies in rural Derbyshire. Flanked by Yorkshire in the north and east, Staffordshire to the west and Cheshire and Greater Manchester to the northwest.

On three sides, the horseshoe-shaped exposure of the Millstone Grit Series provides a rough, rounded, often pebbly and hard, coarse, angular grained siliceous sandstone of impeccable quality. To the north, at round 500 to 600 metres above sea level, this underlies the wide plateaux of Kinder Scout, Bleaklow and Black Hill and the valleys of Edale, Longdendale, Crowden and the Chew. These northern moors are known as the Dark Peak. To the east, overlooking the Derwent Valley, runs the escarpment of the Eastern Edges. Here the great gritstone edges of Stanage, Froggatt and Curbar turn their backs on Sheffield and face the afternoon sun. The western flank of gritstone is revealed as a dinosaur-like ridge of the Roaches and Hen Cloud which looks out west, over to the Cheshire and Staffordshire plains. There now only remain the two outliers in the south: the very rounded Black Rocks and the mystical Cratcliffe Tor, both of which lie deep in the limestone country of the White Peak.

The gritstone edges of the Peak District that are lovingly detailed in this book are a nationally important climbing area and the rock is much relished by all climbers, among whom it has almost cult status and is often referred to as 'God's own rock'.

Liam Postlethwaite about to embark on the lonely crux of Millstone's Great Arête, E5 5c (page 214), one of the many great arêtes on this fabulous quarry. ◘ Mark Rankine

TOOLS AND TECHNIQUES FOR THE GRITSTONE CLIMBER

One of the good things about grit is you can stand at the bottom of the route, look up, and generally have a very good idea of the gear that you'll need to protect it and make it safe. For grades up to E3, a normal rack consisting of a selection of wires, cams or hexes, and a few slings will provide adequate protection.

Modern micro-cams certainly take the bite out of some routes that were previously considered bold and poorly protected; as do some large cams on the wider cracks. In addition, micro or brass type nuts will be a useful supplement on the peg-scarred routes at Millstone and Lawrencefield.

As with all forms of climbing a helmet is recommended, together with an agile and attentive belayer (perhaps more so on grit, because of the hard starts and even harder landings). Grit is not a good place for skinny and slick ropes. The fatter the better, you're hardly going to feel the weight on a gritstone edge.

The best training for climbing on grit is to climb on grit! It's available all year round, so you have no excuses. One thing you learn pretty quickly is that clean and squeaked-up boots certainly give you a fighting chance. But there are also other techniques with the feet that certainly make a difference. Deft footwork, dropping the ankles, and getting as much flat foot rubber on the rock as possible are all things that you learn over time.

Crack climbing is something that can't be learned on an indoor wall. It is something that is picked up through hard graft over the years. Good jamming techniques for feet, fingers and hands can make the difference between one climber's nightmare and another climber's joy. At least cracks are generally well protected and therefore relatively safe.

It's always a sobering thought as you clip your well-placed Cam #4 above your head that most, if not all, of the wide cracks were climbed by pioneers who were bold, strong and very well practiced in the art. They used some techniques that modern climbers nowadays just shy away from.

Does size matter? Well height can be an advantage on some routes but a disadvantage on others. Both John Allen and Johnny Dawes are not exactly tall, but that doesn't have seem to have slowed them down at all. Ron Fawcett is tall, but has been heard to complain that he can't get his fat fingers into small holds. It's all swings and roundabouts; learn to use what you've got to its best advantage.

Perhaps one thing that you do need to endure and learn to love is some pain. A finger-lock that leaves your pinkie numb for a week, or a good old bloody flapper on the back of your hand caused by pivoting a baggy hand-jam in a horizontal break. But the best one of all is grinding the skin off your ankle bones whilst locking your feet deep in a pebbly crack: they just take weeks to heal. Modern jamming gloves certainly take away some of the painful skin damage and make those pebbly jamming cracks perhaps easier but more enjoyable for some.

Agility, flexibility and not being afraid to 'throw some shapes' are all skills that are a definite advantage on grit, as is a modicum of core strength. You definitely have fewer hold combinations on the crux on grit than most other rock types. The ability to use what you've got in front of you, together with balance and even finesse will likely see you through.

The old timers put up some desperately wide and physical affairs, some that nowadays put the fear of God into the modern day climber. To enjoy these routes, you have just got to get engaged and deeply involved; it's no holds barred, everything has to be used to secure progress – shoulders, back, arms, elbows, hips, knees – and in some of the oddest and most contorted combinations you'll ever come across. Please don't shy away from these, but take note and look at the first ascent dates and pay homage to your elders.

And finally, it is worth noting that most, if not all, serious accidents on grit are as a consequence of a ground fall. Extra vigilance by both leader and belayer on the start of your route, together with the belayer not standing too far away from the base of the crag, are both ways to mitigate this particular risk.

GRADES AND STARS

The system of grading for routes is the traditional British style, a combination of adjectival and technical grades, and assumes the leader has a normal rack, including standard camming devices, nuts, slings, quickdraws etc. The adjectival grade gives a sense of the overall difficulty of a climb. This will be influenced by many aspects, including seriousness, sustainedness, technical difficulty, exposure, strenuousness and rock quality. It is an open-ended system, and currently runs from Easy to Extremely Severe. Along the way, and in ascending order, are Moderate (M), Difficult (D), Hard Difficult (HD), Very Difficult (VD), Hard Very Difficult (HVD), Severe (S), Hard Severe (HS), Very Severe (VS), Hard Very Severe (HVS) and Extremely Severe (E), the last category being split into E1, E2, E3 etc.

The second part of the grade, the technical grade, is there to give an indication of the hardest move to be found on the route. They come onto the scale somewhere around 4a and currently run thus: 4a, 4b, 4c, 5a...

This guide is primarily a guide to routes. Where significant boulder problems exist beside routes, and their absence would be an omission, they have been included. The Fontainebleau (Font) system is used in this guide.

Stars (none, one, two or three) have been used in this guide to indicate quality. An un-starred route is by no means a bad route.

SANDBAGS

There's often a healthy online debate about specific route grades, especially routes that climbers refer to as sandbags. These routes often demand a proficiency in a specific technique, skill or strength. An unreadable sequence. Or even a trick; a toe hook, or thumb-sprag or the subtle use of an undercut. Or it's just plain hard: painful, but honest.

Our approach is therefore not to wholesale upgrade these so called 'sandbags', but just to mention in the text that they might be considered hard by some. As Guidebook editors,

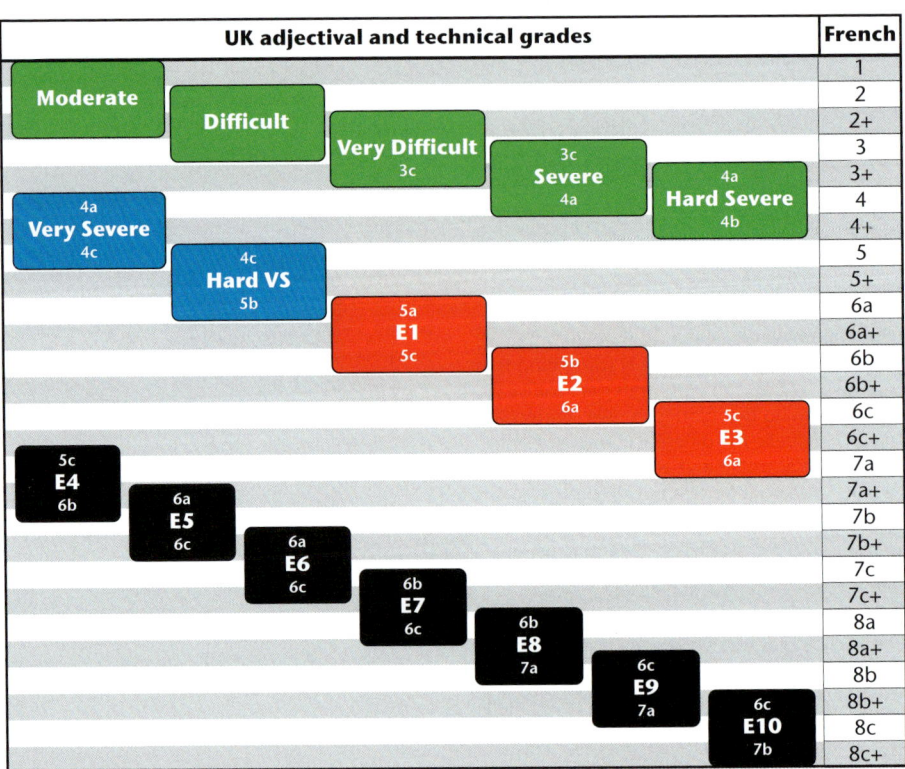

there is a fine balance between disappointing some people with grade-creep and others with tough traditionally graded routes. You just can't please everyone all of the time.

PROTECT THE ROCK AND THE ENVIRONMENT

Gritstone is a precious commodity and as climbers we should cherish and protect the rock and its surrounding environment. Its popularity has resulted in some areas of the crags and edges becoming worn and overused. All we can ask is that people spread out more and visit the less frequented areas instead of heading straight for the honey pots of the popular end of Stanage, Birchen and Froggatt edges.

Through the ages, and in particular the industrial age, the grit has formed a hardened surface. On some very popular routes this surface has been worn away by the passing of thousands of climbers, revealing a softer layer of gritty rock. Gritstone loses its strength when it is damp, so please refrain from climbing these routes. Some of the harder routes rely on protruding pebbles for hand and footholds. Again, these are a precious part of the rock and should be preserved.

It goes without saying that chipping and "improving" holds with a wire brush is highly frowned upon. Over brushing with any kind of brush can damage the rock and this is most apparent on some boulder problems. This practice leaves lasting damage and stands against all modern climbing ethics.

Modern cams are so useful on the grit that they have transformed the protection possibilities on many routes. There are however some routes where overused cam placements are causing severe unsightly wear. If you have to use them, then please remember that weighting that cam can only cause additional damage to the rock.

Finally, we have all done it: pushed a large cam deep into a welcoming break, only to find it stuck and inverted. Overzealous removal of any type of stuck gear has damaged some famous climbs. Look at the tip of the flake on *The Right Unconquerable* and see how much has been lost due to a jammed cam.

NESTING BIRDS

Some of the crags detailed in this book can be subject to voluntary access restrictions during the nesting season. Ring Ouzel nesting sites at Stanage, Burbage valley and elsewhere are clearly marked with BMC signs, as are other regular raptor and Raven nesting sites on other crags in this book. The BMC's Regional Access Database is always kept up to date: load the RAD App on your phone and check your chosen crag before a visit. Otherwise, use common sense and steer well clear of nesting birds and other sensitive wildlife.

MOORLAND FIRES

Over recent years, moorland fires have become a real problem. Managed, unmanaged or malicious, their results have been devastating to areas of the Chew, Longdendale and the Roaches. The serious damage to this unique ecosystem will take decades to repair. There are a number of organisations such as the National Trust and the Moors for the Future Partnership who are actively repairing and regenerating the moors to their former green and boggy glory. If you have any free time, they are always looking for active volunteers to work forming dams and planting grasses and sphagnum moss on our high moorland to restore the moors.

DOGS

When visiting the countryside, dog owners need to keep their canine companions under effective control at all times but especially during the breeding season, so that they do not scare farm animals, birds and wildlife. Take the lead and follow the Countryside Code.

GROUP USE

If you are an organiser or participant in one of these groups, please refer to the BMC's Green Guide for Groups of Climbers. This is a free download from the BMC website.

CLIMBING HISTORY

There is a full climbing history of all the crags covered in this book to be found in the definitive guides. Another great reason to check them out.

THE ACCESS TEAM

The BMC is dedicated to ensuring access to the crags in this book, and throughout England and Wales. The access team, comprising paid members of staff and a network of volunteers, is working tirelessly behind the scenes to make sure your rights to climb are protected.

If you experience any problems, your first port-of-call should be your local access rep. Search the BMC website for your local access reps. Otherwise email access@thebmc.co.uk.

CONSERVATION AND COMMUNITY

Many of the places where we climb are very special too for local communities, other visitors and above all for wildlife and conservation. This is emphasised by the fact that the majority of sites have been given special protection as Sites of Special Scientific Interest (SSSI's), Specially Protected Areas (SPA's) and Special Areas of Conservation (SAC's), which relate to habitats, plants and birds, and include internationally endangered species. Like the guide says, always check RAD for latest updates, and always be mindful of others.

BMC REGIONAL ACCESS DATABASE (RAD)

The BMC's Regional Access Database – or RAD as it's known – is the definitive source of access info on the web. From access restrictions and parking advice, to sensitive approaches and advice on local ethics, from group use to dog restrictions, this is the place to find out whether you can climb on a crag and just how to approach it.

The BMC's RAD app for mobile gives you access information, wherever you are. You can search for crags (or just let your phone show you nearby crags with access information), report an access problem and mark crags as favourites for quick access updates on your dashboard.

MOUNTAIN RESCUE AND FIRST AID

In the event of an accident dial 999 and ask for Police - Mountain Rescue. Briefly describe the nature of the incident and clearly specify your location. The Police will co-ordinate the Mountain Rescue team and, if appropriate the air ambulance that is available for serious medical attention and rapid evacuation.

CRAG CODE
www.thebmc.co.uk

Access	Check the Regional Access Database (RAD) on www.thebmc.co.uk for the latest access information
Parking	Park carefully – avoid gateways and driveways
Footpaths	Keep to established paths – leave gates as you find them
Risk	Climbing can be dangerous – accept the risks and be aware of other people around you
Respect	Groups and individuals – respect the rock, local climbing ethics and other people
Wildlife	Do not disturb livestock, wildlife or cliff vegetation; respect seasonal bird nesting restrictions
Dogs	Keep dogs under control at all times; don't let your dog chase sheep or disturb wildlife
Litter	'Leave no trace' – take all litter home with you
Toilets	Don't make a mess – bury your waste
Economy	Do everything you can to support the rural economy – shop locally

BMC Participation Statement — Climbing, hill walking and mountaineering are activities with a danger of personal injury or death. Participants in these activities should be aware of and accept these risks and be responsible for their own actions and involvement.

Andrew Deacon getting away from the crowds on the Skyline area of the Roaches on Inspiration Point, E2 5c (page 71). This cool route traverses along one of the finest slabs on gritstone. 📷 Mike Cheque

CHOOSE YOUR CRAG

MORNING GRIT
Very few Gritstone edges catch the morning sun. So, for those early risers, the options are limited.

Cratcliffe Tor: page 110
Ramshaw Rocks: page 96
Alderman Rocks: page 417
Laddow Rocks: page 456

THE EASIER STUFF
This might come as a surprise to many, but the grit does actually sport loads of easier routes suitable for the lower grade and novice climber. Listed below are the best venues in this guide to the rounded delights that grit has to offer in the lower grades.

Dovestones Edge: page 428
Rob's Rocks: page 434
Windgather: page 472
Castle Naze: page 478
Wharncliffe: page 398
Yarncliffe Quarry: page 222
Birchen Edge: page 178
Burbage North: page 228
Stanage Edge: page 256

THE CLASSICS: NOT TO BE MISSED
Whilst all the crags in this guidebook are of undoubted quality, there are a few that absolutely must not be missed by the visiting climber. Many would argue that at least one of those listed below is the best crag in the world, although some feel that may be over stating it somewhat... but what do they know? However, in terms of both quality and quantity it is difficult argue against the merits of the following:

Stanage Edge: page 256
Bamford Edge: page 366
Froggatt Edge: page 130
Curbar Edge: page 146
The Roaches: page 44
Millstone Edge: page 206

ESCAPING THE HEAT
In the summer months, the Peak can get very hot. When the weather is like this, the true gritstone aficionado will be hard to spot. In these conditions, they will say, the friction is rubbish... and they may well be right. Mere mortals should not be put off though; a gritstone edge on a gorgeous summer's day is a fantastic place to be. Having said that, those that do want a bit of shade and cooler conditions should check out the following. Most of the crags listed below may need several days of dry warm weather to come into condition:

Ravenstones: page 424
Shining Clough: page 458
Burbage South (morning only): page 240
Wimberry Rocks: page 436
Laddow Rocks: page 456
Kinder Northern Edges: page 500
Kinder Downfall: page 484
Chatsworth Edge: page 190

ESCAPING THE COLD
For hardy souls, as long as it's dry, it is possible to climb on Peak grit throughout the winter months. The gritstone edges, by their very nature, tend to be situated high up and in exposed positions. However, the following venues may offer some respite from the cold for those wanting their gritstone fix. Bouldering is also a good way to enjoy the rock in the winter months when friction is at its best: however climbing or bouldering on damp rock should be avoided, as there is a greater opportunity to damage the rock. As well as taking a big coat, gloves and a hat, give yourself a later start to allow the sun to come round and warm the rock and burn off any overnight dampness.

Rivelin Edge: page 382
Froggatt Edge: page 130
Lawrencefield: page 198
Cratcliffe Tor: page 110
Wharncliffe: page 398
Hobson Moor: page 464
New Mills Torrs (some routes are even rain proof!): page 468

Emmott Baddeley on Snail Crack, HVD (page 201) at Lawrencefield. This is a great venue for getting into leading, with many fine training routes that lead onto better things. 📷 Pete O'Donovan

GRIT FOR THUGS

If you like daintily tiptoeing up perfectly angled slabs or edging delicately on small footholds, then skip this list. The following crags are what many think gritstone is all about and are a way for aspiring climbers to test their mettle. For others however, the routes on these crags can represent a climber's worst nightmare.

New Mills Torrs: page 468
Higgar Tor: page 252
Curbar Edge: page 146
Chatsworth Edge: page 190
Wimberry Rocks: page 436
Ramshaw Rocks: page 96
Black Rocks: page 118
Hen Cloud: page 84

AWAY FROM THE CROWDS

The Peak is a busy place, upwards of 17 million people live with an hour's drive of the National Park so finding some peace and quiet, particularly on a summer weekend, can be very challenging. For the visiting climber however, there are plenty of escapes. Most, unfortunately require a walk of some distance, so for those willing to put the effort in, the edges listed below will offer a quiet day's climbing, often in stunning surroundings.

Standing Stones: page 418
Laddow Rocks: page 456
The Pagoda and Crowden Clough: page 491
Upper and Nether Tor: page 494
Dovestone Tor: page 378
Gardom's Edge: page 164
The Skyline: page 70
Hen Cloud: page 84
Agden Rocher: page 394

BOULDERING

This book is designed for the climber, with ropes. However, on the same crags, is a wealth of bouldering. On a freezing cold day, with optimum conditions, the Plantation Boulders at Stanage will see more mats than ropes on the adjacent crag. The BMC's definitive gritstone guidebooks cover bouldering in detail, including colour coded circuits. Honey pots are Stanage Plantation, Stanage Apparent North, Curbar, Burbage North and South, The Roaches, Robin Hood's Stride and Wimberry.

EVENING CRAGS

One of the advantages the Peak District has over other climbing areas in the UK is the ease of access and the short approach walks to so many of the edges. After a day slogging away in the office, many of the gritstone edges are very well placed for many to enjoy a few post-work routes - a few hours on the likes of Stanage or Bamford can be a magical experience.

Stanage: page 256
Hobson Moor Quarry: page 464
Windgather: page 472
Running Hill Pits: page 444
Burbage North: page 228
Bamford Edge: page 366
Castle Naze: page 478
The Five Clouds: page 80
Robin Hood's Stride: page 116

QUARRIED GRIT

A different beast to the rounded delights of the natural edges; these monuments to the industrial past of the Peak District require fingers of steel and, in many cases, good edging skills: you have been warned.

Tintwistle Knarr: page 454, (in a dry spell)
Millstone Edge: page 206
Lawrencefield: page 198
Hobson Moor: page 464
New Mills Torrs: page 468
Running Hill Pits: page 444

ESCAPING THE MIDGE

During the summer months the dreaded midge can, and regularly does, blight the gritstone Edges - high humidity after a damp start, still air and lots of bracken spells misery for most. Carrying a head-net and various repellents may work for a time, but if they are out and it gets too much, it's probably worth heading south to limestone country (or a pub), where the general absence of their damp moorland breeding grounds means midges are usually less of a problem. If, however, it has to be the grit, choose a crag facing into the wind, and not one with the wind blowing over the top and sheltered below. Dawn and dusk are usually worst. Strong sunshine normally keeps them away. However, it's pot luck of course and nowhere is exempt: again, you have been warned.

Mark Sharratt going deep on the Joe Brown Ramshaw testpiece, Brown's Crack, E1 5c (page 100). This climb may be short, but it's known to take its toll on the unskilled. 📷 Jon Read

Introduction

Area	Crag	Page number	M to HS	VS HVS	E1 to E3	E4+	Total	Approach time	Main aspect	Sheltered from wind
Staffordshire Gritstone	Roaches Lower Tier	46	21	16	16	18	71	10 mins	SW	Sheltered
Staffordshire Gritstone	Roaches Upper Tier	58	31	17	10	2	60	15 mins	SW	E & NE
Staffordshire Gritstone	The Skyline	70	31	21	16	12	80	15 - 30 mins	SW	Exposed
Staffordshire Gritstone	The Five Clouds	80	7	9	5	4	25	10 mins	SW	Sheltered
Staffordshire Gritstone	Hen Cloud	84	14	18	13	16	61	10 mins	SW	Exposed
Staffordshire Gritstone	Ramshaw Rocks	96	24	23	18	12	77	2 - 10 mins	E	W & NE
Southern Gritstone	Cratcliffe Tor	110	5	5	11	8	29	10 mins	SE	Very sheltered
Southern Gritstone	Robin Hood's Stride	116	8	3	0	4	15	10 mins	All	Exposed
Southern Gritstone	Black Rocks	118	16	11	8	11	46	5 mins	N & W	Sheltered
The Froggatt Area	Froggatt Edge	130	27	21	24	17	89	20 mins	SW	E & NE
The Froggatt Area	Curbar Edge	146	21	23	37	31	112	10 - 20 mins	SW	E & NE
The Froggatt Area	Gardom's Edge	164	21	24	17	6	68	10 - 20 mins	W	Sheltered
The Froggatt Area	Birchen Edge	178	67	21	6	5	99	15 mins	SW	E & NE
The Froggatt Area	Chatsworth Edge	190	15	7	11	2	35	10 - 15 mins	NW	Sheltered
Eastern Quarries	Lawrencefield	198	9	11	8	6	34	10 mins	SW	Very sheltered
Eastern Quarries	Millstone Edge	206	12	32	30	21	95	10 - 15 mins	W	Sheltered bays
Eastern Quarries	Yarncliffe Quarry	222	4	11	4	2	21	1 min	SW	Very sheltered
The Burbage Valley	Burbage North	228	58	41	13	5	117	2 - 20 mins	SW	N & NE
The Burbage Valley	Burbage South	240	15	22	9	22	68	15 - 25 mins	NW	S & SE
The Burbage Valley	Higgar Tor	252	5	7	3	9	24	5 mins	SW	Exposed
Stanage Edge	Stanage North	260	19	14	5	6	44	20 - 30 mins	NW	Exposed
Stanage Edge	Marble Wall	266	9	13	7	4	33	25 mins	W	E
Stanage Edge	High Neb	270	39	36	17	7	99	15 - 20 mins	SW	E
Stanage Edge	Count's Area	284	7	5	20	3	35	15 mins	SW	E
Stanage Edge	Stanage Plantation	290	30	35	33	20	118	15 mins	SW	E & NE
Stanage Edge	Left-hand Popular	310	53	54	34	9	150	15 mins	SW	E & NE
Stanage Edge	Right-hand Popular	336	69	54	24	7	154	10 mins	SW	E & NE
Stanage Edge	Apparent North	358	2	8	4	9	23	5 mins	S & SE	Exposed

Character	Conditions	Area
The pride of Staffordshire gritstone. Sheltered and friendly but with a fair share of butch cracks and bold slabs. Lots of bouldering.	Generally quick drying, but can remain damp in the winter.	Staffs Gritstone
Extensive with a host of classics across the grades, very popular with both walkers and climbers.	More exposed, sometimes colder and quicker to dry than the lower tier.	
The continuation of the Upper Tier, a series of compact buttresses giving both variety and solitude.	Quick drying on slabs and faces with some surprisingly sheltered areas. Tree cover.	Southern Gritstone
A string of delightful little gems of craglets. Quieter than the nearby larger crags.	Quick drying in the afternoon sun. Clean exquisite gritstone.	
A massive gritstone fortress of a crag above a steep escarpment. Tamed by good cracks and features.	Although it looks green it is often dryer than you expect. Often colder than its neighbours.	
Gothic, jutting fins and prows. Split by many humbling wide and steep cracks and rounded features. Looks green and dark, but is not, in the right weather.	Dries quickly in the morning sun, cold in the afternoons; a good escape in hot weather.	Froggatt Area
A magical crag, hidden away in limestone country. Impressive prows and walls criss-crossed with juggy breaks.	The exposed faces dry quickly in the morning sun. All year round possibilities.	
A mass of perched block pinnacles and boulders with a mythical ambience. Popular with boulderers.	Sunny side dries quickly, undergrowth holds the dampness in the darker area.	
A bizarre lump of gritstone deep in the heart of limestone country. The most rounded grit crag, demands respect.	Sunny walls are quick to dry and are sheltered. Opposing walls can be green.	
One of the most popular gritstone venues. Rich diversity of climbing styles and grades. Multiple classics, lots of slabs and cracks.	Very quick to dry. The northerly end in the trees can hold some dampness. Very clean.	Eastern Quarries
An impressive edge with a well deserved reputation for toughness. Characterised by some wide cracks, bold slabs and forceful climbing.	Quick to dry, more exposed than Froggatt. Generally clean. Climbing year round.	
Quiet and understated. Multiple characterful buttresses of different styles and aspects. Something for everyone.	Can be slow drying due to trees. Sunnier faces dry quickly. Multi faceted with sun or shade.	Burbage Valley
Delightful and very popular with beginners and groups. Infamous hard undercut starts with lots of slabs above.	Very open and quick to dry. Very clean with some wear and polish.	
A quiet, secluded and shady crag with a tough reputation for hard and fierce cracks, offset by some hidden low-grade gems.	Relatively slow to dry due to aspect and undergrowth. Best in the spring or autumn.	
Millstone's little sister, but with a charm and character all of its own. Something for everyone	Can feel damp after rain, but does dry quickly, some seepage. Clean and polished.	
The main event, one of the most popular crags in the Peak. Smooth soaring walls, cracks and corners at all grades. Many facets.	Quick to dry, but the northerly bays are slower to dry. Very clean. An all-year venue.	Stanage
A popular quarry used by groups. A good place to familiarise yourself with the delights of quarried gritstone.	Clean and worn, can be gritty from washdown after rain. Dusty with ants in summer.	
Close to Sheffield, very popular with multiple buttresses, blends bouldering, soloing and routes together.	Very quick to dry and climbable all year around. Very clean but some signs of wear.	
A darker and quieter alternative to the North. Steeper and technical throughout the grades.	Slow to dry, but later sun makes this a great summer evening venue. Green in winter.	Northern Edges
Powerful and steep routes on the famous Leaning Block that are full of character and history.	Perfect clean, grit. Cold in the wind, but a good place to escape the summer midge.	
The walk is worth it, for all grades. The coldest area; pick a good day, enjoy the walk away from the crowds to bask in a perfect sunset.	The slowest area of Stanage to come into condition due to its exposed location.	
As the name suggests, some superb angular rock in a wild and often lonely location.	Quick to dry with little drainage. Gets late sun. A great afternoon and evening venue.	Chew Valley
A landmark crag. Tall and proud with classy routes of all grades, including a couple of testpieces. Popular.	Very quick to dry, but can be windy and a bit exposed to the elements. Can be cold.	
A relatively quiet and less travelled area of the edge. Known for its highball, bold and technical slabs.	More greenery and less frequented than elsewhere, but still quick to dry.	
Some of the tallest and most angular sections of the crag. Multiple classics litter the area throughout the grades.	Very clean and quick to dry. Some of the deeper clefts and chimneys can be green.	
Tall and classy, with a bit more roundness and weathering than its neighbours. Routes for everyone.	Quick to dry. Some more sheltered areas to get away from the cold. Can be sheltered.	Kinder Bleaklow
Just very popular, with good reason. Some of the most popular routes on the crag for the mid grade climber.	Quick to dry. Clean and perfect rock. A great winter venue with tightly packed routes.	
Separate to the bulk of the main Stanage Edge with its own steep bouldery character.	Very quick to dry; early sun. Can be in the mist when other areas are clear. Exposed.	

Introduction

Crag	Page number	M to HS	VS HVS	E1 to E3	E4+	Total	Approach time	Main aspect	Sheltered from wind
The Northern Edges									
Bamford Edge	366	42	32	17	8	99	15 - 25 mins	SW	Exposed
Dovestone Tor	378	9	12	4	1	26	70 mins	W	Exposed
Rivelin Edge	382	24	22	17	14	77	15 mins	S	N & NE
Agden Rocher	394	2	6	16	3	27	10 - 15 mins	SW	N & NE
Wharncliffe	398	37	18	34	10	99	15 - 30 mins	W	E
The Chew Valley									
Alderman Rocks	417	7	4	2	0	13	20 mins	SE	Very exposed
Standing Stones	418	5	11	13	3	32	25 mins	S	Sheltered
Ravenstones	424	7	6	9	5	27	60 mins	N & NE	Very exposed
Dovestones Edge	428	19	22	13	0	54	60 mins	N & NW	Very exposed
Rob's Rocks	434	12	8	3	0	23	40 mins	S	Very exposed
Wimberry Rocks	436	10	12	8	10	40	50 mins	NE	Very exposed
Running Hill Pits	444	9	16	22	7	54	15 mins	all	Sheltered
Kinder & Bleaklow									
Tintwistle Knarr	454	0	2	6	1	9	25 mins	S	NE
Laddow Rocks	456	6	7	2	0	15	60 mins	E	NW
Shining Clough	458	3	14	5	4	26	50 mins	N	Very exposed
Hobson Moor	464	4	8	12	5	29	1 min	SW	Sheltered
New Mills Torrs	468	4	9	9	4	26	5 mins	S	Very sheltered
Windgather	472	48	9	1	0	58	2 mins	W	Very exposed
Castle Naze	478	30	11	7	2	50	5 mins	W	Exposed
Kinder Downfall	484	13	11	15	3	42	90 mins	S & W	Exposed
Upper Edale Rocks	490	5	5	4	3	17	60 mins	S	Exposed
Crowden Clough Face	492	2	2	4	2	10	60 mins	E	Exposed
Upper Tor	494	10	4	9	0	23	60 mins	S	Exposed
Nether Tor	497	8	16	7	4	35	60 mins	S	Exposed
Kinder North	500	6	12	13	2	33	60 mins	N & E	Exposed

Character	Conditions	Area
A gem, this lofty edge has stunning views and equally as good climbing. Distinct buttresses, with a broad range of routes.	Very quick to dry due to aspect and altitude, but can be cold in the wind.	Staffs Gritstone
A classy moorland buttress best savoured in high summer. Characterful routes in a lonely situation.	Windy and fresh, dries quickly. Cold. Can be gritty and green.	
High quality climbing on this relatively small edge. Great in the winter.	Low lying and very quick to dry. Very reliable in poor weather.	Southern Gritstone
A long and seldom visited crag set amid beautiful pastoral scenery above Agden Reservoir.	Quick to dry with an open outlook. Seldom visited with some friable rock.	
A huge collection of dark buttresses on a long quarried edge. Overlooking post-industrial Sheffield.	Often dry due to its sunny, low level aspect. Takes little drainage. Quiet.	
A very lofty viewpoint overlooking the Chew and Dovestones valleys. Short, sharp routes in the morning sun.	Dries very quickly, no drainage. Very clean, can be a little gritty and friable.	Froggatt Area
A hidden gem with not so easy access. An ancient landslip above a chaotic boulder field. Classy and unspoilt.	Needs a day or two after rain. Relatively clean, can hold summer heat.	
Monolithic, lofty, an elusive moorland venue with a long approach. The routes are unspoilt and will not disappoint.	Takes a day or two to dry after rain, best in the summer.	
A classic edge for low- and mid-grade routes with lots of variety at those grades.	Needs a day after rain. Best in the afternoon and evening.	Eastern Quarries
A small crag with lots to offer in the low- and mid-grades. Lofty and fresh with good views.	Proud and quick to dry. Clean and often shiny on the historical routes.	
The finest moorland crag. Impressive lines at all grades. A string of 'last great problems' to feast on.	Dries quickly, but remains green due to its northerly aspect. Best in summer.	
A charming collection of 'holes in the ground'. A mass of quality climbing on sunny or dark walls.	Dries quickly, some seepage. Can be green during and after winter.	Burbage Valley
A steep angular quarry on the moor's edge that unfortunately suffers from seepage and a lack of traffic. Good routes when dry.	Takes a lot of drainage. Corners stay damp. Can get overgrown.	
An essential moorland crag with lots of history and a reasonably long approach that keeps the crowds away.	Morning sun dries the crag. The classic buttresses dry quickly.	
A brilliant steep and angular crag, the best on Bleaklow. Prized for the essential VS and HVS moorland experiences.	Needs a day or two to dry. Receives little sun. A shady summer delight.	Stanage
Convenient roadside quarry. Great when time is short early or late in the season. Typical crack and edge climbing.	Semi urban. Mostly quick drying; the back wall can be seepy and ferny.	
A semi-urban quarry, sheltered deep in a river valley. Steep strenuous routes where a positive attitude pays dividends.	Reliable. Can stay dry even in rain, can also hold humidity from the river.	
The beginners crag par excellence, vying with Birchen for top spot. Steep and positive climbs abound.	Quick to dry with little drainage. Very clean. An all year round venue.	Northern Edges
A friendly crag in a great setting with a character of its own. A fine collection of lower grade routes. Great views.	Clean and quick drying with lots of evening sun. Can be cold.	
A grand place to visit in high summer, something for everyone from brutally rounded to gentle and serene.	Lots of sun, so a day or two after rain will see the crags dry in the summer.	
Diminutive yet perfectly formed moorland gritstone outcrops.	Quick to dry. Can be green and gritty early in the season.	Chew Valley
A cool and shadier crag on Kinder's southern rim. Best combined with a visit to the other crags around.	Relatively quick to dry in the morning sun, but with some greenness.	
Classic routes in a wonderful moorland setting. Expect roundness and wide brutal features.	A couple of dry days and a breeze are usually needed to dry the crag.	Kinder Bleaklow
Steep and uncompromising walls formed by an ancient landslip and quarrying. High quality routes.	Quick drying faces, but seepage can be an issue in the deeper cracks.	
Essential summer gritstone. A number of quality buttresses dot Kinder's northern rim. Linking them gives a classic moorland day out.	Aspect and altitude give slow drying rock, often green even in summer.	

GRADED LIST

Crag Key: A Alderman Rocks; **AR** Agden Rocher; **BE** Bamford Edge; **BIR** Birchen Edge; **BN** Burbage North; **BR** Black Rocks; **BS** Burbage South; **BSQ** Burbage South Quarries; **C** Curbar Edge; **CE** Chatsworth Edge; **CN** Castle Naze; **CT** Cratcliffe Tor; **DE** Dovestones Edge; **DT** Dovestone Tor; **F** Froggatt Edge; **FC** The Five Clouds; **G** Gardom's Edge; **HC** Hen Cloud; **HMQ** Hobson Moor Quarry; **HT** Higgar Tor; **KD** Kinder Downfall; **KN** Kinder North; **KS** Kinder South; **L** Lawrencefield; **LR** Laddow Rocks; **M** Millstone Edge; **POP** Stanage Popular; **RE** Rivelin Edge; **RHP** Running Hill Pits; **RHS** Robin Hood's Stride; **RLT** Roaches Lower Tier; **ROB** Rob's Rocks; **RR** Ramshaw Rocks; **RS** Ravenstones; **RUT** Roaches Upper Tier; **SCA** Stanage Count's Area; **SAN** Stanage Apparent North; **SC** Shining clough; **SHN** Stanage High Neb; **SKY** Roaches Skyline; **SN** Stanage North; **SP** Stanage Plantation; **SS** Standing Stones; **TK** Tintwistle Knarr; **W** Windgather; **WH** Wharncliffe; **WR** Wimberry Rocks; **Y** Yarncliffe

E10
Baron Greenbank (WR)
Doctor Dolittle (C)
Equilibrium (BS)
Sleepy Hollow (RLT)
Parthian Shot (BS)

E9
The Groove (CT)
Dangermouse (WR)
Dynamics of Change (BS)
Black Out (BS)
Harder Faster (BR)
Knockin' on Heaven's Door (C)
Appointment with Death (WR)
Meshuga (BR)

E8
Captain Invincible (BSQ)
Marbellous (SN)
Superstition (BN)
Sectioned (WR)
Soul Doubt (F)
The Promise (BN)
Loose Control (KD)
Simba's Pride (BS)
Gaia (BR)
The End of the Affair (C)
Nah'han (G)

E7
Slab and Crack (C)
Smoked Salmon (BE)
Groove is in the Heart (SAN)
The Angel's Share (BR)
Unfamiliar (SP)
Balance It Is (BS)
Messiah (BS)
Shine On (POP)
Avoiding the Traitors (BE)
Beau Geste (F)
Paralogism (RUT)
Clippity Clop... (RR)
The Mentalist Cupboard (KS)
Silent Scream (BSQ)
White Lines (C)
Toploader (M)
B4XS (HC)
Master's Edge (M)
Dangerous Crocodile Snogging (RR)
Braille Trail (BS)
Never, Never Land (RR)
Black Mountain Collage (RS)
The Bad and the Beautiful (M)
Appointment with Fear (WR)
Kaluza Klein (RHS)
Three Blind Mice (BN)

E6
Sad Amongst Friends (SAN)
Flight of Ideas (SP)
Thing on a Spring (RLT)
Against the Grain (RLT)
Janus (C)
Wall of Sound (POP)
Neptune's Tool (WR)
Mother's Pride (M)
Master of Reality (HC)
Velvet Silence (BR)
Adam Smith's Invisible Hand (M)
Perplexity (M)
Narcissus (F)
Ulysses (SP)
One Step Beyond (C)
Linden (C)
Mickey Finn (G)
National Acrobat (RR)
A Fist Full of Crystals (RLT)
Masters of the Universe (BSQ)
Piece of Mind (RLT)
Bloodrush (SC)
Barriers in Time (RLT)
9 O'Clock Watershed (SP)
Caricature (HC)
Double Take (WR)
The Crypt Trip (SHN)
Crème de la Crème (Y)
Linkline (HT)

Art Nouveau (SKY)
Painted Rumour (RUT)
No Time to Pose (RS)
Nosferatu (BS)
Jasmine (BE)
Desolation Angel (WH)
Make it Snappy (G)
Salmon Left-Hand (BE)

E5
Scoop de Grace (RHP)
Shirley's Shining Temple (SCA)
Offspring (BSQ)
White Wand (SP)
London Wall (M)
Ulysses or Bust (C)
Hairless Heart (F)
Moon Crack (C)
Moonshine (C)
Curving Arête (BR)
Pebble Mill (BS)
Perfect Day (G)
Over the Moors (RS)
Sagittarius Flake (RHP)
Green Death (M)
Saucius Digitalis (SC)
Edge Lane (M)
Consolation Prize (WR)
Great Arête (M)
Profit of Doom (C)
The Thin Air (RLT)

E5 (cont)

Entropy's Jaw (SKY)
Bat Out of Hell (HT)
Goosey Goosey
  Gander (SN)
Strapadictomy (F)
Track of the
  Cat (SKY)
Pool Wall (L)

E4

Nectar (SN)
No More
  Excuses (SHN)
Off With His
  Head (POP)
Snug as a Thug
  on a Jug (SAN)
Caesarian (HC)
Borstal Breakout (HC)
Peaches (BIR)
Ramshaw Crack (RR)
Old Friends (SHN)
Edale Bobby (KS)
Nettle Wine (CT)
Flute of Hope (HT)
The Knock (BS)
Usurper (C)
Downhill Racer (F)
Calamity Crack
  (RHP)
Goliath (BS)
Chameleon (HC)
High Street (L)
Silent Spring (BSQ)
Acid Drop (SKY)
Calvary (SP)
Moon Walk (C)
The Death
  Knell (RLT)
The Dark Side of the
  Moon (KD)
Auto da Fe (RE)
Don (SP)
The Brush Off (RE)
High Plains
  Drifter (L)
Autumn Wall (WH)
Wings of
  Unreason (SKY)
The Strangler (SP)
Jetrunner (BE)

E3

Demon Rib (BR)
Ontos (BE)
Saville Street (M)
The Asp (POP)
Comedian (HC)
Ascent of Man (RLT)
Sleeping Sickness G)
Traveller in Time (RR)
Tippler Direct (POP)
Bionic's Wall (NMT)
Corinthian (HC)
Requiem (CT)
Emerald Crack (CE)
Hunky Dory (RLT)
The Lamia (SN)
Censor (POP)
D.I.Y. (SCA)
Cave Wall (F)
Right Eliminate (C)
Appaloosa Sunset
  (FC)
The Crocodile (G)
Twikker (M)
Final Judgement
  (KD)
Moribund (SP)
Exit (RE)
Dextrous Hare (M)
The Archangel (SP)
Boulevard (L)
Great Slab (F)
Gates of Mordor (M)
The Swan (RLT)
Black Hawk
  Bastion (POP)
Wall End Slab
  Direct (SP)
Waterloo Sunset (G)
San Melas (SKY)
Great West Road (M)
Time for Tea (M)
Boot Hill (CT)
Mangled Digit (RHP)
True Grit (RS)
Smear Test (RLT)
Charm (WR)
Long Johns Slab (F)

E2

Easy Pickings (RE)
The Boggart (BS)
Fidget (C)
Golden Days (BR)
Daydreamer (SCA)
Big Brother (KN)
Cave Eliminate
  (POP)
Sentinel Crack (CE)
Foord's Folly (RR)
Billy Whizz (L)
Vibrio Direct (CE)
Cave Crack (F)
The Plain Sailing
  Midshipman (BIR)
Regent Street (M)
Tom Thumb (CT)
Silica (SP)
The Rasp (HT)
October Arete (WH)
Crack of Gloom
  (RLT)
Elegy (RLT)
Synopsis (F)
The Dangler (POP)
Electric Circus (NMT)
Lichen (CE)
Arabia (KS)
Topaz (SKY)
Quietus (SHN)
Mordaunt (CT)
Handrail (RR)
Count's Buttress (SCA)
Ruby Tuesday (RUT)
Piety (WR)
Apollo (C)
Insanity (C)
Knightsbridge (M)
Suspense (L)
Five Finger
  Exercise (CT)
Undercut Crack (BE)
Robert (KS)
Firebird (BR)
Blasphemy (WR)
Spanner Wall (RHP)
Sorb (BS)
Zeus (BSQ)
Pearls (CE)
Fern Hill (CT)
Orang-Outang (SN)
Elder Crack (C)
Wombat (RUT)
Hanging Crack (DE)
The Arête (TK)
The Last Fling (KD)
Commix (M)
Gumshoe (RR)
Heavy Duty (NMT)

Brimstone (M)
Erb (M)
The Big Crack (F)
Auricle (BE)
Vaya Con Dios (G)
Hanging Slab (HMQ)
Mather Crack (NMT)
The Sentinel (BN)
Wuthering (POP)
Commander Energy
  (RLT)
Promontory
  Traverse (BR)
Original Route (RE)
Pot Black (SP)
Savage Messiah (CT)
Brown's Eliminate (F)
Tower Face
  Direct (SP)

E1

Trojan (KN)
Kremlin Wall (SS)
Smoke ont'
  Watter (C)
Teck Crack (RLT)
The Toy (C)
Desperation (POP)
Brown's Crack (RR)
The Vice (SN)
The Left
  Eliminate (C)
Nonsuch (RE)
Asteris (AR)
Galileo (SC)
The Eye of Faith (G)
L'Horla (C)
Brutality (KS)
Pollux (AR)
Dark Continent (POP)
The Unprintable (POP)
Fallen Heroes (SS)
Strapiombo (F)
Naaden (SC)
Ocean Wall (SS)
Tower Chimney (SP)
The Tippler (POP)
Embankment 3 (M)
Encouragement (HC)
Kayak (C)
Millwheel Wall (BSQ)
Mickey Thin (RHP)
Great Peter (L)
Time for Tea
  Original (M)

dmmclimbing.com

climb now
work later

DMM

your better half

Ben Bransby, 1st ascent of How Many Roads... (E7/8 6c), Millstone, Peak District. 📷 Ray Wood

Increase your placement options with DMM's new **Halfnuts**. These single wire lightweight nuts have the same tapered faces and sides as our popular Wallnuts. The reduced width makes them ideal for shallow cracks, pin scars and situations where every gram counts.

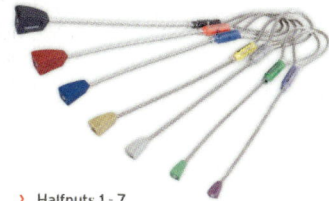

› Halfnuts 1 - 7

› Halfnut 7

E1 (cont)

Embankment 4 (M)
Chicken (HC)
Slowhand (HC)
Moyer's Buttress (G)
Biven's Crack (G)
Flying Buttress
  Direct (POP)
The Ivory Tower (KS)
Left-Hand Pillar
  Crack (G)
Dexterity (M)
Shortcomings (SKY)
Raggald's Wall (KD)
Safety Net (SKY)
The Press (RR)
Mississippi Variant
  Direct (POP)
Kirkus's Corner (POP)
Millsom's Minion (SP)
Billingsgate (M)
Hawkwing (RLT)
Intestate (KN)
Long Tall Sally (BN)
The Left
  Unconquerable (SP)
Conjunctus
  Viribus (AR)
Saliva (POP)
Masochism (RR)
Pulpit Ridge (RS)
Great Buttress Arête (WH)
Strapiombante (F)
The Link (POP)
Easter Rib (POP)
The Trouble With
  Women Is... (SS)
Three Pebble Slab (F)
Lancaster Flyby (DT)
Nemmes Pas
  Harry (BE)

HVS

Matinee (RLT)
Chequers Crack (F)
Blue Lights Crack (WR)
Ackit (RLT)
The Puppet
  Crack (CE)
Tower Crack (SP)
The Trident (WR)
Valkyrie Direct (RLT)
Bachelor's Left-
  hand (HC)
Freddie's Finale (WR)
The Mincer (RLT)
Surgeon's Saunter
  (SN)
Kelly's Overhang
  (SHN)
Suicide Wall (CT)
Hen Cloud
  Eliminate (HC)
The Peapod (C)
Terrazza Crack (SN)
Whillans' Pendulum/
  Black Magic (POP)
Twisted Smile (KN)
Good Friday (POP)
Green Crack (C)
Congo Corner (POP)
The Blurter (SHN)
Cave Arête (POP)
Eliminator (POP)
Herford's Route (KS)
Eros (M)
The Scoop (POP)
Roof Route (RE)
Great Portland
  Street (M)
Scimitar (TK)
Whitehall (M)
The Sloth (RUT)
The Crippler (RR)
Plexity (M)
Fina (SP)
Valkyrie (F)
Prostration (RR)
Maupassant (C)
Blizzard Ridge (RE)
Brooks' Crack (BS)
Great Buttress (DT)
Great North
  Road (M)
Goliath's Groove (SP)
The Right
  Unconquerable (SP)
Right-hand
  Tower (SN)
Sorrell's Sorrow (C)
The Happy
  Wanderer (BE)
Nowanda (G)
Delstree (HC)
Zapple (Y)
Rubberneck (FC)
Titanic
  Direct (SHN)
Avalanche Wall (C)
Legacy (KN)
Crabbie's Crack (FC)
Pisa Super
  Direct (SC)
Priscilla Ridge (LR)
Saul's Crack (RUT)
Cave Innominate/
  Harding's
  Superdirect (POP)
East Rib (SC)
Neb Buttress (BE)
Lyons Corner
  House (M)
Alcove Crack (NMT)
Bond Street (M)
Mississippi Variant
  (POP)
Crew Cut (M)
Croton Oil (RE)
Chequers Buttress (F)
Queersville (POP)
Tower Face (SP)
Tody's Wall (F)
Jester Cracks (KN)
Old Salt (SN)
BAW's Crawl (POP)
Scoop Face (CN)
Knight's Move (BN)
David (BS)
Parker's Eliminate
  (HMQ)
Sunset Slab (F)

VS

Flash Wall (KS)
Cleft Wing (POP)
Altar Crack (RE)
Main Crack (HC)
Fern Crack (SP)
Moneylender's Crack
  (KS)
Fairy Nuff (SS)
Wedgewood Crack
  (RS)
Valkyrie (RLT)
Ornithologist's
  Corner (WR)
Rainbow Crack (HC)
Lean Man's
  Climb (BR)
Birch Tree Wall (BR)
Two Pitch Route (C)
Bachelor's Climb (HC)
Reunion Crack (HC)
The File (HT)
The Crank (RR)
Obscenity (BN)
Tower Face (LR)
Hawk's Nest
  Crack (F)
Great Harry (L)
Embankment Route
  2 (M)
Gardom's
  Unconquerable (G)
Excalibur (L)
Wall End Slab (SP)
The Mall (M)
Womanless Wall (SS)
Route 1 (DT)
Titanic (SHN)
Sand Buttress (BR)
Bilberry Crack (BE)
Quien Sabe? (BE)
North Buttress
  Arête (W)
Hargreaves' Original
  (POP)
Phoenix Climb (SC)
Count's Crack (SCA)
Byne's Crack (BS)
Ellis's Eliminate
  (POP)
Fall Pipe (Y)
Plumb Line (RHP)
Mississippi Buttress
  Direct (POP)
High Neb
  Buttress (SHN)
Great Slab (A)
Himmelswillen (WH)
Extinguisher Chimney
  (KD)
Dunsinane (KN)
The Delectable
  Variation (L)
The Brain (C)
The Whittler (AR)
Barney Rubble (DT)
Nozag (CN)
Wrinkled Wall (BE)
Milton's Meander
  (SP)
Inaccessible Crack
  (SHN)
Hell Crack (POP)
Milton's Meander
  (SP)
Crew's Route (HMQ)
Heather Wall (POP)

Black Diamond

BD Athlete Babsi Zangerl | Caderese, Italy 📷 Andy Earl

BLACKDIAMONDEQUIPMENT.COM

THE ALL-NEW CAMALOT™ Z4

Born from a heart-to-heart with our top trad-climbing BD Athletes Babsi Zangerl, Hazel Findlay, Carlo Traversi, and Sam Elias, the Camalot™ Z4 is the realization of their dream: to have a single-stem cam that stays rigid in-hand, but flexes when you climb past. Behold, our game-changing RigidFlex stem, an innovation that creates a new standard for small cams

VS (cont)
Inverted V (POP)
Misty Wall (KN)
Via Dolorosa (RLT)
Martello Buttress (POP)
Cave Arête (LR)
Gargoyle Flake (BE)
Twin Crack Corner (SS)
Covent Garden (M)
Technical Slab & The Neb Finish (RUT)
Fairy Steps (SP)
Bel Ami (C)
Via Media (POP)
Gargoyle Buttress (POP)
Topsail (BIR)
Fox House Flake (BSQ)
Elliott's Buttress Direct (G)
Apple Arête (G)
Layback Crack (DE)

HS
Central Climb (HC)
The Mermaid's Ridge (KD)
Tango Buttress (SHN)
Jeffcoat's Buttress (RUT)
Crack and Corner (RUT)
The Great Chimney (KD)
The Coign (SP)
Mutiny Crack (BN)
The Left Monolith (RS)
Kestrel Crack (RLT)
Boulder Climb (RHS)
Porthole Direct (BIR)
Nelson's Nemesis (BIR)
Brown's Crack (BE)
Route I (WR)
Paradise Wall (SP)
Upper Tor Wall (KS)
Christmas Crack (POP)
Nasal Buttress (DE)
Manchester Buttress (POP)

Modern (HC)
Hollybush Crack (RUT)
Sail Buttress (BIR)
Terrace Crack (F)
Byne's Route (POP)
Brooks' Layback (BN)
Eartha (M)
Diamond Crack (F)
P.M.C.1 (C)
Amazon Crack (BN)
Kelly's Eliminate (SN)
Robin Hood's Right-hand Buttress Direct (POP)
Dover's Wall, Route 1 (POP)
Sunset Crack (F)
April Crack (POP)
Powder Monkey Parade (BIR)
Nil Desperandum (RS)
Tower Face (WH)
Three Tree Climb (L)
Ant's Wall (Y)

Sev
Crack and Corner (POP)
Green Gut (F)
K2 (HC)
Bertie's Bugbear (WR)
Vivien (SS)
Amazon Crack (POP)
Emma's Dilemma (BIR)
Twisting Crack (SHN)
Root Route (RE)
Campsite Crack (AR)
Great Chimney (HC)
Green Crack (W)
Phallic Crack (RR)
Flying Buttress (C)
Bamford Wall (BE)
Right-Hand Trinity (POP)
Balcony Buttress (POP)
Puttrell's Progress (WH)
Black Hawk Hell Crack (POP)

Beta Crack (WH)
Paradise Crack (SP)
Via Principia (SC)
Black and Tans (RUT)
The Crab Crawl (SN)
Slab and Arête (SKY)
Bishop's Route (POP)
Lone Tree Gully (BR)
Horatio's Horror (BIR)
North Climb (CT)
Ash Tree Wall (BN)

HVD
Long Climb (LR)
Pedestal Route (RUT)
Answer Crack (DE)
Central Buttress (BR)
Sail Chimney (BIR)
Fern Crack (RUT)
The Arête (HC)
Rib and Face (A)
Tower Ridge (DE)
Nose Direct (W)
Heather Wall (F)

VD
Flying Buttress (POP)
N.M.C. Crack (G)
Leaning Buttress Crack (POP)
Jeffcoat's Chimney (RUT)
Right Route (RUT)
Hollybush Crack (POP)
Boomerang (RR)
Maud's Garden (RUT)
Heaven Crack (POP)
Emperor Flake Climb (CE)
Ash Tree Crack (BN)
Zigzag Climb (KD)
Dovestones Wall (DT)
Ylnosd Rib (ROB)
Crack and Cave (POP)
Central Tower (DE)
Pulpit Groove (L)
Chockstone Chimney (KD)

Trapeze (F)
The Pinion (SN)
Mississippi Chimney (POP)
Letter-Box (ROB)
Mississippi Crack Variant (W)

Diff
Black Hawk Traverse Right (POP)
Fat Man's Chimney (BR)
October Crack (SN)
Professor's Chimney (KD)
High Buttress Arête (W)
Slab Recess (F)
Left Twin Chimney (POP)

M
Downfall Climb (KD)
Trinnacle Chimney (RS)
The Promenade (BIR)
Great Slab Chimney (A)
Castle Chimney (POP)
Martello Cracks (POP)

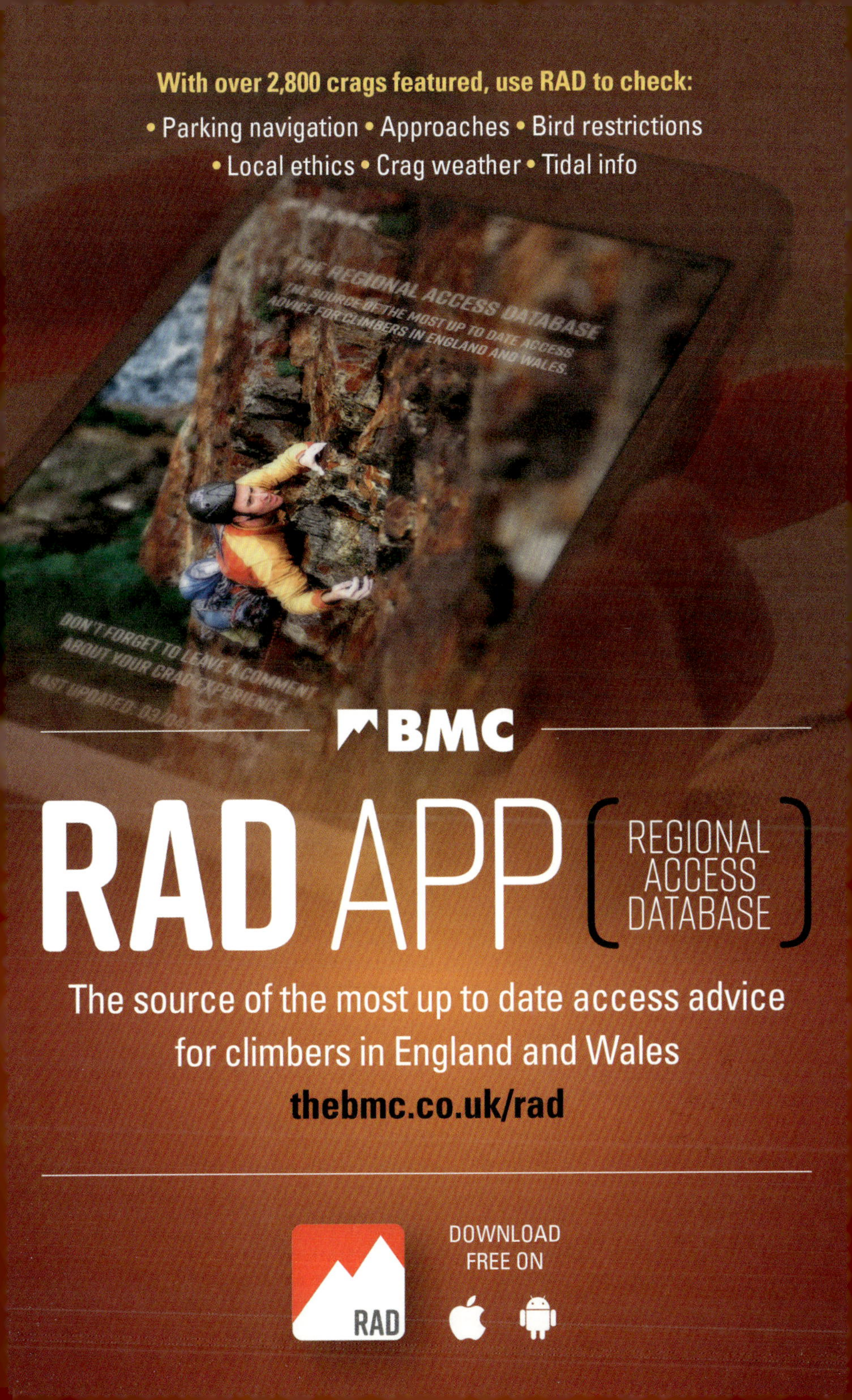

With over 2,800 crags featured, use RAD to check:
- Parking navigation • Approaches • Bird restrictions
- Local ethics • Crag weather • Tidal info

RAD APP (REGIONAL ACCESS DATABASE)

The source of the most up to date access advice for climbers in England and Wales

thebmc.co.uk/rad

DOWNLOAD FREE ON

VISITOR INFO

CAMPSITES
There are many excellent camp sites for those coming to sample the delights of Peak Grit. Those of most interest are detailed below:

North Lees Campsite
Tel: 01433 650 838
A superb campsite situated in woods about a mile and a half from Hathersage and a 25-minute walk from Stanage Edge. Excellent facilities.

Eric Byne Memorial Campsite
Tel: 01246 582 277
A basic campsite about a mile from the village of Baslow. Park next to the Robin Hood Pub on the Chesterfield Road, from where a 10-minute walk gets you to the camping – toilets plus a cold tap.

Upper Booth Farm Campsite Edale
Tel: 01433 670 368
A superbly located campsite at the western end of the Edale valley, about a 20-minute walk from the village itself.

Fieldhead Campsite Edale
Tel: 01433 670 386
Situated in Edale village.

Roaches Campsite
Tel: 01538 300 419
A pleasant site situated in a field beneath Hen Cloud. There are no facilities but there are toilets plus fresh water at Homestead Farm, the site's owners, about ¼ mile down the road.

Well-i-Hole Farm
Tel: 01457 600 208
Situated in Greenfield, convenient for all the Chew Valley crags.

Camping and Caravanning Club site at Crowden
Tel: 01457 866 057
Best for Laddow, Shining Clough & Tintwistle Knarr. Toilet block with showers, dishwashing, drying room, and a small shop and cafe.

Camping and Caravanning Club site at Hayfield
Tel: 01663 745394
Very convenient for the Downfall Crags and the Northern Edges. On Kinder Road, to the east of the village.

BUNKHOUSES
There are numerous bunkhouses and independent hostels dotted around the National Park. Details can easily be found by a web search for 'Peak District Bunkhouses' or by looking on the Independent Hostels website.

Don Whillans Memorial Hut
Rockhall Cottage is managed by the British Mountaineering Council (BMC) and can be hired by individual BMC members, BMC affiliated clubs and overseas national federations. It sleeps 12 people in two bunk rooms. Full details including booking form at www.donwhillanshut.co.uk

CAFES
There are hundreds of good cafes situated in the Peak District National Park: most Peak District villages will have one. For climbers visiting the Peak the following may be of interest:
Outside Cafe (Hathersage)
Tel: 01433 651 936
Cintra's Tea Rooms (Hathersage)
Tel: 01433 651 825
Colemans Deli (Hathersage)
Tel: 01433 650 505
The Pool Cafe (Hathersage)
Tel: 01433 651 159
Grindleford Station Cafe
Tel: 01433 631 011
Yondermann Cafe (Wardlow Mires)
Tel: 01298 873 056
Penny Pot Cafe (Edale)
Tel: 01433 670 688
Roaches Tea Room (Upper Hulme)
Tel: 01538 300 345
Hassop Station Cafe
Tel: 01629 815 668
For the Chew Valley visitor, Uppermill is very well supplied with numerous cafes.

PUBLIC HOUSES

As with cafes, there are hundreds of great pubs situated throughout the National Park. Those listed below are well placed for climbers looking for a post-climbing pint, a selection of others are marked on the individual area maps.

STAFFORDSHIRE GRITSTONE

The Lazy Trout (Meerbrook) A cosy atmosphere and tasty food or an excellent view of the Roaches from the beer garden.
The Winking Man (Upper Hulme) Beer, pub grub and sometimes live bands. Their website includes a webcam which is particularly useful as an indication of local weather conditions.
The New Inn (Flash) Located in the highest village in the British isles, with good beer.

SOUTHERN GRITSTONE

Druid Inn (Birchover) Tasty beer and food a stone's throw from Cratcliffe & Robin Hood's Stride.
The Flying Childers (Stanton in the Peak) A traditional country pub with a focus on good beer and light bites.
The Boat Inn (Cromford) After sampling the delights of Black Rocks discover a tucked away pub with a friendly atmosphere.

FROGGATT AREA

The Grouse Inn (Longshaw) A good selection of beer plus good food.
The Derwentwater Arms (Calver) Local village pub with a terrace and beer garden, to lick your wounds after a day at Curbar.
The Moon (Stoney Middleton) Beer food and atmosphere and also useful if you have succumbed to the local limestone.
Robin Hood Inn (Baslow) Ideal for after Gardom's, Chatsworth or Birchen Edge and those saying at the nearby Eric Byne campsite.

EASTERN QUARRIES

The Millstone Inn (Hathersage) A large pub with plenty of seating, good beer and food.

BURBAGE VALLEY

Norfolk Arms (Ringinglow), good food and beer, and **The Fox House** (Longshaw) is convenient for those Sheffield bound.

STANAGE

The Little John Hotel (Hathersage) A large pub with plenty of seating with good beer and huge food portions.

The Scotsmans Pack (Hathersage) The smallest of the three pubs in Hathersage. Again, great beer and pub grub with a small beer garden next to the river.

NORTHERN EDGES

The Anglers Rest (Bamford) A community-owned pub, cafe and post office, serving good beer, cakes and wholesome local food.
The Strines Inn (Bradfield Dale) For refreshment after a hard day at Dovestone Tor.
Old Horns Inn (High Bradfield) Excellent beer and food, a satisfying accompaniment to Agden Rocher in a lovely location.
The Wortley Arms (Wortley) Outlying but useful for Wharncliffe, serving food.

CHEW VALLEY

Saddleworth and the Chew Valley area host a number of good pubs including. **The Wellington**, **King William** and **The Clarence** in Greenfield and the **Cross Keys Inn** and **Church Inn** in Uppermill on the road up to Running Hill Pits.

KINDER BLEAKLOW

The Bull's Head (Tintwistle): Hidden away on the back road through Tintwistle and ideal after a session on the Knarr, Shinning Clough or Laddow.
Glossop has a number of good pubs including: **The Star Inn** near the station, **The Bulls Head** in Old Glossop and **The Globe**, which is both a micro-brewery and serves vegan food.
The Swan (Kettleshulme): For a celebratory pint after your first lead at Windgather? It serves good food.
Beehive Inn (Combs) A traditional country pub with dining, a perfect reward after a day at Castle Naze.
The Lantern Pike Inn (Little Hayfield) Grand pub, great food and beer.
The George Hotel (Hayfield) A large pub with many beers and ales together with good food and a large outside area. Popular with climbers and walkers.
The Old Nags Head (Edale) A large climber friendly pub, famous for being at the start of the Pennine Way. Great beer and great food; brilliant setting in the summer months after a day out on the southern Kinder Edges.
The Rambler Inn (Edale) As above but with a massive outside garden / seating area; fabulous on a warm summer's evening.

GEAR SHOPS

There are relatively few gear shops located in the National Park itself but of particular interest to climbers are:

Outside (Hathersage)
Tel: 01433 651 936
A large, superbly stocked independent climbing shop stocking pretty much everything a modern rock climber could possibly want - and then some.

Jo Royle Outdoor (Buxton)
Tel: 01298 25824
A small, well stocked independent climbing shop.

Cotswold Outdoor (Bakewell)
Tel: 01629 812 231
Well stocked with climbing and camping equipment.

CLIMBING WALLS

Surprising as this may seem, it does, occasionally, rain in the Peak District. Should you be unfortunate enough to be visiting on such a day, The surrounding areas have several climbing walls, enough to keep you busy. Most of the crags in this book are, at most, 50-minute drive from one of the following:

The Foundry
Tel: 0114 279 6331
Sheffield's original wall, with leading, top roping, bouldering and shop.

Awesome Walls
Sheffield Tel: 0114 244 6322
Stockport Tel: 0161 494 9949
Stoke Tel: 01782 341 919
State of the art climbing facilities – loads of leading lines, bouldering and top roping and cafes.

The Climbing Works
Tel: 0114 250 9990
The original UK modern bouldering wall (for many years it was the largest bouldering facility in the world) – handily situated on the 'Peak' side of Sheffield. On the same site there is The Mini Works with a focus towards kids, groups and beginners and Unit E a dedicated training facility and gym with an emphasis on competition climbing.

The Depot
Sheffield Tel: 0114 327 1948
Manchester Tel: 0161 848 9495
Modern state of the art bouldering facilities with walls in Sheffield, Manchester, Leeds, Birmingham and Nottingham. There's also a Big Depot with lead and top roping in Leeds. Acres of space with loads of bouldering for all abilities. Together with shops and cafes.

The Matrix
Tel: 0114 222 6999
Small Bouldering facility part of The University of Sheffield.

Manchester Climbing Centre
Tel: 0161 230 7006
For those heading back towards central Manchester. Loads of leading, bouldering and top roping. Together with a shop and cafe.

Rock Over Climbing
Tel: 0161 288 1218
Bouldering, kids' play area and a cafe in Manchester.

Rope Race Climbing Centre
Tel: 0161 426 0226
Lead and top rope climbing in Marple.

The Substation
Tel: 01625 440 144
A new compact bouldering wall, yoga centre, cafe and shop in Macclesfield.

The Climbing Unit
Tel: 01332 265 864
Climbing and bouldering wall in Derby.

Alter Rock
Tel: 01332 367 200
Lead climbing, activity centre and cafe in Derby.

The Face
Tel: 01629 824 717
Wirksworth
Leading and bouldering wall in a leisure centre.

The Adventure Hub
Tel: 01433 695 544
Small bouldering and training wall in Bamford.

Gus Hudgins getting groovy on Black Rocks' Lone Tree Groove, VS 5a (page 124), one of the crag's great VSs.
David Simmonite

STAFFORDSHIRE GRITSTONE

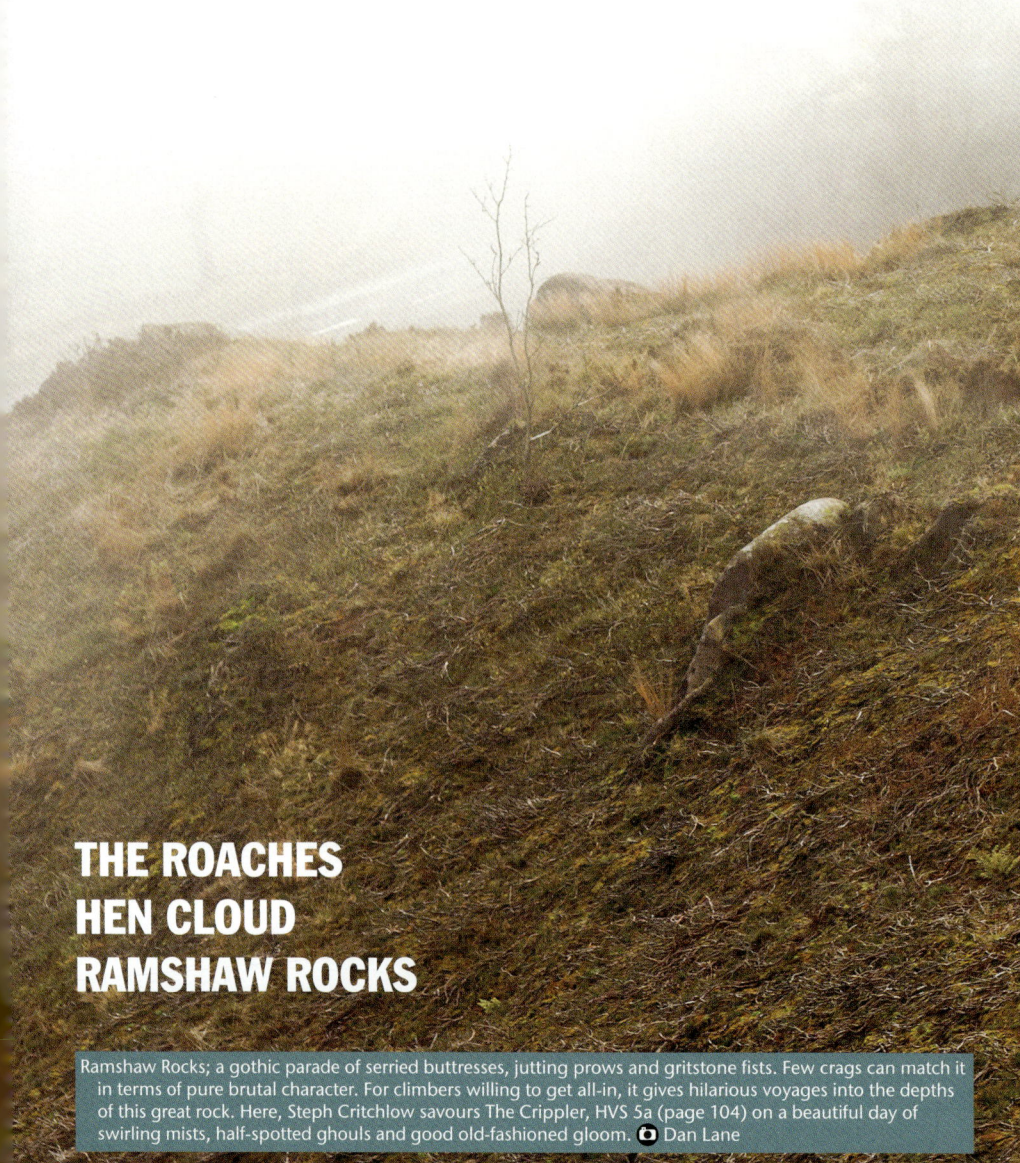

**THE ROACHES
HEN CLOUD
RAMSHAW ROCKS**

Ramshaw Rocks; a gothic parade of serried buttresses, jutting prows and gritstone fists. Few crags can match it in terms of pure brutal character. For climbers willing to get all-in, it gives hilarious voyages into the depths of this great rock. Here, Steph Critchlow savours The Crippler, HVS 5a (page 104) on a beautiful day of swirling mists, half-spotted ghouls and good old-fashioned gloom. ⓑ Dan Lane

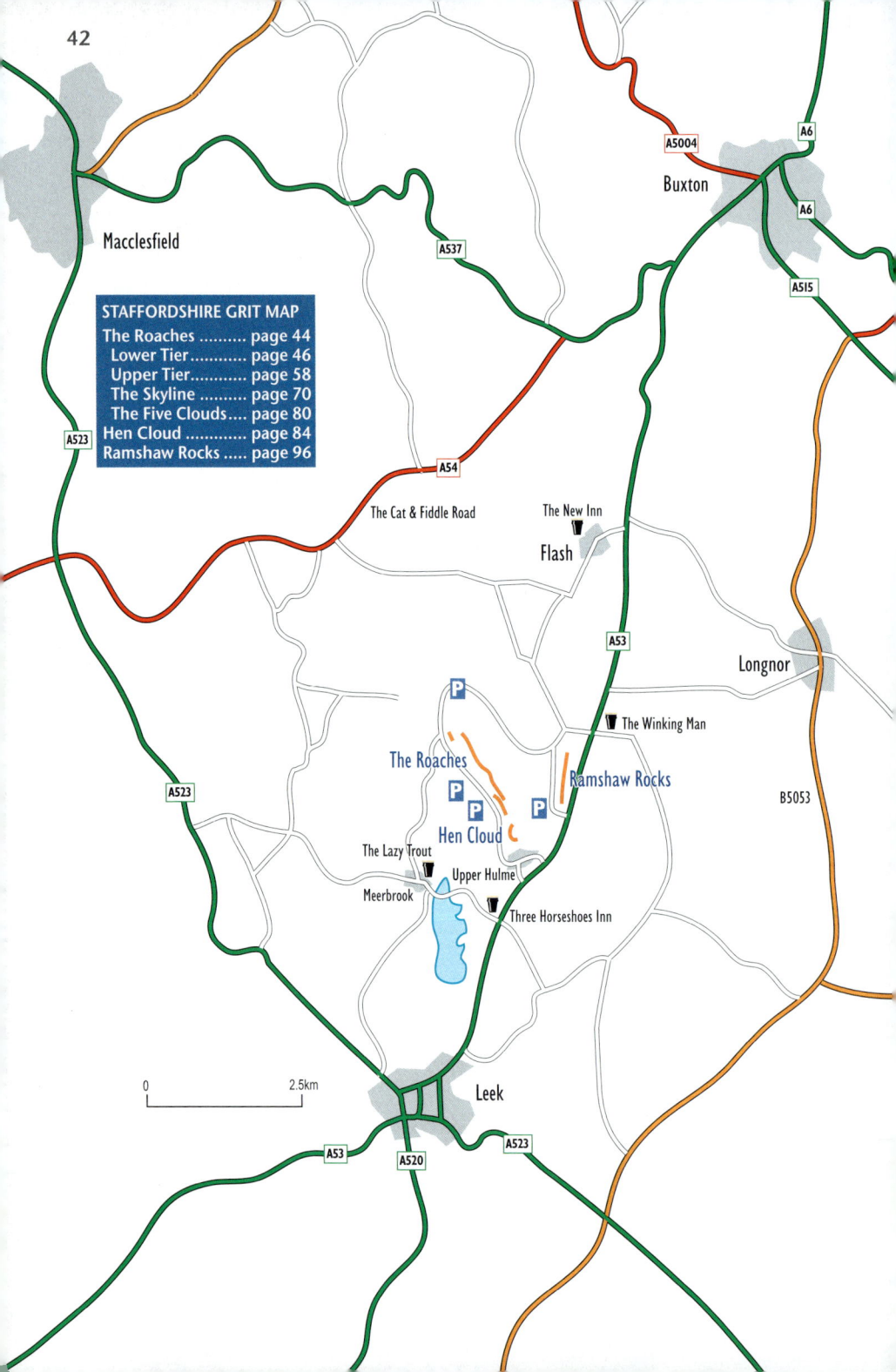

Helen Oughton stepping out above the void on Right Route, VD (page 66). Luckily, despite the space snapping at her heels, generous holds ease the journey. 📷 Paul Evans

THE ROACHES

Gritstone royalty.

The Roaches are the western front of 'God's Own Rock' and offer climbs, landscapes and light as good as any in the land. A firm favourite among gritstoners.

Under the Roaches umbrella sit four discrete sectors, each with their own vibe. The Lower Tier is a commuter train packed to the gills with side-by-side classics from D to E10. Above this, the Upper Tier sits high above the world and specialises in full-size pitches up stately slabs. Fresh and open.

Beyond the Upper Tier, The Skyline has a secretive air and along its dozen buttresses are compact and varied technical climbs as well as some of the best rock on grit. Below here, The Five Clouds offer secluded and peaceful climbs and great lines.

All crags face south-west and get loads of sun. For specific notes on conditions, see the individual sections.

Approach: See map opposite. From the A53, follow signs to Upper Hulme. Drive through the village and continue under Hen Cloud. After about 500m, far below the hooded overhangs of the Upper Tier, park only in designated roadside bays. Read parking signs: incorrect parking often gets ticketed.

For the Lower Tier, go through the access gate (the Upper Tier is directly above). Follow the track up to the crags. See map on page 46.

For the Upper Tier, follow the steps between the Lower Tier Left and Lower Tier Right. See map on page 46.

For the Skyline, carry on up the steps at the left of the Upper Tier or approach from Roach End. See map on page 70.

For the Five Clouds, go through the access gate and turn immediately left along small tracks. Go left along a small path as the track ascends towards the Upper Tier, just by a small quarry.

Pure heaven. Pete Wilson on Appaloosa Sunset, E3 5c (page 83). Wilson collection.

ROACHES LOWER TIER

OS Grid Ref: SK 005 623 to SK 006 621
Altitude: 400m

Upper Tier
- The Skyline
- Upper Tier Left-Hand
- Main Area
- Calcutta Buttress
- Blushing Buttress
- Upper Tier Boulders
- Lower Tier Left
- Lower Tier Right
- steps
- Lower Tier Boulders
- Rockhall Cottage
- Spring Boulders

SEE MAP ON PAGE 45

← Upper Tier
← The Five Clouds
roadside bays
access gate
Upper Hulme 1.5km →
← Roach End

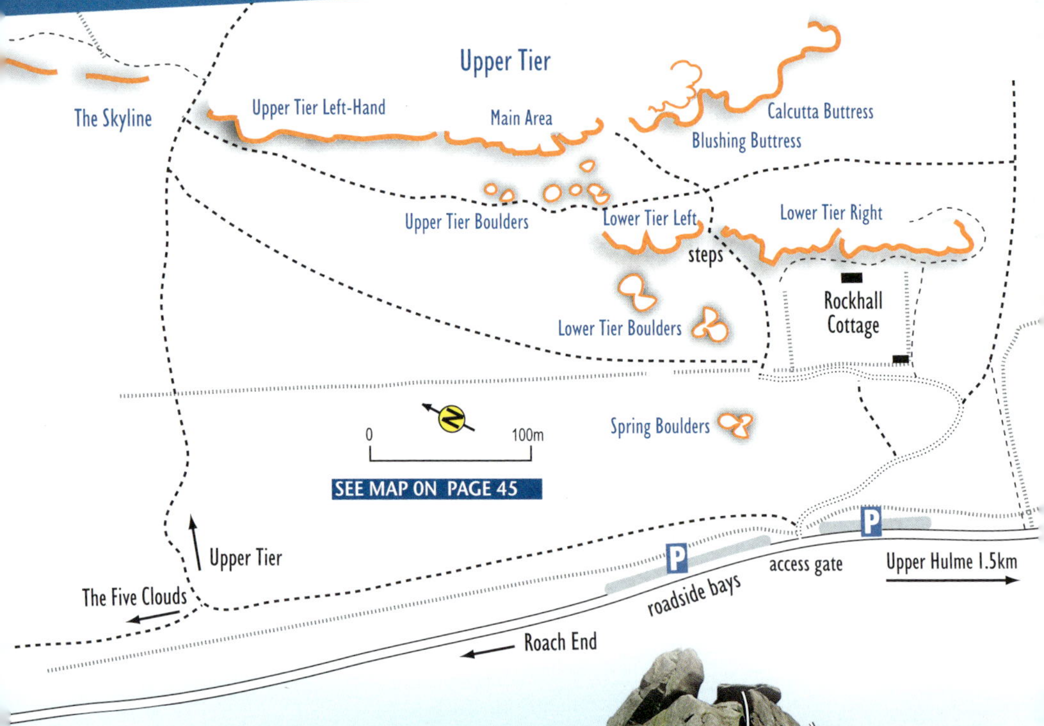

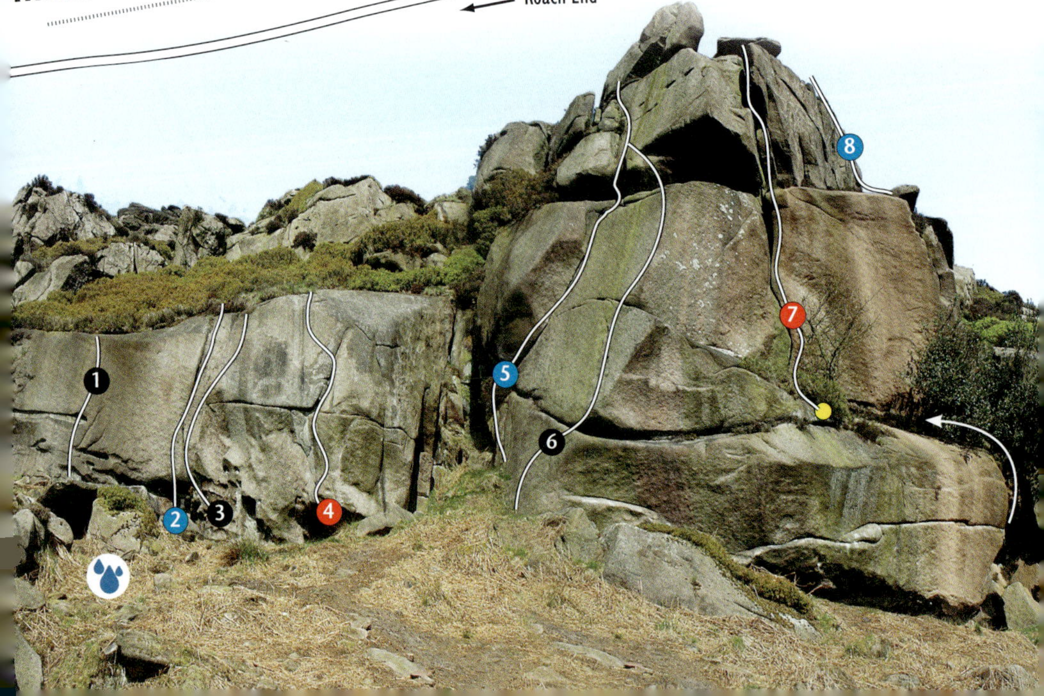

Roaches Lower Tier | 47

The Lower Tier tends to be fairly sheltered, not being as high up the ridge, and with many trees nearby to break the wind. This shelter also makes some of the faces slow to dry and sometimes green, although, surprisingly, this green doesn't always affect the climbing.

LOWER TIER LEFT
These are the buttresses left of the ancient steps, centred around the tall and robust Teck Buttress.

1 Catastrophe Internationale
8m   E5 6b   ★★
Pure pebble climbing at an uncomfortable height.
Nick Dixon, 1985

2 Slippery Jim   7m   HVS 5a   ★
Climb the corner crack to its heathery conclusion. A Rock and Ice Club classic.
Don Whillans, 1958

3 Bareback Rider   8m   E4 6b   ★★
The bouldery arête leads to a sketchy mantel onto the slab. Continue easily.
Dave Jones, 1980

4 Ascent of Man   10m   E3 6a   ★★★
Bold, fingery climbing. Make a hard move to reach a good break and then the fine flake above. Place wobbly runners and make a committing step left onto the pebbly ramp. Mantel onto the top as soon as you dare.
Andrew Woodward, Jonny Woodward, 1974

5 Ackit   15m   HVS 5b   ★★
The hanging corner. A strenuous start and then some tough laybacking lead to a welcome rest below the tricky final bulge.
Don Whillans, 1958

6 Barriers in Time   16m   E6 6b   ★★★
The impressive arête marked a major breakthrough for its time. Climb the scalloped wall to the second break and protection. Proceed thoughtfully up the rounded arête as the runners recede alarmingly. Traverse left into *Ackit* at the top and finish up this.
Simon Nadin, 1983

7 Teck Crack   26m   E1 5c   ★★★
A toughie, with steep laybacking in an impressive situation. Gain the ledge below the crack from the gully on the right (4b). Attack the crack with gusto. Finish up the continuation crack to a historic bolt and seat belay.
⦿ page 57
Joe Brown (lpt), 1958

8 Lightning Crack   20m   HVS 5c   ★
1 8m 5c After a puzzling entry, layback the crack to reach a tree.
2 12m 4c Move up behind the tree and climb the triangular-shaped wall behind. From the sloping ledge either finish direct or, better, by a leftward-rising pod.
Don Whillans, Joe Brown, 1958

9 Crystal Grazer   11m   E5 6a   ★
From the ramp, pull up left to attain a standing position on the lip of the overhang. Foot traverse past a shallow groove until it is possible to move up to gain the obvious ramp-like hold directly above the holly. Unprotected.
Phil Burke, 1982

10 A Fist Full of Crystals
12m   E6 6b   ★★★
Brilliant, balancy and bold climbing on smears and pebbles. From the ramp, pull left and foot-traverse the lip as far as a shallow groove. Climb this and either step left onto a finishing foothold or continue direct.
Nick Dixon, 1983

11 Doug   12m   E8 6c   ★
A historic route, the country's first E8. Hard, blind and unprotected pebble-pulling up the shallow scoop on the right-hand side of the slab. Start as for the two previous routes then climb immediately up the right-hand side of the front face of the buttress to finish up the hanging scoop.
Nick Dixon, 1986

LOWER TIER RIGHT
The first route is just right of the steps.

12 Yong Arête 7m S ★
An interesting route climbing the blunt rib. Protection arrives too late for the leader, but may be appreciated by the second.

13 Yong 9m HVD 4a ★
The crack in the shallow corner is climbed on superb jams throughout, and is excellently protected. A perfect route for beginners.

14 Something Better Change 9m E2 5b
The chipped slab right of *Yong*. A side-runner reduces the grade to HVS.
Gary Gibson, 1978

15 Wisecrack 8m VS 4c
The slanting crack in the left side of the buttress.

16 Hypothesis 11m E1 5b ★★
The excellent cracked arête is technical, sustained and only just protectable.
Colin Foord, Dave Salt, 1968

17 Cannonball Crack 11m S 4b
Slither up the crack in the face until a move left onto a boulder allows the top to be gained.

18 Dorothy's Dilemma 18m E1 5a ★★
Climb the exposed arête by a series of absorbing moves in a serious situation.
Joe Brown, Slim Sorrell, Dorothy Sorrell, 1951

19 Bengal Buttress 30m HVS 4c ★★
An inspired production from ancient times, being exposed, delicate and, even today, poorly protected. Move up to a grassy ledge, then go right up to a break, runners. Traverse right to gain an airy position on the right of the arête where a trying move leads to the top of *Raven Rock Gully*. Step left and go up the short crack.
Ivan Waller, c1920

A Lower Tier classic first climbed over a century ago, Via Dolorosa, VS 4c (page 50), is one of the great passages in the area where cunning sidestepping allow that fabulous Raven Rock to be climbed at a reasonable level. Here, Rebecca Ting slinks leftwards under the roof. Paul Evans

VALKYRIE AREA

To the right, a large tower of rock protrudes out above the trees. Amongst its routes are two of the finest routes of their grade on gritstone, combining magnificent varied climbing, with building atmosphere and great positions. The climbs tend to be steep; by devious and inventive route-finding they usually manage to weave their wonderful ways upwards by guile rather than brute force.

The first routes are in the gloomy gully to its left.

20 Crack of Gloom 23m E2 5b ★★★
A superb, dark and shadowy climb, with a character all its own, taking the mighty gloomy looming crack in the left wall of the recess. Exit left around the chockstone.
Joe Brown, Don Whillans, 1958

21 Raven Rock Gully Left-Hand 20m VS 4b
Ascend cracks and grooves in the left side of the gully, exiting through the skylight above.
Dave Salt, 1969

22 Raven Rock Gully 20m D ★
Follow the flakes in the back of the gully until it is possible to squirm through the manhole above.
Kyndwyr Club, 1901

23 Via Dolorosa 33m VS 4c ★★★
A great historic climb, one of the very best of its grade in the area.
1 8m 4c Ascend a narrow glassy slab, then move up left through the holly to a ledge.
2 10m 4a Traverse left to the rib and follow a short crack, then a slab around to the left. Belay at a block.
3 15m 4c Climb boldly up right to a flake. Surmount this then move right round the arête and go up to the top. page 49

24 Via Dolorosa Variations 33m HS 4a
By avoiding the polished corner by starting higher, and finishing left into *Raven Rock Gully* to avoid the last pitch, this superb climb can be enjoyed at a much lower standard.

25 Valkyrie Direct 25m HVS 5a ★★
A superb gritstone fight. From the holly on *Via Dolorosa*, climb up and right to the huge flake on *Valkyrie*. Struggle over this and step left to battle up the wide crack to regain the original route on the front face of the buttress.
Joe Brown, Don Whillans, 1951

26 Matinee 23m HVS 5b ★★★
A magnificent exercise in jamming, this climb takes the huge, beautifully ugly crack.
1 15m 5a Climb the sometimes green crack on jams to a belay on the fine ledge.
2 8m 5b Continue up the widening crack to the final bulge - a technical flounder.
Joe Brown, Don Whillans, 1951

Roaches Lower Tier | 51

30 Valkyrie Corner 25m HS 4b ★
The major corner. Follow it all the way, or escape through the tunnel or, better, climb the flake on the left to the top.

31 Pebbledash 21m HVS 5a ★
1 12m 5a Climb the chimney and crack. Scamper across the slab leftwards to belay.
2 9m 4b The flake, corner or ramp above.
Dave Salt, 1969

32 Against the Grain 20m E6 7a ★★★
A stunning fingery sequence above a relatively safe fallout zone. Easy ground leads to good cracks. From the cracks, step leftwards and climb on tiny edges diagonally leftwards to gain a sloping ramp. Finish up this.
Simon Nadin, 1985

33 Thing on a Spring 20m E6 7a ★★★
One of Simon Nadin's most technical creations with some of the hardest climbing in Staffordshire. From the cracks step right onto the ramp and foot traverse this to its end. Now compose yourself and pop for the sloping break above. From here, romp confidently to the top.
Simon Nadin, 1986

34 The Swan 24m E3 5c ★★★
Manageable climbing in outrageous positions. From the cracks (high runners), finger traverse out right, culminating in a tough move to the rounded break. Follow the wide crack above.
John Gosling (1pt), 1969. FFA Ron Fawcett, Geoff Birtles, 1977

35 The Mincer 20m HVS 5b ★★★
A steep route with many cruxes. Climb the crack through the stepped overhangs. All that remains is the wide crack.
Joe Brown, Don Whillans, 1951

36 Smear Test 20m E3 6a ★★
A good introduction to the harder slabs hereabouts. From *The Mincer*, traverse horizontally rightwards to finish up the bottomless crack.
Gabriel Regan, 1977

37 Pincer 20m VS 5a ★
Follow the groove (crux) into *Guano Gully*. Ascend this until it is possible to step back left onto the slab to reach the crack.

38 Bloodspeed 19m E6 6b ★★
From *Pincer*, move up to a difficult move thought the overhang to become established on the slab. Smear confidently up the bald slab above to reach the salvation of a thin crack. Finish up this or the slab to the right.
Simon Nadin, 1984

27 Valkyrie 38m VS 4c ★★★
Simply one of the best routes on gritstone – intricate, exposed and varied, and while it is only VS, it definitely climbs through HVS territory.
1 15m 4b Follow the corner then traverse left to a fine belay. A nondescript pitch; the start of *Pebbledash* is a better choice.
2 23m 4c Climb up and then down the huge flake to its base. Intimidating moves lead left onto the front face of the buttress where one final worrying move, out of the sight of your second leads to a large ledge. Finish easily. Careful ropework advised, especially to protect the second.
Peter Harding, A Bowden Black, 1946

The next two routes start from Valkyrie's stance.

28 Northern Comfort 10m E6 6c ★★
Reachy climbing with a safe fall-out zone. From the top of the flake on *Valkyrie*, follow a series of thin flakes leftwards towards a notch on the arête then the easier flake above.
Niall Grimes, 1996

29 Licence to Run 10m E4 6a ★★
A fingery wall climb with some obscure moves. Protection is good but exhausting to place. From the belay on *Valkyrie*, step right and climb a layback flake until it is possible to break out right to another flake. Tricky moves up and right gain a finishing jug.
Gary Gibson (1pt), 1980. FFA Pete O'Donovan, Gary Cooper, 1980

Roaches Lower Tier

39 Guano Gully 13m HS 4b
Start in the corner. Follow this then undercut leftwards to gain the main upper corner.

40 Elegy 16m E2 5c ★★★
An absorbing route of the utmost quality, with a tough crux followed by a sizzling runout. Follow *The Bulger* over the overhang. Pull left around the bulge (technical crux). Follow the flake left to its end then climb the slab above on smears and slopers (psycho crux).
Mike Simpkins (1pt), 1960. FFA John Yates, 1969

41 Clive Coolhead... 16m E5 6b ★★
Amazing friction climbing up the steep slab High side runners in *The Bulger* at this grade.
Nick Dixon, 1983

42 The Bulger 16m VS 4c ★
The crack. More difficult than it would first appear and strangely rewarding.
Joe Brown, Don Whillans, 1951

43 Fledgling's Climb 13m S 4a ★
A bold and balancy route. The wall is followed first left, then back right, to finish up the arête above. Protection is awkward, and the route is precarious when damp, so fledglings beware.

44 Wing Wing 9m HS 4a
A bolder variation on the last climb follows the groove in the middle of the wall before a couple of pulls gain the diagonal flake. Rock right onto the triangular ledge above to finish.

45 Little Chimney 9m M
The little chimney can provide a quick way down for the competent.

46 Battery Crack 11m VS 4b
The wide crack just right, with a taxing exit out of the sentry box. Finish up the chimney.

47 Lucas Chimney 11m S 4a ★
A good traditional thrutch up the wide chimney in the corner, swinging left to finish.

48 Goldcrest 20m E7 6c ★★
The left arête of the buttress direct all the way.
Pete Whittaker, 2010

49 Hawkwing 20m E1 5b ★★
This weaves up the face giving sustained climbing, with protection that requires some thought. Follow a curving crack rightwards to join *Kestrel Crack*. Climb this then traverse left via the slanting cracks to finish up the left arête. ◉ opposite page
Al Simpson, Dave Jones, 1978

50 Carrion 19m E3 5c ★
Good climbing, and while it is low in the grade technically, it has an exposed feel. Fun, protectable moves lead over the lower roof to the ledge on *Hawkwing*. Follow the centre of the face above via long stretches between nice rounded breaks.
Gary Gibson, 1980

51 Kestrel Crack 20m HS 4b ★★
A great rounded gritstone tester, varied and well-positioned. Climb a groove with stiff gymnastic moves (or a wedge and a squirm) to gain a ledge. The grand upper crack is made harder or easier depending on which way you face.

Gareth Williams about to embark on the airy traverse of Hawkwing, E1 5b (opposite page), a cocky swagger up the front of a proud bastion of Roaches grit. Photo: Paul Evans

Roaches Lower Tier

52 Sleepy Hollow 10m E10 7a ★★★
Staffordshire's hardest lead. Climb the very blunt arête to reach the triangular roof. With gear on the left, pull directly over the overhang and layback the arête to finish.
Pete Whittaker, 2013

53 Flimney 18m S 4a
Climb a large flake left of the bushes and finish up the crack and corner behind.

54 The Death Knell 10m E4 5c ★★★
One of best Extremes of its type in Staffordshire. Cool route finding, memorable climbing with no room for mistakes. Climb daintily up the slim arête until a committing stride right can be made to the foot of a thin, unhelpful crack. Fine delicate moves with minimal protection lead up this to a gradual easing and the top.
John Yates, Colin Foord, 1970

55 Rhodren 11m HVS 5b ★★
A great climb taking the stepped corner, with constricted undercutting.
Joe Brown, 1958

56 Flake Chimney 14m D ★
A great adventurous little route. Take the edge of the fallen flake, then 'walk the plank' into the corner on the right. The chimney leads to the top.

57 Straight Crack 11m HS 4a
Bridge against the flake to start, then climb the crack just right of *Rhodren*.

58 Punch 11m E3 6b ★
Pure thuggery. Pull into the groove and climb the crack above.
Jonny Woodward, 1978

59 Choka 11m E1 5c ★
The large roof is overcome by gymnastic finger-jamming. Only the small detail of the offwidth above remains.
Joe Brown (1pt), 1958

60 Hunky Dory 10m E3 6a ★★★
A steep Roaches classic that requires a bit of effort. Climb the snaking crack until it is possible to move up and right to a ledge. Commit to the rounded edge up and to the left, from where one or two tricky moves gain easier climbing.
Gabe Regan, 1975

61 Prow Corner 11m VD ★
The corner is a good climb. Climb the tall crack and finish up the spectacular 'flying' crack.

62 Corner Cracks 10m HVD 4a ★
A good variation on the last climb is to stick to the twin cracks on the right all the way, with a well-protected crux. All classic stuff.

Roaches Lower Tier | 55

63 Chalkstorm 10m E3 5c ★
A bold route requiring some concentration. Climb the centre of the slab on sloping holds and rockovers. Traditionally climbed with a side-runner, which reduces the grade to between HVS and E2 depending on how high you place it.
Ian Johnson, Dave Jones, 1977

64 Prow Cracks 11m VD ★
Ascend using both cracks and a variety of technique. If you can't jam, you'll need to bridge and if you can't bridge, then learn to smear. A good first lead. Either crack can be climbed independently at HVD.

65 Commander Energy 12m E2 5c ★★★
A route of tremendous exposure up the 'out there' arête. Climb the rounded right arête of the slab to the triangular roof. Pull over this on a good flake (spike runner) and layback dramatically up the flying arête above.
John Allen, Mark Stokes, 1975

66 Rocking Stone Gully 8m VD
The chunky corner to the right lives up to its name. Elegant semi-layback moves avoid the half-way grovel.

67 Captain Lethargy 8m VD
Climb the well-formed crack right of the corner. Finish on the left.

68 Sifta's Quid 9m HS 4c ★★
An entertaining climb. Climb to the ledge. Now either climb out over the bulge, or for much more fun, squeeze through the tunnel by the huge boulder under the roof. The scene of much amusing thrutching, most of it 'on the spot'. A classic Roaches rite of passage.
John Amies, 1968

69 Obsession Fatale 11m E7 6b ★
The unprotected centre of the slab is climbed direct to its utterly blank and unforgiving crux at the very top. Very high in the grade and with nothing to grab if things aren't going well.
Julian Lines, 1992

70 Piece of Mind 11m E6 6b ★★★
The blunt central arête is a very serious proposition demanding the cleanest of technique and the coolest of heads. Balance up via scoops until a precarious step right can be made onto a faith-in-friction foothold and so the top. One of the first routes of its type on gritstone, well ahead of its time.
Jonny Woodward, Andrew Woodward, 1977

71 The Thin Air 9m E5 6a ★★★
Quality climbing on the right-hand side of the slab, above a serious landing. Starting in a scoop on the left, climb rightwards to a distinctive ripple whence an airy rockover gains the rounded and easily-fluffable top.
Gary Gibson, 1980

STAFFORDSHIRE GRITSTONE
THE ROACHES
The definitive guide to routes and bouldering

Staffordshire has always held a special place in the hearts of climbers in the Peak District and beyond. A place where towering leads, world class boulder problems and favourite solos live in the same neighbourhood as obscure classics, elf-ridden dales and exfoliating horror shows.

Whether you are a first-time visitor after the famous climbs, or a long-time local after something new, this guide will take you to the places you want to go, and show you so much along the way. A guidebook as bright and as lovely and as warm as the golden sunsets that light this, the most beautiful of gritstone counties.

Here is a book that strives to put across that very special feel that Staffordshire has. The popular bits, the secret bits, the big and the small, the terror and the fun. There is an attention to detail here that brings the gritstone to life and makes the book shine brighter than the golden Roaches sunset.

With full coverage of routes and boulder problems from the main area including **The Roaches**, (including the Lower Tier, the Upper Tier, the Skyline and the Five Clouds), the towering terrifying challenges of **Hen Cloud**, and the roughshod joys of **Ramshaw Rocks**. Beyond these are lovely micro-crags delivering Staffs-grade bouldering and micro-routes (Baldstones, Newstones, Gib Torr, Gradbach Hill, Hanging Stone and Back Forest). Also Wingather, Castle Naze and Bosley Cloud. The furthest-flung joys of Staffordshire lie in the **Churnet Valley**, a wild experience like none other.

Featuring:
1,600 routes from Mod to E8
800 boulder problems
5 Font-style bouldering circuits
140 full-colour action shots
The definitive climbing history of the area

Get it from the BMC shop for a lifetime of gritstone action.

http://shop.thebmc.co.uk/

ISBN 978-0-903908-18-4

Front cover: Leanne Callaghan on The Sloth, HVS 5a, Roaches Upper Tier (page 66). Photo: Mike Hutton

Jack-knife laybacks, marginal smears, blind gear and feral jams all come together to make Teck Crack, E1 5c (page 47), among the toughest of the ticks on The Staffordshire Nose. This is the marathon link-up of all the Joe Brown and Don Whillans routes on the Roaches, Hen Cloud and Ramshaw. Few complete this test as it generously offers so many places to give up. Andi Turner climbing. 📷 Dan Lane

ROACHES UPPER TIER

OS Grid Ref: SK 005 625 to SK 006 622
Altitude: 425m

The biggest, most classic and most popular section of the Roaches, with a height and big feel rarely available on any other grit crag. The central sections are all very clean, and sometimes polished. Smaller sections to the left and right are a little quieter.

One of the most impressive aspects is the stature of climbs and, whatever the grade, some of the most memorable days out on grit are on offer here.

Very exposed and quick drying apart from some climbs on the left-hand section that are sheltered by trees. Faces south-west and gets the sun in the afternoon and evening.

Approach: See page 44. The Upper Tier is approached via the steps, through the Lower Tier, to Great Slab; or via a gentle woodland walk under the Lower Tier to a path up to Fern Buttress

LEFT-HAND SECTION
This is the string of smaller buttresses that stretch leftwards from the Main Area. Trees generally come right up to the crag along this section. This gives it a lot of shelter from the wind but means that some climbs are slow to dry.

Descent: There are various scrambling descents along the way but the easiest is skirting the left end of the crag, left of *Rooster*.

Fern Buttress: The leftmost buttress of the Upper Tier, just before the path to the moors above.

1 Rooster   12m   HVD
Climb up sloping holds from leaning blocks to the ledge and tackle the jamming crack above.

2 Chicken Run   12m   S 4a   ★
A bold route. From the blocks, climb up on worrying, polished rock. From the right side of the large ledge, and gear, finish leftwards.

3 Fern Crack   18m   HVD 4b   ★★
A powerful start gains a crack and a flake. Follow these to ledges. Shuffle leftwards round the corner, to follow sloping holds up the right wall of the recess. Bring lots of slings.
AS Pigott, 1931

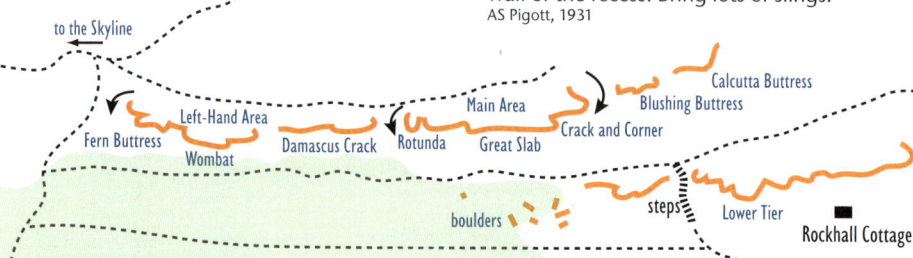

SEE MAP ON PAGE 46

Roaches Upper Tier | 59

Wombat Buttress: To the right lies an area of dramatic overhanging territory, set in tree-enclosed surroundings. The wooded nature of this area affords shelter in windy conditions, the price being some dampness after wet weather.

④ Capitol Climb   14m   HS 4a
A miniature mountain route. Climb the short corner near the left-hand side of the buttress. Step right between the roofs to gain the protruding nose, crux. Move round this to follow the crack on its right then the slab above.
R Handley, Nat Allen, 1954

⑤ Wombat   20m   E2 5b   ★★★
A rapid approach will pay dividends on this, the hard classic. Attain the break below the roof. Good protection is available here, and in the flake early on, but is more dubious further out. Climb to the lip, and pull round on reasonable holds to the wide crack and easy slab above.
Mike Simpkins, 1960

⑥ Walleroo   20m   E2 5c   ★★
More bulging pleasure. Neatly layback the crack to the great block. From the right side of this, difficult, fingery moves lead leftwards through the bulge into a faint groove. Finish easily above.
Mike Simpkins, 1960

⑦ West's Wallaby   23m   HVS 5a   ★★
A great climb that negotiates steep terrain at a modest standard. Climb to the block, then swing dramatically along the break and tackle the obvious steep challenge above. The route originally escaped into the gully at 4c.
Graham West, 1960

⑧ Late Night Final   20m   S 4a
Squirm, curse, and grunt up the overhanging chimney, and continue up the stony gully.
John and Tony Vereker, Graham Martin, 1950s

⑨ Beckermet Slab   15m   HVD 4a   ★
From the foot of the gully, bridge out to gain the horizontal break on the left wall. Swing onto this with difficulty, then move left to the arête. Gain a ledge above and finish up the slabby arête.
A Bowden Black, 1945

⑩ Maud's Garden   21m   VD   ★★
A tricky start that has been bold for nearly 75 years and a thrilling finale, with interesting climbing in between. Follow the well-trodden path up the centre of the slab. This leads to a crack and protection. Press on to the sandy alcove and a possible belay. Wriggle up the chimney then step out left onto the wall, where good holds lead to exposed territory and the top.
A Bowden Black, 1945

Roaches Upper Tier

11 Contrary Mary 15m VS 4b
A tricky pull over the low overhang gains easier ground among a sea of heather. This leads to a break above where the angle changes (not for the better!) and a bold finish up the headwall.

12 Reset Portion of Galley 37 12m HS 4a
Ascend the corner until forced awkwardly right below the roof. Finish up the crack.
Geoff Sutton, 1958

13 Broken Slab 12m VS 4b
A bold start leads to easier climbing with spaced protection. Ascend the wall direct, then bear right to reach a crack. A difficult move starts the crack, which is then followed to the top.
A Bowden Black, 1945

14 Dawn Piper 7m HVS 5b ★
A worthwhile problem up the sharp arête, followed by easier climbing.
John Codling, 1978

15 Runner Route 11m HS 4b ★
From the corner, pad delicately rightwards across the slab. Mantelshelf onto the break (good runner), then move left to the holly and continue up the crack behind it.
Nat Allen, D Campbell, 1955

16 Damascus Crack 12m HS 4b ★★
The polished crack provides excellent protection and good climbing. After reaching the ledge, follow slightly suspect flaky rock up the buttress above. A finish up the short crack in the tower up and left is VS 4b, making a superb exposed finish.
G W S Pigott, W H Craster, 1955

17 Libra 14m HVS 4c ★
The technical crack becomes increasingly tricky near the top. From here, the route wanders left and up a small tower on some awesome pockets.

Aqua Buttress: This is just right of the trees.

18 Central Massif 15m HD
Climb to a large protruding flake on the right, then go direct in the same line to the top.
G Stoneley, R Desmond-Stevens, 1945

19 Aqua 12m VS 4b ★★
One of the better routes in the area. The obvious crack-line through the roof yields easily to finesse. The rest is often covered in an assortment of vegetation but is luckily a lot simpler.
Joe Brown, Don Whillans, 1954

20 Quickbrew 12m E2 5c ★
Stiff! A massive jug in the hanging right arête enables protection to be placed before a cunning move or a desperate pull round the roof on brick edges.
Fred Crook, Ian Barker, 1981

21 Tealeaf Crack 12m HS 4a ★
Climb up to the square overhang. Move around this on the right to a crack. A difficult move up and a step left gain the arête above.

There's something about the Upper Tier of the Roaches that gives the feeling that you ar at the highest point of the earth. With everything beneath him, fresh air and sunshine all about, Josh Plimbley takes three steps to heaven on The Neb Finish, VS 4b (page 64). Pete Wilson

Roaches Upper Tier

GREAT SLAB AREA
A towering bastion of top quality grit, giving routes up to 30m in height, where soaring slabs are punctuated by small ledges and unlikely overhangs. All the routes here have a big feel about them, with lots of splendid multi-pitch adventures and some of the most spectacular roof climbs to be had anywhere. High and exposed, it catches the wind and dries quickly.

㉒ Rotunda Buttress 18m VS 4c
Follow a wide crack for 3m. Move up and left to a ledge. Ascend rightwards, then left to another ledge. Climb the steep final wall.
A Bowden Black, 1945

㉓ Bachelor's Buttress 18m VS 4b ★
Climb the slab leftwards to a ledge on the edge of the gully. The wall to the right is crossed in a very bold diagonal line passing a mantelshelf and enhanced by the exposure below.
A S 'Fred' Pigott, 1922

㉔ Saul's Crack 18m HVS 5a ★★★
Joe Brown's first addition to the Roaches; perfectly protected, but it makes you work for it. Amble up the crack to a niche and make an easier-for-the-short move (at last!) to pass this. Jam the crack above then do the final intimidating bulge. ☉ opposite page
Joe Brown, 1947

㉕ Humdinger 18m E1 5b ★
Climb the wall to a overhang, and a jug on the lip. From here, a tormenting move gains the obvious yet distant hold above.
Mick Guilliard, 1969

㉖ Jeffcoat's Chimney Variations
24m HS 4c ★
The unprotected wall left of the chimney is followed to the cave. Gain the left arête and climb this and the left wall above to the ledge. Boulder up the wall from the right to escape left.

㉗ Jeffcoat's Chimney 24m VD ★★
A historic and cavernous classic of considerable character, one of the Upper Tier's first climbs. The slippery chimney is followed to a ledge (traditional belay). From the left-hand edge of the ledge, move right by a long step and go up to the overlap. Move left to an easy finish.
Stanley Jeffcoat, 1913

㉘ Jeffcoat's Buttress
27m HS 5a ★★★
A tremendous example of pre-War crackcraft, with consistently difficult, varied and enjoyable climbing. A bouldery start (crux) leads to better holds and an easier corner. Follow this, then traverse right above the roof to a ledge (traditional belay). Finish up cracks above.
Stanley Jeffcoat, 1913

㉙ Ruby Tuesday 30m E2 5b ★★
A big undertaking involving both bold and plain hard climbing. A fantastic route.
1 12m 5b Climb directly up to the overhang. Bold moves over this lead to a niche. Delicate climbing leads rightwards to the belay.
2 6m 4c Move left and up to the next belay.
3 12m 5b Follow cracks, then leave these for a bold traverse to gain and climb an overhanging arête and chimney.
Mick Guilliard, John Yates, 1971

When Joe Brown and the Rock and Ice Club first visited The Roaches, they wasted little time before getting stuck into the most appealing lines about, with little respect for steepness or technical difficulty. Here Dominic Oughton gives a bit of modern-day muscle to Saul's Crack, HVS 5a (opposite page), Brown's first addition to the Roaches in 1947. 📷 Paul Evans

Roaches Upper Tier

30 Black and Tans 30m S 4a ★★★
Fred Piggott's stylish swagger up this mighty slab is a righteous climb, classic in every sense.
1 12m 4a Climb a shallow corner to a ledge, then shuffle left to belay in the next corner.
2 18m 3c Climb the corner above and follow a good break left onto the nose. Continue directly via exposed mantelshelves and pockets.
A S 'Fred' Piggott, 1922

31 Black Velvet 27m HVD 4a ★★
Classy climbing taking a good direct line up some impressive terrain. Climb to the first hanging corner, as for *Black and Tans*. Pull steeply up the cracked wall above, and continue to pass the roof on the right.

32 Hollybush Crack 26m HS 4b ★★
The major crack is a fine big pitch with a straddling crux in a prickly situation. Shimmy up cracks left of the holly then step rightwards across (or onto) it. Continue to gain the crack then blast up this to finish up the corner.

33 The Neb Finish 25m VS 4b ★★
Reasonable though rousing climbing, crossing the hanging sidewall. Once over the overhang on *Hollybush Crack*, arrange a high runner. Step down and traverse boldly rightwards to a finish near the arête. 🅾 page 61

34 Technical Slab 23m HS 4a ★★
A brilliant exposed route, high in the grade due to its technicality and seriousness. Ascend the slab, with delicate stretches between well-spaced holds, and distant protection. From below the roof, swing left into *Hollybush Crack*. From here, gaining and finishing up *The Neb Finish* makes for a three-star combination.
A Bowden Black, 1945

35 Pedestal Route 27m HVD 4a ★★★
An outstanding adventure for the grade.
1 12m 4a Climb by any means to the large ledge at 4m. From the centre of this, layback either side of the flake (4a on the left, 3c on the right) to a dainty mantel onto the pedestal, and belay.
2 15m 3c Shuffle leftwards and use the break to gain a standing position. Continue left into *Hollybush Crack* and finish up this, taking care with runners to keep the ropes clear of the infamous rope lock in the crack.
Morley Wood, 1922

A climber leading the bold Central Route, VS 4b (page 66), one of the many ancient tests of bottle to be found on the revered Great Slab. The roof in the background is dominated by the hungry gash of The Sloth, one of the most inspiring and unlikely mid-grade routes in Staffordshire. Niall Grimes

Roaches Upper Tier

36 Painted Rumour 26m E6 6a ★★★
This mighty route attacks the gigantic overhang at its widest, wildest point by some strenuous and scary yarding. Start from *Pedestal Route*. Move up to the roof (gear) then blast outwards to the lip and a rest in the cave (spike runner). This is not a particularly relaxing kind of rest. Pull out leftwards and move up the headwall on sharp rugosities (crux) to finish.
Simon Nadin, Martin Veale, 1985

37 The Sloth 24m HVS 5a ★★★
Superb, intimidating and steeped in legend – a route to bring out your inner Whillans. Climb to The Pedestal. Move up and launch out across the juggy flakes to the lip and wide crack above. ◉ page 56
Don Whillans, Joe Brown, 1953

38 Central Route 15m VS 4b ★★
Serious climbing on small, and rather shiny, holds. Follow the slab directly, then traverse under the overhang to the belay ledge of *Right Route*. High in the grade. ◉ page 65

39 Right Route 24m VD ★★
Morley Wood's early addition is one of the most popular routes on the crag.
1 15m Follow a line of pockets to the roof. Make nervous moves left and then up more easily to the large ledge.
2 9m Balance leftwards above the void to reach the crack. Initially precarious, the climbing soon eases. ◉ page 43
Morley Wood, 1922

40 Right Route Right 15m VS 4b ★
As for *Right Route* to the roof. Thrutch over this to gain the corner and the top.

41 Kelly's Direct 15m E1 5b ★
Climb the thin crack to a ledge. Taking some care to place protection here, move precariously up, right and out to reach a thin flake before making an impressive lunge to a large pocket. Take further pockets from here in a direct line to the top. ◉ opposite page

42 Kelly's Shelf 17m S 4a ★
Using excellent handholds, make an elegant step or graceless flop (delete as appropriate) onto the shelf, then caterpillar along it to a finish up a crack. A fun alternative finish over the bulge to gain pockets is HS 4a.
Harry Kelly, c1930

43 Paralogism 15m E7 6c ★★
Awesome! This Nadin masterpiece is widely acclaimed as one of grit's hardest roofs, featuring blind slappy bouldering in a position of great danger. Starting at the right arête, make committing moves to gain the hanging coffin-shaped feature. A blind slap gains small holds on the left, before crossing the roof leftwards on better holds. From the lip, move right to a careful finish.
Simon Nadin, 1987

Great Slab

Garan Comley on the weaving intricacies of Kelly's Direct, E1 5b (opposite page). David Simmonite

RIGHT-HAND ROCKS

To the right of the lofty Great Slab there lies a string of smaller, friendly buttresses.

Crack and Corner Buttress: Tucked just right of Great Slab is a fun and friendly little buttress with one of the area's great lower-grade classics.

44 Easy Gully Wall 21m S 4a ★
Bold to a ledge, then trend right to a crack and bulge. Move up, then left below the overhang to finish up a wide crack.

45 Jelly Roll 23m VS 4b ★★
A grand outing.
1 8m 4b Climb a thin crack to belay on the block.
2 15m 4a Boldly follow the wall to a spectacular hanging groove. Follow this to finish as for *Crack and Corner*.

46 Roscoe's Wall 11m HVS 5b ★★
Impressive but amenable once the bouldery start is solved. A stiff pull above a worrying landing gains a niche. Swing right and up on fantastic holds and wish that there were more. *Round Table* makes a superb continuation.
Don Roscoe, 1955

47 Crack and Corner 35m HS 4c ★★★
A classic long expedition where you should spare a thought for the original pioneers with tweeds, plimsolls, and no belays.
1 12m 4c Jam, layback and curse your way up the polished, undercut crack.
2 8m Wander left along the ledge to a belay.
3 15m 4a Pockets above lead to a ledge on the left. The corner then leads to a superb and thrilling final overhang.
Morley Wood, 1922

48 Babbacombe Lee 11m E1 5b ★
A broken line, but giving good exposure. Boulder up the left hand end of the undercut wall, and follow a short crack to a contorted rest. A bold and reachy finale over the protruding nose ensues.
Dave Jones, 1978

49 Hangman's Crack 11m S 4a
An interesting climb. The right-hand side of the wall leads to a large black roof flake. Step left to attack the wide crack. Small cams useful.
G W S Pigott, C Topping, 1949

The next route starts from the upper ledge and makes a great combination with Roscoe's Wall.

50 Round Table 11m E1 5a ★★
A route of surprisingly low grade taking the impressive crack and finishing at the highest point of the buttress. Steep and committing moves lead into the wide crack. Swing right across the bulge to an easy finish.
John Allen, Nick Colton, Steve Bancroft, 1974

Crack and Corner

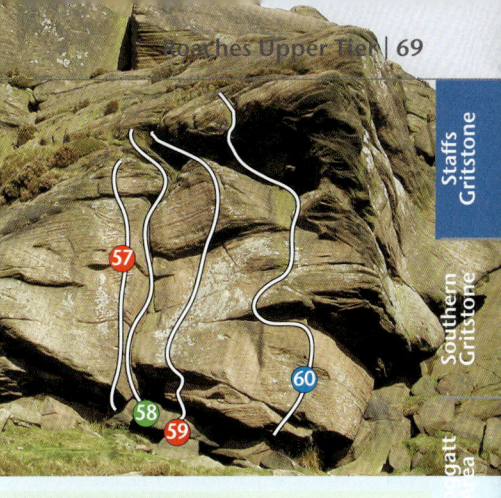

BLUSHING BUTTRESS
Down and to the right is a fine buttress with good routes based on strong cracks and friendly flakes.

51 Scarlet Wall 11m HS 4b
Crank up the crack on the left of the buttress and move right to a large ledge. Move carefully up to a thread runner and precarious exit.
G W S Pigott, C Topping, 1949

52 Left-Hand Route 13m HVD 4a ★
Good climbing, steep at the start then delicate above. Layback the hanging flake past the left-hand end of a roof, then trend upwards.
Lindlay Henshaw, 1924

53 Right-Hand Route 13m S 4b ★★
An elegant line, steep and clean. A hard layback start on shiny footholds leads to a ledge. From here tackle the roof crack above.
Lindlay Henshaw, 1924

54 Gully Wall 9m VS 4b
Trend steeply left up the fun flakes.

55 The Rib 8m M
The right-hand rib of the gully, and started by coming in from the gully. HS 4b if started direct.

56 Rib Wall 8m VD
Climb the front wall of the buttress in a good position passing a niche and a large ledge in as direct a line as possible.

CALCUTTA BUTTRESS
The next pert little buttress is again home to a clutch of fine steep routes on good rock.

57 Sign of the Times 8m E1 5c
Boulder up the arête and continue easily.
Dave Jones, 1978

58 Calcutta Crack 6m S 4b ★★
An awkward start leads to steep satisfying climbing on ideal jams.
G W S Pigott, C Topping, 1949

59 Mistral 6m E2 6a ★
A fierce boulder problem start leads to a short wall and bomber gear in a large break. From here, tackle the small prow on small holds.
Gary Cooper, Fred Crook, 1987

60 Calcutta Buttress 11m VS 5b ★
Hard pulls up and then left gain a mantelshelf. Continue right to a niche, then escape left.

Blushing Buttress

THE SKYLINE

OS Grid Ref: SK 001 636 to SK 005 625
Altitude: 480m

Peace, solitude and some of the best slab routes on gritstone can be found at the Skyline. It is effectively a continuation of the Roaches crag along the moor's edge beyond the Upper Tier. A series of short but perfectly formed isolated buttresses, as well as awesome views, will greet you. The lack of visitors, however, is definitely not an indication of the quality of climbing, and make no mistake about it, here you'll find some of the best routes about.

The crag consists of a number of individual buttresses. These can offer surprising shelter from the wind due to the close proximity of trees, but are otherwise very open to all other weather. Lots of afternoon and evening sun.

THE FAR SKYLINE
Three diminutive but sublime slabs lie below the path, in the final reaches of the Skyline. From left to right these are the fabled Hard Very Far Skyline, Very Far Skyline and Art Nouveau, all within 200m of each other. Coming from Roach End, the path goes past a small outcrop, with another outcrop just below. Hard Very Far Skyline Buttress is about 100m after this, its rocky top visible from the path. 80m after this is Very Far Skyline Buttress, and 100m after this is Art Nouveau. This is also identified by a clump of boulders perched atop it. About 15 minutes from Roach End and 30 from The Roaches parking.

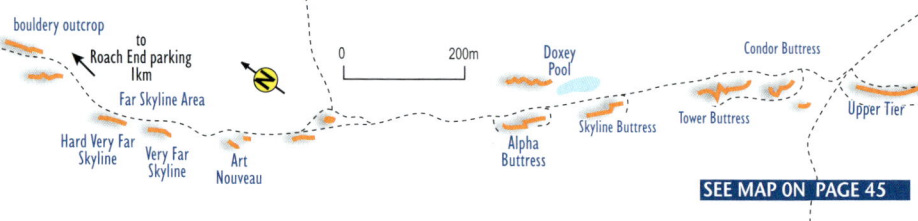

Approach: See page 44. Park as for the Roaches or at Roach End, depending on where you are going. Approach times are given throughout the text and are (left) from Roach End and (right) from the Roaches parking. It is best to return to the top path when moving between areas.

Hard Very Far Skyline Buttress: Totally awesome, mega, wow! Belays are hard to find on the top.

❶ Willow Farm   10m   E4 6a   ★★
On the left side of the buttress is a neat little slab capped by a sloping gangway. Gain the right edge of this slab from the left and move up on tiny edges. A long reach over the top of the gangway may find a good hold, but some precise footwork is required to reach easy ground. Worth three stars on any other buttress!
Chris Hamper, 1977

The Skyline | 71

Hard Very Far Skyline Buttress

❷ Track of the Cat 12m E5 6a ★★★
One of the finest E5s on grit, based on the left arête of the slab. From around the corner slightly to the left, powerful moves lead into a groove and small protection. Careful climbing rightwards from here leads to a pull round onto the slab and twin pockets. The immaculate arête above culminates in a exhilarating final move, with the gear a distant memory.
Jonny & Andrew Woodward, 1977

❸ Inspiration Point 14m E2 5c ★★
A great way to see this slab at a more reasonable grade starting up *Track...*, traversing the slab with hands in pockets, then down slightly to gain and finish up *Prelude...* page 19
Gary Gibson, 1979

❹ Nature Trail 11m E5 6b ★★
Cool smearing. A strenuous direct start through the roof leads onto the slab and protection in *Wings...* and *Track...* From a standing position in pockets, smear directly to the top of the crag.
Simon Nadin, 1985

❺ Wings of Unreason 11m E4 6a ★★★
A brilliant climb, and appropriately named, taking the centre of the beautiful slab direct via unusual pockets. A powerful start gains the slab, then pockets (cams). Stand in these then use all your skill, commitment and intuitive understanding of the sheer magic of gritstone to fly to the cragtop jugs, an experience unlike anything else ever. Or lank it.
Jonny & Andrew Woodward, 1977

❻ Counterstroke of Equity 11m E5 6c ★
The hardest climbing on the slab. Follow *Wings...* to the pocket. Step down and right on a thin horizontal seam and smear fiercely to a scary top move.
Richard Davies, 1985

❼ Prelude to Space 10m HVS 4c ★★
A sample of the quality on offer, at a more reasonable price. The right edge of the slab is unprotected, technical and far too brief. page 73
Andrew & Jonny Woodward, 1977

Alpha Buttress · Skyline Buttress · Tower Buttress · Condor Buttress

Very Far Skyline Buttress: A worthy twin, not as tall, not as wide, but just as good.

8 Triple Point 7m E1 5c ★
Start as for *Wild Thing* then step left and climb the arête.
Andrew & Jonny Woodward, 1982

9 Wild Thing 7m E1 5c ★★
From the large jug pocket, gain a distant edge. The groove provides perfect delicate movement for the confident. Beautiful.
Andrew & Jonny Woodward, 1977

10 Entropy's Jaw 7m E5 6b ★★★
From the standing position on *Wild Thing*, step right to climb the thin seam by even thinner smearing, thumb sprags, and magic footwork.
Andrew Woodward (solo), 1982

11 Script for a Tear 7m E6 6c ★
Ultra-thin smearing up the steep, blank slab.
Simon Nadin, 1985

12 Mild Thing 7m D
Climb the propped-up flake then the little crack above.
Andrew & Jonny Woodward, 1977

Art Nouveau Buttress: A fine gallery containing a gritstone masterpiece. One of the best features on grit.

13 Art Nouveau 7m E6 6c ★★★
The perfectly-formed overlap provides the perfect gritstone experience. When the solution is unlocked it gives one of the best sequences on grit and is one of the great trophies of Staffordshire climbing. Very highball Font 7B.
Simon Nadin, 1985

Art Nouveau Buttress

Don't tell any one, but this is possibly the best slab of gritstone anywhere. The rock here on Hard Very Far Skyline Buttress, along with that on Very Far and Art Nouveau Buttresses, and on the Clouds below, is gold standard gritstone. The slabs bequeath climbers just a few gems across the grades. Here Dave Hudson solos Prelude to Space, HVS 4c (page 71), on a beautiful gritstone evening. 📷 Pete Wilson

ALPHA BUTTRESS

A fine quiet area packed with quality lines and a varied mix of grades. While the crag is not that tall, the routes here definitely pack a punch. It sits below the path about 50m on the Far Skyline side of Doxey Pool, the pool of dark water beside a small bouldering outcrop.

14 Melaleucion 7m HVS 5a ★
Steep climbing over the bulges on the front face. A tough, though honest little gem.
Steve Dale, Barry Marsden, 1976

15 Devotoed 7m VS 4c ★
The crack to an awkward sloping finish.
Gary Gibson, 1979

16 Alpha 7m D
The groove is hard work but well-protected.

17 Alpha Arête 7m HVD
The blocky right arête. Sweet.

18 Formative Years 7m E3 6a
The cute narrow slab looks temptingly escapable. Oddly, it is an altogether different story when high up above the unfriendly landing!
Howard Tingle (solo), 1982

19 Breakfast Problem 7m VD ★
The merging twin cracks provide tons of protection, and good climbing. A good first lead.
North Staffs. M.C., 1950s

20 Days Gone By 7m S 4b
The right-hand of the three parallel cracks. Quite hard if done strictly, but suffers from its interfering easier neighbour.
Gary Gibson, 1978

21 San Melas 8m E3 5c ★★★
A classic of the area. Climb the lower slab to gain the break. Take a deep breath, and commit yourself to a series of high steps and rockovers, with very little in the way of handholds. Pleasant balancy exercise for gritstone divas.
Andrew & Jonny Woodward, 1977

22 Hallow to our Men 9m E4 6b ★
A harder, right-hand twin to *San Melas* via the shallow scoop on the smallest of edges and smears.
Gary Gibson, 1981

23 Mantis 8m E1 5c ★★
The arête, started on the right, is hardest on its unprotected lower section.
Andrew Woodward, 1974

24 Sennapod 7m D
The deep grassy corner.
Gary Gibson 1978

25 Sennapod Crack 8m VD
Climb the crack just right of *Sennapod*.

26 Wallaby Wall 10m S 4a ★
An awkward start leads to an excellent series of moves up the wall to a ledge and then across to the left-hand of the two upper flakes.
North Staffs. M.C., 1950s

27 Definitive Gaze 10m E1 5c
Balance up into a scoop and make a tricky exit on the left. Finish direct avoiding the flakes of neighbouring routes.
Gary Gibson, 1979

28 Right-Hand Route 12m S 4a ★
Climb the crack and chimney until a traverse left leads to the right-most of two flakes.

29 Looking for Today 8m HVS 5b ★
Nice climbing following the line of the thin seam up the slab.

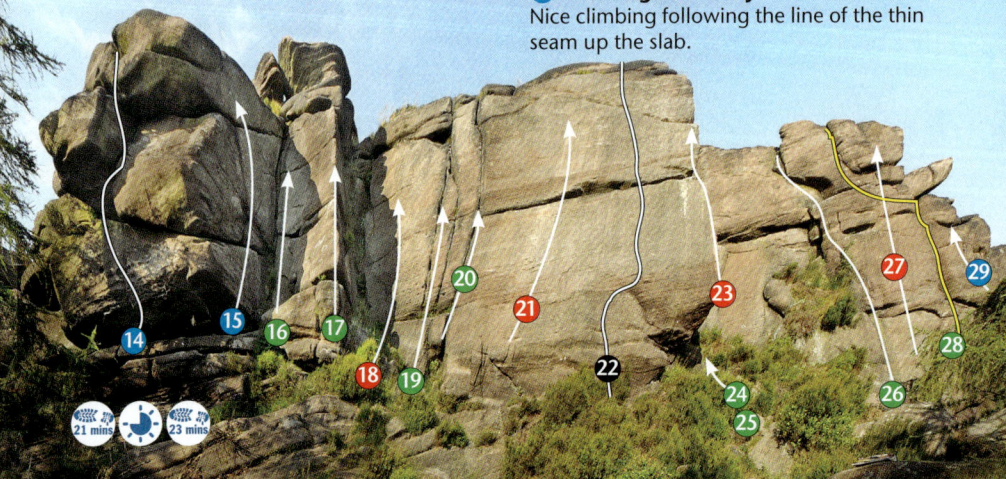

The Skyline

SKYLINE BUTTRESS
The tallest face that the Skyline has to offer. It has a good mixed grade selection of long classics, guaranteed not to disappoint. It is directly below the dark waters of Doxey Pool.

30 Mantelshelf Slab 10m VS 4b ★
A character-building slab climb requiring some conviction. The central line up the slab involves a technical mantelshelf and continues into bolder and bolder (though easier and easier) territory.
Karabiner Club members, 1947

31 Enigma Variation 10m E1 5a ★★
A bold but well-behaved route. Balance across to the right arête and follow it by straightforward moves in a bold position to a useful knobble and a gear placement a little too far round the arête for comfort. Move up and then break out left onto the slab.
Andrew & Jonny Woodward, 1976

32 Karabiner Chimney 12m HVD ★
The pleasant chimney gives good climbing right to the very end.
R Desmond-Stevens, 1945

33 Karabiner Slab 12m HVS 4c
The central line on the narrow slab.

34 Karabiner Cracks 12m M
The cracks and chimney.
Karabiner Club members, 1945

35 Acid Drop 15m E4 5c ★★★
A gem that could have escaped from Bosigran. Continue up above the traverse of *Slab and Arête* to the arching overlap. Make a height-dependent move to gain a good hold and 'thank-God' gear under the roof, which provides a baffling but enjoyable contrast.
Jonny Woodward, 1979

36 Slab and Arête 18m S 4a ★★★
A classic route that builds to an exposed crescendo. At this grade, avoid the now-polished and desperate start up the pocketed slab (5a), by moving in from the left. Traverse the half-height break all the way to a memorable finish up the right edge of the buttress.
G Stoneley, R Desmond-Stevens, 1945

37 Skytrain 10m E1 5b ★
The leftwards-leaning crack provides a pleasantly technical outing leading onto *Slab and Arête* to finish. The original continued rather artificially up the slab to a bold finish at E2.
Jerry Peel, Tony Barley, 1973

38 Slips 8m E3 6b ★
The undercut right arête has hard-as-nails moves to reach the sloping crack and easier arête of *Slab and Arête*. The *Strapadictomy* of western grit!
Gary Gibson, 1982

39 Sidecrack 13m VS 4c
The crack in the sidewall, finishing up the wall.

TOWER BUTTRESS AREA

An excellent concentrated selection of low- and mid-grade routes can be found here. The longer routes on the Tower will bring a smile to the face of any jaded mountaineer. Almost all the routes are clean and quick drying.

40 Tower Eliminate 15m HVS 5b ★
Around to the left, a steep disjointed crack near the arête leads to a niche. From here, either finish up another crack or, better, or up the arête.
Colin Foord, Dave Salt, 1967

41 Curiosity Kitten 15m E3 6a ★
Climb the arête left of *Tower Face*, over a roof to a break, and a meeting with *Tower Eliminate*, gear. Move right and follow the bold arête.
Graham Cole, Kenny Atherton, Alison Trinder, 1999

42 Tower Face 15m E2 5b ★★
A classic hard route. The flaky crack leads to a slanting break and protection. The awkward short crack leads to a bold stretch to sloping holds. Finish directly up another flaky groove.
Al Simpson, Dave Jones, 1977

43 Tower Chimney 18m D ★
The flaky frontal chimney of the tower is a long, traditional treat.
A Simpson, R Desmond-Stevens, 1945

44 Perched Block Arête 15m VD 4a ★★
The arête, climbed largely on its right, from its lowest point to the top block from where a short deviation becomes necessary. Gain a final chimney on the left (VS 4b direct).

45 Thrug 10m VS 4c ★★
The steep jamming crack splitting the right wall has a macho air about it.

46 Bad Poynt 7m D
Start at a perched block and climb up it to a slab and crack.
Ray Baddley, Terry Pointon, 1968

47 Oversight 10m VD
A good climb at the grade. The left arête of the gully, without sticking to any particular side.

48 Ogden 10m VD ★
The well-trodden path up the crack gives good practice for the harder lines in the area.
John & Tony Vereker & NSMC members, 1950s

49 Ogden Arête 8m HS 4b ★★
The left side of the clean-cut arête has a steep, technical start and an airy finish.
◉ page 79

50 Ogden Recess 8m VD
Follow the chimney in its entirety. Good fun.

51 The Black Pig 8m VS 4c ★★
Use the chimney to make initial vertical progress but forsake this as soon as is possible in favour of the thin, rightwards-slanting crack. The VS climber's *London Wall*, but not as well protected!

52 Spare Rib 8m VS 4b ★
The rib left of the gully, started from its base on its left side, gives technical climbing requiring a bold approach, to reach and leave the mid-height protection.
Jonny & Andrew Woodward, 1977

Tower Buttress

53 Bad Sneakers 8m E2 5c ★
The slab just right of the gully requires balance, bottle and actually quite good sneakers. Purists will climb direct up the middle (E3 5c), pragmatists will trend slightly left.
Dave Jones, 1977

54 Spectrum 8m VS 4c
Quite a technical route, which gains the final layback crack via a faint groove.
Jonny & Andrew Woodward, 1977

55 Middleton's Motion 10m VS 5a ★
A tough lead via an obstinate crack.

56 Strain Station 12m E4 5c
Extremely bold, even for the grade. Climb the roof and blunt arête to the left of *Topaz*. It is gained direct or from the right.
Gary Gibson, 1981

57 Topaz 10m E2 5b ★★
A fun runout with a safe fall-out zone. The rib leads straightforwardly to the roof. The slanting crack above provides good holds and protection. Fire on to the ramp and up this with excitement.
Gary Gibson, 1979

58 Letter Box Gully 10m M
Climb up and under the huge jammed block.

59 Letter Box Cracks 7m VS 4c
From the gully, attack the block direct using cracks on either side.

60 Paul's Puffer 10m E4 6b ★
Hard labour. Climb up to the roof and over this via the wide crack.
Paul Mitchell, 1989

61 Safety Net 10m E1 5b ★★★
Classic, with a bit of everything. The blunt rib beneath a roof is gained via a powerful start. A thought-provoking but well-protected move gains the roof. From here layback to glory!
John Allen, Steve Bancroft, Tom Proctor, 1975

62 Shortcomings 10m E1 5c ★★
The attractive wall and beckoning flake provide a superb challenge. However, the route is well-named and the crucial moves to the flake are height-dependent.
Gary Gibson, 1978

63 Left Twin Crack 8m HS 4a
The groove and crack on the left of the chimney.

64 Square Chimney 8m D
The chimney in the left-hand corner.

65 Trio Chimney 8m VD
The chimney in the right-hand corner. Start inside the cleft and remember to exit before it closes off.

66 Substance 8m VS 4c
The left arête on its steep left-hand side.
Gary Gibson, 1978

67 Lighthouse 10m VD ★
After a tricky start, follow a beckoning line of shallow grooves in the centre of the buttress.
John & Tony Vereker & NSMC members, 1950s

68 Ralph's Mantelshelves 8m S 4a
From the bottom right-hand end of the buttress, trend up and left by a series of ledges.

The Skyline

CONDOR BUTTRESS
A great introduction to the Skyline. From the Upper Tier, follow a small climber's path that breaks off from the main path, under a subsidiary buttress and via a rickety fence, to the foot of the wall. The routes are clean and on sound rock.

69 Condor Slab 12m VS 4c ★
A bold and very rewarding route requiring some faith in your ability. Start up a short crack and make tenuous moves up and left to the obvious hole, whence a trying move leads upwards to a ledge. Step right and finish centrally.

70 A.M. Anaesthetic 14m VS 4c ★
The blunt rib gives testing climbing.
Gary Gibson, 1978

71 Cracked Arête 15m HVD 4a
A pleasant two-tier route. Starting from a lower level, opposite the large boulder, climb the arête. From the ledge, follow the slab and flake crack above.

72 Condor Chimney 8m VD ★
The chimney gives the impression of offering a deadly struggle, but a confident approach transforms it into a pleasant bridging exercise.

73 Nosepicker 8m HVS 5b ★
Move delicately up to the overhang and, for once, take the easy way out, avoiding it to the left by delicate moves. Finish directly.
Jonny Woodward (solo), 1975

74 Time to be Had 8m VD
Just right of the easy corner is a cracked wall.
Gary Gibson, 1978

75 Tobacco Road 8m VS 4c ★
Take a direct line up the wall.

76 Wheeze 8m HVS 4c ★
Climb the initial arête to a break and runners, then use both balance and reach to move onto the upper arête.
Jonny Woodward, 1976

77 Bruno Flake 8m VS 4b ★
The corner leads to steep, awkward and powerful climbing through the roof/flake crack (large cam useful). Tough, but a good trophy.

78 Navy Cut 7m VD
Climb the niche to the left to a chimney above. Either wedge yourself in and battle to make vertical progress or, for the claustrophobic, move slightly right and apply a somewhat more open approach.

79 Chicane 7m S 4a
The clean, blunt arête. Very tough moves lead straight off the block (or, better, start up the crack just right) and pass to the left of a small roof. Finish past a shallow pocket.
Gary Gibson, 1978

80 Lung Cancer 7m S 4b
Starting just right of a block, climb left under a roof. Move up, then go back right below another overlap using a crucial jam to contort through an awkward move.
Jonny & Andrew Woodward, 1977

The Skyline; beautiful name, beautiful part of the world. Leave the popular delights of the Upper Tier behind, take yourself up to the edge of things. In less than 200m you can be here, by yourself, above it all. Ogden Arête, HS 4b (page 76). Rebecca Ting on the airy finish. 📷 Paul Evans

THE FIVE CLOUDS

OS Grid Ref: SK 000 627
Altitude: 420m

The Five Clouds are the string of outcrops punctuating the subsidiary ridge below the Skyline area of the Roaches, clearly visible from the road leading to Roach End. These are little gems of crags that are similar to, and rank with the best to be found on the Skyline. Only the Third, Fourth and Fifth Clouds are included here.

The setting gives the crags a delightfully peaceful and isolated ambience, heightened by almost guaranteed solitude, making the area feel a hundred miles from the hectic Roaches nearby. Very clean, compact rock. Quick-drying and relatively sheltered; climbing is possible all year round. Faces south-west, getting sun from late morning.

Approach: See map on page 45. Once inside the access gate, turn immediately left along a quarry track. Where the track turns uphill into the quarry and towards the Upper Tier, follow a smaller track straight on, passing under the First and Second Clouds (not described) to reach the Third Cloud in around 10 minutes. Do not approach directly from below the crag.

Access: Occasional bird restrictions will be clearly sign-posted. Please observe these restrictions. Generally, although nominally in the designated 'quiet area' exclusion zone, there have been no problems as long as the proper approach is used. Please respect the privacy of the cottages and the atmosphere of the place by keeping the noise down.

THE FIFTH CLOUD
Starting with the furthest of the clouds. It's quite small but the rock is peerless.

Fifth Cloud

1 Cloud Nine 10m E2 5b ★
A little sweetie. Swing up right onto the arete (or go direct at 6a) to a ledge. Continue up the slab above with crisp moves.
Jonny Woodward, Andy Woodward, 1977

2 Fifth Cloud Eliminate 10m HVS 5a ★
From the ledge on *Cloud Nine*, Move across the slab to gain and follow a scoop.
John Yates, 1969

Graeme Hammond savours the peerless Clouds gritstone on Private Display, E1 5b (page 82). For lovers of solitude, a day of classic-bagging along these gorgeous bluffs, with a cool breeze and a bright sun as your companions, will live long in your gritstone heart. 📷 Paul Evans

THE FOURTH CLOUD

Not as big and impressive as its neighbouring Third Cloud, but it still offers fine technical climbs on the best of rock. Mostly, the landings are superb and therefore ideal for a picnic or for falling on to!

3 Meander 8m HVD ★
A pleasant route starting up the slab on its right-hand side, then moving leftwards on the upper slab to the top. If only it were longer!

4 Smun 9m VS 4c ★
Climb the crack, bypassing the overhang on the left, and continuing up the corner above to a demeaning finish onto the grassy ledge.

5 Left Block Crack 5m HS 5a
The left-hand twin.

6 Right Block Crack 9m HS 4c
The right-hand twin.

7 Private Display 9m E1 5b ★
An intimidating route; tough with obscure, absorbing moves. Start on the rock on the left and climb the vague rib and thin crack above.
page 81
John Yates, 1970

8 Boysen's Delight 9m HVS 5c ★★
Getting into the groove is pleasantly tricky and the protection is guaranteed to make you smile. Finish up the crack above.
Martin Boysen, 1968

9 Mirror, Mirror 10m E5 6b ★★
Lovely rock. Climb the sharp iron-rich rugosities to the sloping break (place nuts up and right here). Skip left into the undercut arch and gain the thin crack. Finish more easily.
Andrew Woodward (solo), 1979

10 Mantelshelf Route 8m VD 4a ★
Rock up and up to the top via the ledges.

11 Chockstone Corner 6m VD
Every crag needs one!

12 Roman Candle 7m HVS 5b
Stride left off the block and pull into the well-protected thin crack.
John Bull, Dave Garnett, 2002

13 Roman Nose 7m E2 5b
Bold and hairy. Step off the block and climb the middle of the slab on little bendy flakes to the top. Protection is minimal, and the holds might snap off.
Dave Jones, Ian Johnson, John Gilbert, 1977

THE THIRD CLOUD

The largest and finest of the Clouds, with an imposing sheer face and a clutch of excellent routes spread across a range of grades. Sunny, great climbs and perfect rock. The first two routes are accessed across the ledge from the left.

14 Glass Back 5m HVD 4a
The steep crack at the left end of the terrace.

15 Elastic Arm 5m HVS 5b
Gain the wide crack from the left and scrabble up it using all points of contact.

16 Cloudbusting 8m E4 6b ★
A real boulder problem in the sky. Start as for *Rubberneck*, place a high runner, then climb the sickle-shaped flakes on the left to their termination. Sketch rapidly leftwards across the slab, mantel up and clutch at the grass.
Simon Nadin, 1986

Fourth Cloud

The Five Clouds | 83

17 Rubberneck 15m HVS 5a ★★★
An exemplary route, sustained, technical and well-protected; the classic of the crag. Start at the base of the scoop, dislocate your femur from your pelvis, and move up to the crack above (crux), where superb runners can be placed. Swarm up the crack and finish up the slab above, elated.
Robin & Tony Barley, 1967

18 Appaloosa Sunset 16m E3 5c ★★★
An exquisite solution to the 'blank' slab. Climb *Rubberneck* or it's right arête, and at 3m, launch rightwards along the diagonal line of holds, until a series of delicate and precise rockovers leads towards a jug. This is hard to gain and even harder to leave! Wander to the top past an obscure circular hole. Gear is placed high in *Rubberneck* at this grade.

⊙ page 44
Dave Jones, Ian Johnson, John Gilbert, 1977

19 Laguna Sunrise 15m E6 6c ★
A hard and serious start to *Appaloosa*. Climb just right of the cave to stand in a break. Move up onto a flake, then scamper, scrape and slip up left to the *Appaloosa* jug.
Simon Nadin, 1984. Without side-runners, Andi Turner, 2007

20 Crabbie's Crack Left-Hand
   16m   HVS 4c ★★
A fine alternative to the mother crack follows flakes leftwards at the steepening.
John Yates, 1968

21 Crabbie's Crack 15m HVS 5a ★★★
Crack climbing of the utmost quality, at the upper limit of the grade. Climb the perfect jamming crack to arrive, exhausted, on a ledge. Finish up a little crack or, for an excellent delicate contrast, climb up and right to finish up the arête – the **Flaky Wall Finish**, HVS 5a ★★★.
Bob Downes, Nea Morin, 1950s. Flaky Wall Finish, Colin Foord, 1968

22 Flower Power Arête 15m E2 5c ★
From the rib left of the windy cave, climb to a small ledge. Balance up into the rounded flaky scoop, make a long move to a layback flake and follow it to the ledge above. Jam yourself in the tight chimney and squirm to the top.
Martin Boysen, 1968

23 Icarus Allsorts 15m E4 6a ★★
A wonderful name for a wonderful climb. Pull through the roof of the cave to gain the top of the jutting block. Step back across left to gain a flake and get onto the slab above the roof, and follow this to the ledge at the base of the wide corner crack. Step left and climb the arête in an exhilarating position, taking care not to fall off, as the gear leaves something to be desired.
Al Simpson, Dave Jones, 1977

24 The Little Flake 8m HVS 5a
Overcome the small overhang with a hard pull.

25 The Big Flake 7m HS 4c ★
Wriggle, wiggle and writhe up the chimney. Superb.

Third Cloud

HEN CLOUD

OS Grid Ref: SK 008 617
Altitude: 380m

The massive gritstone fortress of Hen Cloud is without doubt one of the most noble and majestic crags in the whole of the Peak District. Proudly guarding the summit of a steep hillside, its impending walls rise abruptly from the escarpment and, to those unused to the crag, project the forbidding impression of a grim fortification. On closer acquaintance, the crag will indeed be found to be steep; however, it is far from impregnable. Get to grips with the climbs here and you will tend to find good holds and generally sound protection, making them welcoming, while still retaining a formidable level of challenge.

With its elevation and aspect, Hen Cloud is a superb crag to visit when the sun shines and, especially on summer evenings, is a great place to watch the sun set. In colder, and especially windy weather its exposed position can be keenly felt and sometimes, in the wetter months, parts of the crag become green.

Approach: See map on page 45. Parking is available in the lay-bys on the road below the crag, but beware the restrictions on parking on the verges, which are periodically ruthlessly enforced. From the gate on the road, walk along the unmetalled lane that runs under the crag. A track leads to the Central Area from the first bend or, a little further on, a larger one runs up to the middle of the crag. Both are steep warm ups (10 minutes).

Access: In recent years Peregrine Falcons have taken a liking to parts of the crag and have reared young successfully thanks to climbers' co-operation. Notices will be placed on site to advise climbers and mark out any restricted area. This will normally be in force from early March to mid-June. Up-to-date information can be found on the BMC's Regional Access Database.

For the confident E4 leader, Hen Cloud has a hat-trick of absolute blockbusters at the grade which severely test the leader's skills in gunning it out when the pressure is on, albeit with good protection in case you run out of ammo. Chameleon, Caesarian and this one, Borstal Breakout (page 90). Mega. Lisa Rands climbing the first pitch. 📷 Alex Messenger

Hen Cloud

PINNACLES AREA
The first area of crag is a distinctive row of pinnacles. The rock on some of the areas can be sometimes a bit scratchy and the routes a little shorter than on the main sections, but they are great routes nonetheless.

① November Cracks 12m HS 4b
Climb the cracks on the front face to the ledge, then the corner crack behind. Good stuff!
Arthur Burns, 1927

② Bulwark 12m E1 5a ★
Exposed situations combined with thoughtful protection and some rather soft and sandy holds make for a memorable lead. Start on the right wall of the tower, and tiptoe out to the arête, whereupon a tricky move gains a scratchy ledge. Delicate climbing now leads up to an awkward finish on good flutes.
Clive Shaw, 1957

③ Slowhand 11m E1 5b ★★
Bulwark's smarter brother which follows the scoop just right. From the recess near the gully, pull out left and move up to a deep flake crack. The blind flake above is used to gain the airy summit.
Dave Jones, Roger Bennion, Gary Gibson, 1978

④ Master of Reality 11m E6 6c ★★★
A contender for the best E6 in the county; a stunning route with consistently fine climbing, based on the dinosaur's spine of grit running up the front of the pinnacle. Work up the lower wall on positive features and marginal pro. At the break, place good medium nuts and cams, take a deep breath, and let rip, aiming for the next break. Inspirational.
Simon Nadin, 1983

⑤ Chicken 12m E1 5b ★★
A really good route with plenty of variety. Follow the steep crack that cleaves the buttress to a break. Swing right to a ledge, then back left up an unnerving scoop to the top.
Tony Nicholls, 1960s

⑥ The Mandrake 10m E5 6a ★
From *Victory* (and a runner level with the overlap), make a powerful hand-traverse leftwards to the brittle flake on the arête and finish boldly up this. Seldom repeated.
Jonny Woodward, 1979

⑦ Victory 9m VS 4c
The crack to the right; nice climbing.

⑧ Electric Chair 9m E3 5c ★★
The line of least resistance. Climb the right edge of the wall to a ledge, then traverse left to a crack and the first protection. From here, good moves lead up and right into a final scoop. Bold.
Jim Moran, Simon Horrox, 1978

⑨ Gallows 8m E2 5b ★
The hanging arête is bold and tricky. Climb the arête on its left to a disappointing break. Swing quickly right and gain the summit using a pocket.
Jim Moran, Simon Horrox, 1978

The Pinnacles

⑩ Recess Chimney 7m VD
Climb the chimney, then either exit to the top.

⑪ Black Eyed Dog 8m E6 6b ★
The rounded arête right of the chimney, gained from the ledge, leads with greater and greater difficulty to a rounded finish. Unprotected.
Andy Popp, 1987

⑫ The Sorcerer 8m E3 6a ★
The wicked crack on the front has a bouldery start, then a continually technical and rounded battle all the way to the top. A good climb.
Jim Moran, Al Evans, 1978

⑬ High Tensile Crack 8m HVS 5b ★
The little corner crack just right has a strenuous start on stiff hand jams, but soon relents.
Colin Foord, 1962

Black Wall: The flat wall at the lower level is home to a number of fingery climbs. Unfortunately, it seeps badly, but when dry, the routes offer excellent climbing.

⑭ A Flabby Crack 10m E6 6c ★★
A line of hopeless seams and nothing finger-pockets is followed to a desperate final move. Well protected, but desperate.
Neil Travers, 1992

⑮ The Stone Loach 10m E5 6b ★★
A very good climb combining a powerful and technical first half with something altogether different in the second. Cracks lead upwards with difficulty and good protection, to the wide break. Finish up the prehistoric gash above; longer than it looks.
Gary Gibson, 1981

⑯ Myxi 10m E6 6c ★
Climb the wall between *Anthrax* and *The Stone Loach* with a fingery crux a long way above any protection. Finish up *The Stone Loach*.
Andi Turner, 2008

⑰ Anthrax 14m E4 6a ★★
A varied battle up two very different sizes of crack. The thin bit; a bouldery start leads to nice holds and protection. The crack above is steep and tough to the very end. Now the thick bit; at the break, traverse left and climb the tough upper gash of *The Stone Loach*.
Steve Bancroft, John Allen, 1975

⑱ Bantam Crack 10m VS 4c ★
Fine jamming up the varied hand crack. Less pleasant when the top is dirty, although a prior inspection and cleaning is easy.

Black Wall

88 | Hen Cloud

> **DELSTREE AREA**
> Big, strenuous cracks on sound rock. Steepness gives a continually challenging feel to the routes, although they also tend to be well-protected and superb.

19 Chockstone Crack 11m HVD
A deep and meaningful experience up the rocky cleft.

20 The Better End 11m E3 6a ★★
A forceful crack climbs a leaning wall. Ascend said crack to a sloping ledge. With protection placed, set sail on the butch leaning layback – somewhat alarming – which leads to the surface. Excellent.
Dave Salt (1pt), 1962. FFA John Allen, Steve Bancroft, 1975

21 En Rappel 12m HVS 4c ★★
A couple of exposed mantels lead into a ramp-line. Follow this to a good ledge. From here, pull out left onto the crest of the crag, and over onto the heather above.
Arthur Burns, 1927

22 Caesarian 12m E4 6b ★★★
The centre of the steep wall is brilliant; top of the range, in every sense, with just about every move being 5c or more. Boulder up past vertical flakes to reach slanting breaks and good gear. An almighty move from here gains the next break, and a still tricky finishing crack. One of the big three E4s on the crag.
Martin Berzins, Bob Berzins, 1978

23 Catharsis 12m E7 7a ★★
Boulder up the shallow flake to the long break. Somehow cover the next 2 metres of blank rock before placing large cams and heading up and left on pockets to join *Caesarian* at the top.
Andi Turner, 2006

24 Main Crack 12m VS 5a ★★
Men have disappeared for days in this fissure. Some have never returned. The big crack is mean to start, but then relents with fine jamming. However, dimensions once again turn nasty near the top, and knees may be called for. A must for the hairy trousered adventurer.
Joe Brown, 1950s

25 Delstree 20m HVS 5a ★★★
The superbly positioned corner perched on the front of the face is a real gritstone classic. Start under an awkward overhang. Negotiate this, surprisingly gymnastic, then move delicately left to the base of the shallow corner. Jamming ecstasy follows to a rounded finish. 5a every magnificent step of the way.
Joe Brown, 1950s

26 Reunion Crack 20m VS 5a ★★
The overhanging corner/flake is impending and strenuous; however the gear is plentiful, and the holds are as friendly as can be. It is gained by surmounting the overhang as for *Delstree*, then following the ramp rightwards to the base of the corner. A brisk layback follows.
◐ opposite page
Joe Brown, 1950s

Hen Cloud has a reputation for steep crack climbing, most of it the legacy of the Rock and Ice Club. Here, Craig Harwood muscles up Reunion Crack, VS 5a (opposite page). 📷 Niall Grimes

Hen Cloud

CENTRAL AREA
The biggest section of rock on Hen Cloud is the complex fortress of the Central Area. Numerous corners and ledges break this section up, although the climbing in between the ledges tends to be forceful.

㉗ Roof Climb 30m VS 4b ★★
1 20m 4b The square-cut corner is followed, first on the right, then the left, to The Terrace.
2 10m 3b Climb the easy gully right of the arête, or much better, do *Final Crack*.

㉘ The Long and the Short 30m E1 5b ★
1 20m 5b The elegant groove is bridged romantically to The Terrace. A quality HVS.
2 10m 5b The thrutchy crack. Escape right at half-height, and finish up an open groove.
Tony Nicholls, 1960s

㉙ Borstal Breakout 33m E4 6b ★★★
The sublime first pitch features meaty bouldering in safe situations.
1 23m 6a Attack the steep hand-jamming crack above the grassy ledge, and climb this to a little roof. Above, the crack peters out. Move up and execute a superb and very testing sequence on big open holds to gain salvation.
2 10m 6b On the wall above ledge, stand on a ledge, and make a desperate move to a poor finger-jam and continue direct to easy ground. An unbalanced pitch: seldom climbed.
⊙ page 85
Jim Moran, Al Evans, Simon Horrox, 1978

㉚ Final Crack 10m HS 4b ★★
Magnificent jamming on perfect rock. Starting on the ledge (gained from *Roof Climb* or *Central Climb*), take the obvious crack right of the flat wall with the final bulge being the crux.

31 Central Climb Direct 30m VS 5a ★★
A series of variations on the original.
1 8m 5a The sinuous fissure below the fine arête is a classic example of the gritstone udge.
2 11m 4b Climb the middle pitch of the parent route, or the exposed flakes to the right.
3 11m 4a The noble groove just to the left is followed to the summit.

32 B4XS 10m E7 6b ★★★
Crikey! An all-out lead of the highest order up the dominating rounded arête. Thin, smeary and serious.
Simon Nadin, 1986

33 Central Climb 32m HS 4c ★★★
A route with a superb line and flawless historical pedigree. The belays are all magnificent.
1 10m 4c The cantankerous crack to a ledge.
2 11m 4b The corner has a very awkward polished slot. Struggle up this to a second ledge. Steep cracks above lead to The Terrace.
3 11m 4a Follow well-used cracks above. Or, the right hand cracks (4b) to a fluted finish.
John Laycock, AR Thompson, 1909

34 Encouragement 30m E1 5b ★★★
A beautiful and balanced climb, with a thoughtful first pitch, and a steep second.
1 15m 5b Gain the square-cut hanging groove. Follow this to a handsome belay ledge.
2 15m 5b The crack above succumbs to a satisfying series of hand and finger jams.
Tony Nicholls, 1960s

35 K2 30m S 4b ★★
A great expedition, demanding on the arms.
1 12m 4a The corner leads steeply to a ledge.
2 18m 4b Follow the steep Y-shaped crack. Above, an easier groove leads to the summit ridge.
Arthur Burns, 1927

36 The Arête 30m HVD 4a ★★★
Follow the exposed stepped ridge all the way to the summit of the mountain. ⊙ page 93

37 Easy Gully 35m M
The moderately easy gully.

38 Modern 18m HS 4b ★★
A super climb that heaves its way up the chunky flake on the front of the face. Once on the ledge, climb the right-hand crack.

39 Ancient 18m HVD 4a ★
Gain the niche on the right, then pull left and follow a line just left of the arête to the ledge. Follow the left-hand crack above.

40 Small Buttress 6m HVS 5a ★
Monkey up the front of the little buttress.
Gary Gibson, 1979

41 The Driven Bow 8m E7 6c ★★
A thrilling sequence, a long, long way above the safety net, up the centre of the overhanging wall left of *Solid Geometry*. Climb the short crack in the steep wall left of the arête and fiddle in some pro at its apex. From here, fingery cranking leads upwards past an alarming slap and a desperate pull onto the top.
Jon Read, 2002

42 Bow Buttress 8m HVD 4a ★★
Climb the rising right-trending line, which intersects the arête, as far as the wide crack. Move up this then finish up left under the capstone.

43 Solid Geometry 8m E1 5b ★★
The fine arête followed direct all the way. Exciting but positive, and difficulties are short-lived.
Dave Jones, 1980

92 | Hen Cloud

BACHELOR'S AREA
To the right lies one of the finest walls on gritstone. The bulging wedge-shaped wall is home to many strong lines, and many required the strengths of the Brown/Whillans and Allen/Bancroft teams to subdue them. Belays are limited above some of the routes. There is a hidden thread and cam beyond the crag top path above *Corinthian*.

44 Slimline 9m E1 5b ★
The crack, with most of the activity centred around getting to the widest section.
Joe Brown, 1950s

45 Fast Piping 11mm E5 6b ★★
Some tough moves well above a good runner. Gain a short crack and make desperate moves up left to the next crack. More hard moves gain a brittle flake then a final, easier crack.
Gary Gibson, Jon Walker, 1981

46 Hedgehog Crack 11m VS 4c ★★
The steep crack, with superb jamming leading to a slightly wide finish.

47 Comedian 12m E3 6a ★★★
A superb route with tough, technical moves. Climb the crack until stiff moves lead right to a horizontal break. Nibble back left to the crack, which is followed on helpful jams to an entertaining groove through the final bulge. Large cams useful.
Steve Bancroft, John Allen, 1976

48 Second's Retreat 15m HVS 4c ★
The steep V-groove heaves and bulges.
Joe Brown, 1952

49 Second's Advance 15m HVS 5a ★
Follow steep cracks and grooves to a ledge. Traverse left to the chimney crack to finish.
Bob Hassall, 1962

50 Corinthian 17m E3 5c ★★★
A fine steep crack climb, where the holds and protection are never quite as good as they would appear. Climb to the base of a faint bulging crack containing a rusty peg. From here, grapple up the rounded, pumpy crack. Testing, but still the easiest of Bancroft and Allen's 'C' routes.
Steve Bancroft, John Allen, 1976

51 Hen Cloud Eliminate
  18m HVS 5b ★★★
A stout second-in-command to *Bachelor's Left-Hand*, similarly positioned at the very top of the HVS grade. The discontinuous cracks give hard jamming, but the finish, struggling into the groove where the rock lies back, gives the crux. Prudent mountaineers will carry two large cams for this section. ⊙ page 95
Joe Brown, 1950s

52 Rib Chimney 20m S 4b ★★
This soaring and confident line gives a fine chimney outing, with a particularly technical bridging section in the middle.

It's all about the positions! The Arête, HVD 4a (page 91), is a great little adventure. Jon Morgan is seen here on the crux high step, while Matt Griffin enjoys the view. 📷 Paul Evans

Hen Cloud

53 Caricature 22m E6 6b ★★★
John Allen's western masterpiece sees very few repeats, and takes a tortuous and sustained line up the big wall with distant, fragile gear. From a ledge on *Rib Chimney*, place a high runner, and make a difficult traverse right, using small holes for the hands, to the front face. Tough moves lead into a scoop, followed by continually demanding moves right to the very top.
John Allen, Steve Bancroft, 1976

54 Bachelor's Left-Hand 25m HVS 5b ★★★
A big lead, continually steep and challenging, and as good as anything on grit. It takes a sweeping line up the right side of the wall, starting from below a prominent crack. Gain this crack with difficulty. At its terminus, make a powerful swing right to a horizontal flake crack then move up to the rounded ramp above. From here, the major crack to the right is taken, which, while still steep, is less taxing than what has gone before.
Don Whillans, 1950s

55 Bachelor's Climb 27m VS 4c ★★★
A carnival of jamming up the butch crack leads to a possible stance. Traverse left and finish up *Bachelor's Left-Hand*.

56 Night Prowler 18m E6 6a ★★
From the ledge, head straight up the lonely arête with committing moves from the word go.
Mark Sharratt, 2005

57 Great Chimney 18m S 4a ★★★
An excellent climb of the old type. Any combination of the corner cracks can be used although starting in the left one and transferring to the right at mid-height is the most obvious.
Siegfried Herford, Stanley Jeffcoat, 1913

58 Rainbow Crack 18m VS 4c ★★
The confident flake crack. Gain a ledge at half-height by either of the two starts. Both are strenuous and awkward. The superb jamming of the upper half makes it all worthwhile.

59 Chameleon 12m E4 6a ★★★
The handsome line on the steep wall is everything E4 should be. Climb to the overhang, then make an exacting traverse left to a deep flake in the roof. Determined pulls from here gain the upper flake, which still needs a bit of huff and puff. Magnificent.
Steve Bancroft, Nicky Stokes, Al Manson, 1977

60 Left Twin Crack 9m HS 4b ★
The left of the twin cracks. Short-lived, but fine laybacking or jamming after a problem start.

61 Right Twin Crack 9m VS 4c
The right crack has a spectacular finish.

The big HVS cracks on Hen Cloud often raise a questioning eyebrow from leaders who are usually solid at the grade, and none more so than Hen Cloud Eliminate (page 92). But rest assured, E1 leaders don't find it easy either. Graeme Hammond on the lower moves. Paul Evans

RAMSHAW ROCKS

OS Grid Ref: SK 019 622 to SK 020 625
Altitude: 440m

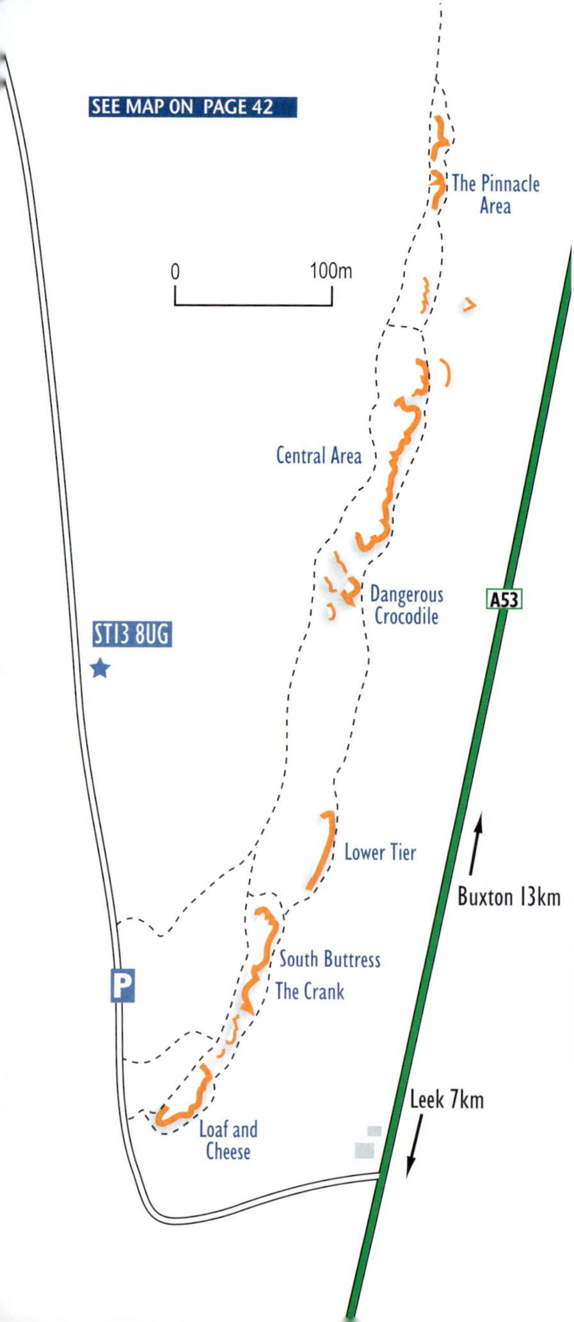

SEE MAP ON PAGE 42

The Pinnacle Area

Central Area

Dangerous Crocodile

ST13 8UG

Lower Tier

South Buttress
The Crank

Loaf and Cheese

Buxton 13km

Leek 7km

A53

Ramshaw Rocks has a character and atmosphere all of its own. Viewed from the road below, the rocks present a Gothic nightmare: vast jutting fins and prows of rock, mainly overhanging, split by many wide, steep cracks and fissures.

The plane of the rocks, combined with the brutal weathering, has accentuated the roughness of the larger grained grit, leaving a coarse, pebbly and, in places, less compact skin.

The climbs at Ramshaw favour those with technique (the cracks), confidence (the slabs), and sheer bloody-mindedness (the weird offwidths). Even more than at most gritstone crags, the effort expended and satisfaction gained are certainly at odds with the length of the routes. These attributes, combined with Ramshaw's odd aesthetics and its relative unpopularity, provide a gritstone experience which a climber of any grade is unlikely to forget, whether later basking in the glow of success, or ruefully licking their (often bloody) wounds.

Predominantly east facing, at its best on a sunny morning. Sitting proudly atop the ridge, the crag catches the wind. This means that buttresses dry quickly. Shady afternoons can also be a welcome escape from summer sun. This exposure can, however, make for a cold day out in winter.

Approach: Parking is on a minor road just off the A53 which runs behind the crag and which is easy to miss the turning for. Look out for a small entrance next to two small buildings at the South end of the crag.

Ramshaw Rocks | 97

> **LOAF AND CHEESE BUTTRESS**
> Sounds tasty. The first rocks have a bunch of friendly low-grade routes and some top-class crack-wrestles.

1 Loaf and Cheese 11m HVS 5a ★
Difficult, but thankfully short-lived, moves up the rather crumbly crack lead to a ledge. A further ledge is gained by a mantel. From here the pinnacle can be climbed at the front or the back to give a pleasant finish.
North Staffs M.C., 1970s

2 Green Crack 8m HVS 5c ★
Despite appearances, a superb route epitomising the Ramshaw experience in miniature. Climb the green groove into the wide crack, where difficulties force a welcome, but almost certainly ungracious exit onto the slab above.
Pete Harrop, 1972

3 National Acrobat 11m E6 6c ★★★
The short non-crack on the left of the buttress was at one time the cutting edge of crack desperation; it isn't much easier today. The crux section, getting established in the hanging groove, is one of the meanest sequences on grit.
Jonny Woodward, 1978

4 Traveller in Time 11m E3 5c ★★★
The features to the right give a less-difficult but equally fine climb. Climb the steep groove until a stretch left gains a smaller flake and small gear. Shuffle left and mantel up, then address the slabby scoop directly. Low in the grade with a Friend 5, high in the grade without.
Andrew & Jonny Woodward, 1977

5 Body Pop 11m E4 6b ★★
Short but committing. From the top of the groove, the right arête is gained adventurously. Luckily, as height is gained, the climbing eases enough to keep you moving in the right direction.
John Allen, Mark Stokes, 1984

6 Wall and Groove 9m S 4a
Starting beneath the prow (or direct), move up to gain the chimney. Better than it looks.
North Staffs M.C., 1970s

7 The Arête 9m S
Climb the arête on tongue-like flakes.
North Staffs M.C., 1970s

8 Louie Groove 8m E1 5b ★
The square-cut groove is easy at the bottom but more intimidating as height is gained, and has seen a few wobblers. Sneaky gear for those who look.
John Yates, Colin Foord, 1968

9 Leeds Slab 8m HS 4a
Ascend the centre of the cutaway on 'chippers' to finish up the notched rib.
Nick Longland, 1980

10 Leeds Crack 6m D
The short crack gives introductory jamming.
North Staffs M.C., 1970s

11 Honest Jonny 5m D
The short little groove just right of the rib.
Jonny Woodward (solo), 1976

Ramshaw Rocks

THE CRANK AREA
This is the series of jutting buttresses starting across to the right. These give many striking climbs.

12 The Great Zawn 8m HVS 5a ★★
The wide crack, in the deep V-slot, just screams to be climbed! Initially wide and tricky, a good hold at mid-height provides welcome relief; then it gets tough again.
Joe Brown, Don Whillans, 1950s

13 Broken Groove 8m D ★
The striking feature provides a good, easy route with a big feel.
North Staffs M.C., 1970s

14 Gully Arête 6m E1 5c
The arête, climbed strictly on the right, is harder than it looks.
Richard Davies, 1986

15 Wellingtons 8m VD ★
The wide crack to the right invites a 'get-stuck-in' approach. Big boots may help. Good fun.
North Staffs M.C., 1970s

16 Masochism 9m E1 5b ★★
Aptly named. The disconcertingly steep hand-to-fist crack leads with venom to a large ledge. The second bulge is less savage but with 'chockstone et al' it still maintains interest to the end. Well protected fun which stops many Extreme-grade leaders.
Joe Brown, Don Whillans, 1950s

17 Sneeze 8m E1 5b ★★
The incipient crack is gained from the left and, though protectable, seems best savoured without the encumbrance of a rope. A fine climb.
Nick Longland, Dave Jones, 1979

18 The Crank 8m VS 5a ★★
Some real Joe Brown jamming, and delightful with it. Climb the crack on sinkers until a step right forces a bit of thought and leads to a wider finish.
Joe Brown, Don Whillans, 1950s

19 Ultimate Sculpture 8m E8 7a ★★
The incredible blank arête provides the sternest challenge at Ramshaw. Climb it using faith, friction, and immense talent. Very minimalist!
Justin Critchlow, 1994

SOUTH BUTTRESS
The most substantial buttress on the edge. It is particularly good for its easier routes, which cover impressive terrain at a moderate standard.

20 Chockstone Chimney 8m VD
The chimney quickly gives in after a short spar with the obvious chockstone.
North Staffs. M.C., 1970s

21 Waiting for the Lions 14m E3 5c ★
A butch start allows you to reach the biggest single hold in the UK. Monkey along this and mantel into it. From here, careful footwork and a hidden sidepull will get you into the upper reaches of *Tally Not*.
Martin Kocsis, 2009

5 mins — The Crank

Ramshaw Rocks | 99

㉒ Gumshoe   14m   E2 5c   ★★★
One of the best routes at Ramshaw, with a disconcertingly obscure crux. Start up the shallow green groove to arrange some rather disappointing protection. Move up left to better holds and a more reasonable finish.
Martin Boysen, 1977

㉓ Tally Not   14m   HVS 5c   ★
Follow the lower corner up and right. Make a difficult move out left to the second corner, which still needs all your attention for a couple of moves until the climbing eases.
Bob Hassall, Norman Hoskins (1pt), 1972. FFA. Martin Boysen, 1972

㉔ Battle of the Bulge   9m   VS 4b   ★
A superb little crack climb. Not half as tricky as the name implies.
North Staffs M.C., 1970s

㉕ The Cannon   13m   VS 4c   ★
Start up friable flakes to gain a short shallow crack, and use this to gain the main groove above. Alternatively, and just as logically, climb the wall left of the short crack at HS 4b before moving right to the same point. Above, pass the 'cannon', and step right to a direct finish.
North Staffs M.C., 1970s

㉖ Whilly's Whopper   12m   VS 4c   ★
From *Phallic Crack*, either step in above the low roof or, better and harder (5a) pull in steeply from below to gain a short hanging groove. Finish direct via a grapple with the, shall we say, prominent feature?
Dave Jones, Gary Gibson, Nick Longland, 1979

㉗ Phallic Crack   12m   S   ★★★
Wide at the bottom, thrutchy at the top, with fine climbing in between. Follow the crack, wrestling the large knob on the way, to finish up the obvious groove. Very good sport.
North Staffs M.C., 1970s

㉘ Alcatraz   12m   HVS 5b   ★★
A fine climb, if a tad green at the start, following the stepped crack. Initial tricky moves lead to a wider crack.
Dave Salt, 1968

㉙ Juan Cur   12m   E5 6a
Follow the wall and arête right of *Alcatraz* as far as possible, until a step left can be made to join the final 3m of that route.
Seb Grieve, 1991

㉚ The Untouchable   11m   E1 5b   ★★
Just right of the arête, a finely positioned crackline snakes up the buttress edge. It is gained from the right.
Colin Foord, John Yates, 1968

㉛ Corner Crack   8m   S 4a
The crack to the right is short but sweet.
North Staffs M.C., 1970s

㉜ The Rippler   8m   HVS 5b
Intricate and fingery climbing. Starting round to the right of the previous route, use ripples to reach a better rail at mid-height. Finish slightly right on very good edges. Bold.
North Staffs M.C., 1970s

South Buttress

THE LOWER TIER
Approximately 50m down and right, is a short but very steep buttress; a mini crag in its own right, and home to a number of superb routes.

33 Crab Walk 20m S 4a ★
A long traverse covering interesting terrain. Start near the centre of the buttress and climb up left via good holds to gain a ramp which is followed leftwards to finish up a short crack.
North Staffs M.C., 1970s

34 Brown's Crack 14m E1 5c ★★
A gem from the master. Gain some giant holds, then fight, fist and furkle your way up the unhelpful crack. Short and plain 'ard. page 23
Joe Brown, Don Whillans, 1950s

35 Prostration 14m HVS 5a ★★
A good climb. Follow the short crack to the roof, somehow gain the ledge, struggle upright (crux), and scuttle up the secondary crack. Not to be taken lying down!
Joe Brown, Don Whillans, 1950s

36 Colly Wobble 11m E4 6b ★★
The wall, passing four small holes. A half-sized Tri-cam in one of the holes protects.
Simon Nadin, 1987

37 Don's Crack 11m HVS 5b ★★
Notably difficult for the pint-sized climber, the steep crack provides another test of crack technique.
Don Whillans, Joe Brown, 1950s

38 Tierdrop Font 7A+ ★★★
Reach the blobby pinches, then using determination, finger strength and burl, get to a chipped runnel on the lip. From here, crimps two feet away tantalise... but can you commit?
Nick Longland, 1980

Dangerous Crocodile

DANGEROUS CROCODILE
The tall buttress 90m right.

39 Camelian Crack 6m VD ★
The crack on the left is short and sweet.
North Staffs M.C., 1970s

40 Dangerous Crocodile Snogging 12m E7 6c ★★★
Hard Grit royalty. Gain the wide break from below and swing left (Friend 6). Pull up and make a crux stretch left to a hold in the face then up to a sloping topout.
Simon Nadin (solo), 1986

41 Clippety Clop, Clippety Clop, Clippety Clop 12m E7 6c ★★★
One of the great lines on grit: the immaculate and ludicrous arête. Start as for *Dangerous Crocodile Snogging*, then rock onto the ramp on the right of the arête. Reach the arête and haul up this.
Seb Grieve, 1991

Lower Tier

Andi Turner on the fine upper flake of Flaky Wall Direct, VS 4b (page 102). This sits high on the dinosaur spine of the Ramshaw ridge and is one of the freshest spots in Staffordshire. David Simmonite

Ramshaw Rocks

CENTRAL AREA
A long stretch of great quality with routes across the grades. There are some steep and brutal challenges hereabouts.

42 Wriggler 6m HS 4b
Severely wide but very short lived. Fun.
North Staffs M.C., 1970s

43 Arête and Crack 13m VD
Climb the short blunt arête left of the cave and follow the crack above to a wide exit left.
North Staffs M.C., 1970s

44 Handrail 12m E2 5c ★★
As the crack of the previous route peters out step up and place gear in the prow on the right, then boldly swing round the arête to follow the obvious traverse line. Carry on fearlessly to an exit up the wider crack. Intense.
Martin Boysen, 1977

45 Handrail Direct 9m E4 6a ★
Climb a scoop on smears and pebbles to join the original before the swing right.
Simon Nadin, 1984

46 Assegai 11m VS 5a ★
The knobbly, sharp, gritty corner is harder than it looks, especially moving onto the slab.
North Staffs M.C., 1970s

47 Bowrosin 12m VS 4c ★
Climb the slab to where a step across leads to a crack, which is followed with a hard move as the angle changes.
Barry Marsden, 1969

48 Boomerang 12m VD ★★★
The wide crack is a great gritstone feature and makes for a superb and well-protected climb. Finish left or via a short steep crack on the skyline (better but harder).
North Staffs M.C., 1970s

49 Little Nasty 14m E1 5b ★
The crack is pretty grim for 3m but then relents to give pleasant climbing to a ledge. Finish up the thin groove in the middle of the wall.
Dave Salt, 1970s

50 Ramshaw Crack 7m E4 6a ★★★
The strangely beguiling and ridiculously steep crack moves from hand to fist to arm-bar width all within twenty feet. One of grit's great cracks and still an intimidating lead today.
Joe Brown (some aid), 1964. FFA Gabe Regan, 1976

51 Never Never Land 12m E7 6b ★★★
A serious lead up the sidewall. Start up a short, wide crack. Leave this rightwards and climb the wall, passing a flake, to a rounded exit.
Simon Nadin, Richard Davies, 1986

52 Imposition 8m E2 5c ★★
The wide crack always seems just too wide and provides a difficult exercise. Very good.
North Staffs M.C., 1970s

53 Iron Horse Crack 6m D
The tiny jamming crack.
North Staffs M.C., 1970s

54 Tricouni Crack 6m HS 4a ★
A pleasant exercise for fat fingers or thin hands.
North Staffs. M.C., 1970s

55 Rubber Crack 6m VS 4c ★
A short crack and corner.
Steve Dale, Dave Salt, 1973

56 Flaky Wall Direct 14m VS 4b ★
A good solid climb. Just to the left of the prow is a green streak which is followed to a ledge. Step left then go straight up past some large spikes into a groove that certainly maintains interest to an airy perch. ⓞ page 101
North Staffs M.C., 1970s

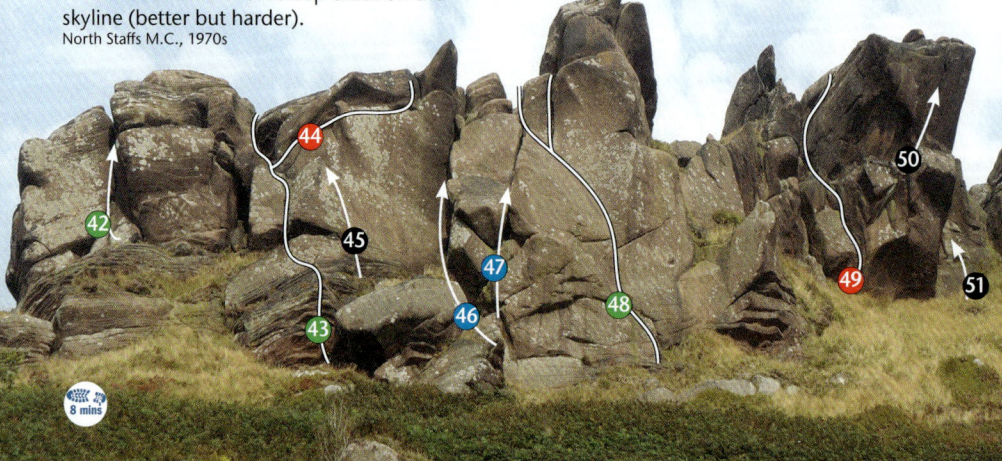

Ramshaw Rocks | 103

57 Flaky Wall Indirect 16m VS 4c ★
Follow the *Direct* to the ledge, move up and right via some flakes and move round the corner. Finish up the front face (crux).
North Staffs M.C., 1970s

58 Cracked Gully 14m D
The wide blocky groove.
North Staffs M.C., 1970s

59 Arête Wall 9m D
Take the V-shaped groove for 4m then finish up a slightly steeper, flaky crack.
North Staffs M.C., 1970s

60 Crystal Tipps 7m E1 5c ★
Climb the wall 1m right of the left arête making a committing move to gain the flake.
Andrew Woodward (solo), 1976

61 Magic Roundabout Direct 7m HVS 4c ★
Take the final shallow groove, crux, to the break. Trend right and aim for the luminous slot directly above the start of *Magic Roundabout*.
North Staffs M.C., 1970s

62 Magic Roundabout 7m S 4a ★
A fine delicate route. Start at the small broken niche on the right of the buttress. Follow the lowest break to finish at a black flake.

63 Port Crack 14m D
The pleasant crack.
North Staffs M.C., 1970s

64 Time Out 9m E2 5c ★★
The central crack. Moving right to a subsidiary upper crack provides the crux.
Gary Gibson, Ian Barker, 1979

65 Starboard Crack 9m E1 5b ★
Vile but fun: the right-hand crack is like jamming porcupines.
North Staffs M.C., 1970s

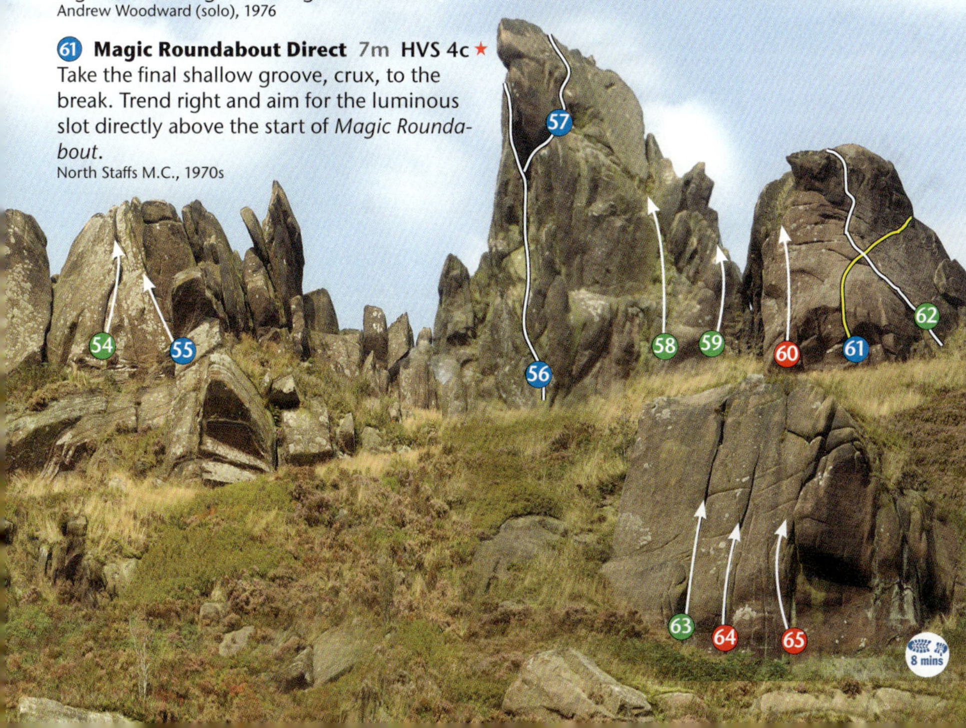

PINNACLE AREA

Two buttresses jut from the moorland further right, Roman Nose Buttress and The Pinnacle. They give very Ramshaw experiences.

66 Big Richard 10m VS 4c ★
Start under a prominent spike at 3m. Gain the spike – either direct, strenuous, or via the ramp to the right, technical. The chimney above is most difficult to enter; exit to a ledge and finish up the wall/groove on the right.
North Staffs M.C., 1970s

67 The Proboscid 10m E1 5b
Do the start of *Big Richard*, then layback the exposed and serious nose above.
Nick Longland, 1980

68 The Crippler 10m HVS 5a ★★★
A route to inspire. Climb from the back until forced left and make difficult moves to gain a groove. Getting stood at the top of this is also entertaining, from where a slabby finish can be made. ⊙ page 40
John Yates, 1969

69 Mantrap 8m HVD 4a
The chimney.
North Staffs M.C., 1970s

70 Great Scene Baby 10m S 4b ★
The smart crack to the left is gained from 2m up the groove. Climb the crack on good jams onto a slab and finish over a small neb.
North Staffs M.C., 1970s

71 Groovy Baby 10m HS 4b
Guess where this goes? Short and green.
North Staffs M.C., 1970s

72 Pile Driver 17m VS 4c ★
A good route with an exposed finish. From the groove, join the crack on the right, which is climbed to its end. A step right leaves one below the final crack. ⊙ opposite page
North Staffs M.C., 1970s

73 The Press 15m E1 5b ★★
Another belter, which is solid at the grade. Where *Pile Driver* goes up, continue right along the obvious break until a beefy pull can be made into the steep crack. This is followed round the arête to an easier finish.
Bob Hassall, 1971

74 Night of Lust 12m E4 6b ★
Make hard moves into the niche, and gear. Grope over a bulge then pull up and left to join *The Press*.
John Allen, 1984

75 Curfew 12m HVS 5b ★
So very Ramshaw. Another burly pull off the ground is the main feature of the steep corner crack. The rest is merely pleasant.
North Staffs M.C., 1970s

76 Foord's Folly 10m E2 6a ★★★
Valiantly attempt to climb the exasperating crack without wrecking digits. If successful, move out to an easier finish up the thin hand crack above.
Colin Foord (aid), 1968. FFA John Allen, 1973

77 The Swinger 13m HVS 5a
Takes the right edge of the buttress with a difficult start on a couple of sloping ramps. From the ledge continue up the arête above.
Martin Boysen, 1972

Roman Nose Buttress — The Pinnacle

Dan Barbour and Claudia Amatruda being attacked from all angles on Pile Driver, VS 4c (opposite page).
Pete O'Donovan

SOUTHERN GRITSTONE

CRATCLIFFE TOR
ROBIN HOOD'S STRIDE
BLACK ROCKS

Andy Earl on Fern Hill, E2 5c (page 112). After a tough, early crux, the climb relents slightly and the cruisy cracks and juggy overhang that follow are a pure joy to climb. Andy Birtwistle

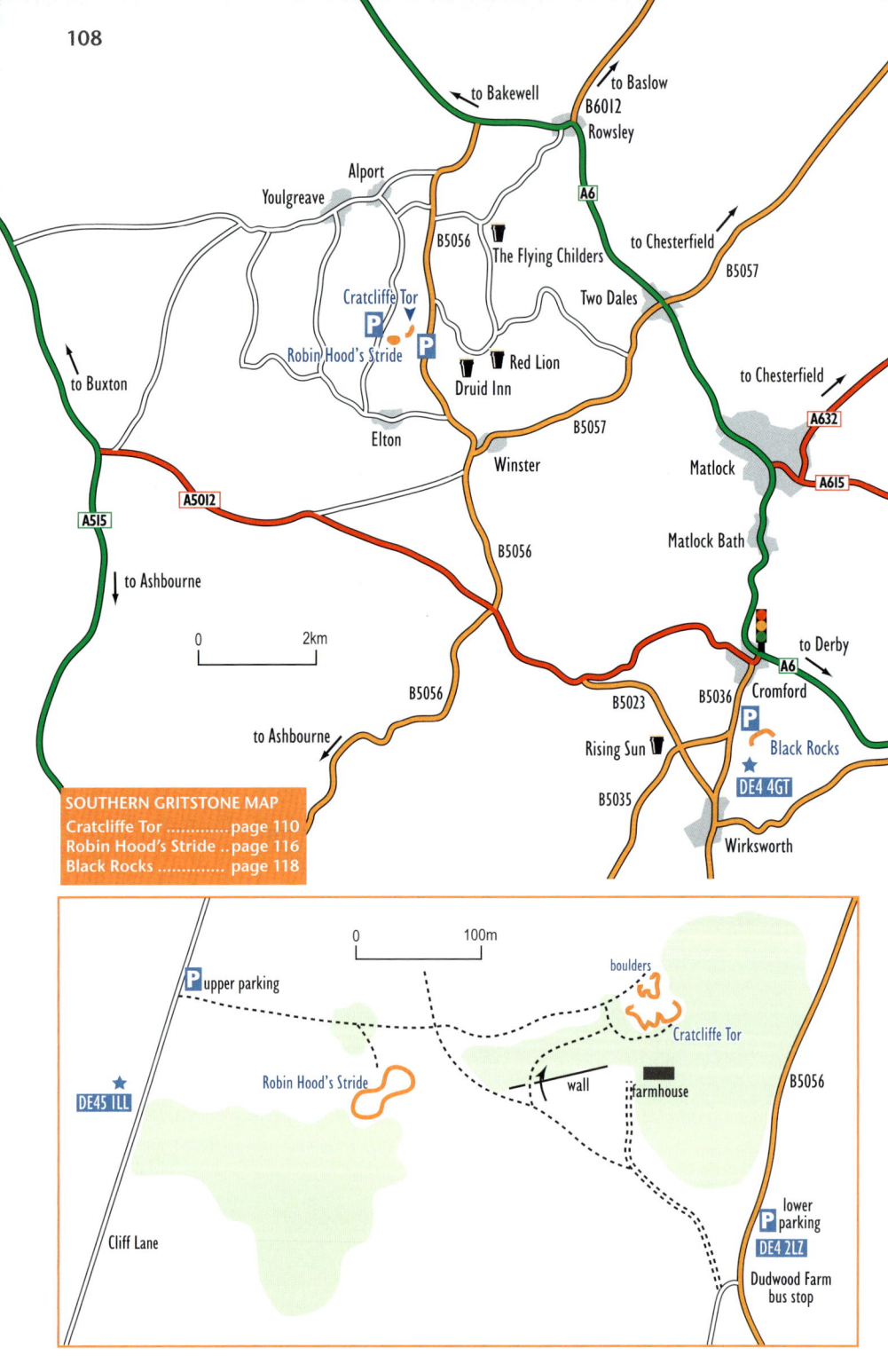

Cratcliffe has some of the best E2s on grit, blockbusting climbs with fistfuls of character - Mordaunt, Tom Thumb, Savage Messiah. But it is the twins in Owl Gully that stand out from the crowd; Fern Hill and this one, Five Finger Exercise (page 113). A technical wall leads to all-out moves up the flying upper flake, an unforgettable passage for anyone on the lower extremes. Jamie Sparkes climbing. Andy Birtwistle

CRATCLIFFE TOR
OS Grid Ref: SK 228 623
Altitude: 240m

One of the finest crags in the Peak, somehow made better by having a limited number of climbs. The rock and the moves are superb, and every route is to be savoured. The perfect, plumb-vertical walls, criss-crossed by juggy breaks, give a unique style of climbing of unrelenting quality. Routes are usually well protected.

This is an all-season crag, facing south-east. Mainly sheltered, takes little drainage and dries quickly. The deep gullies mean sun or shade can usually be sought as seasons dictate.

Approach: Lower Parking – See map on page 108. Park in a small layby on the B5056 (Haddon to Winster road). The crag is just visible above the trees. Go through the gate and follow the farm track for 200m to where it bends right. Continue up the left side of the field then go through the wall and along the tree-covered hillside. After crossing a fence the crag is slightly downhill on the right past a Hermit's cave with metal railings. There is no approach direct via the farmhouse. **Upper Parking:** Alternatively, follow minor roads between Elton and Alport to roadside parking on Cliff Lane near Robin Hood's Stride.

The first two routes sit high on the crag and are gained along ledges from the left or down a chimney on their right.

❶ Reticent Mass Murderer 8m E5 6b ★★
A seventies jamming tour-de-force. Make a hard, bouldery pull (crux) to gain the short, steep and initially unwelcoming crack.
John Allen, 1976

❷ Genocide 8m E6 6c ★★
A cheeky little climb with a tough crux in a position of some concern. On the wall right of *Reticent...*, follow the chunky flake to its end. Move up and make dynamic crux moves to reach the salvation of the break above.
Jerry Moffatt, Neil Foster, 1983

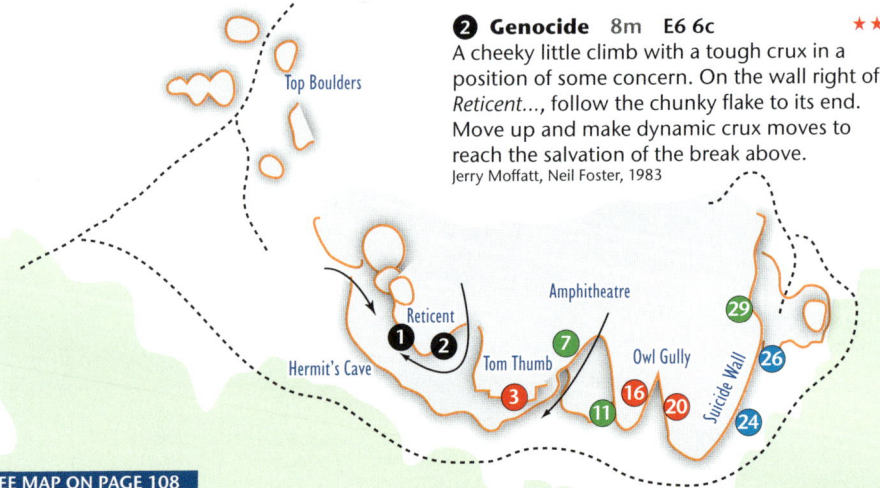

SEE MAP ON PAGE 108

Cratcliffe Tor | 111

> **THE AMPHITHEATRE**
> These are the walls around the broad, open gully. The routes on the left get lots of sun. An easy climb, **Amphitheatre Crack**, Mod, funnels up the left-hand side with awkward sections and is the best descent.

3 Tom Thumb 18m E2 5b ★★
A grasping tussle with lots of exposure. Gain and follow the thin crack on the lower slab, then past ledges to get established below the jutting neb. Arrange protection, then launch out to a heart-in-mouth position in the flake up and right. Ride this to the top.
Tom Proctor, Keith Myhill, 1971

4 Giant's Staircase 18m HVS 5a ★★
An entertaining series of polished mantelshelves leads rightwards to a crack and corner, which quickly lead to more mantelshelves back leftwards, crossing *Tom Thumb*, and an easier exit up a chimney further left.
Fred Pigott, Morley Wood, George S Bower, 1922

5 Beanstalk 15m E2 5c ★★
A characterful route taking a varied line up the right of the pillar. Climb to the tree stump, then stretch up the tricky wall behind it to gain small holds on the right, then a break and the pleasant arête above.
Mike Hardwick, Andy Edgar, 1976

6 Bramble Groove 15m VS 4c
Follow the groove that breaks out from the foot of *Amphitheatre Crack* to a ledge. Climb the groove on the left or steep crack on the right to another ledge. The overhanging crack above gives the crux.
JN Millward, Peter Harding, 1947

7 Oblique Chimney 9m VD 4a ★
From *Amphitheatre Crack*, trend up and left to gain a clean-cut cleft. Shimmy up this.

8 Darren Hawkins' Invisible Neck
  9m E4 5c ★
A short, bold climb up the hanging arête on good rock.
Malcolm Taylor, Darren Hawkins, 1986

9 Elliott's Unconquerable 9m HVS 5b ★
The left-slanting crack is short, but still a fine testpiece.
Frank Elliott, 1933

10 Elliott's Right-Hand 9m E1 5b
The wall just right is sweet, if a little short. Pull over the overhang and follow friendly cracks.
Chris Hunter, Mike Browell, 1977

11 Weston's Chimney 15m VD
Back on ground level, and just left of the arête that bounds *Owl Gully*. A historical polished grovel up the obvious chimney leads to cleaner rock and a large ledge. Finish up the wide crack.
Owen Glynne Jones, 1897

The Amphitheatre

OWL GULLY

The thrusting open book corner is one of the cathedrals of gritstone. Its steep, crack-riven walls are swarmed over by a plethora of routes. The classics are of course the originals, but the climbing is so good that any of the pitches are worth doing. The walls can be very hot in the sun.

12 Boot Hill   18m   E3 5c   ★★★
The first of the great Owl Gully routes, and one of the best, based on the left arête. From 6m up *Weston's Chimney*, hand traverse right to gain a small ledge on the arête. Short climbers will layback up the left side of the arête to a break, while the tall can stretch up the slab above the ledge. Further moves up the left arête lead to the roof and a surprising finish up the wall above.
Tom Proctor, Al Evans, 1971

13 The Groove   15m   E9 7b   ★★
The beautifully sculpted shallow groove gives the hardest route on the crag. Gain and magic up it to the break, crux. Continue up the disappearing continuation groove and ascend the blunt rib to join *Fern Hill* below the roof.
James Pearson, 2008

14 Nutcracker   18m   E3 6a   ★★
From the first ledge a few metres up *Owl Gully*, launch leftwards along the horizontal break and follow it to the arête. From here, more reachy moves lead up the slab (*Boot Hill*) then finish rightwards as for *Fern Hill*.
Vin Ridgeway, Peter Harding, 1951

15 Fern Hill Indirect   22m   E4 6a   ★★
Extend *Fern Hill* with a superb arm-draining, rope-tangling zigzag out along *Nutcracker* and then back along the next break up. However, the crux for most will still be the start.
Ron Fawcett, Pete Livesey, 1976

16 Fern Hill   14m   E2 5c   ★★★
A magnificent route, the classic of the wall. Climb up the gully until about 2m above the third ledge. Gain the diagonal crack and follow it out left, moving up just before the arête is reached; the holds improve (hopefully) quicker than the arms tire! A step left gains a good rest below the roof; above this is a shelf which provides a precarious exit. ⓞ page 106
Keith Myhill, Tom Proctor, Al Evans (1pt), 1971

Owl Gully

Cratcliffe Tor | 113

17 Owl Gully 18m VD ★★
One of gritstone's great pitches at the grade, with the crux at the top.
JW Puttrell, WJ Watson, 1890

18 Tiger Traverse 15m E2 5c ★
Traverse the break to reach the big ledge on *Five Finger...* Easier climbing leads up shelves and ledges.
Peter Harding, Vin Ridgeway, 1951

19 Nettle Wine 18m E4 6b ★★
A superb well protected route. From the start of *Tiger Traverse* make tricky moves up to the next break. Just right, even trickier moves lead up a poor flake-line to a hole and glory.
John Hart, 1978

20 Five Finger Exercise 23m E2 5c ★★★
A varied and absorbing climb with an almighty climax. Easy cracks lead up the right wall to a break below a blank wall. Thin crimping up improving flakes gains the ledge at half height. The grand finale is the hanging flake to the left; gaining this is awkward and climbing it intimidating, so just as well the gear is good.
⊙ page 109
Andy Edgar, Mike Hardwick, 1976

21 The Bower, Route 1 10m HS 4b ★
From just right of the arête, alternate steps up and right lead to a shallow corner. This gains the tree, a superbly-positioned belay and, sadly, the end of the route. Abseil off.
Fred Pigott, Morley Wood, George Bower, 1922

22 Requiem 22m E3 5a, 6a ★★★
A Grit classic – superb positions and a mean crux. Surmount the jutting tongue and climb the wall direct to The Bower (possible belay). Without using the tree, climb the crack splitting the right-hand side of the roof, crux. Follow the break leftwards for a couple of metres then up to a hole. Press on direct veering slightly leftwards to a delightful fluted finish.
Paul Nunn, (2pts) 1970. FFA John Allen, Peter Meads, 1975

Cratcliffe Tor

23. Long Distance Runnel 18m E5 6c ★★
Desperate. Do the roof of *Requiem* then lay off the pod to gain the next break. Make crux moves via the shallow runnel to jugs.
Neil Foster, 1996

24. Suicide Wall 22m HVS 5b ★★★
Deservedly touted as the best HVS on grit, boasting varied well-protected climbing in superb positions. Gain the remains of the oak and swarm over it into a niche. Awkward jamming up the left-slanting crack leads to The Bower. Hand traverse rightwards, a bit intimidating, to climb a thin crack leading to the superb flake and a tricky finish.
◐ opposite page
Peter Harding, Veronica Lee, 1946

25. Stihl Life 18m E5 6a ★★
Follow a thin flake to a shallow hole and pass this to gain the next break. Undercut up to gain *Sepulchrave* and finish up *Savage Messiah*.
Neil Foster, 1996

26. Sepulchrave 18m HVS 5a ★★
Big fun. Follow lovely cracks as they zig up to a cave on *Suicide Wall*, then zag back right to finish up a short, wide crack.
Paul Nunn, 1970

27. Savage Messiah 14m E2 5c ★★
A great line with a fine technical crux. Climb direct to the finishing crack on *Sepulchrave* via superb, technical moves past a hole.
Rob Burwood, Rob Ferguson, 1975

28. Mordaunt 58m E2 5c ★★★
The best girdle traverse on grit with four brilliant pitches. Follow *Sepulchrave* and continue left into *Requiem* where a tricky move down gains another traverse line to a fine belay on the arête (5c). Down-mantel to the *Five Finger* ledge and reverse *Tiger Traverse* into *Owl Gully*, belay (5c). Climb up to gain the traverse line above *Fern Hill* and follow it to a junction with that route just before the arête. Move up to the roof and belay (5b). Move across below the roof to gain *Boot Hill's* arête, then across the final wall to finish up *Weston's Chimney* (5b).
Paul Nunn, 1970

29. North Climb 18m S 4a ★★
A great wee climb up the smart corner just to the right. Climb it direct all the way or, better, step left at half height to finish with joy up the fluted arête.
JW Puttrell, WJ Watson, 1890

This is quite possibly the best flake on gritstone; a great sail of flawless rock, greedy for hands and easily romped by confident leaders. Suicide Wall, HVS 5b (opposite page), was the finest route of its era, and it's as good today as it's ever been. Rebecca Ting climbing. Paul Evans

ROBIN HOOD'S STRIDE

OS Grid Ref: SK 224 622
Altitude: 250m

'The Stride' is one of the coolest outcrops in the Peak District, with an ancient magic that appeals to Victorian alpinists and bouldering mystics. It contains a handful of routes in the lower and higher grades that are prized ticks for the cognoscenti. Brilliant bouldering also.

Known locally as Mock Beggar's Hall, it vaguely resembles an ancient fortification. The twin summits of the jumble are the Inaccessible Pinnacle (or Stoat) and Weasel Pinnacle.

The Stride is exposed to the elements, and generally clean, is quick to dry and can be a great winter venue, especially when rain or low cloud affects the higher eastern edges. It can be miserable in high winds.

Approach: See Cratcliffe parking and map on page 108. Park at the upper parking on Cliff Lane. The crag is clearly visible. Easily approached from the lower parking by continuing up the main track.

1 Zigzag Climb   15m   S 4a
A ramble up the ridge has a surprisingly alpine feel. Gain the ridge from the slab left of the chipped holds and scamper up this to ledges. The wide crack in the wall above is gained by traversing in awkwardly from the gully. This lands you below Weasel Pinnacle which makes for a second pitch.
Henry Bishop, 1907

2 Straight Crack   4m   S 4a   ★
The offwidth gives a fine struggle.

Weasel Pinnacle: The fine tower is fluted, fissured and furrowed. Descend by reversing *Letter Route*.

3 The Crucifix   4m   S 4c
The dark north-east face is tackled by stretchy moves up the flutings near the right edge.

4 Letter Route   4m   D
The north-west face proves the easiest way up and down. Putting the evils of chipping aside, the 'S' at the top is a genuinely impressive piece of work.

5 Stonnis Wall   5m   HVS 5a   ★
The pinnacle's hardest route is also the best. Make stiff moves up from a flat hold. At the break gain the flutings and more testing moves to the top.
Reg Schofield, 1936

6 Long Climb   6m   VS 4c   ★
The face opposite *Letter Route*. A hard start gains a chipped hold. Continue via flutings.
JW Puttrell, 1890

7 Muscle Crack   6m   S 4b
The crack is thankfully furnished with a large hidden hold where the steepness kicks in.

Robin Hood's Stride | 117

Inaccessible Pinnacle: Routes to the summit are all escaped by reversing *Short Climb*, so you may want to check that out first.

8 Crack and Furrow 15m HS 4b ★
A stiff start, pulling into the crack from the left, is followed by a glorious upper wall.
Henry Bishop, 1907

9 Boulder Climb 15m HS 4c ★★
A splendid expedition. A thrutch up the lower crack can be avoided by elegantly smearing up to its right. Once on the boulder, saunter up and right through some wonderful formations on great holds and protection.
Henry Bishop, 1907

10 Path of the Righteous Man
11m E7 6c ★
The arête just right of the boulder. An intense sequence leads to easier ground.
Sam Whittaker, 1998

11 Byne's Traverse 8m HVS 5b ★
From the toe of the pinnacle, a shallow groove leads delicately rightwards. From its end a break leads thuggishly back left. A good climb.
Alf W Bridge, 1930

12 Short Climb 4m HVD 4a
Well named. The short dark face is climbed on beautiful flutings. Pay attention on the way up, this is also the way down.

Kaluza-Klein Area: There is a trio of desperate routes on a large block on the opposite side of the Stride from *Boulder Climb*.

13 Kaluza-Klein 6m E7 6c ★★★
The arête feels bigger than it should, yet you will be all too aware of how close the ground is if you slip off. A tenuous rockover and blind grope provide the fun. Utterly desperate for the short, and quite possibly an entire grade easier for the very tall.
Johnny Dawes, 1986

14 Captain Calamity 6m E7 6c ★
Wild stuff. From a standing position in the break on *Kaluza*, shuffle rightwards to a desperate rounded layback and a right-trending finish.
Pete Whittaker, 2008

15 My Prune 6m E5 6c ★
The steep right arête of the wall. The move to the break is powerful and insecure. Another hard move leftwards brings jugs to hand and an easy slab to pad up. Font 7C.
Ben Bransby, 2007

Inaccessible Pinnacle

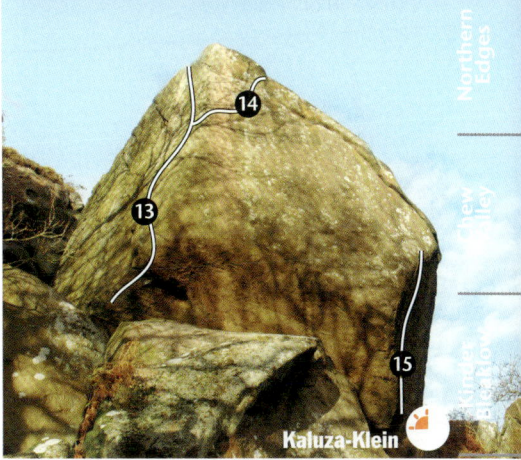
Kaluza-Klein

BLACK ROCKS

OS Grid Ref: SK 294 557
Altitude: 250m

A bizarre crag, a bit like the mad auntie locked away in the attic, tucked away down south with all that nasty limestone threatening. Round. Steep and rounded; vertical and rounded; slabby and rounded. Sometimes bold, but usually protectable routes of the utmost character and historical value. Quite rounded. Whatever your grade, there will be a classic rounded challenge here. Although for the VS climber, Black Rocks has routes that easily outclass the climbs at the more basic crags in terms of dark charisma and character. Somewhat rounded.

The crag is set at two aspects: the West Wall gets loads of sun and the rock is totally clean. The series of protruding buttresses that stretch off on the Northern side get much less sun – a bit on summer evenings – although they are still generally clean. However, deep chasms and the east side of the Promontory, can take a while to dry. The left-hand end of these buttresses, particularly around the Queen's Parlour area, gets virtually no sun, and is also prone to having grassy sections on the routes.

Approach: From Cromford, follow the B5036 towards Wirksworth. Near the top of the hill, a sign points towards Black Rocks, where a road leads to car parks (p&d), and public toilets. A 5-minute walk leads to the crag.

QUEEN'S PARLOUR AREA
Follow the path at the bottom of the crag to the left-hand-most series of buttresses. Great for easier routes. Due to trees and northerly aspect, routes can remain damp after wet weather, so allow some time for them to dry.

1 Mental Pygmy 7m E3 6a ★
Climb easily to the roof crack and tackle it.
Steve Bancroft, Paul Howarth, John Allen, 1976

2 New Year Buttress 17m VD ★
Climb broken rock heading for the small hanging groove high and left. This makes for a fine finish.

3 Queen's Parlour Slab 17m VS 4b ★★
Nowhere are the destructive ancient chippings more appreciated than on this climb. From the gully, punch out right along the break to the front face of the projecting buttress. Above, the narrow slab is easier, but very, very run-out.
Bernard N Simmonds, Len Chapman, 1939

4 Queen's Parlour Gully 27m VD ★★
A great, exciting big route. Follow broken rock to the niche under the large overhang. Thrilling moves lead right into the main shaft which is followed airily to the top.
JW Puttrell, WJ Watson, 1890

5 Queen's Parlour Chimney 27m HS 4b ★
Some spacey back and footing. From the start of the last route, continue up and right to climb the chimney splitting the steep rock.
JW Puttrell, WJ Watson, 1890

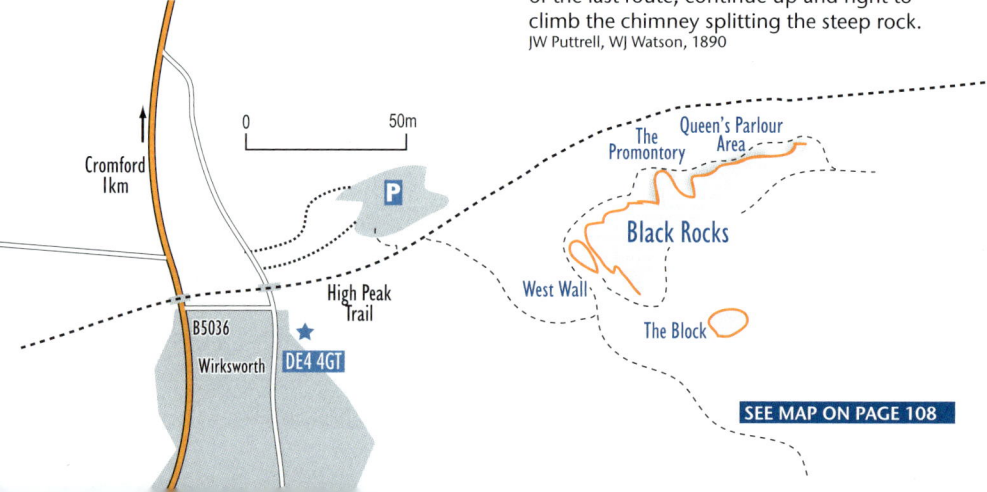

SEE MAP ON PAGE 108

Black Rocks | 119

6 Black Crack 10m VS 4c ★★
The steep flake-crack is a superb test of jamming and laybacking, and is almost as easy as *The File* on Higgar Tor. page 121
George Bower, Fred Pigott, 1923

7 Central Buttress 25m HVD 3c ★★★
A great and classic route, from Morley Wood no less, swerving up through some fantastic terrain. Start round to the left of a pinnacle. Follow dank cracks up and right onto the front face. Climb directly to the pinnacle and a possible belay. Step up the perched slab above until forced left at a steepening to battle up a short thick crack (atop *Black Crack*).
Morley Wood, Fred Pigott, 1923

8 Central Buttress Direct 23m E1 5a
Old, and bold. Gain the original route by climbing the lower broad rib in its entirety.
Polaris Club, 1938

9 Blind Man's Crack 17m HVD 4a ★
Quite steep, despite being so slabby. Make stiff moves up the short lower crack to gain and follow the rampy crack.

10 Blind Man's Buttress 17m HVD
Traverse out from the gully, along the awkward break, then pull up onto the slab. The exposed arête above is followed with less difficulty.
Henry Bishop, Douglas Yeomans, 1913

THE PROMONTORY
Like the great hulk of a mighty battleship, bold, thrusting and indestructible, you almost expect to see barnacles on its rust-hued flanks. The starboard side can remain a bit damp after rain, but the extra foot-skating will only add to the fun.

11 Left Promontory Gully 23m M
The scrambly gully. Often used as an awkward descent, as well as somewhere to put your empty cans and bottles. Shame.

12 Rope Trick 20m E2 5c ★
A great horizontal hand-gallop. From the gully, hand traverse the lowest break all the way to a ledge on the arête. Finish up the bulging crest.
Roy Leeming, 1969

13 Longships 12m E2 5c ★
Follow *Rope Trick* for 4m, and from the double break, stretch up the wall on distant jams.
Gary Gibson, Alison Hargreaves, 1981

14 Firebird 20m E2 5c ★★
The classic of this wall, taking a fine, exhausting sweep. Scuttle merrily along the middle horizontal break until it is possible to udge up to the spike. Follow the flake and thin crack above to the top.
Dave Humphries, 1977

15 Meshuga 18m E9 6c ★★★
Awesome. For many years the last great problem on gritstone, the almighty prow finally fell in a surreal blaze of denim, knees, hair gel and psychobabble to Seb Grieve, putting him amongst Black Rocks' champions. Climb the prow direct.
Seb Grieve, 1997

16 Promontory Traverse
27m E2 5b ★★★
Harding's celebrated crossing of the Promontory is one of the finest ornaments on the mantelpiece of gritstone climbing.
1 13m 5b From the gully, crank along the lowest break to a niche, up a fat crack, then left again to a brilliantly-positioned belay.
2 14m 5b Step down and continue left, with crux moves to gain the spike. Continue traversing in this line all the way to the gully.
Peter Harding, Tony Moulam, 1945

17 Right Promontory Gully 24m M
The deep gully: simple up, simple down. A few harder variations are possible.
Henry Bishop, Douglas Yeomans, 1913

Graeme Hammond giving it hell on the barnstorming Black Crack, VS 4c (page 119), as pure a piece of crack as you'll find this side of Yosemite. Pete O'Donovan

18 Stonnis Arête 30m HVD 4a ★★
Start down at the base of the buttress and climb a steep, juggy wall. Continue *à cheval* up the obvious blade of rock. The left side of the arête above provides a good continuation.
Henry Bishop, Douglas Yeomans, 1900

19 Stonnis Crack 10m HS 4b ★★
Once considered an unjustifiable lead, the fissure still gives remarkable food for thought. Finish up the left side of the arête above.
JW Puttrell, 1900

20 Sand Buttress 20m VS 4c ★★★
A grand, big route; very fulfilling. Follow the crack on the right of the smooth wall to the second horizontal break. Jug left along this to a tree. From here, blast up steep cracks above to a wild, over-the-top finish on atomic jugs.
Fred Pigott and party, 1920

21 Untoward 18m E5 6b ★★
A funky trifle, safe, but still with big fall-potential. From *Sand Buttress*, continue up to a thin crack, with good small gear. Use this and the arête to slap steeply to good holds above.
Johnny Dawes, 1986

22 Sand Gully 20m D
The third of the alpine gullies on the north face of Black Rocks.
JW Puttrell, WJ Watson, 1890

23 Camel Hot 20m E6 6b ★★
The right arête of the gully is arguably well protected for the grade, but placing protection (small/medium cams) is pretty butch. Usually in need of a good brush.
Johnny Shepherd, Tom Kelly, 1986

24 Lean Man's Climb 22m VS 4c ★★★
A technical start up the slippery flake leads to a ledge (possible belay). Above, buster cracks lead to superb positions, the short hanging corner on the left, and a stretch for the top.
Fred Pigott and party, 1920

The next climbs start in the gully to the right.

25 Superstitious Start 10m HVS 5b ★
A trickier start to the *Superdirect*. From the *Superdirect*, climb leftwards to reach a twisting crack, which leads to the belay ledge.
Peter Harding, Tony Moulam, 1949

26 Lean Man's Superdirect 20m VS 4c ★★
The upper crack gives terrific climbing, making up for a thrutchy beginning. Climb the curving corner-crack just left of the parallel chimney to the ledge, and possible belay. Above this the crack and wall 1m left of the arête gives technical moves in a shadowy situation.
Alf Bridge, Ivan M Waller, Jack Longland, 1930

27 Fat Man's Chimney 12m D ★★
Do this. The parallel, clean slot at the back will give you a good lesson in squeeze-voodoo.
JW Puttrell, WJ Watson, 1890

The next route starts on the ledge above.

28 Lean Man's Eliminate 10m VS 4c ★
A cracking little pitch, a good place to see if you're up to speed with the joys of climbing big rounded breaks. Follow the steep fissure-riven wall with a fun stretch for the top.
Peter Harding, Tony Moulam, 1945

For the VS climber, Black Rocks is a big hitter, with a handful of stout classics at the grade as good as any on grit. The sunny side of the crag hosts a few of these, punchy voyages on great gritstone features. Here, Chris Hardy gets ready for some action on Birch Tree Variant, VS 5a (page 124). Paul Evans

WEST WALL

The first rock arrived at is the perfectly clean, sunbasking, purple-hued West Wall. Almost all the routes are worth doing.

29 Gaia 13m E8 6c ★★★
The slim, hanging groove in the centre of the face is a true member of gritstone royalty. Beautiful moves, perfect danger, history and aura, are all woven together in the subtly sinuous line. Climb the groove to a rightward exit.
Johnny Dawes, 1986

30 Harder Faster 13m E9 6c ★★
This murderous brute forsakes the easy(!) exit of *Gaia*, instead to head directly into nightmare territory. Full on at the grade, real E9.
Charlie Woodburn, 2000

31 Curving Arête 10m E5 6b ★★★
An all-out sizzler, climbing the unprotected arête on its right-hand side. A hard starting move leads to a gradual easing with height.
Derek Bolger, Ted Wells, 1976

32 Birch Tree Variant 10m VS 5a ★★
The left-hand of these two classics. Climb thin cracks to reach deeper cracks above. Follow these as they curve left, and either hand traverse the lowest break (containing the tree), or foot traverse at a gentler 4c.
◉ page 123

33 Birch Tree Wall 14m VS 5a ★★★
Classic. A roughshod pummel up cracks, jugs and breaks, sweeping a majestic line up the cliff. Crank out the thin lower crack (or start up the *Variant* and traverse in at a delicate 4c), and climb to a niche. From here follow a delicate traverse left along wide breaks to finish.
Jack Longland, Ivan M Waller, 1928

34 Demon Rib 15m E3 5c ★★★
The stuff of legend, which will test modern day bottle to the limit. Bold bouldering gains the flake on the arête. Take time to arrange good gear then continue up the arête in a position of great reverence. High in the grade.
Peter Harding, Tony Moulam, 1949

35 Lone Tree Groove 14m VS 5a ★★
A lot of climbing in one move. Move up to the cave in the gully on the right. From here, make a cack-handed jellywrestle onto the polished ramp on the left – dig those smears – and simple continuation above. ◉ page 39
Ivan M Waller, 1928

36 Lone Tree Gully 10m S 4a ★★
A fantastic, big steep route, full Black Rocks value. Jug up into the shallow cave then blast on up the crack and big features above. Well-protected joy.
Fred Pigott and party, 1920

West Wall

㊲ Pseudonym 11m E5 6b ★★
A cheeky little test of your grit technique. Follow the friendly ramp leftwards to its end (gear). Make urgent moves onto the hanging slab, then a delicate teeter left to the salvation of the break. From the gully, step back right to climb the easier arête above.
Nick Plishko, 1977

㊳ The Devil is in the Detail 11m E7 7a ★★
The largest dyno on a grit route? Follow *Pseudonym* to the break. Move right and make an all-out turbo for the pocket above. Conventional climbing leads to the top. Safe, but utterly desperate.
Tom Briggs, 2004

㊴ South Gully Rib 8m HS 4b ★
Technical fun. From the gully, make a contorted circumnavigation of the flake on the left to gain and finish up the short crack.

㊵ South Gully 8m HVD 4a ★
Tricky enough, in a full-body kind of way.
John Laycock, 1913

㊶ South Corner 8m HVS 4c ★
Tricky climbing with some cool moves, and not easy to protect. From the gully, swing right onto the flake, then finish rightward.

㊷ End Slab 8m D
A gentle route up the clean slab, often on chipped holds.

THE BLOCK
The last routes hereabouts are on the squat lump over on the right. Technique is the currency on this buttress, although it will buy you nothing without boldness.

㊸ Golden Days 8m E2 6b ★★
Fond. Climb the beautiful flake to the break then make easier moves to the top.
John Allen, Steve Bancroft, 1976

㊹ Jumpin' on a Beetle 8m E6 6c ★★
Boulder up to get stood in the chipped gutter. Step left and tickle up the blunt arête.
Johnny Dawes, 1994

㊺ The Angel's Share 8m E7 7a ★★
A visionary masterpiece with scant regard for anything that could be considered a hold in any real sense of the word. With commitment and magic feet, fall straight up the slab above the gutter.
Johnny Dawes, 1994

㊻ Velvet Silence 8m E6 6c ★★★
The Essence. From the ugly rockover, float over to, and up, the rounded arête. A route of great beauty, encapsulated perfectly in the name.
Gabriel Regan, 1986

The Block

The Block

The Block

THE FROGGATT AREA

**FROGGATT EDGE
CURBAR EDGE
GARDOM'S EDGE
BIRCHEN EDGE
CHATSWORTH EDGE**

Some routes have an extra quality about them that makes them stand out in climbers' memories, a personality that makes them more than the grade or the line. One of these routes is Froggatt's Tody's Wall. It has a cheeky smile, it plays tricks on you, it makes you huff and puff, but all the while you know that it's your friend. Felix James on one of grit's favourite HVSs (page 137). ◐ David Simmonite

On your knees, pilgrim! There is something prehistoric about the joy of being deep inside a gritstone chimney, a mixture of the twin horrors of enclosure and exposure. Here, Jon Winter is executing a textbook example of the crawl on Froggatt's Swimmer's Chimney, S 4a (page 135). Ian Parnell

FROGGATT EDGE

OS Grid Ref: SK 248 764 to SK 250 762
Altitude: 280m

Top-quality gritstone climbing, perhaps only eclipsed by the mighty Stanage and the Roaches. With a rich diversity of climbing styles and grades, the numerous classic lines offer an experience among the best to be found on gritstone.

The fine grit is of immaculate quality, with virtually every climb taking perfectly solid rock, giving home to some of the country's most sought after ticks. These range from amply-protected Moderates to poorly protected E9s, with most of the routes clocking in at reasonable grades. Arguably Froggatt's greatest showpiece is the Great Slab, containing perhaps the highest concentration of top-quality slab climbs anywhere on grit. Whilst these are mainly sparsely protected, there are plenty of better protected slab, wall and crack climbs on offer at all grades.

This magnificent southwest-facing edge stands proud above the Derwent Valley. It is a virtually continuous face of clean and quick-drying rock. Due to its sunny aspect, and excellent spread of routes, the crag is very popular throughout the year. It can be can be very hot on summer afternoons and evenings.

Approach: Park in the long, sweeping roadside bays 500m below the Grouse Inn on the A625, or in the National Trust car park (p&d) just uphill.

From the White Gate, on the long sweeping bend, the track leads for 750m to a gate; the crag starts 500m south of this gate, with an easy descent past Strapadictomy Buttress. An easier descent can be made at the southern end of the edge down the broad gap between the Froggatt and Curbar Edges.

An alternative approach is via a footpath starting just below the Chequers Inn; the path emerges beneath *Downhill Racer* between The Pinnacle and Great Slab areas of the crag.

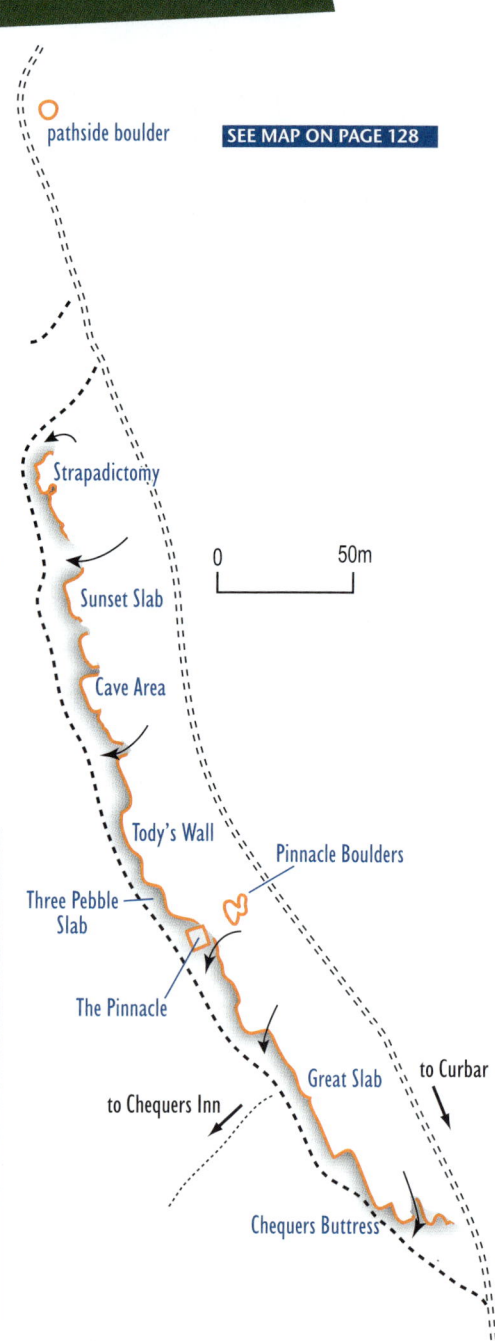

Froggatt is rightly famed, along with the Roaches in the west, as the capital of gritstone slab climbing. As it is often the way with this medium, protection is often either poor or, as in the case of most of Froggatt's harder offerings, totally absent. Ben Bransby cruxing out on the most celebrated of these, Downhill Racer, E4 6a (page 140). 📷 Ian Parnell

Froggatt Edge

> **STRAPADICTOMY BUTTRESS**
> The crag starts proper with a bunch of confident, rounded classics. Scrambling descents are possible to the left and right.

1 Strapiombante 8m E1 5b ★★
A chunky, easily protected climb. Follow the zigzag crack on good holds. Make a tricky exit leftwards, or finish direct. Highly satisfying.
Dave Brearly, Paul Nunn, 1962

2 Strapadictomy 9m E5 6a ★★★
One of the most unforgettable routes on grit. Boulder up the cheeky arête to the break. Crucify your way out to the flake on the arête and pull desperately up into a layback position. Now gun for the top. ⓞ page 144
John Allen, Steve Bancroft, 1976

3 Strapiombo 9m E1 5b ★★
The classic roof crack is the scene of many a mêlée. Traverse stylishly outwards until the easier finishing groove is gained with relief.
Don Whillans, Joe Brown, 1956

4 English Overhang 9m VS 4c ★
The friable flake to the right is gingerly used to gain the flared crack, which is followed direct.
Dave Gregory, Charles Darley, 1978

5 Scarper's Triangle 9m E1 5b ★
Climb a steep groove in the middle of the outside face, then press on boldly, direct up a crack.
John Fearon, Dave Gregory, 1957

6 Oss Nob 9m E4 6a ★
The bold arête, climbed on its right-hand side.
Colin Banton (solo), 1978

7 Left Flake Crack 8m S 4a ★
The corner crack to the right is a fine test in jamming skills but is sadly becoming polished.

8 Right Flake Crack 8m HS 4b
The crack widens awkwardly towards the top.
Wilf White, Slim Sorrell, 1949

9 Parallel Piped 8m E3 5c ★
The left arête of the slab has a couple of quick, smeary moves. Easier for the tall.
Graham Hoey (solo), 1986

10 Benign Lives 7m E6 6c ★★
A good tick for people who can think on their feet. Smear up the middle of the slab direct (harder) or using a flake on the right (logical).
Johnny Dawes, 1984

11 Mild 9m E4 6b ★
From the start of *Benign Lives*, tiptoe along the slab then smear more easily up the arête.
Julian Lines, 1992

Strapadictomy

There's not a lot of point in dragging ropes up there, but they look nice. Sunset Slab, HVS 4b (page 134), is the classic mid-grade Froggatt testpiece of how well leaders can think on their feet. The moves are easy, but seldom positive and the gear is sparse, so the ability to relax, layback and enjoy the ride, is crucial.
Ian Parnell

CAVE AREA

Sixty metres right, past a small square buttress, is the chunky Cave Area. This features the slabby, bold technicalities of *Sunset Slab* and steeper, quarried challenges around the cave itself.

12 Science Friction 12m E6 6a ★
The left arête of the slab will appeal to lovers of long terrifying falls.
Mark Miller, Bill McKee, 1980

13 North Climb 12m S 4a ★★
It's over 100 years since Puttrell first scaled this classic route. Go on, feel the history contained within this awkward crack.
JW Puttrell, Henry Bishop, C Douglas Yeomans, 1906

14 Sundowner 12m E2 5a ★
A cracking bold start and finish to *Sunset Slab* on smears and poor pockets. HVS with side-runners to the right.
John Allen, Neil Stokes, 1972

15 Sunset Slab 14m HVS 4b ★★★
Deservedly one of Froggatt's most famous routes. The first and the easiest in a long line of bold slabs along the crag. Follow the curving crack until it peters out. A smeary traverse leftwards leads to the base of a blind flake, up which faith and friction will be your only friends. ⊙ page 133
Joe Brown, Tony Hyde, Wilf White, 1948

16 Sunset Crack 10m HS 4b ★★
The thin crack is well protected throughout. Once over the crux bulge at the beginning, the rest should be plain sailing.
Len Chapman, Bob Tomsett, 1948

17 Turret Crack 10m S 4a ★
The crack just right puts up a stern fight at its beginning and end.
Don Chapman, Nat Allen, 1948

North Gully Descent: Immediately right of *Turret Crack* the gully provides a polished way down, with just a slightly awkward move to start the descent.

18 Slab and Crack 8m D ★
The ramp in the corner to the right provides a worthwhile though polished outing.
Nat Allen, Don Chapman, 1948

19 Soul Doubt 11m E8 6c ★★
The incredibly bold sidewall, direct, passing the base of the ramp.
Adrian Berry, 2000

20 Beau Geste 11m E7 6c ★★★
Jonny Woodward's era-defining ascent of the big left arête of the buttress really set the stage for hard gritstone climbing. Fiddle up the groove in the arête (RPs) to the break. Cams out right. Move left and make a desperate stretch for the tiny crack above. Slap up the pumpy arête above.
Jonny Woodward, 1982

Froggatt Edge | 135

㉑ Holly Groove 11m VS 4c ★
The twin-cracked corner is a fine climb.
Slim Sorrell, Nat Allen, 1948

㉒ Hawk's Nest Crack 11m VS 4c ★★★
A fabulous frolic up the well-positioned crack. From the large ledge, the flying flake on the left gives an optional, exposed climax.
Joe Brown, Slim Sorrell, 1948

㉓ Cave Crack Indirect 12m HVS 5a ★
Climb *Hawk's Nest Crack* to the chockstone, then traverse delicately right to finish up *Cave Crack*. An enjoyable little combo.
Dave Fooks, Alan Haigh, 2005

㉔ Cave Crack 11m E2 5c ★★★
Summon all your reserves! This strenuous route is a thuggish way up the archetypal gritstone roof-crack leaving the left side of the cave. Easy if you can do it, desperate if you can't; either way, a massive cam is useful.
Joe Brown, Slim Sorrell, 1950

㉕ Cave Crawl 16m HS 5a ★★
Deep fun. Starting from the back left-hand corner of the cave, layback up to gain a 'Journey to the centre of the Earth' type passage leading into *Swimmer's Chimney*. From just below the top of this, squeeze back leftwards to finish. Best soloed.

㉖ Cave Wall 11m E3 5c ★★
A Whillans special: bold and balancey, and at the top of the grade. Surmount the bulge to gain a small ledge. A hard move brings easier climbing but no protection. From the ledge move off rightwards, or tackle the direct finish (more 5c) through the intimidating roofs.
Don Whillans, 1958

㉗ Swimmer's Chimney 12m S 4a ★
The polished chimney is quite a classic of its type and not easy at all. ⊙ page 129
JW Puttrell, 1900s

㉘ Brightside 14m E2 5c ★★
A great wall climb with good protection. Go up *Swimmer's Chimney* for 3m. Swing rightwards round the arête and down to reach slanting finger slots in the centre of the wall. Long moves on good slopey edges remain.
Phil Burke, Paul Nunn, John Sheard, 1980

㉙ Greedy Pig 13m E5 6b ★
Battle up the steep thin crack before scurrying into *Brightside* at the earliest opportunity.
Paul Mitchell, 1981

㉚ Avalanche 11m E2 6a ★
The square-cut groove is tough for 6a; fortunately well protected by small wires.
E Emery (aid), 1967. FFA John Allen, 1975

136 | Froggatt Edge

31 **Mean Streak** 12m E6 6b ★★
The centre of the wall demands utmost respect and steely fingers. After a protectable crux, move rightwards and soldier on up the imposing wall on gradually improving holds.
Dominic Lee, 1981

32 **The Gully Joke** 15m E3 5c ★★
Climb the flake and groove, usually with a side-runner in *Terrace Crack*. From a ledge place small wires in the crack on the right and launch out leftwards and up on hidden holds.
John Allen, Steve Bancroft, Mark Stokes, 1975

33 **Terrace Crack** 13m HS 4b ★★
The well protected crack provides a juggy start and a thought-provoking finish.
Freda Rylett, Jack Macleod, 1940s

TODY'S WALL AREA
To the right is a tall clean buttress peppered with good slab climbs across the grades. The routes are deservedly popular, with some famous low and mid-grade classics.

34 **C.M.C. Slab** 10m HVS 5b ★
The narrow eliminate slab right of the arête is gained awkwardly, and climbed up its centre by great moves, placing gear in the next route (E2 without side-runners).
Members of the Castle Mountaineering Club, 1960s

35 **Heather Wall** 16m HVD 3c ★★★
A classic and perhaps the most popular route on the edge. A good start for beginners learning the art of jamming. Climb the thin lower crack, then blast up the joyous crack just to the right. Once over the polished crux bulge at the start, the rest is simply delightful.
Dick Brown, 1940s

36 **Ratbag** 9m E2 5b ★
Another bold slab climb. Step out from *Heather Wall* and climb the slab between the arête and the upper crack of *Tody's Wall*. HVS with side-runners.
John Allen, Steve Donnelly, Steve Bancroft, 1974

Tody's Wall

Froggatt Edge | 137

37 Tody's Wall 18m HVS 5a ★★★
Another of Froggatt's classics – never has grovelling been so much fun. From the centre of the bay climb to a projecting block. Somehow gain the top slab and, with whatever dignity remains, finish up the fine crack above.
⊙ page 126
Joe Brown, Slim Sorrell, 1948

38 Motorcade 10m E1 5a ★★
Brilliant slab action that can be combined with the start of *Tody's* to give one of the best E1s on the edge. From the ledge on the right, climb the centre of the slab. Protection feels distant when tackling the maze of slopey pockets towards the top. ⊙ page 139
D Warriner, G Johnson, 1969

39 Silver Crack 10m HS 4c ★
Starting just right, climb directly to the forked-lightning crack which is followed on ever-widening jams and joyous thrashing.
JW Puttrell, c1900

40 Bollard Crack 10m VS 4c ★
The leftward kinked crack is a bit of a struggle and requires big gear.
Slim Sorrell, 1948

41 Two-Sided Triangle 11m E1 5b ★
Climb the slab immediately right of the shallow groove using some shallow slopey pockets.
Gary Gibson, 1978

42 Three Pebble Slab 10m E1 5a ★★★
One of the great slab climbs on grit, guaranteed to give you a buzz. The route is at the bottom of its grade, although the top 4c slab can easily reduce the strongest to tears and raise muttered calls for top ropes. Climb up the lower slab to a weird pocket (runner). Delicate crux moves lead up and right to a sloping shelf. Pad straight up to finish. ⊙ page 13
Joe Brown, Wilf White, Tony Hyde, 1948

43 Four Pebble Slab 9m E3 5c ★
The sister route is considerably harder, and just as dangerous. Climb rightwards (but not too far right) through the steep ground, before gathering your thoughts, moving leftwards and pressing on up the committing upper slab. The **Direct Start** is E4 5c, involving a *Tody's Wall*-type manoeuvre.
John Allen, Neil Stokes, 1972. Direct, Gary Gibson, 1978

44 Grey Slab 13m HS 4a ★★
Butch moves on big holds lead up the right side of the slab until a large ledge is reached. The crack above is difficult to protect, difficult to climb, but seems even more difficult to fall out of!
Jack Macleod, Freda Rylett, 1940s

Three Pebble Slab

Froggatt Edge

RIGHT-HAND AREA

The right-hand area is the showpiece of the crag, where a hundred metres of quarried walls and slabs hold a peerless collection of testpieces across the grades. Starting with the famous Froggatt Pinnacle, perhaps the finest pinnacle on grit, then passing many slab climbs, both bold and safe, and finishing with the last natural hurrah by Chequers Buttress. All routes are clean and quick-drying.

There is a convenient scrambly descent behind the pinnacle and a very easy one at the end of the crag.

45 Valkyrie 20m HVS 5a, 5a ★★★
'The' essential mid-grade tick on the crag with two contrasting pitches and a wonderfully positioned belay. Pummel up the jam-crack then hand traverse right to a belay on the arête. Step right again and go up to a short crack, then move left on to the sloping nose and more easily to the summit. Abseil from ring bolt to descend.
Joe Brown, Wilf White, 1949

46 Narcissus 9m E6 6b ★★★
The lower arête of the pinnacle is home to one of the best routes of its grade on grit with sustained, hard bouldering all the way. Finish up *Valkyrie* or traverse off.
Steve Bancroft, 1976

47 Oedipus! Ring Your Mother 9m E4 6b ★★
Proctor's bold testpiece. From the gully, make a fierce, fingery traverse leftwards along the thin break to good holds near the arête. From here, climb the blind flake in the wall above, with an ankle-worrying stretch for the ledge. Finish up *Valkyrie*. The direct start is easier.
Tom Proctor, 1968

Back of the Pinnacle: The next two routes start by scrambling up the start of the descent gully. They are based on the backmost arête, opposite *Narcissus*.

48 Chapman's Crack 11m HS 4b ★
From the arête, traverse a shelf leftwards to a mantel leading to a tricky finishing crack.
Len Chapman, Bob Tomsett, 1948

49 Route One 8m VS 5a ★
Henry Bishop's original route goes direct from the start of *Chapman's Crack* via an awkward mantel.
Henry Bishop, Douglas Yeomans, 1912

50 Diamond Crack 8m HS 4b ★★
The polished cracks in the centre of the wall are climbed by some fierce jamming, with increasing difficulty, but excellent protection throughout.
Henry Bishop, Douglas Yeomans, 1913

51 Corner Crack 9m HD
The corner-crack from a crux start.

Froggatt Pinnacle

Dave Hinton thinking on his feet on Motorcade, E1 5a (page 137), one of the many tests of footwork and confidence on the edge. 📷 Paul Evans

Froggatt Edge

Sickle Buttress

52 Left Broken 9m VS 5a ★
Don't underestimate the awkwardness of this short, frustrating climb. Tussle with the initial groove/chimney before finishing more easily.
Slim Sorrell, Nat Allen, 1953

53 Broken Crack 9m VS 5a ★★
Another Joe Brown route; a well-protected brute. The slanting crack really packs its punch in the top half, where a choice is to be made. To jam or to layback, that is the question?
Joe Brown, Wilf White, Slim Sorrell, 1948

54 Sickle Buttress 10m S 4a ★★
Gain the halfway ledge in the centre of the buttress, then move right through a scoop, to finish in a groove on the arête. A butch route for the grade.
RE Davies, RA Brown, 1945

55 Sickle Buttress Direct 9m VS 4c ★
From the ledge, continue directly up the wall with some fine climbing.
Nat Allen, Don Chapman, 1948

56 Performing Flea 9m HVS 5a ★
The bold right arête tackled on either side.
Matt Boyer (solo), 1985

57 Congestion Crack 10m HS 4c
The slim groove bounding the steep slab.
Nat Allen, Slim Sorrell, Wilf White, J Morgan, 1948

58 Long John's Slab 11m E3 5c ★★
A good introduction to the harder slabs, with a low crux. From the block, gain a narrow ledge then make crux pulls (very reachy) to better holds. At the steepening, swing right to finish.
Paul Gray (1pt), 1968. FFA Al Rouse, 1969

59 Downhill Racer 14m E4 6a ★★★
Livesey's infamous creation, tracing a lonely and uncompromising line up the right side of the slab. From the right, climb up and left to make desperate moves to get stood on a thin break. Follow better holds along a ramp, until a final committing move to the top.
◎ page 131
Pete & Alex Livesey, 1977

60 Slab Recess Direct 14m HS 4b ★
Determination is needed to overcome the initial steep and polished groove. If the large upper groove is reached, climb this more easily to the top.
Joe Brown, 1948

61 Slab Recess 18m D ★★
The most popular beginner's route on the crag. Climb *Gamma* for a few metres before strolling leftwards to the base of a large flake. A short layback past this brings easier ground, finishing leftwards.
Sandy Alton, J Morgan, 1948

Downhill Racer

Froggatt Edge | 141

62 Gamma 12m D ★
A great beginner's route following the crack.
Nat Allen, Wilf White, 1951

63 Allen's Slab 19m S 4a ★★
A great climb – technical and balancey – just don't expect too much protection. From *Gamma* follow the diagonal break to a ledge. Continue delicately right to finish on good holds just left of *Trapeze Direct*.
Nat Allen, Wilf White, 1951

64 Trapeze Direct 15m VS 5a ★★
A popular VS lead, containing mainly easy climbing, with only one source of well-protected difficulty. Follow the large crack direct.
Wilf White, Chuck Cook, 1948

65 Trapeze 14m VD ★★
Follow *Trapeze Direct* to the bulge, thank goodness you're not heading straight up, and traverse right to a short left-trending groove. Excellent climbing through steep ground, on more than adequate holds.
RE Davies, Dick Brown, 1945

66 Nursery Slab 9m M ★
The aptly named broken rocks at the left side of the large expanse of slabs.
JW Puttrell, Henry Bishop, Douglas Yeomans, 1906

67 Heartless Hare 11m E5 5c ★★
Technically harder than *Hairless Heart*, but a bit less scary. After a few thin moves, a small positive edge leads more easily to the break.
Steve Bancroft, John Allen, 1975

68 Jugged Hare 13m E6 6a ★★
From *Heartless Hare*, a delicate move right on poor holds leads to an uncomfortable position at the break. Another very worrying move allows better holds on the steep headwall to be gained.
Johnny Dawes, 1983

69 The Great Slab 19m E3 5b ★★★
Joe Brown's sweeping line – first soloed on sight in Woolworths' pumps (think about that on the crux) – remains the classic of the slab. Trend rightwards up the slab to a small, all-too-comfortable ledge. Cool your boots here, and grasp rightwards along a line of well-used footholds (crux) until awkward but juggy holds lead to the top and a great feeling of euphoria.
Joe Brown, Wilf White, 1951

70 Hairless Heart 16m E5 5c ★★★
An exquisite and haunting pitch with no hiding places, guaranteed to scare the bejesus out of you. From the little ledge on *The Great Slab*, move up to the blank left-facing flake. Smear up this then quickly exit rightwards.
John Allen, 1975

71 Artless 16m E5 6b ★★
The bouldery slab has fabulous climbing, and has the safest crux. Gain a small ledge then make a series of decisive moves up the ramp to eventually gain the better holds at the end of the traverse on *The Great Slab*. Finish up this.
John Allen, 1976

72 Toy Boy 15m E7 7a ★★
"A route with no holds and long reaches in between." A ferocious solo.
Ron Fawcett, 1986

73 Synopsis 13m E2 5c ★★
The once-pegged crack at the right side of the slab is a good climb, but with slightly awkward holds and fiddly protection. Smooth and high in the grade.
Nat Allen, D Carnell, R Handley (5pts), 1952. FFA Steve Bancroft, John Allen, 1974

74 Beta 12m VD ★
The deep chimney and broken corner are taken direct.
Nat Allen, Wilf White, 1951

Great Slab

Froggatt Edge

75 Brown's Eliminate 17m E2 5b ★★★
A great wall climb from the Master with thoughtful, crimpy moves which, although bold, are still inside the safety net. From a few metres up the corner, traverse left to gain a big ledge (gear at foot level on the left arête). Thin moves, that are showing sign of wear, allow the wall right of the arête to be climbed on slowly-improving holds.
Joe Brown, Slim Sorrell, Wilf White, 1948

76 Armageddon 14m E3 5c ★★
The harder, but well worthwhile sister route to *Brown's Eliminate*. A problem start left of the corner leads to the ledge. Continue in a direct line, in an increasingly serious position, but on reasonably good holds. E2 with side-runners.
Alec Burns, Andy Brown, T Wilkinson, 1977

77 Green Gut 13m S 4a ★★★
The fantastic corner line gives honest and classic bridging with a crux where it should be – near the top. Can give a real tussle if you don't think.
Nat Allen, Wilf White, 1948

78 Pedestal Crack 12m HVS 5a ★★
The long steep and awkward crack is climbed direct. The innocuous crux arrives whilst passing the overlap towards the top.
Joe Brown, Nat Allen, 1948

79 The Big Crack 14m E2 5b ★★★
A fine outing up the steep wide crack in the headwall. Gear is reasonable, which is more than can be said of the holds in the upper section. Butch moves on good slots lead to the base of the deep, dark crack. This succumbs to a somewhat different approach.
Don Whillans (1pt), 1955. FFA John Syrett, 1973

80 Stiff Cheese 13m E2 5c ★
The short crack is short, but definitely stiff. Worth placing the awkward protection before committing to the crux moves onto the ledge. Finish up the easy groove as for the next route.
Steve Bancroft (solo), 1974

81 Beech Nut 13m E1 5c ★
A tough nut to crack. The increasingly difficult crack saps your energy, before handing out one final move to reach the ledge, and an easy finish up the groove.
Don Whillans, Nat Allen, 1951

82 Chequers Crack 12m HVS 5b ★★
A local testpiece. The smooth, though well protected crack succumbs to a combination of laybacks and jams. From a breather at the half-way ledge, the delightful upper crack is cruised on perfect jams.
Don Whillans, Joe Brown, 1951

Brown's Eliminate

Froggatt Edge | 143

83 Chequers Buttress 15m HVS 5a ★★★
Pure joy, with exposure, protection and great moves: a route you'll do again and again. Follow the ramp rightwards, then traverse the wall up and left until a long move brings a huge jug on the arête into reach. The spectacular finishing arête eases considerably.
John Gosling, Mike Simpkins, 1962

84 Chequers Climb 18m VS 4c ★★
The original, and the true start of the Chequered history, combining the easy bits of *Chequers Buttress* and *Crack* with an exposed traverse. From the ledge on the buttress traverse under the roof to gain the delightful finish of the crack.
Joe Brown, Wilf White, Nat Allen, Don Chapman, 1949

85 Bacteria Cafeteria 12m E1 5b ★★
An eliminate line, but with good climbing. From the foot of the ramp, follow a tiny groove, crossing the leftward traverse of *Chequers Buttress*, to finish up cracks right of the arête.
Gary Gibson, Jon Walker, Paul Bird, 1979

86 Solomon's Crack 14m VD ★
Follow the starting ramp of *Chequers Buttress* to it's top. Finish up the corner above stepping right at the top. There are three harder variations at around S 4a: the wide 'Victorian' crack in the left wall; the overhanging top corner; or the deceptive slot on the right.

87 Jankers Crack 10m HS 4b ★★
Very good climbing which presents a series of puzzles that can dispirit the unbeliever. Climb the blocky groove and wider undercut crack directly above. Jamming ability is a big plus for this route.
Joe Brown, Don Chapman, 1949

88 Jankers Groove 11m VS 4c ★
Follow the last route to the roof then step right to take the next crack. If you keep your cool this one is a real soft touch; if you bury yourself in the back of the climb and ignore your feet, expect a struggle.
Joe Brown, Don Chapman, 1949

89 Jankers End 14m VS 4b ★
Continue the traverse of *Jankers Groove* until once round the arête (a direct start limits the fun too much). From here a shallow groove is climbed, before stepping back leftwards to finish up the slabby arête.
Slim Sorrell, Nat Allen, 1949

Chequers Buttress

FROGGATT TO BLACK ROCKS
The definitive gritstone guide

The range of crags that stretches from the mighty Froggatt and Curbar in the north to the fantastic oddness of Black Rocks in the south, is arguably the finest and most varied collection of outcrops on gritstone.

Everything is here, from big leads on mighty classics to tucked-away ticks on quiet wooded buttresses. From top-level highballs to gentle bouldering circuits. From Victorian tweed-wrecking classics to the latest nerve-testing desperates.

Here is a guide that lays out these myriad joys as never seen before. Where first-time visitors will find the classics and locals will find endless surprises. Where inspiration and information come together perfectly to give a lifetime's worth of climbing. Whether you know what you want or are in search of something new, this guide will show the way.

Pick up the definitive guide for details of every route on the crags selected here as well as a great number of crags for users of this book who get the bug and want to find out more.

With full coverage of routes and boulder problems on crags from the **Northern Area** (including Froggatt, Curbar, Yarncliffe, Baslow, Tegness, Gardom's, Chatsworth, Birchen), obscure gems in the **Beeley-Matlock Area** (including Harland Edge, Hall Moor Quarry and the Upper Matlock Quarries), gems in the **Cratcliffe Area** (Cratcliffe, Robin Hood's Stride, Eagle Tor, Rowtor Rocks and Stanton Moor), **The Amber Valley crags** (Eastwood, Turning Stone Edge, Cocking Tor), and finally the **Cromford Area** (starring Black Rocks, along with the shy joys of Bauston Tor, Robin Hood Quarries, Leashaw Brow, Chasecliffe and Shining Cliff).

Featuring:
2,200 routes from Mod to E9
1,100 boulder problems
130 full-colour action shots
The definitive climbing history of the area

Get it from the BMC shop for a lifetime of gritstone action.

http://shop.thebmc.co.uk/

ISBN 978-0-903908-09-2

Front cover: Richard Buswell on Strapadictomy, E5 6a, Froggatt (page 132). Photo: Mike Hutton

Big cracks, wide cracks, steep cracks, technical cracks. All these give the true spice of Curbar and, much like Hen Cloud in the West, grades will never tame the experiences on these. Andy Gardner on Peapod, HVS 5b (page 162). Pete O'Donovan

CURBAR EDGE

OS Grid Ref: SK 253 756 to SK 258 750
Altitude: 310m

One of the most impressive crags on grit with a well-deserved reputation for tough climbs, usually requiring boldness, determination and power.

Situated high above Curbar village, with magnificent views overlooking the Derwent Valley. The edge faces south-west and gets plenty of sun, with wonderful evening light. It is also exposed to the wind and the cold. The rock is extremely clean and quick drying.

Approach: The usual parking is the pay and display carpark at Curbar Gap. A path leads off from here along the top of the cliff all the way to Froggatt and beyond. There are a few other opportunities on the road 250m below this, from where a path leads to the Right-Hand Area.

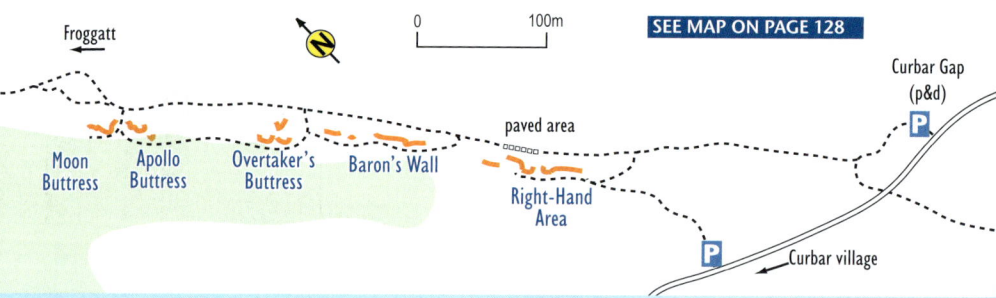

MOON BUTTRESS AREA

A tight-knit collection of powerful buttresses. The climbs are characterised by rounded, aggressive bulges, and all provide forceful routes at the top of the quality ladder. Moon Buttress is clearly visible from the approach path. Drop down the easy gully to access all areas. The approach is around 20 minutes from Curbar Gap.

1 Mastiff Wall 7m VS 4c ★
The parallel cracks are started with some difficulty and finished steeply on good holds.
Nat Allen, Derek Burgess, 1964

2 Rat Scabies 11m E3 6b ★★
The undercut wall provides an excellent micro-route. Mantel over the lower bulge with gusto, a move you will remember ten years later, followed by a still-tricky finish up the wall.
Gabe Regan, 1970s

3 Bulldog Crack 11m S 4a ★
The corner, moving right to a ledge at midway.
K Brindley, Wilf White, 1950

4 John's Arête 11m E1 5c ★
Climb the bold arête on its left to the ledge. Finish up the front of the buttress above.
Steve Bancroft, John Allen, Con Carey, 1975

Curbar Edge | 147

5 Derwent Groove 10m HS 4a ★
The groove has a hard start and a harder finish.
Nat Allen, E Burton, 1950

6 Cool Moon 12m E7 6c ★★
A bold, technical outing up the sidewall, starting from the block on the left. Make hard moves to good holds and then an overlap. Further hard, scary moves gain an S-shaped crack and an easier finish.
Daniel & Dominic Lee (pre-placed runners), 1981

7 Moon Walk 12m E4 6a ★★★
One of the best E4s on grit: the ride up the top arête, as the gear recedes, is religious. Start steeply up flakes and follow the arête to the top ledge and easier finish. The very definition of grit E4 6a.
John Allen, Nicky Stokes, Mark Stokes, 1976

8 Moon Crack 14m E5 6b ★★★
A cantankerous and powerful route which regularly spanks the hopeful. Strenuously attack the crack until through the bulge. Continue to reach a flared break, then delicately move right to an easier finish up the groove.
John Allen, Steve Bancroft, 1975

9 Sorrell's Sorrow 12m HVS 5a ★★
The wide central crack provides a superb gritstone fight. After a steep and desperate entry, the climb is merely awkward, to an easier-angled finish. Modern climbers will require some big cams at the grade.
Joe Brown, Slim Sorrell, 1950

10 The End of the Affair 13m E8 6c ★★★
A route with pedigree. The impending arête gives a sensational route which captures the essence of hard gritstone; elegant, technical, and precarious climbing in an outrageous situation. Starting on a block on the right, climb the arête direct with a crux top move. A low cam and rapid belayer protect.
Johnny Dawes, Nick Dixon, 1986

Curbar Edge

Moon Gully: Up the gully from Moon Buttress lie some shorter climbs.

12 Twin Crack 8m HS 4b ★
The wide left-hand crack doesn't give up easily.
Slim Sorrell, Nat Allen, 1950

13 Straight Crack 7m VD
The right-hand crack has a hard start.
Slim Sorrell, Nat Allen, 1950

14 Ulysses or Bust 7m E5 6b ★★★
A perfect gritstone solo. The arête is climbed mostly on its right-hand side. As the landing gets further away, the moves get thinner, until a precarious crux gains the break.
Neil Foster (solo), 1984

15 The Unreachable Star 7m E2 6a ★★
A mini-classic up the tenuous crack, with a committing move to gain the break.
Mark Stokes, 1980

11 Amphitheatre Crack 8m S 4a ★
The wide crack, with a difficult start and easier finish.
Slim Sorrell, Nat Allen, 1950

16 Dog-Leg Crack 5m S 4b ★★
One of the best easy jamming cracks in the Peak, perfection for its size.

APOLLO BUTTRESS AREA
Like a malignant boxing glove, this mighty buttress calls out its challenge to all. The routes are all tough and brilliant, taking powerful cracks and jutting overhangs. Get ready for a rumble.

Curbar Edge | 149

17 Buckle's Sister 7m HVD 4a ★
The first corner crack has a steep juggy start.
Nat Allen, Sandy Alton, Bob Kerry, 1950

18 Buckle's Brother 7m HVS 4c ★
The next crack to the right is wide and awkward.
Nat Allen, Sandy Alton, Bob Kerry, 1950

19 Buckle's Crack 6m HVS 4c ★
Get deeply involved in the corner crack.
Nat Allen, Sandy Alton, Bob Kerry, 1950

20 Soyuz 10m E2 5c ★★
A great route fitting the Curbar mould, that feels surprisingly urgent for its size. Follow the flake to sloping breaks. Move right to a short flake where a stretch gains the top. The direct is reachy and a wee bit harder.
John Allen, Neil Stokes, 1972

21 Dark Entries 10m E4 6a ★
A good but tough route. Pull through the roof to the left of the arête, trending left to a short crack then back right and up to an easier finish.
Ron Fawcett, Gill Fawcett, 1980

22 Forbidden Planet 11m E5 6b ★★
A great route – beefy, big and bruising – which swaggers up the front of the tower. From the ledge, pull over the overhang to a deep break. A hard move up gains a standing position below the roof. From here, either move left and grasp up the arête, or do the original method and claw up the wall. Big cams are useful.
John Allen, Mark Stokes, 1984

23 Apollo 19m E2 5c ★★★
A very butch, brilliant and exposed pitch. From the big ledge, shuffle right until halfway along the shelf. Pull through the centre of the roof to gain the base of a short crack. Struggle up the crack then delicately trend rightwards in a superb position up the upper wall.
John Gosling, Mike Simpkins, 1969

24 The Beer Hunter 17m E3 6a ★★
A fine, technical and grasping route, although a little short-lived. Climb the cracks in the sidewall to reach the main ledge. Move steeply up then make hard moves out left, past a very short crack, to reach a hidden pocket around the arête. Move up the arête to a short break and swing back onto the sidewall to finish.
Steve Bancroft, Tim Rhodes, 1979

25 Two Pitch Route 15m VS 5a ★★★
A fabulous pitch if started up *The Beer Hunter* at solid HVS. Otherwise start off the ledge. The twisting crack on the steep sidewall above is a brilliant exercise in crack climbing. The original and scrappy lower pitch traversing in from the left is not described here.
Joe Brown, 1950

Apollo Buttress 20 mins

Brain Buttress: The jutting tower taken by the Curbar classic *The Brain* is easily seen from the top path. It is approached from the wide gully between Moon and Apollo Buttresses.

26 The Brain 20m VS 4c ★★
An excellent and varied adventure. Traverse the lower slab rightwards from the bottom left to gain a possible stance in the corner. Climb the corner on the right of the tower with increasing difficulty, or, better and easier, step left from halfway up to a lovely exposed arête finish. ⓘ opposite page
Slim Sorrell, Nat Allen, Wilf White, 1940s

27 Mensa 14m E6 6b ★★
A protectable but committing route up the exposed left arête. Climb the lower slab directly, then follow the arête direct to the top, with the crux being just above the half-height break. Very reachy.
Neil Foster, Martin Veale, 1993

28 Birthday Crack 7m VS 5a ★★
In the corner right of *The Brain* is a chimney system (HS). This butch route takes a steep fissure in the angles just right of the upper chimney. Bridge up to make a difficult pull on jams to gain the upper groove and an easier finish.
Joe Brown, 1950

29 Diet of Worms 9m E4 5c ★★
A classic Curbar frightener, good for people who don't worry enough. Start a few metres left of the arête and climb up to a committing traverse right to join the arête at the break (big cam). Finish up the arête with difficulty.
Paul Mitchell, 1978

30 Slackers 9m E6 6b ★★
An excellent direct start to *Diet of Worms* up the sharp arête on its left-hand side. The poor landing puts a cowardly expression on all but the bravest faces.
Robin Barker, 1997

31 Birthday Groove 9m E1 5c ★
A tricky, reachy and worrying entrance gives access to the attractive groove. Things soon ease.
Valkyrie Mountaineering Club, 1950

Memorable leads lie along the whole length of this mighty crag, providing moments and memories for all climbers, whether the E8 leader on End of the Affair or the VS climber on The Brain (opposite page). They are all brilliant. Tom Luff climbing. ◉ Mike Cheque

152 | Curbar Edge

OVERTAKER'S BUTTRESS AREA
Some neat craglets sit below the edge. The jutting prow of Triplet Buttress can be seen just below the path.

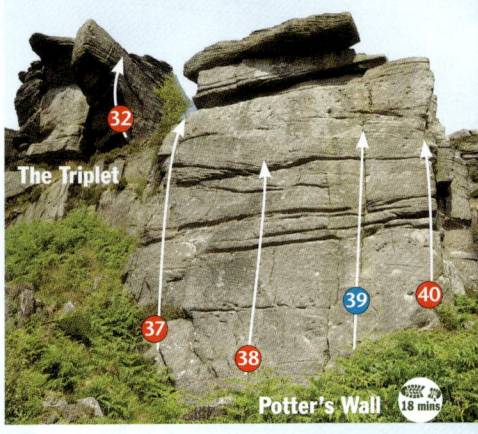

The Triplet: The wall facing Curbar Gap holds a mini-classic:

32 Fidget 6m E2 6b ★★
Climb the short downhill arête to the overhang and press on to the short, steep flake-crack.
John Allen, 1979

Overtaker's Buttress: This is on a lower level, below Triplet Buttress.

33 Overtaking on the Outside 6m S 4a
Takes the front of the fun rib on the left.
Steve Clark, Lynn Robinson, 2003

34 Overtaker's Buttress 18m HVS 5b ★
Move easily up and right on jugs and ledges. From their end, duck under the lower overhangs and teeter across the slab to the gully (sensible belay, 4c to here). Finish with tricky crux moves on the right wall of the nose.
Don Chapman, Nat Allen, 1954

35 Overtaker's Direct 10m E2 5c ★
Climb the groove on the left of the buttress to a ledge. Move up and left past some creaking holds to a final bulge. Mantel this bulge with difficulty.
Mike Simkins, John Gosling, 1970s

36 White Lines 13m E7 6c ★★★
Essential Dawes, with brilliant moves on the lower wall. Move up until forced right to a small undercut. More hard moves lead to the break. Climb the upper overhangs direct via a shallow pocket to a frightening top out.
Johnny Dawes, 1984

Potter's Wall: This pleasant buttress lies just right at the same lower level, past the descent.

37 Gone to Pot 11m E1 5c ★
The groove on the far left of the wall gives some delightfully bold climbing. Finish over the capping block (or slink off left at E1 5b).
Paul Harrison, Dave Simmonite, 2002

38 Mad Hatter 12m E2 5c ★★
Go direct up the middle of the buttress until below the centre of the protruding capstone at the top. Attack this direct to a puzzling finish.
John Gosling, 1966

39 Potter's Wall 10m VS 4b ★★
The cracks on the right of the face. Sustained and more pulse-raising than you might expect.
⊙ opposite page

40 Circus of Dinosaurs 9m E1 5b
The right arête; avoid the crack as much as you can.
Roy Bennett, Dave Simmonite, 1989

Curbar is less well-known for its more gentle routes but they are there for those who know where to look. A leader on one of the best of these gems, Potter's Wall, VS 4b (opposite page). 📷 Neil Foster

BARON'S WALL AREA
Back on the edge, some 200m right, is this steep and clean-cut wall. This holds a great collection of vertical face and crack climbs that always manage to put you under a bit of pressure. There are lots of variations and boulder problems around the start of the routes.

41 Smoke ont' Watter 9m E1 6a ★★
A problem start in the centre of the wall leads to the obvious and difficult finger crack.
Nicky Stokes, John Allen, 1976

42 Baron's Wall 9m HVS 5b ★★
Hard initial moves up the right of the wall soon gain good holds. Move up and left to a break and the rewarding jamming crack above.
Joe Brown, Nat Allen, 1950s

43 Sweet Gene Vincent 10m HVS 5c
Hard bouldery moves gain the break. Step left and power up the juggy crack. Eliminate fun.
Gary Gibson, 1979

44 Saddy 9m E2 5c ★
A nervy little test of technique. The crack is followed direct. High in the grade.
Steve Bancroft, Nicky Stokes, Neil Stokes, 1977

45 Wall Climb 9m VS 5a ★★
This classy, slanting, shallow groove gives surprisingly sustained climbing, so a positive approach pays dividends. It does ease towards the top if you have any strength left to celebrate getting there.
Valkyrie Mountaineering Club, 1950

46 Top Secret 9m E1 5c ★
Climb the right arête of the wall on its left side, past a break and hard move, to an easier finish.
T Nicholls, 1966

47 Calver Chimney 9m D
The chimney is a good climb if dry, or a slip-sliding acquired taste if not.

48 Calver Wall 8m VS 5a ★★
Climb the groove above the block to the ledge. The impressive crack, directly above, gives considerably more trouble than estimated from below. It's your choice: hard and safe finger locks or easier but precarious layaways.

49 Brindle Crack 10m HS 4b ★
From the same start, walk right to climb the delightful shallow corner-crack.

50 Polar Crack 9m VS 4b ★
Lower down and right; a wide crack, with helpful holds on the outside, leads to a ledge and strenuous moves up the crack above.

51 Arctic Nose 8m HS 4b ★
Boldly climb the right arête of the wall to a ledge. Finish direct up the bulging crack above and left with difficulty.

Curbar Edge | 155

Flying Buttress: Just over to the right is a jutting buttress.

52 The Corner 9m HVS 5b ★
Hard initial moves and an easy upper section.
Joe Brown, Joe Smith, 1955

53 Flying Buttress 12m S 4a ★★
A peach. Start up either side of the jutting rib and romp the upper cracks. Sticking strictly to the left crack is a pleasant HS 4b.

54 U.F.O. 7m S 4a
The crack and grooved arête on the right.

Quarry Face: The right-hand end of this section has some fierce walls and cracks.

55 By George 7m E3 6b
The thin crack on the left has a tough sequence past the small groove to gain the break.
Keith Sharples, Graham Hoey, 1984

56 Culture Shock 11m E1 5c ★
The thin cracks to the right past hard moves to an uncomfortable position at the break. Once adjusted, the climbing eases.
Ian Riddington, Keith Sharples, 1982

57 Confidence Trick 11m E2 5c ★
Easily climb through the loose blocks to the ledge, then climb the flaked wall above to the break. Finish direct. A side-runner in *Culture Shock* protects the initial moves on the upper wall.
John Russell, Doug Kerr, 1985

58 Ling Crack 11m HS 4c ★
Gains the testing deep crack from cracks right of the ramp; the easier original start up the ramp is now rather overgrown.
Slim Sorrell, Nat Allen, 1949

59 Incestuous 11m E2 6a ★
The thin crack to the right is gained from a ledge. A long reach is followed by hard moves to the grassy break and then an easier finish. Harder for the short, or is it just shorter for the hard?
John Allen, Nicky Stokes, 1976

60 Cardinal's Backbone II 11m E3 5c ★
Nice face climbing. Starting on the right, reach the break, then move left and up the discontinuous flakes, trending leftwards. The direct start is 6a.
Nicky Stokes, John Allen, 1976

61 Vain 11m E3 5b ★★
A great line, with climbing to match. The arête, starting on the left, before swinging round for a committing final move on its right side.
John Allen, 1976

Curbar Edge

Kayak Slab

RIGHT-HAND AREA
There now begins the most popular set of walls and buttresses on the crag, with almost 200 metres of fearsome vertical and bulging rock, with sheer walls, holdless slabs, searing corners, thrusting cracks and brutal arêtes, all giving flawless lines and unforgettable challenges. The quarried wall holds some of the biggest routes on the edge. They are generally ferocious, fingery, technical and bold.

Kayak Slab: One of Curbar's few true slabs. But what you lose in angle, you gain in everything else: the routes are bold and technical, with hand and foot holds often feeling a bit unhelpful. Be brave, and be good.

1 Kayak 9m E1 5c ★★
The brilliant and original route on the slab. Move up, then rightwards to gain good holds in the middle of the slab. Move right again to a tricky finish or go straight up (both reachy).
Colin Mortlock, 1964

2 Finger Distance 9m E3 6b ★★
The middle of the slab is an elegant problem. Thin moves on shallow scoops and pockets gains the finish just left of *Kayak*.
Gary Gibson, 1980

3 El Vino Collapso 8m E5 6a ★
More technical delights. The rounded flake is climbed to worrying moves for the break and flutings at the top. The final crux move may feel a little stiff if you can't reach the fluting.
John Allen, 1985

4 Canoe 6m E2 5c ★
Drummond's classy addition. Climb the pocketed left side of the slab with difficult moves to reach and move up from the break and a sandy topout that might require a clean.
Ed Drummond, 1970s

5 Stopper 8m E4 6a ★★
The centre of the slab is a seriously reachy affair, climbed on rounded pockets to the appalling break. From there, a stretch gains the top.
Ron Fawcett, 1987

6 White Water 7m E6 6c ★★
A little gem, first climbed ground-up and pre-pads. Start beneath a flake. Make a hard move off the flake to reach good pockets. Leave the security of these past an insecure mantel to finish.
Johnny Dawes, 1984

7 Done Years Ago 7m E3 6b
Climb the crack and bulge then trend rightwards to finish up the arête.
Johnny Dawes, 1984

Quarry Face

Kayak

Curbar Edge | 157

8 Avalanche Wall 12m HVS 5a ★★★
A Curbar classic that can feel hard for the grade. Pummel the fabulous cracks as they converge to reach the wider upper crack. Thankfully this soon eases.
Joe Brown, 1950

9 One Step Beyond 20m E6 6b ★★★
Fawcett's original line up the blank wall. Climb rightwards to good edges. Make a tricky move up then traverse rightwards to a gear slot. Hard moves then lead right to a good edge and the end of the major difficulties.
Ron Fawcett, Phil Burke, Chris Gibb, 1980

10 Doctor Dolittle 20m E10 7a ★★
A hideously technical slab climb with very marginal protection. The crux is gaining the high overlap.
John Arran, 2001

11 Slab and Crack 15m E7 6c ★★★
An awesome line up the middle of the wall is about as hard as E7 ever gets. Climb direct to gain a halfway slot and protection. Now it gets hard! Follow the hairline crack above.
Johnny Dawes, 1986

12 Owl's Arête 15m HS 4c ★★
The right arête of the wall feels exposed but is well protected. Follow the groove until holds on the left allow the slabby face to be followed.
Slim Sorrell, Nat Allen, 1949

13 Predator 13m E2 5c ★
The thin crack left of the corner is not a thing of beauty, but it's a fine test of crack skills.
Joe Brown, Ron Moseley (aid), 1957. FFA, John Allen, 1976

14 Argosy 14m VS 4c ★
The corner gives some classic action.
Slim Sorrell, Chuck Cook, 1940s

15 P.M.C.1 15m HS 4a ★★★
Awesome terrain. Climb steep, deep cracks past some marvellous jamming to a ledge and an airy finish on flakes leading rightwards. Exit right or step back left for more fun moves.
Bob Tomsett, Len Chapman, 1948

Curbar Edge

ELDER BUTTRESS
A big, bruising and brilliant buttress, one of the great Curbar buttresses.

16 The Fall 16m E6 6b ★★
The big sidewall holds a heart-stopper. Start just right of centre and climb straight up, past a pocket, until forced rightwards to a resting place on the arête of *Profit*. Climb the wall left of the top arête to a terrifying last move.
John Allen, Dave Fearnley, 1987

17 Profit of Doom 16m E5 6b ★★★
The hanging groove in the arête is the very definition of grit technicality. Trend easily rightwards to a ledge on the arête and right again to the base of the groove. Bridge up the perplexing groove to a hard exit. Small protection in the groove is often pre-placed at E4.
John Allen, 1975

18 Rigid Digit 16m E5 6b ★★
Outmoded maybe, but still brilliant, and hard. Climb the lower groove to a junction with *Profit* and its fiddly protection. Span out right and monkey-up-a-stick to reach the final groove of *Janus*, which ensures a battle all the way.
Ron Fawcett, 1980

19 Janus 18m E6 6b ★★★
The immaculate changing grooves on the front of the buttress is one of the best lines on the edge; subtle, until you're on it, and high in the grade. Climb to the base of the groove, and let the battle commence.
Johnny Dawes, 1986

20 Elder Crack 18m E2 5b ★★★
The wide central crack is a must for every crack climber and provides a good warm-up for the Eliminates. ⦿ opposite page
Joe Brown, 1950

21 Knockin' on Heaven's Door 18m E9 6c ★★★
A desperately serious route, proper nightmare material. Gain the lip of the slab with relative ease (good cam low and left). Climb the slab passing a possible hand-placed peg out left.
Andy Pollitt, 1988

22 Keeper's Crack 15m HS 4b ★
Bounding the big wall on the right is an awkward wide crack (VS without big cams). The continuation corner is a little easier.
Slim Sorrell, Wilf White, 1949

It's strange to imagine today, where cracks can easily be seen as hostile and intimidating features, that they were once considered the easier plums to pick. Despite its early vintage, Elder Crack E2 5b (opposite page) can still cast its heavy shadow over climbers today. James Pearson showing it some style. 📷 David Simmonite

L'HORLA BUTTRESS
Another star-studded buttress with lots of steep, round and rough challenges.

㉓ Slab Route 9m S 4a ★
Climb the lower slab to welcome runners in a slot, which protect the steeper crux above.
Chuck Cook, Ray Handley, 1948

㉔ Bel Ami 20m VS 4b ★★
A VS classic: jam the corner to the big ledge (possible belay). The final exposed pinnacle arête, on its right, is delightful.
Wilf White, Chuck Cook, 1948

㉕ Green Crack 11m HVS 5b ★★★
The curving flake on the sidewall gives brilliant climbing with increasing difficulty, effort and trepidation to a stylish finish on the right arête.
Joe Brown, Morty Smith, 1957

㉖ Usurper 12m E4 6a ★★★
A brilliant brutal bully of a route, the scene of many a dogging session. Follow the crack to, and over the bulge, then force left to struggle up the arête to reach a fluted finish.
John Gosling, Dave Little (2pts), 1967. FFA Nicky Stokes, Al Manson, 1977

㉗ Moonshine 13m E5 6b ★★★
Get everything right, and this classic feels okay. However... from *Maupassant*, step left and pull through the first crack to good pro. Continue styling leftwards to gain the upper crack and crux moves, right at the top.
Tim Leach, Graham Desroy, 1980

㉘ Maupassant 11m HVS 5a ★★★
The easiest of an outstanding triplet. The crack leads to jams just before the crack widens. Initial fears of an overhanging offwidth experience are soon dismissed with a strenuous layback. The top is then surprisingly close.
Don Whillans, Joe Brown, 1955

㉙ L'Horla 10m E1 5b ★★★
Plenty of jugs but it ain't no jug-fest. Climb the awkward groove to the roof. Move around this with a cavalier swing left to a jug before lunging up the arête, or finger-lock the crack and bridge up the hanging corner. Either way this is glorious stuff. front cover
Joe Brown, 1957

Perhaps the most renowned of all Curbar's cracks, The Right Eliminate, E3 5c (page 163), mixes body-width action, steep, low-friction rock and holdlessness together to form a merciless brew. Alex Hughes showing it who's boss. 📷 Ian Parnell

Curbar Edge

30 Insanity 9m E2 5c ★★★
The crack just left of the arête is the stuff of glory, laybacked by thugs or sneakily jammed by those with thin hands.
Hugh Banner, 1958

31 Committed 8m E6 6b ★★
A bold and fingery route up the blank sidewall. After a hard start on the right, move left to the centre of the wall; finish direct via a long move past a diagonal crack. Easier for the tall.
Johnny Dawes, 1984

32 The Toy 7m E1 5c ★★
A mini classic that is very good value. The thin crack on the wall has a hard move low down and an even harder one higher up.

33 Plaything 7m E2 5c ★
Start up the wall just left of the chimney which gradually leads to the arête and a bold finish.
Gary Gibson (solo), 1983

34 Pretty Face 7m E1 5b ★
An unprotected gem up the wall right again, with several reachy cruxes.
Paul Mitchell, 1975

35 October Crack 7m HS 4b ★
The steep cracks are climbed via a variety of techniques and as much calm as you can muster.
Wilf White, Slim Sorrell, 1949

36 Shallow Chimney 10m VD ★
The chimney is clean and enjoyable; hardest, as it should be, at the start and finish.

37 Grey Face 9m VS 5a ★
The fierce crack right of the chimney is tamed slightly by the presence of a jug to the right.
Dennis Gray, Nat Allen, Des Hadlum, 1964

38 Thirst for Glory 9m E1 5b ★
The centre of the wall is climbed direct.

39 Pale Complexion 8m VS 4c ★
The right arête of the wall on its left-hand side, using a thin crack on the face.

THE ELIMINATES WALL
Tigers only need apply. Forceful, bullying cracks or terrifying, technical face climbs ram upwards along its length. Powerful stuff - you'd better be on form.

40 The Left Eliminate 12m E1 5c ★★
The first of the major cracks on this wall. *Right Eliminate's* little brother is just as awkward but much less sustained.
Joe Brown, Slim Sorrell, 1951

41 The Zone 15m E8 6c ★
A tough eliminate with F8a climbing in a bold situation. Technical, crimpy climbing drifts rightwards, past some skyhook runners, to the arête, near the top of the pod. Stride back left to a flake, then inch up the slab above.
John Arran, 1998

42 The Peapod 18m HVS 5b ★★★
One of the Peak's essential HVSs but, like a lot of routes on Curbar, will feel a lot harder if you don't climb it well. Gain the pod. This leads, with increasing difficulty to a hard exit onto a ledge. The upper crack is easier, though can be cruel to tired arms. ⊙ page 145
Joe Brown, Slim Sorrell, 1951

Curbar Edge | 163

43 The Right Eliminate 18m E3 5c ★★★
The offwidth crack, which splits this steep wall down the middle, is the pride of Curbar and one of the Peak District's most renowned cracks – big, steep and impressive, and very unlikely to show you any pity. ⓞ page 161
Joe Brown, Slim Sorrell, 1951

44 Drummond Base 20m E8 6c ★
Follow the slim groove immediately left of Linden, crossing rightwards past another groove to gain Linden either at its niche or, harder and more independently, a little higher. Finish up that route.
Johnny Dawes, 2003

45 Linden 23m E6 6b ★★★
A proper biggie. An awesome and intimidating line up the flakes in the centre of the wall with hard and very bold climbing. From a flake, gain the flaky niche with difficulty. Move back rightwards ever so slightly before moving back up and leftwards past more hard and committing climbing which gets progressively easier but scarier until the sanctuary of a ledge is reached. Finish more easily.
Ed Drummond, Hamish Green-Armytage (2pts), 1973. FFA Mick Fowler, John Stevenson, 1976

46 Salix 23m E7 6b ★
A harder finish to Linden going up and rightwards from the flake to gain Hurricane. Finish direct..
Pete Whittaker, 2016

47 The Grey Area 23m E8 7a ★★
Just as serious as Linden, but with harder climbing. Follow the parent route through the steep scoop as far as the poor runners. Technical and tenuous climbing leads rightwards to gain Hurricane. Continue direct, as per Salix.
Charlie Woodburn, 2003

48 Hurricane 21m E4 6a ★★
The exposed ramp line shows little mercy. From Scroach, step left and make a teeter of terror up and left to gain the easy finish of Linden. A good cure for hiccups.
Mick Fowler, John Stevenson, 1977

49 Scroach 21m E2 5c ★★
A fierce route, at the Curbar end of E2 and hard for the short. From the large block, squeeze desperately into the slim groove (small nuts). Grasp upwards towards a wider crack and the relief of a ledge, then trend diagonally left to finish.
John Gosling, M Emery, (1pt), 1967. FFA Ed Drummond, 1975

50 Hercules 11m E1 5a ★★
The wide crack is a strenuous and serious traditional outing; desperate for all but the greatest offwidth heroes.
Chuck Cook, Nat Allen, 1949

51 Alpha 12m S 4a ★
The shallow recess right of the rib provides testing climbing for the grade to the pointing block but eases a little above.
Chuck Cook, 1949

Eliminates Wall — 10 mins

GARDOM'S EDGE

OS Grid Ref: SK 274 738 to SK 273 726
Altitude: 260m

Gardom's is the quiet, understated crag of Peak gritstone. It's not brash and noisy like some crags, it just gets on with it, and with varied climbing, pockets of seclusion and good views who can blame it? It can offer peace and quiet, which can be a blessing on busy weekends, when all the popular crags are teeming. Yet, in case you're feeling lonely, there's always a couple of parties around Apple Buttress.

The climbing can be affected by the trees and vegetation. Some of the north-facing climbs need a few dry days to come into condition, whereas the cleaner south-facing climbs can dry quickly and provide sheltered winter sun-traps. It is perhaps best to visit in the afternoon and evening when the sun has swung around. It's a big, rambling crag, over a kilometer long with about 230 routes in the BMC's definitive guidebook. Only the best, cleanest and largest buttresses are described here. On your first visit, locating your selected buttress can be difficult. Once found, moving between buttresses is usually best by returning to the top of the crag.

Approach: Roadside parking just off the A621 on Clodhall Lane. Walk back down the road and go through the gate and take the right-hand path. Continue to a second gate and emerge from the trees at the top of the crag above Black Wall Area.

The edge can also be approached from the south. A stile on the A619, 200m west from the Robin Hood Inn, leads to the crag. See map below.

NORTHERN ROCKS
The approach path passes the classic Gardom's North Boulders, after which there is a fence. One hundred metres beyond this, the edge begins with three tidy buttresses. The first of these is Black Wall.

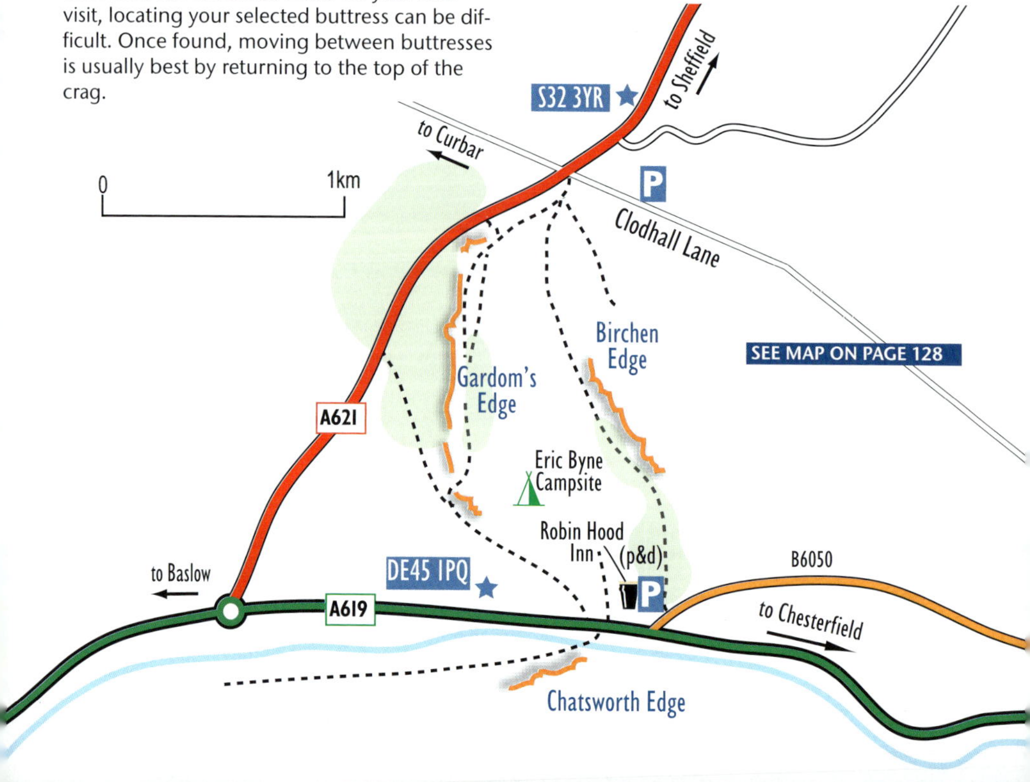

It's the trees that make Gardom's Edge such a special place, and in this respect it feels unlike any other crag on the Eastern Edges. Bex Shearring amongst the old oaks on the lovely Elliott's Buttress Direct, VS 4b (page 172). 📷 Mike Cheque

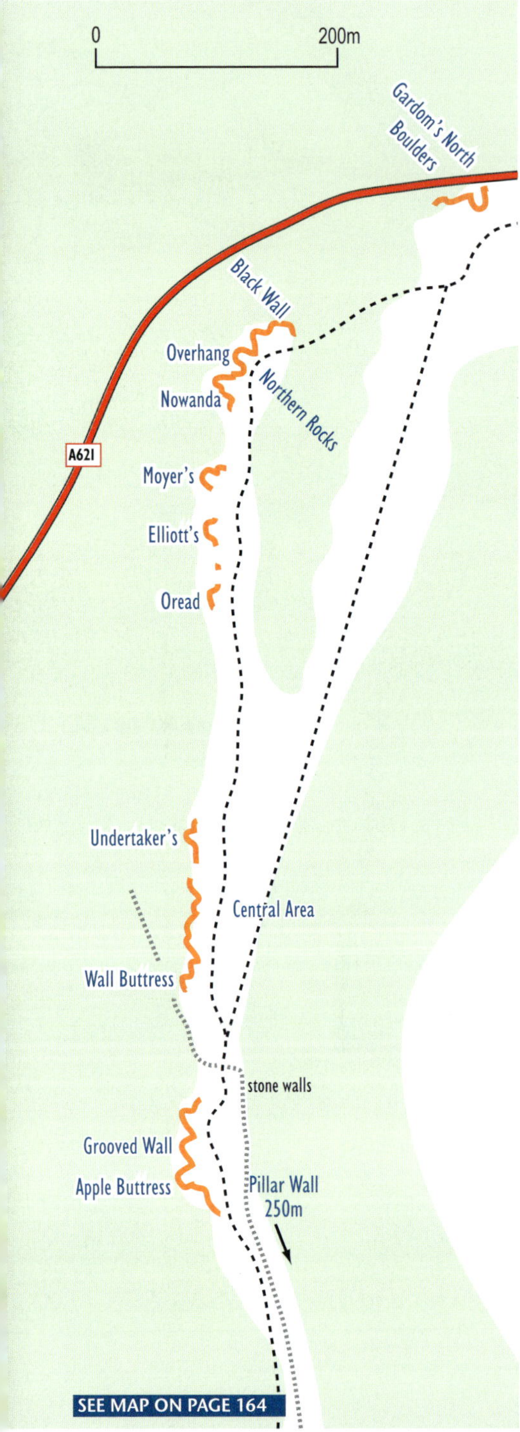

166 | Gardom's Edge

Black Wall: At the end of the trees, drop down to the right. The wall can stay damp after rain as it only gets late sunshine.

❶ Mickey Finn 15m E6 6b ★★★
A stylish and protectable route at the grade. Climb easily to the lower overhangs. Hard, protectable moves gain the flake under the next roof. Climb this via some via some brutish moves to the finish of *Sleeping Sickness*.
Paul Mitchell, 1990

❷ Sleeping Sickness 10m E3 5c ★★★
A brilliant route making the most of steep and very exposed terrain. From the ledge climb the thin crack in the left wall. Traverse left to an exciting position above the main roof, then battle up the steep rounded wall. The first of the Big Five Gardom's E3s. (The others are *Landsickness*, *Stormbringer*, *Crocodile* and *Waterloo Sunset*. A big day out!)
John Allen, Chris Addy, 1975

❸ Brown Crack 18m S 4a ★★
Gardom's first route, from none other than Puttrell himself and a cracker at that. The corner/chimney gives a classic struggle.
JW Puttrell, WJ Watson, 1890

Any E3 leader will know about Gardom's 'Big Five' at the grade, each testing climbers in a different (usually bold) aspect of the grade. Here Anna Gilyeat tests her form on terrible gritstone slopers on Landsickness, E3 6a (page 169), and gets her results back (ouch!). 📷 Mike Cheque

168 | Gardom's Edge

OVERHANG BUTTRESS
This powerful buttress to the right has got something for everyone, but demands a tough, positive approach.

4 Four Horsemen 15m E2 5b ★★
A fine route with good runners and a worrying finish. Start in the middle of the left wall of the buttress. Climb a crack then step right to a niche. Continue direct on layaways and rounded holds.
Gary Gibson, Hazel Carnes, 1981

5 Lightning Wall 15m HVS 5a ★★
A great line which keeps you guessing all the way. Follow *Four Horsemen* to the niche. Take the descending break to the arête; continue delicately to the top from here.
Nat Allen, Don Chapman, 1951

6 Spanish Fly 15m E7 6c ★★
An extremely powerful route. Cross the roof and make hard moves to gain the break above. A small wire pre-placed above the lip reduces the grade to E6!
John Allen, 1985

7 Vaya Con Dios 20m E2 5c ★★
An unforgettable pilgrimage, and an essential Gardom's experience. Move up the short chockstoned crack, invoke any deities you can think of, and propel your body leftwards along the wide break, around the arête, and struggle into a standing position. Finish with ease.
Allan Austin, Ernie Marshall, Brian Evans, 1956

8 Overhang Buttress Ordinary 12m VS 4b ★
Start up *Vaya...* then follow the short crack.
Eric Byne, 1934

9 Infirmary Groove 12m VS 4b
Up one crack then right to the next.
Ernie Marshall, 1956

NOWANDA BUTTRESS
To the right, a series of tower-like walls give a fine collection of routes.

10 Corner Crack 10m D
The aptly named crack up the corner.
Richard Brown, 1951

11 Grey Crack 10m VD
The doglegged crack in the wall to the right.

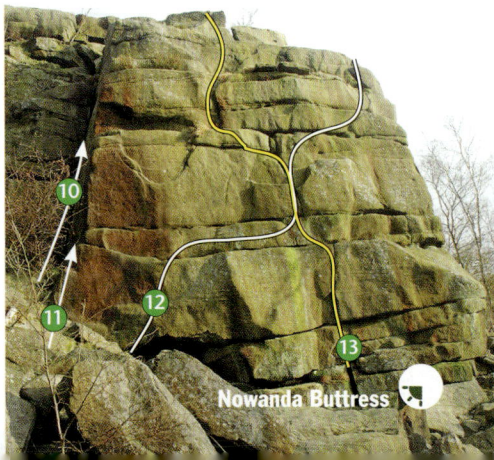

Nowanda Buttress

12 Moyer's Climb 15m HS 4b ★
A diagonal route with a hard start and a harder finish. Start at the left side of the buttress, climb up and rightwards to some gear. A long stretch brings the finish at the right-hand edge.
Clifford Moyer, Eric Byne, 1930s

13 Moyer's Variation 12m S 4c
A more direct line. After a hard start climb more easily up the centre of the face.

14 Nowanda 12m HVS 5a ★★★
Fun fun fun. The crack at the left of the wall gives a classic jamming test.
Ernie Marshall, 1953

15 Landsick 13m E1 5b ★
A tester. Follow the series of cracks to a small overhang at two-thirds height. Carefully arrange protection before a tough, rightwards finishing traverse.
Peter Biven, 1953

16 Landsickness 10m E3 6a ★★
The second of the crag's great E3s which will test your ability to crank on slopers. Follow *Landsick* to the overhang, then lurch directly for the top. ⓘ page 167
Ian Riddington, 1981

To the right of this buttress is a deep, capped chimney. Starting on its left-hand wall is:

17 Cave Gully 8m HD
The deep gully.

18 Cave Gully Crack 10m S 4b
The crack system just right of the gully is quite steep and pushy: tough for the grade.

19 Chockstone Climb 12m HS 4a
The chocked crack leads to a constricting chimney. The crux may be deciding which way to face before you enter.

20 Garden Face Crack 15m HS 4b ★
Grunting guaranteed. Start with a move on to a platform on the left, and gain the crack by an awkward move, with protection from monster cams (VS without). Climb the crack to finish.
Clifford Moyer, Eric Byne, c1930

21 Garden Face Direct 10m VS 5a ★
Start up the previous route and swing rightwards on to the face and follow it to the top. There's a couple of reachy moves which aren't too bad once you work them out. A direct start is only just harder.

22 Garden Face Indirect 10m D ★
Another ancient Puttrell pitch. A short corner leads to dogleg cracks up the wall above.
JW Puttrell, WJ Watson, 1890

To the right is an easy way down.

Nowanda Buttress

MOYER'S BUTTRESS AREA

Moyer's is a magnificent buttress, the showpiece of the edge. The reputation of the routes precede them. Undercut and smooth, the compelling steep upper slab gives an impression of isolated impregnability.

23 Cave Arête 18m HVS 5a ★

A climb of two contrasting styles. First fight your way out of the cave up the crack, then teeter up the arête.
Wilfred White, Joe Brown, Slim Sorroll, 1950

24 Stormbringer 20m E3 6a ★★

Great God Almighty: E3 number three, and as fierce a test of mantelshelving as you will ever get at the grade. With a side-runner in the chockstone up and left, get the flat hold above the roof. Make a brave mantel onto this – the living end – and continue up the wall above.
Dave Morgan, Bill Briggs, Richard Hasko, 1976

25 Moyer's Buttress 21m E1 5b ★★★

One of the top E1s on grit – historically significant, with interest and variety every step of the way. Climb up the cracks in the slab and swing right to a niche on the steep sidewall. Move up to a sloping break and make crux moves to get established on the front face. Climb the slab with help from the arête to the top.
⊙ opposite page
Peter Biven, Trevor Peck, 1955

26 Biven's Crack 22m E1 5b ★★

On the face to the right is a steep crack. Jam this to its end and finish rightwards with sustained difficulty.
Peter Biven (aid), 1955. FFA Jack Street, 1966

27 Perfect Day 22m E5 6b ★★★

A great route, with good gear, but with a committing and technical crux sequence. Follow *Biven's Crack* until it fades. Swing left and make bouldery crux moves past a diagonal crack (runner) to reach the deep slot above. Don't dally here, as the rounded finishing moves, passing a pocket, are still tricky.
Andy Parkin (1pt), 1979. FFA Steve Bancroft, 1979

28 Keith's Corner Crack 10m HS 4b

The steep corner on the right to a ledge. Climb the slanting groove on the left to the top.
Keith Axon, 1949

10 mins Moyer's Buttress

Definitely one of the best E1s on grit. Emily Huzzard on Moyer's Buttress, E1 5b (opposite page). Flakes, cracks, knee-bar rests and a weaving line all lead to great exposure on the final sizzling slab. This can go from gentle padding to runout scratching, depending on how you feel on the day. 📷 Paul Evans

Gardom's Edge

ELLIOTT'S BUTTRESS
Around 50m right of *Moyer's* lies this tall narrow-fronted buttress.

29 Elliott's Buttress Indirect 15m VS 4c ★
From the gully, shuffle along the break to the ledge. Continue more easily up the arête before moving back to finish up the wall above.

30 The Eye of Faith 22m E1 5c ★★★
Climb the roofed corner and move leftwards to gain a thin crack in the nose, crux. At the top of the thin crack move right to the arête and follow it magnificently to the top. A slightly easier, more popular, HVS 5b start is possible by moving in rightwards from the gully to gain the thin crack. ⓘ opposite page
Peter Biven, Trevor Peck, 1956

31 Rhythmic Itch 22m E1 5b ★★
Start up the roofed corner. Exit right and climb to the second roof. Either make a massive reach directly into *Elliott's* or traverse left to the arête. Move up rapidly before your arms fail.
Gary Gibson, Hazel Carnes, 1981

32 Elliott's Buttress Direct 22m VS 4b ★★
Another Gardom's gem. Start down in the depths and emerge out onto clean soaring rock. The corner and crack bring you to the top of a huge flake. Step off the polished foothold and climb the upper wall trending rightwards to gain the final crack. ⓘ page 165
Frank Elliott, 1934

Oread Buttress

Oread Buttress: After some smaller buttresses, about 50m right of Elliott's, is the last significant buttress of this section.

33 Nymph's Arête 12m VS 4c ★
The overhanging crack is followed to the ledge. The arête above is followed on its steep right-hand side.
Ernie Marshall, 1962

34 Oread 12m VS 4b ★★
One of the finer VSs on the edge. The central crack, moving left on the upper bit.
Cyril Machin, 1949

Elliott's Buttress

Sublime technicality, a subtle line and great gear make The Eye of Faith, E1 5c (opposite page), one of those routes you'll go back to time and time again. Anna Gilyeat enjoys the bomber jams and cool positions.
Mike Cheque

174 | Gardom's Edge

Undertaker's Buttress

Gardom's Unconquerable

CENTRAL AREA
After a gap of 200m or so (best walking along the crag top), the crag gets going again. This area is characterised by less continuous rock, with more sporadic buttresses strung out among the trees.

Undertaker's Buttress: The next area is identified by locating the very conspicuous capping overhang of *Hearse Arête*.

35 Undertaker's Buttress 18m VS 4c ★★
A great route that cleverly manages to avoid the steep ground. Start up a crack to the chockstone, teeter right and climb the delicate wall. A tricky move around the arête leads to an easier finish up a short crack in the sidewall.
Joe Brown, Slim Sorrell, 1951

36 Hearse Arête 16m E1 5b ★★
The striking overhang yields a spectacular route. Start up the rounded arête. A bit of bold wall climbing leads to below the steep overhang. Arrange some gear, take a breath and tackle the roof on good holds.
Peter Biven, Trevor Peck (1pt), 1956

Gardom's Unconquerable: This tall buttress sits 60m to the right.

37 Bilberry Buttress 16m VS 5a ★
A couple of tricky moves up the arête lead to a ledge. Continue up the right-hand edge of the wall above in an exposed position.
Ernie Marshall, 1953

38 Crottle 16m E1 5b ★
Climb the thin finger-crack on the sidewall to join *Bilberry Buttress*.
Chris Jackson, Bob Conway, Adey Hubbard, 1983

39 Stepped Crack 18m HD ★
The rising line of steps is followed up to the right to an escape rightwards.

40 Gardom's Unconquerable 14m VS 4c ★★
Bring along some big arms for this one. The leaning corner is best laybacked, probably. From the ledge escape easily to the right.
Joe Brown, Slim Sorell, Wilfred Wright, 1950

41 Whillans' Blind Variant 14m E1 5b ★
From the ledge on *Gardom's Unconquerable*, follow a break leftwards to a swing round the arête. Finish up the right-hand wall.
Don Whillans, 1951

Wall Buttress: This is the steep tower of rock to the right with a fine south-west facing wall containing a collection of bold testpieces.

42 Nah'han 13m E8 6b ★★★
The wild arête of *Make it Snappy* on its left-hand side. Gain the break and protection, as for that route. Climb steeply up following rounded holds on the left of the upper arête.
Tom Randall, 2013

43 Make it Snappy 13m E6 6b ★★★
The exposed arête of the buttress is gained by a traverse from the right. It has super bouldery

APPLE BUTTRESS AREA
The set of buttresses to the right are probably the cleanest, sunniest and most popular on the edge, centred around the magnificent Apple Buttress. They are about 100m from Wall Buttress.

Grooved Wall: Across the grassy gully is a striking arête marking the start of a fine wall.

46 Waterloo Sunset 16m E3 5c ★★
The last of Gardom's E3s. Exciting, bold and balancy climbing. Start on the right and climb to runners. Follow the arête above on the left.
Martin Boysen, 1977

47 Finale Groove 16m VS 5a ★
The bulging crack on jams and layaways.
David Penlington, John Fisher, 1951

48 Babylon's Groove 15m VS 4c
Follow the crack to a small roof. Step right and mantelshelf to a crack just left of the chimney. Finish up the crack or the chimney.
Don Chapman, Nat Allen, 1951

49 Central Groove 15m VS 4c
The next groove is harder than it looks.
Clifford Moyer, Eric Byne, 1934

50 Tree Groove 12m VS 4b ★
Pleasant climbing up the groove leads to a tree. Either move rightwards to the narrow chimney or use the tree and continue up the 4c wall.
Clifford Moyer, Eric Byne, 1934

moves, and with decent protection and a long fall zone, it makes a great, safe ground-up prospect for the budding E6-er.
Neil Foster, Alan Rouse, 1984

44 The Crocodile 12m E3 5c ★★
The penultimate classic Gardom's E3, a great test of your cool and wall-technique. Climb up to a good flake and arrange as much psychological gear as you can. Now all you have to do is climb the bold wall to the good break.
Gabriel Regan, 1975

45 Right-Hand Crack 10m VS 4c ★
The corner has a few tricky moves.
Eric & Ivy Byne, 1940s

APPLE BUTTRESS
Here are some of the best lower- and mid-grade climbs in the Gardom's area. They are popular, get lots of sun and are reliably clean and quick drying.

51 Layback Crack 7m VS 5a ★
Well up the bank on the left is a steep and strenuous, straight crack. Jamming is allegedly sinful. Tough for the grade.
Wilfred White, Joe Brown, Slim Sorroll, 1950

52 Flake Crack 11m HS 4b ★
The steep, wider, right-hand crack has an awkward bulging move.
Eric Byne, 1934

53 N.M.C. Crack 18m VD ★★
The classic VD of the crag. The fine wide crack-line with a mountaineering feel. A flake leads to a ledge then a corner to a wide platform. Finish up the tough slanting hand-crack.
Frank Elliott, 1930

54 Apple Arête 18m VS 4b ★★★
The classic VS of the crag. With good gear and moves that aren't too hard; so why does it feel so bold? Start up *Apple Crack*, move left at the first break and follow the arête to the top.
David Penlington, Ernie Marshall, R Hardy, 1952

55 Apple Crack 12m HD ★
The wide crack in the front of the buttress leads to a large ledge just below the top.

56 Cider Apple 18m S 4a ★
Climb the arête and slab to the ledge. Finish boldly up the right edge of the final tower.
P Knapp, Eric Byne, SG Moore, 1950

57 Giant's Staircase 14m HVD 4a ★
The obvious large steps lead with increasing difficulty to the ledge. Gain the top using the short, difficult crack behind.
Clifford Moyer, Eric Byne, 1930s

58 Bitter 6m VS 5a ★
Ascend the crack with the help of a small spike and a gymnastic move.

59 Master of Thought 8m E2 6a ★
This bold slab gives technical fingery climbing with an on/off move to gain the break.
Gary Gibson, 1979

60 Velvet Cracks 8m HS 4b
The twin thin cracks with no cheat start using its neighbour.
Ernie Marshall, 1963

61 Apple Jack Crack 9m VD
The two well-polished cracks in the centre of the slab. A start from the far right is also possible along a slippery traverse.

62 Cydrax 9m HVS 5b ★
Good balance, nerve and technique will allow you to climb the centre of the slab to the right and then the flake-crack above.
Eric Finney, Peter Fieldsend, 1957

Gardom's Edge | 177

63 Cider 9m VS 5a ★
More delightful balance and technique. The arête and slab to the right lead to a steeper wall above. A 5b variation start is possible up the flake in the left-hand corner of the pit.
David Penlington, Eric Byne, J Adderley, 1950

64 Blenheim Gully 9m HS 4b ★
The undercut corner of the pit has an awkward start. Continue up a crack and corner and finish up the wall on the right.
David Penlington, Eric Byne, J Adderley, 1950

PILLAR WALL
The final rocks of note lie further to the south, about 250m from a high stone wall that crosses the path. Despite the walk, it is an essential Gardom's buttress.

65 Charlotte Rampling 10m E6 6b ★
A weaving line based on the slanting ramp that would potentially make a good highball although the landing is not too clever. Gain the ramp and follow it leftwards, almost to the arête, before moving upwards.
Johnny Dawes, 1984.

66 Left-Hand Pillar Crack 8m E1 5b ★★
A classic and well worth the walk, the leaning crack will leave you spent. Furious laybacking may, or may not, reward you with the top.
Allan Austin, Brian Evans, 1956

67 Right-Hand Pillar Crack 9m HVS 5a ★
Prepare to be humiliated. Using arms and legs and any other spare appendages thrutch your way up the crack.
Frank Elliott, 1930

68 Elliott's Crack 10m S 4a ★★
Fine, more amenable climbing up the crack and flake system on the right-hand side of the wall to a ledge. Finish leftwards.
Frank Elliott, 1930s

Pillar Wall — 25 mins

BIRCHEN EDGE

OS Grid Ref: SK 278 732 to SK 281 726
Altitude: 300m

A delightful crag on an open moorland edge. It is very popular, especially with beginners and groups. The crag is famous for its large number of friendly low-grade routes following slab, crack and chimney lines. However, it is infamous for hard starts, where the inexperienced (and sometimes the experienced) can struggle to get off the ground. There is a handy pub adjacent to the parking, the approach is pleasant and there is a very handy campsite just minutes away, all this adds to the many attractions of the climbing.

The crag faces south-west, and gets the sun from late morning to sunset. The rock is clean, fast drying and climbable year round. Midges can be a problem on grey, humid and windless summer days.

Approach: Park in the National Trust pay & display car park adjacent to the Robin Hood Pub. From a stile just up the road, a well-used path heads north. After a few hundred metres a minor path leads off diagonally right through the wood to Kismet Buttress (10 mins); although most carry straight on to the main edge (15 mins). It is reached from the north, from roadside parking on Clodhall Lane, in 15 - 20 minutes.

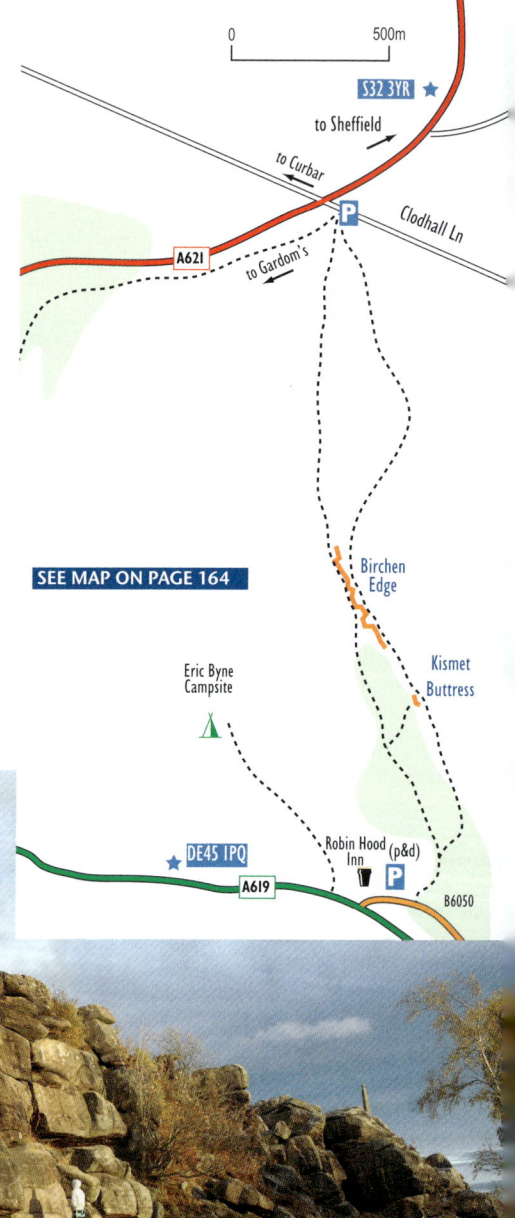

Runout slab climbing, open moves on rough flat holds where you need to keep your head about you; this is the classic Birchen experience. Here Spenser Gray is cruising the upper slab of The Crow's Nest, VS 4c (page 180), the scene of many shipwrecks. Hold fast! 📷 David Simmonite

Birchen Edge

1 The Crow's Nest 13m VS 4c ★★
This bold classic slab feels somehow out of place on the edge. The initial low step right after the 'piggish crack' is often (but should not be!) avoided; whatever way you approach, the superb upper slab is the main event and the site of many a wobble. ◉ page 179
Frank Elliot, Gilbert Ellis, Harry Dover, 1928

2 Lookout Arête 12m S 4a ★
After the awkward corner start, bridge out of the depths of the chimney to gain the delightful hanging slab arête.
Gilbert Ellis, 1956

3 The Funnel 11m HD 3c ★★
Take the technical and polished corner, or the reachy, unprotected wall to the right on pockets to the right, to land with some relief on the ledge. Fortunately, the chimney above is a worthy reward.

4 Kiss Me Hardy 11m VD 4a ★
Initial moves right of the corner lead to the awkward cleft where exposed elegance will reap rewards.
Eric Byne, Clifford Moyer, 1930s

5 Victory Crack 10m HS 4b ★★
The excellent upper crack gives a well-protected jamming test. Low in the grade but if you can't jam it will feel a good deal harder.
Eric Byne, Clifford Moyer, 1930s

6 Victory Gully 10m S 4b
A good 'traditional' climb to an awkward though protectable finish.
Eric Byne, Clifford Moyer, 1930s

7 Emma's Slab 10m VS 4b
Worthwhile climbing once established on the face, with a well-positioned crux stretch (and a moving block above).
Ernie Marshall, David Penlington, 1952

8 Emma's Dilemma 11m S 4b ★★★
The crack gives great climbing and an introduction to routes where you really should jam. The slippery lower crack, just right of the undercut gives access to the upper crux.
Eric Byne, Clifford Moyer, 1930s

9 Emma's Temptation 10m HVD 4b ★
Delightful climbing with sustained interest, providing you can get off the ground (a bypass is available in the groove on the right).
Jack Macleod, 1930s

10 Emma's Delight 10m HS 4b ★
More tempting slab climbing heading for the short crack to finish.
David Penlington, Ernie Marshall, 1952

11 Deluded 10m HS 4b
Compressed moves out of the cave lead to a nice variation above; this will feel a lot harder if you miss the hidden holds.

12 Emma's Delusion 10m HVD 4a ★
An awkward but protected move to leave the cave and impressive above. It originally started up *The Prow* at the same grade and is still best this way.

13 The Prow 10m VS 4c
Another good climb at the lower end of the grade, more reachy than hard.
Chris Craggs, Colin Binks, 1993

Emma's Buttress

All hands on deck! Gowry Sisupalan gets shipshape on the big grasping exit of Topsail, VS 4c (page 182), one of the more physical of the VSs on the edge. 📷 Paul Evans

Birchen Edge

14 Captain's Bunk 9m VS 4c ★
Crux starting moves lead to a bold mantel and two more of the same above; very reachy. Traditionally finished up the short 5a wall.
Chuck Cook, 1951

15 Telescope Tunnel 12m HD 3c ★
From the gully, exposed moves gain the short chimney on the left. Pull up this then squirm tightly inwards, to an exit through a hole at the back.

16 Porthole Buttress 10m HVD 4a
A fine wander. Start up the gully then make a long traverse right to finish up *Nelson's Slab*.

17 Porthole Direct 10m HS 4b ★★
A three-course experience with a delicate starter, a traditional main course and some gut-busting afters. Deliciously top-end HS fare but those not used to the menu may regret their overindulgence.
Gilbert Ellis, 1951

18 Blind Eye 13m HS 4b
From the cave recess, gain the easy slab on the right. The obvious direct finish is HS 4b.
Gilbert Ellis, 1952

19 Dead Eye 10m HVS 6a
Technical trickery up the cutaway leads to a jug. The climbing soon eases above.
John Allen, 1986

20 Nelson's Slab 12m HS 5a ★
A protectable if perplexing problem start, with a nervous rock left above; after this it eases.
Frank Burgess, Eric Byne, 1930s

21 Left Ladder Chimney 10m HVD 4a
Compelling stuff for chimney fans.

22 The Plain Sailing Midshipman 13m E2 6a ★★
A classy, bouldery route up the steep wall. From the middle of the three flakes, yard up and slightly left to a thin crack. Press on to a good break and a massive span to gain the capstone finish.
Len Millsom, 1963 / Gary Gibson, 1982

23 Sail Buttress 14m HS 4b ★★
An excellent exposed route zigzagging up the impressive prow, with a well-positioned crux traverse left.
Bert Smith, Byron Connelly, 1934

24 Ratline 11m HVS 5a ★★
If you spot the sequence to leave the ledge this is just a reachy one move wonder: best started up the technical wall left of *Sail Chimney*.
Len Millsom, 1963

25 Sail Chimney 13m HVD 4a ★★★
An outstanding chimney climb. A tricky start leads to exploratory wandering inside for the easiest moves. Normally finished, with maximum exposure, stepping right onto the rib wall above the start. It can also be finished inside with maximum effort.
Eric Byne, Clifford Moyer, 1930s

26 Topsail 11m VS 4c ★★
Romp up to the roof which is overcome by a wonderful sequence; low in the grade for most but tough for the short. The big worn cam placement on the roof is eroding rapidly; please don't use it. ⓘ page 181
David Penlington, Ernie Marshall, 1951

Nelson's Buttress

27 Spinnaker 12m VS 5a
From the slab, pull left onto the rib to gain a ledge. A tricky sequence up and right under the roof lands one on a block in the chimney.
Graham Wilding, Barry Knox, 1963

28 Monument Chimney Crack 11m VD 3c ★
From the chimney a hard sequence gains the hanging crack that gives good easier climbing.

29 Monument Chimney 11m D 3a ★★
Not really a chimney and don't be put off by the greenness or polish: this is a must-do route with some excellent sustained climbing.
Henry Bishop, 1910s

ACCESS: Please do not use the monument as a belay.

30 The Bow 12m S 4a
From the slab, traverse diagonally right to the arête. A little green but with good moves and exposure; much easier once on the arête.

31 Orpheus Wall 12m HVS 5c ★★
Great technical climbing. Bouldery moves up the scoop and crack gain the break and protection. The crux bulge is best climbed quickly before your arms give way. Easier climbing remains. At the top of the grade and only recommended for experienced HVS 5c leaders.
Joe Brown, Slim Sorrell, 1950

32 Peaches 12m E4 6b ★★★
Near perfection in hard grit climbing. Climb the slab to better holds on the overhanging wall (thread runner). Move left and climb the steep wall to a break then move left slightly and up, on poor holds, to a ledge where the tricky climbing ends.
Gary Gibson, 1980

33 Monument Gully 12m VD 3c ★
A great test where the gully narrows at its exit, especially so for the short. If you get out of the trap, reward yourself with the pleasant slab arête above on the left.
Henry Bishop, 1912

34 Monument Gully Buttress 7m VS 5a ★
The arête is a stiff test piece with trick moves.
Ken Wright, Keith Axon, 1951

35 The Keel 7m HVS 5b ★
The wall just right gives an even trickier problem, if arguably more obvious.

36 Naughty Nauticals 6m E2 6b
The wall right of *The Keel*, using the flake on the lip is deliciously technical.
John Allen, Paul Williams, 1985

184 | Birchen Edge

The Promenade

37 The Promenade 15m M 2c ★★
The initial arête gives bold climbing for the grade. From the break, the remaining wander right and finish up the arête right of the gully is a protectable delight.

38 Promenade Direct 9m HVD 4b ★
The centre of the slab has a perplexing crux start and no protection to the break. Continue over the edge of the overlap then take the testing arête finish (or escape left).

39 The Chain 12m S 4a ★
Good holds arrive to help you swing onto the slab just as you feel you need to start tunnelling. Move right to the easier finishing slab.
David Penlington, Eric Byne, 1951

40 Gritstone Megamix Font 7A ★
The bulge and wall give a classic problem but it feels pretty high.
John Allen, 1986

41 Anchor Traverse 13m HS 4b ★
Take the gully then the protected, but scary, traverse left. Finish up the wall (easy) or staying right, next to the arête (more sustained).
David Penlington, John Fisher, 1952

42 Hollybush Gully 9m VD 4b
The fissure. There are numerous ways to reach the chockstone, with squirms, jams, laybacks, arm-bars and foot-locks being common.

43 Powder Monkey Parade 15m HS 4b ★★★
Delightful stuff. After the awkward start, buck up courage for the intimidating hand traverse; the upper slab is bold but much easier.
David Penlington, Eric Byne, 1951

Trafalgar Wall

Birchen Edge | 185

44 Oarsman Font 6B+
Burly layback moves on the right of the thin crack get you over the bulge.
Mark Stokes, 1984

45 Hornblower Font 6C ★★
An old and tough classic following the short seams and small flake in the scoop.

46 Obstructive Pensioner Font 7A+ ★
A cool problem tackling the nose direct.
Nic Jennings, 2000

47 Jumpers for Trousers Font 7C+ ★
Totally nails. Climb the bell-shaped scoop in the right wall. The hardest move on Birchen?
Ben Bransby, 2009

48 Admiral's Progress 9m D 3b ★
Good, traditional chimney climbing with a an exposed finish which can be bypassed using the obvious through route.

49 Camperdown Crawl 11m HS 4c ★★
The technical start leads to a delicately bolder upper section; excellent contrasting climbing.
Eric Byne, Charles Ashbury, Winifred Hill, 1951

50 Barnacle Bulge 11m HS 4c ★
The crack with help from holds on the left, gives a tricky start but soon eases to a slightly bold finish right of *Trafalgar Crack*.
Stan Moore, Harry Pretty, 1950

51 Trafalgar Crack 12m VD 4a ★★
A renowned beginner's testpiece which eases considerably if you can get off the ground.
Eric Byne, Clifford Moyer, 1930s

52 Trafalgar Wall 11m S 4b ★★
The technical crux is getting started; the mental crux is the finish, especially serious for the short; big cams and confidence help.

53 Sailor's Crack 7m HS 4c ★
Great fun and low in the grade for those who can jam, desperate for those who can't.

54 Reef Knot 8m S 4a
A good route, initially bold, with a tricky rounded finish; fortunately protectable.
Richard Brown, P Carr, 1951

55 Sheep Bend 8m HVD 4a
The slab left of the arête is artificial but fun.

56 Nautical Crack 8m VD 3c
The niche is entered easily enough but getting out the top in a dignified fashion is a different proposition. Very well protected.

57 Yo-Ho Crack 8m VD 3c ★
The dogleg crack gives a very safe steeper route.
Reg Schofield, 1933

58 Rum Wall 8m VD 3c
A reachy route from a hard start.

59 Stoker's Break 8m VD 4a
A climb with a rest midway.
E Clegg, Dick Brown, 1951

60 Stoker's Hole 8m HS 4a
A reachy start leads to a bold but fun move past the hole.
Colin Binks, Chris Craggs (both solo), 1993

61 Stoked 7m VD 3c
The thin crack has good pro.
C White, Dick Brown, 1951

62 Stoker's Wall 7m HD 3a
The far right of the wall gives good, polished, balance climbing.

Stoker's Wall 15 mins

Birchen Edge

Copenhagen Wall

63 Copenhagen Corner 5m HVD 4a
The flake just left of the arête is a good problem, which feels easier when you know how.
David Penlington, John Fisher, 1952

64 Scandiarête 6m VS 5c
An excellent technical problem up the arête, which can be done in a variety of ways.

65 Dane's Delight 6m VS 5a
A reachy move between two breaks at the start.

66 Dane's Disgust 6m VS 5b
The undercut wall past the vertical flake.

67 Copenhagen Wall 10m HS 5a ★
A nifty problem; from the block, hard moves gain the wall just left. Easier moves lead to a sting in the tail, gaining the hanging slab.
Norman Kershaw, 1951

68 Wonderful Copenhagen 10m VS 5a
A sustained start heading right from the block on slopers. Finish up the hanging slab as for *Copenhagen Wall*.
Richard Brown, 1951

69 Mast Gully Ridge 10m S 4a
A good route with some nice moves though protection is merely adequate. Normally started from the gully on the right; the harder left-hand start requires a cool head.

70 Mast Gully Wall 12m VD 4a ★
A green, polished and tricky start up the sidewall soon leads to a niche; a pull onto the slab brings a good exposed finish.

71 Mast Gully Crack 10m HS 4b ★
The bottom crack is better than it looks; the top gives superbly positioned moves on jams or laybacks.

72 Mast Gully Buttress 10m VS 5b ★★
This teasing classic has a perplexing and reachy start. Above, the climbing eases.
Gilbert Ellis, Ray Kerry, 1950

73 Fo'c'sle Wall 10m VS 4c ★
Balance quickly up the cracked ramp to steep moves between breaks and holes, hopefully leaving some strength for the reachy finish.
David Penlington, John Fisher, 1952

15 mins The Fo'c'sle

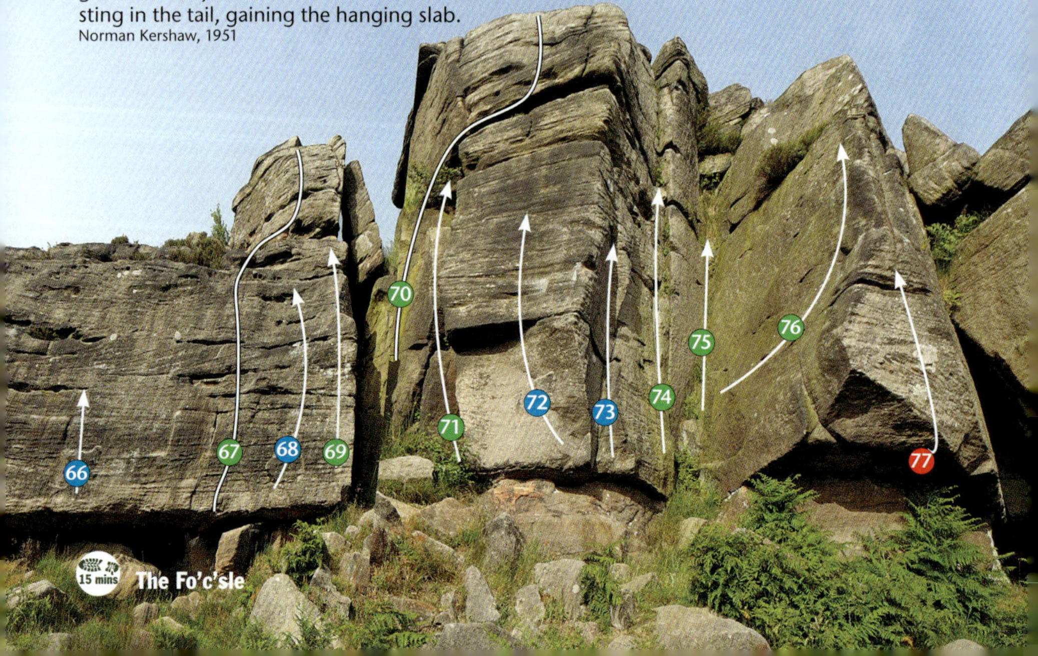

Birchen Edge | 187

74 Fo'c'sle Crack 10m S 4a ★
A lovely little route climbing the shallow V-corner with holds on the wall to the left; steep, sustained and protected.
Reg Schofield, George Walker, Reg Damms, 1930s

75 Fo'c'sle Chimney 10m HD 3c
The back of the V-slot can be climbed facing in, out, right or left at varying degrees of difficulty.

76 Fo'c'sle Arête 10m HS 5b
Stretchhhh across to the large hole from holds on the left; a few more moves up the arête and it's all over.

77 Broadside 10m E2 6a ★
Climb up the undercut arête with long stretches past open holds to an easier finish.
G Warren (solo), 1988

78 Cave Gully 12m S 3c ★
Above the cave is an intimidatingly polished, green, good old fashioned chimney groove.
Richard Brown, 1951

79 Ta Very Much 8m VS 5a
A steep, protected start leads to unprotected technical interest on flakes and crimps; a good eliminate climb but unfortunately it's all too easy to drift right to easier ground.
Chris Craggs, 1993

80 Tar's Arête 8m VD 4a ★
A steep start up the sidewall provides the usual challenge of speed versus protection; interest is fairly sustained up the arête above.

81 Ta Ta For Now 8m HS 5a
An interesting boulder problem start over the overhang.
Chris Craggs, Graham Parkes, 1993

82 Tar's Crack 7m VD 4a
A good bouldering start leads to moderate climbing above.

83 Tar's Wall 7m HVD 4b
Starting from the block, a good, protected boulder problem leads to pleasant padding.

84 Tar's Traverse 12m D 3a
A slight starting lunge from a boulder in the gully leads to many possibilities for the traverse and exit as for *Tar's Arête*.

85 Tar's Gully 6m M 2b
Finish right or left (harder) of the upper prow.

86 Pig Head 6m HS 4c
Stubborn application helps when climbing the smart arête.
Ken Holton, 1982

87 Pigtail 6m HS 4b
Precarious and reachy moves heading for the shallow groove.
Dick Brown, P Carr, 1951

Emma's Buttress

KISMET BUTTRESS

The final buttress is well worth a visit, especially for the classic climbs on the highest central section. It lies 300m across to the right. From the main edge it is best approached along the crag top path.

88 Powder Keg 11m HVD 4a
The undercut corner has an explosive mantel.

89 Fuse 11m HS 4b ★
Brilliantly committing, with scary moves over the overlap onto the central slab. The optional flake finish up on the left is interesting as well. Top end of the grade and nasty for the short and inflexible.

90 Gun-Cotton Groove 11m HD 3b ★
A cute little route, with more interest than you might expect.

91 Cook's Rib 11m E1 5c
Climb the front of the narrow rib, using the left arête. Avoiding the arête is tougher.

92 Horatio's Direct 11m VS 4c
An awkward test taking the narrow corner: steeper and reachier than it looks. Small wires useful.

93 Horatio's Horror 13m S 4a ★★
A local gem, well worth searching out. A tricky polished corner crack leads to a protected but intimidating step across left to easier climbing.
Keith Axon, 1949

94 Nelson's Nemesis 14m HS 4b ★★
The tricky corner crack leads to a committing traverse and excellent exposed climbing above; a great little route.
Keith Axon, 1949

95 Tom's Arête 14m E5 6b ★
The unprotected right arête of the corner above a very bad landing.
Paul Mitchell, 2001

96 Victory Vice 9m VD 3b
Traditional chimney climbing. If you make it to the chockstone be careful as it can move; a fair bit harder for the short.

97 For Queen and Country 11m VS 4b
An artificial weave, first on the right arête, then the left arête of the chimney to finish up a finger crack on the right.
Izzy Stewart, 2001

98 Device 7m VS 4c
A tough little number: the slab, via pockets, and a blind crack has good moves but fiddly protection, a round finish, and can be dirty. Moving right to the arête is cheating but you might not care!
Ernie Marshall, 1963

99 Gunpowder Gully Arête 7m S 3c
The delicate arête has good but unprotected moves that require plenty of confidence.

Amongst the sometimes-lichen-bothered corners of Chatsworth Edge lie some true jewels, rare ticks for gritstone connoisseurs. Here, Andy Long is on one of these jewels, Pearls, E2 5c (page 192). Cheeky technicalities above small gear gives this route its character. David Simmonite

CHATSWORTH EDGE

OS Grid Ref: SK 275 721
Altitude: 200m

Chatsworth is a quiet crag. A reputation for fierce cracks, green walls and swarms of midges has always kept the majority at bay. A reputation it has to be said, that's not entirely undeserved. However, when conditions are favourable, Chatsworth is home to some great gritstone experiences. The scene of many battles, the crag's renown stems from its trophies being hard won. A visit is a must for anyone nearing the end of their grit crack apprenticeship. That said, there are also plenty of delicate and hugely enjoyable climbs.

A series of north-west-facing buttresses that get little sun leaving them inhospitable in winter, yet providing welcome shade in summer. The eastern end only receives the sun from late afternoon in summer, whilst the western end receives more. The trees filter the noise from the nearby road and the crag has an atmosphere of quiet seclusion. It is fabulous in spring after a dry spell. It is worth bringing a soft brush to bring your chosen route into condition if need be.

> **Approach:** From the car park next to the Robin Hood Inn, walk down the main road towards Baslow for 200 metres. On the left side of the road is a stile. Cross this, then the river via a bridge and follow a path (that can get boggy) to join a gated track bearing rightwards to the crag. Follow small tracks under the buttresses, or direct. The first climbing is ten minutes from the car.

SENTINEL BUTTRESS AREA
The first rocks reached are centred around the steep buttress. Not much sun.

① Sidewinder   10m   HVS 5b   ★
The left arête is worthwhile and has a testing crux towards the top.

② Mort Wall   10m   HVS 5a   ★★
The centre of the wall is an appealing line. Well protected to boot.
Colin Mortlock, 1958

③ Slip Arête   10m   E2 5b   ★★
The right arête is delightful but bold and reachy.
Gabriel Regan, 1975

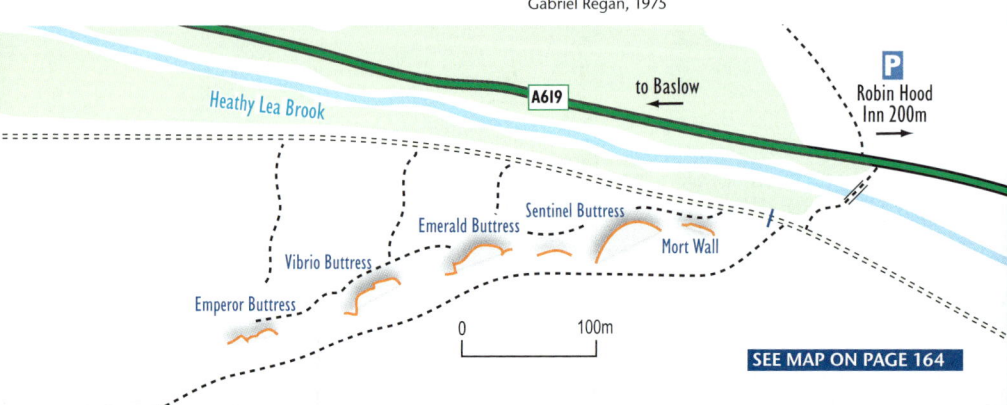

Chatsworth Edge | 191

4 Strangler's Groove 10m S 4a ★
Pleasant climbing leads to an awkward step onto a sloping ledge. Above this things get more constricted.
Don Chapman, Nat Allen, 1951

5 Strangler's Crack 10m VD
The crack right again is a fine climb.
Don Chapman, Nat Allen, 1951

6 Throttled Groove 10m S 4a ★
Gear, jugs and jams abound in the dusty corner lurking in the back of the bay.
Don Chapman, Nat Allen 1951

7 The Puppet Crack 15m HVS 5b ★★
The steep crack just right of the corner. A difficult start gives way to superb jamming and jug pulling. The top is arduous.
Joe Brown, Slim Sorroll, 1951

8 Sentinel Crack 16m E2 5c ★★★
Stunning, savage and tough. The groove leads to the roof. Butch undercutting leads rapidly to the lip. Entry into the tantalising groove above involves a world of pain. A full-bore sandbag, one of the best on grit.
Don Whillans (solo!), 1959

9 Sentinel Buttress 15m E3 5c ★
From the rest under the roof on *Sentinel Crack* traverse right along the break until a bold mantelshelf gains ledges. Finish up *Cave Climb*.
Mick Fowler, 1977

10 Sentinel Groove 15m E6 6c ★
Archetypal Dawes. The beautiful hanging groove isn't furnished with an abundance of 'grips,' so expect a lesson in tenuous bridging and contortions. Oh, and terror.
Johnny Dawes, 1990s

11 Cave Climb 15m VD ★
The corner is a struggle, especially when passing the chockstone tightly on its inside.
Eric Byne, Clifford Moyer, 1928

12 Cave Crack 12m S 4b ★★
The crack is a struggle to get established.

13 Sloping Crack 7m VD
The crack in the right side of the gully.

14 Lichen 35m E2 5c ★★★
One of the grit's classic traverses, best enjoyed when clean (add a grade if battling lichen).
1 10m 5b Start up the gully of *Sloping Crack* and traverse the break to belay in *Cave Crack*.
2 10m 5c Step round the rib and demonstrate your ability on slopers to gain *Cave Climb*.
3 15m 5c Traverse the rounded break across the face, with a unique 'hammered-in machine nut' runner, then a long step down leads to an easier finish on the arête.
Keith Myhill, B Haley, J Crown, 1971

15 Tree Crack 7m S 4b
The wide crack is for offwidth connoisseurs, being green, hard to start and tricky above.
Eric Byne, Clifford Moyer, c1930

16 High Step 10m E1 5b ★
From the centre of the wall, climb diagonally left to a tricky high step. Move left and mantel onto the ledge with relief. Finish up the crack on the right.
Ernie Marshal, 1959

17 Price 10m HVS 5a
A bold parallel line heading left to the niche and then to the sloping ledge.
Eric Price, 1959

Sentinel Buttress

Emerald Buttress

20 Pearls   12m   E2 5c   ★★
An elegant route. Climb the flakes which get progressively smaller with height. When they finally run out, a dainty teeter gains what looks like the top. ⊙ page 189
Keith Myhill, 1971

21 Double Cave Climb   12m   VD   ★
The crack and chimney right of *Pearls*. The start and the finish of the climb can be avoided (tightly) on the inside by troglodytes.
Frank Burgess, Rupert Brookes, 1930s

VIBRIO BUTTRESS
This is 30m right again, a fine clean and sunnier buttress with a good spread of grades.

22 Step Buttress   13m   HVD   ★
Start 1m right of the left arête, using a helpful sidepull, and mantel to gain fun steps and the mid-way ledge. The wide upper crack is not so hard as offwidths go.
Byron Connelly, Bert Smith, 1930s

23 Good Vibrations   15m   E2 6a   ★
Take the lower wall direct, or avoid it on the right to reduce the grade to 5c. From the roof follow the crack in the left sidewall. When this runs out an exposed traverse leads to the arête.
Chris Craggs, Jim Rubery, 1990

24 Vibrio   15m   E1 5b   ★★
A good little adventure with an open feel to it. Climb the crack to the roof. An awkward grovel over the lip lands you at a runner slot. Scuttle leftwards to the easy arête. **Vibrio Direct**, E2 6a ★★, takes the obvious finish above and slightly right of the gear slot.
Black and Tans CC, 1963. Direct, Keith Myhill (1pt), 1971. FFA John Allen, 1976

EMERALD BUTTRESS
Across the descent slope is the second of the crag's major buttresses. It has a much sunnier aspect than the previous buttresses and is therefore more often in condition.

18 Left Twin Crack   11m   HS 4b   ★★
A feisty thrutch left of *Emerald Crack*.
Eric Byne, Clifford Moyer c1930

19 Emerald Crack   14m   E3 6a   ★★★
Another beast. Involving, but steady climbing leads to a niche near the top and helps build optimism. However, the brutish crux diminishes the spirit of most.
Joe Brown (1pt), 1957.
FFA Jim Campbell, 1967

Vibrio Buttress

Chatsworth Edge | 193

Emperor Buttress

25 Twisted Reach 10m E4 6b ★★
The desperate hanging groove. Better than it looks, with a stopper move, especially for shorties.
Bob Berzins, Martin Berzins, 1979

26 Step Buttress Crack 8m HVD
The crack bounding the right of the buttress leads to a character building grassy finish.
Byron Connelly, Bert Smith, 1930s

27 Broken Buttress Climb 8m VS 4b ★
The crack bounding the right of the buttress leads to a grassy finish.

EMPEROR BUTTRESS
This lies 50m right. It contains the best low-grade routes on the edge.

28 Emperor Flake Climb 12m VD ★★★
A stunning climb at the grade. Climb the left-hand sidewall until an awkward move gains a ledge. Lean rightwards to the juggy arête, revelling in the exposure, to finish. From the flake it is also possible to finish straight up the wall at VS 4c.
Eric Byne, Ivy Byne, 1940

29 Emperor Crack 12m VS 4b ★
Steep and satisfying. From mid-height you can either, get in and wriggle or, if wearing shorts and a vest, layback the right-hand edge.
Eric Byne, Clifford Moyer, c1930

30 Despot 12m E1 5c ★★
A lovely climb with a strenuous start and stretchy top wall. From the corner, ape leftwards along the thin break and move up to better holds. Finish direct up the wall.
Tim Leach, Ian Millward, 1977

31 Empress Crack 12m S 4a ★
Wonderful corner climbing. An awkward yet perfectly protected move at half height constitutes the crux.
Eric Byne, Clifford Moyer, c1930

32 Prince's Crack 14m S 4b ★
A fun boulder problem start. The upper crack often looks dirty but gives good corner crack climbing.
Eric Byne, Jack Macleod, 1930s

33 Up the Establishment 12m E1 5b ★
Undercut the flake crack to reach the arête and climb this on its left with some delightful technical balance moves.
Chris Craggs, Graham Parkes, 1990

34 Anarchist's Arête 12m VS 4c ★
From the corner on the right, move left along a wide horizontal break to near the arête. Make teetery moves to stand up and continue, pumpily.
Don Chapman, Nat Allen, 1951

35 Emperor's Struggle 12m S 4a ★
The corner is a misnomer, as despite all appearances the holds are good.
Eric Byne, Clifford Moyer, c1930

EASTERN QUARRIES

**LAWRENCEFIELD
MILLSTONE EDGE
YARNCLIFFE QUARRY**

Billy Whizz, E2 5c (page 200), takes pride of place on the steep blasted walls that surge out of the dank darkness of the Lawrencefield pool. The climb forces ever upwards in an out-there position to give one of the Peak's great quarry climbs. Harry Lewis making the most of the jugs. Pete O'Donovan

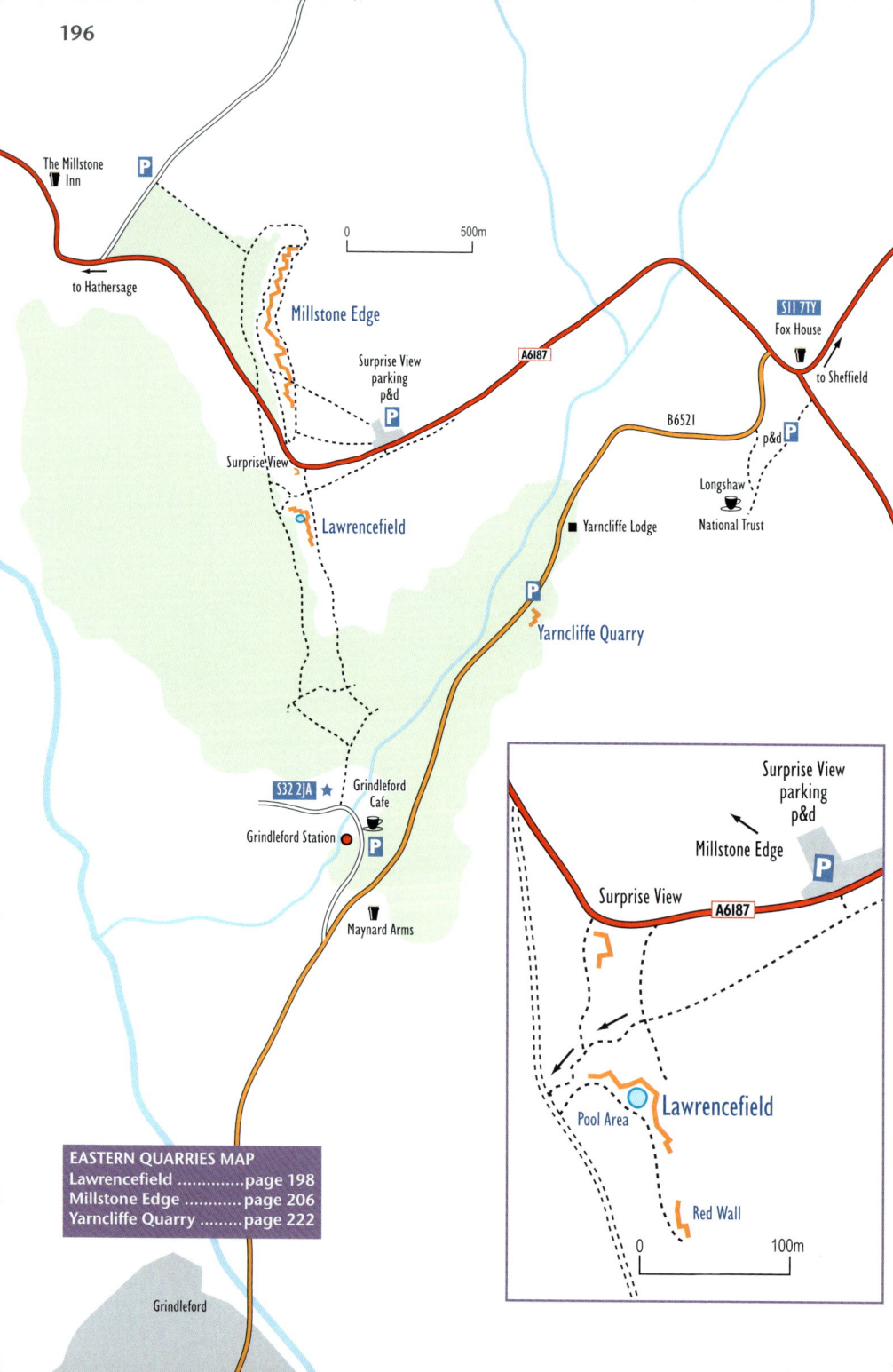

The arêtes at Millstone offer few hiding places, no matter what the grade. Psyche, skill and commitment must be your security. Here, Yuji Hirayama applies all three to Edge Lane, E5 5c (page 214), one of many tests of such skill at Millstone. 📷 David Simmonite

LAWRENCEFIELD

OS Grid Ref: SK 249 798
Altitude: 300m

Lawrencefield is an impressive quarry lying just under Surprise View. It exists slightly in the shadow of Millstone, and although it lacks the grandeur of its neighbour, it has enough good points to make it a very worthy destination. These include a friendly aspect, better easier climbs, the dark and mysterious pool, and a very sheltered and cosy setting.

The routes tend to be fairly steep corners and cracks, with some fine examples of peg-pocket-pulling to rival Millstone. There are also good slab climbs, especially on the unfortunately polished Gingerbread Slab. The climbs above the pool have a fine situation. However, some suspect rock exists and care is needed at the top of routes, especially in the Great Harry Area. There are a number of stout stake belays dotted around the top of the quarry.

The crag generally faces southwest, is very sheltered and is a great option on cold, windy days. However, in summer it can be like an oven. Generally, the quarry is still fast drying but the routes behind the pool can be green after rain and take longer to dry in winter.

Approach: Park as for Millstone Edge (see map on page 196). Cross the road and walk to just before Surprise View. A grassy, gated path leads to the quarry lip. Follow the path rightwards to an easy descent. 10 minutes.

GREAT HARRY AREA
This is the steep walls and corners to the left of the main areas around the pool. Good routes, despite some wear.

1 Summer Climb 15m HS 4b ★
A fun little climb in any season. From the square platform, make a tricky move right into the large, clean corner. A thrilling layback and a perplexing move gain easier terrain.

2 Three Tree Climb 21m HS 4b ★★
A fine climb with an exposed, exciting finale. Stiff pulls on a polished crack gain a series of grooves. Follow these and, near the top, grope

right to a crack round the arête. Layback this to the ledge and a finish off to the left.
Albert Shutt, Reg Pillinger, 1952

3 Great Peter 18m E1 5b ★★
A pumpy classic with reasonable but fiddly gear. Attack the thin crack directly. The lower direct start is 5c.
Peter Biven, Trevor Peck, 1956. FFA Clive Jones, Jim Reading, 1976

4 Pulpit Groove 27m VD 4a ★★
A great multi-pitch journey, with a refreshing sense of space. After a tricky start (variations possible), follow the leaning groove to a well-positioned pulpit (potential belay). Deep breath, and launch right across the void, then follow the leaning scoop to a large shelf. Belay here or exit onto the top if rope drag allows.
Albert Shutt, Reg Pillinger, 1952

5 Great Harry 21m VS 4c ★★★
A stout line with brilliant, sustained climbing. The corner-crack is jammed and bridged to the pulpit. Continue to the large ledge with difficulty. Tackle the corner direct to a friable finish.
Harry Hartley, Reg Pillinger, 1953

Tracy White on Excalibur, VS 4c (page 201). This Arthurian corner feels big and exposed although jugs and valour soon bring glory. 📷 Pete O'Donovan

THE POOL AREA

The centrepiece of Lawrencefield with its infamous dark pool. Surrounding this is a steep cauldron of superb routes, most of which present tough, physical challenges.

6 Scoop Connection 22m E3 5b ★
Worrying ledge-shuffling. Follow *Suspense* to the arête. Step up, and left onto the sloping shelf and follow this to finish up *Pulpit Groove*.
Keith Myhill, 1970s

7 Suspense 21m E2 5c ★★★
A local testpiece that will live long in the memory. Trend rightwards up the slab to the arête. Move boldly right around this to follow cracks and edges to the ledge.
Peter Biven, Trevor Peck, 1956. FFA John Allen, Nicky Stokes, 1975

8 Pool Wall 21m E5 6b ★★
A fantastic wall climb just about protected by wires and small cams. Step down, then climb up to a thin break. Move right (crux) then back left to finish up *Suspense*.
Alan Clark (aid), 1958. FFA Roger Greatrick, Alan Carn, 1980s

The following routes are all approached leftwards along the ledge system; don't fall in.

9 Cascara Crack 9m HS 4a
The chimney crack. From ledges, finish up the second corner above.
Dick Brown, 1953

10 Lawrencefield Ordinary 22m VD ★
A scenic ramble taking a rising set of steps.
Albert Shutt, Reg Pillinger, 1952

11 Austin's Variation 9m VS 4c ★
The fourth corner gives an alternative finish to the previous two routes. Big cam useful.
Alan Austin, 1956

12 High Plains Drifter 20m E4 6a ★★
Quality climbing; not easy! Climb a groove to the break. Ascend the wall above via a short ramp to an old peg. Move left then go up to the large ledge, crux. Drift off left to finish up the wall to the right of the flake.
Jim Reading, Rob Mallinson, 1977

13 Boulevard 18m E3 6a ★★
Brilliant crackcraft. Start up shallow corners, then attack the thin peg-scarred crack with conviction. Low in the grade with good pro.
Peter Biven, Trevor Peck (aid), 1956. FFA Ed Drummond, 1975

14 Von Ryan's Express 18m E6 6b ★
A serious route. Start directly up the slab to gain the break. Gain a small ledge in the centre of the face. Continue passing a thin crack.
Tony Ryan, Mick Ryan, 1985

15 Billy Whizz 18m E2 5c ★★★
A Peak testpiece. Ferociously pumpy, at the top of its grade. Follow the slabby groove to a break (peg). Strike on, heading for the slanting crack. Follow this, then make hard moves up the wall to finish. Dynamite! ⊙ page 195
Geoff Birtles, Ernie Marshall, Tom Proctor, Giles Barker, 1975

Lawrencefield | 201

16 High Street 20m E4 6a ★★
More thrilling finger-jamming. Start as for *Billy Whizz* to the break. Move right to a peg-scarred crack and crank up this to glory.
Peter Biven, Trevor Peck, (aid) 1956. FFA Jim Reading, 1975

17 Excalibur 21m VS 4c ★★★
The tough corner-crack rising up from the lake. Layback to the top in fine style in a superb position, with plenty of jugs and gear.
page 199
Peter Biven, Trevor Peck, 1955

GINGERBREAD SLAB
The most popular piece of rock in the quarry and is often festooned with ropes. From the top of the slab, scramble carefully to the top of the crag using a chimney on the left.

18 Once Pegged Wall 9m VS 5a ★
Climb the scars direct to the ledge on the left. Gain this and move round the arête to the top.
Don Morrison, 1950s

19 Limpopo Groove 9m VS 4b ★★
Grapple with Gregory's 'Great, Grey, Green Greasy Groove', with care at the top. Bomber protection but it can be a bit slippery.
Dave Gregory, 1955

20 Gingerbread 9m VS 4c ★★
A lovely climb. Follow the delicate left-hand arête of the slab arranging the only protection on the right at half height.
Albert Shutt, Reg Pillinger, 1952

21 Meringue 9m HVS 5a ★
After a polished start, the thin awkward crack is climbed to a shallow break. A small poorish cam might just protect the top move.
Albert Shutt, Reg Pillinger, Tony Davies (1pt) 1953. FFA John Fearon, 1955

22 Éclair 10m E1 5b
The unprotected slab on smooth holds.

23 Vanilla Slice 10m E1 5c
Another slippery slab climb but with small wires for protection where it counts.

24 Snail Crack 18m HVD ★★
The polished crack is climbed direct to the ledge. A good beginner's route. page 21
Albert Shutt, Reg Pillinger, 1953

25 Nailsbane 20m VD ★
The leftward-slanting crack is followed to an awkward mantel. Another good starter route.
Albert Shutt, Reg Pillinger, 1952

26 Tyrone 18m VS 4c ★
Climb the cracked wall to an awkward move to the ledge. Move a little right into the groove and take the upper curving crack to a ledge. From here, a worthwhile second pitch takes the bulging wall above.

27 Nova 18m HS 4b ★
Take the line of choice right of *Tyrone* to twin cracks high in the wall, then an awkward move to a shelf, to gain the large ledge.
Don Morrison, John Fearon, 1956

Gingerbread Slab

RED WALL
Fifty metres right is a steep reddish wall with a shallow sandy cave at half-height.

28 Rattus Norvegicus 15m E5 6b ★
Bouldery moves up the lower slab gain the break. Climb the upper wall past two tricky sections.
Gary Gibson, Neil Harvey, 1981

29 Delectable Direct 15m HVS 5b ★★
Excellent, well-protected climbing that takes the peg-scarred crack to the 'Red Cave' and continues direct up the headwall, past a small sentry box.
Peter Biven (aid), 1956. FFA Don Morrison, Les Gillot, 1964

30 Red Wall 17m VS 4b ★
Follow the groove and flakes rightward to the ledge in the corner. Finish up the main corner groove. A good E1 5b variation takes the wall left of the top corner.
Don Morrison, John Fearon, 1956

31 Delectable Variation 22m VS 4c ★★★
A wildly exposed outing. Follow *Red Wall* to its ledge, then traverse left, all the way across the wall, treating holds with care, to finish up the fine arête. ⊙ opposite page
Don Morrison, 1950s

32 Cordite Crack 15m HS 4b ★
From a corner 2m right, move up to the obvious steep corner-crack. Blast up this to the top.
Peter Biven, Trevor Peck, 1955

The next routes are all gained from the right along a huge sloping ledge below the wall.

33 Skyline 12m E3 5b
The well-positioned crack is a tad loose.
Daniel Lee, 1981

34 Block Wall 12m E4 6b ★
The best line on the wall gains the pegged-out crack on the upper wall. Finger-knackering cranking on peg holes leads to an easier finish.
Daniel Lee, 1981

A little journey to the edge of the world... ish. Rebecca Ting swashbuckling her way up the arête on Delectable Variation, VS 4c (opposite page). ◉ Paul Evans

BURBAGE, MILLSTONE AND BEYOND
The definitive gritstone guide

Covering, amongst others, the crags of the Burbage Valley, Higgar Tor, Millstone, Lawrencefield, Rivelin, Bell Hagg, Wyming Brook, Bamford, Derwent Edges, Agden Rocher and Wharncliffe this truly is a bumper guide.

It details all the routes and boulder problems to be found in these areas. It features full-colour topos, fantastic clear maps, and a dazzling array of superb contemporary and historical photos. It has a fine mix of historical, amusing and inspirational information and anecdotes. Plus graded lists, first ascent lists, even a highball list, information to get people away from the usual haunts, information on conditions and the best, most accurate, most up to date information on the routes and boulder problems.

Pick up the definitive guide for details of every route on the crags selected here as well as a great number of crags for users of this book who get the bug and want to find out more.

With full coverage of routes and boulder problems on the crags from the **Burbage Valley** (including Burbage North, Burbage South, Burbage Quarries, Carl Wark, Higgar Tor, Higgar Tor East and Burbage West), the **Millstone area** (including Millstone Edge, Lawrencefield, Mother Cap and Secret Garden), gems in the **Rivelin area** (Rivelin Edge and Quarry, Bell Hagg, Wyming Brook), the **Derwent to Bamford area** (Hurkling Stones, Wheel Stones, White Tor, Back Tor, Howshaw Tor, Dovestone Tor, Ladybower Quarry, Bamford Edge) and finally the **Wharncliffe Area** (Wharncliffe Edge, Agden Rocher, and Stannington Ruffs).

Featuring:
2,700 routes from Mod to E10
700 boulder problems
120 full-colour action shots
The definitive climbing history of the area

Get it from the BMC shop for a lifetime of gritstone action.

http://shop.thebmc.co.uk/

ISBN 978-0-903908-77-8

Front cover: James Pearson on The Sentinel, E2 5b, Burbage North (page 234). Photo: David Simmonite

Alex Hull on Time for Tea Original, E1 5b (page 216), one of Millstone's many great mid-grade crack pitches. 📷 Mike Cheque

MILLSTONE EDGE
OS Grid Ref: SK 248 801 to SK 248 806
Altitude: 320m

The king crag of quarried grit. Big, steep and clean with row upon row of walls, arêtes, overhangs, grooves and cracks of all sizes. From fists to fingertips, it's all here. Three-star routes litter the crag from VS to E7. Fill your boots!

The crag is exposed and mostly west-facing, and the majority of its walls get lots of sun from the early afternoon. These faces are clean and sound and dry quickly. The North Bays are in the shade till late afternoon. The crag is climbable all year round, although on cold grey days, it can feel a bit bleak. On wet days, the Keyhole Cave area stays remarkably dry.

Approach: Park in the Surprise View pay & display car park on the A6187. Take one of the paths across the moor to the crag.

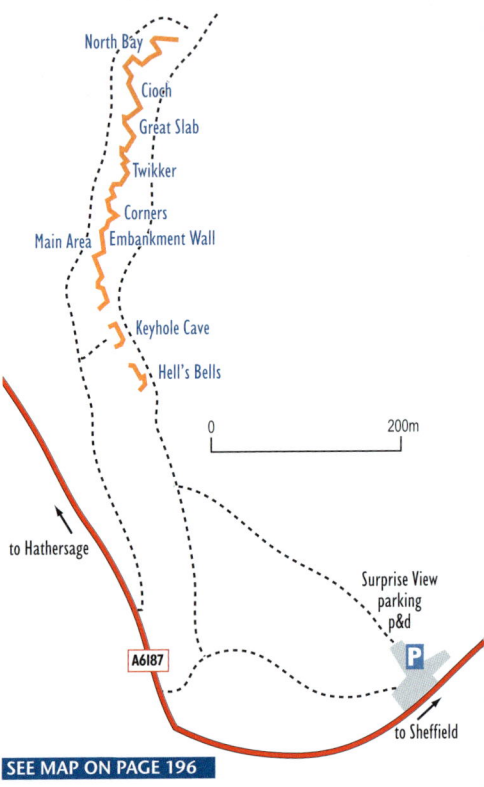

NORTH BAY AREA
The leftmost area has a character all its own. Shadier and more gothic. It's a cool spot.

1 Brimstone 16m E2 5b ★★
The fine overhanging crack will pump you into the middle of next week. Fantastic.
Keith Myhill, Nick Elliott (aid), 1969. FFA Henry Barber, 1973

2 Satan's Slit 16m E1 5b ★
The wide, kinky crack is tough low down.
John Loy, 1964

3 Gates of Mordor 16m E3 5c ★★
A genuine thunderpump. Climb the groove and the perfectly protected hand crack above.
Hank Pasquill, 1969

4 Hacklespur 16m HVS 5b ★
The wide chimney / groove.
Alan Clarke, 1960s. FFA John Loy, 1962

5 Cauldron Crack 16m E3 5c ★★
Good chunky climbing. The right side of the arête is followed, hollow but mellow, to a jug beneath the overhang. Swing left to gain and follow the nut-friendly crack to the top.
Mick Fowler, John Stevenson, 1976

6 Estremo 16m HVS 5a ★★
Climb the wide fissure as far as a niche, then the corner above in a position of exposure.
Ted Howard, 1960s

Millstone Edge | 207

7 Gimbals 18m HVS 5a ★
Climb the corner as far as a niche. Step right and tackle the bulging wall into the skylight.
Mick Fowler, John Stevenson, 1976

8 Mother's Pride 24m E6 6b ★★★
A superb, long and sustained pitch, fairly well protected. Climb the steep crack and groove feature in the narrow face, passing some pegs.
Mike Lea, 2001

9 Perplexity 24m E6 6b ★★★
A superb climb, taking a stately line up the arête. Boulder up the arête to the first bulge. Crux moves up and right lead to the overhang. Climb the groove and wall above.
Johnny Dawes, 1984

10 Plexity 22m HVS 5a ★★★
A big route for the HVS leader, with thrilling climbing up the central crack system. The high overhang is negotiated on the right.
Joe Brown, Morty Smith, 1957

11 Remembrance Day 20m VS 4b ★
Jam joyously up the wide crack in the main corner of the bay, passing a ledge.
Ted Howard, c1960

12 Southern Comfort 22m E3 5c ★
Very Cumbrian. From the right end of the ledge, take a line up the dark groove; good steep moves. Beware loose rock near the top.
John Stevenson, Mick Fowler, 1976

13 Commix 20m E2 5c ★★
Very fine and well-protected climbing with a trying crux. From 3m up *Southern Comfort*, move right to a crack. Follow this to a ledge and an easier, though hollow, finish.
John Loy (aid), 1960s. FFA John Stevenson, Mick Fowler, 1976

14 Toploader 28m E7 6c ★★★
Top notch cranking up the steep wall, almost a sport climb. Follow a crack then carry on past pegs to a junction with *Saville Street*. Step back left and climb past old bolts to the top.
Mike Lea, 2001

15 Saville Street 28m E3 6a ★★★
A tough Millstone classic with continually forceful climbing and good protection. A short awkward crack gains a ledge. From here, follow the fine crack to the overhang. A very determined attitude is now needed to gain a standing position above. Hard for E3, and 6a.
Reg Pillinger (aid), 1960s. FFA John Allen, 1975

16 Shape Shifter 28m E6 6b ★
The steep arête, passing a couple of poor pegs.
Tom Randall, 2008

17 Soho Sally 28m E1 5b ★
A great little route with lots of character. Climb the crack to the ledge. Step boldly left above the void to a groove and move up to good gear. Careful, easier climbing remains.
Geoff Birtles, Tom Proctor, 1975

THE CIOCH
A great area for more moderate climbs with clean, sunny and quick-drying rock.

18 April Arête   16m   HVS 4c   ★
A *Master's Edge* for the enthusiast. From the ledge, climb the main arête. Fine exposure.
Alan Clarke, c1960

19 March Hare   16m   E2 5c   ★★
A worrying solo up the arête.
Gabe Regan, 1975

20 Dextrous Hare   16m   E3 5c   ★★
A fine route which climbs the sneaky little pegged wall with a committing crux moving left to the tiny, hanging groove. A bit sketchy; RPs useful.
Martin Taylor, 1976

21 Dexterity   20m   E1 5b   ★★
The splitter crack. Superb, straight-in jamming leads exhaustingly to a slap-in-the-face crux at the top. Those of lesser moral fibre have been known to scurry out left below this, but you wouldn't do that, would you?
◉ opposite page
Harold Drasdo, 1957

22 Cioch Corner   22m   S
Climb the corner left of the Cioch to the ledge, then climb any of the easier finishes to the top.
Alan Clarke, Ben Wilson, Ted Howard, 1956

23 Mayday   22m   HVS 5a   ★
A technical exercise up the arête of the Cioch. Finish up the upper arête.
Alan Clarke, 1960s

24 Supra Direct   20m   HVS 5b   ★
Climb the peg-scarred crack, with a couple of thin pulls, to the ledge. Finish up the corner.
Parnassus Climbing Club (aid), 1957. FFA Pete Brayshaw, 1975

25 The Hacker   20m   VS 4c   ★
Follow the little pegged crack as it curves right to join *Close Shave*. Finish up this or the upper arête of *Mayday*.
Brian Mosley, Tony Eady, 1983

26 Close Shave   30m   HVD 4a   ★
A good route following the sweeping groove formed at the right side of the Cioch. From the ledge, finish up the back corner.
Alan Clarke, Ben Wilson, Ted Howard, 1956

27 Boomerang   24m   S
The easiest route up the steep wall is unfortunately a bit loose. It climbs leftwards until half-height, then slightly rightwards to a ledge. Traverse right and finish up the corner.
John Loy, 1960s

28 Only Just   15m   E1 5a   ★
Gain the ledge and climb the clean open groove to the left of the wall. The climbing is easy, but protection limited (side-runners sometimes used in *Eartha*).
Ernie Marshall, Wilfred White, 1959

29 Eartha   16m   HS 4b   ★★
Fine climbing up the attractive flake system in the centre of the slab. It is gained by climbing delicately up near the left side of the lower wall. Among the best HSs on the edge.
Al Parker, Peter Bamfield, 1957

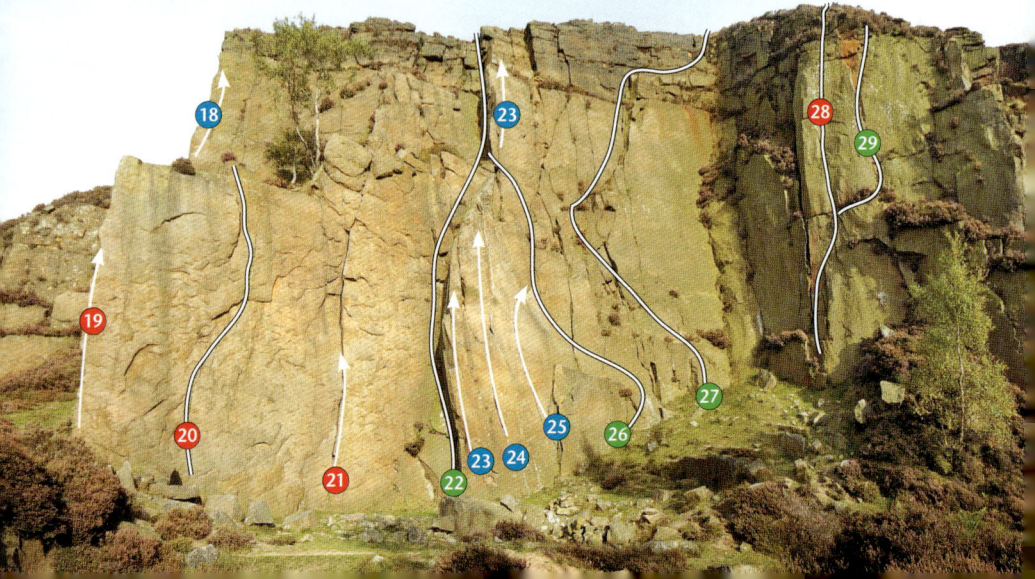

Steph Ward laybacking with verve up one of Millstone's proudest cracks, Dexterity, E1 5b, (opposite page). Other methods of climbing this wide-hand crack are available. Andi Smith

GREAT SLAB
Well, maybe not great, but it's good. A fine venue for some adventurous mid-grade climbs.

30 Evening Premiere 19m VS 4c ★
Good steep crack climbing. Climb the thin crack on jams and finger locks. Avoid the loose finish by heading for the crack on the left.
Mick Fowler, John Stevenson, 1976

31 Svelt 20m HVS 5a ★
The smooth corner has a couple of slippery bulges. From the top of the slab trend left and up a steep juggy corner.
Al Parker, Martin Boysen, 1962

32 The Snivelling Shit 10m E5 6a ★★
This unique test of nerve and footwork climbs the bald slab on the smallest of holds, passing a deep slot high on the slab. Finish up or down *Great Slab*.
Jonathan Lagoe, 1977

33 Greasy Chips 10m VS 4b ★
An alternative start to the next route can be made up a line of chips. Unprotected.

34 The Great Slab 28m HS 4b ★★
A good big route, with an adventurous feel. Climb the crack with slippery difficulty to the top of the slab. From here, climb straight up via a wide crack and a careful topout, as the rock is a little hollow. ⓞ opposite page
Alan Maskery (aid), 1952. FFA Al Parker, Peter Bamfield, 1957

35 Sex Dwarves 10m E3 6b
Painfully thin climbing up the slab on razor blades and polished smears leads to the break.
Mark Millar, 1982

36 Lorica 20m VS 4c ★
Climb a crack to the top of the slab. Above and left is a right-curving flake. Follow this, then the hand crack above.
John Conn (aid), c1960

37 Bun Run 20m HVS 5a
Follow *Lorica* to the top of the slab. Gain a hanging corner to the right and follow this steeply to a final wide crack.
Al Evans, Nick Elliott, 1969

38 Windrête 14m E2 5b ★★
The arête, climbed face-on, is a pretty full-on affair. Some gear can be had at a third height, and while this will cover the crux, it still feels a long and lonely way to the top. On a more positive note, it is neither strenuous nor pumpy, which allows you plenty of time to worry about each move.
Al Evans, Z Dyslewicz, 1969

Great Slab, HS 4b (opposite page), is one of the few great routes below VS at Millstone. Here Cherelle Fielding stretches up the fine technical slab section below the chunky top half. 📷 Mike Cheque

Millstone Edge

39 Eros 15m HVS 5b ★★
Pummel up the ramshackle flake in the centre of the wall with great joy and care. Fine chunky climbing in a great position. ☉ opposite page
Paul Grayson, 1960s

40 Lyon's Corner House 30m HVS 5a ★★★
A fantastic rock climb based on the fine arête. Gain the cave, then continue up the corner to the roof. Swing left around the arête and up to a ledge. Trend up and left to gain and follow the juggy arête in a superb position. A direct start is up the lower arête is HVS 5a.
George Leaver, Kit Twyford (aid), 1956. FFA unknown

41 Erb 28m E2 5c ★★
Another good route, serving up a delightful smorgasbord of strenuous thuggery and delicate technicality. Follow the previous route to the swing left to the ledge. From here, a line leads up and right to a hungry gash in the lip of the roof. Beef through this to a rest, then still surprisingly difficult going to the top.
Alan Clarke (aid), 1960s. FFA Tom Proctor, Geoff Birtles, 1975

42 Twikker 28m E3 5c ★★★
This awesomely steep route gives one of the best E3 challenges on the edge. It takes the big roof crack, both exhausting and exciting, and then continues to a niche below an overlap. A disappointingly difficult manoeuvre over this on pin scars leads more easily to the top.
Dave Johnston, 1956. FFA Tom Proctor, Geoff Birtles, 1975

43 Pinstone Street 28m E2 5c ★★
A testing route; well-protected but with a sense of urgency. Climb a corner to a crusty cave under the overhang. Heave up and right and climb the peg-scarred crack to a ledge. The finishing crack retains interest.
Dave Johnston (aid), 1956

44 Flapjack 24m VS 4b ★
Climb the stepped feature, until a mantelshelf gains the ledge. From here, a series of bold stretches leads up the shallowest of grooves as far as another ledge, and the top.
Jack Soper, 1956

45 S.S.S. 18m VS 4b
The stepped corner has good bridging moves.
Jack Soper, 1956

46 Winter's Grip 17m E6 6b ★
Fine, scary climbing up the arête. A couple of poor blade pegs can be hand-placed en route.
Neil Foster, 1983

47 Keelhaul 17m VS 4c ★
Gain the flake and climb it. Finish on the right, as the direct is a bit loose.
Alan Clarke, John Loy, 1960s

48 Billingsgate 17m E1 5b ★★
The classic corner 10m right of *Keelhaul* gives absorbing moves, with small runners, to an exit left.
Steve Chadwick, 1969

Twikker Bay

If you stray only a little beyond the popular delights of the main area of Millstone you will be rewarded by many cool climbs with a less-travelled feel about them. These are every bit as memorable as the celebrity pitches. Here, Hulda Norstein tackles Eros, HVS 5b (opposite page). ◐ Andi Smith

214 | Millstone Edge

THE MAIN AREA
Now we're talking. A series of walls, corners, arêtes and slabs that are the gold standard of quarry climbing. Clean, sunny and popular.

Corners Area: The area starts with some gritstone skyscrapers. Awesome.

49 Crew Cut 20m HVS 4c ★★
The salivating fissure features some medieval thrutching, or bold laybacking.
Alan Clarke, 1963

50 Great West Road 35m E3 5c, 5b ★★★
Two contrasting pitches, one strenuous and the other serious, combine to produce a class route. Follow the corner to the ledge (belay), then the bold arête above.
Dave Johnson (aid), 1956. FFA Al Evans, 1969

51 Edge Lane 18m E5 5c ★★★
The square-cut arête. Nowhere is the climbing more than 5b/c and the crux is only the crux because it is at the top. ⊙ page 197
Richard McHardy, 1974

52 Green Death 18m E5 6b ★★★
The corner provides a stern test of technique and nerve. The 6b bit comes right off the deck and a 5c crux is just below the high peg.
Tom Proctor, 1969

53 Master's Edge 18m E7 6c ★★★
Fawcett's masterpiece. The stunning arête gives one of the finest hard challenges in the Peak, with sustained difficult climbing and painfully limited protection.
⊙ opposite page
Ron Fawcett, 1983

54 The Bad and the Beautiful 16m E7 6b ★★★
A fabulous route needing utter commitment. From the mid-height ledge, follow the slabby flake just left of *Great Arête*.
Mark Leach, 1987

55 Great Arête 16m E5 5c ★★★
The hulking upper arête. The climbing is fairly steady, although you could fall the height of Millstone - and survive. From the ledge, follow the arête on the right. ⊙ page 14
Tom Proctor, 1975

56 Knightsbridge 35m E2 5b, 5c ★★★
A fabulous climb, somehow both sustained and cruxy - work that one out! Climb the lower corner, or scramble up *The Scoop*. Climb the thin pegged-out crack above.
Tom Proctor, Geoff Birtles, 1973

57 Scoop Crack 32m VS 4b ★
Climb a shallow corner then the crack above.
John Loy, c1960

58 The Scoop 35m D
Disjointed climbing with some good positions up the slab, ledges and corner.

59 Great North Road 35m HVS 5a ★★★
This, the *Cenotaph Corner* of grit, climbs the fantastic stepped corner. Everything that HVS should be, and then some. ⊙ page 217
Peter Biven, Trevor Peck (aid), 1956. FFA Joe Brown, 1957

One of the most prized ticks for many committed gritstoners. Master's Edge, E7 6c (opposite page), is perhaps the ultimate E7 on Peak grit. The moves are technical, the gear barely sufficient, the position outrageous and the last lunge will live long in the mind. Stuart Honick climbing. 📷 David Simmonite

Millstone Edge

EMBANKMENT WALL
The pristine walls are a treasure chest of cracks in the VS to E3 range.

60 Technical Master Font 6B ★★★
The left arête, on its right.
Keith Myhill, 1960s

61 Embankment Route 1 10m VS 4c ★
Follow the short crack to a horizontal flake, then swing awkwardly right and up past a helpful iron bar. Belay. A second pitch is E2 5c.
Peter Biven, Trevor Peck (aid), c1960. FFA John Allen, 1975

62 Embankment Route 2 25m VS 4c, 4b ★★
Twin cracks, lead to the belay ledge. The second pitch follows a loose groove (poor).
Peter Biven, Trevor Peck (aid), c1960

63 Scritto's Republic 18m E7 6c ★★
Hard, thin and technical, a searing test of technique and finger strength.
Ron Fawcett, 1982

64 Embankment Route 3 25m E1 5b, 5b ★★
The perfect peg crack. Straightforward Millstone quality, making up for the sore feet. The second pitch takes a short steep crack just left of the groove of *Embankment 2*.
Peter Biven, Trevor Peck (aid), c1960s. FFA Ed Drummond, 1975

65 Time for Tea 20m E3 5c ★★
A tasty runout. Climb the crack, and with good gear at its apex, move left to a ledge in the middle of the wall. Balancey climbing on flat holds leads up and left to the ledge. Short people would like to upgrade this, but tough.
Ed Drummond, John Young, 1974

The direct finish is **Tea for Two,** E4 6a ★★.
Time for Tea Original, E1 5b ★★, gains *Embankment Route 4* from the top of the crack.
⊙ page 205

66 Embankment Route 4 22m E1 5b ★★★
The tall crack is as good an example of peg-pocketeering as gritstone has to offer.
Peter Biven, Trevor Peck (aid), c.960s. FFA Chris Addy, 1975

67 Whitehall 25m HVS 5a ★★
The major corner provides a fine test of lay-backing technique.
Keith Myhill, 1969

68 Lotto 25m E1 5c ★
Varied climbing in an exposed position. Ascend a faint groove which curves up, past a thin section, to the arête. Swing right to follow *Covent Garden*. At the roof, go back left along the wide break and beef the overhang at a slotted crack.
John Loy (aid), c1960. FFA Tom Proctor, 1975

For many climbers, Great North Road is one of the top five HVSs on grit. Boasting 35 metres of sublime climbing, great holds, perfect protection, a stunning line and mounting exposure, it's not hard to see why. Here Dave Hinton styles the hooded corner heading for the overhang and final glory romp (page 214). 📷 Paul Evans

Millstone Edge

69 Covent Garden 25m VS 4b, 4b ★★
A mellow first pitch is followed by the delightfully exposed second pitch. Climb easy ledges then the crack up the left side of the pedestal to a big ledge and belay. The top section of this pitch can be climbed up the left arête, more in keeping with the second pitch. Cross a narrow terrace to the left arête and balance up this with glee. Finish direct. 🔘 page 221
Peter Biven, Trevor Peck, 1956

70 Scruples 22m E5 6b ★
A cool deviation. From the sentry box on *Bond Street*, move left and up the bulging slab.
Paul Evans, Neil Buttle, 1987

71 Bond Street 22m HVS 5a ★★★
Cancel your trip to Yosemite. This Millstone classic has it all. Climb the perfectly formed jamming crack. Scramble off the finishing ledge or finish up *Covent Garden*.

72 Monopoly 22m E7 6b ★
A very bold climb following shallow features up the wall between the two cracks.
Johnny Dawes, 1983

73 Great Portland Street
20m HVS 5b ★★★
Another brilliant HVS! This cool groove is guarded by a desperate mantelshelf. The upper groover is bridged with sustained interest.
Alan Clarke, 1963

74 White Wall 22m E5 6b ★★
A worthy sister route to *London Wall* takes the pegged crack in the smooth face left of *The Mall*. While not quite as fine, being less sustained, it still has great climbing and impressive situations. Climb steadily up kinked cracks until a desperate move gains a standing position below the overlap. From here, thrilling cranking over the small roof leads to a poor peg and less difficult climbing to finish.
Steve Bancroft, Jim Reading, 1976

75 The Mall 22m VS 4c ★★★
Heave-ho your way up the big chunky corner. This contains a lot of climbing, all of it enjoyable, although it can be sandy post-monsoon.
Joe Brown, Morty Smith, 1957

76 London Wall 22m E5 6a ★★★
This classic product of the '70s free climbing revolution is also one of the best lines on grit. Finger lock your way up the searing pocket-studded seam with never-ending difficulty. One of the greatest trophies on gritstone.
Peter Biven, Trevor Peck (aid), 1956. FFA John Allen, 1975

77 Lambeth Chimney 22m HS 4b ★
Follow the broken chimney, then the easy arête above, until an exacting straddle to the left gains a smart little groove leading to the top.

Millstone Edge | 219

KEYHOLE CAVE
A favourite spot for steep crack climbs. It is 100m right of *London Wall*.

78 Adam Smith's Invisible Hand 20m E6 6b ★★★
At last! Sport climbing without the safety. The desperate arête, past three ancient bolts.
Johnny Dawes, 1984

79 Oxford Street 22m E3 5a, 6b ★
A lovely HVS crack leads to the sandy cave; belay. Beef over the roof crack to the right then saunter up the easy wall above.
Peter Biven, Trevor Peck (aid), 1956. FFA Phil Burke, 1969

80 Piccadilly Circus 25m E2 5a, 5c ★
Climb the delightful HVS finger crack to the sandy cave. Belay. Beetle leftwards to a thin crack which leads to a ledge and an easy finish.
Steve Bancroft, Nicky Stokes, 1976

81 Coventry Street 22m E5 6b ★★
Tricky finger-jamming gains the cave (E4 6b). Muscle over the roof crack with determination, and wobble directly to the top.
Steve Bancroft, John Allen, 1976

82 How Many Roads 22m E7 6c ★★
A desperate and fingery wall-climb with F8a/F8b climbing and decent peg-protection, after a bold start.
Ben Bransby, 2019

83 Jermyn Street 25m E5 6a ★★
Climb the crack and groove into the cave. Move right and scuff your way up the right arête of the cave. Hand-traverse the lip leftwards, and pull into a standing position. Migrate leftwards in relative security to a common finish.
Peter Biven, Trevor Peck (aid), 1956. FFA Tom Proctor, Geoff Birtles, 1975

84 Regent Street 20m E2 5c ★★★
One of the best Extremes in the Peak, with superb protection and sufficient rests making up for its uncompromising steepness. Follow twin cracks then move right to a ledge below the headwall crack. Attack this with gusto.
Pete Bevin, Trevor Peck (aid), 1956. FFA Terry King, 1968

85 Shaftesbury Avenue 20m HVS 5a ★
Climb the straight, wide crack past an overhang. Enjoyable open climbing remains.
Pete Bevin, Trevor Peck (aid), 1956. FFA Jim Campbell, 1967

86 The Whore 20m HVS 5b ★
Follow jams to the little overhung corner. Overcome this strenuously, good solid 5b, then follow finger locks to an easier finish.
Jim Reading, Clive Jones, D Hayes, 1975

87 Gimcrack 20m VS 4c ★
Romp up the jamming crack and finish up the corner above. Beware looseness on the exit.
Baz Ingle, 1962

HELL'S BELLS AREA
A final section, 80m right of Keyhole Cave, has a friendly nature.

88 Flank Crack 8m VD
The short corner to the ledge. Walk off right or take the direct finish up the sandy wall at S.

89 Chiming Cracks 8m HS ★
The steep cracks are short but pumpy.

90 Hell's Bells 8m HS 4b ★★
The best route hereabouts taking the tall corner.
Alan Clarke, 1963

91 Juniper 8m E1 5b
The arête, with good balancy moves. Often climbed with side-runners at HVS.
Nick Halliday, Tony Sawbridge, 1978

92 Midrift 7m VD
A good beginner's route up the short corner.

93 Giant's Steps 8m D
A gentle frolic up large features. The crack systems in the upper wall are VD, providing a good finish.

94 Street Legal 8m E2 5c ★
Climb the wall with stiff moves passing a hanging flake. Little protection until after the crux.
Paul Cropper, Nadim Siddiqui, 1978

95 Blood and Guts on Botty Street
  8m E5 6b ★
Hard and unprotected slapping up the right arête of the buttress.
Allen Williams, 1987

Holly Peristiani on the thrilling upper pitch of Covent Garden, VS 4b (page 218). The protection is sparse and the climbing precarious, but the holds are positive enough to keep you moving in the right direction.
Paul Winder

YARNCLIFFE QUARRY

OS Grid Ref: SK 255 794
Altitude: 250m

Yarncliffe Quarry is a popular roadside venue, especially with outdoor groups and low-grade climbers. With such intense traffic over its relatively short years the popular routes are ageing before their time.

The quarry is very sheltered with the left-hand slabs getting the sun. Further right, the walls receive less sun and can be green and slow to dry. Some routes can be sandy after rain and plagued by wood ants in summer.

Approach: The quarry is beside the B6521, just below Yarncliffe Lodge, with a small but obvious parking bay adjacent to two gates with just enough room for four cars. The quarry is within spitting distance. To approach the crag, follow the footpath round to the right of the gate.

SEE MAP ON PAGE 196

The first climbs are on the series of sunny slabs immediately on your left as you approach. The descent is down the path leftwards following the fence line.

1 Ant's Arête   16m   VS 4b   ★
Pleasant arête climbing with limited protection.
Nat Allen, Don Chapman, 1950

2 Aphid's Wall   16m   E1 5b
The line of least resistance. Bold, sandy climbing.
Dave Gregory, Dave Eyles, 1972

3 Latecomer   16m   VS 4b   ★
Move up left to the thin crack and niche. Trend left to a bold finish (or bail out right).
Don Morrison, 1964

4 Soldier Ant   16m   E3 5c
Starting as for *Latecomer*, continue direct up the very narrow slab. E1 with side-runners.
Malcolm Slater, Bruce Barnes, 1978

5 Ant's Crack   17m   S 4a   ★
The crack is well protected but often sandy.
Nat Allen, R Kerry, 1950

6 Ant's Wall   17m   HS 4a   ★★
The slab and crack has good holds and gear.
Dave Gregory, Dave Eyles, 1972

Yarncliffe Quarry | 223

7 Angular Climb 17m HVD
The crack system, first on the right then the left.

8 Cardinal's Arête 20m VS 4c ★
Follow the arête in its entirety. Stepping right to protect the final steepening feels sensible.
Don Chapman, Nat Allen, 1951

9 The Outdoor Centre Route 20m VD ★
The shallow parallel feature right of the arête.

10 Cardinal's Slab 20m VS 5a ★★
Ascend the slab rightwards to a thin crack. This gives a few well-protected technical moves.
Dave Gregory, Dave Eyles, 1972

11 Threatened 20m E1 5a
The thin slab, starting on the right then trend left to a more direct line to finish.
Graham Hoey, 1974

12 Cardinal's Crack 20m VS 4b ★
The fearsome crack eats feet and fists. Small holds on its edge give hope to those with smaller hands. Move leftwards around the final blocks to a large tree belay.
Don Chapman, Nat Allen, 1950

13 Chalked Up 20m E1 5a ★
The slab and thin crack. Scant protection.
Giles Barker, 1978

14 Sulu 20m VS 5a ★
Technical. Take the thin, slanting crack left of the arête to a ledge. Finish direct or shuffle onto its right at the top.
J R Barker, P Brown, W Phillips, 1971

15 Rhythm of Cruelty 20m E4 5c ★
The bold arête is laybacked on its right to a ledge and the easier finish of *Pedestal Arête*.
Phil Wilson, Gary Gibson, 1979

16 Capital Cracks 20m VS 5a ★
The thin cracks 2m right of the arête. A hard start leads to a ledge then juggier cracks above.
Dave Gregory, Geoff Milburn, 1971

17 Pedestal Arête 22m VS 4b
From a small corner 4m right of the arête, follow a series of left-trending steps, crossing *Capital Cracks*, to the top of the pedestal. Finish direct up the arête as for *Rhythm of Cruelty*.
Nat Allen, Don Chapman, 1951

From the corner, a series of walls zigzag off towards the eventual undergrowth at the end of the quarry. The quarry now succumbs to nature until a prominent arête appears.

18 Crème de la Crème 16m E6 6b ★★★
The magnificent ship's prow vies for the best route in the quarry. Start by laybacking the left side of the lower arête to the large ledge. The upper section is protected by small gear.
Ron Fawcett, Geoff Birtles, 1977

A short way right is a clean, cracked wall.

19 Fall Pipe 16m VS 4b ★★
The well-protected groove and jamming crack is taken direct. A must if the start is dry.
Ted Howard, 1964

20 Zapple 18m HVS 5b ★★★
The must-do climb in the quarry, steep and well protected. Climb the right-hand crack (or left, 5a, but not quite as good), to the break. Follow the cracks and breaks to the top.
J R Barker, W Phillips (aid), 1969. FFA, P Brown, W Phillips, 1971

21 Trised Crack 15m VS 4c
Good laybacking up the flaky crack.
Don Cowan, Don Chapman, Nat Allen, 1951

THE BURBAGE VALLEY

Burbage North
Burbage South
Burbage Quarries
Higgar Tor

The Ash Tree Wall area at Burbage North is a great venue for lower-grade leads. The rock is clean and quick drying, the routes are cool and far enough from the road that their natural essence is a true part of the experience. Liz Asquith on Bilberry Crack VD (page 232), with the autumnal joys of Burbage as her witness.
Niall Grimes

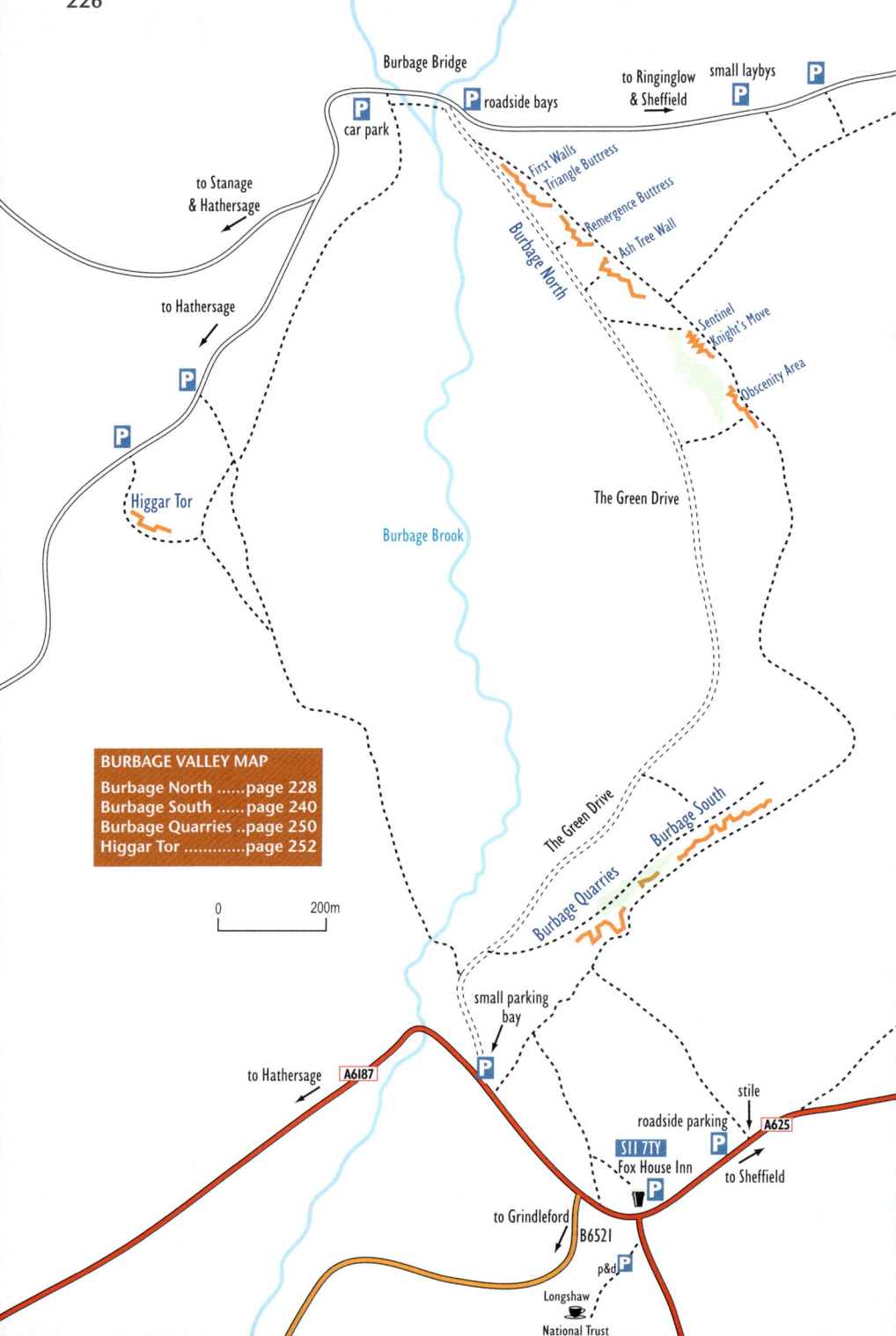

Rebecca Ting on Fox House Flake, VS 4b, catching the sun in the sometimes shadowy quarries of Burbage South (page 250). 📷 Paul Evans

BURBAGE NORTH

OS Grid Ref: SK 263 828 to SK 268 823
Altitude: 400m

Burbage North fills a wonderful niche in the Peak gritstone collection of crags. It is less imposing and impressive than the other major crags hereabouts but, on closer acquaintance, it's a wonderland of small buttresses crammed full of high-quality routes, micro-routes and boulder problems.

The crag is perhaps best loved as a soloing venue. Many of its lines exist in the grey area between highball problems and short routes. These micro-routes can be enjoyed either as bold solos, as well padded and spotted boulder problems, or with rope and runners.

The rock is all extremely clean, quick-drying and is climbable year-round. Lots of sunshine, although it can be a bit midgy on summer evenings and tends to catch any wind hurtling up or down the valley. The crag faces south-west and receives the sun from late morning onwards, providing some welcome warmth when other crags are cold.

Approach: See map on page 226. Park on the roadside or in the car park by Burbage Bridge and follow the Green Drive to below the buttress of your choice or along the muddy crag top path. Approaches from 2 to 20 minutes.

FIRST WALLS
Popular as a bouldering and soloing warm-up above mats. There are many variations and traverses so just go wherever your fancy and fingers take you.

1 Route 1   6m   HS 4c
The arête has a polished start and a fluttery finish.

2 Route 1.5   6m   VS 5b
The wall above the start of the slanting crack has a polished start to a positive finish.

3 Route 2   6m   S 4b   ★
A difficult start leads into a juggy triangular niche and easier finish.

4 Route 2.5   6m   VS 5a
The fingery wall between the two cracks eases with height.

5 Route 3   6m   S 4a   ★
A little cracker of a route. A polished start leads to a zigzag jam crack.

6 Route 3.5   6m   E1 6a
A contrived line with a long move high up.

7 Route 4   6m   VS 5b
The wall left of the arête has a poor landing.

Burbage North | 229

8 Cranberry Crack 6m HD
A gentle introduction to wide crack technique.
Albert Shutt, 1951

9 The Chant 6m HVS 5a
Climb the left-curving overlap to the break; step right to a tricky but protectable finish.
Alan Clarke, 1950s

10 Twenty-Foot Crack 6m S 4b
Could a crack this high be better? The start is unfortunately as polished as gritstone gets.

11 The Curse 6m HVS 5c
The wall has a super boulder problem start. A parallel line just right is slightly harder.

12 Lost in France 6m VS 5c
After a tough start, the wall eases above.

Triangle Buttress: Not much of a triangle.

13 Little Plumb 5m D
The cracked groove.

14 Base Over Apex 6m VS 4c
The in-between wall has a long reach.
Chris Craggs, 1991

15 Baseless 7m VD 4a
The crack, starting in a widening, has a gutsy finish pulling between two jutting blocks.

16 Triangle Buttress Arête 7m VD 4a
The blunt arête is pleasant after the sloping horrors of the start.
Eric Byne, Rupert Brooks, Jack Macleod, 1932

17 Triangle Buttress Direct 7m VS 5b
The even-blunter arête has a powerful start.

18 Triangle Crack 8m HVD 4a
The corner-crack is quite tough to start.

19 Leaning Wall Direct 8m VS 5b ★★
Gain the wide crack at the top via some steely pulls on polished holds.
Ron Townsend, M Padley, 1957

20 Little White Jug 9m VS 5a ★★
A smashing route that blasts straight up the ever-steepening wall and finishes with a scuffling mantel over the vague nose.
Andy Hall, Keith Sharples, 1977

21 Big Black 'Un 9m HVS 5a ★
Another arm-blaster up the steep wall with a similar grovelling finish.

22 Steptoe 8m M
The wide stepped crack.

Triangle Buttress

Monkey Wall: The undercut slab 30m right.

23 Monkey Corner 8m VD ★
From the undercut groove in the left arête, swing right at a jug onto the upper slab.

24 Banana Finger 8m Font 6A ★★
A Burbage gem. Move up and fidget leftwards along the crease until the crux move up can be made. The direct start is Font 6C.
Ed Drummond, 1971

25 Monkey Wall 8m M ★
An unprotected right-to-left romp up ledges.

26 Monk On 6m E1 5b
A bold little problem. Climb the overhung arête on its left-hand side.
Steve Bancroft, 1982

27 Ad Infinitum 14m S 4a ★
A left-to-right traverse above the roof; exposed.

28 Wednesday Climb 8m HVS 5b ★★
The big, baggy, undercut crack with a very steep start. Long trousers, a kneebar and some determination may provide the key.
Pat Fearnehough, 1960s

29 Overhang Buttress Direct 8m S 4a ★★
A fine route that climbs directly past a shiny start and the right-hand end edge of the roof.

30 Overhang Buttress Arête 8m M ★★
The right-hand arête of the buttress is a little delicate but quite lovely.
Eric Byne, Rupert Brooks, Jack Macleod, 1932

31 Burgess Face 6m HS 4c
The smart face left of the arête.

32 Burgess Buttress 6m M
The right arête.
Frank Burgess, 1930s

33 Burgess Street 6m HD 3c
The small corner 2m right of the arête.

Busker Buttress: The sweet slab just up and left of Remergence Buttress.

Remergence 5 min

34 The Busker 7m VS 5a ★
The bulging slab is mighty fine.
Steve Bancroft, 1982

35 Bracken Crack 7m S 4a ★
Quality wide-cracking.

36 Green Slab 7m VS 5a ★
Another gem, steep 'n' sweet.

Remergence Buttress: A powerful, overlapping buttress just right.

37 The Grogan 8m HVS 5c ★★
A fierce little finger-ripper. Climb the slanting crack if you think you're 'ard enough.
Dave Gregory, 1964

38 Wollock 8m HVS 4c ★
Saunter stylishly rightwards into the centre of the fine wall on spaced but good holds.
Dave Gregory, 1964

39 Pulcherrime 8m VS 4b ★★
The obvious crack is a wicked hand jammer with the crux near the top.
Dave Gregory, 1950s

40 Slanting Crack 8m VD ★
The dark crack in the alcove.
Dave Gregory, Andrew Brodie, 1977

41 Chockstone Climb 8m D
Another tortuous treat. Climb as far inside the dark chimney as you dare. How to tackle the chockstone? That's your decision.

42 Stomach Traverse 13m VS 4c ★
Move up from the gully and traverse the break rightwards (big cams) to finish up *Mutiny Crack*.
Eric Byne, Rupert Brooks, Jack Macleod, 1932

43 Tiptoe 13m VS 5a ★
The lower traverse line is much more delicate, and is best finished up *Mutiny Crack* (VS 4c).
Chris Craggs, 1972

44 Mutiny Crack 12m HS 4c ★★★
An all-time favourite. A steep and pushy start, leads into a series of honest jams and big jugs.
Eric Byrom, Douglas Milner, 1934

45 Meddle 12m HVS 5a ★
The right-hand side of the slabby rib is followed before moving right to climb with a touch of bravado through the overhangs.
Dennis Carr, Jon de Montjoye, 1976

46 Detour 12m S 4a ★
Go up the corner to the capping roof then decide, wisely, to scuttle off left, crossing *Meddle*, and pulling round the arête until a step up can be made.
Ron Townsend, M Padley, 1957

ASH TREE WALL
Home to a bunch of brilliant micro-routes and some grand lower-grade leads.

1 Beach Tea One 7m HVS 6a ★
Gymnastic fun. Move up the arête to the break, move left to the centre of the wall and lurch upwards.

2 Ivy Tree 7m HVS 5b ★
The arête all the way.
Dave Gregory, Andrew Brodie, 1977

3 All Stars' Goal 7m E1 5c ★
Sweet. Climb the bulging left-hand side of the wall with some long moves on good holds.
Colin Banton, 1978

4 Evening Wall 7m E1 5b ★★
Trend up and right to the arête. The big breaks above are rounded and insecure.
Dave Gregory, Andrew Brodie, George Kitchin, 1964

5 Wall Chimney 8m HVD ★
Full-bore squeeze action up the chimney.

6 Wall Corner 9m S 4a ★
A miniature classic up the small V-corner in the arête of the buttress.

7 Ash Tree Variation 12m HVS 5c ★
Climb the centre of the wall to the break then step right to finish up the delicate slab.

8 Ash Tree Wall 12m S 4a ★★
A great wandering route up the line of least resistance. Start up the slippery crack then traverse left to gain the 'staircase' which leads to a ledge. Finish up the open groove.
 opposite page
Eric Byne, 1932

9 Ash Tree Crack 12m VD ★★
The major crack gives well-protected, physical climbing. Getting slightly harder due to the polish.

10 Bilberry Crack 12m VD ★★
The second major crack is again well protected and very classic. From the big ledge finish steeply, slightly to the left. page 224

11 Bilberry Face 12m S 3c ★
The narrow little face just to the right is delicate and bold. Finish right of the nose.

The Leaning Block: This is a miniature version of the big daddy over on Higgar Tor and is home to some of the crag's hard power routes.

12 Living in Oxford 10m E7 7a ★★
Hard and strenuous weirdness up the inhospitable blunt arête.
Johnny Dawes (solo), 1989

13 Superstition 10m E8 7a ★★★
This and the next route are the hardest on the crag so far. Gain the break from the left and then make extremely powerful moves on tiny holds to a high crux, a good way above protection.
Miles Gibson, 1999

14 The Promise 10m E8 7a ★★★
The blunt, bold and technical right-hand arête has very limited protection.
James Pearson, 2000

15 Green Chimney 10m VD ★
The cleft on the right-hand side of the block has a desperate start onto a chockstone. Well-protected and satisfying climbing above.

8 min Ash Tree Wall

Burbage North is a crag of sunlight, from the bullying brightness of an August afternoon to the caressing crepusculars of a snatched winter evening. The colours, the valley and the climbs vary so much with the season that no two visits ever feel the same. Kyung-Ha Park staying warm on Ash Tree Wall, S 4a (opposite page). 📷 Mike Cheque

THE SENTINEL AREA
The fabulous Sentinel area begins with a characteristic set of pointed arêtes and grooves, and is home to the route The Sentinel itself.

16 Stepped Crack   7m   M
The deep crack.

17 Black Slab Arête   8m   S 4a
Swing around the arête to the right at the obvious line of holds to finish up an easy groove.

18 Black Slab   8m   VS 4b   ★
Bold, and quite thin. Start up the slab and trend left to finish up the arête.

19 Black Slab Variation   8m   D
The slab by the easiest line.

20 Green Corner   8m   VD
The deep dark.

21 Now or Never   8m   E1 5b   ★
Intimidating. Start up a flake to a difficult move round the arête to a ledge on the right-hand side. Make plucky moves up the arête.
John Allen, Neil Stokes, 1971

22 Sentinel Chimney   8m   VD
An unusual, but protectable, route which will severely test those climbing without proper thought or technique.

23 The Sentinel   8m   E2 5b   ★★
Taken direct, the biggest arête is steep and very exposed. A super route although a little escapable in places and with only adequate gear.
⊙ opposite page, and page 204
Dennis Carr, Ted Rogers, Tony Cowcill, 1977

24 Sentinel Crack   8m   VD
The crack to the right of the big flying arête.

25 High Flyer   8m   E3 5b   ★
The unprotected bulge right of the crack is tentatively climbed trending diagonally leftwards.
Gary Gibson, 1978

26 The Grazer   8m   VS 4c   ★
An obvious short-lived jamming crack splits a bulge. With a big cam above your head you can afford to really 'give it some'.

27 Lie Back   8m   HS 4b   ★
A great little layback flake breaches the bulge just to the right of The Grazer. If only it was three times as long.

28 Ringo   8m   S 3c   ★
A pleasant and sustained climb.

29 Ring Climb   8m   HVD 4a
The short crack is quite cruxy.

30 Ring Chimney   8m   M
The wide cleft.

31 Agnostic's Arête   8m   VS 5a   ★
The blunt arête on its right-hand side.
Clive Jones (solo), 1977

12 mins The Sentinel

There isn't much in the E2/E3 grades on Burbage North, but from that range, this is definitely the classic. The Sentinel, E2 5b (opposite page), is an intimidating line but, if climbed with confidence, things soon fall into place to give a great sequence. 📷 Mike Cheque

KNIGHT'S MOVE AREA
The biggest buttress at Burbage North and is home to some great varied routes

32 The Keffer 8m HVS 5a
The blunt rib on the left side wall is delicate and bold. Finish up the rib or the slab.
Kevin Thaw, 1986

33 Still Orange 10m S 4a
A jolly route with an exciting finish. Climb the corner to the ledge before making an intimidating step right to finish up the well-protected jam crack.
Dave Gregory, Ron Townsend, 1956

34 Green Crack 10m VD ★
An excellent route with good protection.

35 Dover's Progress 12m HVS 5a
A bold undertaking up the narrow wall. Side-runners are fair play.
Harry Dover, Gilbert Ellis, 1932

36 Hollyash Crack 12m VS 4b ★★
A really absorbing route up the smooth wide crack. It can be thrutched or climbed on the outside. A large cam is useful at the grade.
Harry Dover, Gilbert Ellis, 1932

37 The Knight's Move 14m HVS 5a ★★★
A classic of the crag. Use the big holes to gain the flake-line and continue straight up to its end at a bulge. Step left, up, and then right (the 'knight's move') and continue straight up to the top.
Gilbert Ellis, Harry Dover, 1933

38 Peter's Progress 18m VS 4c ★★
Much fun. Climb *The Knight's Move* until a long and airy traverse can be made on a break above the big roof. Finish up *Great Crack*.
Peter Biven, 1953

39 Great Crack 14m VS 5a ★★
A chunky one for crack monkeys. From behind the severely pruned holly, climb the corner to the roof. Hand-traverse out until a stiff pull gains the enjoyable upper crack.
Harry Dover, Gilbert Ellis, 1932

40 The Big Chimney 12m HVD ★
Climb direct to the capping stone at the top. Escape right or take it on the left at Severe.

41 Windjammer 12m E1 5b ★★
Start at a cutaway in the middle of the buttress and pull boldly out right to gain a stance and a break close to the right arête. Traverse left along the break all the way to the left arête and bomber cam. Make a lovely move up the arête before finishing easily. A really satisfying route.
Gary Gibson, 1980

42 Big Chimney Arête 10m HS 4b ★
A fine exposed climb with good protection.

Knight's Move

Burbage North throws up some fine examples of the deep joys of crack climbing, and some of the finest of these lie at the crag's far reaches. The Obscenity area is perhaps the finest section of the edge, with Obscenity itself and this one, Amazon Crack, HS 4a (page 238), taking pride of place. Nina Stirrup climbing. 📷 Pete O'Donovan

Tharf Buttress

Brook's Layback

OBSCENITY AREA
The last climbs described are at the far end of the woods (there are lots of nice climbs in the woods, not described here). These are about 20 minutes from the parking, and are well worth the walk. Perfect clean rock and strong lines combine to give a great number of very high-quality routes.

Tharf Buttress: The first climbs lie 30m to the left of the main area.

1 First Crack 8m S 4b ★
The crack eases after a hard start.

2 Tharf Cake 8m VS 5a ★
The slabby wall to the right is thin and feels rather bold in its mid-section.
John Parkin, Dave Gregory, 1977

3 Left Twin Crack 8m S ★
A good climb with weird moves.

4 Right Twin Crack 8m S ★
Well-protected, technical climbing.

5 Farcical Arête 8m HS 4a ★
The unprotected right arête of the buttress.

Brooks' Layback Area: These are the left-facing corners on the left of the main area.

6 The Irrepressible Urge 6m E1 5b ★★
A little beauty up the middle of the wall. Precision and a cool head are mandatory.
Colin Banton, 1978

7 Arctic Mammal 6m E3 6a ★★
The left-hand side of the right arête is pure grit magic, but with a poor landing.
Dave Musgrove, 2001

8 Ace 6m VS 4b
The prow.

9 Thralls' Thrutch 6m S
The tight chimney is well-named.

10 Brooks' Layback 8m HS 4b ★★
The green corner crack has perfect jams and is over all too fast. Otherwise layback if you must.
Rupert Brooks, Eric Byne, Jack Macleod, 1932

11 Wobblestone Crack 8m HVD ★
A lovely route up the obvious crack in the front of the buttress, with a thought-provoking start.

Obscenity Area: More classic corners and cracks.

12 Hollybush Gully 8m VD
Traditional climbing above the holly.

13 Obscenity 11m VS 4c ★★★
The solid, old-fashioned crack. Pull on your corduroys, grab some hexes and let rip.
Nip Craven, Rowland Pitts, 1948

14 Amazon Crack 11m HS 4a ★★★
A classic of its grade on grit. The perfect jamming crack is more sophisticated than its bully of a brother. ⓞ page 237
Jack Macleod, Rupert Brooks, Eric Byne, 1932

15 Amazon Gully 10m M
The deep cleft.

16 Long Tall Sally 10m E1 5b ★★★
The attractive curving groove yields to delicate footwork and a touch of blind faith.
Jack Street (aid). FFA Alan Clarke, 1960s

Burbage North | 239

17 Three Blind Mice 10m E7 6c ★★
Beautiful but dangerous climbing up the smooth slab. Move left into a scoop from the large pocket. Desperate slapping up pockets above leads to a harrowing mantel on the slab.
Dave Pegg, 1994

18 Greeny Crack 10m VS 4b ★
An enjoyable old school romp up the corner crack, with a tricky move to an abrupt finish.

19 Left Studio Climb 10m VD
Follow a thin crack to a ledge. Climb the arête on the right, bold, and a crack above to finish. A good and varied challenge.

20 Rose Flake 8m VS 4b ★
Good gear and burly jamming. Growl up the left of the two cracks on the left side of the fin.
SUMC, 1958

21 The Fin 8m E1 5b ★★
The ferocious hanging crack is superb. You can place high gear before the crux, but it will probably occupy the best handholds.
Tony Barley (aid), 1969. FFA Neil Stokes, John Allen, 1971

22 Ai No Corrida 8m E5 6b ★
The attractive arête gives a technical and committing climb. Traditionally led with runners on *Right Fin*, although these feel distant on the hard moves.
John Allen, 1984

23 Right Fin 8m HVS 5a ★
Follow the attractive flake on the right wall. It's a bit of a soft touch but only has one runner.

Last Slab: The short slab on the right has a few sweet micro-routes/solos.

24 Nicotine Stain 8m Font 6B ★
The thin seam is a brilliant extended problem. Hardest at the start but it keeps coming.
Al Rouse, 1983

25 April Fool 8m VD
The deep crack.

26 Approach 8m Font 6A
Thin moves up the narrow face. No arêtes.
Colin Banton, 1978

27 Spider Crack 6m Font 5 ★
The thin crack is more devious than it looks.

28 The Be All 6m HVD
The wide, left-hand crack.

29 The End All 6m HS 4a
The less wide, right-hand crack.

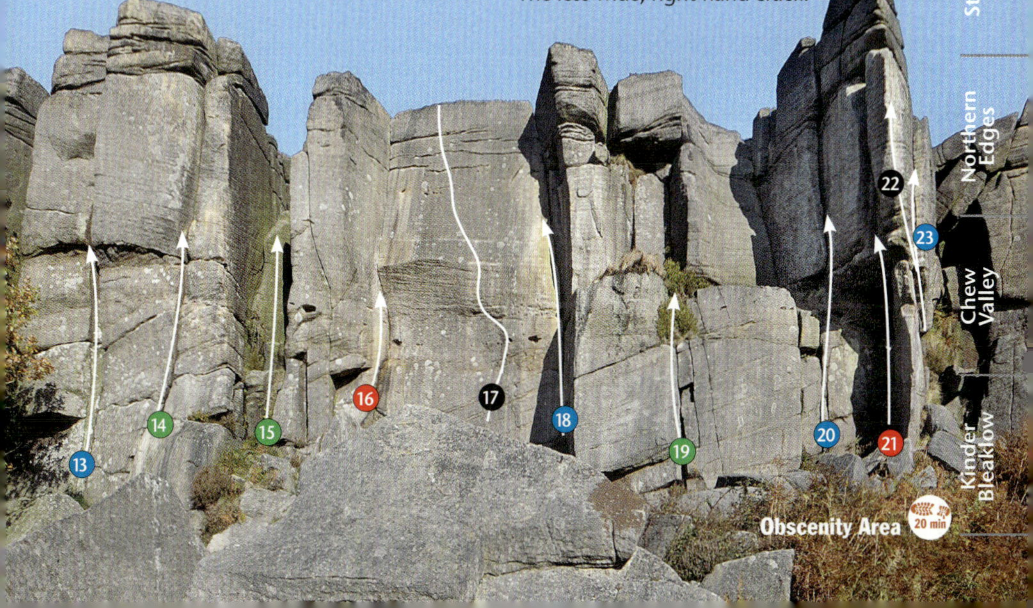

Obscenity Area

BURBAGE SOUTH

OS Grid Ref: SK 265 809
Altitude: 380m

Burbage South could easily be overlooked among the great crags of the gritstone area. The edge, although long, seldom has great stature, and is often quite broken. It gets less sun than most, and often appears dark and dank. However, whilst it is perhaps not the greatest edge, it somehow manages to have a huge collection of many of the most beautiful and challenging routes on grit, as well as some of the best rock anywhere.

Tall, powerful challenges are to be found along the main central section, especially on The Tower and The Keep, giving phenomenal, exposed routes. Endless short and ferociously technical challenges are to be unearthed everywhere, and – especially in these days of pads – these will give some of the most memorable days out. The routes are pure gems, and even the most ardent Burbage fan will never run out of inspiration.

The crag faces mainly north-west and gets summer sun from around 4 or 5pm. Despite its lack of sun, the rock is clean: it can become a little green but this presents surprisingly little problem. For all the above reasons, Burbage South makes a great escape from the summer heat. The crag is often sheltered.

Approach: See map on page 226. Ample parking is available on the roadside above the Fox House. Cross a wall at a stile 250m above the Fox House, then strike straight across the moor to the top of the quarries (15 minutes), from where all parts of the crag can be approached in about 10 minutes. Alternatively, approach from the Fox House or the small parking spot at the end of the Green Drive.

❶ **Simba's Pride**   8m   E8 6b   ★★
An utterly bold route taking the fine left arête of the leaning tower direct, with the final moves forming the crux.
Toby Benham, 2005

❷ **Black Out**   8m   E9 6c   ★★
The arête is ultra-serious with poor holds. Step out of *Roof Route* to follow the arête and holds leading to the vague scoop on the lip.
Toru Nakajima, 2009

❸ **Roof Route**   8m   VS 4c   ★★
Shimmy up the fine wide crack in the angle, wearing the stoutest trousers you can lay your hands on. Sustained.
Jack Macleod, 1934

❹ **Gable Route**   8m   HVS 4c   ★★
A real gem of a route which climbs the right arête via a wide crack and a horizontal break, using a variety of techniques.
Mark Vallance, Clive Jones, Dave Gregory, 1977

❺ **The Gutter**   8m   HVS 5a
Climb a short crack to a ledge and continue up the corner.
Dave Gregory, Mark Vallance, 1977

❻ **Charlie's Crack**   10m   HVS 5b   ★
The very attractive sickle-shaped crack is gained steeply and followed with great joy to a slabby finish up the arête.
Charlie Curtis, 1961

❼ **Life Assurance**   10m   E6 6b   ★
From the flake on *Charlie's*, pad nervously up the steep slab on smears and poor pockets. Bold, but potentially survivable, and only E5 once you've done it.
John Dunne, Dean Eastham, 1986

Roof Route   The Tower   The Keep   Dowel Crack

Burbage South | 241

Roof Route
The Tower

8 Tower Climb 12m HS 4b
Gain the deep chimney by the leftmost crack and finish up a flake on the right wall.
Byron Connelly, Bert Smith, 1934

9 Tower Crack 12m HVS 5a ★
The steep thick crack leads to a small ledge. Finish with a thrilling layback.
Geoff Sutton, Tony Moulam, 1957

10 Balance It Is 12m E7 6c ★★★
This is one of the safer routes of its grade on grit, although it is utterly desperate. You can't have it all your own way. Crank up the steep wall to gain a thin crack and follow it to just below the niche. Place good protection, then skedaddle left, and layback powerfully up the right side of the arête.
Neil Foster, Keith Sharples, 1995

11 The Boggart 12m E2 6b ★★
Technically testing. A worn and frustratingly desperate crack leads up to a horizontal break. From here, traverse left to a better crack that leads to the well-positioned niche at the top of the tower.
Alan Clarke (aid), 1960s. FFA John Allen, 1975

12 Equilibrium 12m E10 7a ★★★
The living end. The arête features powerful bouldering combined with an unjustifiable level of danger to produce a lead of gargantuan proportions. Begin by climbing the short lower arête to the ledge. From there, gear can be placed out left. This is sound, and will just about protect the crux. Suitably psyched, launch up the arête via an unforgiving series of powerful snatches.
Neil Bentley, 2000

13 Tower Chimney 12m M
Start this old sandbag if you can: a real damp day challenge!

Nosferatu
The Drainpipe

Burbage South

14 The Braille Trail 10m E7 6c ★★★
One of Johnny Dawes's first big grit routes, an audacious journey on nothing smears across a shady slab with the bare minimum of protection. Begin on a ledge halfway up the gully. Smear desperately across the hanging slab (very thin gear) to a harrowing rest on the arête. A further hard move leads to the bottomless crack, and an easy finish.
Johnny Dawes, 1984

15 Dynamics of Change 15m E9 7a ★★★
An outrageous lead that gains the delicate finish moves of *Braille Trail* from directly below. A wild dyno, one of the world's grimmest mantels and distant protection all go to give the route its charm.
Pete Whittaker, 2008

16 Parthian Shot 15m E10 6c ★★★
One of grit's great routes, this beast bludgeons its way up the mighty prow left of *Brooks' Crack*. Since the demise of the legendary flake the route is pumpier and the protection is worse. It remains awesome. Begin up *Brooks' Crack* then finger-traverse left. Gain the broken flake (small gear). Press on towards the crux moves below the final slab. A harrowing rock-over onto this brings the final easier moves.
John Dunne, 1989. Ben Bransby, 2013 after crucial flake broke.

17 Brooks' Crack 14m HVS 5a ★★★
A phenomenal route for the 1930s – the *Parthian Shot* of its day. Climb the left-hand crack directly to the top. The route is strenuous and sustained for its entire length.
⊙ opposite page
Rupert Brooks, 1934

18 Byne's Crack 14m VS 4b ★★★
The right-hand crack is steep, strenuous and intimidating, although with its good protection it's easy to enjoy the fantastic jamming and positions that it offers.
Eric Byne, 1934

19 The Knock 9m E4 5c ★★★
This top-notch frightener up the blunt arête is John Allen's most elegant addition to the crag. Sloping shelves lead to some reachy crimping before a good hold is reached below the break. Make crux moves to gain the top.
John Allen, 1975

20 Keep Crack 11m VS 5a ★
The stout crack in the corner is fairly tough. Once on the ledge, follow the thin crack in the groove above.
Alan Clarke, 1960s

20 min — The Keep

The shaded sentinels of Burbage South have always been a tough forcing ground for the standards of the day on gritstone, whether that is the mighty Brooks' Crack, HVS 5a (opposite page), a mightily steep route for 1930, or Parthian Shot behind. Gareth Williams climbing. Paul Evans

244 | Burbage South

Dowel Crack — 20 min

21 Captain Sensible 8m E1 5b ★
This route is on the short dark wall, facing *The Knock*. The vague flake on the right is satisfying, although bold for the grade.
Steve Webster, 1977

22 Slow Ledge 11m VS 5a
Follow the fine bouldery wall to a bold mantel onto the sloping ledge. Finish to the left.

23 Ladder Gully 8m M
The gully has a tricky low move.

24 Recurring Nightmare 8m E4 6a ★
Absorbing climbing, technical and somewhat bold, up the ever steepening rib.
Andy Barker, 1982

25 Macleod's Crack VD
An honest bit of crack-work.

26 Crikey 8m E5 6a ★
Climb the bookend rib face on, with a bold lunge for the high pocket. Finish up and left.
Niall Grimes, 2001

27 Dowel Crack 8m VS 4c ★★
A fine wrestle up the steep enclosed crack. Good hand jams lead pumpily to a wider crux.
Dave Gregory, Andrew Brodie, George Kitchin, 1964

28 The Iron Hand 8m S 4b
The little crack, starting off a pedestal, is short but gives some action.

29 Pollux 8m HS 4b
A slight climb up the left-hand crack.

30 Castor 8m VS 4b
The right-hand crack is slightly harder.

31 Movie Star 8m E1 5b ★
A good climb on the right of the clean face. Boulder up to a good jug on the arête, then stand on this. Follow the face just left of the arête with a bold grope to finish.
Colin Banton, 1978

Nosferatu — 20 min

Burbage South | 245

32 Surprise 6m S 4b
The left corner of the recess on the right.

33 Pythagoras 8m HS 4b
The right-hand corner of the recess.

34 Sorb 9m E2 5c ★★
The left edge of the buttress is quite technical, and is much less willing to take protection than it would appear.
Dennis Carr, Al Parker, D Sinclair, 1976

35 Nosferatu 11m E6 6b ★★★
Bold climbing up the elegant rib. From the boulder jumble, snatch and crimp manically upwards to the salvation of a horizontal break and protection. Finish directly, or up the right arête. Low in the grade.
Andy Barker, Pete Lowe, 1980

36 Reginald 9m VS 4b ★
A pleasant voyage into the depths. Steep, but good holds lead to a narrowing which is passed on the right.
Nat Allen, Nip Underwood, 1951

37 Nathaniel 9m HVS 5b ★
The wide crack is fantastic – a proper battle.
Nat Allen, Nip Underwood, 1951

38 The Knack 8m E1 5c ★
A great little micro-route which gains the shallow hanging groove from below and left. The crux is getting established in the crack, although this still feels steep and pressing.
John Allen, Neil Stokes, 1971

39 Nick Knack Paddywack 8m E2 6b ★
A Burbage beauty, oft-ignored. A fierce flake gains the break (Font 7A). Swing left and climb the beautiful wall on flatties (5b).
Andy Barker, Paul Mitchell, 1982

40 Less Bent 6m S
Follow the mellow arête and at the break, move a bit left to finish (or go direct at VS).

41 No Zag 8m HVS 5b ★
Climb the right-curving flake to the break. Climbing-wall bunnies will quiver here, while the well-rounded will make a couple of brisk jams up the short crack.

42 Ribbed Corner 9m M
Follow either of the cracks up the stepped corner, and bridge up the shallow chimney above.
Joe Brown, 1951

43 Unfinished Symphony 8m HVS 5b ★
Lots of fun can be had tackling the short hanging offwidth crack.
John Allen, Steve Bancroft, 1974

44 Left Bannister 9m HS 4a
Mantel up the face just right of the shallow groove.

45 The Staircase 9m HS 4b ★
The impending wall left of the arête is climbed using a series of bold features. page 247

46 The Drainpipe 9m HS 4b ★★
Beautifully simple. Climb the clean crack in the major corner.

The Drainpipe

Stanage, Froggatt and Curbar might hold more classics, but there's something about just being at Burbage – perhaps on a late-summer evening, as the light peeks below gathering clouds, with nobody else about, that will warm the heart of a gritstoner unlike any other place. A climber on The Staircase, HS 4b (page 245). 📷 Dan Lane

Pebble Mill

47 Wazzock 9m HS 4b ★
The tall crack yields to some fine deep green jamming.
Dave Gregory, Andrew Brodie, George Kitchin, 1964

48 Pebble Mill 11m E5 6b ★★★
A Burbage classic, a great test of technique and nerves, based upon the arête. Layback the lower arête on its slabby left side, until a swing right on a good hold allows a standing position to be reached. From here, tinkle up the wall above in a position of heightened anxiety.
John Allen, 1976

49 Above and Beyond the Kinaesthetic Barrier 6m E4 6b ★★
Although in some ways a boulder problem, the height and difficulty mean that the E4 is well-earned. Gain the left arête of the buttress from a hole on the left wall or the slab below, then follow the arête direct via a beautiful and committing sequence. Highball Font 7A.
John Allen, 1976

50 Goliath 8m E4 6a ★★★
This brutal and uncompromising line is the perfect metaphor for its first ascensionist, Don Whillans. As such, you'd better be ready for a scrap! Climb the offwidth, starting with difficulty and getting worse near the top. Those in possession of very large cams, two pairs of trousers, a leather jacket and fists the size of Higgar Tor will lose an E point.
Don Whillans, 1958

51 David 8m HVS 4c ★★
The major dog-legged gash, while apparently of the most terrifying dimensions, yields to a positive, airy and satisfying layback.

52 Messiah 8m E7 6c ★★★
A mighty challenge up the immaculate right arête of the buttress. Beautifully sculpted and overhanging all the way, it calls for first bold, then brutally powerful climbing.
Jerry Moffatt, 1984

53 Saul 9m VS 5b ★
A satisfying solo, with a tough low crux, following the fingertip crack. At the ledge, move left and finish direct.
Dave Gregory, Andrew Brodie, 1964

Goliath

A cheeky little pumper that catches out a lot of climbers. It is not unusual to see things take a turn for the urgent, especially if not warmed up enough, as forearms swell and fingers start to fidget. A great route. Rebecca Lounds on Zeus, E2 5b (page 350). Niall Grimes

Burbage South

BURBAGE QUARRIES: NORTHERN QUARRY
The Burbage Quarries swap the friendly technicality of the edge for strong foreboding battles. Their smooth, vertical and overhanging walls call for a determined approach. Amid some scruffy routes are some peerless tests of fitness and nerve.

54 The Great Flake Route 23m D
A fine ramble. Ascend the chimney and go across the ledge to a blocky belay. Climb the blocky corner above.

55 Zeus 11m E2 5b ★★★
A relentless battle from the word go. The superb crack will pump E2 climbers into the middle of next week, but at least it's well-protected, if you have the strength to hang on. ⓘ page 249
Jack Street, 1969

56 Fagus Sylvatica 11m E8 7a ★★
The sharp arête slopes in more dimensions than physicists have dreamed of. With gear in the very low slot, power up the arête with great determination, skill, technique, and all those other things that you haven't got.
Miles Gibson, 2002

57 Hades 11m HVS 5b ★
The corner gives a tight, technical and slippery struggle.
Gerry Rogan, 1960s

58 Fox House Flake 14m VS 4b ★★
A very fine climb. Follow the fine friendly fissure and finish up the corner. ⓘ page 227
Frank Burgess, George Walker, 1934

59 Fox House Fake 12m HVS 5a
A counter-diagonal to the flake with a steep finish up the wall.
Leon Zablocki, Cathy Meads, 1999

60 The Cock 11m VS 4c
The steep blocky corner and crack.
Gerry Rogan, 1960s

Millwheel Slab: This is just right of the entrance to the Northern Quarry.

61 Dunkley's Eliminate 9m VS 4c ★★
Great exposed climbing on positive holds. Trend left to the arête, and follow it.

62 Pretzel Logic 9m E3 6a ★
Thin slab climbing following the green streak with crux moves to gain the horizontal breaks.
Dave Jones, John Codling, 1979

63 Millwheel Wall 10m E1 5b ★★★
A superb route for confident E1 leaders. Starting at the centre of the clean slab, trend right to a steep juggier finish.
Len Millsom, 1958

Northern Quarry

Burbage South | 251

The Cioch

SOUTHERN QUARRY
The right-hand quarry is dominated by The Cioch, the huge hanging, undercut looming block.
The next two routes traverse the hanging slab on the dark side of The Cioch. Start from the top left and drop down to a belay ledge on the left of the face. A hanging rope is useful for the belay.

64 Silent Spring 16m E4 5c ★★★
An exposed and highly adventurous traverse of The Cioch's dark half. From a belay ledge on the top left, make an exposed traverse right to a detached block in the middle of the face, and a reverse mantelshelf. Finger-traverse right to the arête with better protection, and finish up this in a great position. Old bolts offer dubious protection on this pitch.
Steve Bancroft, John Allen, 1975

65 Silent Scream 16m E7 6c ★★
A hard remix of *Silent Spring*. From the belay drop down and traverse with feet above the lip. to join and finish up *Masters of the Universe*. Gear is placed in the block at the midway point.
Pete Whittaker, 2009

66 Masters of the Universe
12m E6 6c ★★
The arête of The Cioch. Abseil to a foothold just above the lip and just left of the arête and, having clipped some old bolts (backed up by the abseil rope), climb the arête.
Andy Pollitt, 1988

67 Offspring 11m E5 6b ★★★
A brilliant bouldery route in a position of barely justifiable exposure although, ironically, probably the safest route on grit. Abseil to a hanging stance on the arête, by deep cracks. Make a fingery traverse rightwards to a deep slot and cams. From here, give it all you've got, blasting up the slim groove.
Johnny Dawes, 1985

68 Captain Invincible 15m E8 6c ★★★
The awesome front face has F8b climbing as well as some spicy cranking above dubious pegs. Start at the very bottom of the face, and climb to two poor pegs at the base of the groove. Pass these, and pull out left past two good pegs onto the face. Climb a series of thin cracks, past another peg and small wires, heading towards the relatively easy finish of *Offspring*, and glory.
Sean Myles, 1991

The Cioch

HIGGAR TOR

OS Grid Ref: SK 254 819
Altitude: 420m

A very powerful crag, with lots of character. The routes are generally fierce and physical, although generally well protected. The front face of The Leaning Block is among the steepest bits of grit around.

Higgar Tor's exposed position provides little protection against the wind and rain, but ensures that the crag dries quickly after poor weather. It faces south-west and gets sun from late morning.

Approach: See the map on page 226. Park in the large bays by the side of the road. Ignore the obvious stile and walk down the road for 200m to another stile, climb over this and take the steady path trending around the hill: 5 minutes.

1 The Warding 6m VD
The crack, starting from a block. S 4b without using the block at the start.

2 Aceldama 8m E4 6a
Serious. Climb the steep fingery wall first direct, then slightly left, to a small flake and a hideously difficult crux finish.
Gary Gibson (solo), 1980

3 The Mighty Atom 8m E2 5c ★
A good route with a distant exit. Starting at parallel cracks, climb direct to good cams. An exciting, difficult finish follows.
Steve Bancroft, John Allen, 1975

4 Brillo 8m E1 5c
A deceptively difficult route starting on the arête of the cave and taking thin cracks above.

5 The Riffler 8m HVS 5a ★
From the centre of the small cave climb the overhang direct, finishing up a small corner.

6 The Cotter 8m HVS 5a
Climb the wall to a break and huge jugs, then make a difficult move to the next break. Finish up the crack above, with a tricky top move.

7 The Rat's Tail 8m VS 4c ★
Steady, well-protected climbing leads to a testing fist jamming crack and the top.

8 The Reamer 8m VS 4c ★
The arête and wall lead, via a curving crack, to a large ledge and the top.
Dave Gregory, Andrew Brodie, 1964

9 Leaning Block Gully 9m VD
Ascend the gully on its left side. Exit outside the first chockstone and finish up the flake on the left wall.

10 The Sander 12m E4 6b ★
The steep left wall of the Leaning Block. Start by bridging up the gully and get established on the left side of the arête at an awkward break. Climb direct up the wall on the left of the arête via rugosities and a break to a large ledge.
Jerry Peel, 1976

First Walls

When you arrive beneath the front face of the Leaning Block it is easy to imagine the steepness is an illusion. It's only the moment you pull on that you realise it is actually steeper than it looks. James Turnbull in the ring with The Rasp, definitely one of the top five E2s on gritstone (page 254). David Simmonite

254 | Higgar Tor

THE LEANING BLOCK

The essence of Higgar. Steep and ferocious. Descend via a Diff scramble at the back of the block.

11 Block and Tackle 12m E6 6c ★★
A brutal but safe route, tackling the front arête of the block. Start as for *The Sander*, then swing round to the front face from a good jug. Continually difficult climbing leads to a final ledge. The direct start is Font 7B+.
Neil Foster, Howard Lancashire, 1994

12 Surform 15m HVS 5b ★★
A superb climb, spoilt only slightly by the ledge at two-thirds height. Climb the prominent flake until it is possible to move left into a shallow recess. Leave this by climbing a short corner and continue diagonally leftwards up ledges.
Joe Brown, 1958

13 The Rasp 14m E2 5b ★★★
A Brown and Whillans masterpiece, simply one of the best routes on gritstone. Start as for *Surform*, and follow the line of flakes to below the roof. Traverse right with difficulty to finish. Strenuous from the word go. ⊙ page 253
Joe Brown, Don Whillans (1pt), 1956. FFA Unknown

14 The Rasp Direct 12m E4 6a ★★
An even harder version of *The Rasp*! After a difficult start up thin cracks, climb straight up to join *The Rasp* at its crux, and continue to the cave. Climb directly over the roof above to a scary nose-grinding mantelshelf.
Steve Bancroft, John Allen, 1975

15 Flute of Hope 20m E4 6a ★★
A fine expedition taking a rising traverse of the Leaning Block with sneak previews of other hard routes (if you're not too pumped to look). Climb the short corner and thin crack. The impending flake above leads to the next break. Traverse left with difficulty to gain and follow

The Leaning Block

The Rasp to the cave. Exit left and finish with great determination.
Ed Drummond, Hamish Green-Armytage (2pt), 1971. FFA Ron Fawcett, Geoff Birtles, 1977

16 Bat Out of Hell 12m E5 6a ★★★
An excellent, well-protected route up the front of the face, which sees its fair share of air time. Follow *Flute of Hope* to the top of the flake. Hard moves up the wall above (possibly 6b for the short) gain the next break. Finish slightly rightwards, as for *The Rasp*.
Paul Bolger, 1979

17 Linkline 12m E6 6c ★★★
An outstanding climb – powerful, technical and safe – the equal of anything on the Tor. Start as for *Bat*... then traverse right to gain a prominent rugosity and stand on this to reach the next break. Continue direct (crux – totally desperate), and straight up to the niche above. Finish as for *Bat Out of Hell*.
Neil Foster, 1993

18 Pulsar Direct 11m E6 6b ★★
A quality route that takes the right arête of the block. Reasonable moves up the right side of the arête lead to good cams in the mid-height break. Swing left and climb the left side of the arête to the next break, and on to the top.
Pulsar – Jonny Woodward, 1980. Direct – Ben Moon, 1990s

19 The File 10m VS 4c ★★★
One of the classic cracks of the Peak – probably the best of its type on grit, and one that sees a good few blood-infused failures. Just right of the arête is a fine continuous crack; jam this with determination.
Don Whillans, Joe Brown, Nat Allen, 1956

20 The Raven 10m HVS 5a
The arête, gained from the right.
Gary Gibson, Dave Tempest, Richard Kerr, 1980

21 Paddock 7m HVD ★
A thoroughly pleasant route climbing a series of cracks on the face just right of *The Raven*.
Dave Gregory, George Kitchin, 1964

22 Greymalkin 7m S 4a ★
Climb the cracks right again, finishing over the obvious bulge.
Dave Gregory, George Kitchin, 1964

23 Hecate 7m HVD
Climb a tricky shallow corner left of a large slabby boulder to gain a ledge and finish on the right.
Dave Gregory, George Kitchin, 1964

24 Rock Around the Block 37m E4 6b ★★
A girdle traverse.
1 10m 5a Start on the block below *The Warding*. Step right passing *The Mighty Atom* and climb thin cracks. Continue to belay on the arête.
2 10m 6b Move up and 'fall' across the gully to the prominent break. Traverse on good holds to the arête and move across the Leaning Block to gain the shallow recess of *Surform*.
3 10m 5c Move right along the break on improving holds to the arête and belay around the corner before *The File*.
4 7m 4c Follow the excellent break and dismount at the back of the block.
Chris Craggs, Colin Binks, 1982

STANAGE EDGE

OS Grid Ref: SK 225 865 to SK 252 830
Altitude: 420m

Of all the gritstone edges, it is Stanage that feels closest to Heaven. The feeling of cruising the perfect rock with so much space all around remains an unforgettable experience, no matter how many times you go. Here, George Gilmore treads gently on High Neb Variation, VS 5a (page 277). Paul Evans

The finest gritstone crag on earth. Three miles of the best rock, where climbers of every level come to pay homage. Leads, micro-routes, solos and bouldering are packed into every metre.

The crag is divided into discrete sections, each with its own character and outlook. Some are busy, some give solitude. Some have nationally famous routes standing side by side, others have shy gems.

Approach: The areas are aproached from a number of parking spots, depending on your destination. See the map above and area introductions.

STANAGE EDGE MAP

Stanage North	page 260
High Neb	page 270
Count's Area	page 284
Stanage Plantation	page 290
Stanage Popular	page 310
Apparent North	page 358

Cleft Buttress racks up a series of corners and cracks in the HS to E2 range. These climbs may not look like much, nor are they very tall, but know this – you will have to fight for every inch of these climbs. For it seems to be a fact, the further a climb is from the car park, the harder the grades get. Here, George Gilmore is on Richard's Sister, HS 4b (page 267), which is a solid 25 minutes from the car. 🄾 Paul Evans

STANAGE NORTH

OS Grid Ref: SK 225 865 to SK 224 857
Altitude: 430m

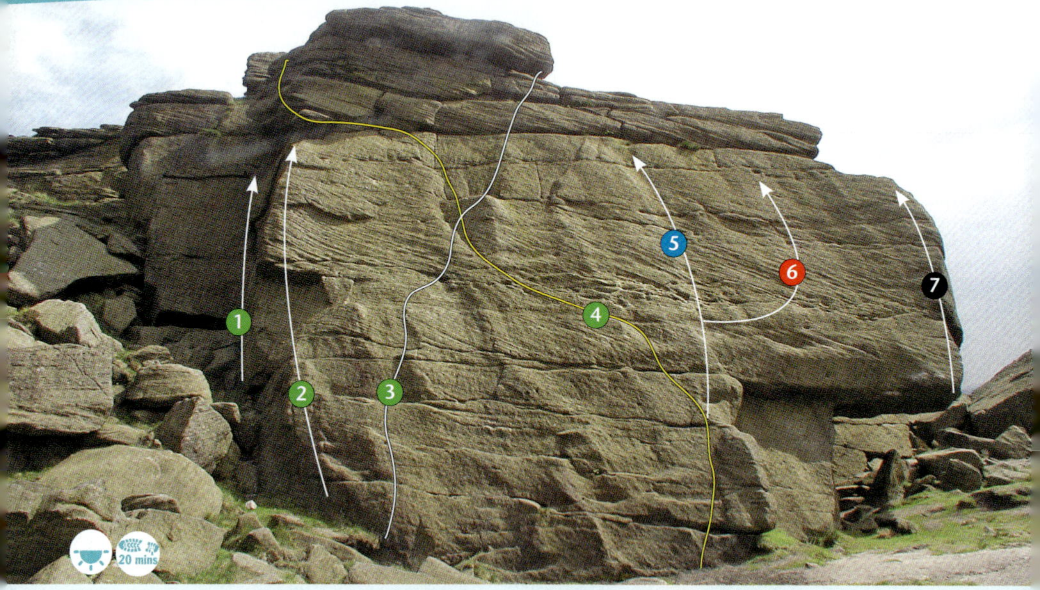

The section of crag that runs from Stanage End and down to Marble Wall and Crow Chin, represents the northern-most reaches of this fine edge, and amongst them are some of the really classic destinations. The crags feel remote and have a fine sense of wilderness about them – for Stanage.

Approach: See map on page 258. Two approaches are possible. From the High Neb (Dennis Knoll) parking, follow the approach to High Neb (see page 270). Continue along the well-worn path towards Crow Chin, the section of cliff visible on the skyline; 20 minutes to here. Continue for Marble Wall (a further 5 minutes) and Stanage End, 30 minutes from the parking.

Alternatively, from a small pull-off car park on the A57, 100m west of the Sheffield/Derbyshire border sign, follow the path to Stanage End (20 minutes).

STANAGE END
A good a way as any to get things going. Great for climbs with lots of character and individuality, all in a very peaceful setting.

End Slab: The main slab gets less sun than most of Stanage and hence has a green appearance, this green doesn't affect the climbing at all if it is dry. It may, however, take some time to dry in still weather.

1 The Rack 11m D
The wide crack in the corner of the slab leads to a finish up the short arête on the left.

2 Another Turn 11m HS 4b ★
The left arête is climbed directly. The lower section is delicate and unprotected, and the steeper upper part has good runners and large holds.

Stanage North | 261

3 The Pinion 14m VD ★★
Fine slab climbing. Climb up for 3m, make a long stride to a hole and move up to the ledge. Continue in a diagonal line to the large ledge.
Harry Kelly, George Bower, Rice Kemper Evans, 1921

4 The Ariel 15m VD ★★
Move up left of the cutaway, then move diagonally left up the slab. At the break, traverse left around the corner and finish close to the arête.
Rice Kemper Evans, c1920

5 The Green Streak 12m VS 4c ★★
A cheeky little test of your faith in friction. Start as for *The Ariel*, and streak confidently up the shallow green groove.
Rice Kemper Evans, c1920

6 Incursion 13m E1 5b ★★
A bold route with a memorable smeary crux. From *The Ariel*, foot-traverse right above the lip for 2m before climbing the centre of the slab.
Paul Nunn, Oliver Woolcock, Dave Roberts, 1962

7 High Flyer 11m E4 6a ★★
A gymnastic start leads to a classy finish. Take off from the block under *Chip Shop Brawl* and swing leftwards to gain a jug. Step round onto the slab and follow the arête above, with an unforgettable move to the ledge; unprotected.
Lee Bower (solo), 1979

8 Chip Shop Brawl 7m Font 7A+ ★★★
A John Allen micro-route that has gained classic status with the advent of pads. Power up to the sloping shelf then continue direct or up the face on the left. A terrible beauty.
John Allen (solo), 1987

9 Caliban's Cave 11m HS 4b ★
The dark recess can be climbed in a very traditional back-and-foot manner.
Harry Kelly, George Bower, Edgar Pryor, Rice Kemper Evans, 1921

10 Prospero's Climb 12m VD ★★
A delicate start leads to a great layback finale. Start at a crack. Follow this to the first ledge and move left to gain the layback flake.
Harry Kelly, Edgar Pryor, Rice Kemper Evans, 1921

11 The Crab Crawl 11m S ★★
A direct and well-protected slab climb giving a deservedly popular route.
Fred Pigott & friends, c1920

12 Crab Crawl Arête 11m VS 4c ★
Follow the arête as closely as possible.
Andy Parkin, Giles Barker, Bill Briggs, 1976

13 The Vice 9m E1 5b ★★★
A ferocious climb that will eat you up and spit you out. Bulldoze your way up the leaning, widening fissure. A beautiful sandbag.
Clive Rowland, 1962

SURGEON'S SAUNTER AREA

The delicate delights of the End Slab are well and truly left behind with this next buttress, where steep walls and cracks call for forceful climbing.

14 Cripple's Crack 12m S 4a ★★
The steep slanting crack that splits the centre of the sidewall gives an enjoyable climb.

15 Which Doctor? 18m E5 6a ★
Climb to the right-hand edge of the ledge then make an intricate traverse out to the arête and slap wildly up this to reach safety.
Martin Veale, Chris Craggs, 1991

16 Doctor's Chimney 18m S 4a ★★
The tall chimney gives a long, steep and sustained climb. Climb up the left side of the pillar to reach the narrow soaring chimney which is followed without deviation to the top.
Fred Pigott, Morley Wood, Rice Kemper Evans, 1919

17 Doctor's Saunter 19m HVS 5a ★★
This is the original way of accessing the fine upper cracks of *Surgeon's Saunter*. It obviously lacks a direct line, but gives fantastic, gutbusting climbing all the way. Begin up the right side of the pillar, then hand-traverse the deep break into the parent crack. Follow this upwards, ever upwards.

18 Surgeon's Saunter 18m HVS 5b ★★★
A great climb, perhaps the best of the classic HVSs at this end of Stanage. Powerful laybacking leads up the steep lower cracks to the easier, though sustained, upper cracks. At the top, tackle the final bulge direct, or sweep out left on a flake. Well-protected.
Peter Biven, 1953

19 Kelly's Corner/Niche Climb 18m S 4b ★
The corner-crack leads to a broad amphitheatre (VD). At the back left-hand corner of the amphitheatre is a niche. Climb this to the top.

20 Heath Robinson 16m E6 6b ★★
The bulging arête leads to a final, holdless top-out, where you would probably sell your soul to the devil for one tiny crimp.
Johnny Dawes, 1984

21 Manhattan Arête 6m VD
The little arête is quite bold for the grade. Finish up *Niche Climb* at the back left side.

22 Manhattan Chimney 6m S 4a ★
The square, capped chimney is a back-and-foot cocktail of considerable vintage. Passing the capping flake is the crux, though an escape can be made through a skylight.
Fred Pigott, Morley Wood, Rice Kemper Evans, 1919

23 Manhattan Crack 6m VS 4c ★
A little layback gem, quite physical. Climb a steep crack in the corner to reach a rocky platform where there are a variety of ways off.

The area from Stanage End to Old Salt has a fistful of outstanding climbs in the HVS/E1 bracket. If you think you have the juice, head along here on a fresh, sunny day and see if you can tick off The Vice, Surgeon's Saunter, The Wobbler (pictured here - page 264), Old Salt, Valediction and Microbe. What a day that would be! Graeme Hammond climbing the classic E1 5c. 📷 Paul Evans

264 | Stanage North

OLD SALT AREA
Quality climbing continues with a series of steep cracked walls just 40m right of the Surgeon's Saunter Area. The steep walls between *The Wobbler* and *Valediction* give a good supply of stiff challenges in the HS to HVS range, with some real gems, as well as a couple of significantly harder offerings. To the right of *Valediction* is an ancient quarried area which provides some classic technical, highball walls.

24 Concept of Kinky 9m E6 6c ★
The hanging flake in the arête is climbed by a variety of techniques including a dynamic move. A nerve-testing tiny wire is supposed to offer protection.
John Allen, 1989

25 Good Clean Fun 9m E5 6b ★★
A pushy, fingery and technical route climbing the flat wall. From a couple of metres up *The Wobbler*, lean out to the deep pocket on the wall. Hard moves lead up to slightly better holds, but the climbing is sustained all the way.
John Allen, Mark Stokes, 1984

26 The Wobbler 9m E1 5c ★★
An exhausting crusade up the cracks. The holds promise much but often disappoint, especially on the start, where the ability to remain technical under fire will bring reward.
⊙ page 263
Pete Crew, 1962

27 Avril 6m HS 4b ★
The crack gives short-lived but quality jamming.

28 Mai 6m VS 4b
Follow the thinner, right-hand cracks.
Dave Gregory, John Street, 1992

Stanage North | 265

㉙ **Mars** 6m VD 4a
The slanting flake-crack is awkward to start.

㉚ **February Crack** 6m HS 4b ★★
Ascend the fine well protected crack in the main angle to a tough finish.

㉛ **Old Salt** 10m HVS 5a ★★
A brilliant combination of climbing styles come together to give a very satisfying, well-protected climb. Climb the front of the buttress to gain a small ledge. Move leftwards to climb flakes in a superbly exposed position.
Paul Nunn, Al Parker, 1963

㉜ **Valediction** 9m HVS 5a ★★
The steep, smooth-sided crack is climbed through overhangs.
Geoffrey Sutton, G F Mansell, 1959

㉝ **Monad** 6m E2 6b ★
A classic problem. Start by bridging the corner, then swing left onto a fingerhold. A mercilessly strenuous move allows a standing position and an easier, though still interesting, finish. Font 6C+ direct.
Steve Bancroft (solo), 1979

㉞ **Boomerang Chimney** 6m S 4b
The aptly named cleft.

㉟ **Twin Cracks** 6m VD
Just to the right of a corner is a crack with jammed blocks. Surmount the blocks and take either or both cracks to finish.

㊱ **Quiver** 6m HVS 5c
Climb the left crack, which fades out at 3m, to reach a poor break. The finish is hard and reachy.
Graham Hoey (solo), 1981

㊲ **Arrow Crack** 6m VS 5b
The straight, right-hand, thin crack yields to good technique and a layback move or two.

㊳ **Blinkers** 6m VS 5b
Climb the wall right of the right-hand crack to a horizontal break and finish past a thinner break, with a long reach for poor holds.

㊴ **Balance** 6m D
The shallow leftward-slanting ramp/groove has one awkward move.

Balance Descent: The giant steps give a descent route with a tricky drop at the bottom.

㊵ **Thin Problem Crack** 6m VS 5b ★
The thin crack is started on finger jams and slippery footholds. It eases rapidly: Font 5.

㊶ **Microbe** 6m HVS 5c ★★
Start at a small cutaway below a thin crack with an obvious pocket to its left. Climb directly, linking the features. Classic highballing. Font 5+.
Steve Bancroft (solo), 1975

㊷ **Germ** 6m E2 6b ★★
A classic highball, featuring a technical lower wall and harrowing finishing moves. Font 6B.
Chris Sowden (solo), 1980

㊸ **Crumbling Crack** 6m HS 4b
Use thin parallel cracks to gain a dirty cleft. Grovel up this to an easier exit

㊹ **Problem Corner** 5m VS 5a
The thin bridging corner. Font 4+.

MARBLE WALL

Marble Wall is home to some fierce technical challenges. Its quarried smoothness and plumb verticality make for some very powerful climbs. Everything feels hard here.

45 Marble Arête 11m VS 4c ★★
Follow the arête. Excellent climbing up exposed rock, with a bold central section.
Paul Nunn, Al Parker, 1960s

46 Sceptic 11m HVS 5b ★★
A worrying lower wall leads to ape-like relief at the top. Start from a block, then move out right and up on flat holds to ledges. A spectacular finale leads over the capping roof.
Al Parker, 1970s

47 The Lamia 27m E3 5c ★★★
A superb girdle of the most continuous section of wall with an exhausting second pitch.
1 12m 5b Start as for *Sceptic* but move right to a developing horizontal break and follow it to *Nectar* and continue traversing to take a hanging belay on *Orang-Outang*.
2 15m 5c Beef along the break until a hard move gains the roof. Move right again and finish up the tough roof-crack to the left of *Goosey's* final crack.
Steve Bancroft, John Allen (alt), 1975

Meisner's Link-Up, E3 5c ★★★, links *Orang-Outang* into the second pitch of *The Lamia* in one super-pumping pitch.
Mike Meisner, 1990s

48 Terrazza Crack 10m HVS 5b ★★★
A classic romp for crack addicts. The seductive crack gives brilliant jamming and laybacking.
Joe Brown, Don Whillans, 1952

49 Harvest 5m E3 6b ★★
The short and savage roof crack above *Terrazza Crack* has quite a bite to it. Desperate.
John Allen, Tom Proctor, 1975

50 Nectar 15m E4 6b ★★★
The trouser-busting corner and savage crack.
1 11m 6b Severely technical bridging, protected by small nuts and RPs, leads up the corner to reach a welcome rest and belay under the roof.
2 4m 6b Reach into the roof-crack above the corner. Shuffle towards the lip then follow the final section of the crack with great difficulty.
John Allen, Steve Bancroft (alt), 1976

51 Orang-Outang 12m E2 5c ★★★
A Marble Wall classic, with a fairly fierce crux. Start to the left of the arête. Climb up the cutaway and layback around the overhang to a poor rest. Follow a thin crack to ledges.
Pete Crew (2pts), 1962, FFA Terry King or John Allen, 1970s

52 Marbellous 12m E8 7a ★★★
The crag's hardest route doesn't see many successes. Climb a ramp to the break and traverse left to place small cams in an obvious horizontal slot. Move back right and, and use undercut flakes to make hideously hard moves to an easier finish. A more direct left-hand start is even harder - **Mother of Pearl**, highball 7C.
Robin Barker, 1997 / John Welford, 2004

25 mins Marble Wall

53 Goosey Goosey Gander 12m E5 6a ★★★
A ferocious, steep and technical crack-pitch. Follow the crack direct. The pitch is well protected, but some effort is required to place it.
Gabe Regan, Al Evans, 1976

54 Don's Delight 8m E1 5b
At last, a delicate route. Start up a slab and trend rightwards. A bold layback leads into a shallow groove. Climb this to easy ground.
Don Whillans (solo), 1962

CLEFT BUTTRES
Just right is a rounded buttress that holds a set of cracks, which are evidence of how routes farther from the car park are always harder for the grade.

55 Left-Hand Tower 18m HVS 4c
The steep deceptive offwidth where the only way to face is the wrong way. From the top of the tower step right and finish up the arête.

56 Slap 'n Spittle 14m E4 6a ★★
Boulder up the arête to a break. Balancy climbing and improving protection leads to the top.
Andy Lewandowski, Colin Brooks, 1983

57 Vena Cave-In 16m E3 5c ★
An entertaining trip with good protection from large cams. From the top of the initial crack on *Right-Hand Tower*, trend gradually leftwards up well-spaced breaks to stretchy final moves.
Gary Gibson, 1981

58 Right-Hand Tower 16m HVS 5b ★★★
A spooky classic with a baffling collection of sloping ledges and flared breaks. Begin at a thin crack just to the left of the arête and continue straight up on its left-hand side to the final break. Move right round the arête on to the south face, with precarious moves to finish.
Peter Crew, c1958

59 Wild and Woolly 16m E2 5b ★
From the top of the collapsing wall, move out leftwards to good holds in a break. Climb straight up a bulging wall, keeping just to the right of the arête, to reach the ledge of *Right-Hand Tower*. Move left round the arête and finish with a long reach. Many finish right at E1.
Chris Craggs, Dave Spencer, Angela Soper, 1995

60 First Sister 12m VS 5a ★★
A lovely route, with a technical start. Start under the left-hand continuous crack. Make pleasing moves up the thin lower section to reach and follow the more continuous, and deeper, upper section of the crack.
Richard McHardy, Al Parker, 1958

61 Second Sister 10m HVS 5a ★
The crack to the right. Like all the cracks here, it takes a surprising amount of concentration.
Richard McHardy, Al Parker, 1961

62 Richard's Sister 8m HS 4b ★
The next deeper crack, heading for the wider cleft. page 259
Richard McHardy, Al Parker, 1961

63 Not Richard's Sister Direct 8m E1 6a ★
The first crack from the right leads up to a bulge and ends there. Stepping left would be easy but unfortunately the true way is straight on and is very tough.
John Allen, 1989

Cleft Buttress

CROW CHIN
To the right is a cracked wall made of some of the nicest rock on Stanage. It is seldom busy.

64 Jim Crow   9m   HVS 5a
Start in a small overhung niche and climb a roof using a thin crack, then continue up a short wall and a shallow groove.
Terry Bolger, Steve Punshon, Chris Astill, 1979

65 Perforation   9m   HVS 5b   ★
From a flat block, pull over the centre of an overlap and make hard moves to stand in a break. The slab and wall above are easier.
Chris Craggs, Colin Binks 1985

66 Feathered Friends   10m   VS 4b   ★
Start at a blunt rib to the left of *Kelly's Crack* and trend left, before climbing the steepening slab to an awkward exit. Good bold climbing.
Terry Bolger, Dave Dunn, 1979

67 Kelly's Crack   10m   S 4a   ★★
The stout crack is as good as it ever was. A steeper section at half-height gives the crux.

68 Kelly's Eye   10m   HS 4a   ★
Climb the left-hand side of the face to enter a shallow, flaked groove. Finish directly.
John Street, Dave Gregory, 1993

69 Kelly's Eliminate   10m   HS 4a   ★★
A direct line up the centre of the face. The start is steep and strenuous, though on good holds, whereas the upper section is delicate.

70 October Crack   10m   D   ★★
A brilliant pummelling crack at a very affordable grade. Ascend the crack with joy.

71 May Crack   10m   VS 5a
Climb above the left-hand edge of the triangular niche and continue up a thin crack above the overlap. Not that well protected.
Chris Craggs, Colin Binks, 1985

72 October Slab   10m   HS 4b   ★★
One of the better routes in the area, with absorbing climbing. Ascend the right-hand arête of the niche and follow the thin seam above, finishing over a stepped overlap.
⊙ opposite page

73 Big Al   10m   HVS 5a
The centre of a steep slab is followed delicately. Start just left of the corner and climb leftwards, and then back rightwards on small holds to enter a shallow groove. Finish up the slab.
John Street, Dave Gregory, 1993

74 Bent Crack   10m   VD   ★
Climb the corner-crack to ledges and follow an easier corner to below a capping roof. Traverse out left to finish up a small corner.

75 New Year's Eve   10m   HS 4b
Climb the awkward left-hand arête to the left of cave, then step right and climb the flat wall to ledges. Step left to climb the left edge of the tower on great holds.
Lee Bower (solo), 1989

76 The Marmoset   6m   VS 4c   ★
A quality struggle. Climb over the centre of the roof of the cave using jammed blocks with care. Scramble easily up the chimney above.

77 Autumn Gold   10m   HS 4b   ★
Climb a flat wall right of the main cave to a ledge and finish up a crack.
D Leversidge, M Ellis (both solo), 1983

There is a distinctive essence to Crow Chin, almost as if it was revered by the ancients, like a stone circle or a confluence of two rivers. Add to that the singular nature of the rock, the fact that the crag's earliest visitors climbed here, and a particular solitude, and you have a unique outcrop. Nadine Fecht on October Slab, HS 4b (opposite page). 📷 Paul Evans

HIGH NEB

OS Grid Ref: SK 226 854 to SK 229 852
Altitude: 430m

Ultra-classic Stanage quality with a lofty aspect and a great sense of history. One of the finest sections of the edge. It consists of the main buttress and a bunch of cool, smaller buttresses to its left.

Approach: From the High Neb car park (Dennis Knoll), follow the broad track, Long Causeway, for 500m, until a choice of stiles lead over the fence on the left (first stile for Blurter and buttresses to the left, second to High Neb). From here, smaller tracks lead to the crags. Approach times from 15 to 20 minutes.

HIGH NEB LEFT-HAND

This is the scattering of smaller buttresses that stretch left from the main High Neb area. Approach along the bottom of the rocks or along the good path below the edge that runs toward Marble Wall.

1 Exodus 10m HVS 5a ★
The first of the steep cracks is entered awkwardly and followed religiously to its end.
Richard McHardy, Al Parker, Paul Nunn, Bob Brayshaw, 1959

2 Deuteronomy 10m HVS 5b ★★
Possibly the fiercest of this fierce quartet. Climb the left-slanting crack. Step left and climb the thin crack that springs from the lip of the roof.
John Allen, Steve Bancroft, 1974

3 Leviticus 10m HVS 5b ★
The twin cracks are followed in tandem.

4 Missing Numbers 8m HVS 5b
The thin crack on the right side of the wall.
Graham Hoey, 1981

5 E.M.F. 7m HVS 5a ★
Although small, the arête has good moves.
Gary Gibson, 1979

6 Sudoxe 8m E1 5b ★
A fairly pushy route up the centre of the tower.

7 Pup 8m HVS 6a
Start below a flake in the arête. Gain the flake and use it to climb the arête past another flake.

8 Puss 8m HVS 5c ★
A short problem with an entertaining couple of moves. Climb the centre of the wall.
John Allen, Neil Stokes, 1974

9 Kitten 8m VS 5b ★
Start in the centre of the wall and move slightly right, then go up with less difficulty.
Al Parker, Peter Bamfield, 1959

10 Lucky 7m VS 5b
The right-hand arête of the wall.
Dave Simmonite, 1991

COSMIC BUTTRES
Fifteen metres right is a buttress containing a good collection of routes.

11 Pulse 6m VS 4c
The thin crack.
Dave Gregory, John Street, 1992

12 Beanpod 6m S 4a
A well-protected route with some interesting moves. Climb into the small sentry-box at half-height and finish up the thinner crack.
Al Parker, Bob Brayshaw, Peter Bamfield, 1959

13 X-Ray 7m HS 4b ★
Technical and well-protected moves following the thin crack. A good warm-up for the VSs.
↪ page 273
Al Parker, Bob Brayshaw, Peter Bamfield, 1961

14 Electron 8m VS 5a ★
Easyish climbing up the crack leads to technical and enjoyable moves to pass the final roof.
Alan Clarke, Mike Parkin, 1964

15 Quantum Crack 9m HVS 5a ★★
A fantastic varied line that gives pressing moves to pass both overhangs. It still manages to feel quite friendly, all the same.
Alan Clarke, Mike Parkin, 1964

16 Cosmic Crack 9m VS 4c ★
A great route. Swing steeply up to gain the main crack. Follow this easily until steep moves lead to the top of the crag.
Al Parker, Bob Brayshaw, 1959

KNUTTER BUTTRESS

The steep walls 40m right are a true delight for the connoisseur. The best routes here are fiercely technical, and are often enjoyed as exacting solos.

17 Heather Crack 6m HVD ★
Solid, flaky holds and good pro make this a very enjoyable route.
B Platt, Al Parker, 1958

18 Flipside 6m E2 5c ★
A grasping highball problem up the wall to the left of *Travesties*, with a crux to reach a horizontal break.
Gabe & John Regan, 1984

19 Travesties 7m HVS 5b ★★
Excellent moves lead into and up a shallow left-slanting groove. With stiff climbing and uninspiring gear, it feels high in the grade.
Robin Miller, Pete Steward, Steve Cannon, 1976

20 Pig's Ear 7m E1 6a ★
Superb climbing, despite a lack of line, on tiny holds just right of the centre of the face.
Jonny Woodward, 1978

21 Deep Chimney 7m D
The wide, awkward cleft.

22 Suitored 8m E4 6a
Start under the overhang (as for *Crew Pegs Diffs*), but pull straight over the roof using a wafer-thin flake and continue by laying away from the left-hand arête.
Steve Bancroft, Sue Bird, 1987

23 Crew Pegs Diffs 8m E3 6a ★
A tough little route that is difficult to protect. Move up the arête, then step rightwards using a small flake. Another hard move gains entry into a hanging groove. Gibber up this on better holds to reach a wide, horizontal break and finish up a short wall.
Steve Bancroft, Nick Stokes, Pete Lowe, 1977

24 No More Excuses 10m E4 6b ★★★
A technical delight that will suit a cold day. The centre of the wall is climbed past a sloping hold to an easier, but still tricky, finish.
Graham Hoey, Giles Barker, 1982

25 The Knutter 10m HVS 5b ★★
The broad, flaky groove gives a route of similar character to *Travesties*, albeit with a low, short lived crux.
Don Whillans, 1962

26 Hearsay Crack 10m E1 5a ★
This thin, attractive crack doesn't give protection as easily as you would imagine.
Al Parker, B Platt, 1958

27 Pure Gossip 8m HS 4b
Start 1m to the left of a perched block and climb the wall, initially trending slightly rightwards, and then directly.
Gary Gibson, 1979

The string of little buttresses that dribble leftwards from the main bastion of High Neb Buttress give off a modest, undemanding air. But get involved and they reveal themselves to be little plugs of character, each with its own vibe. Enchaining these buttresses is one of the great High Neb experiences. Here, Anna Hammond rattles off X-Ray, HS 4b (page 271). Paul Evans

BLURTER BUTTRESS
A stout big buttress 30m right of Knutter Buttress.

28 Undercoat 10m HS 4b
Climb the left-hand arête of the pillar to the large ledge. Traverse left round the corner and go up the centre of the sidewall.
Al Parker, Richard McHardy, Peter Bamfield, 1997

29 Lucy's Slab 10m E1 5b
Climb the left side of the pillar to its top. Step left and cross the overlap at a scoop and finish up the slab above.
Al Parker, Richard McHardy, Peter Bamfield, 1978

30 Stairway Crack 10m M
Your basic rocky cleft.

31 Meddle 18m E2 5c ★
A good climb with a reckless-feeling crux. Climb the arête on its right-hand side, until level with the bottom of *The Blurter's* groove. Swing leftwards around the arête and continue via a disconcerting barn-door to reach a large ledge. Finish directly.
Paul Millward, Jon de Montjoye, 1976

32 Youth Meat 18m E4 6b ★
An extended boulder problem, using a poor pocket for the left hand, leads into the base of the groove of *The Blurter* (variations to the left are easier). From the groove, step right and yank over the roof to finish direct.
Johnny Dawes, 1984

33 The Blurter 21m HVS 5b ★★★
An excellent and crafty climb. Start up the chimney then traverse left and follow the groove to a small ledge. Step right and pull over a bulge before trending leftwards round the arête and up the steep wall.
Al Parker, B Platt, 1959

34 Overhanging Chimney 16m S 4a ★★
The central chimney is a bit of a beast to climb.
Harry Kelly, 1915

35 Wolf Solent 16m E4 5c ★★
The bulging wall right of the chimney. While the moves aren't too difficult, the gear is slightly depressing. Teeter leftwards up the slab under the overlap to a position just to the right of the chimney. Pull over the overlap, first rightwards then leftwards, with difficulty and a poor pocket. Continue warily up the slab to a large ledge and an easier finish.
Martin Berzins, Nic Hallam, 1978

36 Typhoon 12m VS 4c ★★
Action-packed. Follow *Aries* to half-height, then step left to follow a curving crack to a sloping ledge. Rounded rock leads directly to the top.
Al Parker, B Platt, 1959

37 Aries 10m HS 4b ★
The square-cut groove leads to a short roof-crack which gives a real struggle.
Al Parker, Richard McHardy, Peter Bamfield, 1957

Stanage High Neb | 275

DUO SLAB
The laid-back slab 20m right has a good set of low-grade routes, well suited to the bold.

38 Pleasant Slab 6m D
The slight slab leads to a heathery ledge and a juggy steepening below the top.
Bruce Goodwin, 1993

39 Ono 8m S ★
Go directly up the slab immediately to the left of the crack and finish through a juggy bulge.
Brian Cropper, Paul Cropper, 1976

40 Uno Crack 9m D ★
Climb the wide crack towards the left-hand side of the slab.

41 Fate 9m E2 5c ★
The slab is climbed directly, with difficult initial moves and serious final moves; reachy.
Gary Gibson, Ralph Hewitt, Derek Beetlestone, 1978

42 Rinty 9m VS 5a ★
The thin shallow seams, with delightful moves, and always just in balance. Keep off the easier parallel cracks on the right.
Clive Rowland, Al Parker, 1961

43 Duo Crack Climb 9m VD ★
A good testpiece, with technical moves on finger-jams. Climb the parallel cracks.
Harry Kelly, George Bower, Edgar Pryor, Rice Kemper Evans, 1921

44 Solo Slab 9m HVS 5b
A good, bold eliminate, avoiding the arête on the right and the crack on the left.
Dave Gregory, John Street, 1992

45 Staircase Rib 9m D
The projecting rib. Precarious.
Dave Gregory, John Street, 1992

YOUTH BUTTRESS
Twenty metres to the right is another slab, riven by cracks with some pleasant easier routes.

46 Side Plate 8m S 4b
Climb the arête, starting over a small nose, and continue up the enjoyable arête above.
Dave Gregory, John Street, 1992

47 Ice Cream Flakes 8m VD
Climb the right-hand arête of the tower and follow the rightward-slanting flakes above.
Dave Gregory, John Street, 1992

48 Warm Afternoon 9m VD
Nice climbing with no nasty surprises. Start up the left-hand arête, then step rightwards and climb the centre of the narrow pillar.
Dave Gregory, John Street, 1992

49 Frosty 9m D
Climb the open peapod-shaped groove, followed by the V-shaped groove above.

50 Icy Crack 9m VS 4c
A route with a very good start and finish, but an aimless middle, following a thin crack and blunt arête 2m to the right of the deep groove of *Frosty*. The protection leaves a lot to be desired.
Bill McKee, Rob Jarret, 1978

51 Youth 8m VD ★
The thin crack matures towards the top and gives a pleasant climb.
Clive Rowland, Al Parker, 1961

Duo Slab

Youth Buttress

HIGH NEB BUTTRESS

To the right lies the main area of High Neb, with a stretch of tall classics of all grades. This continuous line of jutting buttresses is delightfully situated close to the highest point of the edge and in a commanding position above the surrounding moorland.

52 Gunter 10m VS 5a
The thin, dog-legged crack.
T Norcliffe, C Smith, 1966

53 Straight Crack 12m HS 4b ★
The tall crack is followed with a bit of a jam, a bit of a wedge and a bit of a wriggle.

54 Eric's Eliminate 14m S 4a ★
A good crack pitch – lots of variety, and never savage. Ascend a short crack in the face. Continue to finish up the vertical crack.

55 Twisting Crack 14m S 4a ★★
A great route covering fine terrain. Climb the corner-crack; step left on to the exposed arête and make a hard pull to gain and climb the excellent cracks above.
Harry Kelly and party, 1915

56 Kelly's Overhang 15m HVS 5b ★★★
Many grades are offered for this climb, with HVS representing the lowest of them. Climb *Twisting Crack* and struggle out rightwards past a protruding block, then make a hard move up and right to reach good holds. ⊙ page 279
Morley Wood, 1926

57 Mouthpiece 15m E1 5b ★★
Climb to the overhang, stretch leftwards and swing boldly to a block at the lip (junction with *Kelly's*). Finish straight up the wall above.
Steve Bancroft, John Allen, Neil Stokes, 1973

58 Overflow 15m E1 5b ★
Climb *Inaccessible Crack Direct* to below its final bulge. Hand-traverse out above the lip of the overhang to finish up the exposed arête.
Chris Calow, 1983

59 Inaccessible Crack 16m VS 4c ★★
A great, solid VS, swaggering up the cliff. Follow a crack rising from the recess and balance leftward to below a corner-crack. Climb the glorious corner above. **Inaccessible Crack Direct**, VS 4c, goes up the lower crack and arête, and is almost as good.
Harry Kelly, 1915

60 Impossible Slab 15m E3 5c ★★
The slab, 2m left of the chimney, has thin and sketchy moves, a long way above good gear.

61 Eckhard's Arête 14m HS 4b
The left arête of the chimney.
Rucksack Club, c1913

62 Eckhard's Chimney 14m VD ★
A good climb, muscling up the chimney.
Rucksack Club, c1913

63 Quietus 14m E2 5c ★★★
The all-time great gritstone roof – powerful and exposed with a historic pedigree. Climb a curving groove and slab to the overhang. Cross this, with hard moves rounding the lip.
Pete Biven (1pt), 1953. FFA Joe Brown, Don Whillans, 1954

Stanage High Neb | 277

64 Quietus Right-Hand 14m E4 6a ★★
Space! From the ledge on *Norse Corner Climb*, make a wild hand-traverse along the lip to the arête (cam) and haul your way to glory.
Ian Maisey, 1981

65 Norse Corner Climb 15m HS 4c ★★
A feisty start leads to steady climbing above. Use a large pocket to pull desperately onto the slab. Laybacking the crack just right gains the same point, and is no easier. Follow the slab rightwards, under the overhang, and up to a ledge; finish up the corner above.
Rucksack Club, c1913

66 Kelly's Variation 14m S 4a ★
Pull up into the scoop, then saunter delicately leftwards to finish up *Norse Corner Climb*.

67 King Kong 12m E3 6a ★
Bridge up a shallow scoop leading up to an overhang. Reach over this for a good hold on the upper wall. Progress from here is by means of a decisive and monstrous mantelshelf.
Al Parker, Graham Fyffe, 1978

68 Sogines 11m HVS 5b ★
Bridge the corner to reach the thin flakes in the wall just to the left (5c direct). Strenuously follow them to a steep finish up the bulging rib left of the shallow cave.

69 Neb Corner 11m D
The corner. A bit polished, but still fun.
Rucksack Club, c1913

70 Boyd's Crack 12m VD ★
The offwidth crack.

71 Limbo 14m S
Climb the lower slab. Cross the diagonal break and finish up the slab. Not well protected.
Chris Craggs, 1978

72 Tango Crack 14m VD ★
A fun climb, with a good, wide beginning. After that, continue up the easier cracks above.
Rucksack Club, c1913

73 Tango Buttress 14m HS 5a ★★
A fine technical exercise up the slab. The initial moves off the ground form a definite crux.
Rucksack Club, c1913

74 Where did my Tan Go? 14m HVS 5b
Start at the base of the gully and climb a tricky wall to the first break. Move rightwards and climb the arête. Poorly-protected,.
Chris Craggs, 1989

75 High Neb Gully 18m M
The deep, block-choked gully.

76 High Neb Buttress 20m VS 4c ★★★
Exposed, delicate climbing up the centre of one of the best bits of rock on the crag. Start up a projecting rib and gain the ledge above. Continue to a good ledge (runners) then move right and climb the centre of the slab by a crucial mantelshelf. Finish more easily.
Ivar Berg, 1915

77 High Neb Variation 20m VS 5a ★★
A lesser variation on a very good theme. Start up a thin crack to the break. Continue in the same line to a standing position on a good ledge and traverse left to runner slots. Mantelshelf to reach better holds and finish up the left side of the face above. ↻ page 256

Stanage High Neb

78 High Neb Edge 20m HVS 5c ★
Start up the shallow groove. Continue on the right-hand side of the arête until it is becomes imperative to move round on to the front face.

79 The Crypt Trip 19m E6 6b ★★★
A thrilling and pumpy climb of the highest calibre. Climb up and left through the notch in the overlap to gain the first proper break. More difficult, though protectable, moves lead past a pocket to the main horizontal break and an easier finish.
Ron Fawcett, 1983

80 Old Friends 19m E4 5c ★★★
The ultimate E4 tick on the edge that has been known to take a few scalps, as well as a few ankles. From the corner, make a tricky move left to gain a tiny groove which leads up and left to the central hanging groove. Stretch to reach the horizontal break. Step back right and finish up the easier upper wall past a lovely pocket.
John Allen, Neil Stokes, Steve Bancroft, 1973

81 Ami 14m M
The awkward slabby corner.

82 The Dalesman 22m HVS 5a ★
A very fine bit of sightseeing, although you may be a bit too pumped to enjoy the view. Climb *Ami* and hand-traverse along the break to a finish up the left side of the far arête.
Roger Greatrick, Keith Ainsworth, 1983

83 Mantelshelf Climb 14m VD ★
Go up the slabby face by a line of obvious ledges. Finish up a shallow right-facing corner.
Rucksack Club, c1920

84 It's a Cracker 12m S 4b
Climb the centre of the face with an awkward, but well-protected, move to get established in the thin crack. Finish in the same line.

85 Typical Grit 10m HS 4a
Climb the narrow slab and up easier rock above; poorly protected.

86 Cave Buttress 15m S 4b ★★
A devious route. After a tricky undercut start, climb the buttress to the large overhang. Move right around the corner and finish awkwardly up rounded holds. ⊙ page 283. **Cave Buttress Right-Hand**, HS 4b, goes up the dog-leg crack on the right wall.
Rucksack Club, c1920

87 Jeepers Creepers 15m E1 5b ★★
An esoteric masterclass in roof jamming. Follow *Cave Buttress* to the overhang and attack the crack that splits the edge of the roof.
Joe Brown, 1958

Dave Thomas enjoying the fresh air on the mighty Kelly's Overhang, HVS 5b (page 276). This big climb with its bullying crux dates from 1926. Even today, with cams and sticky rubber, very few climbers operating at the HVS grade will cruise it (confession time: it might actually be a grade or two harder). But still, it's all good, clean fun. 📷 David Simmonite

Stanage High Neb

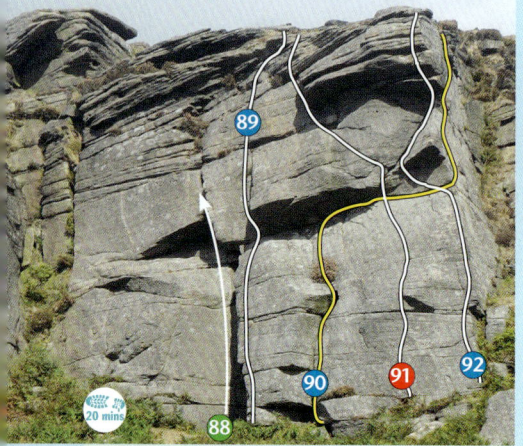

91 Gypsy Moth 12m E1 5b ★
Climb the slab using a pocket. From the diagonal crack, climb the bulges leftwards.
Malc Baxter, Simon Royston, 1997

92 Titanic Direct 12m HVS 5a ★★
A delicate start leads to buster moves above. Ascend the delicate edge of the slab to gain sinker jams in the slanting crack. Finish straight over the spectacular prow. Considered by some to be better than the original.
⊙ opposite page

93 Angus 9m S
The undercut, narrowing chimney.
Al Parker, Paul Nunn (both solo), 1959

94 Sinew Stretch 8m HVS 5c ★
The left-hand arête has a technical start to gain a good hold. A long move leads to easier ground.
Bill Sutton, Steve Bancroft, 1979

95 Blockhead Direct 8m E1 5b ★★
The right arête gives an inventive route.
Bob Brayshaw, Al Parker, 1959

96 Headbanger 7m E1 5c ★
The narrow, undercut front face, gained from the right, is short and sharp.
Keith Ashton, Dave Allsopp, 1985

97 Prairie Dog 6m HVS 5b ★
The crack on the left gives a bit more trouble than you'd expect.
Jim Rubery, 1992

98 Scavenger 8m VS 4c ★
The thin crack in the middle of the wall leads to a delicate finish.
S Thorpe, 1977

99 Sneaking Sally through the Alley 10m VS 4c ★
Gain and follow the leftward-rising break to finish up the left corner of the face.
Keith Ashton, Dave Allsopp, 1985

TITANIC BUTTRESS AREA
A great little outcrop 250m right of High Neb. It is usually very quiet. Approach from High Neb Buttress, or direct from Long Causeway (bracken-jungle in summer).

88 Lusitania 12m VS 4b
A memorable voyage through dark waters. The gloomy corner leads to a bulging crack.
Al Parker, Peter Bamfield, B Platt, 1958

89 Q.E.2 12m VS 4c ★
Boulder up the arête to the right-angled groove. Leave it by tricky moves to finish steeply above, taking care with loose rock.
Bill Birch, Al Parker, 1972

90 Titanic 14m VS 4c ★★★
A fine route, with a big feel about it. Take the central groove to the first overhang. Move rightwards to the arête then swing round onto the right side and, using the arête above, gain and follow the rightward-slanting crack.
Al Parker, Hugh Banner, Lew Brown, 1958

Wouldn't you just love to be there, grabbing those jugs, placing those runners, feeling all that space! Neil Foster on the shy delights of Titanic Direct, HVS 5a (opposite page), on the rarely-visited Titanic Buttress.
Clare Reading

STANAGE
The Definitive Guide

Stanage. Queen of the Eastern Edges. The finest crag on grit. Where beginners come for their first grapples, and the top performers crank the hardest problems. Mile after mile of perfect rock, containing some of the best routes and boulder problems in the country, whatever the grade. Where busy VDiffs, heart-in-mouth highballs, desperate power problems, lonely leads and warm summer solos all sit shoulder to shoulder. The country's favourite crag.

And here is a guidebook to match. A guide that reflects the richness and diversity of this great crag. Whether you are a first-time visitor after the famous climbs, or a long-time local after something new, this guide will take you to the places you want to go, and show you so much along the way.

Never has so much love for Stanage been crammed into one book. Never has a book brought you more information, inspiration and fun.

Featuring:
- 1300 routes from Moderate to E8
- 400 boulder problems from V0 to V13
- 140 full-colour action photos
- 5 Fontainebleau-style bouldering circuits
- Over 200 full-colour photo-topos
- Old-school black and white pictures of the pioneers stretching back as far as first ascents in 1915
- A full first ascents list
- A series of essays and yarns that give the story and climbing history of Stanage
- Original contributions from 40 authors

Get it from the BMC shop for a lifetime of gritstone action.

http://shop.thebmc.co.uk/

ISBN 978-0-903908-0-85

Front cover: Adam Long on Don, E4 5c (page 295).
Photo: Pete O'Donovan

For high summer grit, High Neb's fresh setting makes it a great choice. John Smith jugging skyward on the surprisingly steep finish of Cave Buttress, S 4b (page 278). 📷 Paul Evans

COUNT'S AREA

OS Grid Ref: SK 238 845
Altitude: 400m

The next section is a compact collection of well-formed buttresses lying between the Long Causeway track on the left and the Plantation path on the right.

Despite sitting under the very noses of the crowds at the Plantation area, these buttresses are often deserted.

Approach: See map on page 258. The area is best reached from the Plantation (Hollin Bank) parking. Follow the Plantation path until it reaches the top of the edge. Follow the path further along to drop down at your chosen buttress. Approach takes 15 minutes.

COUNT'S BUTTRESS
The showpiece of the area is the bastion of Count's Buttress, with its tall, burly crack and face climbs. Either side are some of Stanage's best slab climbs.

Nightmare Slab: A steep, rectangular slab, home to a series of routes to delight technicians and frustrate thugs. A drop below the ledge that runs across the base of the routes means that they are best treated as short routes, rather than just boulder problems; don't jump off without a spotter.

❶ Nightmare Slab   9m   E2 5c   ★★
A classy route, where you'll find yourself asking questions of balance at a spicy height. Gain and follow the left-hand edge to a precarious high step to reach a good break. Pass the bulge above by a long reach followed by either a stride out right or, slightly harder and better, continue directly.
Al Parker, Peter Bamfield, Paul Nunn, Richard McHardy, 1959

❷ Dream Boat   9m   E3 6b   ★★
Cool your boots, sunshine! A slabtastic route where difficulties diminish as height is gained (but not as quickly as you'd like). Climb the technical and sustained slab midway between the polished start of *Daydreamer* and the left arête. Highball Font 6B.
Alan Doig (solo), 1986

❸ Daydreamer   9m   E2 6b   ★★★
The original smear test on this brilliant slab. Start in the centre of the slab at well-buffed footholds and a short vertical flake. Make intricate crux moves near to the limit of adhesion to gain an obvious but sloping ledge, then continue direct. Highball Font 6A+.
Bob Brayshaw, Al Parker, 1960

❹ Nightrider   9m   E3 6b   ★★
A sustained, enjoyable eliminate. Go up the green streak and line of pebbles just right of the line of *Daydreamer*. Highball Font 6B.
Chris Hamper (solo), 1980

❺ Sleepwalker   8m   E2 6a   ★
Follow the lesser green streak, 2m left of the corner, passing a couple of tiny overlaps early on. Highball Font 6A.
Chris Calow, Tim Carruthers, 1977

Count's Area | 285

Count's Face: The front face of the buttress is home to a number of tightly-packed routes. On first acquaintance these appear to be too close for real independence, but once embarked upon they all prove to be separate enough to ensure that there is no chance of straying onto another climb.

6 Out for the Count 15m E4 6a ★
The left arête has some naughty moves and tricky protection.
Chris Calow, Tim Carruthers, 1977

7 The Cool Curl 15m E6 6b ★★
A typically bold Dawes addition tracing a lonely route up the centre of the clean slab. Climb the lower buttress just left of its right edge to the first ledge (gear). Step up and left to make a cruel pull and crucial high step to get established on the central slab. Easier above.
Johnny Dawes, Nigel Slater, 1984

8 Count's Chimney 14m D ★
The classic fissure splitting the cliff is of true Puttrell vintage. Named after Count Orloff.
JW Puttrell, 1900s

9 Count's Wall 17m E1 5b ★
A nice wall climb based around the thin crack. Climb easily up the lower wall. Climb the crack above, with a hearty, reachy move to gain the break above. Continue more easily.
Al Parker, B Plat (1pt), 1959. FFA Dave Mithen, Dave Morgan, 1976

10 Counterblast 16m E3 5c ★
Climb the right-hand edge of the cave and gain the ledge above. Step left again to a point directly above the centre of the cave. Climb the slab via a pocket and a small vertical crease then continue straight up the wall above, passing a small bulge.
Gary Gibson, 1981

11 Abacus 16m E3 5c ★
Follow the previous route to the ledge. From here step left and climb straight up the poorly-protected wall above the right-hand edge of the cave, using spaced holds and a pocket, to reach a horizontal break. Finish direct.
Dave Mithen, Dave Morgan, Jim Worthington, 1976

12 Count's Buttress 16m E2 5c ★★★
A classic and historical route, fierce for its time, tracing a devious but logical path up the front of this commanding buttress. Climb the blunt rib to a ledge. A tough traverse right gains the main arête. Stretch up delicately for the horizontal break above, before traversing back left to a short final crack.
Joe Brown, Slim Sorrell, 1955

13 Count's Buttress Direct 14m E3 6a ★
The direct line to the finishing crack has some tough moves.
Al Parker, B Platt, 1959

Count's Area

14 The Count 14m E2 5c ★★
A great route, with a slightly worrying start and grand beefy climbing above, that follows the right-hand arête of the buttress. Climb to a suspect flake under the roof. From this, gain holds just over the roof, then a fierce pull out right brings the sanctuary of the deep break on *Count's Buttress*. Make the moves up, as for that climb, then strike directly up the wall above with long and satisfying moves.
Dave Morgan, Dave Mithen, Jim Worthington, 1976

15 Count's Crack 12m VS 4c ★★★
An absolute classic, with continually steep, solid jamming, giving one of the truly great VSs of the crag. The big crack is gained from the right and once entered provides classic jamming, leading to a steep, juggy finish. The **Direct Start** is HVS 5c and the **Left-Hand Finish** is a fine HVS 5a ★★.
◉ opposite page.
Eric Byne, Clifford Moyer, 1930s

16 B Crack 9m S 4a ★★
The smooth, right-angled corner provides a sustained route in a good setting.

17 Dracula 9m HVS 5b ★
The shapely arête feels a little too easy for the tall and a little too hard for the short. Compelling, whatever height you are.
John Gosling, Mike Simpkins, Eddie Thurrell, 1967

18 Scraped Crack 8m HD
The somewhat scruffy right-angled corner.
Les Gillott, Alan Clarke, 1960s

19 Basil Brush 9m HVS 5b ★
Climb straight up the steep slab with sketchy moves to reach the ledge, and a direct finish.
Nigel Slater, Alistair Ferguson, 1984

20 Mop Up 12m E1 5c
The centre of the slab.
Tony Nicholls, 1994

21 Lino 12m VS 5a
From just left of the arête, go up to a block and move left to a vegetated ledge. Finish directly.
Al Parker, Peter Bamfield, 1959

22 Prickly Crack 9m VD
The twin cracks lead to a prickly finish.
Les Gillott, Alan Clarke, 1960s

23 Shirley's Shining Temple 9m E5 7a ★★★
A bit of technical wizardry from the shiny-headed master himself, taking the centre of the blank slab. Start at a small overlap and get established on the slab with difficulty. More hard moves allow a direct ascent of the upper section of the slab, keeping always to the left of the vertical flake. Highball Font 7C.
John Allen (solo), 1984

24 Shock Horror Slab 9m E3 6b ★★
A frustrating test of pebble-savvy. Scratch and smear desperately up the right-hand side of the bulging wall, crux, to gain the scant flake leading to an easier finish. Highball Font 6C.
◉ page 289
Steve Bancroft (solo), 1980

The Count's Buttress area has two sides to it: super-thin slab highballing in the higher grades and blockbusting crack climbs in the mid-grades. Here, Jim Symon is on the latter, the classic VS of the area, Count's Crack (opposite page). 📷 Paul Evans

D.I.Y. AREA
This small area has a brilliant clutch of routes, balanced beautifully on the cusp 'twixt route and boulder problem.

25 Black and Decker 9m E2 6b ★
The left-hand side of the wall is climbed with difficulty to reach a sloping ledge. Step left and finish up the easy arête: Highball Font 6C.
Greg Griffith (solo), 1985

26 D.I.Y. 10m E3 6a ★★★
The local classic, with exciting, technical climbing. The centre of the wall is climbed via a vague shallow groove. An ingenious crux move is required to pass the one good flake hold at mid-height: Highball Font 6B.
Graham Hoey (solo), 1981

27 Torture Garden 10m E3 6b ★★
The wall to the left of the crack is climbed directly, initially reaching the prominent slot and passing it with difficulty. Highball Font 6C+.
Greg Griffith (solo), 1985

28 Grime 8m HS 4b
Jam the crack to the wider upper section.
Les Gillott, Alan Clarke, 1960s

29 Sithee Direct 8m E1 6b ★★
A great problem. Start from a small flat block and make hard technical moves directly up the wall. Highball Font 6B.
Graham Hoey (solo), 1981

30 Sithee 8m E1 5b ★
The original start, gaining the centre of the wall by starting from a block on the right.
Jim Lawrenson, Giles Barker (both solo), 1977

31 Toxic 6m D ★
Climb the sharp flake to its top and then move right to a pleasant finish.
Les Gillott, Alan Clarke, 1960s

Tom-Cat Slab Area: This is just to the right.

32 Dot's Slab 8m D ★
Climb the left side of the slab on steps. Traverse along a ledge to the arête and finish up a corner on the right.
Al Parker, Peter Bamfield, 1959

33 Tom-Cat Slab 8m E1 5b ★★
A neat little test of confidence. From just left of centre, flaky holds lead to a difficult move at half height and a delicate finish.
Alan Clarke (solo), c1962

34 Skin Grafter 8m E3 5c ★
A delicate climb up the unprotected right arête.
Gary Gibson, 1982

35 Surprise 8m HVS 5b ★
A disjointed route, but with its huffy start and puffy finish, you'll be glad of the rest at half way. Overcome the left edge of the lower tier using a tight crack and holds on the left. Wander up slabs then wage war on the short upper crack.
Al Parker, Peter Bamfield, 1959

D.I.Y. Slab

The Count's Buttress area holds many great slab testpieces, usually unprotected and at an exciting height, but where bouldering pads can render them safer. Jon Wells is on Shock Horror Slab, E3 6b (page 286).
© Mark Rankine

STANAGE PLANTATION

OS Grid Ref: SK 239 844 to SK 242 839
Altitude: 400m

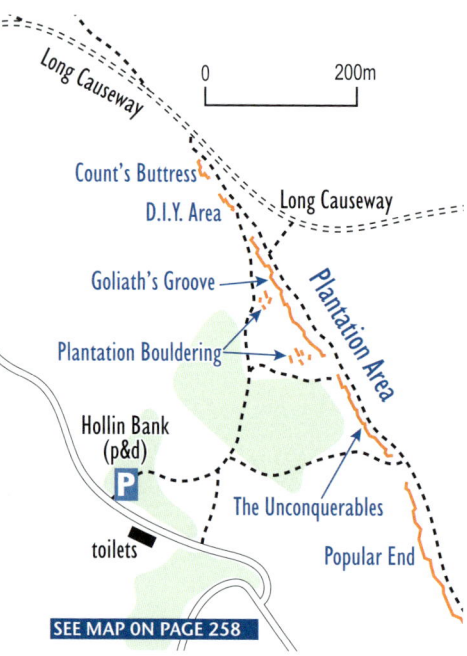

FERN CRACK & WALL END SLAB
A pair of fine buttresses containing a fistful of high-calibre slab and crack routes across a good spread of grades.

❶ Argus 8m E2 5b ★
An exposed highball problem. Starting from a ledge on the left. Layback the arête in a somewhat dramatic fashion on its left-hand side.

❷ Silk 16m E6 6c ★★
A brutal boulder problem leads to the thinnest of thin slab climbing above. Powerfully overcome the lower bulge, avoiding the crack, then trend up and left on smears and tiny pebbles to poor but gradually improving holds. A wicked highball, Font 7A+.
Johnny Dawes (solo), 1984

❸ Fern Crack 16m VS 5a ★★★
A splendid crack-climb with tough, awkward sections and good rests. Climb the steep, slippery crack to a ledge. Make a tricky move to enter the wider upper crack till a step left gains a shelf. Finish up the scoop above.

❹ Fern Groove 17m E2 5c ★★
Powerful, perplexing and pressing climbing based around the fine hanging groove. Climb the lower slab and arête to the break. Swing leftwards along this and battle into the groove (crux) above. Once established, climb the incipient crack with continued difficulty.
Pat Fearneough (2pt), 1960s

❺ Virginia Calling 14m HVS 5a
The left-hand arête of the slab is climbed throughout, with the final rounded section providing the crux. *Bridge's Variation* makes the best finish.

The buttresses along the edge behind the beech plantation lie at the centre of the edge. This is pure Stanage, where it appears that every groove, crack, slab and wall host amazing climbs across the grades. The area is unsurprisingly popular. Magic stuff.

The bouldering areas, one concentrated below *Goliath's Groove* and the other just below The Pinnacle, are among the best in the country.

Approach: See map above. Park in Hollin Bank and follow the main path through the trees to your chosen buttress. 10 to 15 minutes.

Stanage Plantation | 291

6 Wall End Slab 22m VS 5a ★★★
A devious but venerable classic. Climb the tricky lower slab then press on over the bulges to reach a large triangular ledge. Step down and traverse across the slab to reach the right arête. Follow the right-hand side of the arête to the top. Protection is spaced, although the upper moves are relatively steady.

7 Bridge's Variation 20m VS 5a ★
Follow the regular route to its triangular ledge and then climb the crack that rises from the back of this to the top of the slab. Stride across the gap to the main face and finish up this.

8 Wall End Slab Super Duper Direct 14m E3 5c ★
A good route, despite a squeezed-in appearance. Climb the centre of the lower slab and then continue over the middle of the bulge above on pleasantly surprising pockets. The final broad rib is the main challenge of the route, where a side runner to the left reduces the grade to E2.
Chris Craggs, Jim Rubery, 1991

9 Wall End Slab Direct 15m E3 5c ★★★
The ancient direct start to *Wall End Slab* – an astounding effort for 1930 – is combined with a newer direct finish to give a good bold route. Climb the lower slab to a break. Continue boldly with great moves to pass an undercut flake, and gain *Wall End Slab* (this gives a good E2 5b in itself). Continue carefully up the scoop in the steepening final wall, a long way from any runners. page 271
Frank Elliott, Harry Dover, Gilbert Ellis (Start), 1930. Chris Craggs, Martin Veale (Finish), 1985

Pure gold! A climber enjoying Wall End Slab Direct, E3 5c (page 291), as the setting sun turns Stanage's winter coat the colour of fire. The crisp clean air draws special friction from the rock which will be much appreciated on this bold classic. 📷 David Simmonite

GOLIATH'S GROOVE AREA
One of the most impressive parts of the edge. A collection of stunning corners, grooves and arêtes that provide some of the finest and most historic routes on the edge.

10 The Coign 16m HS 4b ★★
The left arête of the slabby wall is a fine route with a couple of tasty run-outs.
Geoffrey Sutton, 1958

11 Outlook Slab 16m VS 5a ★
An enjoyable eliminate. From the top of the short crack, follow the steepening slab.
Martin Veale, Bill Lucas, 1978

12 Wall End Crack 16m S 4b ★★
A good, raunchy crack-climb. Start up the fabulous hand-crack (or the wider crack to the left), then follow the wider fissure direct.

13 Death and Night and Blood
16m E1 5b ★★
From *Wall End Crack*, climb the exposed arête, passing a rickety flake, to a final long reach.
Gary Gibson, 1978

14 Wall End Flake Crack 20m VS 4c ★★
A great climb in a tight position. Start up *Wall End Crack* until it is possible to traverse right up the sloping ramp to the foot of the two flakes. Climb the left-hand flake on jams and laybacks.

15 Wall End Holly Tree Crack
18m HS 4b ★
The right-hand of the two flakes can be reached by the thin, scratched crack below and is then followed by jamming and bridging.

16 Helfenstein's Struggle 18m HVD ★★
The wide rift has a good historical pedigree, featuring a hellish final squeeze; success depends more on your diet than your technical ability. Climb the cleft to the large boulder which corks the rift. Squeeze through or navigate it on the outside. Great fun.
Helfenstein (not quite), 1930s

17 Saul's Arête 22m VS 4b ★★
Gain the upper section of *The Archangel* by a hand-traverse along the horizontal break.
G Dimmick, H Richardson, 1965

18 The Archangel 20m E3 5b ★★★
One of the great rites of passage for any ambitious gritstoner. Follow the arête on its left side. Any doubting will be severely punished.
Ed Drummond, Hamish Green Armitage, 1972

19 Don 20m E4 5c ★★★
A fine piece of climbing forever doomed to live in the shadow of its superb opposite. Layback the arête on its right side. A bit longer than the original, purer and arguably better. ⓞ page 282
Ed Drummond (solo), 1985

20 Goliath's Groove 20m HVS 5a ★★★
A famous Stanage struggle that gives a good test of a climber's gritstone ability. Shuffle up the lower crack with or without elegance to gain a shelf on the right. Now move left and climb the upper groove with relative ease and a refreshing sense of exposure.
Peter Harding, J N Millward, Ernest Phillips, 1947

21 Ulysses 20m E6 6b ★★★
The epitome of hard gritstone arêtes, requiring good technique, deft footwork and total commitment. Layback the ever-steepening arête on its right, with each move getting harder than the last. Finish easily. Very highball Font 6C+.
Jerry Moffatt (solo), 1983

22 Holly Bush Gully Left 20m HS 4b ★★
A good route up a big classy line. Start up the left-hand crack to gain the easy upper section of the gully. Either move left to the short crack or squeeze through a skylight.
JW Puttrell, c1900

23 White Wand 22m E5 6a ★★★
The most technically interesting of this trio of sublime arêtes. Start easily. Now switch on the magic. Style up and left towards the sharp arête – the moves to gain this giving some of the finest moments on grit. Layback this with relative ease but significant terror to gain the ledge above. The upper arête is a formality. Very highball Font 6B. ⓞ page 270
John Allen, Steve Bancroft, 1975

24 Holly Bush Gully Right 20m S 4a ★★
The Puttrell-vintage gully contains joyous climbing deep in its heart. The gully is reached either by climbing the twin cracks or by an exciting VD traverse from blocks just right.
JW Puttrell, c1900

25 Fairy Steps 15m VS 4a ★★
A great bold voyage across the vast wall. From the corner, teeter dizzily leftwards across the narrow ledge, until a line of better holds leads to the top. Bold, but simple; take some micro-protection if you have it. ⓞ page 273
Alan Clarke, Les Gillott, 1960s

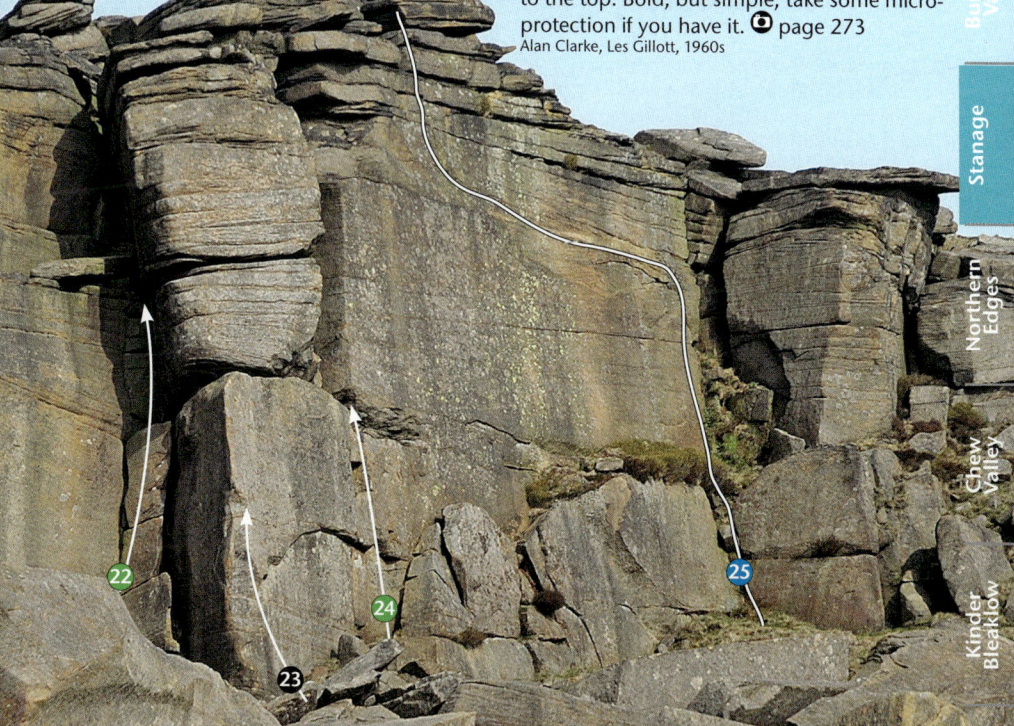

TOWER BUTTRESS AREA
Further right are the tall delights of Tower Buttress with its lofty classics. Beginning to its left are some shorter beauties.

26 Fina 15m HVS 5b ★★
A smashing climb, following a series of neat moves with solid protection. Follow the juggy hand-traverse right to the arête, then savour the sequences leading up the wall and arête above. The direct start, **Four Star**, is Font 6C.
Al Parker, Peter Bamfield, 1958 / Simon Horrox, 1982

27 Centaur 8m E2 5c ★★
A true beast – a powerful and extremely technical route, requiring stacks of inventive climbing ability, and the first of many testing wide crack routes in this area. From the cave, battle up to tackle the narrowing.
Don Whillans, Morty Smith, 1958

28 Additive Chimney 10m HS 4b ★
Enter the chimney and get to work. You will be a better climber at the top of this than you were at the bottom.
Al Parker, Peter Bamfield, 1958

29 Cinturato 14m E2 5b ★★
A fine little buzz. After a tricky start, climb the slabby arête to a delicate final move.
John Gosling, Mike Simpkins, Eddie Thurrell, 1967

30 Grace and Danger 15m E6 6c ★★
A quick and technical route in a worrying position. Climb the wall past a tiny overlap and a pocket to a rounded hold. Continue more easily to join *Cinturato*.
John Allen (solo), 1986

31 Esso Extra 16m E1 5b ★★
A memorable effort. Swing left from the cave into a cramped niche. Jam the short-lived but strenuous overhanging crack.
Joe Brown, Wilf White, 1957

32 Tower Crack 24m HVS 5b ★★★
The leaning corner-crack is as good a test of hand-jamming as you'll get in the area. Well protected but fierce. Jam the crack to a testing grope onto the ledge. Traverse up and right along the wide break, to finish on the ledge round on the front face.
Joe Brown, Slim Sorrell, Wilf White, 1950

33 Tower Chimney 20m E1 5b ★★★
This bell-bottomed brute offers the willing and adventurous an almost Tolkienesque adventure. Climb the easier lower section to the mid-height chamber. Now it's time to get old fashioned. A full-bodied approach encompassing much back-and-footing and thrutching will gain the narrower upper section and an easier exit. Large cams are available in the depths of the recess.
Eric Byne, 1933

34 Flight of Ideas 22m E6 7a ★★★
A great route – obscenely technical but with good runners below the crucial upper arête. Climb up past a crusty overlap to a horizontal break. Move left and climb the ever-more-holdless arête to a heart-stopping finale, which gives one of the most outrageous and technical sequences on the edge.
Simon Jones, 1994

Adam Long rides the sharp upper arête of White Wand, E5 6a (page 295). The technical crux is just below and the situaion, gunning for the ledge, gives one of the most exciting situations on gritstone.
 Niall Grimes

Stanage Plantation

35 Tower Face 25m HVS 5a ★★★
A popular Stanage classic with open climbing leading to the superb central flake. However, a brittle flake on the lower section means the climb should be treated with respect. Climb up to the right-facing flake. Move right to another flake at a lower (easier) or higher (better) level and move up to the break above. A short traverse left allows the magnificent flake to be gained and swarmed up with great delight.

36 Tower Face Direct 25m E2 5b ★★★
The short hard section allows the natural line to be climbed. Avoid the excursion rightwards by trucking directly on to reach the big flake.
Pete Biven, Trevor Peck, 1956

37 Stretcher Case 10m E2 5c ★
The steep crack in the left wall is taken to the final break. Traverse rightwards around the arête for 3m and lurch for the top.
Chris Jackson, Roy Small, Andy Kassyk, 1981

38 Nuke the Midges 10m E1 5c ★
A delicate start is followed by a frisky finale on this fun route. Start at the right-hand side up easy ledges. Traverse left on a break to a hard move up to gain a big flat jug. Mantelshelf on this to reach the top.
Al Manson, 1977

Tower Buttress Upper Tier: These are the short walls above and right of *Tower Face*, gained by a scramble. Running out to the left is a narrow ledge that is actually the top of the Tower Buttress. Starting from this are several small but worthwhile offerings in a relatively remote setting.

39 Miserable Miracle 8m E2 5b ★
The left-hand arête of the face, from the ledge, features unprotected and exposed moves on slopers.
John Allen, Neil Stokes, 1976

40 The Mangler 10m E1 5c ★★
Whillanstastic. The wide, undercut crack is a real climbing delight, and is only slightly easier than *Centaur*. Overcome the roof to get established in the wide crack and an easier finish. A runner in *Crescent*, or a large cam is fair at this grade.
Don Whillans, Audrey Whillans, Nat Allen, 1959

41 Crescent 10m VS 5a ★
The curving, well-protected crack.
Don Whillans, Audrey Whillans, Nat Allen, 1959

Fairy Steps, VS 4a (page 295) is a wonderful route. As the grade suggests, the climbing is not hard for VS. However, with its exposed journey across a great sheet of Stanage grit, where good runners are not always to hand, it certainly isn't somewhere to throw a wobbler. Holly Peristiani climbing. 📷 Charlotte King

STRANGLER AREA
A series of smaller walls and corners stretching right from Tower Buttress.

42 The Strangler 12m E4 5c ★★★
A fine bold route, without being nasty, making this a good introduction to the classic grit grade. Climb the left-hand arête of the front face all the way. The smeary crux, some way above good pro, is memorable.
Gabe Regan, Al Manson, Steve Webster, 1977

Upper Tier: The routes above are gained by scrambling round to the right.

43 Grooved Arête 8m S
Starting round to the left of the arête, move right and climb the nicely exposed arête.
Les Gillott, Alan Clarke, 1960s

44 Anji 10m VS 4c ★
Start 3m to the right of the arête and climb a short wall to the overlap. Move up and left to finish just right of the arête.
D Constable, Angela Illingworth, Terry Bolger, 1970

45 Obstinance 14m VS 4c
At a slightly lower level is a buttress with a holly bush. Climb the cracked heathery slab, 5m to the left, to an overlap. Go over this and make a long reach to gain the arête.
Al Parker, Peter Bamfield, 1960

46 Gardener's Groove 10m HS 4b
Struggle past the painfully-positioned holly bush and climb the pleasant corner.
Al Parker, Peter Bamfield, 1960

47 Percy's Prow 8m S
Step off a boulder and climb the arête. Finish up the crack that starts on the left (**Compost Corner**, D).

48 Gardener's Crack 10m D ★
A very good climb following a series of challenging, wide cracks in a good setting.
Al Parker, Peter Bamfield, 1960

49 Pizza Slab 10m HS 4a ★
From the foot of *Gardener's Crack*, climb the slab on the right trending slightly right to finish up its centre. Bold and intense.
Les Gillott, Alan Clarke, 1960s

50 Poor Pizza 10m D
The short straight crack.

51 Scorpion Slab 11m HS 4b ★
An airy little climb. Gain the midway ledge from the left and a move right to climb the right-hand arête of the slab without much protection.
Bob Brayshaw, Al Parker, Paul Nunn, Peter Bamfield, 1960

52 Hercules Crack 14m HS 4b ★
Climb the flake-crack to a ledge and continue up the wider crack above.

53 Mercury Crack 11m VD ★
Start in the corner below the cave. Gain this and after an awkward move to exit it, climb the easier crack above.

Stanage Plantation | 301

54 The Hathersage Trip 10m E4 6a ★★
A good, strenuous route up the centre of the steep wall, somewhat tamed by modern protection. Start on the right but move left to climb the centre of the wall.
Bob Berzins (solo), 1982

55 Overhanging Crack 10m HVS 5a ★
The steep wide crack is difficult to enter, being strenuous and not that easy to escape from.

56 Corner Crack 8m VS 5a ★
The undercut crack is difficult to start.
Al Parker, Peter Bamfield, 1960

The next routes start at a lower level.

57 See-Saw 14m VS 4c ★
Start on a large block, swing right on to the arête and continue directly up the left-hand edge of the buttress.
Al Parker, Peter Bamfield, 1960

58 Margery Daw 14m HVS 5b
Start as for the last climb, then climb the slight depression and passing the overlap.
Neil Stokes, John Allen, 1970s

THE PINNACLE
Just right is a fine pinnacle which contains a small number of uncompromising routes.

59 Crime 6m E4 6a ★
The left-hand side of the arête gives good climbing and a better landing than its twin.
Martin Veale, 1986

60 Punishment 8m E5 6b ★★
The same arête can be climbed on its right-hand side by a harrowing sequence.
John Allen, 1986

The Pinnacle

61 Unfamiliar 9m E7 6c ★★★
The front arête gives a ferocious, powerful yet elegant route. Boulder up the arête to the triangular block, and a slightly easier finish. One of the best hard routes on Stanage and at the top end of the grade.
Robin Barker, 1992

62 Walking the Whippet 8m E3 5b ★
The right-hand arête, gained from boulders on the right, proves to be worthwhile and scary.
John Allen, 1984

PEGASUS WALL
To the right of The Pinnacle is a series of small, steep walls. The first routes are on the smaller faces.

1 Too Cold to be Bold 12m E2 6b
The arête, with a side-runner in *Taurus Crack*.
Keith Sharples, Graham Hoey, Bill Gregory, 1987

2 Taurus Crack 11m VS 4c ★
The flake-crack is a particularly proud line, giving a technical exercise to the swift, and a more challenging lead to the rest.

3 Star Trek 10m E5 6c ★★
A bouldery route which requires careful spotting. From the block on the left, step right and climb the thin flake to the slot and protection. Continue up the wall.
Graham Parkes, Chris Craggs, 1989

4 Klingon 10m E6 7a ★★
Similar to *Star Trek*, but with a harder crux. Climb the thin wall on undercuts to a stretch, or dyno, to the pocket. Finish direct.
Mike Lea, 2000

5 Valhalla 10m VS 5a ★★
The lovely corner-crack is approached from the left via a shorter crack and a heathery ledge.
Wilf White, Chuck Cook, 1948

6 Pegasus Wall 10m VS 4c ★
Just to the right, several thin cracks trend slightly leftwards up the wall. Reach these awkwardly and climb them pleasantly.

7 Pegasus Rib 12m HVS 5a ★
Follow the short crack directly below the angular arête, then climb the arête on its left-hand side by pleasantly exposed moves.
John Allen, Neil Stokes, 1970s

8 Flake Gully 10m D
The well-scratched corner on the left-hand side of the bay has a steep exit.

9 Flake Chimney 10m S
Take the chimney up the right-hand side of the large flake to a narrow exit.

10 Overhanging Wall 12m HVS 5b ★★
A good, varied route. Climb the thin crack to the left end of the capping overhang. Interesting technical moves lead right under this until a swing round to the right allows a finish to be made up the sidewall.
Joe Brown, Slim Sorrell, 1950

11 Crossover 12m E2 5c ★
A counter-line to *Overhanging Wall*. Start just right of the arête below the overhanging nose and gain the obvious ledge. Climb the slabby right-hand rib of the buttress and balance up this to the roof. Traverse left to a flange and swing left around the corner to finish up the shelving wall, without sneaking off to the left.

12 Passover 8m E1 5c
The short, pocketed, right-hand rib of the buttress has a hard, fingery start but an easier finish.
Steve Bancroft, John Allen, Pete Lowe, 1986

Paradise Buttress gives a cool collection of steep, friendly crack pitches in the HS to HVS range. Jugs and gear are often your companions here. Charlotte King on the classic, Paradise Wall, HS 4b (page 304).
Pete O'Donovan

PARADISE BUTTRESSES
One of the most popular buttresses of the plantation area, with a handful of very friendly routes.

13 Parasite 12m HVS 5a ★
Climb into and up the shallow square corner in the arête (crux). Step right and finish directly up the centre of the wall on an assortment of breaks and poor holds.
Chris Craggs, Colin Binks, 1981

14 Paradise Arête 12m VS 4c ★★
A slightly harder companion to *Paradise Wall*, with more open climbing. Climb the thin crack until it fizzles out. A difficult move up is followed by a shuffle left to a small ledge. Climb the arête directly to the top. Can feel scary for the short.

15 Paradise Wall 12m HS 4b ★★★
A classic and compelling line up the centre of the buttress. Climb the parallel cracks until they merge and take the straight crack to the top. A great, steep route for the grade.
⊙ page 277

16 Milton's Meander 18m VS 4c ★★
A great way to cross the wall at a very reasonable grade. Follow *Paradise Wall* until it is possible to hand-traverse the deep break (all very airy) to finish up the right arête.
Alan Clarke, Les Gillott, 1960s

17 Comet 14m E3 5c ★
Hard scary pocket-pulling up the wall 1m to the right of the cracks (side-runner) leads to some gear in the break. Finish up the delicate, open, upper wall in the same line.
Jonathan Wyatt (solo), 1985

18 Comus 14m E4 6a ★★
A fierce bit of cranking through the overlap on blind pockets, one of which contains a slot for a micro-cam. Once the horizontal break is reached, the upper difficulties can be savoured in relative safety.
Martin Berzins (solo), 1979

19 Paradise Crack 14m S 4a ★★
A nice, hefty challenge with enjoyable, wide-crack climbing. Ascend the major crack to a tricky finish.

20 Sand Gully 14m D ★
The gully-cum-corner. Start either side of the small pinnacle and climb to a ledge. Continue up the corner above using the two cracks.

21 Silica 12m E2 5c ★★
A great little route, where an abrupt transition from strenuous to delicate can cause some trouble. Use the flake to heave over the overhang. Once established, continue precariously and calmly, using the right arête.
John Fleming, John Street, 1977

22 Sand Crack 12m S 4a ★
Quite a tough challenge. To the right is a crack in a corner. Climb this steeply passing the holly bush and finishing up a sandy groove.

Paradise Buttress

BILLIARD BUTTRESS

The routes on the slabby front face are necessary ticks for the Stanage climber, where you will most likely wish the pockets were a bit deeper, your footwork a bit better.

23 Curved Crack 12m HS 4b ★
The crack on the left.

24 Billiard Buttress 22m HVS 5a ★★
A fine and varied line up the left-hand side of the buttress. The bulging wall is climbed boldly on pockets to the break. Step left and climb the delicate arête, finishing up the slab.
Al Parker, Paul Nunn, Bob Brayshaw, 1959

25 Pot Black 22m E2 5b ★★
A great route, bold but mild for the grade. Follow *Billiard Buttress* to the break. Balance up the slab above, continuing directly into a shallow groove to easier rock.
Giles Barker, John Oldroyd, 1976

26 Millsom's Minion 24m E1 5b ★★★
Glorious! Step off the block and make bold moves up to the break. Traverse right then move up delicately rightwards, then back left, via a large shallow pocket to gain a break above. Step left into a scoop and easier finish.
Len Millsom, 1962

27 In-Off 22m E3 5c ★★
An excellent route which gives a good direct way up the face. Climb to the left edge of the overlap. Move rightwards over it on pockets and up to the horizontal break. From here, grope left into a shallow scoop, then finish more easily.
Steve Bancroft, Sue Bird, Adrian Hughes, 1988

28 A Problem of Coagulation
22m E3 5c ★
Climb over the first bulge of *Cue* onto a ramp and make a bold swing onto a flake on the face. Continue until just short of a blunt arête and move up the flat wall.
Gary Gibson (solo), 1982

29 Cue 23m HVS 5b ★★
Good value at the grade, with some exposed, burly climbing. Enter and climb the slanting chimney to the overlap. Hand-traverse left below the overhang until a steep pull gains access to a thin hanging crack. Finish up this.
Bob Brayshaw, Al Parker, 1959

30 Left Pool Crack 8m D
The left-hand crack is just sufficiently independent to be recorded as a separate route.

31 Pool Crack 8m VD
The wider right-hand crack set in a corner.

WALL BUTTRESS
A fine buttress with a good spread of classics across the grades.

32 Boys Will Be Boys 8m E6 6c ★★
A hard and brilliant route, with bouldery and unobvious climbing. Gain the low ledge and follow the wall above, with crux moves to gain the pocket.
John Allen (solo), 1986

33 Capstone Chimney 10m S 4a
The obvious cleft capped by a huge chockstone is a real struggle. VS 4c outside.

34 Badly Bitten 10m E4 6a ★
A tough, pushy route. Climb past the left-hand end of the overlap to reach a horizontal break. Step left above the overlap and climb the rib to reach an obvious 'Thank God' pebble. Using this, gain the next break and finish up the centre of the final wall.
Paul Pepperday, Chris Hale, 1984

35 Moribund 12m E3 5c ★★
A good hard classic, with some fairly intimidating climbing. Climb to the break, then swing right into the centre of the face. Harrowing moves past a poor pocket lead to another horizontal break. A hard pull leads to an excellent flake on the left and easier ground.
Steve Bancroft, Nick Stokes, Pete Lowe, 1980

36 Wall Buttress 12m HVS 5a ★★
A big and fairly butch route demanding a 'get stuck in' approach. Climb either the rightward-slanting flakes on the left or the jamming crack on the right, to gain the offwidth crack in the upper face. Once established, continue to an awkward exit or step left to an easier finish.
Frank Elliott, Harry Dover, Gilbert Ellis, 1930

37 Walrus Butter/Direct Loss 14m E5 6b ★
Climb the wall by a hard dynamic move from pebbles (side-runner, E4 6b to here). At the break, go right and continue up the thin crack above, before moving rightwards (hand placed peg) to finish up the blunt arête.
Paul Mitchell / John Allen, Martin Veale, Steve Bancroft, 1986

38 Improbability Drive 12m E3 6b ★
A fierce and sharp pebble-puller with a hard crux between the breaks. Finish up *Namenlos*.
John Hart, 1978

39 Namenlos 14m E1 5a ★★
A bold route requiring more faith in the feet than ferocity in the fingers. Climb the crack to a ledge. Move left and climb into a narrow ramp-line. Ascend this delicately and finish up the chimney behind the block. Hidden cams under the overlap left of the ramp give welcome security. ◐ opposite page
Joe Brown, Wilf White, 1950

Namenlos, E1 5a (opposite page), is one of those gritstone delights that returns a sense of boldness yet without being too dangerous. Lovely technical moves, requiring trust in smears, with good gear just below you, are the magic ingredients in this Joe Brown gem. 📷 Steve Clegg

40 August Arête 14m HVS 5b ★★
A sweet little route, with a very 'gritstone' feel. Climb the slanting crack to a ledge. Move right and gain the arête by an awkward move. Continue up the arête on rounded holds.
Al Parker, Peter Bamfield, 1959

41 Telli 10m E3 6a ★
Neat, technical moves and straightforward protection make this a popular choice. Climb the centre of the lower slab to the break. Struggle into a standing position, then make exciting, reach-dependant moves to the top.
Steve Bancroft, Robert Carey, Dave Humphries, 1978

42 Rib Chimney 13m VD ★
The black cleft left of the arête.

43 Calvary 18m E4 6a ★★★
The finest E4 on the crag; steep, sustained and intimidating, although perfectly manageable by the competent. Start up the steep crack then hand-traverse left to a difficult move to gain a friable black flake. Go up this and move left to climb the shallow scoop to a ledge near the arête. Place small protection in the break then crimp for all you're worth up the bulging headwall directly. Magnificent!
Mike Simpkins, John Gosling (2pts), 1970. FFA Gabe Regan, 1976

44 Defying Destiny 18m E6 6b ★★
A superb but serious line. Climb the initial crack to a move right and gain the next break with difficulty. Dubious cams, in flared placements to the left, protect moves on tiny brittle flakes, heading for the thin finishing crack.
Bill Turner, Iain Edwards, 1982

45 Chockstone Chimney 12m HVD 3c ★
The chimney. A good line: a beautiful grunt.

46 Cleft Wall Route 1 12m HS 4b ★★
A good traditional exercise. Follow the leftwards-zigging crack all the way to a final wide section.

47 Early Starter 12m E1 5b
Start up the crack in the middle of the wall and continue up the wide crack. Finish up the wall above on sloping holds.
Chris Craggs, Dave Spencer, 1988

48 Cleft Wall Route 2 12m VS 5a ★
Just to the right is a straight crack that runs the full height of this part of the buttress. Follow it throughout, with sustained interest.

49 Ritornel 12m HVS 5a ★
To the right is a thin crack in a rightwards-sloping groove. Follow this to a ledge at 5m. Move up and right to the centre of the wall and traverse right to the arête to finish.
Al Parker, R Stevens, 1972

UNCONQUERABLES BUTTRESSES

The next buttress is gritstone royalty, the throne to two of the country's finest climbs, the mighty Unconquerables. Steep and steeped in history, these climbs, and especially the *Right*, could be among the finest hours in a climber's career, the heart of the gritstone experience.

50 Little Unconquerable 12m HVS 5a ★
The short, wide, steep crack on the left. Start from the platform. Enter the overhanging crack with difficulty and finish with urgency. Thought by some to be the hardest of the trio.
Joe Brown, Wilf White, 1953

51 The Left Unconquerable 16m E1 5b ★★★
Brilliant steep climbing, with perfect protection and a distinct crux. Climb the crack to reach the horizontal break that runs across the buttress. The next moves up and left are the crux to reach monster buckets leading to the top.
Joe Brown, Wilf White, 1949

52 Vanquished 16m E5 6b ★
Follow *The Left Unconquerable* to the good break just below its crux. Hand-traverse right and climb straight up the wall past poor breaks and a small pocket.
Tony Ryan, Gary Ryan, 1988

53 The Right Unconquerable 16m HVS 5a ★★★
Perhaps the most celebrated route on grit, and not without reason. A superb natural line is combined with arm-busting, well-protected climbing, with a generous dash of legend thrown in for good measure. From the short crack, gain and follow the flyaway flake in a spectacular position, all the way to the capstone. A fraught, belly-roll grovel (for most people) onto the holdless top awaits. ◐ page 3
Joe Brown, Wilf White, 1949

54 Monday Blue 16m E2 5b ★
Climb the slabby right arête of the front face without recourse to the right-hand side of the arête. Finish over the final overhang.
Ernie Marshall, Nick Longland, 1981

55 Curving Chimney 15m VD ★★
The sweeping, widening cleft to the right is a great journey back in time. Enter the narrow chimney and climb towards the light.

56 Curving Buttress 16m E2 5b ★
Climb the blunt arête and make committing moves up and rightwards to gain a good ledge in the centre of the wall. Continue above to a narrow ledge and pull over the final bulge to finish. The direct finish is a similar grade.
Eric Byne, 1930s. Direct, Pete O'Donovan, Chris Craggs, 1993

STANAGE POPULAR

OS Grid Ref: SK 244 837 to SK 246 834
Altitude: 400m

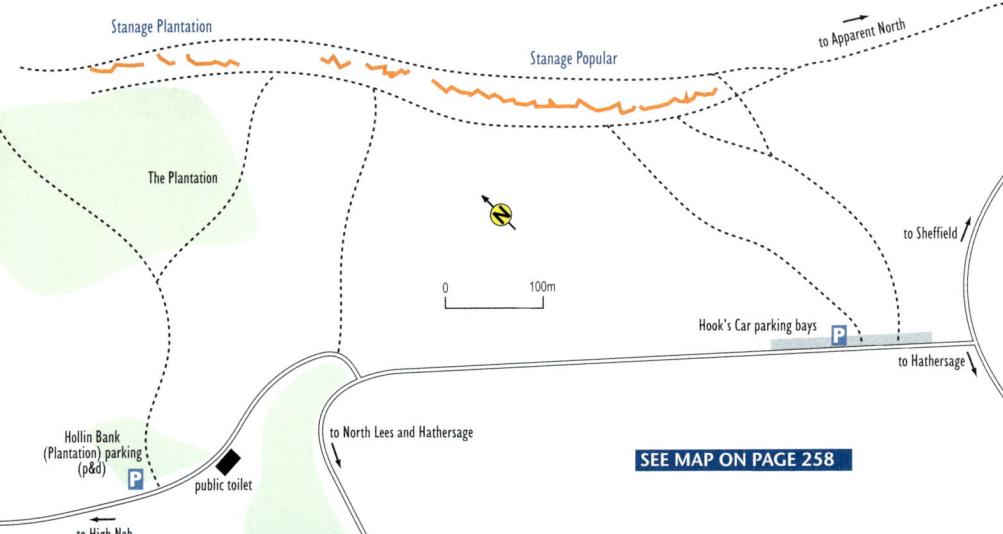

Stanage Popular provides 500 metres of the finest gritstone where hundreds of classic routes jostle shoulder-to-shoulder for attention. It's all just so brilliant. The rock is always clean and quick drying. It can get busy, especially towards the right-hand end.

Approach: Park in parking bays at Hook's Car (a contributions box is cemented into the wall). Follow paths uphill and along to your chosen buttress. The left-hand end can also be approached from the Plantation (Hollin Bank, p&d) parking in a similar time.

ACCESS: Seasonal restrictions for nesting birds may occur anywhere along the edge. BMC signs will be in place to mark out the affected areas. Please respect these by simply moving on to an unrestricted area to climb.

DOVER'S WALL AREA
The Popular End starts with some shorter buttresses. The routes are highly enjoyable, steep and usually well-protected, with the advantage that it is possible to rattle them all off in a short space of time.

1 Bumbler's Arête 7m Mod
The blunt, nose-shaped arête.

2 Beady Eye 6m VS 5a ★
Either side of the square arête, but slightly harder from the right.
Dave Gregory, John Street, 1993

Stanage Popular | 311

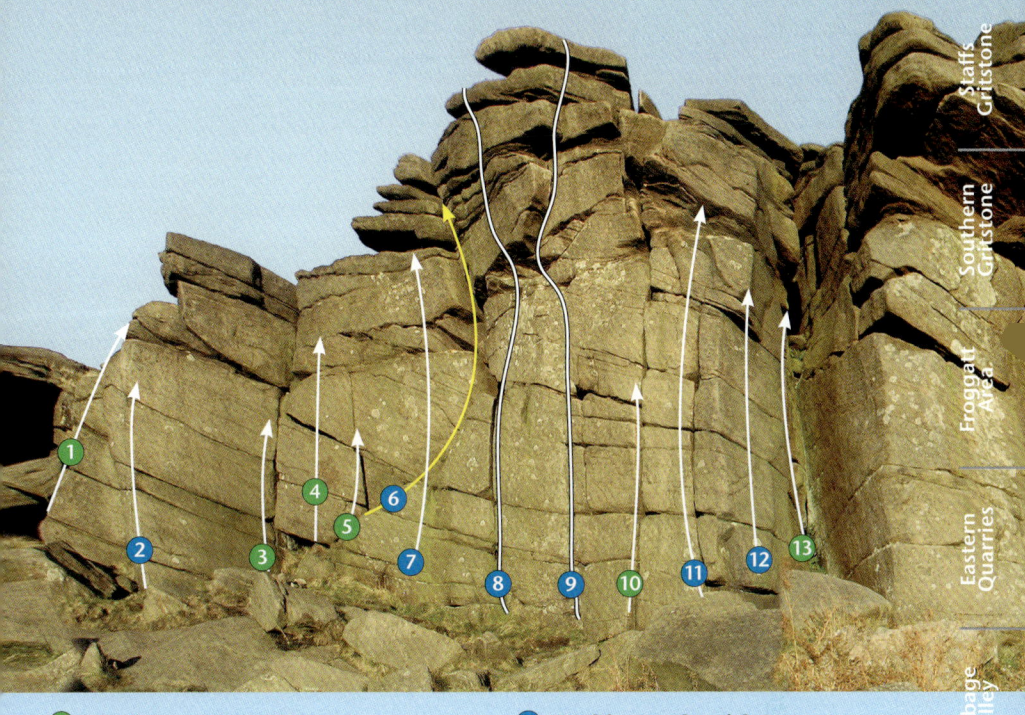

3 Newhaven 7m HD ★
The corner is an enjoyable pitch, with great romping holds all the way.

4 Ramsgate 7m S 4b
The wall 1m right of the corner is pleasant.
Chris Craggs, 1996

5 Dieppe 7m S 4b
From the foot of the ramp, climb the left-slanting crack and finish up the steeper wall.
Dave Gregory, John Street, 1992

6 Dover's Wall, Route 3 12m VS 4b
Ascend rightwards up the ramp. Climb the bulging crack to a difficult finish. 🌐 page 313
Les Gillott, Alan Clarke, 1960s

7 Falaise de Douvre 7m VS 4c
Start just right of the foot of the ramp and cross this to climb straight up the bulging wall left of the steep flake-crack of *Dover's Wall, Route 3*.

8 Nothing to do with Dover 12m HVS 5a ★
A pleasantly gymnastic pitch. Tackle the smooth lower wall and stacked bulges above.
Clive Jones (solo), 1978

9 Dover's Wall, Route 2 12m HVS 5a ★
Climb the thin crack to reach an exciting finish up the overhanging flakes in the centre of the face.

10 Dover's Wall, Route 1 12m HS 4b ★★
Well-protected crack climbing. A narrow crack, second from the right, leads to a small projecting tooth of rock at the top of the buttress.
Harry Dover, 1930s

11 Dover's Wall, Route 4 12m VS 4b
Climb the awkward crack immediately left of the right-hand arête of the wall to reach a ledge. Finish over a bulge.

Mississippi Buttress | Balcony Buttress | Agony Buttress | Twin Chimneys Buttress | Wuthering Buttress | Robin Hood's Buttress

12 The Grey Cliffs of ... 12m HVS 5b
Climb the little facet to the left of *Wing Buttress Gully* to a triangular overhang. Go over this and finish up the arête.
Bruce Goodwin, Dave Gregory, 1999

13 Wing Buttress Gully 12m D
The obvious deep cleft is yet another of those classic grit chimneys.

> **WING BUTTRESS**
> Dover's twin with its distinctive wing of grit that plays host to a few unusual routes.

14 On a Wing and Prayer 12m E1 5c ★
Delicately gain the small ledge 3m up the arête (crux). Continue awkwardly over a nose to finish up the sidewall immediately left of the capping roof. Finish at a rocking stone.
Graham Parkes, Chris Craggs, 1996

15 Wing Buttress 12m VS 5b ★
Start on the left-hand wall of the deep cleft at the well-scratched footholds and make delicate moves to better holds. Swing leftwards along a horizontal break. Go around the arête and climb the steep side wall to finish up a short crack.

16 5.9 Finish 12m E1 5b ★★
A brilliant finish to the previous routes. Gain the roof, then cross the overhang rightwards by means of a thin flake and a couple of strange upside-down moves, to a 'beached whale' landing.
Clive Jones, Ray Jardine, 1977

17 Cleft Wing 12m VS 5b ★★
One of Stanage's more bizarre routes. Start as for *Wing Buttress*, then make sketchy moves to reach the flake crack that runs up to the overhang. Face the opposite wall of the wing and, when suitably psyched, fall across the gap, making sure to catch the holds on the other side. Swing around the arête to reach easier climbing. Magic.
Joe Brown, Slim Sorrell, 1953

18 Cleft Wing Superdirect 12m VS 4c ★
Climb up into the back of the gloomy V-shaped groove, take a deep breath, and hand-traverse the overhanging right-hand wall in spectacular fashion. Swing round the arête and finish up *Cleft Wing* with relief.
Bob Brayshaw, 1958

19 Trimming the Beard 12m E3 6a ★
A wild ride. The hanging arête of the wing is gained directly. Layback boldly up the left-hand side of the arête to reach easier rock.
Chris Horsfall (solo), 1989

20 Wing Wall 12m VD 3c
Climb the shelving right-hand edge of the slabby face, that forms the outside of the wing, to reach a ledge with a prominent holly bush. Walk left along the ledge and finish up a wide crack.

Henry Tyndal on the steep, bulging finish of Dover's Wall, Route 3, VS 4b (page 311). The climbs hereabouts may be short, but the rock is fantastic and the joy is in rattling a load of them out in double-quick time.
Niall Grimes

B.A.W.'S AREA
The rock to the right is dominated by the steepness of B.A.W.'s and Verandah Buttresses.

B.A.W.'s Buttress: A projecting buttress containing a classic and unusual HVS, as well as a couple of modern highball desperates. The first climbs are on the short wall on the left.

㉑ The Nays 5m D
The left side of the face, starting with a mantelshelf.
Bruce Goodwin, Dave Gregory, 1999

㉒ Jon's Route 5m S 4a
The centre of the face.
Jon Street, Dave Gregory, 1992

㉓ Eyes 5m VS 4c
The right arête, climbed on its left.
Dave Gregory, Jon Street, 1992

㉔ The Punk 10m VS 4b ★★
An exciting little number with good exposure. The crack in the front face is gained from the gully on the left by a worrying hand-traverse above jagged boulders.
Steve Bancroft, John Allen, Neil Stokes, 1973

㉕ Cemetery Waits 9m E6 6c ★★
A good ground-uppable E6 for talented uberbeasts with lots of pads, or snow (Font 7A+). Powerful, committing bouldering leads up the left side of the lower arête to the break, and an easier finish.
Joe Brown, Tim Hulley, 1995

㉖ Shine On 9m E7 6c ★★★
A modern classic featuring powerful campussing on poor pockets above a worrying landing. These are gained by traversing the thin expanding flake in the roof. Font 7A above a stack of mats.
Robin Barker, 1992

㉗ B.A.W.'s Crawl 10m HVS 5a ★★★
An absolute blast of a route which, although it ascends a steep piece of rock, can only just be described as climbing. Start from a boulder below the centre of the big roof. The object is to install yourself, or at least your feet, in the slot high on the right. Once ensconced, shuffle along the slot until a standing position on the face on the right is achieved. Finish with a long reach and a grin.
Joe Brown, Nat Allen, Don Whillans, 1952

㉘ Punklet 8m E1 6a ★
A tasty micro-route taking the centre of the vertical wall, with fingery bouldering leading to breaks and more open climbing above.
Steve Bancroft, John Allen (both solo), 1976

㉙ Green Chimney 10m VD
The narrow chimney is tricky to enter. Exit through a hole.

Joyous Stanage soloing, where the sun warms the rock just right, where the autumn air cools it off just perfect. To wander the edge, grabbing all those holds, making all those moves, chatting with all those other climbers. Could anything be better? A soloist enjoys Greengrocer Wall, HVS 5c (page 317). Niall Grimes

Pedlar's Buttress: Between the two steeper buttresses is a smaller face with some cool mid-grade testpieces.

30 Pedlar's Rib 10m E1 5c ★★
The elegant arête with a low crux, but then unprotected 5a all the way to a deep horizontal break. Swing rapidly rightwards to finish.
Jim Perrin, 1967

31 Pedlar's Arête 10m HVS 5b ★
Only a little tricky and only a little bold. Climb the flaky scoop to a ledge. Traverse right and finish near *Pedlar's Slab*.

32 Keep Pedalling 10m E2 5c
The rib leads through *Pedlar's Arête* to a rounded finish. It is hard to keep off the more natural routes.
Chris Craggs, Jim Rubery, Dave Spencer, 1991

33 Pedlar's Slab 10m HVS 5c ★★
A classic test of slab knowledge. Follow the smooth slab to better holds and an easier finish.
Barry Pedlar (solo), 1960s

34 Top Block Rock 10m S
The sharp rib.
Bill Taylor, 1992

35 Corner Crack 10m D
The corner.

36 Recess Rib 10m VD
The rib in the back of the recess.
Dave Gregory, Bill Taylor, 1992

Verandah Buttress: The big, steep and stepped buttress holds a good number of routes that will bring a smile to the faces of bicep merchants. Steep, pumpy Extremes force complex ways through the overhanging shelves on the left side, while the right walls hold delicious mid-grade wall-climbs, and one unique lower-grade wrestle.

37 Plastic Dream 10m E3 6a ★
The undercut left arête of the buttress. Once established follow the rest of the arête throughout, tackling the last steep section on the left.
Ed Wood, Colin Banton, Nigel Riddington, 1977

38 Headless Chicken 12m E5 6b ★★
Climb the wall using a line of juggy flakes before stretching up left to the ledge below the obvious worrying flake. Climb the wall just right of this to the top overhang, step left and cross the roof with difficulty. Finish more easily leftwards.
Neil Foster, Steve Hartley, 1994

39 Off With His Head 14m E4 6b ★★★
A steep and exciting journey, taking the best line on the wall. Follow *The Guillotine*, but trend up and left, left of a rock scar to a jug on the lip. An almighty move gains the break under the top roof.
Andy Barker, 1982

40 The Guillotine 14m E3 5c ★★
An exciting and arduous trip. Start in the centre of the overhanging face and climb to a small ledge. Step left and go up to the lip of the first overhang, before swinging right below a prominent scar, to reach a good ledge on the right-hand edge of the buttress. Make a cramped traverse leftwards until just around the arête and surmount the overhang just to the left of the prow.
Ed Drummond, Hamish Green Armitage (1pt), 1971. FFA John Allen and Neil Stokes, 1973

41 The Old Dragon 14m E2 5b ★
Start under the groove on the right-hand side of the overhanging face and climb to a small ledge. Climb the steep groove on better-than-expected holds to reach the ledge on *The Guillotine*. Escape right at E1 or, better, finish up the overhanging crack just to the left.
Bill Birch (1pt), 1968. FFA John Allen, Neil Stokes, 1973

42 Fit as a Butcher's Dog 12m E1 5c
Do battle with the hideous meat-eating roof-crack to reach the centre of the shelf. Climb over the smaller overhang and finish with a long reach.
Graham Parkes, Chris Craggs, 1997

43 Verandah Buttress 14m HVD 5b ★★
A uniquely graded route, with a desperate grovel leading to more conventional climbing. The sloping shelf of the verandah is gained by devious manoeuvres (crux). From the scoop walk left to finish up the exposed arête of the buttress.

44 Butcher Crack 12m HVS 5b ★
A well-protected, meaty route stretching up the steep wall. Start as for *Verandah Buttress* to reach the shelf. From there climb directly to the top by two short cracks and long stretches.
Peter Biven, 1954

45 Greengrocer Wall 10m HVS 5c ★★
The wall to the left of the corner. A fierce, bouldery start, using a thin crack, leads to easier climbing up the steep wall. page 315
Ray Burgess, 1950s

46 Verandah Crack 8m VD
The left-hand of the twin cracks in the angle.

47 Verandah Wall 10m VS 4c
The steep wall to the right of the corner is climbed on a series of rounded holds. Reachy.

48 Cocktails 10m VS 4c ★
The rounded rib in the centre of the wall proves to be juggy and excellent. Start from the cutaway and trend leftwards over the initial bulges before continuing directly.
Dave Gregory, John Street, 1993

49 Verandah Pillar 8m HS 4b ★★
Brilliant fun. Climb the left-facing flakyness to a tricky finish.
Dick Brown, Eric Byne, 1951

50 The Confectioner 10m VS 5a ★★
A sweet climb taking the short wall on the right, via a shallow niche, a couple of long reaches and a rounded exit.
Bob Brayshaw, Al Parker, 1959

Verandah Buttress

MARTELLO AREA

Take a deep breath. From here on, there is not going to be a gap in the quality for 400 metres.

Roundabout Buttress: The first climbs are to be found on the fine rounded joys of Martello Buttress.

51 Intermediate Buttress 10m S 4a ★
The left edge of the face of the tower is climbed passing a square flake to a fairly rounded finish, which requires some care.

52 Jaygo's Pipe 10m HVS 5a
Start as for the next climb and, after a couple of pulls, continue up past rounded breaks.
Bruce Goodwin, John Street, 1994

53 The Nose 10m VS 4b ★★
A good climb with a muscular start and a pensive finish. Starting low at the blunt rib, swing up to deep cracks, then traverse rightwards, on the two lowest breaks to the arête. A rounded pull over a bulge is tricky to protect, but better holds and runners arrive immediately.
Joe Brown, Don Whillans, 1954

54 Second Wind 10m HVS 5c ★
A good climb with a bouldery start, and a notable depression in the ground below. Traverse the low break leftwards and pull up to gain the short crack. Continue up the right side of the arête to the top.
Tony Ryan (solo), 1986

55 Swings 12m HVS 6a ★
A sweet, direct way up the wall with a bouldery start. From the centre of the face move up past a very vague ramp, with a fingery crux gaining a deep pocket. Continue to the shallow groove, which is followed enjoyably to, and over, the capping roof.
Tony Walker (solo), 1983

56 Little Tower 8m VS 4c
A surprisingly tough route up the square arête. Long reaches are required between measly breaks with scant protection before a deep horizontal is reached and an easier finish.
Dick Brown, 1951

Martello Buttress: To the right is a broad tapering buttress, with great big rounded holds all over it.

57 Zel 12m VS 4c
Follow *Byne's Route* to the start of the traverse and climb the wall, trending leftwards to finish up the left-hand arête of the face.
Gary Gibson, 1979

58 Byne's Route 15m HS 4b ★★
A cracking route, with some sloping action to add to the excitement, which saunters stylishly up and right across the fine wall. Start round to the left of the buttress and climb into a recess. Traverse right to a short crack and continue in a direct diagonal line to the top corner of the wall and a rounded finish.
Eric Byne, Clifford Moyer, 1930s

Roundabout Buttress   Martello Buttress

59 Another Game of Bowls Sir Walter?
15m E1 5b ★
An enjoyable route for those comfortable on rounded holds, and a good lesson for those who aren't. To the left of the start of *Martello Buttress* is a short flake just right of the arête. Climb this to its end, then make troublesome moves to better holds. Continue steeply, keeping right of the upper arête throughout.
Chris Craggs, Brian Rossiter, 1992

60 The Scoop 15m HVS 5a ★★★
A great route, with continually demanding climbing on big, open holds; an absolute delight. Start in the middle of the buttress and make steep and awkward moves on the left or right of the jammed block – leaning in every direction – onto a ledge. Move up into a shallow scoop, where a long move left reaches rounded breaks which lead to the top. The original starts of *The Scoop* and *Martello Buttress* have been swapped to give more balanced routes.
Rodney Wilson, Al Parker, 1959

61 Martello Buttress 15m VS 4c ★★★
The original route of the buttress has a real sense of class about it. Start at the bottom right-hand corner of the buttress at a projecting tooth of rock. Step off this and pull steeply up and left to a ledge. Continue, trending left and up, to a good ledge and an impressive finish up the left-hand side of the final arête.
Fergus Graham, 1922

62 Bloodshot 15m E3 5c ★
From *Martello Buttress*, trend up and right into a shallow, leaning corner and climb the overhang using spaced and rounded holds, via a harrowing sequence of reaches. Finish up the easier arête on the left.
Gabe Regan, John Regan, Steve Webster, 1979

63 Martello Cracks 10m M ★★
A cracking voyage up the parallel cracks in the big corner, that will bring a smile to beginners and tigers alike.

Saliva Buttress: A steep buttress sits just right of the deep crack.

64 Phlegethoa 12m E1 5c ★
A fierce start to the arête, requiring a bit of bouldering power and/or a long reach. From the blocks under the roof, reach right, aiming for a shallow groove just right of the arête. Gain this, then move up to gain and follow the arête with ease.
Jim Perrin, 1967

Martello Buttress

Stanage Popular

65 Fading Star 12m E2 6a ★★
Technical maestros and funky gibbons alike will enjoy this well-positioned trip up the buttress. Start down and right from *Phlegethoa* and make savage moves from the arête up and right to a sidepull, which leads to a shallow groove and roof above. Move right, and make absurdly technical moves onto the upper face, using a shamefully long reach. Finish relatively easily.
Gary Gibson, 1979

66 Saliva 14m E1 5b ★★
A brilliant, thoughtful and committing route. The moves on the traverse are unprotected, but hand and footholds just keep coming, so it never feels that bad. Start by climbing a thin crack with some difficulty, until it is possible to traverse leftwards to the arête; finish up this.
Peter Biven, 1955

67 Ashes 12m E3 5c ★★
Start as for *Saliva*, then make a series of difficult and unprotectable moves directly up the wall above to reach the security of a large horizontal break (crux) and protection. From here, a series of satisfying, rounded reaches lead to the top.
John Fleming, John Street, 1981

68 Devil's Chimney 12m VD ★★
An atmospheric delve into the beating heart of the crag.

69 Step-Ladder Crack 14m VS 5a ★★
Despite its good gear and solid, friendly jams, this route is still guaranteed to get the blood pumping. From the pedestal on the left, make a difficult stride right to the thin crack. Climb this and move right to a deeper flake-crack, which is followed by a move right again to finish up the rib, or shallow cracks just right. A direct start followed by a direct finish makes the route a fierce HVS 5c.
Ted Howard, 1950s

70 Hell Crack 12m VS 4c ★★★
A great route – your archetypal gritstone VS tussle, with bazooka hand-jamming on some of the roughest, toughest rock on the cliff. The black bulging crack is taken directly.
Eric Byne, Clifford Moyer, 1930s

71 Heaven Crack 10m VD ★★★
Pure, unadulterated gritstone joy. The inviting flake-crack at the lower end of the descent gully is climbed by a laybacking jug fest to a final delicate move. ⊙ opposite page

Saliva Buttress | Heaven Buttress

To feel the holds on Heaven Crack, VD (opposite page), really is one of the most special experiences on gritstone. The line is beautiful, the climbing is quick and straightforward. For many climbers wandering below, its allure is almost impossible to resist Aide Jebb enjoying its delights. 📷 Niall Grimes

MISSISSIPPI BUTTRESS

This proud bastion is one of the greatest buttresses on the whole of Stanage, with steep, juggy climbs on the best of grit. Some of the routes in the VS to E1 category are the very definition of what three star routes should be, but there's quality here through all the grades.

1 Acheron 16m E1 5b ★

An exciting route which climbs the left-hand arête, starting up a short crack.
Jim Perrin, R Bowker, 1967

2 The Louisiana Rib 18m VS 4c ★★

A quality route, finding a sneaky way up the narrow buttress. Climb the short crack of *Acheron* until a delicate traverse rightwards leads to the arête. Climb this on its left for 3m to a move leftwards on to the front face to finish.
Dick Brown, 1950

3 Finger Licking Good 18m HVS 5a ★

Climb the middle of the wall on a series of perfectly spaced, positive crimps.
Graham Parkes, Chris Craggs, 1998

4 Mississippi Chimney 18m VD ★★

A fine blocky scramble up the accommodating cleft. The chimney is entered by a short difficult crack and followed more easily.
JW Puttrell, 1890s

5 African Herbs 18m E3 5c

Follow *Mississippi Chimney* to half-height then move rightwards to attack the bold wall and easier rib above. No stars, but you know it's going to be good.
Al Rouse, Richard Hazsko, 1985

6 Dark Continent 20m E1 5c ★★★

A sublime route, with exposed, demanding moves. Cross the overhang by a crack to join *Congo Corner* and follow it left to the end of its traverse. The wall directly above this point is climbed with a very long reach (and a big cam). Move slightly left, then finish directly.
Phil Burke, John Yates, 1978

7 Congo Corner 24m HVS 5b ★★★

A sensational route with continually steep and interesting climbing. The thin crack is hard to start. Follow this then skirt the overhang leftwards until a move up enables a second traverse line to be reached. Follow this back rightwards to the arête and mantel onto a ledge. From this, a precarious move leads to a good horn, and a sensational finish.
Pete Biven, Trevor Peck, 1954

8 The Link 22m E1 5b ★★★

An excellent direct on *Congo Corner*, which tackles the flake crack through the roof to join the original at its mantel. ⊙ opposite page
Chris Craggs, 1974

Mississippi Buttress

It's as juggy as hell, which is just as well. Mike Hutton getting to grips with some steep terrain on The Link, E1 5b (opposite page). The quality of the rock on Mississippi Buttress is fabulous, making all the routes gems at the grade. 📷 David Simmonite

Stanage Popular

9 The Mersey Variant 22m E2 5c ★
A worthwhile eliminate line starting up the initial stacked roofs between the two cracks to reach a horizontal break. Climb up and left, with difficulty, before continuing up the smooth slab and juggy breaks to the top.
Trevor Pilling, Ian Carr, 1980

10 The Mississippi Buttress Direct
22m VS 4c ★★★
One of the great climbs on gritstone, the definition of Stanage quality, with more jugs, bulges and gear than you can shake a stick at. Gain and follow the leftward-trending flake-line that splits the centre of the buttress.
Albert Hargreaves, Roy Horsman (TR), 1929

11 Mississippi Variant 22m HVS 5a ★★
A classy route following a strong line. Start as for the *Direct*, and above the mid-height bulge, step out right to reach a flake. Climb this to an overhang and make a difficult move out right to gain a small ledge and an easy finish.
○ opposite page
Bernard Simmonds, 1930s

12 Mississippi Variant Direct
22m E1 5b ★★
Even better than the *Variant*, and with a distinct crux. Climb a groove and bulge to reach a good ledge. From the left-hand end of this step awkwardly up and left to reach a sloping ledge, and join *Mississippi Variant*.
Bill Birch, T Norcliffe, 1968

13 Stanleyville 22m E4 5c ★★
A harrowing lead with worrying pro. From the ledge on *Variant Direct*, make committing moves to gain a vague horizontal break and a crucial mantelshelf. Continue trending left to finish over the overhang above the *Variant*.
John Allen, Neil Stokes, Steve Bancroft, 1973

14 Morrison's Redoubt 18m E1 5b ★★
An excellent climb, with a worrying start up the centre of the smooth wall. Climb onto a block and, with little in the way of protection, teeter leftwards up the wall (crux) to reach a good horizontal slot and bomber gear. Continue more easily up a very short vertical crack then follow a wider crack to a steep finish.
Don Morrison, 1960s

15 Amazon Crack 12m S 4a ★★
A great little warm up for those biceps. The undercut flaky crack is hardest at the start, and soon eases.

16 Fallen Pillar Chimney 10m VD
The deep chimney gives an archetypal grovel.

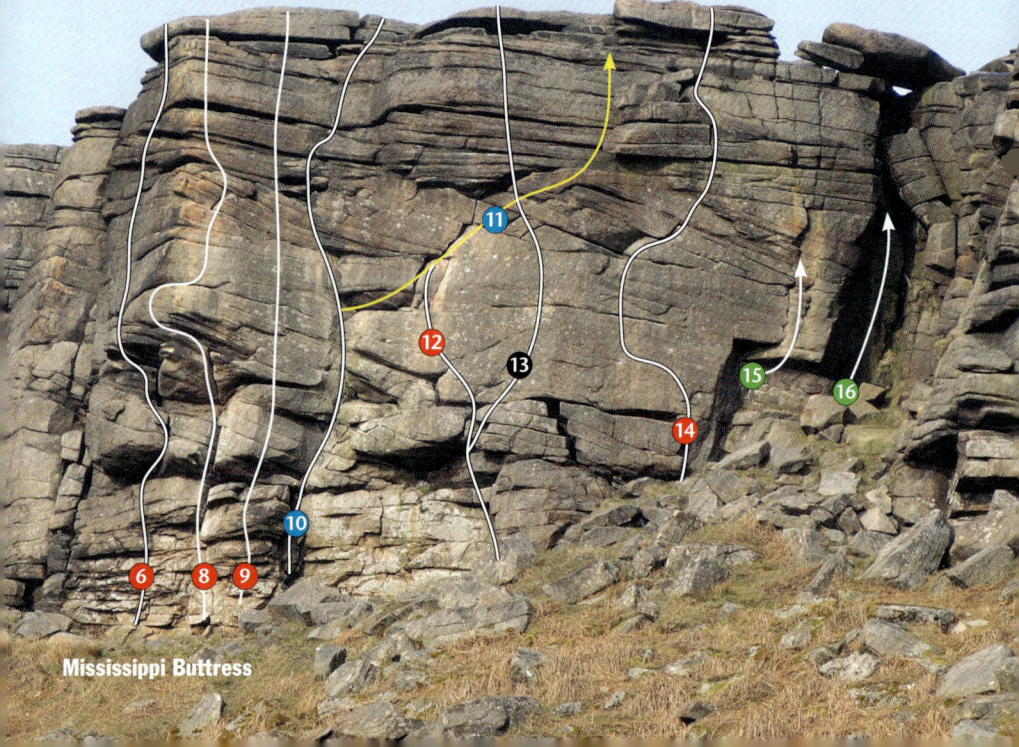
Mississippi Buttress

The holds are big, but rounded enough that they never feel like jugs. Chris Hardy putting his foot down to cover the steep and committing crux of Mississippi Variant, HVS 5a (opposite page). 📷 Niall Grimes

BALCONY BUTTRESS AREA
The next feature is a fine tall buttress containing a ledge, 'The Balcony', at half-height.

17 Fairy Castle Crack 10m HD
Ascend the crack to the right of the chimney, passing around the right-hand edge of a protruding square block with some difficulty.

18 Fairy Chimney 10m D
The chimney is blocked at mid-height by a protruding rib which can be passed on either side.

19 Balcony Climb 12m S 4b ★
Struggle into the niche, then follow the sustained, slanting, left-hand crack to the top.
Fred Piggott & friends, c1922

20 Balcony Cracks 14m S 4a ★
Gain the first, then the second niche, then follow the left-hand arête and pull awkwardly over the bulge to finish directly via a series of well-positioned shallow flake cracks.

21 Exit Stage Left 20m E1 5b ★
Climb over the roof to ledges. Tackle the next bulges directly, then finish up the wall around to the left of the flake of *Balcony Buttress*.
Chris Craggs, Dave Spencer, 1993

22 Centre Stage 18m HVS 5a ★★
A great climb, despite an uninspiring line. Cross the awkward initial bulges then head straight up the face. From the ledge pull powerfully through the roof to finish at a notch.
Chris Craggs, Dave Spencer, 1993

23 Balcony Buttress 20m S 4a ★★★
A fine, old-style route with a spectacular finale. Start at the flat ledge and trend up to reach a wide crack. Climb this to the ledge, then traverse to the left edge of the buttress and finish via a swift layback up the flake on the arête.
Lewis Coxon, Cyril Ward, Rice Kemper Evans, 1922

24 The Flue 14m VD
Climb the straight left-hand crack to a ledge and continue up an awkward chimney.

25 Scoop Crack 14m HS 4b ★
Climb a left-facing right-hand corner crack to a ledge and the undercut continuation crack above, which is awkward to start. Crucial hidden holds tame the crux.

26 Rib and Face 12m VS 4c
Climb the narrow face, or broad rib, to a ledge and continue up the broader face above.
Mike Snell (solo), 1993

Balcony Buttress

27 Balcony Corner 8m VD
Move up to the left-facing corner and follow this, with particularly pressing moves to pass the overhang.

28 Upanover Crack 8m S 4b
Climb the straight crack, with the overhang at one-third height providing all the fun.

29 M Route 10m VS 4c
Climb the left arête of the buttress on its left (bold), finishing rightwards under the fang.
Reg Pillinger, 1952

30 N Route 10m VS 4b ★
Tricky moves gain the shallow, protectionless groove on the front face. Follow this, until it eases just below the top.

31 Agony Crack 10m HVS 5a ★★
A traditional gritstone grinder for meatheads, or a fluffy laybacking delight for intellectuals. Climb the crack to an undercut ledge then attack the well-named continuation crack above.
Len Chapman, Bernard Simonds, 1940

32 Big Dave's Wall 10m E3 6a
The slab, roof and wall between the two cracks provide a few thin moves, with a runner in *Agony Crack* to protect the tough overhang.
Percy Bishton, David Simmonite, 1996

33 Thrombosis 10m VS 5a ★
The friendly-looking crack turns out to be a bit of a trial, especially at the rounded top-out. Climb a short corner-crack to gain and climb the steep, narrow left-hand crack.
Don Morrison, 1960s

34 Rigor Mortis 12m VS 4b ★
The even friendlier-looking right-hand crack is not much easier. Start as for *Thrombosis* then climb the wider right-hand crack, to finish up the arête. Bold, in its own little way.
Don Morrison, 1960s

35 Paralysis 12m VS 4c
The difficult to protect rounded scoop leads to a ledge. The wall above is much more open and better protected.
Don Morrison, 1960s

36 Boris the Bold 10m HVS 5a
The wall to the right provides a predictable eliminate, with a somewhat scary, bouldery start and a reachy top.
Chris Gilbert, Dave Woolgar, 1985

Twin Chimneys Descent: To the right, easy rocks lead into the cave, although the bottom crack is bloody awkward and it's probably worth taking some care on the polished rock.

Agony Buttress

TWIN CHIMNEYS BUTTRESS

A fine buttress with a good collocation of climbs, mainly in the lower grades.

37 Via Roof Route 8m HVS 5b ★
A spectacular bit of roof-work. Climb the thin awkward crack in the slab to gain the cave. From a stance, gain flakes in the roof and swing rightwards to the arête where awkward moves lead to an airy finish up the wall above.
Eric Byne, Charles Ashbury, 1951

38 Don't Bark, Bite 18m E2 5c ★
Pushy roof climbing. Climb the polished slab right of the last route then tackle the thin cracks in the roof and follow these leftwards to a finish up the hanging left-hand arête.
Gary Gibson, 1980

39 Crack and Cave 18m VD ★★
A delightful route, especially if you like to jam. Climb the wide crack into the cave then make a tricky traverse rightwards to finish as for *Twin Chimneys Buttress*.
Eric Byne, Charles Ashbury, 1950

40 Twin Chimneys Buttress 18m VS 4c ★★
The blunt arête has steady, balancy climbing, and it's best not to rush it. Follow the arête from the left to a detached block. Step off this onto better holds and flakes to finish.
Lewis Coxon, 1922

41 Lucy's Joy 14m E1 5b
Climb the steep slab to the mid-height bulge. Pull over the right-hand end of this and continue up the narrower buttress above.
Brue Godwin, Guy Fox-Kelly, Alan Cowburn, 1995

42 Left Twin Chimney 14m D ★★
An enjoyable, roomy chimney climb, taking the left-hand branch of the prominent Y-shaped chimney system.
JW Puttrell, c1900

43 Right Twin Chimney 10m VD ★★
Go pleasantly up the rib just right of the chimney (starting the chimney directly is easier and no less pleasant) and continue up the chimney as it leans away to the right.
JW Puttrell, c1900

44 Bobsnob 14m E1 5a
An enjoyable solo, even if it does feel a little artificial. Climb the slab keeping a couple of metres right of the wide crack.
Chris Craggs, 1983

45 Little John's Step 25m S 4b ★
A rambling expedition with some pleasant moves and situations. Start at the large detached block that stands in front of the cliff and pull leftwards over the initial roof (crux), to climb the left-hand side of its sharp outside edge. Then cross the slab behind leftwards and work your way up and left to a choice of finishes.

There often seems little respite from the steepness along this part of Stanage, especially in the mid grades. Luckily, great holds are usually your passport through these hostile lands. John Smith feeling the space on Harding's Superdirect Finish to Cave Innominate, HVS 5a (page 333). 📷 Paul Evans

46 Little Slab 12m S
Start up a blunt rib to an easy finish.
John Street, Dave Gregory, 1992

47 Awl 12m HVD ★
The left-hand arête of the buttress finishing up the face on the left.
John Street, Bruce Goodwin, 1992

48 Bean 15m VS 4c
The narrow slabby wall just to the right, finishing over a small overhang via a thin crack.
Bruce Goodwin, John Street, 1992

49 Dun 15m HS
The blunt left-hand arête of the central groove. Finish as for the previous route.
John Street, Bruce Goodwin, 1992

50 Bee 12m D ★
The central groove proves to be a pleasant beginner's route.
John Street, Bruce Goodwin, 1992

51 Four 12m VS 4c ★
Climb just right of the right-hand arête of the central groove and continue up the wall using flakes to reach a ledge. The upper arête is climbed over a couple of small overlaps and can be started on the left or the right.
Bruce Goodwin, John Street, 1992

WUTHERING BUTTRESS
The fine stepped, undercut and cleft buttress to the right holds many fine climbs, and one of the best E2s on the edge.

Asp Descent: The stepped gully behind *Wuthering* provides an easy descent from the cliff top and from the ledge where *Wuthering* and *The Asp* finish.

52 The Asp 10m E3 6a ★★★
A classic pitch, a must for the aspiring E3 leader, taking the slim crack in the steep wall. Enigmatic moves gain the initial pocket, from where sustained finger-jamming/laybacking leads to an easier, bolder finish.
Ed Drummond, John Young, 1975

53 Boc No Buttress 14m E5 6a ★★
A well-positioned climb that has just enough protection. Climb *The Asp* until it is possible to make a thin traverse out to the right along a line of poor pockets to reach a small ledge on the arête. When suitably composed, climb the arête, which is daunting, but all there.
Steve Bancroft, Nick Stokes, Pete Lowe, 1979.

Wuthering Buttress

Dave Hinton, with the trouser-splitting crux of Wuthering, E2 5b (page 332), behind him. Now, in the middle of that great big wall, he can savour the position of one of the finest spots on Stanage. The holds here are rounded but good; the protection is limited, but there's enough to keep you safe. Few people who have been here will look at this photo without a warm smile on their face. 📷 Paul Evans

54 Wuthering 20m E2 5b ★★★
An elegant climb, providing one of Stanage's best experiences, with unlikely moves covering unlikely ground at a reasonable grade. Climb the chimney and place high protection around a chockstone. Climb back down, then bridge out along the lowest line of holds to make a groin-busting move to gain the arête. Swing round onto the front face and traverse delicately left and up to a welcome gear slot. Now, either climb the groove above direct, or trend up and left on flakes to the top. ⓘ page 331
Ed Drummond, Hamish Green Armitage, 1973

55 Dithering Frights 18m E2 5b ★
Follow *Wuthering* to the runners in the centre of the slab then reverse back to a position just left of the right-hand arête. Climb straight up the slab on poor pockets and finish up the well-positioned left-hand edge of the wall.
Chris Craggs, Graham Parkes, Dave Vincent, 1995

56 Robin Hood's Chockstone Chimney 16m S 4a ★
The main chimney. It is also possible to finish to the right up an easier groove. Alternatively, **Connolly's Variation**, S 4a ★, provides a better finale, moving left above the chockstone to climb the exposed upper arête.
Fred Piggott & friends, c1920

57 Paucity 16m HVS 5b ★★
A route with great varied and technical climbing, following a lovely, subtle line. Climb to a shallow depression and up this to the left-hand side of a narrow roof. Make forceful and fingery moves up and left, then some contrastingly delicate step-ups into the shallow scoop above to eventually gain ledges. Finish up the wall above.
Don Morrison, 1960s

58 Robin Hood's Crack 18m HVD ★★
Climb the flaky crack in the groove, passing the overhang on the right. From the ledge climb the face left of the cave. A direct start climbs the arête at VS 4c.
Eric Byne, Clifford Moyer, 1930s

59 Tea-Leaf Crack 16m HVD 4a ★
In the left wall of the gully is a flake crack. Follow the flake to the ledges in front of the cave, step left and climb the face just left of the cave.
Alpha Club, 1959

Out on the left, part way up *Robin Hood's Cave Gully*, is the legendary Robin Hood's Cave, which has been used as a perfect, weatherproof bivouac site for generations. Please leave it as you'd like to find it.

60 Robin Hood's Cave Gully 14m VD
The big, deep and slippery V-groove.

Wuthering Buttress

ROBIN HOOD'S BUTTRESS

Square like a boxer's jaw, jutting forward in challenge to see how hard you can punch.

61 Cave Gully Wall 14m HVS 5a ★★
A brilliant route culminating in joyous yarding up the upper scoop. From the boulders in the gully, tense climbing up the lower slab leads to the right-hand cave. Continue up the left-hand edge of this and follow the steep shallow groove above to finish at a rocking block.
Alf Bridge, 1932

62 Cave Innominate/Harding's Superdirect 14m HVS 5a ★★★
A brilliant combination. The thin, polished crack at the right end of the gully wall is reached by a precarious toe-traverse from the left or harder, 5b, directly up the arête. The crack leads all too soon to the Balcony Cave (VS 5a to here if you escape rightwards). From the cave, step left and make a long grope round the roof followed by an exposed pull over on superb holds. Climb the short wall above. ⊙ page 329
Alf Bridge, 1932 / Peter Harding, J Greaves, E Phillips, 1946

63 Carpe Diem 14m E6 6c ★★
A fierce classic. Climb to a hollow block at 3m. Continue up, making a step left, then go up to good holds beneath the roof. Stretch rightwards to a pocket on the lip and make a desperate move to get established on the headwall. Finish directly and more easily.
Neil Foster, Howard Lancashire, Huw Perkins, 1994

64 Cave Eliminate 16m E2 6a ★★
A bulging problem start (Font 6A+), leads past a pocket to a good ledge at 5m. Above is a step in the overhang. Pull past this with difficulty and finish leftwards up the easier wall.
John Allen, Neil Stokes, 1973

65 Cave Arête 12m HVS 5b ★★
Well-positioned and well-protected climbing on memorable holds, following the right arête of the buttress. First, gain the ledge below the overhang and make long reaches to gain better holds and an easing in the angle. The upper section is followed delicately on the right to a stance in the caves.
Don Morrison, 1960s

66 Robin Hood's Balcony Cave Direct 20m S 4b ★★
Climb the large, imposing, V-shaped cleft on polished holds to reach the balcony and optional belay. Move left and go through the ledgey overhang above by unlikely-looking moves on big jugs.
Fred Piggott & friends, 1920s

67 Broken Arrow 5m E1 5b
The roof-crack directly above the chimney.
Graham Parkes, Chris Craggs, 1999

68 Constipation 12m E4 6a ★★
The arête is tough, but it does contain just enough gear. Climb onto a block then make hard crux moves up just right of the arête to get stood on a sloping ledge. The upper part of the arête is easier, unless you are short.
John Allen, Neil Stokes, 1973

69 Pacific Ocean Wall 12m E5 6b ★★
Desperate crimping. Climb *Desperation* and place side-runners in its crack, then reverse to the ground. Start up *Constipation* then move right and climb the wall. This features hard climbing on tiny holds and has the potential for a major flier from the final hard moves. Climbed direct, without side-runners, is E7.
◉ opposite page
John Allen, Mark Stokes, 1983

70 Desperation 10m E1 6a ★★
A technical treat. A reachy start gains the break. Move left and make tough moves to get established in the crack; righteous jugging follows.
Bob Brayshaw, Al Parker, 1959

71 Robin Hood's Staircase Direct
8m VS 4c
A direct line on nice holds.

72 Robin Hood's Staircase 9m HVD
The diagonal weakness is poorly protected.

73 Rubber Band 18m VS 4b ★
A brilliantly positioned journey. Follow *Robin Hood's Staircase Direct* until 2m from the top of the cliff. Traverse left along the horizontal break on superb jams, crossing the upper wall of *Desperation* to finish with a touch of *Constipation* or, more easily, round to the left of the arête.
John Allen, Neil Stokes, 1972

74 Titbit 8m HS 4c ★
The crack on the north-facing side-wall gives a good little exercise in steep jamming.
Don Morrison, c1960

75 Muesli 10m HS 4c
The square arête is pleasantly technical.
Bruce Goodwin, John Street, 1992

76 Cornflakes 10m HS 4c
The centre of the flaky wall.

77 Boot Crack 10m VD ★
The wide crack with an awkward start.

78 Soft Shoe 10m HS 4b
The narrow wall just right of the crack.
Bruce Goodwin, John Street, 1992

79 Shuffle 10m VD ★
The crack is climbed passing to the left of the cannonball-sized porthole. Polished fun.
John Street, Dave Gregory, 1993

Dan Cheetham on Pacific Ocean Wall (opposite page). This gives some of the crimpiest wall climbing on the entire edge. Luckily this can be enjoyed in relative safety, with side-runners in Desperation (at E5), or in utter terror without (at E7). Choices, choices... Mike Cheque

INVERTED V BUTTRESS
The crack-riven bastion gives classic leads with big strong lines and lots of stars.

1 Twin Cracks 12m HVD ★
Ascend the left-hand crack all the way to the ledge under the capstone, and escape left.

2 Right Twin Crack 12m VS 4c ★
The right-hand crack is followed directly, giving good climbing with great nut protection. Finish to the right at the huge capstone.
Rodney Wilson, c1960

3 Ellis's Eliminate 20m VS 4c ★★
Buster jams and rising footholds in a great position give this route its charm. From *Right Twin Crack*, traverse airily rightwards along the horizontal break to finish up the arête.
Gilbert Ellis (tr), 1950

4 Good Friday 15m HVS 5b ★★
Enjoyable climbing on thoughtful holds. From the middle of the traverse of *Ellis's Eliminate* make a series of stretches up the centre of the steep wall.
P Green, Mike Nugent, 1977

5 Inverted V 20m VS 4c ★★★
A big line with classic climbing; a good introduction to gritstone VS. Follow the crack and groove to the cave. Continue up to the roof and traverse right (thread) before finishing up the exposed crack that splits the roof.
⊙ page 335
Cyril Ward, 1922

6 Retroversion 21m HVS 4c ★★
A great route, with strong, confident climbing in a fine position. Gain the hanging arête from 5m up *Inverted V*, and follow this with steep spectacular climbing between horizontal breaks. Finish up the rounded arête.
Don Morrison, c1962

7 Robin Hood's Right-Hand Buttress Direct 22m HS 4a ★★★
One of Stanage's finest features, the impressive head-sized crack splitting the face. Climb a wide crack up to the large overhang, then shuffle out right to reach a small ledge. The crack above, if taken steadily, is easily tamed.
Cyril Ward, 1922

8 Cold Turkey 20m HVS 5a ★
An intimidating climb, with slopey holds and tricky gear; very fine, nonetheless. Start up the flake in the left rib of *Straight Crack*. Step left onto the face and climb directly up to and over a small capping roof.
John Allen, Steve Bancroft, 1973

9 Straight Crack 20m VS 4b ★★
The crack gives great challenging climbing, especially in its lower half. Climb up into the wide chimney and follow this to the roof. Shuffle left under this to the exposed relief of the front face, whereupon a move allows access to the wide crack above, then the chimney above.

10 Robin Hood Zigzag 24m S 4a ★★
A classic line, deviously following many strong features to give a very memorable climb of only modest difficulty. Climb the chimney then traverse right to a good ledge. Ascend the crack to the left of the holly to a ledge and continue up the fine wall to a niche. Step right and climb the face to the top.
Cyril Ward, 1922

11 Spring into Action 20m HVS 5b ★
Bridge the chimney to gain flutings on the right-hand arête above the overhang. Pull onto the ledge, then climb a short wall to another ledge. The centre of the steep wall above provides the main substance of the route.
Graham Parkes, Chris Craggs, 1996

12 The Actress 10m E2 5c
Tackle the overhang directly, to gain the halfway ledge. Select any way, up or down.
Alan Clarke, Mike Parkin, 1965

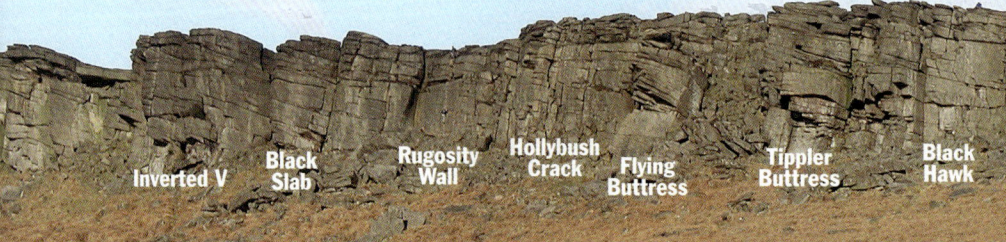

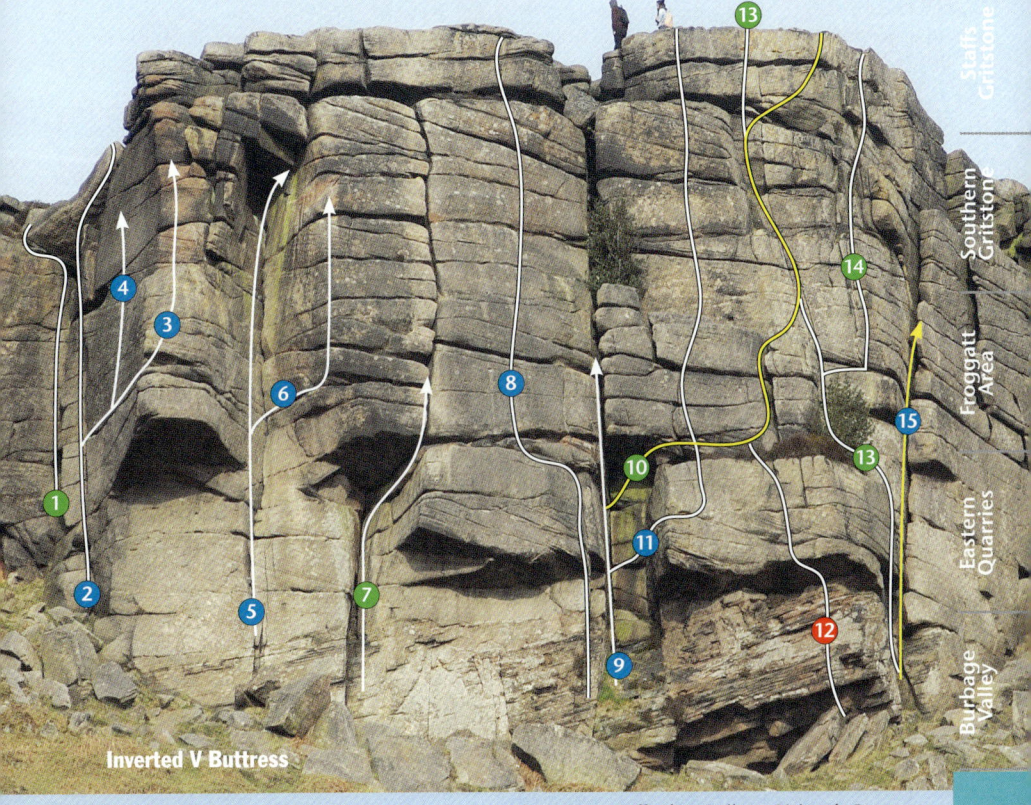

Inverted V Buttress

13 Bishop's Route 24m S 4a ★★★
A brilliant wandering expedition that gives the longest and easiest way up the buttress. From the base of the big flake, follow a left-slanting crack to a platform. This feels stiff due to polish, but is quickly passed. Continue up the corner-crack to the right of the holly to a higher ledge. Gain and follow flakes to a niche and finish reachily direct (or escape left).
Henry Bishop, c1920

14 Zagrete 20m HS 4b ★★
A good route in a fine position up the arête. The initial moves are strenuous, but above things ease off a lot. Follow *Bishop's Route* to the holly, then swing out along a break and yank up steeply into the crack. Continue on using this and the arête to a fine finish on flutings at the top.
John Loy, c1962

15 Zigzag Flake Crack 18m VS 4b ★★
The impressive flake is serious due to some precarious and poorly-protected climbing. Layback the edge of the flake all the way. From the small ledge on its top, finish up the easier short wall behind. Safer with big cams.
Herbert Hartley, 1929

16 Coconut Ice 18m E2 5b ★
An urgent eliminate. Moving up past a small nose in the lower section is the crux (6a for the short). Above the break the route is a bit more contrived, but still enjoyable.
Gary & Hazel Gibson, 1981

17 Ice Boat 20m E1 5c ★
Climb the wall to the horizontal break. Step up and traverse rightwards almost to the arête before finishing up the wall with a long reach.
Gary & Hazel Gibson, 1981

18 The Little Flake Crack 18m VS 5a ★
Starting from the chimney make a hard traverse left, using polished footholds, to attain the base of the flake, which is climbed directly.
Frank Elliot, 1930s

19 Flake Chimney 15m HVD ★
The chimney gives classical grunting as far as the jammed boulder. Pass on the inside, or outside at HS 4b. The upper section is steep but much easier.

20 Hybrid 15m E1 5b
Climb directly up the narrow rib. At the overhang, use the flake to gain the ledge above.
Don Morrison & friends, 1960s

21 Pedestal Chimney 15m D ★
The right-hand chimney is entered by climbing the polished crack on the left-hand side of the pedestal at its base. Continue up the chimney and finish under the huge 'corking' boulder.

22 Wright's Route 16m VS 4c ★
A frisky little climb in a shy setting. Climb the overhanging corner-crack right of the pedestal to gain its top and the base of the chimney above. A short exposed traverse leads out rightwards across the steep wall and into the bottomless corner, up which the climb finishes.
Don Morrison & friends, 1960s

23 Wall of Sound 16m E6 6b ★★★
A hardcore little number, with forceful and powerful climbing, based on the steep, scooped wall with little in the way of inspiring protection. Start up the thin crack (poor wire at the top) then continue up the wall and use a pocket to finish left towards *Wright's Route* (better) or right to gain and finish up the right-hand arête.
John Allen, Mark Stokes, 1983

Inverted V Buttress **Black Slab**

Inverted V Buttress has got more than its fair share of mega features and probably chief amongst them is its eponymous VS. Inverted V (page 336), funnels up one of gritstone's proudest grooves. giving a great combination or restriction and exposure. Dave Hinton climbing. Paul Evans.

> **BLACK SLAB**
> Despite the name it is the same colour as all of this section of the cliff. Although it can be climbed virtually anywhere, its three main routes are all independent and brilliant.

24 Whillans' Pendulum/Black Magic
16m HVS 5b ★★★
The athletic start and delicate finish combine to produce a fine lead. From under the overhang, swing right to gain a ledge on the front face. Move up, then step left on to the narrow side face of the slab and ascend this delicately.
Don Whillans, 1958 / Giles Barker, John Oldroyd, 1976

25 Hargreaves' Original Route
16m VS 4c ★★★
One of the best VSs on the edge, giving a long, exposed and delicate climb. Start from boulders under the right edge. Pull up and leftwards to the centre of the slab. Trace an intricate line upwards trending slightly left (easier) or right (longer and harder).
⊙ opposite page
Albert Hargreaves, 1928

26 The Flange **16m HVS 5b** ★★
A fun and highly muscular start gives access to more conventional slabbing above. Steep pulls through a cracked overhang gain a niche at 4m. Above, layback up 'the flange' then press onwards by delicate moves between rounded breaks to a finish up a short crack.
Peter Biven, Trevor Peck, 1956

27 April Crack **16m HS 4b** ★★★
The major corner-crack has everything you could want from a grit route at the grade – big holds, big moves and a big situation.
Herbert Hartley, 1928

28 Easter Rib **16m E1 5b** ★★
A delicate classic. Climb a shallow undercut groove just to the left of the nose then swing right and go up to a horizontal break. Balance up the rounded rib to gain the final juggy rib.
Peter Biven, Trevor Peck, 1956

29 Christmas Crack **16m HS 4b** ★★★
A brilliant route, packing in an amazing amount of quality, variety and fun. Wriggle up the groove into a friendly crack. The final leaning corner gives an airy climax. The only route in the country where a queue is normal on December 25th whatever the weather.
George Bower, 1926

Stanage must have at least a dozen VSs that could call themselves amongst the best in the country but first amongst these must be Hargreaves' Original Route on Black Slab (opposite page). The slab feels tall and the position feels exposed and it has testing moves up its whole height. Just magic. 📷 Niall Grimes.

30 Central Trinity 16m VS 4c ★★
A well-positioned route with a classic pedigree and a short crux section. Climb the right-hand crack, then make a strenuous traverse left to gain the left-hand crack. Follow this to the summit. The **Direct Start** is 5a.
Herbert Hartley, 1929

31 Right-Hand Trinity 12m S 4a ★★
A cracking big old-fashioned Severe, with continually chunky climbing and a big feel. The long crack in the wall is climbed directly, initially via a shallow rightward-facing corner.
Herbert Hartley, 1928

32 Fergus Graham's Direct Route 14m HVS 4c
The poorly protected wall immediately to the right of the crack is followed throughout. Start slightly on the left side and gaini and follow the centre from midheight.
Fergus Graham, 1920s

33 Topaz 12m E4 6a ★
The sharp arête is laybacked on its right to an alarmingly long reach above a nasty landing. Swinging left for the top arête reduces the grade to E1 5b.
Gary Gibson, 1979

> **RUGOSITY WALL**
> To the right is a flat, off-vertical wall, containing a good number of technical climbs. The harder ones are poorly protected but, as they tend to have their difficulties at the start, make for popular solos.

34 Green Crack 12m VS 4b ★
The square-cut corner is well-named and best avoided after rain. When dry it is usually laybacked until good jams arrive.
Herbert Hartley, 1928

35 Rugosity Wall 12m HVS 5c ★
The wall 2m right of the corner has a difficult and fingery start leading to marginally easier-angled climbing, with one more tricky pull before things ease. Finish up the short wall.
Chuck Cook, 1948

Rugosity Wall

Stanage Popular | 343

36 Rusty Wall 12m HVS 6a ★
The wall immediately left of the left-hand crack has hard starting moves on slowly-vanishing 'rusty excrescences'. Once the first good hold is reached things relent. Finish up the short wall immediately to the left of the chimney.
Herbert Hartley, 1928

37 Rusty Crack 12m HVS 5b ★
The left-hand crack on the wall has a tough start, using polished rusty footholds and a thin crack. Finish up the short chimney above.

38 Via Media 10m VS 4c ★
The right-hand crack gives a sustained climb. Perfect nut placements make this a good first VS lead.
Ron Townsend and members of the Peak Climbing Club, 1949

39 Via Dexter 10m E1 5c ★
Ascend the wall directly. Purists will attack the centre of the wall with conviction and will doubtless enjoy the experience.
Tony Moulam, 1951

40 Oblique Crack 10m HVD ★
The crack. The lower section gives good jamming and leads to a loose chockstone and a finish up the rounded face directly above.
Herbert Hartley, 1928

41 Oblique Buttress 12m VS 5b
The narrow face can be ascended at 5b by strictly ignoring the arêtes on either side. Or the whole thing becomes much easier if one or both arêtes are employed: VS 4c.
Don Morrison, John Loy & friends, 1960s

42 Straight Chimney 12m VD
The obvious chimney widens in its centre and narrows to a crack just below the top.

43 Albert's Pillar 12m HS 4c
The bulbous pillar has a boulder problem start and easier climbing above.
Don Morrison, John Loy & friends, 1960s

44 Albert's Amble 12m HVD
The crack has an awkward move to start but soon eases.
Bruce Goodwin, John Street, 1992

Rusty Descent: The broken rocks on the right are frequently used as a descent. There are various ways down the top section and these all unite in an easy blocky chimney in the lower section, immediately to the left of *Narrow Buttress*.

Rugosity Wall

HOLLYBUSH CRACK AREA

The twin towers of Narrow and Leaning buttresses stand sentinel over the next section of cliff.

45 Narrow Buttress 14m VS 4c ★★
Good, interesting climbing. Start up the right arête then move to the left-hand edge briefly before traversing back rightwards again to finish spectacularly on the large flutings on the tip of the final overhang. The true '**Straight and Narrow**' is HVS 5a, avoiding the arêtes.
Ron Townsend & members of the Peak Climbing Club, 1949

46 Hollybush Crack 14m VD ★★★
The holly has long since gone but this corner-crack remains superb, leading to a thrilling finale. ◉ opposite page
George Bower, 1926

47 Queersville 16m HVS 5a ★★★
A sublime climb, one of the sweetest about, with continually technical climbing and sufficient protection. Start up the 'dinosaur's spine', then stretch out left to reach flat ledges. Climb up to a broken flake below the roof and make a thrilling reach to the ledge above. Continue up the pleasant wall above.
Alan Clarke, Mike Parkin, 1965

48 The Nose 16m E4 6a ★
Very bold. Climb the arête on good finger-holds to the ledge on *Yosemite Wall*. Step left and tackle the more precarious upper section with some tenuous laybacking.
Andy Bailey, 1985

49 Yosemite Wall 16m E2 5b ★★
A bold route. Climb into a small recess. Leave this by difficult moves leftwards to gain the ledge above (crux). Step up right and teeter up the slab to reach ledges and easier climbing.
Alan Clarke, A Watson, 1965

50 Leaning Buttress Gully 16m VS 4c
Climb up to the left side of the overhang in the gully and surmount this. Easier rock leads to the top, passing the final overhang on the left.
Jim Lomas, 1930

51 Hangover 16m VS 4c ★
Climb the right-hand crack of the gully past the awkward bulge. Continue up the easy corner above and exit right at the final overhang.
Bob Brayshaw, NKT Froggatt, GS Kitt, 1957

One of the best lower-grade climbs at the Popular End with great rock to match a great line. Gemma Stocks on Hollybush Crack, VD (opposite page). 📷 Niall Grimes.

52 Leaning Buttress Direct 16m HVS 5b ★
The narrow runway up the front of the buttress is taken direct, with a steep boulder problem start and a worrying move to leave the ledge.
Fergus Graham, 1922

53 Leaning Buttress Indirect 16m VD
Climb *Leaning Buttress Crack* to the 'window' then traverse out left on to the front of the buttress proper and climb its left-hand edge.

54 Leaning Buttress Crack 15m VD ★★
The well-protected, right-angled, corner-crack. It offers varied moves up a strong line

55 Right On 14m HS 4b ★
Climb a corner and make an awkward move to get on top of a pedestal. The continuation crack gives pleasant moves to easy ground.
Dave Gregory, Chris Craggs, 1997

56 Garden Fence 14m HS 4a
Climb the wide crack in the corner behind the projecting block, then go straight up using the large pocket and a long reach.
Simon & Maggie Pape, 2004

57 Space Junk 14m HVS 5a ★
The short arête at the front edge leads to the platform. Move right and finish up the wall right of the chimney, initially up a short crack and continuing direct on rounded holds.
Gary Gibson (solo), 1979

58 Garden Wall 14m S 4a ★
Climb the chunky crack and narrow chimney above to the level of the large rounded chockstone. Surmount this with a bit of a huff and a puff.
Cyril Ward, 1922

59 Birch Tree Wall 14m HS 4b ★
The moves on the upper wall are reminiscent of the best bits of *Heaven Crack*. Climb the short crack to a large platform. Gain the obvious flake by a long reach and a quick pull to ledges. Another long reach gains the top.

60 Wild West Wind 14m S
Climb a flake to the midway ledge at a perched block. Move right and climb the upper wall midway between the flake of *Birch Tree Wall* and the easy gully on the right.
Chris Craggs (solo), 1997

61 Scrappy Corner 12m D
To the right is an angular corner that leads to block-strewn ledges. The upper continuation of the corner is easier.

Stanage Popular | 347

FLYING BUTTRESS AREA
One of gritstone's great features now comes in the hunched and hooded form of The Flying Buttress, jutting its confident challenge forwards for all to see.

62 The Wedge 14m VS 5a
Ascend the front of the buttress directly.
Bob Brayshaw, Al Parker, 1959

63 Wedge Gully 12m S 4a
Bridge up the chimney, then move right around the outside of the block.
Don Morrison, John Loy & friends, 1960s

64 Wedge Rib 14m VS 5a
Climb the arête on either side, avoiding any cracks. Finish up the broad arête above.
Don Morrison, John Loy & friends, 1960s

65 Flying Buttress Gully 16m D
The gully with the jammed blocks is awkward.

66 Flying Buttress 22m VD ★★★
A classic and varied route, weaving its way through magnificent positions. Climb the slab leftwards. A steep groove on the left leads to an exposed slab which is climbed rightwards to a large ledge and a finish on monster jugs.
Fergus Graham, 1922

67 Goodbye Toulouse 18m E1 5b ★★
An exciting route crossing the left-hand side of the overhang. Climb the slab, then over the first roofs, passing left of the concave flake, pressing on to finish just right of the final nose.
Gary Gibson, Ralph Hewitt, Derek Beetlestone, 1978

68 Flying Buttress Direct 16m E1 5b ★★★
One of the most photographed routes on the edge, yarding along massive steepness on equally massive jugs. Guaranteed to make you feel like a hero. Climb the slab to the roof. Climb this, with an initial long reach, using a mixture of heel-hooks and brute force to a leg lock rest. One final long haul remains.
D A Lomas (4pts), 1956. FFA Paul Grey, David Johnson, 1966

69 Kirkus's Corner 16m E1 5b ★★
Fine climbing culminating in bold and delicate final moves. From the slope on the right of the slab, swing left using a good diagonal crack above the lip. Move up and step left into a shallow scoop from which a delicate rounded exit is made to the welcoming final crack.
Colin Kirkus, 1934

Flying Buttress Descent: An scrambling descent path is found behind the buttress.

348 | Stanage Popular

TIPPLER BUTTRESS
Now here's a buttress guaranteed to raise a pump. Starkly overhung, holding a great collection of Extreme routes, where big biceps and the ability to push on when under fire will pay dividends. The great routes here – *The Tippler, The Unprintable, The Dangler, Tippler Direct, Black Hawk Bastion* and *Censor* – are essential ticks for the Stanage devotee, and all mark memorable milestones on the long and winding road that is a gritstone life.

1 Jitterbug Buttress 12m S 4a ★
Climb the front face to the capping overhang and avoid this by sneaking off to the right.
Eric Byne, 1950

Jitterbug Gully Descent: The steep gully to the right is easier than it looks.

2 The Kirkus Original 12m HVS 4c ★
Start on a block to the right of the base of the gully. Go directly up the face to harder moves at 6m, which lead to a mantelshelf and then easier ground above; unprotected.
Colin Kirkus, 1930s

3 Jitter Face 12m HS 4a ★
A good route for bold climbers. Start below the centre of the face. Trend up and right then back left to join *The Kirkus Original* at its mantel. Finish up this.

4 Townsend's Variation 14m HVS 4c ★★
Unprotected, but never desperate. Take a line up the right-hand edge of the face, and at mid-height move round on to the exposed front face before making committing moves up the rib to reach superb finishing jugs.
Ron Townsend & members of the Peak Climbing Club, 1949

5 Censor 15m E3 5c ★★
A classic frightener, with brilliant, gymnastic climbing above small gear. Start up a shallow corner. Climb to the roof, swing right and commit to the bulge before making strenuous and then delicate moves to gain a standing position on the nose. Do a tricky move up then finish up the wall above.
Jim Perrin, 1967

6 The Unprintable 16m E1 5b ★★
A brute, a struggle for all but the most technically adept, with more than a whiff of Whillans about it. The left-hand crack is difficult but gives a perfect opportunity to display your breadth of knowledge of four-letter words.
Don Whillans, Joe Brown, Nat Allen, 1952

7 The Dangler 16m E2 5c ★★★
Gymnastic thuggery taking the right-hand roof crack, best suited to squat, post-war plumbers.
Joe Brown, Ron Mosely, 1954

8 Tippler Direct 16m E3 6a ★★★
Well-protected roof-play. Start in the centre of the wall and weave through the overhangs using some mighty pulls to meet and finish up the original. So much fun.
Jim Reading, Clive Jones, 1976

9 The Tippler 20m E1 5b ★★★
A classic – steep, technical, exposed and demanding a bit of 'go for it'. Climb the right edge of the buttress to the overhang. Make an exciting traverse left, to a crack in the lip of the overhang. Grope up and left for a horizontal break then make the crux moves to get established on the final wall.
Barry Webb, 1964

10 The 9 O'Clock Watershed
15m E6 6c ★★
The right arête gives a powerful and scary lead. Starting from a shelf, climb the side-wall to the main break and step left into *The Tippler*. Stretch round to a flat hold at the base of the arête. Finish up the arête.
Neil Foster, 1994

11 The Y Crack 18m VS 4c ★★
The cleft is often green, though in dry weather it gives a good direct line. Climb the corner steeply to ledges and finish either left or right.

12 The Z Crack 18m VS 4c ★
Climb the hand crack that runs up the back of the hanging groove.
Joe Brown, Nat Allen, Don Whillans, 1953

13 Castle Chimney 20m M ★★
A deep and atmospheric journey to the depths of the chimney. Enter it over blocks and progress Sheffield-wards until it is possible to bridge up to daylight at a large platform. A variety of routes lead to the top.
JW Puttrell, 1904

14 Black Hawk Tower 24m HVD 4a ★
A devious but pleasant climb. Ascend *Castle Chimney* until a traverse along a ledge on the right leads round the arête and onto the front face. Continue rightwards around the next arête and climb the final shallow corner groove of *Elliott's Eliminate*.

15 Master of Disguise 16m E6 6c ★★
A short but exciting problem up the hanging arête. Start to the left of *Chameleon* at a white marked wall. Climb this and make a cramped traverse right under the roof to the undercut on *Chameleon*. Stretch round to a disappointing break leading left to the arête. Slap up this to easier ground.
Neil Foster, 1994

16 Chameleon 16m E4 6a ★★
An excellent route, with forceful, technical climbing in an intimidating position. Climb the narrow lower wall to the overhang. This is crossed with difficulty and commitment to reach a rightward-slanting ramp. Hand-traverse up this, then move rapidly to the right-hand arête and better holds.
Ed Drummond, John Young, 1975

17 Black Hawk Bastion 16m E3 5c ★★
An essential E3 tick; commitment required. The stepped, overhung groove is followed forcibly to an exposed finish up the hanging left arête of the final groove.
Dick Brown (1pt), 1952. FFA John Allen, Steve Bancroft, 1975

Stanage Popular

BLACK HAWK

The bay is one of the most popular areas on Stanage. Its good collection of easier routes, pioneered by the ancients, makes it a fine venue for lower-grade climbers. The routes have a well-worn feel about them due to heavy traffic, but are still fine passages.

18 Eliminator 15m HVS 5b ★★★
A popular and technical climb with good pro. Climb the arête and move right to a short crack. Follow this, to finish up a groove.
Alan Clarke, Mike Parkin, 1965

19 Castle Crack 18m HS 4b ★★
A great big corner-line with solid protection makes this an understandably popular lead.
Henry Bishop & friends, c1912

20 Elliott's Eliminate 18m HS 4c ★
Good moves and exciting positions. Climb the flake then traverse leftwards into *Castle Crack*. Climb this to a good ledge on the left and traverse leftwards to finish up the exposed groove.

21 Black Hawk 15m HS 4c ★★
A good direct line. Follow the flake on *Elliott's Eliminate*, then continue rightwards to follow a shallow crack which leads to a good ledge. Finish up the right-hand crack above.
Eric Byne, Clifford Moyer, c1932

22 Providence 15m E1 5c
Climb a small groove to a niche. Climb directly above the niche passing the diagonal crack.
Gary Gibson, Ralph Hewitt, Derek Beetlestone, 1978

23 Black Hawk Traverse Left 17m VD ★★
A great route, stylishly covering some fine terrain. Climb a groove to a niche, and move left round a bulge. Continue up and leftwards to a good ledge. There are various finishes, with the crack on the right being the best.

24 Black Hawk Hell Crack 14m S 4a ★★★
An excellent route taking the crack just left of the chimney. It feels steep and exposed, but with bags of holds and gear.
Eric Byne, Clifford Moyer, c1932

25 Black Hawk Traverse Right 16m D ★★
Excellent sustained climbing with an exposed finish. From the base of *Hell Crack*, follow polished footholds rightwards to a crack; climb this to bulges. At the level of these, step right and climb the main fissure to the capping overhang, which is skirted on the left.
Fred Pigott & friends, c1912

Stanage soloing; oh Joy! racing up and along classic after classic on sound rough rock. So many brilliant moves and unique holds and special moments. The best. Graeme Hammond on Gargoyle Buttress, VS 4b (page 352). 📷 Becky Hammond

26 Gargoyle Variant 14m HS 4b ★
Begin under the hanging left arête of the buttress and climb the wide crack to the overhangs. Alternatively take the less thrutchy unprotected rib to the right. From the right end of the overhang, move up to the unattached boulder and follow the rib above.

27 Gargoyle Buttress 14m VS 4b ★★
Start at the right-hand toe of the buttress and follow a horizontal crack out to the left. Pull up, and definitely not out, on a slightly suspect perched boulder and finish up the wall to the right with some concentration. ⦿ page 339
Ron Townsend & members of the Peak Climbing Club, 1949

28 Dry Rot 14m E2 5b ★
From *Gargoyle's* traverse pull up and right with difficulty before following the precarious and poorly protected right-hand edge of the slab to finish over the capping stone.
Gary Gibson, Derek Beetlestone, Dave Light, 1981

29 Physiology 12m VD ★
The left-hand crack is followed throughout; good quality.

30 Sociology 12m S
The centre of the narrow face is best climbed directly, initially up the front face of a block.

31 Anatomy 12m VD
The right-hand corner is climbed with a move left at the overhang. Finish up the continuation corner.

32 Tinker's Crack 12m VS 4c ★
The narrow wall is split in its upper part by an indefinite crack. Pull over a bulge to gain the crack and follow it with a couple of tricky moves in the middle.
Don Morrison, John Loy & friends, c1962

33 Beggar's Crack 12m VS 4c
The wider crack with an overhang. The main difficulty is getting established in the upper crack. A bit bold and a bit awkward.

34 Tip Off Right 14m E1 5b
Climb a blunt rib just right of *Beggar's Crack* to a move to the right, then head up the hanging flake directly above the point where *Manchester Buttress* swings round the corner.

35 Manchester Buttress 15m HS 4b ★★★
A magnificent lead for the competent, with devious, demanding but never desperate climbing. Head up the crack before moving left in an exposed position underneath the overhang. Go up to a deep horizontal break, then make an exciting traverse back to the right and around the nose to get established on a ledge. Finish directly. **Manchester United**, HVS 5b, avoids the detour.
Maurice Linnell, Alf Bridge, Eric Byne, Clifford Moyer, c1932 / Chris Craggs, 1988

Manchester Descent: There is an awkward descent just right.

HEATHER BUTTRESS

The glossy classic that is *Crack and Corner* dominates the steep walls to the right. On either side can be found solid mid-grade excursions with *Heather Wall* being a classic, as well as the ever-popular *Grotto Slab*.

36 Cakestand 9m S 4b
Follow a narrow buttress with the occasional long reach, to a narrow ledge in a corner just below the top. The true finish up the rounded buttress is tough, though there is an easier (VD) corner immediately to the left, climbed from the narrow ledge.
Don Morrison, John Loy & friends, c1962

37 Cool Groove 10m S 4b
An open groove leads easily to a capping overhang, the passing of which provides the fun.
Don Morrison, John Loy & friends, c1962

38 Lancashire Wall 12m HVS 5a ★
The centre of the wall to the right has a delicate start from a block and a moderately thrilling finale up the leaning front face of the final, detached block. Fortunately, the good holds keep on arriving. Bypassing the top block on the right gives a fun VS 4c.
Dave Kenyon, Paul Cropper, 1978

39 Crack and Corner 15m S 4b ★★★
A classic sandbag, taking the snaking grooveline in the well-positioned arête. The corner is started with difficulty, using a variety of polished holds. Continue up the excellent groove to a comfortable platform below an overhanging block. This is overcome at its left-hand corner by an ungainly move.

40 Heather Wall 12m VS 4c ★★
A fun, steep route with brilliant protection. After a polished start, climb the face using a series of short cracks, to a flat ledge. A right-trending scoop leads to a finish just right of the big capping block. The right-hand start is 5a.

41 Chimp's Corner 12m VS 5b
The overhanging corner is climbed in a rather simian fashion to eventually grasp onto the ledge above. Climb to the ledge, then move left to pull over the final roof using a superb jug on its rim.
Don Morrison, John Loy & friends, c1962

42 Grotto Slab 14m D ★
A gentle, rambling route best enjoyed by beginners. Start at the toe of the slab (or, even easier, by the right side of the slab), and ascend to its apex by any one of a series of variations. A couple of short corners then lead to the top.
Henry Bishop, Douglas Yeomans & friends, 1910s

Heather Buttress

43 Jersey Boys   14m   E1 5a
Climb the easy corner to the top of the slab, then take the blunt rib on the right. Move right to pass the roof and continue up the wall on large sloping holds.
Chris Craggs, Kevin Eloury, Phil Brown, 1989

44 Grotto Wall   14m   HVS 4c   ★★
A bold test of confidence, harder for the short. Start immediately right of the slumped flake. Gain the shallow groove and climb this to its top. Exit awkwardly and finish up the wall trending rightwards on adequate, but elusive, holds.

45 Reagent   12m   E5 6a
An unprotected route up the smooth wall. From just left of the start of the flake of Green Wall, rock up and stretch left to reach a good hold. An enormous span from this gains small holds followed by a further reach for better ones. From the break climb, more easily, up the often dirty wall above.
Al Rouse (solo), 1984

46 Green Wall   10m   VS 4b   ★
Climb a flake-crack until a traverse right gains the final, usually green, chimney which is awkward to enter.
B Platt, Al Parker, 1958

47 Capstone Chimney   10m   D   ★
The wide, capped chimney forms a delightful introduction to chimney techniques.

48 Little Ernie   8m   S 4b
Start at the left-hand edge of the small buttress and climb on to a ledge, before trending rightwards to reach easier ground.
Don Morrison, John Loy & friends, c1962

49 Big Chris   10m   E1 5b
The centre of the face is climbed directly, starting up a thin flake and finishing up the crack splitting the final overhang.
Chris Craggs, Dave Gregory, 1993

50 In Earnest   10m   HVS 5a
The square left-hand arête of the recess has an awkward short wall for starters, followed by a couple of delicate moves before it eases.
Chris Craggs, Dave Gregory, 1993

51 Recess Wall   10m   HVD   ★
Climb the right-hand edge of the steep slab that forms the left-hand side of the recess, passing the left-hand edge of the capping overhang.

52 Right Wall Route   10m   HVD 4a   ★
Small, but perfectly formed. A steep slab forms the right-hand side of the recess. Climb this and move right to finish up a crack that cuts round the right edge of the roof.

Lena Drapella on Rugosity Crack, HVS 5b (page 356), a great test of technical 5b cranking. Good gear can be had, protecting a tough, short section. 📷 Pete O'Donovan

RUGOSITY CRACK AREA

From here the height of the crag starts to diminish and the area gives a bunch of quick climbs that get slabbier the further right they go... mostly. Descend on the far right.

53 Randolf Cheerleader 10m E3 6a
Climb the rib at the left-hand edge of the wall to a bulge. A mean rock-over and a long reach bring the short crack to the left within reach. Easier ground remains.
Mark Stokes, 1983

54 Gullible's Travels 10m E1 5b ★
Start in the middle of the wall and trend right with reachy moves at mid-height. Good technical climbing, protectable with small cams.
Brian Pallet (1pt), c1962. FFA Alan Clarke, 1963

55 The 3-D Wall 8m E2 6a
Ascend the wall from the right side of the platform and keep between one and two metres from the chimney.
Gary Gibson, 1979

56 Black Chimney m D
Plumb the depth of the chimney behind the tower. Not for the faint-hearted claustrophobic.

57 Rugosity Crack 9m HVS 5b ★★
Pure technical joy. The thin crack which splits the tower is a little gem. ⓞ page 341
Pat Fearneough, c1962

58 Niche Wall Direct 10m S 4b ★
Climb the crack into and over the niche to a good finger crack.

59 Nicheless Climb 9m S 4b
The steep wall to a finish up the wide crack.

60 Right Edge 9m S
Climb the stepped arête to reach ledges on the right, just below the top. Finish up a short, awkward crack close to the chimney.

61 Hoaxer's Crack 7m HS 4b
Immediately right of the chimney, climb the steep finger crack to a reach for solid jams.
Don Morrison, John Loy & friends, c1962

62 Blunt Arête 6m HS 4c
Climb directly to a ledge, continue straight up past a suspect flake to an awkward finish.

63 Small Crack 6m VD
Climb the straight crack.

64 Ground Glass 7m HVS 4c ★
Ascend the shallow niche to the right, with a tricky move onto the upper wall.

65 Plate Glass Slab 7m VS 4c ★
The centre of the slab has a glassy start from a boulder up two well-scratched flakes.

66 Carborundum 7m VS 5a
The slab just right of the well-scratched start of *Plate Glass Slab* has a couple of long reaches.
Chris Craggs, 1993

67 Mantelpiece Crack 7m M ★
The crack that bounds the right-hand side of the steep slab, with a hard start.

68 Mantelpiece Buttress 7m D ★
The slanting flake. It is most easily reached by starting under the roof and traversing left to the base of the flake, though a more direct start has one polished move of 4b to reach the initial ledges. A good, easy route.

Stanage Popular | 357

69 Mantelpiece Buttress Direct
8m HVS 5b
Start under the triangular roof, stretch around this passing a thin crack into the deep break. Another strenuous move allows your knees and then feet to regain contact with the rock.
Don Morrison, John Loy & friends, c1962

70 Fragile Mantel 7m HS 4c
Climb the wall, passing the right edge of the disappearing roof. Gain the ledge; finish easily.
Chris Craggs, 1993

71 Mantelpiece Right 7m HVD
A bit steep and scary. Climb the depression just left of the right-hand edge of the buttress to a ledge and continue up the wall above.

72 Zip Crack 7m M
The V-shaped cleft to the right is a fun little climb on good holds.
Don Morrison, John Loy & friends, c1962

73 Button Wall 6m VD
The crack to the right of the left-hand arête is pleasantly situated.
Dave Gregory, John Street, 1993

74 Toggle 8m HS 4b
The centre of the narrow face has a tricky move just below the top.
Dave Gregory, John Street, 1993

75 Velcro Arête 6m S 4b
Lovely moves lead up the right-hand arête of the buttress.
John Street, Dave Gregory, 1993

76 Square Chimney Arête 6m S 4b
It is possible to climb the arête just to the left of the chimney on its right-hand side, using a finger crack to the right.

77 Square Chimney 6m M
Climb the chimney and escape out left at the capstone.

78 Monkey Crack 6m VD
The shallow, undercut corner crack is awkward to start and remains steep throughout.

79 Square Buttress Direct 7m HVS 5b
The centre of the front face. Font 5.

80 Square Buttress Arête 6m VS 4c
The right arête is climbed mostly on its right-hand side. It has a few pushy moves, and variations are possible to make it feel harder.

81 Square Buttress Wall 6m HS 4b
Climb the centre of the right-hand wall of the buttress. It is steep and pleasant.

82 Square Buttress Corner 6m D
Climb the short corner on the right.

83 Gashed Crack 7m VS 5a
The crack on the left-hand side of the buttress eases above the bulge.

84 Ding Dong 8m HVS 5b
A lovely start from under the roof gains holds on the front face and, thence, powerful moves to and up the arête. Font 5.
Don Morrison, John Loy & friends, c1962

85 Suzanne 8m HVS 6a
Brilliant. From under the roof, gain the lip and crank on positive holds to the ledge. Continue to the top up shelving rock. Highball Font 6A.
Reg Addey (solo), 1965

APPARENT NORTH

OS Grid Ref: SK 250 830 to SK 253 831
Altitude: 440m

The southern reaches are a sometimes fun and sometimes physical but always an underappreciated area of Stanage.

Despite being very close to the road, Apparent North tends to be visited by a more savvy clientele, those that value the technical over the big, exploration over habitual, and the apparent over the popular. The area has several distinct styles. There is a great string of bouldering to be had, all on small outcrops along the line of the edge. These are covered in the BMC's *Stanage* definitive guidebook.

Easy Jamming Buttress: A friendly buttress sitting just left of Apparent North Buttress.

1 Sleasy Jamming 5m S 4b
The left-hand crack. The flake to the left is D.

2 Easy Walling 6m HVS 5c ★
Climb straight up the centre of the wall between the cracks with a tricky start. Font 5+.

3 Easy Jamming 6m VD 4a
The crack just left of the arête isn't that easy at all.

4 Trainer Failure 6m VS 5a ★
A satisfying series of lock-offs up the arête.

5 The Real 20 Foot Crack 6m VS 4c ★★
The sweet crack, and a worthy twin to its Burbage brother.

6 Twin Cam 6m E4 6c ★
A series of desperate moves up the wall passing three horizontal breaks. Font 7A.
Johnny Dawes, 1984

7 Scary Canary 6m HVS 5b
The right-hand arête of the buttress.
David Simmonite, Alex Thackway, 1993

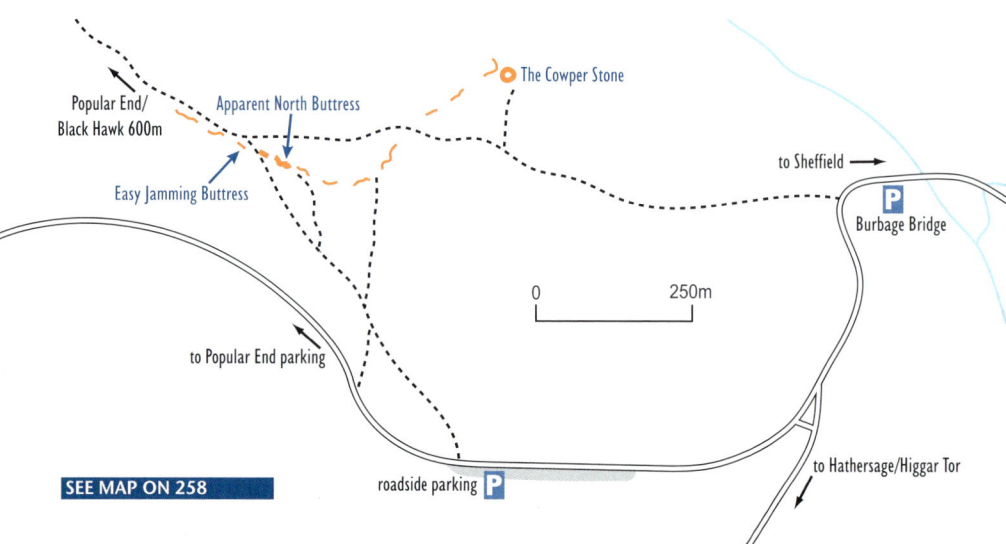

SEE MAP ON 258

Apparent North | 359

APPARENT NORTH BUTTRESS
This buttress stands proud, an architecturally stunning piece of rock that crowns this whole area. Severely undercut and overhanging, it is home to the highest concentration of hard climbs on the whole escarpment.

8 Apparent North 15m HVS 5b ★★
A great little-big climb with space below the feet. Start round left of the arête and stride across a gap to a bottomless crack. Follow this to the roof. A horizontal rightwards skedaddle onto the front face and a fun finish.
Len Millsom, c1962

9 Skinless Wonder 9m E6 6c ★★
Gain a short, horned crack at 3m, and undercut up and slightly left to the break and gear. Move right and keelhaul your way on to the shelving top.
Richie Patterson, 1993

10 Stanage Without Oxygen 9m E5 6c ★★
Climb the vague rib, with a fierce pull on a sloper that is barely discernible from the vertical rock that surrounds it. Highball Font 7A+.
John Allen, Mark Stokes, 1983

11 Little Women 10m E7 7a ★★
An intense, bouldery route up the hanging arête, that is fortunately protected. Move up to a deep horizontal break, and protection. Several slaps on slippy slopers lead to a monkey's bum on the arête. If successful, a long lock-off will hopefully bring relief.
John Welford, 1997

12 Groove is in the Heart 8m E7 7a ★★★
The line of the buttress taking the shallow central groove. Small, pre-placed RPs protect a series of technical and fingery moves through the stacked overlaps to a rounded finish.
Neil Bentley, 1998

13 Black Car Burning 9m E7 6c ★★
Scary bouldering. Start below the groove, and trend rightwards to a poor hold under the roof. Make a hard move to a hold on the lip and finish more easily by long reaches.
Robin Barker, 1993

14 Magnetic North 9m E3 5c
Climb the arête on its left-hand side using the diagonal crack, with a hard move to gain a projecting ledge on the right. Continue up the arête with a hard swing left at the overhang to an easier finish.
Simon Horrox, 1982

15 True North 9m VS 4c
Climb on to the large boulder jammed in the gully and continue up the right-hand side of the blunt arête to the left. Finish up the final short wall by a long reach.
Len Millsom, c1962

16 Mating Toads 9m HVS 5c
A bold little climb up the front face.
Andy Barker, 1982

17 Massacre 9m E1 5b ★
Climb the short grove. Swing wildly along the break to finish on the arête.
Andy Barker, 1982

THE COWPER STONE

Facing east, The Cowper Stone guards the southern end of Stanage Edge. The rock here is rougher, grainier and coarser. Its rounded black bulges attract an entirely different personality and mood from those on the nearby Popular End. Yet to many devotees, this ugly lump is the very essence of gritstone climbing, for without the requisite amounts of balance, technique, power and determination, the climbs will be impossible. However, for those in possession of these qualities, the Cowper Stone will provide some of the most perversely satisfying moments on grit.

18 Bodypopping 7m VS 5a

From a small cutaway just left of the arête, climb the left side of the arête and the wall above to a rounded finish.
Nick Taylor (solo), 1997

19 Whatever Happened to Bob? 7m E3 5c

Start at the left-hand side of the overhanging face and follow flakes initially rightwards, then back left to finish. One of the easier routes on the buttress - but still no pushover.
Bob Berzins (solo), 1983

20 Sad Amongst Friends 8m E6 7a ★★★

A prized tick for the true Stanage cognoscenti, climbed by a series of desperate, bulging contortions. Follow the central section of the face to finish past a protruding iron carbonate blister on the lip of the final overhang. The lower section is bold but the finish is well-protected and quite unique. ◉ opposite page
Johnny Dawes (solo), 1984

21 Snug as a Thug on a Jug 8m E4 6b ★★★

Every metre of this route would be worth five on a regular cliff. Fight up the non-crack to gain flutings on the left. Grasp right to a short, flared corner and pull up. Only the stoutest of minds will handle the sight of the top-out, although it comes easy with a little commitment. The direct finish is **Warmlove**, E6 7a ★.
Paul Mitchell, 1983 / Johnny Dawes, 1995

22 Happy Amongst Friends 7m E6 6c ★

A tough eliminate up the bulging wall to the left of *Breakdance*, finishing as for *Snug*...
Johnny Dawes (solo), 1996

23 Breakdance 7m E3 6a ★★

The bulging right-hand arête of the buttress is climbed by a series of weird contortions that prove strangely satisfying. The finish is rounded but not markedly more than the rest of the route.
Johnny Dawes, 1985

The very essence of hard gritstone - holdless, powerful, balancey, technical, committing — and utterly weird. Mark Rankine on Sad Amongst Friends, E6 7a (opposite page). 📷 James Thornton

THE NORTHERN EDGES

BAMFORD EDGE
DOVESTONE TOR
RIVELIN EDGE
AGDEN ROCHER
WHARNCLIFFE

The routes at Wharncliffe often cover steep ground for their grade, thanks to positive holds for the hands and hungry cracks for nuts and cams. Here, Paul Harrison enjoys a spot of autumn yarding on Tower Face, HS 4b (page 408). David Simmonite

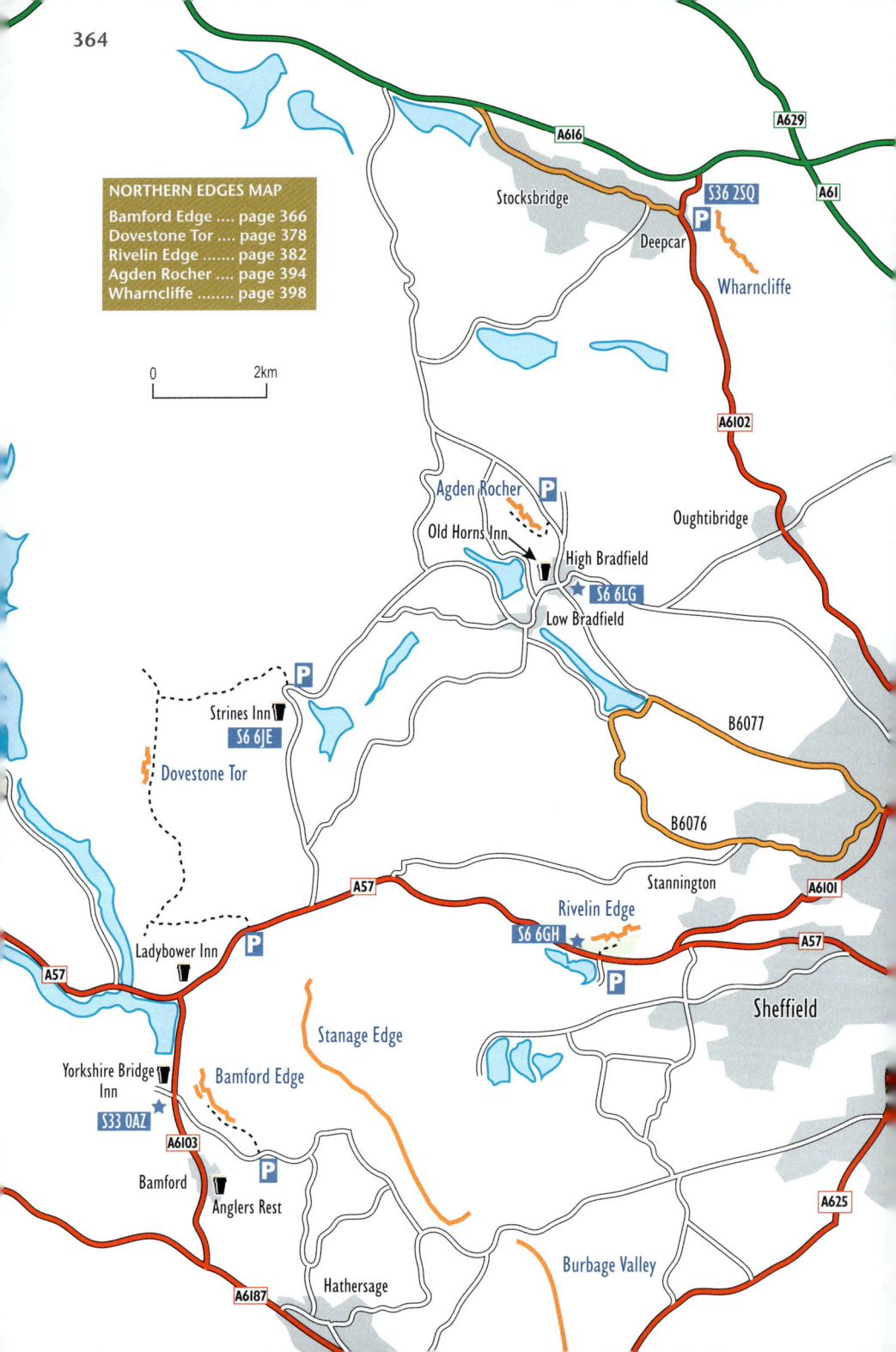

Some of the best routes at Agden Rocher use its distinct positive, crimpy nature to overcome otherwise foreboding walls, often helped along with good protection. It gives a special day out to bucolic crimp-hounds. Here, Dominic Oughton cruises Asteris, E1 5c (page 395), one of the crag's finest routes. 📷 Paul Evans

BAMFORD EDGE

OS Grid Ref: SK 208 849
Altitude: 390m

Bamford Edge is truly one of the gems of Peak grit. It sits majestically on a wild hillside, with its back turned on the busy popularity of the Eastern Edges, looking instead, longingly, towards the wildness of Kinder and Bleaklow. A happy crag, full of rough gritstone and rousing views.

As with any crag in such an exposed situation, there are two things to note about Bamford. One is that it will catch any inclement weather going, the other is that it will dry out in no time. It can be impossible to climb there on a very windy day. The crag faces southwest, and gets sun for most of the day.

ACCESS: No dogs. The crag is on open access land, but the landowner can restrict access for up to 28 days per year (often used on public safety grounds for shooting in moorland areas). Please check the BMC's Regional Access Database (RAD) before a visit. Closures will also be posted at the access point.

Approach: Near the top of the hill on New Road is a patch of trees and a footpath leading down to Bamford Village. Park in the roadside bay that starts just uphill from these trees. At the top of the bay is a gate and stile – this is the only permitted access point to the crag. Cross the stile and follow the path to the crag – a 15 to 25 minute walk.

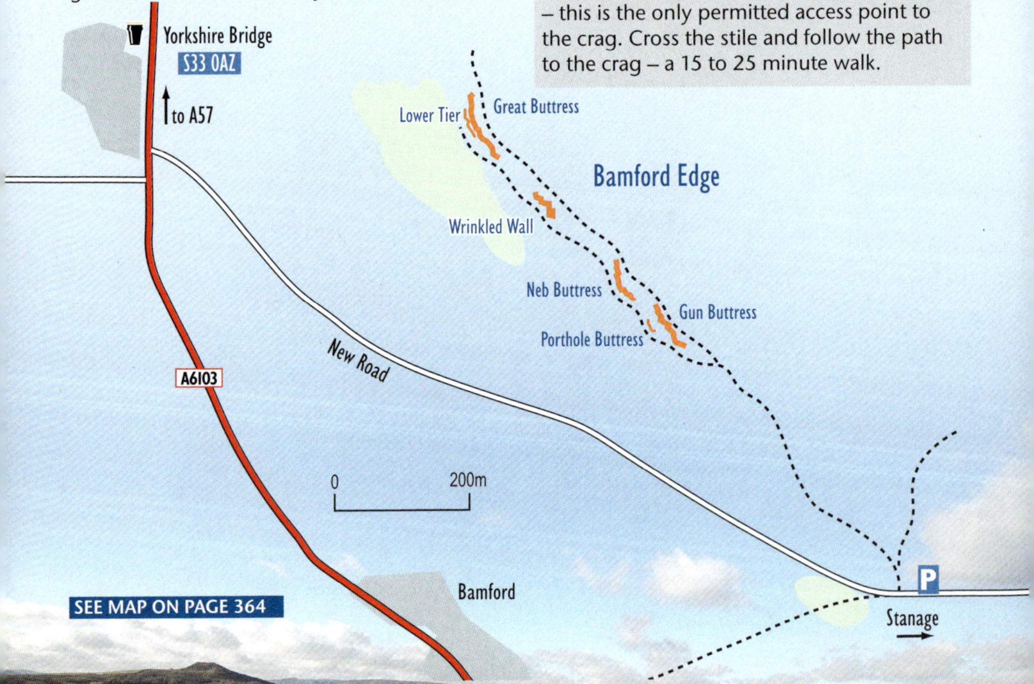

The finest of the many fine buttresses on Bamford must surely be Neb Buttress. The climbs here have a loftiness that befits the already fine setting, routes punching up the steep walls where jugs and gear are usually constant companions. Oh! for summer days, hands full of gritstone, that rolling landscape at your heels. Simon Watchorn-Rice on Neb Buttress, HVS 5a (page 374). 📷 Andy Birtwistle

GREAT BUTTRESS

Few crags can match the grandeur of its setting, perched high on the hillside, guarding the tranquil village of Bamford, looking across onto Win Hill, and of course, along to the dams and reservoirs of the Derwent Valley. Added to this is a great collection of routes in the mid-grades, and you are left with one of the great venues on grit.

It has two tiers, one of the highlights being the beautiful Salmon Slab, one of the great slabs on grit, and a superb testing ground for the lover of high-end smearing.

Lower Tier – Quien Sabe? Area: This is found down and to the left of the Salmon Slab.

1 Hasta La Vista 8m HVD
A good honest thrutch. Start a few metres left of the corner of *Bilberry Crack*. Climb the wide crack and step right onto the upper slab. The finish is easier but does feature a short grovel.
Geoffrey Sutton, Geoff Roberts, 1957

2 Bilberry Crack 10m VS 5a ★★
A little gem. The left-hand corner-crack gives good well-protected climbing.
Dick Brown, 1952

3 Recess Crack 10m VD
Climb the stiff right-hand corner of the recess.
Dick Brown, 1952

4 Nemmes Pas Harry 10m E1 5b ★★
A little artificial but still with quality climbing. Follow the disappearing crack over the bulge to gain ledges and finish up the reachy scoop.
Gary Gibson, Phil Gibson, 1982

5 Quien Sabe? 14m VS 5a ★★★
Guaranteed to brighten your day; safe and technically absorbing. From *Brown's Crack*, swing up the scoop to a crack in the nose above. The crux is overcoming this.
Brian Evans, Allan Austin, 1958

An excellent sustained HVS 5b, **Nemmes Sabe** ★★, can be had by linking the start of *Nemmes Pas Harry* with the more natural finish of *Quien Sabe?*

6 Brown's Crack 12m HS 4b ★★★
A tremendous route taking the straight crack. It proves tricky to begin and the rest is pure crack-climbing delight.
Dick Brown, David Sampson, 1951

Lower Tier – Salmon Slab: The showpiece of the area is the smooth slab, one of the top five slabs on grit.

7 Jetrunner 12m E4 6a ★★
A great introduction to the local slab delights, with a couple of tidy runouts. Climb the wall to the break then finish up the left arête.
Andy Bailey, 1984

8 Salmon Left-Hand 12m E6 6b ★★★
A first-rate route, friendly at the grade. Climb *Jetrunner* to the break. Step up and follow pockets until a lunge gains the ledge.
Nick Dixon, 1995

9 Smoked Salmon 12m E7 7a ★★★
Slab climbing at its most tenuous. Gain the break. Very small smears and miniscule pebbles mark the way up towards a group of small pockets. If you reach here, via the three consecutive 7a moves, you truly are a slab master.
Johnny Dawes, 1995

10 Curving Crack 10m VS 4c ★
Meanwhile, back on planet Earth... Follow the bold curving feature with great jams and increasing difficulty to a delicate step into *Sandy Crack* and a still interesting finish.
Allan Austin, Brian Evans, Doug Verity, 1958

11 Quebec City 30m VS 5a ★
An easy drive through stunning scenery. Start up *Sandy Crack* and keep heading leftwards along the break to finish up *Quien Sabe?* or easier, (HS 4b) continue to *Recess Crack*.
Chris Crags, Graham Parkes, 1981

Palpitation Buttress   Undercut Buttress   Gargoyle Buttress   Tinner Buttress

Lower Tier

Bamford Edge | 369

12 Sandy Crack 8m S 4b ★
The corner gives good climbing to a ledge. The offwidth crack above gives an awkward finish.
Eric Byne, Clifford Moyer, 1930

13 Fizz 7m E1 5c ★
A remarkably joyous little climb, guaranteed to give a buzz. Boulder up to the ledge then climb the wall past two sets of threadable pockets. Reachy.
Martin Veale, 1980

Great Buttress Upper Tier: The crown of the buttress has a collection of fresh routes.

14 Palpitation 7m HVS 5b
Power up the undercut arête with difficulty.
Eric Byne, Clifford Moyer, 1930

15 Initiation 6m S 4b
The short V-corner leads to a layback overhang. A stiff pull leads to the top.

16 Beer Matters 6m VS 5a
The arête climbed on its right-hand side to a steep finish. The block at the top 'appears' solid enough.
Paul Harrison, 1997

17 Deep Chimney 10m M
Chimneys were all the rage in 1900, apparently. Classic stuff.
JW Puttrell, WJ Watson, 1900s

18 Kelly 10m S 4a
Another ancient addition from one of the Peak's great pioneers. Starting down and right, move up to gain the shelf. Take a short crack in the sidewall above and move round right to finish.
Harry Kelly, 1918

19 Astronaut's Wall 10m HVS 5a ★
Grunt up to the overhang and go through the weakness before things get easier above. Take care with protection in the hollow rock beneath the overhang.
MP Haston, John Robson, 1963

20 Possibility 12m S 4a ★
A fine juggy ramble. On the left wall of *Primitive Chimney*, go up to below the upper bulge. Move left round the corner in a great situation and a leftwards finish.
Bob Downes, Harold Drasdo, Philip Gordon, 1957

21 Primitive Chimney 10m D
Another fine Puttrell thrutch. The obvious V-cleft where the huge overhang ends is climbed passing a moving chockstone.
JW Puttrell, H Smithard, 1901

Undercut and Gargoyle Buttress

22 Undercut Crack 10m E2 5c ★★★
Thuggery at its best. This is where a gritstone crack climbing apprenticeship will pay off. Attack the major fissure with gusto.
Allan Austin, 1958

23 MAy35 10m E6 6c ★★
A forceful route climbing up and through the big scallop feature in the roof.
Joe Brown (aid), 1958. FFA Ben Bransby, 2006

24 Avoiding the Traitors 10m E7 6c ★★
An elegant addition to the great roof. The splendid dish and runnels feature powerful, dynamic and bold climbing. ⓒ opposite page
Johnny Dawes, 1995

25 Terrace Trog 14m M ★
The leftwards-slanting weakness is climbed easily with increasing exposure.

26 Terrace Wall 13m VS 4b
From *Terrace Trog*, take a diagonal weakness rising up the steep wall on the right.
MP Haston, John Robson, 1963

27 Gargoyle Flake 13m VS 4c ★★★
An excellent, photogenic route with reasonable climbing in thrilling positions. Climb the lower arête to a ledge and layback the large flake above to an exhilarating finish over the gargoyles, using the biggest jugs possible.
MP Haston, John Robson, 1963

28 Gargoyle Gully 10m D
The gully can be climbed in a variety of ways.

29 Sunset 10m HVD
The short offwidth and juggy wall above.

30 Bum Deal 10m E1 5c ★
Cross the cruxy overhang via the helpful 'bum' then the easier crack above.
Chris Craggs, 1981

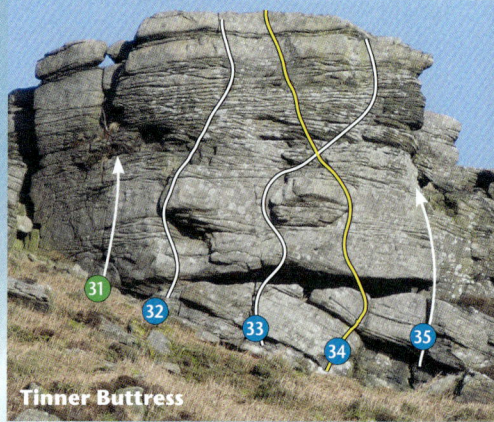

Tinner Buttress

Tinner Buttress: Sat to the right is an isolated buttress, the last of the upper buttresses.

31 Left Wing 8m S 4a
The broken cracks passing a heathery niche.

32 Tinner 10m HVS 5b ★
A bold lead, where a steady approach is the key. Use the flake to surmount a bulge and continue precariously to a ledge, then the top.
Allan Austin, Brian Evans, 1958

33 Right-Hand Twin 12m HVS 5a ★
Gain the chunky flake and follow the rightwards-slanting line. Protection takes a little finding.
Allan Austin, Brian Evans, 1958

34 Private Practice 10m HVS 5b ★
A direct line up the buttress gives more of the same quality and boldness.
John Allen, Mark Stokes, c1990

35 Solstice Arête 10m VS 4c ★
The arête is escapable, but has good moves.
Peter Stone, 1997

Mark Rankine on the Johnny Dawes roof-buster, Avoiding the Traitors, E7 6c (opposite page). Bold, uncompromising climbing, great rock and a cool line combine to make a classic Bamford pitch. It's a bit harder to enjoy the view on this one all the same. 📷 James Thornton

WRINKLED WALL AREA
These are the rocks around the Easter-Island-style feature, 70m right of Tinner Buttress.

36 K Buttress Slab 6m D ★
A nice climb up the right edge of the slab.

37 K Buttress Crack 8m S 4a ★★
A deep and dark voyage up the spooky, slanting chimney. It offers a variety of positions.

38 Wrong Hand Route 9m E1 5c ★★
The very definition of the grade. A short, hard and well protected sequence, tamable by masters, a struggle for most.
John Gosling, 1971

39 Skarlati 9m E2 5c ★
Long reaches above distant protection. From the right, gain a small ledge on the right arête. Go over the bulge above, trending slightly left.
Martin Boysen, 1969

40 Fern Chimney 9m D
The wide voyage.

41 Bracken Crack 9m VD ★
Follow the crack, moving right over the bulge.
Pete Hatton, 1963

42 Dead Mouse Crack 7m HS 4a ★
The exposed and reachy left-slanting crack.
Allan Austin, 1958

43 Jasmine 10m E6 6b ★★
Maybe E5 for super-confident pad monsters, E7 for careful traditionalists. The centre of the wall is climbed on poor breaks. No protection.
Ron Fawcett, 1990

44 Access Account 10m E3 6a
Committing climbing leads to the wide break, then more easily up the left side of the arête.
Allan Austin, 1958

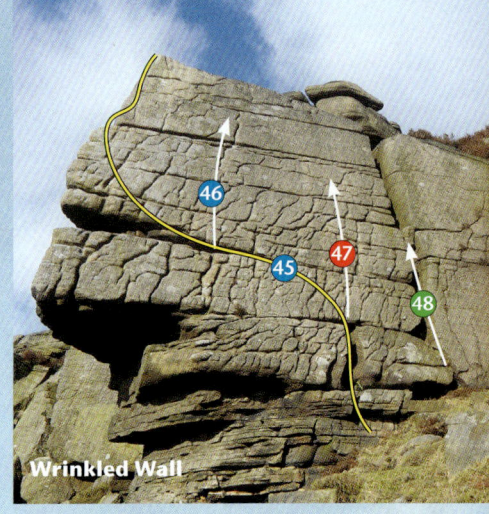
Wrinkled Wall

45 Wrinkled Wall 14m VS 4c ★★
An absolute must for any VS leader, with solid moves and spaced protection. Start up a vertical slot, then go left to the arête. An airy finale up this concludes a tremendous route.
⊙ opposite page
Allan Austin, 1958

46 Old and Wrinkled 14m HVS 5a ★
Start as for *Wrinkled Wall* then follow some bold and balancey climbing up the wall slightly left of centre.

47 The Crease 12m E1 5a ★★
A distinct lack of protection gives the E grade (just) and makes this an exciting outing. Head straight up using shallow cracks and without recourse to the arête on the right.
Mark Davies, 1979

48 Sinuous Crack 10m D ★
The crack.

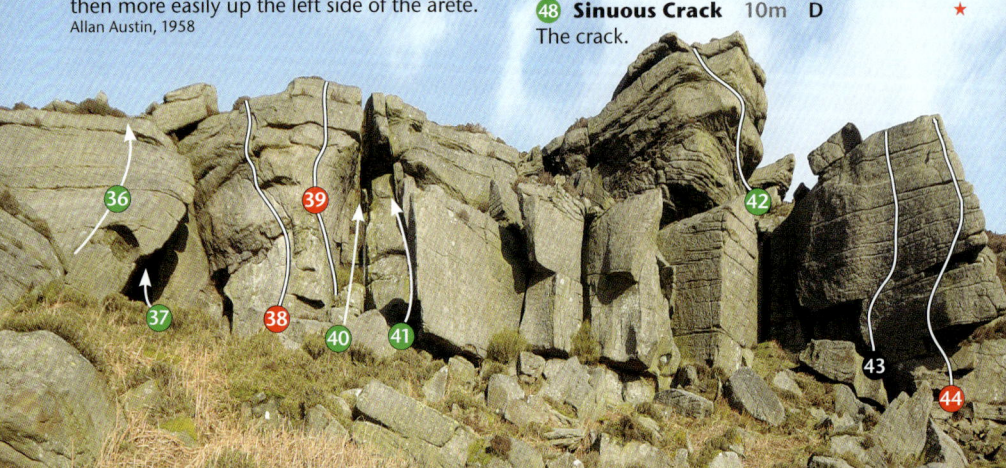

Wrinkled Wall, VS 4c (opposite page), gives a quick and scenic voyage to confident VS leaders. The rock is unique and the setting a delight. Here John Smith prepares to set off up the runout arête, as a cold wind howls down from Win Hill. Brrrrr. 📷 Paul Evans

NEB BUTTRESS

Twenty metres to the right sees the beginning of the Neb Buttress area, containing some of the longest and best climbs on Bamford Edge.

49 Cleopatra 10m VS 4c
A burly, hanging crack rising from the corner on the left side of the arête.

50 Sampson's Delight 10m HS 4c ★
A gem. Climb the overhanging arête then follow the strenuous crack on hidden holds.
MP Hatton, John Robert, 1958

51 Dirty Stop Out 10m E2 5b ★
A fierce little crack leads to delightful moves over the upper bulge.
Chris Lawson, Trevor Pilling, 1981

52 Delilah 10m HS 4a ★
The wide crack. A big cam can help.

53 Short Curve 10m VD ★
Steep, awkward fun.

54 N.B. Corner 8m M
The corner.

55 Big Ben 10m VS 4c ★
The left-hand of twin cracks in the sidewall.
Chris Lawson, Trevor Pilling, 1981

56 Parliament 10m HVS 5b ★
The right-hand crack in the sidewall, artificially avoiding the left-hand crack.
Chris Craggs, 1981

57 Auricle 16m E2 5c ★★
A tremendous route, with good holds, bomber gear and, if you have long arms, very gentle for the grade. Climb the steep and technical face direct, with reachy moves to pass the mid-height overlap. Escape right at the top overhang: the direct finish is **Jumping Jack Longland**, E3 5c ★★.
John Gosling, Arthur Robinson, B Carus, 1971

58 Neb Buttress 20m HVS 5a ★★★
A classic and varied climb to rival any on grit. Climb the thin crack, then traverse left on good holds to the arête. Step round left to follow the steep crack to the overhang, then the wall above to escape strenuously right along the wide crack and mantel over the nose to finish.
⊙ page 367
Allan Austin, 1958

59 Bamford Rib 17m HVS 5a ★★
A fine companion to *Neb Buttress*, this time demanding technique and boldness more than force. Neat moves up the blunt rib lead to a ledge and a prickly rest. Step left and continue up the steeper wall via the obvious lump.
John Allen, Mark Stokes, 1973

60 The Happy Wanderer 13m HVS 5a ★★
An exquisite and well-protected route – satisfyingly steep on generous holds. Climb the square arête on jugs to a reachy move below the top overlaps (5b for the short).
Geoff Morgan, 1967

Bamford Edge | 375

61 Reach 13m VS 4c ★
Climb direct 2m right of the arête (and keeping left of *Bamford Wall*). Good sustained climbing.
Chris Craggs, Graham Parkes, 1981

62 Bamford Wall 13m S 4a ★★
A first-class route, a must for anyone operating at this level. Climb a rightward-slanting flake to the top of a big flake. Move right and go straight up the wall, finishing up the crack.
Hugh Banner, 1960

63 Bamford Buttress 13m HS 4a ★
Starting at a yellow hole, climb up and onto a huge flake at 5m and then slant up and right to finish as for *Twin Cracks*. Not overly-protected.
Brian Evans, 1958

64 Twin Cracks 10m VS 4b ★
A surprisingly graceful route, considering the terrain. From the cave, climb up to follow the right-hand crack by bridging and jamming.
Hugh Banner, 1960

65 Deep Cleft 12m M ★
The chimney is taken in its depths and a tight exit is performed behind the chockstones. A bit harder on the outside of the chockstone (D).

66 Oracle 13m VS 4b ★★
An unsung route with a very traditional feel taking spectacular ground but just meriting the VS tag. From halfway up *Deep Cleft*, take a deep breath and traverse right above the void using a low break to gain the arête at a small roof. Swing round and finish up the arête.
Paul Nunn, Ken Jones, 1971

67 Sterling Moss 18m E4 6b ★★
Easy climbing leads to committing, crimpy moves over the roof.
Johnny Dawes, 1984

68 Ontos 18m E3 6b ★★
A tough bouldery pull over the roof gives the action on this stubborn route. Climb to the roof and use a jug and sloping holds to gain the slab above.
John Allen, 1975

69 Fatal Inheritance 18m E4 6a ★
The roof and wall just right of *Ontos*.
Gary Gibson, 1982

70 Trouble with Lichen 25m HVS 5b ★
A good route crossing memorable territory. Climb the slab on the right of the buttress. Step up and head leftwards on a narrow ledge to its end where a committing step leaves one stood on the jug of *Ontos*. An exposed but protectable foot-traverse on the lowest break gains the left arête up which a finish is made.
John Allen, Mark Stokes, 1973

71 Slanting Slab 10m M
The easy-angled slab.

Porthole Buttress

PORTHOLE BUTTRESS
The lower tier of Gun Buttress.

72 Slab and Crack 8m D
The slab and short layback crack above.

73 Moglichkeit 12m VS 4b
The overhanging chimney and fist crack.
Allan Austin, 1958

74 Plimsoll Line 12m HVS 5a
Reach the hole from the cave on the left and finish directly up the bold wall above.
Colin Binks, 1981

75 Porthole 12m HVS 5a ★
Excellent, tense climbing. Climb easily to the hole. Move left and climb the grasping arête.
Hugh Banner, 1961

76 Portside 12m S 4a ★
The slab and wall, passing the right-hand porthole.
Hugh Banner, 1961

77 Leaning Slab 12m VD ★
The pleasant slab and wall.

78 Trango 2 12m E3 5c ★
The fine unprotected wall, with a high crux.
Martin Boysen, 1987

GUN BUTTRESS
The first proper buttress encountered on the way in is a great spot for lower-grade climbs and beginners.

79 Shadow Wall 12m VS 5a ★
The sidewall is climbed up its centre before moving right below the gun to finish.
Chris Craggs, 1981

Gun Buttress

80 Life During Wartime 12m E2 5c ★
The arête, passing the square roof.
Keith Ashton, 1985

81 Randy's Wall 13m HVS 5a ★★
A tough climb. Climb up to the square roof, move up rightwards to a rest and runners in the centre of the wall. Finish direct, or continue along the traverse towards the right edge of the buttress before moving up.
John Robson, 1960s

82 Magnum Force 13m HVS 5b ★
A more strenuous way up the wall than its randy neighbour. Climb straight over the bulges in the centre of the wall to the mid-height rest on *Randy's*. Move up and leftwards almost to the arête before going up.
Chris Craggs, 1981

83 Gunpowder Crack 12m VS 5b ★
The excellent undercut crack has a hard start and is the scene of some colourful language.
Hugh Banner, 1961

84 Master Blaster 11m E1 5c ★
On the wall immediately left of *Loader's Bay*, haul over a small roof and climb direct. A fine climb with tricky protection (small wires).
Chris Craggs, 1981

85 Loader's Bay 8m D
The corner.

86 Ammo 8m S 4a
Climb the short arête and the wall above.

87 Long John 8m HVS 5b
The undercut arête. A gigantic reach, a gnarly leap or a 5b traverse from the corner on the left gains good holds on the lip of the roof. A pile of stones is useful if lacking in inches, ethics or both.

88 Three Real Men Dancing 8m E2 6a ★
Pull over the overhang left of the chimney and climb the difficult, thin wall.

89 Green Chimney 8m VD
The constricted chimney has a hard start.

90 Artillery Corner 8m D
Green, but straightforward, corner climbing.

91 Gangway 8m VD 4a
The gangway, gained from the left. Or S 4b more directly.

92 Bosun's Slab 8m D
Take the slabby wall trending slightly left.

93 Concave Slab 8m M
Climb the narrow slab from the block.

94 Adjacent Slab 8m D
Follow the centre of the pleasant slab.

95 Hypotenuse 8m M
The corner is a good beginner's route.

96 Opposite 8m S 4a
Climb the wall on good holds.

97 Vertigo 10m HS 4c
The left arête of the buttress. A problem 4c start over the initial overhang starting just to the right of the overhang's arête leads to a stretch for a break on the left. Move back right to finish.
MP Hatton, John Robinson, 1963

98 Dynamite Groove 10m E1 5b ★
Start on the sloping block below a shallow groove (or from the back of the roof). Make a hard pull into the groove and continue direct.
Martin Veale, Chris Craggs, 1981

99 Right Side 8m S 4a
Climb up just left of the blunt arête.

Gun Buttress

DOVESTONE TOR

OS Grid Ref: SK 196 897
Altitude: 470m

VS / HVS heaven. The showpiece of the area. It's no surprise that the early pioneers were drawn to produce great deeds on this section of rock. The centrepiece, The Great Buttress, is most spectacular, giving long, steep and adventure-filled climbs of the highest quality. The rock is intricate and heavily featured on its bulging lower sections, and rough, hard grit at the top. Combine all this with its isolated setting and amazing views, and it becomes one of gritstone's select venues.

The crag gets the afternoon and evening sun. It can be cold and windy, so it is essentially a summer crag. Perfect for midsummer evenings, with a chance of missing last orders in the Ladybower Inn.

Approach: Park in the layby 250m east of Cutthroat Bridge on the A57. Walk down the road to the bridge, cross the road, and take the well-made path onto the moor. At the intersection on the col, turn sharp right to follow the path along the edge, passing several outcrops along the way. The main crag is below you at the highest point of the ridge. Allow up to 70 minutes.

Alternatively, and perhaps slightly quicker, park on the road approx. 400m north of the Strines Inn. Walk through the gate and take the Foulstone Road (bridleway – tarmac initially) to the ridge. Dovestone Tor is about 600m south of the point where the bridleway meets the main ridge. About 60 minutes.

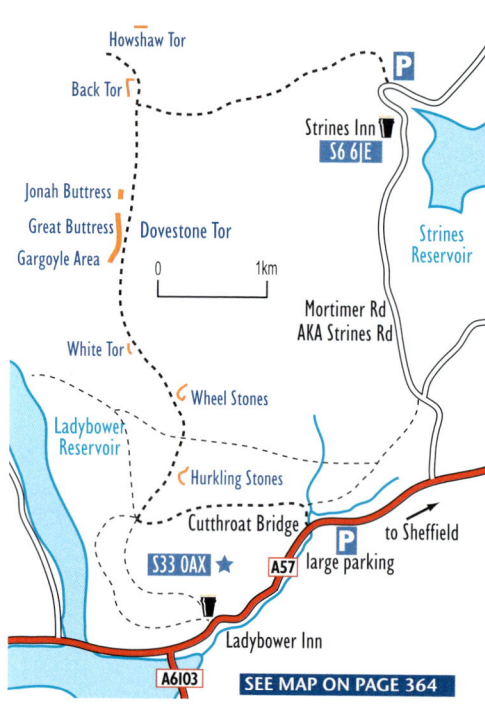

JONAH BUTTRESS
This is 60m left of Great Buttress

① Windblasted 8m D ★
Fine wall climbing, easy for the grade.

② Windblown 8m VD ★
A direct line up the juggy wall.
Ted Howard, 1957

③ Jonah 8m D ★
For full value, finish inside the chockstone.

④ Titanium 9m VS 4c ★
The slab and wall just left of the blunt rib.
Chris Craggs, 1994

⑤ Titanic 9m VS 4c ★
The fun, juggy wall passing the diagonal crack
Chris Craggs, 1996

⑥ Titania 9m HS 4b ★
The slab and juggy wall just left of the arête.
Chris Craggs, 1996

Jonah Buttress

Oh yeah! Great Buttress, HVS 5a (page 380). Honestly, this is one of the HVS treasures of the Peak District. A long walk-in and a shorter season make trips to Dovestone Tor all the more special when they happen. If this visit coincides with a fresh, sunny evening, purple heather, good friends and some solid fitness on steep jugs, then you are in for a feast. Andy Birtwistle climbing the moorland classic. Birtwistle collection

GREAT BUTTRESS
This sits to the right, dominating the edge, a mighty, steep, exposed and juggy buttress. One of the coolest in the book.

7 Dovestones Gully 20m M
The deep chimney is fun. Finish leftwards.
Ted Howard, 1957

8 Dovestones Edge 18m S 4a ★
From the bulging start, continue direct up slabby rock.
Chris Craggs, 1996

9 Dovestones Wall 20m VD ★★
An excellent, exposed climb which unfortunately can be dirty. Climb steep perforated rock to gain a slab. Climb this slightly to the right and then back to the left to finish.
Albert Shutt, Roy Beadham, Ron Ibbotson, 1949

10 A Little Green Eyed God 20m VS 4c ★
A fine climb, steep and exposed for its entire length. Climb onto a large jammed block and carry on fairly direct up holey features to finish out on the arête in an exposed position.
Chris Craggs, 1996

11 Barney Rubble 20m VS 4b ★★★
Excellent sustained climbing on huge holds, full-on VS. Move up into the left-hand sandy cave then climb boldly up the steep wall above on big holds until below the flat roof. Pull through the bottomless corner in the roof to gain a slab and an easier finish directly above.
Paul & Neil Harrison, 1984

12 Thread Flintstone 20m E1 5b ★★
As good as its name. Pull over the low roof, climb between the two caves and continue steeply up on good holds to the capping roof. A big yank over this leads to an easy finish.
Mike Appleton, 1996

13 Great Buttress Eliminate 22m HVS 5a ★★
A fine steep route. Gain and follow the undercut rib to a junction with *Great Buttress*. Continue directly through bulges until it is possible to traverse right and finish as for *Great Buttress*.
Stuart Gascoyne, 1981

14 Great Buttress 20m HVS 5a ★★★
Fantastic! Solid HVS, one of the most thrilling routes of that grade in the Peak. From near the corner, climb leftwards to just past the arête. Go straight up the steep wall then trend right through the bulges, just above the lip of the roof, until a final tricky move gives access to the ledge. Finish up *Central Climb* or the poorly-protected slab to its left (E1 5b). ⊙ page 379
Ted Howard, Barry Pedlar, 1957

15 Sforzando 17m E5 6a ★
A wild route crossing the double roofs.
Alan Monks, 1985

16 Central Climb 25m VS 4c, 5a ★
Climb the corner and trend rightwards to avoid the overhang and reach the corner on its right with difficulty and up to a ledge (possible belay). Move left and make thuggy moves into an undercut flake, up which a finish is made.
Albert Shutt, Roy Beadham, Robert Gratton, Reg Pillinger, 1949

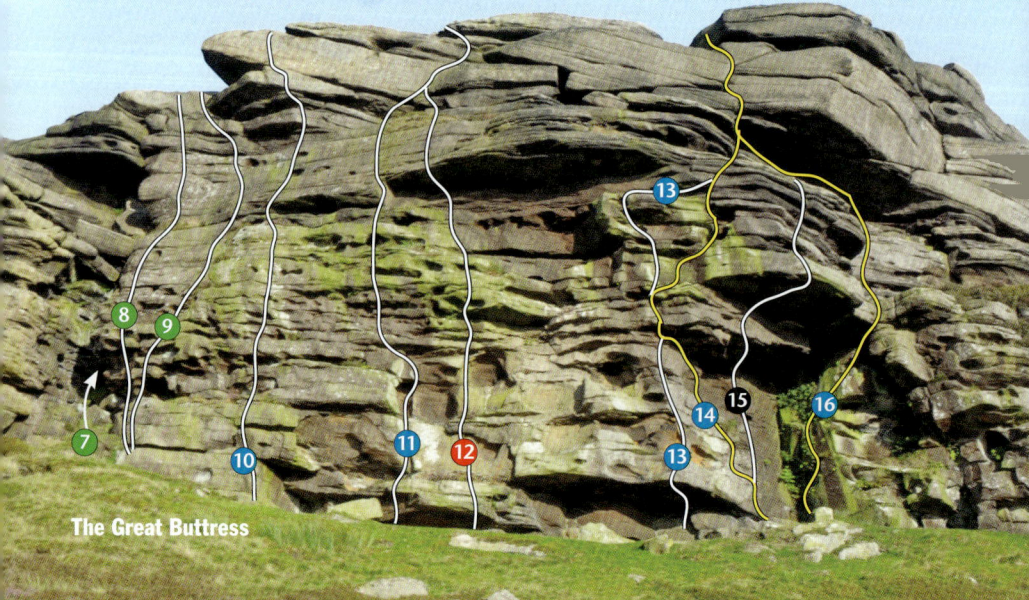
The Great Buttress

GARGOYLE BUTTRESS & BUTTRESS I

The twin buttresses to the right are not as impressive as Great Buttress, but nonetheless are still worth the walk.

17 Gargoyle Traverse 16m S 4b ★
Start up the slab to gain the well-positioned traverse. Finish up the blocky chimney.
Albert Shutt, 1949

18 Stoney Faced 16m E1 5b ★
Climb the arête to a slab then the bulging wall left of the crack to a bold, puzzling finish.
Mike Appleton, 1996

19 Gargoyle Buttress 16m VS 4c ★
A fine climb in good situations. Climb the corner then traverse left to attack the bulging crack.
Geoffrey Sutton, 1957

20 Route I 16m VS 4c ★★★
A brilliant old-fashioned VS, at the top of its grade. Follow the bold square arête. Steep moves lead to a ledge below an overhang. Difficult moves over this lead to a short, ferocious corner-crack. Finish rightwards.
Albert Shutt, Peter Rickus, Peter Todd, 1949

21 The Shylock Finish 16m HVS 5a ★★
An exhilarating leftwards finish to *Route I*. From the ledge, follow the lowest horizontal break out left and finish in a dramatic situation.
Stuart Gascoyne, 1981

22 Blue Velvet 12m E1 6a ★★
A fierce move gains the tiny crack. Continue with the usual ledgey steepness to join the final moves of *Route I*.
Chris Craggs, 1996

23 Claw Climb 14m VS 4c ★
Steep terrain leads dramatically left under the roof. Get established over this, trend up and right more easily.
Ted Howard, Tanky Stokes, 1957

24 Talon 14m VS 4c ★
Go up the recessed corner groove until forced out right onto the front face. A couple of quick pulls leads to slabbier rock.
Ted Howard, Tanky Stokes, 1957

25 Lancaster Flyby 14m E1 5b ★★
A fine route with steep moves and positive protection, generally taking the wall right of the arête.
Chris Craggs, 1996

26 Route II 14m VS 4b ★
From the grassy ledge follow the rising diagonal break out to the left edge (crossing *Lancaster Flyby*) and pull around onto a slab in a great position to finish up the arête above.
Albert Shutt, Peter Rickus, Peter Todd, 1949

OTHER BUTTRESSES

The other rocks marked on the Derwent map, Hurkling Stones, Wheel Stones, White Tor, Back Tor and Howshaw Tor, all give further fantastic exploration with lots of wild bouldering and short routes. Full coverage can be found in *Burbage, Millstone and Beyond*.

Gargoyle Buttress | Buttress I

RIVELIN EDGE

OS Grid Ref: SK 278 872
Altitude: 260m

A gem of a crag with a host of fabulous routes that are bursting with character, giving continually interesting moves on generally very strong lines. Rivelin is worth a visit at any time, but it comes into its own in poor weather when other crags can be out of condition.

Really good climbing on a combination of quarried and natural grit. Tending towards the steep and the technical. Mainly on cracks, arêtes and walls with positive edges. Routes tend to be well protected.

Rivelin is low-lying and often in the rain shadow of the Peak District. The edge faces south and is a sheltered sun-trap, making it an excellent winter venue when other crags are windswept. By the same measure, it can feel unpleasantly warm on sunny summer days. Sun from late morning till early evening.

Approach: Park in the car park across the dam-wall. Return to the A57 and follow the footpath uphill. Turn right, across a small stream. Trend left and wind through the trees to reach the Rivelin Needle area in around 15 minutes. Please stick to existing paths.

ACCESS: Please do not bring instructional groups here. Please check the BMC's Regional Access Database (RAD) before a visit.

LEFT-HAND AREA
Upon reaching the edge, walk left along a series of buttresses amongst the trees. The first routes described here are Birch Buttress, about 100m left of Kremlin Buttress.

Birch Buttress

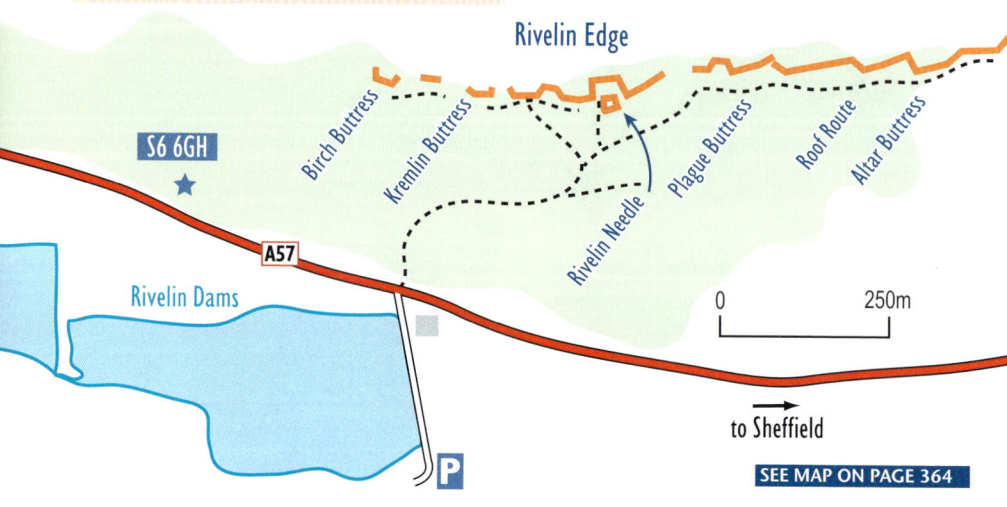

to Sheffield

SEE MAP ON PAGE 364

Kremlin Buttress

1. **Birch Bark** 7m HS 4a
The slight rib then step right to a tricky finish.

2. **Birch Buttress** 7m S 4a ★
Pleasant smearing up the centre of the slab.

3. **Don't Birch the Doc** 7m VS 4c
An eliminate up the vague arête and wall.
Graham Hully, Tony Boreham, 1994

4. **Birch Crack** 7m VD ★
A great route up the central fissure.

5. **Birch** 7m HVS 5a ★
A bold route up the arête.
Al Wright, G Rogan, 1964

KREMLIN BUTTRESS
Strong lines on good rock.

6. **Seville Flake** 7m HVS 5a ★
A lovely little climb. Gain the flake on the sidewall direct and follow it to a rightwards finish.
Al Wright, 1956

7. **Ausfahrt** 11m E3 5c ★★
Exposed and unlikely. From the ledge on the left, swing right and mantelshelf onto the small ledge. Step left and follow the exposed rib, which eases with height.
Chris Craggs, 1991

8. **Exit** 11m E3 5c ★★
A great exposed route. From the niche, mantel over the bulge and continue directly, in a lonely position, up the line of the crack.
Roger Greatrick, Chris Rowe, 1983

9. **Jaded** 11m E4 6b ★
Climb the short wall to the break. A thin pull on slopers allows the centre of the upper wall to be gained and followed, past a nut slot.
Graham Hoey, Nic Hallam, 1986

10. **Kremlin Krack** 11m HVS 5a ★★
One of those routes that a climbing wall can't prepare you for. Ascend the steep crack by strenuous jamming and wedging, along with the occasional hidden hold.

11. **Scarlett's Chimney** 11m VS 4c ★
Enter the widening chimney with some difficulty. Battle and curse your way to the top.
Harry Scarlett, 'Ginger' Wylie, c1928

12. **Left Edge** 11m HVS 4c ★
A good route with a bold move onto the left arête of the slab. The slab direct is E1 5b.
Pete Crew, Al Wright, c1961

13. **Rivelin Slab** 11m M
A wandering line up the broken slab on good holds to the right.

14 Angle Rib   7m   HVS 5a
Climb a crack to a ledge. Step right and back left to climb the right-hand side of the rib.

15 Angle Crack   7m   D
The corner crack has a good finish.

16 Solitaire   7m   VD
Ascend the crack in the wall just right.

17 Isolation   7m   S   ★
The wide deep fissure is demanding.

18 Rodney's Dilemma   7m   S 4a   ★★
The arête is an exposed gem with joyous holds and just enough protection. ⊙ opposite page
Rodney Wilson, c1961

19 Temple Crack   7m   VD   ★
The slanting crack to a juggy exit.

20 Crafty Cockney   7m   E2 5c   ★
Climb the scoop to a thin break. Step right and reach up to small crimps. A stiff pull brings positive holds then, all too quickly, the top.
John Allen, Nick Stokes, 1984

21 Pious Flake   7m   S 4b
A good route up the thin corner crack on the right. A hard but well-protected move gains the ledge below the tree and an easy finish up the blocky cleft.
Al Wright, c1961

22 White Out   12m   E2 5c   ★★
A popular route following the wall 2m left of *Blizzard Ridge*. Move carefully up to a horizontal break at half-height. Stretch past this keeping left of the arête to finish. Straying right at the break reduces the grade to E1.
Bob Bradley, Graham Hoey, 1983

23 Blizzard Ridge   14m   HVS 5a   ★★★
The arête provides a quality climb that is not overly endowed with protection. Gain the arête via a thin flake on the right. Continue airily to welcome protection below a small nose. Move right around this and climb direct.
Allan Austin, 1958

24 The Tempest   12m   E5 6b   ★
A worrying lead up the centre of the slab.

25 Jonathan's Chimney   12m   HS 4b   ★
The fine corner crack has a hard start.
Harry Scarlett, 'Ginger' Wylie, c1930

26 David's Chimney   12m   VD   ★
The wide crack with a tricky chockstone.
Harry Scarlett, 'Ginger' Wylie, c1930

Clever climbers, when the weak sun struggles to warm a winter's day, when Millstone is a Siberian ice box and Stanage is dressed in drizzle, head to Rivelin. It's surprising how often clement conditions can be found when other crags send climbers scurrying to the indoor wall. Marcus Buckley in his shirt sleeves on Rodney's Dilemma, S 4a (opposite page). 📷 Ian Carr

RIVELIN NEEDLE
The landmark of the edge. All its routes are well worth doing. Summit belay and subsequent abseil descent are from a fixed chain down the short back side.

27 Declaration 12m E5 6c ★
Desperate, even for 6c, but protectable. Start down and right of the platform at a thin crack. Climb the crack to gear, then slap up the blunt arête above. Finish direct.
Dave Pegg, 1986

28 Angst 12m E3 5c ★★
A very good route, with an exciting finish. Climb the groove in the arête to the overhang. Move out left and follow thin cracks to the break and a steep finish up the wall above.
Ian Riddington, 1984

29 Original Route 14m E2 5c ★★
Follow *Angst* to the overhang and move up right with difficult long stretches onto the cracked wall. Finish up this and the flake of *Croton Oil*.
Eric Byne, Clifford Moyer (aid), 1935. FFA Joe Brown, 1954

30 Croton Oil 20m HVS 5a ★★★
The route of the crag? Climb a deep, wide crack to a ledge. Balance up the face to a short crack and stretch left for a flake. Follow this to a notch and a finish up a flake. ⊙ opposite page
Dick Brown, Donald Wooller, Frank Fitzgerald (5pt), 1953. FFA Pete Crew, Oliver Woolcock, 1963

31 The Spiral Route 22m VS 4c ★★
Start as for *Croton Oil* and continue up the next crack to the platform. Belay. From its end, traverse out rightwards along the horizontal break and a finish up the flake of *Croton Oil*.
Donald Wooller, Dick Brown, J Renshaw, 1950

32 Jumpey Wooller 12m E6 6c ★
Start from a boulder on the ledge at the back of the needle. Climb the short black wall to the overhang. Round this, with crux moves to get established on the hanging slab.
Niall Grimes, 1998

The Peak's finest pinnacle? Possibly. With the easiest route up it being VS, any summiteer can rightly feel a special sense of place and peace. As such it sits as high on a gritstoner's wish list as Froggatt Pinnacle. Here Stephen Coughlan is on its standout route, Croton Oil, HVS 5a (opposite page). David Simmonite.

Face Climb

33 Face Climb No. 1 7m VD ★
From a head-height shelf, follow a line of square-cut holds passing a ledge.
Frank Burgess, George Walker, 1933

34 Face Climb No. 1.5 7m VS 4b ★
Cool soloing. From the head-high shelf, boldly follow smallish edges up and slightly right.
Geoff Milburn, 1962

35 I'm Back 7m E4 6a ★
A technical solo about 2m left of *Jelly Baby*. The crux is fairly low, but the landing is poor.
Nick Stokes, 1985

36 Jelly Baby 7m E1 5b
The slim corner is a tough exercise.
Chris Addy, Duncan Munroe, 1977

37 Face Climb No. 2 7m VS 4c ★
Go up the narrow face, trending left to a high crux. Lovely moves.
Frank Burgess, George Walker, 1933

38 Crack One 7m S 4a
The corner-crack leads to a steep, reachy finish.
Dick Brown, 1950

39 Oversight 7m VS 4c ★
The narrow wall with some bold climbing.
Clive Rowland, 1963

40 Crack Two 7m HD
The wide crack.

41 Shelf Wall 7m VS 4c ★
A fun mantelshelf, starting at a large flake.
Dick Brown, 1950

42 Easy Picking 9m E2 6b ★★
A superb testpiece. Initial bouldery moves lead to a juggy flake. The upper cracks provide thin, sustained climbing. Considered a sandbag.
Donald Wooller (aid), 1953. FFA Steve Bancroft, 1976

43 Oliver's Twist 9m VS 4b ★
On the right are twin cracks. This is the left-hand fist-wide crack.
Oliver Woolcock, 1963

The Brush Off

44 The Brush Off   10m   E4 5c   ★★★
The slabby arête is a classic adrenaline trip, not for the faint hearted. Simply brilliant.
Pete Crew (solo), 1963

45 Party Animal   10m   E3 5c   ★
A direct line up the narrow slab passing a thin break (small cam).
John Allen, Nicky Stokes, 1985

46 Fringe Benefit   10m   E1 5b   ★★
Memorable, inventive climbing. From *The Brush Off*, move right and pad up the right-hand side of the slab.
Graham Parkes, Nigel Baker, 1980

47 Fumf   5m   VS 5b   ★
The superb bouldery arête. Font 5.
Jack Soper, 1962

48 Wobbly Wall   5m   HVS 5b   ★
The elegant, unprotected groove: Font 6A.
Ed Drummond, 1969

49 Europe After Rain   5m   E4 6b   ★★
This splendid, elongated problem takes the right side of the wall with a distressing lunge for the top. Highball Font 7A.
John Allen (solo), 1984

PLAGUE BUTTRESS
Twenty metres right, a steep buttress sports an overhang and an old bolt (on *Plague*).

50 Outsider   9m   E2 5c   ★★
Consummate gritstone with an exhilarating run-out above good protection. Climb just left of the arête, gain the break, and swing onto the front face. Superb climbing remains.
Bill Briggs, Andy Parkin, 1976

51 Big Al   10m   E6 6c   ★
The edge's most technical climb following the steep wall. The bolt on *Plague* is pre-clipped - E7 without this.
Neil Stokes, John Allen, 1986 / Nik Jennings bolt free, 2000

52 Plague   9m   E4 6b   ★
Climb the front face past an ancient bolt (beware). Elongated monsters may pass the bolt direct, but most will skirt it on the right.
Andy Parkin, Bill Briggs (1pt), 1976. FFA Jonny Woodward, 1981

53 The Crevice   8m   VD   ★
Bridge the corner to the ledge then climb the wall just right of the arête. The top corner is HVD.

54 Lichen Slab   6m   S 4a
Climb the centre of the slab, avoiding the overhang on the left.

55 Palm Charmer   11m   E3 5c   ★★
Only slightly easier than *Auto da Fe* going left to the arête and climbing it on its right side.
Paul Harrison, Neil Harrison, 1985

56 Auto da Fe   10m   E4 6a   ★★★
A stupendous route, one of the best E4s on grit. Climb the crack to the break. Arrange protection then climb the right arête (crux) on its left-hand side to a break. Finish more easily.
Andy Parkin, Bill Briggs, 1976

57 Left Holly Pillar Crack   6m   S 4a   ★★
The left of two cracks in the right wall has good protection and perfect jams.

58 Right Holly Pillar Crack   6m   S 4a
The deep right-hand crack is a bit of a thrutch.

ROOF ROUTE BUTTRESS
To the right, past some lesser buttresses, sits a clean, shapely buttress of great rock.

59 Summertime 9m E3 5c
An enjoyable solo up the bulging arête. The difficulties are short lived.
Dave Morgan, 1976

60 Renshaw's Remedy 9m VD ★★
The corner-crack is a brilliant easy climb.
J Renshaw, c1950

61 Regular Route 9m HVS 5a
Climb the centre of the leaning slab. The upper wall is serious and requires some blind faith.
John Allen, Nick Stokes, 1988

62 Groove Route 9m HVS 5b ★
A good climb, strenuous and technical. Ascend to the overhang but move left to below a cracked shallow groove and climb this past a short lived crux.
Bill Briggs, Andy Parkin, 1976

63 Roof Route 9m HVS 5b ★★
This roof crack will have most climbing wall fans running for cover, whereas the true gritstone connoisseur will love it. Amble up to the roof and enjoy the jamming delights above.
⊙ opposite page
Joe Brown, c1960

64 Root Route 9m S 4b ★★
The corner crack is a superb and strenuous.

65 The Bush Off 14m S 4b ★
From the ledge on *Root Route*, traverse right to finish up near the arête.
Sarah Smart, Steve Clark, Nigel Edley, 2004

66 Dynasty 9m E4 6a ★
Artificial and worrying, but with worthwhile climbing. Start up a flake just right of *Root Route* and climb the wall to the roof. Pull round this and trend right to undercuts below a small overlap. Finish direct.
Andy Parkin, Bill Briggs, 1976

67 April Fool 9m E2 5b ★
A route requiring a strong, confident approach. Climb the wall just left of the arête to an overhang and a scary finish.
Andy Parkin, Bill Briggs, 1976

68 Steph 6m HVS 5a ★
Follow a line up the right side of the arête, with little protection.
Bill Briggs (solo), 1976

Roof Route, HVS 5b (opposite page) is not quite a sandbag at the grade, but it is a route that often crops up in conversations between Rivelin fans, often followed by a tale of struggle. Tom Luff clearly enjoying every minute. 📷 Mike Cheque

ALTAR BUTTRESS
The final buttress is an absolute cracker, with a great selection of routes on the finest of Rivelin grit. The first route starts left of the arête.

69 Altercation 7m HVS 5a ★
Follow a rightwards-trending crack on the left wall to a difficult finish on the arête.
Bill Briggs, Andy Parkin, 1976

70 Raredos 12m E1 5b ★
A secretive belter. Climb *Altercation* then gallop along the high break to finish up *Altar Crack*.
Jonny Woodward, Ian Maisey, 1981

71 New Mediterranean 9m E5 6c ★★
Excellent powerful climbing up the blank wall, protected with side-runners in the adjacent route. Climb *Moolah* to the tricky gear then come back to the ledge (the Altar). Step left and climb the left-hand line past burly undercut moves and a long stretch to a pocket.
John Allen, Nick Stokes, 1985

72 Moolah 9m E5 6b ★★
A fierce, but protectable outing on the right side of the wall. Starting from the Altar climb the flake — committing — and hurriedly place micro-protection in a thin slot up to the left. Continue direct to the top via some viciously thin pulls on a hold the size of a jigsaw piece.
John Allen, 1988

73 Altar Crack 9m VS 4c ★★★
A brilliant climb, every bit as good a test of VS as *The File* on Higgar Tor. Climb the sublime corner-crack by good jams or a thrilling layback to a good resting point near the top. Swing right, or finish direct.
Dick Brown, Donald Wooller, Frank Fitzgerald, John Clegg, c1950

74 Nonsuch 9m E1 5b ★★
Flawless, well protected and strenuous. Gain the thin crack and follow it on jams and sloping holds. ⊙ opposite page
Alan Clarke, Les Gillott, c1963

75 Gettin' Kinda Squirrelly 9m E6 6b ★
An underrated gem climbing the left arête of the chimney on its left.
Mark Hundleby, 1999

76 Vestry Chimney 9m VD
The chimney leads to a prickly exit.

77 Too Much 6m E2 6a ★★
A mini classic, protectable in the right places. The thin slab and crack to an easier finish.
Andy Parkin, Bill Briggs, 1976

A gem of a route at the very end of the crag. Hit it right, get the gear in and it's a cinch. Get it wrong and you'll get pumped and spat off the last move. Ian Milward on Nonsuch, E1 5b (opposite page). 📷 Neil Foster

AGDEN ROCHER

OS Grid Ref: SK 262 934
Altitude: 340m

Agden Rocher has a feel unlike any other crag in the Peak. A long and seldom visited crag, set amid beautiful pastoral scenery above Agden Reservoir. A crag for the rural adventurer. The climbs can feel hollow at times but it is rewarding for those who can handle that.

The climbing is generally steep and positive, following walls and cracks. Belays at the top are scarce and a number of iron stakes are in place above the popular routes. Be prepared to improvise.

Its southwesterly aspect attracts plenty of sunshine and consequently the rock dries quickly after rain. Its position and outlook, above mature oak woodland is unrivalled in the Peak.

Approach: From the Old Horns Inn in High Bradfield, follow Brown House Lane in the direction of Midhope. After about 1km, and about 200m after a road leading off on the right, is a gated green drive (public footpath) with a stile on the left-hand side of the road. Parking isn't great but try to squeeze on the verge somewhere around here.

Follow the track as it winds downhill. After 350m take a right fork then 100m past that, fork off up through the trees to eventually arrive in an open area. The climbs described are left of here. There are climbs here not described in this book - see *BMC Burbage, Millstone and Beyond*.

Alternatively, take the clifftop path and drop down a gully between the Campsite and Whittler areas (probably easier).

GREAT WALL

Great Wall is the showpiece of the crag. Tall and clean. The protection pegs on various route on this and the other buttresses may need checking before an ascent.

❶ The Snip 19m E2 5c ★
Start just left of *Jaffa*. Good holds lead directly to the base of a short corner. Step right and follow the left edge of the wall with the help of a thin crack to the top.
Paul Harrison, Graham Sutton, 1998

A stacked pile of blocks lean precariously against the base of the cliff.

❷ Jaffa 19m E1 5b ★
Start immediately left of the stacked blocks and climb the wall stepping right to a tree atop the blocks. The wall above is taken direct on good but not always obvious holds (peg) to the top.
Paul Harrison, Graham Sutton, David Simmonite, 1999

❸ Ardua 19m E1 5b ★
Just right of the stacked blocks is a thin crack. Ascend the crack to a grassy ledge and a tree. The fine continuation crack (peg) is followed to the top.
Keith Myhill, Al Evans, 1963

❹ Hit and Run Driver 20m E3 5c ★
Climb the wall 3m right of the blocks to a small ledge just left of a tree. Move rightwards up the wall above (peg) to a poor flake, then back left for a direct finish through the overlap on good holds.
Andy Lewandowski, Roger Brookes, 1983

Great Wall

5 S.O.S. 29m VS 4c ★
A route with some worthwhile climbing and plenty of character. At the left edge of Great Wall is a small undercut corner. Climb the corner, move right to a shelf then continue easily to the large tree and a possible belay. Move up above the tree and traverse left to the base of a steep corner. Climb this exiting right.
Roy Briggs, Pete Titterton, 1952

6 Speak Easy 29m E3 5c ★
A wandering line with some anxious moments. Start beneath a rightward-slanting ramp in the left edge of the wall. Climb the wall below the ramp and move up and left to the sanctuary of a large tree. Traverse right for 3m and climb the left edge of the headwall to the top.
Ron Fawcett, Al Evans, 1971

7 Monster Munch 29m E4 6a ★★
A big pitch – protected but intimidating. From 3m up *Asteris* step left (peg), and move left again to an undercut ledge. Difficult climbing on small rugosities (peg), leads to the overlap where exciting moves up and left gain a good horizontal break. Step right (peg), and take a direct line up the centre of the headwall.
Paul Harrison, Neil Harrison, 1996

8 Asteris 29m E1 5c ★★
A fine climb, tackling the impressive crack in the centre of the wall. The initial crack leads to a standing position atop a large detached block. A difficult and fingery section protected by a peg runner gains easier cracks leading to the top. page 365
Neil Mather, Arthur Birtwistle, 1953

9 Conjunctus Viribus 28m E1 5b ★★
An excellent sustained pitch with good protection. Climb directly into a groove and follow it to an overlap. Step right and storm the steep headwall via twin cracks to an easier finish.
Al Evans, Joe Goodison, 1967

10 Ignis Fatuus 22m E3 5c ★
Requires a confident approach. Move up to an overlap and turn it via a thin crack. Step left and climb the wall above direct.
Roger Brookes, Andy Lewandowski, 1983

11 Ocydroma 15m E3 5b
Start as for *Ignis Fatuus* and at the overlap move slightly right and follow the vertical crease on small holds, moving right near the top to finish right of the oak tree.
David Law, 1999

WHITTLER WALL
Further right is a clean-cut wall, home to some of the finest routes at Agden.

12 Pollux 19m E1 5b ★★
The left-hand crack is an excellent pitch, nicely sustained and well-protected with small wires. Follow the crack to a difficult sequence through the overlap (peg), to reach an oak tree. Finish up the arête to the left. ⓘ page 11
Al Evans, Keith Myhill, 1969

13 Wheat Thin 19m E4 6a ★★
An absorbing pitch up the wall between *Castor* and *Pollux*; the small holds may need a brush prior to an ascent. Pull through the overlap 3m left of *Castor* and step up to a peg. Step right and move up and left, crux, to reach a small flake and better holds above. Easier climbing leads directly to the top.
Paul Harrison, Neil Harrison, 1984

14 Castor 19m E1 5c ★
Behind an oak tree is a peg-scarred crack. Climb the wall in the line of the crack and fight past a holly to an easier upper section.
Keith Myhill, Al Evans, 1969

15 The Whittler 18m VS 4c ★★
A good climb, delicate and nicely exposed. Start at a small cutaway just right of an oak tree. Pull over the overhang and climb up and leftwards to reach a grassy ledge and a tree. Finish up the layback crack left of the tree.
Colin Whittle, Dick Brown, Frank Fitzgerald, Donald Wooler, 1952

16 Briggs' and Titterton's 17m HVS 5b ★★
This fine route follows the line of the straight thin crack making good use of holds on its left to the tree. Finish up the wide crack above and right.
Roy Briggs, Pete Titterton, 1952

17 The Avenue 17m E2 5c
A good, if green, eliminate line just right of the crack of *Briggs' and Titterton's*. Climb the wall direct on small holds to a large horizontal break. Traverse left and pull up into a small groove and a junction with *Briggs' and Titterton's*. Finish up this.
Neil & Paul Harrison, 1996

18 Spring Lamb Dopiazza 16m VS 4c ★
Climb the wall to an overlap. Step right into the chimney for a move or two and then back left along a narrow ledge; finish direct.
Warren Trippett, David Law, 1999

Agden Rocher | 397

THE CAMPSITE AREA
This is a good open area, with some short, technical problems, and some long, challenging expeditions.

19 Gemini 18m VS 4c
A thin crack in the slab 4m left of *Campsite Crack* leads to a grassy ledge. Move right to twin sandy cracks and jam and layback steeply to the top.
Keith Myhill, Al Evans, 1968

20 Campsite Crack 20m S 4a ★★
A classic; a varied and sustained pitch at the grade. Climb the corner, moving right after 10m to a large ledge and possible belay. Continue up the corner for an exposed finish.
Eric Byne, Charles Ashbury, 1952

21 Campsite Crack Indirect Finish 20m E1 5c ★
An exciting alternative finish moves right from the upper section of the corner to climb a roof-crack in the final overhang.
Terry King, 1975

22 Scouting For Boys 20m E3 5c ★
An exciting pitch up the arête to the right. Climb the initial arête and jam the roof crack above to a ledge. A sandy corner leads to a break, swing right onto the arête and make difficult moves up its right-hand side to the top.
Paul Harrison, Graham Sutton, 1977

23 Libra 15m HVS 4c
Follow the corner of *Man of God* until level with a large pocket in its left wall. An exposed traverse left gains the arête, which leads to a ledge. The vegetated slab above is taken to the top.
Al Evans, 1968

24 Man of God 10m HS 4b ★
An honest, well-protected pitch up the clean-cut corner crack. Abseil from the tree.
Dick Brown, 1952

25 Artifax Arête 10m E3 5b ★
The left arête of the wall to the right is climbed initially on its left-hand side with a final worrying move on its right. Abseil from the tree.
Dennis Orwin, 1968

26 Are We There Yet 10m E4 6a ★
Start just right of the arête. Take a direct line to the peg on *Dreams by the Sea* then crimp straight up to finish left of the tree.
Warren Trippett, Simon Royston, M Robinson, 1999

27 Dreams by the Sea 10m E2 5c ★
Neat, technical face climbing. Start up a faint crack in the slab that leads to the left end of the long brown pod. Step left at the break (peg) then stand up and finish slightly rightwards to the tree; abseil descent.
Doug Kerr, Paul Harrison, 1984

WHARNCLIFFE

OS Grid Ref: SK 296 977 to SK 303 970
Altitude: 230m

A long edge comprising lots of small buttresses. The climbing is very friendly although the landings are not. Despite this, it has often been used as a soloing and easy mileage venue for locals. The routes are mostly short (with a few great exceptions) and the rock, being finer-grained and less weathered than moorland edges, tends to give incut and positive holds.

The edge faces west and gets lots of afternoon and evening sun. Sitting in the rain-shadow of the Peak District, the edge can be dry when other higher venues are wet. It is very quick drying and takes little seepage. The rock is generally clean and this, combined with a relatively low altitude, makes it a good winter venue. Long John's Stride area takes longer to dry but gives more shade.

Approach: Follow the maps to Station Road and park. On the opposite side of the river from the Lowood Working Men's Club, go through the green gate and fork right uphill. This joins a well-worn track, which leads under two tunnels to emerge on the well-made Plank Gate forestry (cycle) track about 500m from the road. Turn right along this and take a path through a gate on the left, immediately before the huge pylon, which leads up to the edge.

Alternatively, from where the path meets Plank Gate, continue straight uphill until a pond is reached. Turn right and the path gradually ascends out of the wood to reach the edge.

Walking below the crag is very hard-going, and moving between the buttresses is usually best by walking along the path at the top.

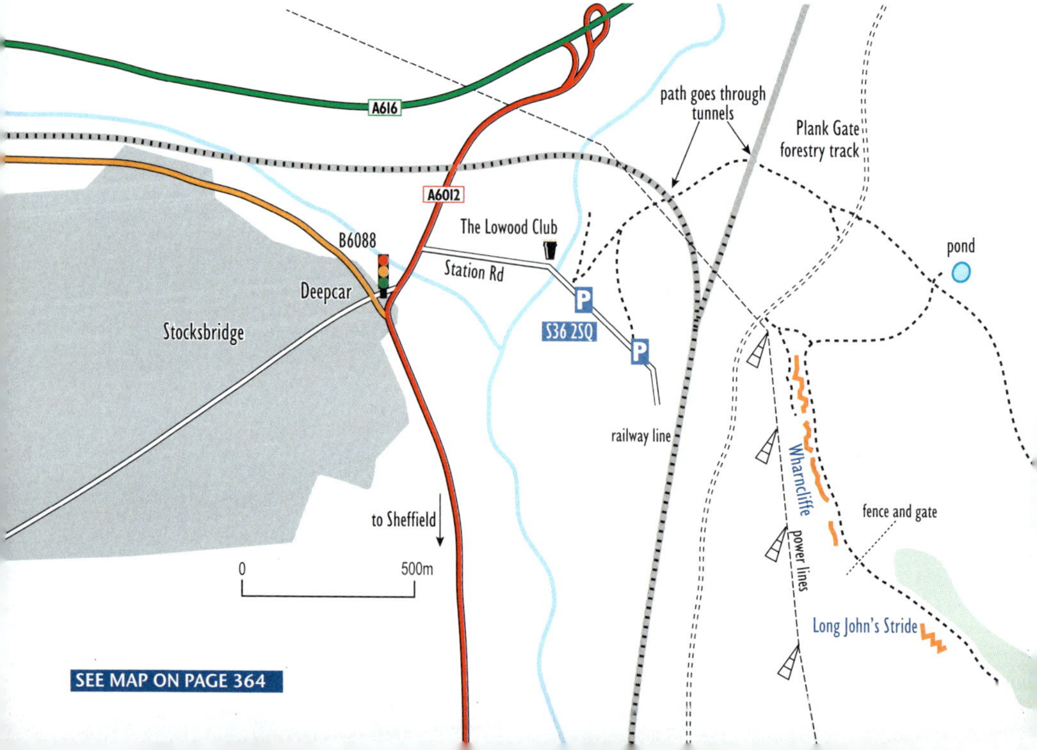

SEE MAP ON PAGE 364

Ian Carr revelling in the sharp winter sunshine on Great Buttress Arête (page 404), one of the best E1s on Wharncliffe. Tall, steep buttresses, proud lines and positive holds are the specialities of this unique crag.
📷 Paul Evans

400 | Wharncliffe

Prow Rock

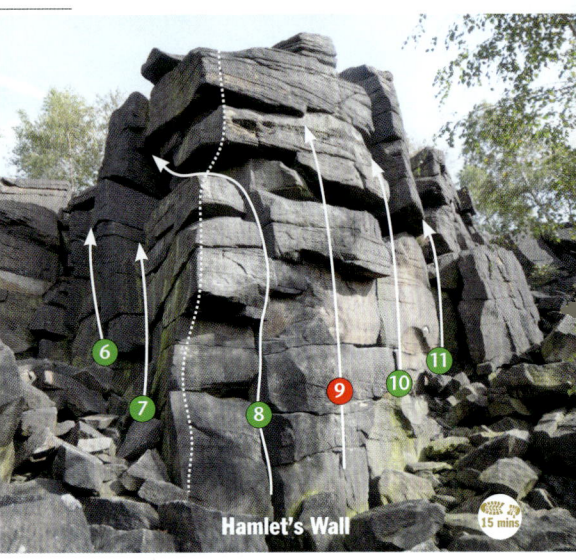
Hamlet's Wall

THE DEEPCAR CRAGS
This is the string of buttresses that stretch out along the first 300m of the edge.

Prow Rock: This is 100m from an old pylon mounting. Descent is by either an unforgiving leap to the main edge or more sensibly by reversing *Inside Route*.

❶ The Moire 9m E5 6b ★
Ascend the arête moving left at the top.
Don Barr, Paul Hallos, 1978

❷ Querp 9m E3 6b
The enticing scoop in the upper wall.
Howie Darwin, 1989

❸ Outside Route 8m HS 4b ★
Move up and traverse diagonally leftwards, via a crack and niche, to the top.
JW Puttrell, WJ Watson & friends, c1900s

❹ The Nose 6m VS 4c ★
Tackle the right-hand arête direct.
Fred Jones, 1933

❺ Inside Route 8m D ★
Climb the centre of the inside face to the crack.
JW Puttrell (solo), 1885

Hamlet's Wall: The area is quite popular and is good for a quick evening fix.

❻ Pylon Crack 8m VD
The leftmost crack, left of a wedged pillar.
JW Puttrell, WJ Watson & friends, c1900s

❼ Quern Crack 8m S
The crack right of the pillar.
JW Puttrell, WJ Watson & friends, c1900s

❽ Hamlet's Climb 12m HVD ★
Climb a thin crack to the gash where a traverse left leads to *Pylon Crack*. The direct finish is VS 4c ★, as is the arête in its entirety.
JW Puttrell, WJ Watson & friends, c1900s

❾ Requiem of Hamlet's Ghost 9m E2 5b ★
A direct line up the buttress. The crux is a poorly protected move above a horrible landing.
Terry Hirst (solo), 1976

❿ The Crack of Doom 8m HS 4b ★
The steep, dark crack; deeply traditional.
JW Puttrell, WJ Watson & friends, c1900s

⓫ Chockstone Climb 7m D
The chimney-groove leads to a step left, on good holds, to gain a crack with a chockstone.

Wharncliffe | 401

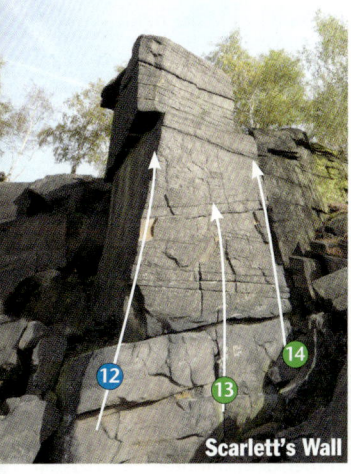
Scarlett's Wall

Tensile Test

Scarlett's Wall: Ten metres to the right is a pillar.

12 Scarlett's Wall Arête 9m VS 4c ★
A good little route following the bold arête.
Reg Addey, 1965

13 Scarlett's Climb 8m HS 4b ★
A bold route straight up the face: reachy.
Harry Scarlett, 1931

14 Scarlett's Edge 8m HS 4b ★
The angular arête to the right.

Tensile Test Area: Most of the routes are usually soloed or bouldered due to a lack of gear.

15 Suspense 6m VS 5b
The enjoyable left-hand arête is hard to start.
Pete Crew, 1950s

16 Mellicious 6m E1 5c
The crimpy wall.
John Camateras, 2000

17 Tensile Test 6m E1 5c ★
The faint groove gives good technical climbing.
Terry Hirst (solo), 1977

18 Elastic Limit 6m E1 5c
Climb the centre of the slab to a break, step left to finish. The direct start is harder and the direct finish is E2 6a.
Michael Anderson (solo), 1977

19 Handover Arête 8m HVS 4c ★
The crux overhang is attacked from the left.
Frank Fitzgerald (solo), 1955

Mantelshelf Pillar: Just right is a pillar.

20 Mantelshelf Pillar 7m HVS 5a
The left edge of the pillar.
John Fearon (solo), 1950s

21 The Mantelshelf 6m HS 4b ★
The right edge via an awkward mantelshelf.
JW Puttrell, WJ Watson & friends, c1900s

22 Back and Foot 6m VD
The deep square-cut cleft can be done in its original manner of back and footing. However, it is more logical to use the corner crack.
JW Puttrell, WJ Watson & friends, c1900s

Mantelshelf Pillar

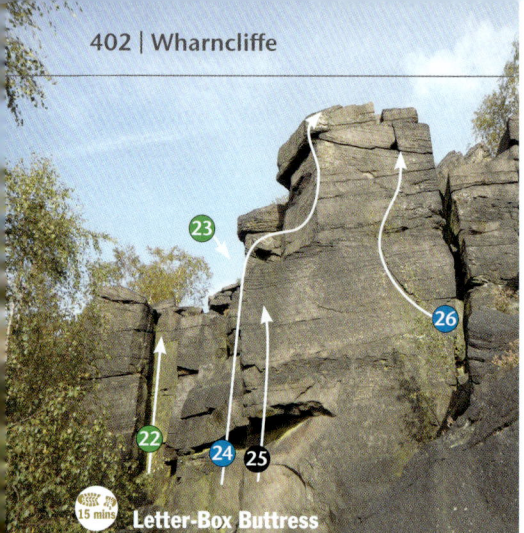

Letter-Box Buttress

Letter-Box Buttress: Just to the right.

23 Rook Chimney 8m D
The corner-chimney on the left side of the buttress is steep and exposed.

24 Post Horn 8m VS 4c ★
Climb the wall just to the right of *Rook Chimney* to a ledge and a finish up a blunt rib.

25 Tears Before Bedtime 8m E4 6a ★
The arête is climbed on its right-hand side.
Jon Darwin, 1987

26 Curved Balls 8m VS 4c ★
Climb the flake, gained from the right.
David Simmonite, Paul Harrison, Graham Sutton, 2001

Rocking Block Slab: Thirty-five metres further on is a slab with a large block on top, which is reputed to rock in stiff breezes.

27 Slab and Corner 8m HS 4a ★
Move diagonally leftwards to a niche on the arête. An awkward mantelshelf leads to the top. The direct start up the arête is VS 4c.
Fred Jones, 1933

28 Photo Finish 9m E1 5b ★
From the niche, go onto the middle of the wall and up to a ledge. Above, surmount the block.
Terry Hirst, Ian Hirst, 1979

29 Dead Heat 8m E5 6a ★★
No gear and a hideous landing. Climb the slab 3m left of the edge to a small overlap. Undercut this and make a thin pull over the overlap before committing to the reach for the break.
Nick White, Steve Yates, 1985

30 Renrock 6m E1 5a ★
Only just E1, but still a bold proposition up the technical blunt right-hand edge of the slab.
Rodney Wilson, 1950s

Rocking Block Slab

Cheese Block: Fifty metres right.

31 Hard Cheese 8m E1 5b ★
The centre of the wall and the small roof to finish up the right-hand side of the arête.
David Simmonite, 2000

32 Cheese Cut 8m D ★
The chimney-crack in the back of the corner.
JW Puttrell & friends, c1900s

33 Cheese Block 7m VS 4b
Pull over the cutaway on its right-hand side and continue up the arête above. A bold route.

34 Cheese Cut Flake 8m VD
Layback the flake-to-hand crack.
JW Puttrell & friends, c1900s

Cheese Block

Imaginary Boulder

Imaginary Boulder: Fifteen metres further on at a lower level, is a rounded buttress.

35 Imaginary Boulder Climb 8m VS 4c ★
A Puttrell sandbag from the 1900s. Climb the steep crack, ignoring the adjacent boulder, and continue up the wall above.
JW Puttrell, c1900s

36 Authentic Boulder Climb 6m VS 4c
A central line starting from a good flat hold on the right that pretends to be a tiny ledge.

Pete's Sake Area: A series of steep and angular features on clean rock.

37 Pinnacle Arête 9m E1 5b
Start up the wall to the right of the deep corner-chimney and move onto the small pillar on the left-hand arête. Delicate and thought provoking climbing remains up the arête.
Pete Crew, John Henry Fearon, c1960

38 Cumberland Crack 9m HVD
The steep fissure to the right offers arduous climbing. The buttress has been traversed.

39 V-Groove 9m VD
The cute groove.

40 Pete's Sake 6m E1 5b ★
An impressive outing. Climb the centre of the face to gain the obvious break where a strenuous move up and right leads to better holds on the right edge.

41 Leftover Chimney 6m D
Climb up to and continue up the narrowing chimney, staying near the outside for maximum enjoyment.

42 Overhanging Chimney 6m HVD
Enjoyable climbing for the chimney freak.

43 Overhanging Crack 6m S 4b ★
A worthwhile route demanding good jamming technique, and big cams if you have them.

44 Pass By 6m E1 5c
The blind flakes near the arête above an awkward landing.
Don Barr (solo), 1978

45 Splitter 6m E1 5b ★
The arête is climbed on its right-hand side and once committed is far from escapable.
Paul Harrison, Steve Coughlan, David Simmonite, 2001

46 Split Chimney Wall 6m HVS 5b ★
The centre of the wall to the right is climbed direct.

Pete's Sake Area

GREAT BUTTRESS AREA
An area of high-quality buttresses, containing some of the best routes on the crag.

47 Alpha Crack 9m M ★
Climb up via flakes to the platform, from where a variety of finishes can be taken.
JW Puttrell & friends, c1900s

48 Beta Crack 9m S 4a ★★
The well-marked flake crack provides a fine, well-protected route at the grade.
⊙ opposite page
JW Puttrell & friends, c1900s

49 Trapezium 9m E1 5c
The steep wall.
Don Barr, Paul Hallos, 1978

50 The Great Chimney 9m HD ★
The cleft. A through route can be climbed at D.
JW Puttrell & friends, c1900s

51 Thrown Away 12m E2 5c ★
Escapable climbing, with good moves, up the wall left of the arête.
Gary & Hazel Gibson, 1981

52 Great Buttress Arête 12m E1 5b ★★★
A classic of the crag. A superb exposed route blazing a way up the arête past a somewhat dodgy spike runner. ⊙ page 399
Pete Crew, John Fearon, 1960s

53 Great Buttress 14m VS 4c ★
Ascend the previous route for 4m then break our right and climb the wall passing a cave (side-runner in *Romulus*; HVS without).
Fred Jones, 1933

54 Just a Minute 12m E1 5b ★
Climb up the centre of the buttress then straight over the rocking block to finish.
Frank Horsman, Bill Phillips, 2000

55 Romulus 8m VD

56 Remus 8m S 4a

57 Leaf Buttress 6m VS 4c ★
Climb the centre of the buttress, trending leftwards and finishing just right of the arête.
Pete Crew, 1950s

Black Slab: Twenty metres further on.

58 Black Slab Left 6m HVD 4a ★

59 Black Slab Centre 6m VD ★

60 Black Slab Right 6m D ★

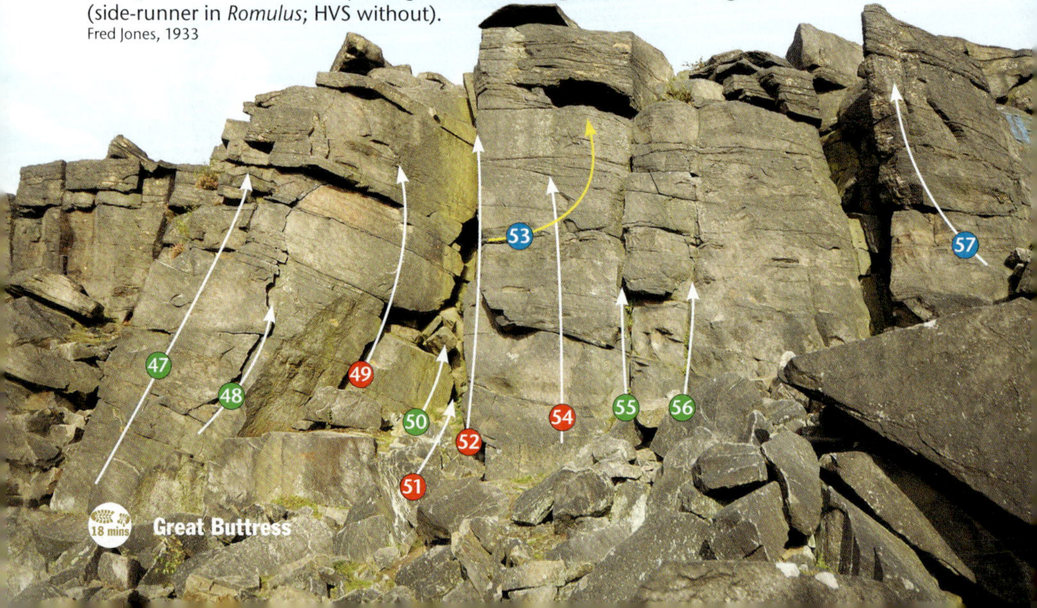

Black Slab

Great Buttress

Chris Hanson and Roberta Spagnul on the fun and flaky Beta Crack, S (opposite page). Paul Evans

PUTTRELL'S PROGRESS AREA
Past a boulder-filled gully there is a square buttress with 'Puttrell's Cave' at its base.

61 Black Finger 9m E3 5c ★
Follow thin cracks leftwards above the cutaway, to reach and finish up the left-hand arête.
John Allen, Neil Stokes, 1973

62 Diamond White 9m E3 5c ★
Climb *Black Finger* to the top of the thin cracks and continue up the thin wall above, trending slightly rightwards to the arête to finish.
David Simmonite, 1992

63 Anzio Breakout/Pilgrimage 12m E5 6b ★★
Boulder rightwards along the lip and pull to easier ground. Climb the roof and wall above.
Jon Darwin (solo), 1987 / Don Barr, Paul Hallos, 1978

64 Puttrell's Progress 12m S 4a ★★
A classic route, covering impressive ground. Climb the right-hand side of the buttress to an awkward entry into the sentry-box. Make committing moves left above the void to reach a finishing crack.
JW Puttrell, WJ Watson, c1900s

65 The Flue 12m HVD ★
Ascend to the sentry-box and venture inwards to the bowels of the earth.
JW Puttrell & friends, c1900s

66 Helping Hand 9m E1 5c ★
Climb the rib right of the sentry-box to the ledge. The blunt arête at the right-hand end of the overhang, climbed mainly on its left side, needs commitment.
John Allen, Neil Stokes, 1973

Twin Pillars: Twenty-two metres further on are twin square pillars.

67 Bolster 8m E1 5b
Climb to the overhang and make bold moves leftwards over it. Finish more easily.
Terry Hirst, 1982

68 Summer Lightning 8m E1 5b
Step off a boulder and climb to a ledge. Continue confidently up the arête above.
Terry Hirst, 1985

69 Flake Climb 8m HVS 5a
Climb steep, loose flakes until the left-hand arête can be gained. Finish up this with difficulty.
Jack Soper, 1950s

70 Schard 8m E2 5b ★
To the right is a groove above half-height. Gain this directly up a demanding wall; bold.
Terry Hirst (solo), 1976

Puttrell's Progress

Some of the crags in this chapter stand out because they offer an experience and an ambience not found on any of the others in this book. Agden Rocher and Dovestone Tor stand out, as does this one, Wharncliffe, the book's northern outlier. Electrically-charged cracklines on sharp, dark rock give this crag an ambience of its own. Here, Naomi Simmonite buzzes up its flagship VS, Himmelswillen (page 408). 📷 David Simmonite

HIMMELSWILLEN AREA
The next buttress marks the crag's most popular area. The climbs around here make a visit well worthwhile.

71 Himmelswillen 15m VS 4c ★★★
A classic of the crag with good open climbing. Ascend the left-hand arête of the front face and move right under the overhang to gain the finger flake. (Or reach the flake from directly below). Climb this, stepping left onto a ledge. Reach the top directly. 🅞 page 407
Tom Stobart (solo), 1933

72 Serrated Edge 15m E1 5b ★
The right-hand arête is climbed directly.
Gary & Hazel Gibson, 1981

73 Teufelsweg 15m D ★
Climb the deep chimney.
Hans Teufel, Heine Sedlmayr, 1936

74 Dragon's Hoard 11m E6 6b ★★
An excellent technical route, climbing the sinuous crack-line near the centre of the wall to a challenging and committing direct finish; very fingery and difficult to protect.
Simon Jones, Roger Brook, 1993

75 Banana Wall 12m E3 6a ★★
Climb the flake to an undercut move to gain the ledge above. Fingery and with mediocre protection to help concentrate the mind. Hard for the short.
Don Barr, Paul Hallos, 1977

HELL GATE AREA
Easily found when walking along the cliff top path due to the well-worn top of the crag, and a stone wall ahead and left of the path. It is also at the summit of the rising cliff top path from the north end.

76 Tower Face 12m HS 4b ★★★
A justifiably popular route with plenty of exposure, up the steep, narrow wall. Start at the base of a cleft, round to the left of the toe of the buttress. Climb up gingerly into a steep scoop. Follow the line of a thin crack on good small holds up the centre of the face.
🅞 page 363
Eric Byne, Frank Burgess, 1933

77 On the Air 12m E5 6a ★★
A committing climb requiring technique and balance. The right arête of the front face is climbed direct, initially on the right-hand side.
Terry Hirst, 1978

78 Journey into Freedom 12m E7 6b ★
The wall to the right of *On the Air* provides the most demanding route on the edge. Start by bridging out of the cleft, then move leftwards off a large flat undercut to slap up the arête for a couple of moves. Move rightwards to gain thin edges and reach the large ledge. Finish up *On the Air*.
Simon Jones (solo), 1993

Wharncliffe | 409

81 Desolation Angel 12m E6 6b ★★★
The majestic, leaning, right-hand arête gives an outstanding route that ranks amongst the finest anywhere on gritstone. Climb the arête to reach the break, where a final awkward move brings the top.
Terry Hirst, 1978. Simon Jones (without side-runner), 1992

82 Hell Gate 15m VD ★
Varied climbing up the deep corner-groove. Stuff yourself in the crack or bridge wide according to taste – awkward at the start for the short.
JW Puttrell, WJ Watson, c1900s

83 Gavel Neese 14m E2 5b ★
Climb the bold arête with a little faith and friction to a ledge. Carry on up the upper arête with interest. Very, very, reach dependant.
Reg Addey (solo), 1960s

84 Hell Gate Crack 12m HS 4b ★
The prominent scarred and polished crack to the right is climbed passing an awkward bulge to gain a recess on the right below the top.

85 Joie-de-Vivre 8m E1 5c ★
Ascend the rib to the break at 6m then make a dynamic move directly for the top with good protection, et trop joie.
Pete Crew, John Fearon, 1960s

79 Hell Gate Gully 12m M
The major gully line.
JW Puttrell, WJ Watson, c1900s

80 News at Zen 11m E3 5c ★
Climb the wall to the left of *Desolation Angel* via a black pocket.
Simon Jones, John Stanger, Barry Clarke, 1993

LONG JOHN'S STRIDE

The next area is some 1km south of where the climbing starts at the northern end of the edge and around 400m beyond a gate and fence running perpendicular to the crag. The top of the pinnacles are easily spotted from the cliff edge path. Can be green.

This excellent buttress is composed of four tower-like pillars. These contain some of the best harder climbing on the edge.

86 October Arête 12m E2 5c ★★
A climb of considerable character. The arête is taken directly with hard initial moves to a small ledge. Above, the moves are still bold but easier.
John Fearon, Dave Gregory, 1955. Direct, Pete Crew, 1960s

87 Autumn Wall 12m E4 6a ★★★
The steep wall right of the arête provides an outstanding route that would make a good introduction into the E4 grade. After a committing start continue direct via numerous breaks, some good, some not so good. Possibly the best hard route on the edge.
Terry Hirst, 1978

88 Deepcar Named Desire 12m E5 6b ★
A squeezed-in but demanding line up the wall to the right of the last route. Side-runners protect the initial moves.
Bill Birch, Roger Birch, 1997

89 Equinox 14m E3 5c ★
Climb the right-hand arête of the wall direct. Good climbing but unfortunately escapable.
Terry Hirst (solo), 1978. Direct, John Hesketh, 1988

90 Grammarian's Progress 12m VS 4c ★★
Climb the left-hand side of the arête, passing the hole at its right-hand end. Reach the huge angular hold higher on the arête and boldly gain a standing position on it, before traversing right on the break across the exposed face to a finishing crack. An odd alternative is to bridge all the way up between the two pinnacles at a similar grade.
Dick Brown, 1944

91 Gwyn 12m E2 5c ★
Climb directly up the centre of the intricate technical face crossed by *Grammarian's Progress*.
Reg Addey (solo), c1960s

92 Grammarian's Face 12m E2 5b
The right-hand arête. Stepping left onto *Gwyn* at 6m gives an easier variant at E1 5a.
Rodney Wilson, c1960s

93 Long John's Eliminate 15m E2 5b ★★
Superb open climbing but with sparse protection. From 4m up the arête, teeter across the face to a groove on the right arête. Ascend this with difficulty to a ledge leading leftwards to a crack to finish.
Pete Crew, John Henry Fearon, 1960s

94 Long John's Super Direct 13m E2 5b ★
To the right of *Long John's Eliminate* is a flake. Climb this, step left into the scoop above and follow this directly to the headwall. Traverse right to finish up the arête.
Bill Birch, Roger Birch, Richard Hyde, 1999

95 Impish 9m E1 6b
The short bulging arête is a scary problem.

96 Long Chimney 9m D ★
Just to the right again is a narrowing chimney.
JW Puttrell, WJ Watson, c1900

97 Inclusion 9m HVS 5b
The right-hand arête of the chimney.
Terry Hirst, Ian Hirst, 1980

98 Richard's Revenge 9m VS 4c ★★
A good exercise in jamming, particularly the upper section. The thin crack is climbed past a niche to a roof and a stiff pull over this on solid jams.
Dick Brown, c1950

99 Lincoln Crack 8m HVD 4a ★★
Exciting stuff. The layback crack on the right leads to a swing rightwards into a chimney crack above.
Dick Brown, c1950

THE CHEW VALLEY

ALDERMAN ROCKS
STANDING STONES
RAVENSTONES
DOVESTONES EDGE
ROB'S ROCKS
WIMBERRY ROCKS
RUNNING HILL PITS

Moorland fires blaze below Wimberry Rocks (page 436). Your arms will appreciate how this feels after a visit to this amazing crag, one of the toughest in the Peak District. *Craig Hannah*

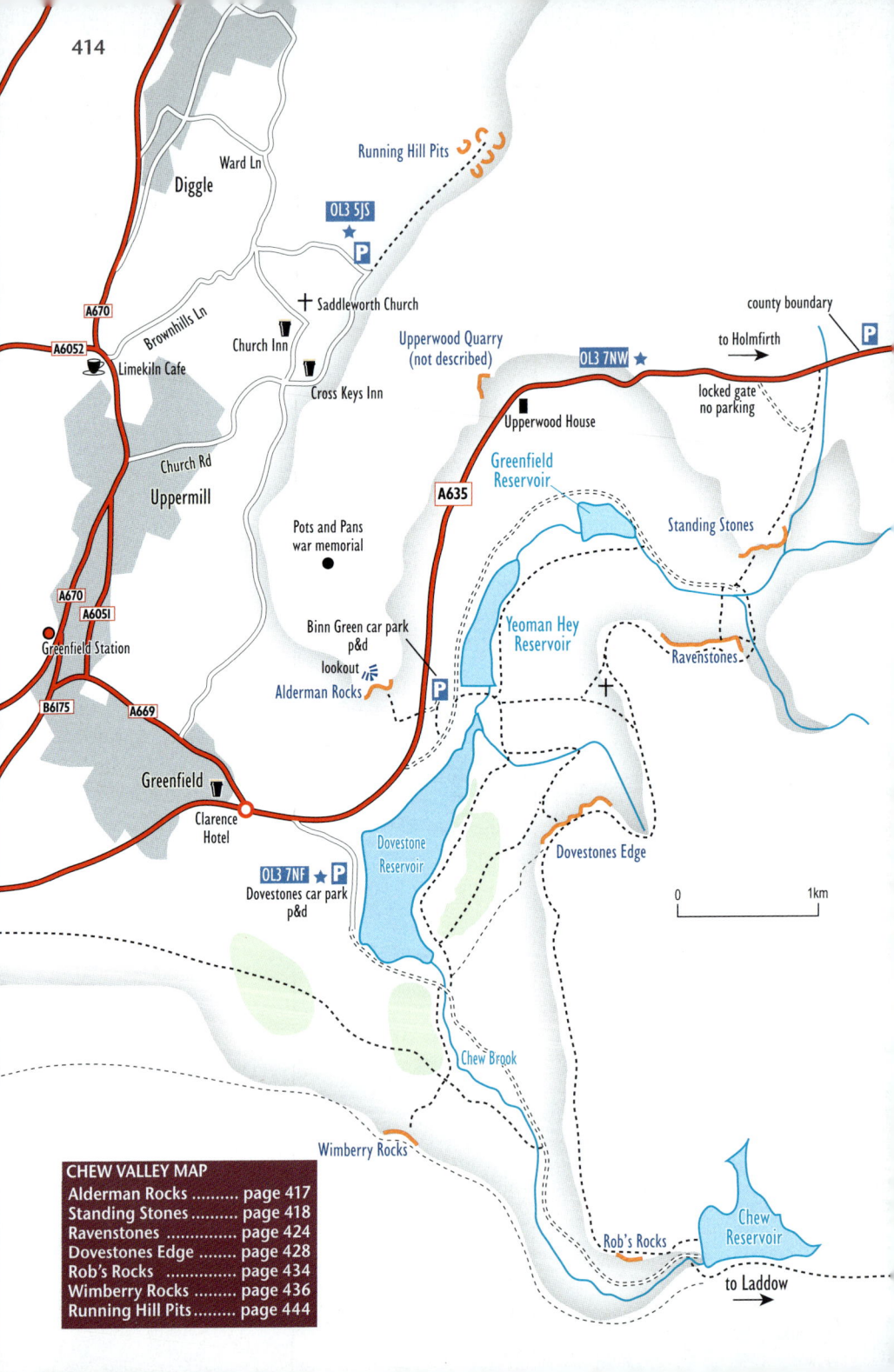

Dovestones Edge provides us with a number of classic VD to VS slab and crack climbs in positions of beauty and solitude. Here, Jo Sunderland demonstrates solid technique on Layback Crack, MVS 4b (page 432).
Ian Carr

OVER THE MOORS
The definitive guide to moorland climbing

The upland gritstone crags that ring the mighty moorlands of Kinder, Bleaklow and the Chew Valley are some of the most noble outcrops in the land. Jagged adventures, breathtaking scenery and sublime routes meet to give the wildest climbing on gritstone, and all within a few miles of the big northern cities.

This book covers them all. Yawning edges to while away perfect summer days, century-old chop routes and deep green chimneys. Crashed bombers, purple heather-clad hillsides and the cry of the curlew. It hardly seems right that such remoteness can be so close to the traffic jams of Manchester and Sheffield.

Pick up the definitive guide for details of every route on the crags selected here, as well as a great number of crags for users of this book who get the moorland bug and want to find out more. With full coverage of crags from the **Chew Valley** (including Upperwood Quarry, Dovestones Quarry, Charnel Stones, Wilderness Rocks, Wimberry Boulders), the **Saddleworth** area (including Den Lane and Pots and Pans), **Marsden** (Pule Hill, Nab End and Shooter's Nab), **Kinder** (Mill Hill, Western Buttress, Great Buttress, Crowden Towers, Chinese Wall) and **Bleaklow** (Yellowslacks, Shelf Benches, Worm Stones).

Featuring:
3,800 routes from Mod to E9
200 boulder problems from V0– to V10
90 full-colour action shots
The definitive climbing history of the area

Get it from the BMC shop for a lifetime of moorland action.

http://shop.thebmc.co.uk/

ISBN 978-0-903908-24-5

Front cover: Paul Fleuriot on Trinnacle West, E1 5b, Ravenstones (page 426). Photo Mike Hutton

ALDERMAN ROCKS

OS Grid Ref: SE 015 045
Altitude: 420m

Alderman is a gentle crag that allows the climber with a few hours to spare the opportunity to climb on gorgeously rough weathered rock. Here you will find pleasant, delicate face and slab climbing, generally in the lower grades. The crag faces south east. It gets the morning sun and dries quickly.

Approach: See map on page 414. Clearly visible high above the Binn Green pay and display car park, the direct approach straight up the hillside takes about 20 lung-bursting minutes. A better way, however, is to follow a dry-stone wall on the left from the start of a deep cut track.

1 Edgehog Flavour 8m E2 5b ★
The bold, gritty arête by laybacking.
Carl Dawson, Cath Dawson, 1985

2 Pigmy Wall 8m S 4a ★
Climb up a crack and tiptoe delicately up on footholds on the lip of a deep cleft.
Tony Howard, Alwyn Whitehead, 1958

3 E Route 9m S 4b ★
The well-scratched slab in the alcove.
Alwyn Whitehead, 1958

4 F Route 9m VD ★
The deep corner chimney of the alcove.
Brian Hodgkinson, 1958

5 Golden Wonder 9m E1 5b ★
The unprotected arête from the left.
Chris Hardy (solo), 1982

6 Crispy Crack 8m HVS 5a ★
Delicately tiptoe the thin crack rightwards.
Tony Howard, Alwyn Whitehead, 1958

7 Rib and Face 15m HVD 4a ★★
Start up the easy-angled rib on the left side of the cleft. A second pitch follows the well-marked crack in the left wall of the upper buttress.
Tony Howard, 1958

8 Cleft and Chimney 15m HVD ★
The V-shaped cleft followed by a second pitch up the short undercut chimney which cleaves the nose of the higher buttress.
Brian Hodgkinson, 1958

9 Great Slab Arête 10m S 4a ★★
Step off a large boulder on to a short rib and ledge. Climb the arête in a fine position.
Brian Hodgkinson, 1956

10 The Great Slab 20m VS 4b, 4c ★★★
The classic of the crag. Climb the centre of the slab to a balancy finish. The second pitch gains a deep jamming crack on the right, swinging left at the top, or finishing direct at 5a.
Alwyn Whitehead, Tony Howard, 1958

11 The Great Gatsby 10m VS 4c ★
The right side of the slab to a tricky exit.
Rick Gibbon, Bill Birch, 1986

12 Great Slab Chimney 10m M ★★
The right-bounding chimney is a fine route.
Brian Hodgkinson, 1958

13 Great Slab Right 10m HVS 5a
A poorly protected excursion on the right-hand edge of the chimney, finish over the prominent knobbly nose.
Rick Gibbon, Bill Birch, 1986

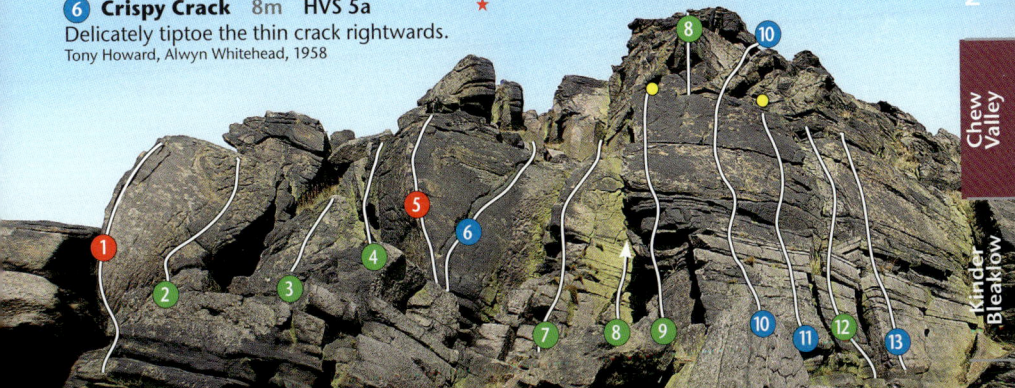

STANDING STONES
OS Grid Ref: SE 039 052
Altitude: 425m

Lovely Standing Stones; the crag for lazy summer days and classic moorland autumns. The setting is serene, gentle and really quite gorgeous. The sound of skylarks and meadow pippets in high spirits overhead is one of the great sounds of moorland climbing. If you climb here on such glorious days as only seem to exist at the Stones, then count yourself lucky.

Top-class climbing in the VS to E1 range harbouring a number of unspoilt Peak classics. The top-outs of many routes can be over steep blocks and grass.

The crag faces south. Can be humid and slippery in the midsummer months. Some of the darker, deeper features can be prone to seepage after heavy rain. Its sunny aspect and sheltered nature means that the climbing season can run from early spring to late autumn.

Approach: Head east out of Greenfield on the A635. Pass Binn Green car park on your right then, 2.8 miles later, there is a large car park on the left (north) side (Grid Ref: SE 051063). Walk 250m back toward Greenfield to an access point just to the right of the first culvert reached. Walk just right of Rimmon Pit Clough to the ruins of Rimmon Cottage. Keep left of the ruins, crossing a subsidiary clough. Follow a faint path leading steadily away from the clough and onto higher ground until the crag is reached. An easy descent is just left of a small rock face visible on the right, leading down between The Lower Right Wall and Left Twin Face. 25 minutes.

Alternatively a pleasant but longer approach can be made from Binn Green or Dovestones car parks.

MAIN FACE
The tall face has lots of classic corners and cracks.

1 Guillotine 15m S 4b ★
Gain the ledge from the left and follow the enjoyable corner to a grassy finish.
Tony Howard, Roy Brown, 1961

2 Fallen Heroes 16m E1 5b ★★★
A superb route that is best climbed quickly. From the ledge, attack the disjointed juggy crack in the steep wall.
Allan Wolfenden, Barry Rawlinson, 1972

3 Brainchild 15m E5 6b ★★
The bulging wall with a long undercut move to pass the blank section. A fine upper crack remains. The upper crack, gained by a loop into *Fallen Heroes*, is a fantastic **E3 5c** ★★.
Gary Gibson, 1982

4 Vivien 15m S 4a ★★
Corner-tastic! The short, steep corner is climbed to a large ledge; the twin cracks above give good, well protected climbing.
Tony Howard, Tony Jones, Paul Seddon, 1960

5 Scratchnose Crack 15m VS 5a ★★
Climb to a ledge; wedge the cleft above with 'interest' into an easier chimney.
Paul Seddon, Brian Woods, Graham West, 1960

Standing Stones | 419

6 Twin Crack Corner 16m VS 4b ★★★
A moorland classic, well protected and sustained climbing following the twin cracks in the rightward facing corner. Enjoy.
Paul Seddon, Brian Woods, Graham West, 1960

7 False Prospects 17m HVS 5b ★
Follow the awkward, hanging groove until a step right joins *Fairy Nuff* at the arête. From the niche, finish directly up the crack.
Con Carey, Nadim Siddiqui, 1982

8 Fairy Nuff 18m VS 4c ★★★
Superb climbing at the upper end of the grade, with few finer examples in the Peak. Start up the large capped corner until a traverse left (don't go too high) gains the first break in the arête. Climb this into a niche and then make a move right into an exposed finishing crack.
Paul Seddon, Tony Howard, 1960

9 Leprechauner 18m HVS 5a ★★
The massive corner can be green but this is compensated for by the roughness of the rock. Be bold, or bring a very big cam.
Graham West, 1960

10 Kremlin Wall 18m E1 5c ★★★
The fingery splitter crack provides hard but well-protected climbing. The short may struggle getting started on the upper crack.
Mike Wrigley, John Lumb, (some aid), 1969. FFA John Allen, Steve Bancroft, 1973

11 Obyoyo 16m HVS 5b ★
Very impressive ground covered by equally impressive masochistic jamming and thrutching.
Tony Howard, Tony Jones, 1961

12 The Trouble With Women Is... 16m E1 5b ★★
Gain the large flake block directly, then place a cam in the left-hand pocket of *Womanless Wall*. Balance up and follow the fine upper wall (crux, small cams useful) just to the left.
Chris Hardy, Brian Roberts, 1985

13 Womanless Wall 18m VS 4c ★★★
A great big steep classic with enjoyable climbing throughout, at the upper end of the grade. Ascend the wall diagonally leftwards to a large flake block. Boldly gain large pockets (good cam). Do not stand up, but hand traverse quickly right to reach the finishing crack.
Tony Howard, Alwyn Whitehead, Vivien Nicholls, 1958

420 | Standing Stones

LOWER RIGHT WALL
This wall has two tiers: the upper one, which contains some short but delightful routes, and the lower which contains longer and steeper cracks. Belays can be awkward in the blocky ground above.

14 Pocked Wall 10m VS 4c ★★
Delicate with a bold middle section and an awkward, protected finish.
Tony Howard, Alwyn Whitehead, Vivien Nicholls, 1958

15 Touch of Spring 10m HS 4c ★
Well protected crack climbing with a tough initial move.
Tony Jones, Tony Howard, 1960

16 Prolapse 10m E2 5c ★
Trend rightwards on knobs and pockets to the arête. Wobble boldly up this on the left.
Gary Gibson, 1982

17 The Slanting Horror 15m VS 4c ★
The right-hand crack is climbed direct.
Paul Seddon, Tony Howard, 1960

18 Wits' End 15m E1 5c ★★
Boulder the start using a small flake. Step left at the break then romp up the wall on interesting holds.
Steve Bancroft, John Allen, 1973

19 Tranquility 15m E1 5b ★
A stiff pull gains the ledge. Pull out of the niche and sprint up the crack and groove above.
Bill Tweedale, Brian Toase, 1971

20 Fish-Meal and Revenge 12m E5 6a ★★
A committing and sequency climb with a fingery crux. Climb the centre of the wall to gain small rounded holds. Blindly place a small cam on the right before slapping for the top.
John Smith, Chris Hardy, 1987

21 The Diamond 12m E3 5b ★
Trend right to the arête, which is climbed on rounded holds.
Paul Cropper, Brian Cropper, 1982

Mention to anyone that you've been to Standing Stones and chances are they'll ask "Did you do Ocean Wall?" Well you should. This E1 5b (page 422) has a beautiful essence about it. Ian Parnell climbing. Jon Winter

 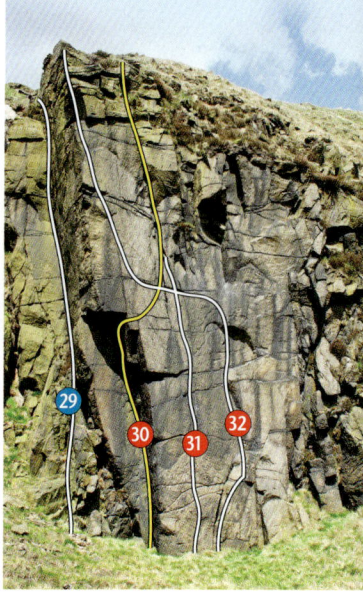

LEFT TWIN FACE
Across an open gully and easy descent, you'll find the next two friendly buttresses.

22 Wobbling Corner 12m S
Narrow cracks lead to sloping ledges and a finishing corner.
Tony Howard, Alwyn Whitehead, 1957

23 Piece of Pie 14m HVS 5b ★★
A steep little number starting up the shallow groove. Step left to the arête, then use the cracks just right of the arête to finish.
Tony Howard, Bill Tweedale, 1964

24 Right of Pie 14m E3 6a ★
A steep and technically baffling little number. Take the thin flake on the right to reach and stand on the only good hold on the route.
Paul Cropper, Brian Cropper, 1982

25 Fat Old Sun 14m E1 5b ★
Walk the plank to the start of the difficult thin crack.
Paul Cropper, Brian Cropper, 1982

26 Jiggery Pokery 14m E1 5b ★
From the base of the ramp, launch up the wall with long moves to the ledge. Continue directly to the top.
Tony Howard, Bill Tweedale, 1964

27 17 Shades 14m S
The slanting chimney to a blocky finish.
Tony Howard, Tony Jones, Paul Seddon, 1960

28 The Annoying Little Man 12m E4 6b ★
An extended boulder problem up the wall from the base of the large flake.
Steve Delderfield, Mike Delderfield, 1993

RIGHT TWIN FACE
At a lower level and down a grassy slope you'll find the next area of crag.

29 Kon-Tiki Korner 14m VS 4b ★
Follow the steep groove to strenuous moves right and a juggy finish.
Tony Howard, Tony Jones, 1961

30 The Ocean's Border 14m E3 6a ★★
Follow the square groove until one hell of a span gains a hold above the roof. Follow a thin crack above.
Gary Gibson (solo), 1983

31 Dredger 14m E2 6b ★★
A direct through *Ocean Wall*. The slippery arête and slab are bouldered-out to gain thin cracks and finish direct, as for *The Ocean's Border*.
Chris Addy, Colin Brooks, 1977

32 Ocean Wall 16m E1 5b ★★★
A classic. Off-balance climbing gains a ledge. Commit yourself on a sneaky traverse left to gain sanctuary and better gear. Move left again to the arête and vault up this to finish carefully.
⊙ page 421
Malc Baxter, Jim Heys, 1960

Oh glory! Is there anywhere you'd rather be on a soft summer evening than up on Ravenstones, a gentle breeze blowing, the world a million miles away, on the final runout of Pulpit Ridge, E1 5a (page 424). Marcus Buckley climbing. 📷 Ian Carr

RAVENSTONES

OS Grid Ref: SE 036 047
Altitude: 450m

Ravenstones lurks in the upper reaches of an enigmatic valley. Victorian tunnels, weird inscriptions, caves and witchcraft are all part of the local scene. The crag is at its best on warm summer days when the tranquillity and solitude is something to treasure. Evening climbing in the middle of the year is a fine end to anyone's day.

The crag faces in nearly every direction except south. Summer is the best time to visit. If it's been dry for a few days then the crag will be fine, but some of the chimneys and cracks will need longer to dry. Routes may need a clean beforehand, especially the harder ones.

Approach: See map on page 414. Park at Binn Green car park (p&d). Follow steps down to the reservoir road, and start walking up the valley. The way is long, but fairly flat. Expect to take 45 minutes to reach the end of the track (Tunnel End). From here it's a steep 15 minutes up to the crag. A mountain bike cuts the approach time down by 20 minutes, and the trip back is a quick 15 minutes.

1 Boy's Own 14m E1 5b
The smart arête.
Ray Duffy, Chris Hardy, Ian Carr, 1982

2 Nil Desperandum 12m HS 4a ★★★
The corner-crack rears up as soon as you get started. From the ledge, pull through the overhangs and finish up the right side of the arête.

3 The Ravenstones Stomach Traverse 45m ★★
An ungradable grovel from *Nil Desperandum* all the way to *Mark I*. Some call it a classic.

4 Pulpit Ridge 16m E1 5a ★★★
The first of the Ravenstones mega classics, which must have been extremely bold back in the day (it still is!). Gained from the right or direct via the steep jamming crack. ⊙ page 423
Arthur Birtwistle, CP Haywood, 1938

5 Over The Moors 16m E5 6b ★★★
A superb and bold climb. From the traverse on *Pulpit Ridge*, climb the wall above, first left, then right, to an easing at the wide break. A pocket on the slab accepts a crucial runner.
Paul Clarke, Colin Matthews, 1994

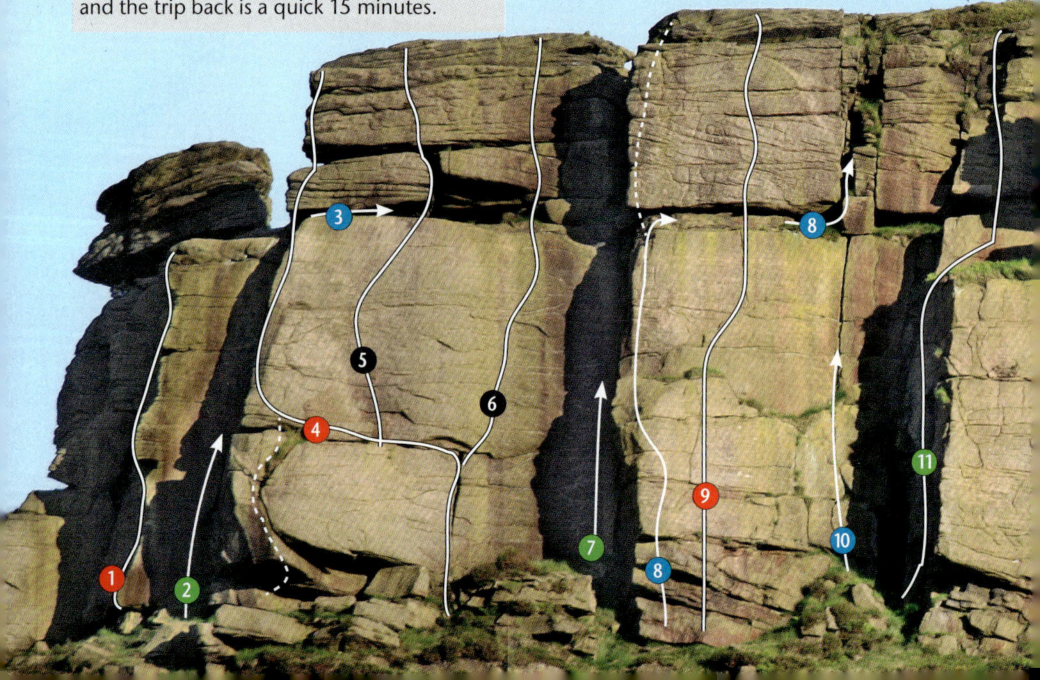

Ravenstones | 425

6 Black Mountain Collage 16m E7 6b ★★
A horror show up the right side of the wall. Absorbingly thin climbing in a very serious position. A classic moorland frightener.
Andy Popp, 1999

7 The Drainpipe 16m HS 4a ★★
The offwidth corner goes more easily than you might expect thanks to help from useful holds.

8 Unfinished Arête 25m VS 4c ★
A bit of an expedition. Follow the arête then stomach traverse right to the finish of *Undun Crack*. The direct finish is **Guerrilla Action**, E2 5c ★★.
Arthur Birtwistle, CP Haywood, 1938 / John Smith, 1981

9 Welcome to Greenfield, Gateway to The Valley 16m E3 6a ★★
Getting to the break is hard enough, but leaving it is preposterous. Try not to succumb to the temptation to climb into the gash.
Mike Chapman, Ian Carr, 1982

10 Undun Crack 16m VS 4c ★
A great little route! At the block, avoid the grass and go straight over it into a juggy finish.

11 Little Kern Knots 16m S 4a ★
Follow the crack and sentry box in the wall right of the deep corner to the grass terrace. Take the knobbly groove above to finish.
George Bower, Fergus Graham, 1920s

12 No Time to Pose 16m E6 6b ★★★
The leaning arête is eye-catching, and it's hard to see where the holds and the gear are.
Dougie Hall, John Smith, 1987

13 Mark I 18m S 4a ★★
A great route taking a grand line up the left-hand side of the bay. After the ledge take the wide crack either direct or to the left.
George Bower, Albert Wood, pre-1924

14 The Derivatives 20m HS 4a ★★
A superb expedition. Start up the chimney right of *Mark I* (**Mark II**, S 4b) and, where forced on to the outside, gain a traverse right to climb a big flake crack. Continue past ledges and finish up the puzzling slab.

15 Rizla 20m HVS 5a, 4b ★
Avoid the initial overhangs by sneaking in from the left. From the corner, move diagonally to the roof, then slink to the ledge (possible belay) and the upper crack of *Wedgewood Crack*.
Paul Seddon, Tony Howard, 1961

16 Roll Up 20m E2 5c ★★
A real challenge with some spectacular exposure at the top. The direct start over the bulge feels bold, and the climbing builds nicely to a technical, frightening, rising traverse to finish up the hanging slab. The short may find it 6a.
Ian Carr, Mike Chapman, Ray Duffy, 1982

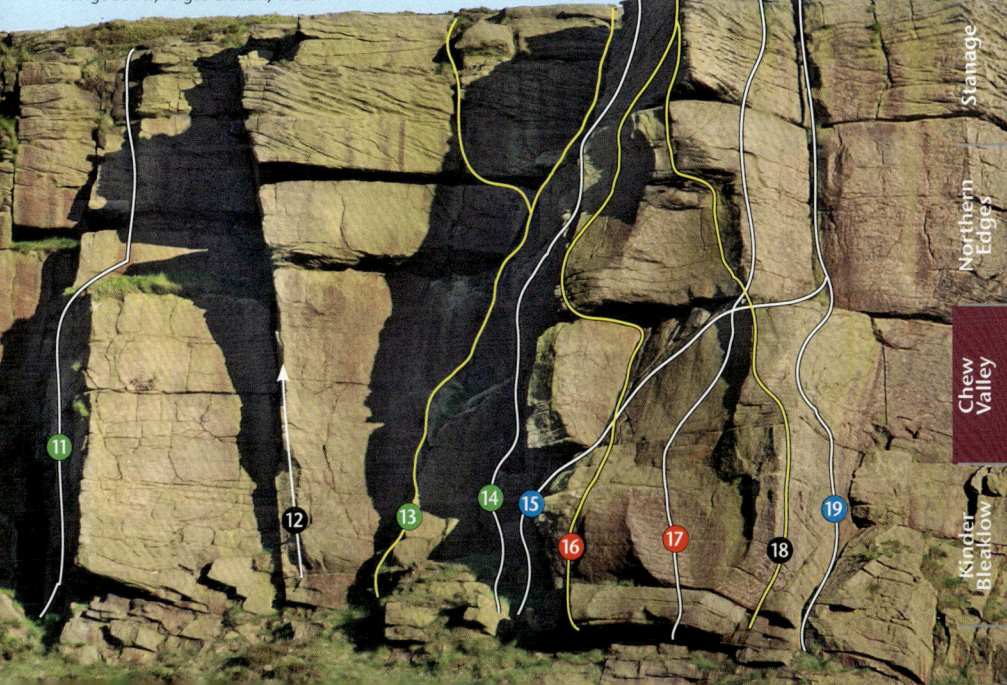

17 Stranger Than Friction 20m E3 5c ★★
This is what Ravenstones is about. Bold, towering and sustained. The first part of the route is perhaps the psychological crux, with little or no gear to speak of. The upper rib, crack and wall are well protected and really enjoyable.
John Smith, Tony Howard, 1981

18 Rough Shag 20m E4 6b ★
Follow the arête on its right to a ledge. Swing left into the overhanging scoop, then use creaking flakes to gain the break via a wild lunge. Finish via *Roll Up*. ⊙ opposite page
Ian Carr, Marcus Buckley, 2007

19 Wedgewood Crack 22m VS 4c ★★★
The objective is the enormous upper corner. Start up a shallow ramp to enter the left-slanting crack. Follow this, then boldly up and right to the ledge. The corner above is just superb.
George Bower, Albert Wood, 1920s

20 Wall of China 20m E5 6b ★
Insecure, reachy, balancy and very out there. From *Wedgewood's* ledge climb rightwards to the arête. Make a hard move up the left side of this then step left to finish up a crack.
Ian Carr, 1987

21 True Grit 16m E3 5c ★★★
Fabulous in every way: big moves, great rock and increasing exposure needing plenty of muscle. A tricky move on a flake gains the first wide break. Layaway and balance to the next break, and a further sloping move to gain the upper wall. Take two extra-large cams.
John Smith, Tony Howard, 1981

22 Sniffer Dog 14m E1 5a ★
A belter of a route, covering big ground with style. Bold moves up the arête lead to a step left to the base of the fab jamming crack and easier upper wall.
John Smith, Tony Howard, 1981

THE TRINNACLE: The fabulous tri-corned feature. The easiest descent lies to its right.

23 Trinnacle East 10m HVS 5a ★★
A steep blast up the tower's sidewall. From the gully, move right to a shallow corner. Follow this, and the wall above, to the top.

24 The Left Monolith 10m HS 4b ★★★
The delightful front face of the pinnacle with masses of exposure. Use the left arête just below the top, otherwise VS.
Herbert Hartley, 1928

25 Trinnacle Chimney 10m M ★★★
Romp up the chimney between the pillars.

26 The Right Monolith 10m E1 5a ★
Bold and absorbing climbing directly up the right-hand front face. Using the arêtes reduces the grade, but only slightly.
Herbert Hartley, 1928

27 Trinnacle West 12m E1 5b ★★
The final route is on the back wall of the pinnacle. A steep, pumpy, rounded thing. Starting from a block, follow the crack up the steep wall to the overhang. Pass the crack above to a tough top. ⊙ page 416
Paul Seddon and the Rimmon Club, 1963

Big country! The towering buttresses of Ravenstones deliver mega-leads with the yawning moorland exposure always snapping at your heels. What a place to be! Ian Carr on Rough Shag, E4 6b (opposite page) 📷 Jon Moulding

DOVESTONES EDGE

OS Grid Ref: SE 028 040
Altitude: 440m

Dovestones Edge is the finest crag in the Chew area for low to mid-grade routes. The situation and superb aspect of the edge is something to savour late in the day as the routes bathe in the glow of the afternoon and evening sun.

Climbing on the Edge will be fine on any good day between April and October, especially in the afternoon. It is however at its best on a summer's day when it catches the sun from the early afternoon 'till sunset. Its lofty and breezy position usually keeps the midges at bay.

Approach: The approach involve a stiff walk of just less than an hour.

The quickest is from the Binn Green car park (p&d). Take the steps down through woods, then turn left along the metalled road to the reservoirs. Cross the dam and follow the track clockwise around Dovestone Reservoir. At the bridge, take the track up by the left side of the watercourse to a footbridge, where a tunnel emerges. From the footbridge a horizontal path leads to Dovestones Quarry (not described). From here walk a few hundred metres and take the second stile then head rightwards, later cutting back left under *The Hanging Crack*.

1 Eyebrow 15m VS 4c
Climb the left side of the buttress via a wide crack, followed by a cheeky traverse right above nose level to finish up the brow.

2 Nasal Buttress 15m HS 4b ★★★
A moorland classic, sustained and excellent throughout in a fine, airy situation. Pick your way up the fine protruding buttress mainly on the left, passing a polished crux foothold at half height. Finish on the exposed crest.
George Bower, 1920s

3 Nasal Buttress Right-Hand
  15m VS 4c ★★
A harder version passes the nose on the right.

4 Eight Hours! 14m E1 5a ★
A route that requires a clear cool head, taking the slim wall on the right of the nose.
Chris Hardy, Chris Dent, 1984

5 The Changeling 15m VS 4b
Follow the deep dogleg crack. Where it joins the chimney, step right onto the next buttress and finish up its left arête.
Tony Howard, 1960s

6 Crack and Chimney 12m M ★★
The deep cleft finishing over the capstone.

7 Palpitation 13m E1 5a ★★
Take the front face of the tower, skirting the overhang on the left. Step back right to finish.
Jim Campbell, Steve Bancroft, 1973

8 Capstone Chimney 12m M ★★
The cleft with a huge block guarding the finish.

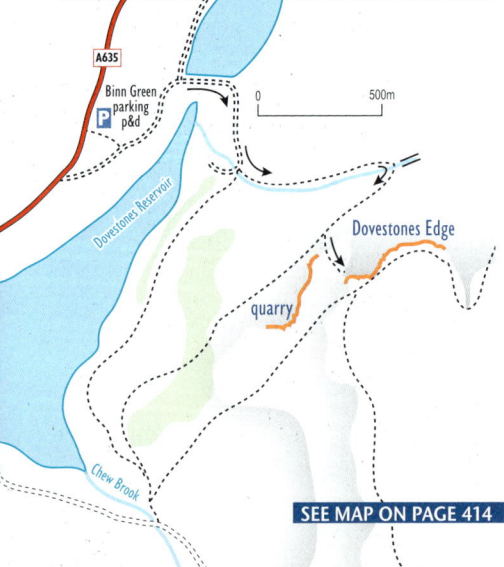

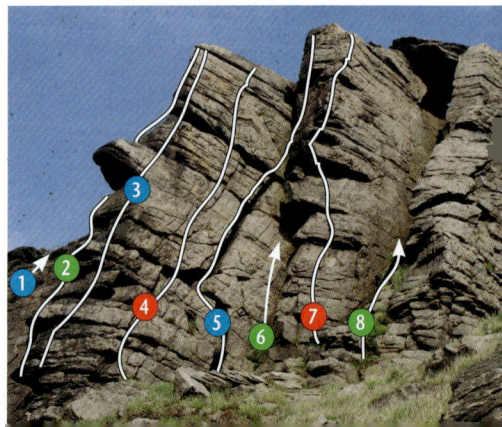

Dovestones Edge | 429

9 Central Tower 18m VD ★★
Justifiably popular, this fine route takes the front face of the buttress finishing up a slab.

10 Tower Arête 18m VS 4c ★
The right edge of the tower passing a difficult bulge near the top.
Rick Gibbon, Bill Birch, 1986

11 Left Embrasure 16m VS 4b ★★
A great honest route up the left-hand of the twin cracks. Good holds and jams appear when most needed. Thankfully not as butch as it looks.
Barry Kershaw, Tony Howard, 1958

12 Right Embrasure 16m VS 5a ★
Grunt your way up the right-hand crack, some poor rock (avoidable).
Tony Howard, Barry Kershaw, 1958

13 Matchstick Crack 10m S 4a ★★
The thin crack in the back wall of the recess give some good climbing after a poor start.
Tony Jones, 1960

14 Maggie 10m HVS 5a ★★
The arête is stylish, satisfying and balancy.
Tony Jones or Eric Flint, c1960

15 Dennis 10m E1 6a ★
Gain the break via a tantalising reach, finish direct.
Ian Carr, Marcus Buckley, 2008

16 Grim Wall 10m HVS 5a ★
The short unfinished crack is started from the platform, then followed rightwards up the wall with some difficulty.

17 Noddy's Wall 12m VS 4c ★★
Good climbing up the narrow front face of the buttress, made all the more exciting by the paucity of protection. Move slightly right at the finish.
John 'Noddy' Hadfield, 1958

18 Swan Crack 14m S 4a ★★
An old-timer's favourite. Start on the rounded arête then head up right to gain and climb the prominent deep, polished crack.

19 Swan Down 10m VS 4c
A tricky route up the wall right of the crack with more than its fair share of sloping holds.
Graham West, 1960

20 Gnome's Wall   14m   VS 4c   ★★
The lower wall is nice and technical. The scrappy finish can be avoided.
Graham West, 1960

21 Rib and Wall   15m   HS 4a   ★
Take the rib and deep groove in the arête to the midway ledge. Take the centre of the wall on the right to finish.

22 Mammoth Slab   16m   HVS 4c   ★★
Worthwhile and varied. Pull rightwards over the bulge to gain the edge of the undercut slab. Easier but bolder padding gains the sanctuary of the big ledge. Trend leftwards up the wall to an awkward sloping finish (crux) on the right side of the arête.
Graham West, 1960

23 Ferdie's Folly   16m   E2 5c   ★★
Make a perplexing move over the overlap using a hollow flake and polished foothold. Alarming friction moves lead (hopefully) to the big ledge. Good climbing but unprotected where it counts.

24 Dust Storm   16m   E3 5c   ★
Precarious and protectionless. Cross the scoop then climb directly to the ledge. Often green and dirty so graded accordingly.
Chris Hardy, Chris Dent, 1984

25 Kaytoo   15m   VS 4c
From the block, step left into the crack and follow this to a ledge. Zigzag the wall above.
Tony Howard, Barry Kershaw, 1958

26 Asinine   8m   E2 6b   ★★
From the boulder, a long stretch right gains slopers. Go straight up connecting a series of poor crimps and smears. Hard for everyone, but especially the short.
Ian Carr (solo), 1982

27 June Climb   14m   D   ★★
The central deep grassy fault is taken to the midway ledges. From the left gain the upper slab and follow it rightwards to the top.

28 Austin Maxi   8m   E2 5c   ★★
Good fingery climbing – the best of the micro-routes.
Chris Hardy (solo), 1982

29 June Wall   8m   VS 5b   ★
A great traditional problem. Step rightwards off the boulder to the break and easier finish.
Graham West, 1960

The next two routes starts just right, around the arête:

30 June Ridge   8m   HS 4c   ★
Gain the sloping shelf and then move left to finish as for *June Wall*.

31 Dogsbody   8m   E2 5c
Stretch up the wall from the start of *June Ridge*.
Chris Hardy (solo), 1986

Amidst the genteel lower-grade joys that relax along Dovestones Edges lies this brute. The Hanging Crack, E2 5b (page 433) just screams to be climbed. The perfect handshake crack busts it out over dramatic overhangs where all but the strongest, slickest and luckiest of E2 leaders will be left scraping the bottom of their barrels. Andy Gardner feeling the pressure. 📷 Mike Delderfield

Dovestones Edge

Across the gully, the first rock encountered is a narrow rib.

32 Rubber-Faced Arête 10m HVS 4c
Take the thin crack in the left wall of the narrow rib until a swing right gains a large foothold. The reachy crux is passing the blanker section above.
Malc Baxter, Jim Heys, 1961

33 Rubber-Faced Wall 10m VD
Follow the rightwards-slanting recessed crack to easier ground.

34 December Arête 12m HVS 5a ★
The bold arête offers a balancy and slightly harrowing finish on the right. Worth doing, but perhaps not in December!
Malc Baxter, Jim Heys, 1961

35 Layback Crack 12m MVS 4b ★★★
A classic route, one of crag's finest: the name says it all. ⊙ page 415

36 Friction Addiction 12m E2 5c ★★
Climb the slab right of the layback crack: a satisfying solo. The crux is unprotected but fairly close to the ground. Above the break the climbing eases.
Chris Hardy (solo), 1984

37 Slip-Off Slab 12m VS 4c ★★
A route which requires a careful approach. Bold but rewarding climbing up the thin initial crack (and your only protection). After this trend leftwards to a seam in the upper slab.
Tony Howard, Barry Kershaw, 1958

38 Double Time Crack 12m S
Wide and deep crack climbing, bounding the right edge of the slab.

39 'Owd on Arête 12m VS 4b ★
The neat curving arête finishing left of the sharp prow, or on the right side at 4c.
Malc Baxter, Jim Heys, 1961

40 Answer Crack 12m HVD 4a ★★★
A moorland classic. Superb climbing and a compelling natural line make this the best easier route around.
Paul Seddon, 1960

41 Question Mark 12m HVD 4a ★★
A fine old-school boot-width crack, moving left to finish.
Paul Seddon, 1960

42 Full-Stop 12m E1 5a ★
The unprotected wall has numerous holds which, at times, aren't quite as good as you'd like them to be. **Pause**, E2 5b ★★, is a scarier but finer direct finish.
Steve Bancroft, Jim Campbell, 1973. Chris Hardy (solo), 1982

43 Third Triplet 12m D ★
The left-hand and widest of three fine fissures.

44 Yellow Crack 12m HVS 5c ★★
Fine clean climbing. Gain the crack from the left arête, via a keyed-in hold. The crack gives a few moves to a tricky finish.

Dovestones Edge | 433

45 Yellow Peril 12m E2 6a ★
Boulder the initial wall to gain a thin seam and micro wires. Technical and very reachy moves past a very small ramp gain the ledge.
Ian Carr, Marcus Buckley, 2008

46 Second Triplet 12m VD ★
The narrower right-hand, polished fissure.

47 Loose End 12m VS 5a ★★
The thin, peg-scarred crack has a difficult but protected start. Finish steeply up the arête on the right.
Duggy Baynes (aid), FFA Paul Seddon, 1960

48 First Triplet 10m HS 4b ★
A short, polished, hand crack stepping right to a juggy finish.

49 Scarface 10m VS 4c ★
The left-slanting and narrowing crack underneath the prow can unfortunately be dirty. Otherwise a fine climb.
Barry Kershaw, 1960s

50 Silly Arête 12m HS 4b ★
Start up the next route from the midheight terrace then break left to follow the exposed left edge of the buttress.
Jim Heyes, Malc Baxter, 1961

51 Tower Ridge 28m HVD 4a ★★★
A climb of two halves. Scramble down below the main edge to start up a crack on the right side of the ridge. Easy climbing gains the terrace below the main edge. The upper part is superb in its own right taking a juggy flake crack on the left side of the main buttress.
George Bower, 1920s

52 The Jester 12m HS 4b ★
The short crack and depression bounding the edge of Hanging Crack Buttress.
Steve Bancroft, Pete Buckley, 1972

53 The Hanging Crack 15m E2 5b ★★★
A classic Chew and Peak testpiece. The crackline snaking through the roofs is one of the best routes of its type on grit. It requires technique, stamina and determination at the lip for a successful ascent. Protection is excellent.
page 431
Joe Brown, 1957. FFA Richard McHardy, Paul Braithwaite, 1967

54 The Gibbet 15m E3 5c ★★
The imposing and bold sidewall. From a low jug and large cam, launch up the wall (crux) via a series of long stretches between gradually improving holds.
Lawrence Francomb, Brian Cropper, 1980

ROB'S ROCKS

OS Grid Ref: SE 030 017
Altitude: 470m

A collection of delightfully isolated south-facing buttresses close to the top of Chew Brook.

Predominantly south facing, with lovely afternoon and evening sun. Can be exposed to the wind, therefore quick drying.

> **Approach:** See map on page 414. Pay and Display parking at Dovestone Reservoir (the charges are 7 days a week 8am - 8pm), from which a 40-minute (gentle) uphill approach is made via the tarmac service road to Chew Reservoir.

1 Snow Crack 8m   HS 4b ★
The pleasant wide crack.
Jeff Sykes, 1961

2 Dormant in the Dormitories 9m   HVS 5b
The right edge of the wall.
Carl Dawson, Cath Dawson, 1985

3 Nice Edge 9m   VS 4b ★
The arête, started on the left, but soon moving round to climb it on its right.
Paul Seddon, 1961

4 Fantastic Edge 8m   VS 4b ★★
The juggy prow is climbed mainly on the left.

5 Cataract 8m   VS 4c ★
At the left-hand side of the wall, start by a block and ascend the wall via a worrying crux at two-thirds height.

6 Torrent 8m   VS 4b ★
The eliminate wall immediately left of *Cascade* with spaced protection.

7 Cascade 8m   HS 4a ★★
Go direct up the centre on reasonable holds (small cams). It gets harder as you go.
Tony Howard, 1961

8 Rapid 8m   HS 4b
The face between *Cascade* and *Zacharias*.

9 Zacharias 8m   VD ★
To the right, easy climbing leads to a crack finish.
Tony Howard, 1961

10 Nameless One 10m   VS 4b ★★
The striking line. The initial crack is climbed to its end where tricky moves left gain the wider finishing crack. **The Direct Finish** is E1 5b ★.
Roy Brown, Jimmy Curtis, 1950

Rob's Rocks | 435

11 Nameless Two　12m　E2 5a　★
Pull rightwards over the overhang towards the arête. Daunting climbing up its airy left-hand side remains. Bold.
Ian Carr (solo), 1983

12 Ylnosd Rib　12m　VD　★★
The undercut crack is a very traditional and quality route. Climb into the crag's innards then make a tough squeeze and shuffle out to daylight and a great finishing crack.
JW Puttrell, Lehmann J Oppenheimer, 1903

13 Letter-Box　11m　VD　★★★
Fantastic and understandably popular. Gain the cut-out ledge then the centre of the slab.
JW Puttrell, Lehmann J Oppenheimer, 1903

14 Cave Crack　10m　HS 4b　★
The chimney crack requires traditional technique or strong arms.
Members of the Rimmon MC, 1961

15 Cripple's Way　10m　VD　★
The slabby face gives a lovely little route.
Members of the Rimmon MC, 1961

16 Ow't　10m　D　★★
The wider left-hand crack and wall using a thin crack is popular with those new to the game.
Members of the Rimmon MC, 1961

17 Cool Rib　8m　VS 4c
The narrow wall leads to a vague, steep rib and a tricky, short wall.
David Simmonite (solo), 2006

18 Ice Crack　8m　VD
Bridge and jam up the corner.
Members of the Rimmon MC, 1961

19 Digital Orbit　8m　E3 5c　★
Spicy for such a short route. From the block a couple of metres left of the roof, jump (gulp!) to a jug at the base of the left arête and finish up this. For less trauma, and a grade easier, pop to the jug from the block beneath the roof.
Paul Moreland, 1990

20 The Nose　7m　HVS 5b　★★
Had your three Weetabix then? Cos you're going to need them! From the right edge of the roof grab a couple of holds and somehow heave your way over to a standing position and an easier finale.
Tony Howard, 1961

21 Nosey　7m　HS 4a　★
From the right, make a couple of moves up then head delicately out above the roof to the left edge of the wall. Suss out the hidden holds and it doesn't feel too bad.
Jeff Sykes, 1961

22 Freebird　8m　E2 5c
Climb the triangular overhang then haul up the hanging arête.
Paul Moreland, 1990

23 Niche Wall　8m　HVD　★
Gain the niche from the left and move on to the arête. Skirt left beneath the top block.
Members of the Rimmon MC, 1961

WIMBERRY ROCKS

OS Grid Ref: SE 016 024
Altitude: 440m

Wimberry Rocks is without doubt the finest of all the moorland crags and is indeed one of the proudest crags on gritstone. Its serrated profile, with great arêtes and deep corners angling along the whole width of the crag, provides some of the fiercest and most satisfying challenges of any grade. It metes out drymouthed terror, bloodletting pumps and never-to-be-forgotten buzzes to the worthy, be that on dark Severes or a holdless E10.

The crag is characterised by a series of strong angular features. Its faces are comprised of large open expanses of highly pebbled, rippled and pocketed rock. Therefore, the climbs are often sustained throughout their length and only succumb to an equally positive approach by the climber. At whatever grade you operate, expect a full-on day. Even the well-protected routes feel bold because of the steeliness they demand.

Facing northeast, the crag receives sun early (before 9am) and late in the day (after 9pm) in high summer. It can therefore be green after damp weather. The crag is at its best between April and October. Altitude and aspect contribute to the fact that good conditions can be found throughout the summer.

> **Approach:** See map on page 414. From the car park below Dovestones Reservoir (p&d, charges are 7 days a weeks between 08:00 and 20:00), walk along the road past the sailing clubhouse until the bridge crossing Chew Brook is reached. Turn right upstream to a large boulder, the Sugar Loaf. A steep path leads directly up to the left-hand end of the crag in around 50 minutes.

Wimberry Rocks

Sugar Loaf boulder

The classic Wimberry E2 5c. Blasphemy (page 442) tempts leaders steadily upwards, with surprising holds and generous runners until, just when you're about to give yourself a pat on the back, this happens. John Crook wondering where all the grips have gone. ◘ Ian Carr

Wimberry Rocks

① Thermometer Crack 8m MVS 4b ★
Layback and jam the overhanging crack. A good warm up route (groan!).
Tony Howard, 1960s

② Short Crack 8m VS 5a ★
The well protected short chimney passing a small overhang by jamming and bridging.
Joe Brown, Don Whillans, 1954

③ Pinball Wizard 9m E1 5c ★★
A smart little classic which feels hard on first acquaintance. Climb the finger-crack to where it curves left. Hard moves straight-up gains a hidden slot (cam) then a final fingery move.
◉ opposite page
Steve Bancroft, 1972

④ Eight-Metre Corner 8m D ★
The pleasant polished corner is often used as a convenient descent.

⑤ Poltergeist 10m VS 4b ★
Climb the arête, with a delicate move to reach good jams in a bottomless crack.

⑥ Blocked Chimney 10m VD ★
Climb the chimney to the overhang then swing left to gain easier ground.

⑦ Ornithologist's Corner 12m VS 5a ★★★
Classic steep climbing, with excellent protection. Bridge up to the roof past a keyed-in wobbly block. Jam strenuously rightwards to the top.
Joe Brown, Slim Sorrell, Wilf White, 1940s

⑧ One-Way Ticket 12m E2 5b ★★
The right-hand side of the arête is climbed to the break. Finish direct with difficulty for the grade or escape left at HVS - **Surprise Arête**.
Chris Hardy, Carl Dawson, 1987

⑨ Surprise 12m VS 4c ★★
An old classic where good gritstone technique pays dividends. Climb with increasing difficulty to an awkward and nose-grinding move around the block.
Joe Brown, Slim Sorrell, Wilf White, 1940s

⑩ Overhang Chimney 12m VD ★
Best tackled facing left, the chimney leads awkwardly past an excellent thread.
Anton Stoop, 1910

⑪ Freddie's Finale 14m HVS 5b ★★★
The first of the big three HVSs. Gain the overhung niche via a baggy fist jam. The upper crack eases and narrows with height with some of the best hand jamming on grit.
Joe Brown, Fred Ashton, 1948

⑫ Double Take 16m E6 6b ★★★
A brilliant and improbable line up the severely undercut arête. From the niche of *Freddie's*, traverse rightwards to the arête. Slap the desperate bulge to finish up a straightforward ramp. Two belayers might curtail a nasty fall.
Dougie Hall, Nick Plishko, Ian Carr, 1987

On a crag as burly as Wimberry tends to be, it's no wonder that the odd delicate outing proves popular. Ian Carr on his toes and tips on the lovely Pinball Wizard, E1 5c (opposite page). Chris Tan

Wimberry Rocks

13 Space Shuffle 18m E5 6a ★★
A wild trip. From the second chockstone on *Hanging Groove* traverse leftwards to the arête. Swing onto rounded holds and shuffle left again to gain the lip. Move up then continue leftwards by foot-traversing a horizontal crack to finish up a hidden ramp line. Ground fall potential from the lip.
Mike Chapman, Ian Carr, 1983

14 Hanging Groove 15m VS 4c ★
Gymnastic and strenuous pulls on good but polished holds give access to the groove, then finish with less difficulty up the wide crack.

15 Coffin Crack 16 VS 4c ★★
A good line and good climbing, giving one of the best VSs on the crag. Gain and leave the sentry-box by a sustained and strenuous layback.
Joe Brown, Merrick (Slim) Sorrell, Wilf White, 1940s

The wall right of *Coffin Crack* contains a fine collection of hard gritstone routes. The routes rely upon the uniquely pebble-dashed, wrinkled and pocketed rock. By chance the centre of the wall, where the routes converge, contains a deep letterbox pocket which gladly accept cams.

16 Berlin Wall 22m E6 6c ★★
A left-to-right diagonal. From a little way up *Coffin Crack*, balance right to reach a pocket (hand-placed peg). Move rightwards, then up on rounded finger-holds which are just left of a faint rib. A semi-lunge follows for a 'thank God' pocket. Step up then slink rightwards by the superb and intricate pebble-dashed wall to reach a hollow-sounding flake below the roof. Finish as for *The Trident*.
Nick Plishko, Chris Hardy, 1987

17 Sectioned 20m E8 6c ★★★
The super direct via the small bulge and pebbled face to gain the twin pockets in the centre of the wall. A runner in the base of *The Trident*, provides little security. Now choose your finish.
Kevin Thaw, 2004

18 Neptune's Tool 20m E6 6c ★★★
The thin curving crack is gained with great difficulty and followed (past a small, hard-to-place wire) to a good rest at mid-height. Continue up the pocketed wall, then trend leftwards to finish over a small bulge just to the right of *Coffin Crack*.
Nick Plishko, Chris Addy, 1986

19 The Trident 20m HVS 5b ★★★
The second of the big three HVSs. Don't be put off by the green as the rock is extremely rough and the protection perfect. The striking groove-line provides strenuous, sustained and unusual back-and-footing.
Joe Brown, Merrick Sorrell, Wilf White, 1948

20 Bertie's Bugbear 18m S 4a ★★★
The central deep feature of the crag gives one of the best easy routes in the Chew.
Anton Stoop, 1910

There are moments on short gritstone leads where you would probably give a significant amount of money just for a single positive crimp to grab. Matthew Nuttall making the most of what he's got on the lovely little runout on Halina, E2 5c (page 443). 📷 Dan Lane

Wimberry Rocks

㉑ The Sick-Bay Shuffle 22m E3 5a ★★
Not for the faint-hearted. From gear in *Bertie's*, traverse rightwards with increasing difficulty to finish up the scooped arête. The transition between good handholds and good footholds plays games with your mind.
Nick Plishko, Paul Drummond, 1987

㉒ Dangermouse 18m E9 7a ★★
The big blunt arête was one of the last great problems of the crag. Low gear does nothing to ease increasing technicalities up the steep, rippled arête.
Miles Gibson, 2009

㉓ Piety 20m E2 5c ★★
Bare your soul and leave *Blasphemy* along the large scoop in an increasingly exposed position. Gain the arête (micro-cam), swing right to finish easily up the left edge of the upper slab as per *Sick-Bay Shuffle*. A fantastic route, worth three stars when completely clean.
Ian Carr, Mike Chapman, 1982

㉔ Blasphemy 16m E2 5c ★★★
A classic E2 of Peak grit. From the platform, step into the peg-scarred finger crack and follow it past a difficult move to a foothold rest. Continue up the fading crackline to a perplexing and oft fallen-off finishing move.
⊙ page 437
Graham West, Michael Roberts (aid), 1950. FFA John Allen, Steve Bancroft, Neil Stokes, 1973

㉕ Blue Lights Crack 15m HVS 5b ★★
The last and maybe the hardest of the big three HVSs, or should that be E1s? The all-too-obvious corner-crack, starting from a sentry-box, can be climbed either by a bold layback or, more usually, by reverting back to wedging at mid-height. A great way to continue the fun into three-star territory is **Green Streak**, (HVS 5a) which traverses right at the top to finish up the short hanging crack.
Don Whillans, Joe Brown, 1948 / Steve Bancroft, 1973

㉖ Sacrilege 22m E2 5c ★★
Gain the traverse line from the chimney. Thumper jams lead to a sticky exit.
Tony Howard, Barry Taylor (aid), 1963. FFA Martin Berzins, Bob Berzins, 1978

㉗ Starvation Chimney 18m HVD 4a ★★
Strip down to the bare essentials and head off into the darkness. Wriggle and thrutch through the narrow opening into a crevasse, daylight and hence the top.

㉘ Baron Greenback 20m E10 7a ★★★
The best line on grit? Like the bow of a ship, the massive prow is climbed direct. The outrageous crux on the steepest section (above three old aid bolts) leads to an easier but very bold finish on the left.
Pete Whittaker, 2014

Wimberry Rocks | 443

29 Appointment With Fear 22m E7 6b ★★★
Precarious and bold, a stunning route in an awesome position. From *Route 1*, move left to a sloping handhold; more hard moves enable a standing position to be attained. An increasingly difficult combination of balance and pebbles gains large footholds just right of the arête. This leads to a scary top-out.
Dougie Hall, Chris Hardy, 1986

30 Appointment with Death 18m E9 6c ★★
A combination of brittle technicalities and mind-blowing seriousness. After the first few moves of *Appointment*, climb the wall via a subtle but obvious line with a high crux.
Sam Whittaker, 2003

31 Route 1 18m HS 4b ★★★
A gritstone classic; clean, well-protected and continuously interesting, with the crux near the top. The open book narrowing crack passing through two scoops. Fantastic. ⊙ page 7
L Kiernan, F Hewitt, 1937

32 Route 2 18m VS 5a ★★
The thin crack has a difficult shiny start. From its top move rightwards to a 'rock-knob', then step left into an exposed blocky crack and the top.
L Kiernan, F Hewitt, 1937

33 Halina 15m E2 5c ★
From the 'rock-knob', gain the hanging ramp by hard moves at the bulge. The ramp is technically easier though rather bold.
⊙ page 441
Barry Rawlinson, Gerry Peel (1pt), 1972. FFA John Allen, Steve Bancroft, 1975

34 Twin Cracks 8m HS 4b ★★
Climb the clean twin cracks; hardest at the start and over all too soon.
Anton Stoop, 1910

35 Squirmer's Chimney 12m S 4b ★★
The deep narrow chimney is a classic of its type.

36 Consolation Prize 12m E5 6a ★★★
Classic grit boldness. Tricky, unprotected arête climbing at its best. A hard start leads to a holding point on the left. Committing but easier moves eventually lead to the top.
Jonny Woodward (solo), 1981

37 Slab Climb 12m S 4a ★★
A bold outing up the left-hand side of the slab on reasonable holds.

38 Herringbone Slab 12m HVS 4c ★★
Another serious proposition for the grade. Follow the centre of the slab with a difficult move to reach a scoop, thereafter an easier finish.
Members of the MGCC, 1950s

39 Groove and Chimney 10m D
The deep, well-named feature.

40 Charm 10m E3 5c ★★★
A popular clean route. Make a difficult rockover past the horizontal break to reach a poor pocket. A bold move leads to the thinner break and a finish up a slight flake.
Jonny Woodward, Nick Plishko, 1982

RUNNING HILL PITS

OS Grid Ref: SE 017 073
Altitude: 400m

Steep walls, steeper cracks and ferocious crimps characterise the climbs. The climbing is typical of quarried gritstone. Good jamming cracks abound in the Pits. These are complemented by some thin and very thin slab and face climbs that rely upon a combination of good friction and tiny crimps.

The west facing walls of the Pits have a sunny aspect and come into their own in the afternoon and evening. In the hot dry days of moorland high summer, the other walls of the Pits can provide a cool and shady escape. It's worth avoiding during mid-winter and after prolonged heavy rain due to seepage.

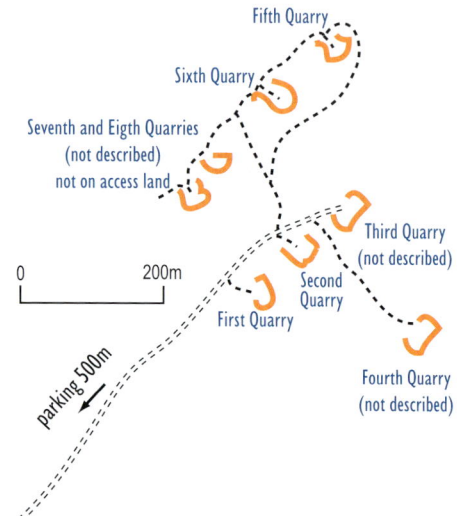

FIRST (CALAMITY) QUARRY
The first quarry is characterised by a combination of steep cracks and walls together with a more slabby area. The walls catch all the afternoon sun going, making it a great evening venue.

1 Acarpous 12m E2 5b
Climb up to and exit right from the large niche. Finish left with ease.
Chris Hardy, Chris Dent, Carl Dawson, 1987

2 Maquis 12m E1 5b ★
Butch jamming leads to the more thoughtful section of the previous route.
Bill Tweedale, Mick Quinn, Pete Oldham, 1966

3 Flush Pipe 10m E1 5c
The problematic arête and mantel can be used to start Maquis or finished via the dirty crack.
Bob Whittaker, Gordon Mason, 1977

4 Oh my Stars and Garters!
12m E3 6b ★
The real McCoy: fingery, steep and with a beast of a finish. Climb directly up the wall after the initial moves of *Flush Pipe*.
Marcus Buckley, Ian Carr, 2006

Approach: From the centre of Uppermill, go east up Church Road that becomes Running Hill Gate at the Cross Keys Inn. Continue along for a further mile to a sharp left where the lane drops back down the hill. Two gated tracks complete the crossroads. Park sensibly in the wide part of the track leading uphill. The Pits are reached in 15-20 minutes along the deeper (northward) track.

Running Hill Pits | 445

5 Old Dog, New Tricks 13m E3 6b ★★
Forceful stuff. Start with difficulty, powering past the flat slot to a slanting jug. Gain the break then reeeeeeach rightwards along the diagonal break and finish left up the higher ramp.
Ian Carr, Marcus Buckley, 2006

6 Gull-Wing 14m E2 5c ★★
Climb the left-hand start of *Mimosa* then hand traverse leftwards, with style of course, along the flat traverse to the impending groove. Finish by tapping into a bit more power to pass the roof on the right.
Paul 'Tut' Braithwaite, Nick Estcourt, 1978

7 Mimosa 12m E2 5c ★
Climb the left-hand crack with a little help from the right, or is it the right with help from the left. Either way you'll be confused and pumped by the time you reach the niche.
Tony Howard, Bill Tweedale, 1966

8 Calamity Crack 14m E4 6a ★★★
This awesome testpiece sorts the wheat from the chaff. Thin hands and bomber gear lead all the way to the crux at the niche. Amongst the best E4 cracks in the Peak. ⓘ page 449
Tony Howard, Alwyn Whitehead (aid), 1962. FFA Steve Bancroft, Pete Buckley, 1972

9 Gargantua 14m E1 5b ★★
More niches, and pure thuggery. Climb the crack to the first, and then puzzle your way into the next. Gibber off rightwards taking care with the rock.
Bill Tweedale, Roger Wynne, 1966

First Quarry

10 Mickey Thin 12m E1 5b ★★
Power the undercut jams then layaway up the hairline crack. Mantel out of it to finish in style.
Mick Shaw, Tony Howard, 1974

11 It Only Takes Two to Tango 12m E2 5c ★★
Take the faint undercut rib (crux) then the bold upper ramp and thin finish. Originally started from the right at 5b.
Gary Gibson, 1982

First Quarry

446 | Running Hill Pits

SECOND (SPANNER) QUARRY
This more open quarry hosts a very fine selection of routes. Its sunny walls are very quick to dry. The classic cracks on the darker walls also dry relatively quickly, but often look green.

12 Tighten Up Yer Nuts 10m E3 6a ★
A feisty finger-traverse along the top break.
Dougie Hall (solo), 1987

13 Iguanodon 10m E6 6b ★★
Powerful soloing at a rousing height. Enter the shallow depression from the left then make a difficult and committing move to the break.
Jonny Woodward, 1980

14 Folies Bergère 12m HS 4b
The awkward crack just right of the corner.
Bill Tweedale, Pete Oldham, 1966

15 Lolita / Shine On 12m VS 4c ★
Climb the wall and crack. Exit right up the shallow bold groove for the finish of *Shine On*.
Pete Oldham, Bill Tweedale, 1966 / Chris Hardy, 1981

16 Harvest Moon 12m E4 6b ★★
Using the right edge of the tiny hanging groove, gain the thin break (pegs). Passing these rightwards is the crux. The upper wall and groove are easier but bolder. **The Connection**, E4 6b ★★, continues after the crux to finish up the next route; well protected.
Chris Hardy, Ian Carr, 1984 / Mike Watson, 1987

17 Spanner Wall 14m E2 5c ★★★
From 4m up *Dead Dog Crack*, hand traverse left to the spanner. Launch boldly upwards for the toothy blocks and a trouser-filling finish.
Dougie Hall, Alan Pierce, 1978

18 Dead Dog Crack 8m VS 4c ★★
The left-hand crack. Easier than it looks.
Graham West, 1962

19 Cave Crack 8m VS 4c ★
The right-hand crack. Harder than it looks.
Graham West, 1962

20 Midsummer 8m S
The arête right of the cave-crack.
Bob Whittaker, 1972

21 Hazy Groove 8m VD
The groove right again.
Bob Whittaker, 1972

22 The Cracks 8m S
The twin cracks just right again.

23 Breakdown 8m HVS 5c ★
The satisfying finger crack is tough enough.
Brian Cropper, Ken Mercer, 1974

24 Problem Arête 8m D
The arête.
Brian Cropper, 1974

25 Yorick's Crack 10m E5 6c ★★
The protectable but desperately thin seam.
Dougie Hall, John Smith, 1988

26 Sagittarius Flake 10m E5 6b ★★★
The flake and hairline crack gives an unrelenting fight with a mighty lunge for the top.
Paul Cropper, Rehan Siddiqui (1pt), 1978. FFA Nick Colton, 1979

27 Scoop de Grace 9m E5 7a ★★★
A desperate highball; Font 7C+.
Dougie Hall (solo), 1987

28 Phaestus 8m E3 5c ★★
Tippy-toe out along the hanging ramp and mantel over the top whilst ignoring the drop.
Bob Whittaker, Geoff Smith, 1972

29 Windbreaker 8m E2 5b ★★
From the base of the ramp, bridge onto the slab and blast up the invisible holds to the top.
Bob Whittaker, Brian Cropper, Ken Mercer, 1974

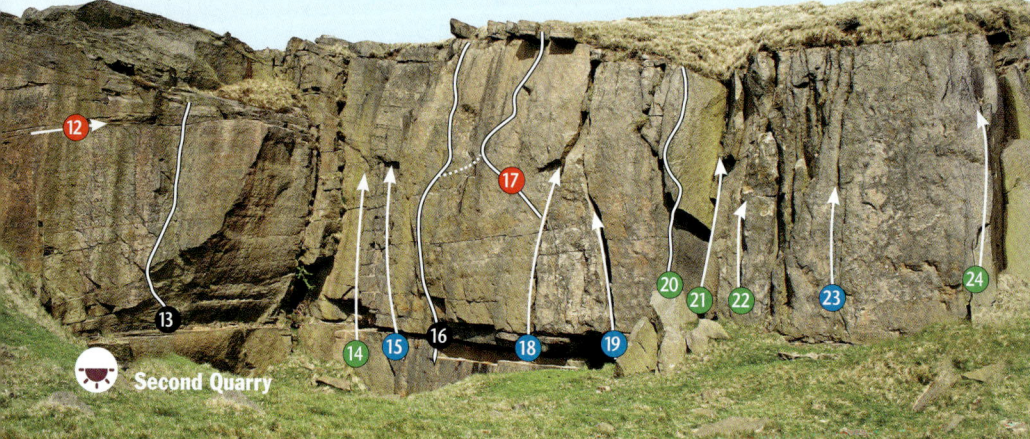
Second Quarry

30 Cochybondhu 6m E1 5c ★
Sketchy. Float up the angular right arête.
Bob Whittaker, Brian Cropper, Ken Mercer, 1974

31 The Mechanic 8m E2 5c ★
The scooped wall.
Chris Hardy, 1988

32 Pipe Spanner 8m E1 5c ★
Climb directly up the thin slab 2m left of the V-groove to a sloping finish or nasty landing.
Dougie Hall, 1980

33 Groove-V Baby 9m VS 4c ★★
A nice little solo. The V-groove with a right-hand finish.
Tony Howard, 1969

34 Paradise Crack 12m HS 4b
The first of the cracks.
Pete Oldham, 1966

35 Cameo 12m VS 4c
The second crack.
Bill Tweedale, Pete Oldham, 1966

36 Riddler 12m HVS 5a ★
Paradise if you like climbing peapods: even better if you can exit them.
Bill Tweedale, 1966

37 Pantagruel 12m HVS 5a ★★
The gruelling twin cracks give a good old-fashioned jamming lesson.
Bill Tweedale, Mile Widdal, 1966

38 Mangled Digit 14m E3 6a ★★★
Aptly named. Sustained, reachy and fingery with some brilliant jamming.
Ian Carr, Chris Hardy, 1982

39 Plumb Line 14m VS 4c ★★★
One of the area's great VSs and a super introduction to quarried grit. The main crack swallows jams and protection with equal aplomb. Enjoy, but don't stop till you reach the top. Extra points can be gained by placing the cams in sequence, Silver, Blue, Yellow, Red, Green!
Mick Quinn, Pete Oldham, 1966

40 Sodom 12m E1 5c ★★
From *Gomorrah* (or direct at 6a) cut leftwards up its wider twin. Classic thin hands.
Bill Tweedale, Pete Oldham (some aid), 1966. FFA Bob Whittaker, 1972. Direct, Chris Hardy, 1982

41 Gomorrah 12m E1 5b ★★
Another great introduction to the quarries with well-protected climbing on solid finger-locks.
Ian Lonsdale, Paul Cropper, 1977

FIFTH (WEAVER'S) QUARRY

This more open quarry hosts a very fine selection of routes. There is an array of walls here that enjoy a variety of orientations and conditions, although the one detailed here is clean and enjoys lots of sun.

42 Swing Up 8m VS 5a ★
From the left, swing onto the arête then pull quickly to finish; a direct start is 6a.
Graham West, 1960s

43 Yarn Spinner 8m E4 6c ★★
No joke. The short crack points the way.
Dougie Hall (solo), 1982

44 Weaver's Wall 8m E3 5b ★★
A Pits classic requiring a peaceful mind and a forthright attitude. Climb the short crack to the sloping break and small cam. Breathe in deeply then weave your way upwards.
Bob Whittaker, Ralph Pickering, 1976

45 Weaver's Crack 8m HS 4b ★★
The excellent offwidth crack. One of the best lower grade routes in the Pits.
Bob Whittaker, Ralph Pickering, 1977

46 Norah Batty 8m S 4a
The left-most of the four cracklines.
Chris Hardy, Ian Carr (solo), 1983

47 Cool Fool 8m VS 4c
The left-slanting crack.
Clive Maybury, Ian Frazer, 1983

48 Kiss My Arm 8m VS 4c
If you came for *Weaver's Crack*, you may as well have a go at this as well. The rightward-curving crack.
Clive Maybury, Ian Frazer, 1983

49 Hardy 7m VS 4c
The corner unfortunately suffers from run-off.
Clive Maybury, Ian Frazer, 1983

Sixth Quarry

SIXTH (POTHOLE) QUARRY

A great sunny playground for some mid-grade climbing.

50 Contents 7m E1 5a ★
Some reachy gymnastic moves. No side-runners at the grade!
Craig Hannah, James Whittaker, 1991

51 Intro Wall 7m HS 4b ★★
The slanting crack has a tricky exit.
Tony Howard, 1960s

52 Summary 7m HVS 5b ★
The right-hand crack is climbed with more guile to a fine upper wall.
Chris Hardy (solo), 1984

53 Seconds 7m VS 4c ★★
Wide hands and fists lead to a break, then step left to the fine upper crack.
Bob Whittaker, Brian Cropper, 1974

54 Matthew's Crack 7m HVS 5c ★
The finger-crack is a good alternative start to *Seconds*.
Paul Moreland, Adam Oglaza, Gareth Farnan-Jones, 1989

Fifth Quarry

One of the finest E4s in the book, Calamity Crack (page 445), is notorious for spitting off pumped leaders. Jason Pickles working hard to get hands to fit into the off-fingers fissure. Ian Parnell

KINDER & BLEAKLOW

TINTWISTLE KNARR
LADDOW ROCKS
SHINING CLOUGH
HOBSON MOOR
NEW MILLS TORRS
WINDGATHER
CASTLE NAZE
KINDER DOWNFALL
KINDER SOUTH
KINDER NORTH

Moorland gritstone is one of the unique experiences of Peak climbing. For those that can endure a one-hour walk through stunning mountain scenery, amidst the soundtrack of grouse and curlew, with the yawning heather hills all around, these routes provide unforgettable climbs. Here, Jules Lane is yarding up gritty jugs on Dunsinane, VS 4c (page 505), one of Kinder North's great classics. 📷 Dan Lane

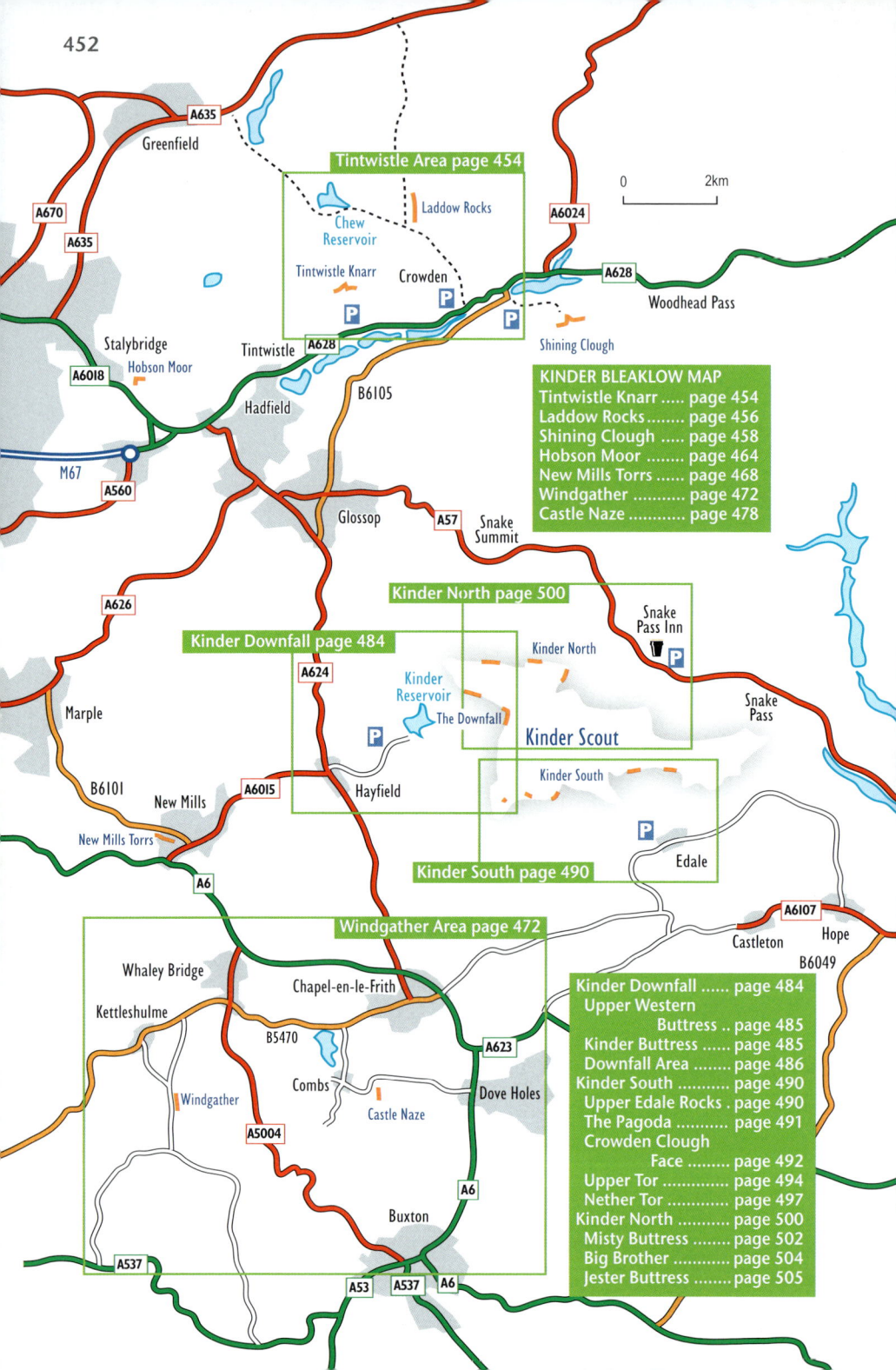

"Venerated for over a century, its holds have the polish of an alabaster saint; it still draws the faithful." For the Victorian climber, Laddow was the place to be. Its climbs wallow in a sense of history, not to mention quality, remoteness and natural beauty. Here, climbers enjoy Long Climb, HVD 4a (page 456). 📷 Pete O'Donovan

TINTWISTLE KNARR

OS Grid Ref: SK 043 992
Altitude: 400m

Tintwistle (known as "The Knarr") is a fine moorland quarry with striking lines. Similar, when clean, to Millstone but with a longer approach. A good crag for those climbing up to E3, with strong lines and one of the Peak's classic arêtes.

The crag faces south and gets good afternoon sun, from midday to about 7pm. There can be a fair amount of seepage, so a few dry days in the summer are needed before the routes are in condition. Utterly miserable in the wrong conditions. Some of the deeper corners can sprout vegetation and may need a quick clean. Can be midgy.

Approach: There is a small, 4-car, parking bay on the north side of the A628 (0.8 miles from Tintwistle, 2.8 miles from Crowden). Park here. There is also a layby on the main road back towards Tintwistle. Follow the forestry track, angling right after 250m, left after 200m, then right again after 200m, then enter the forest. The crag is on the left after a further 1km. The walk takes about 25 minutes.

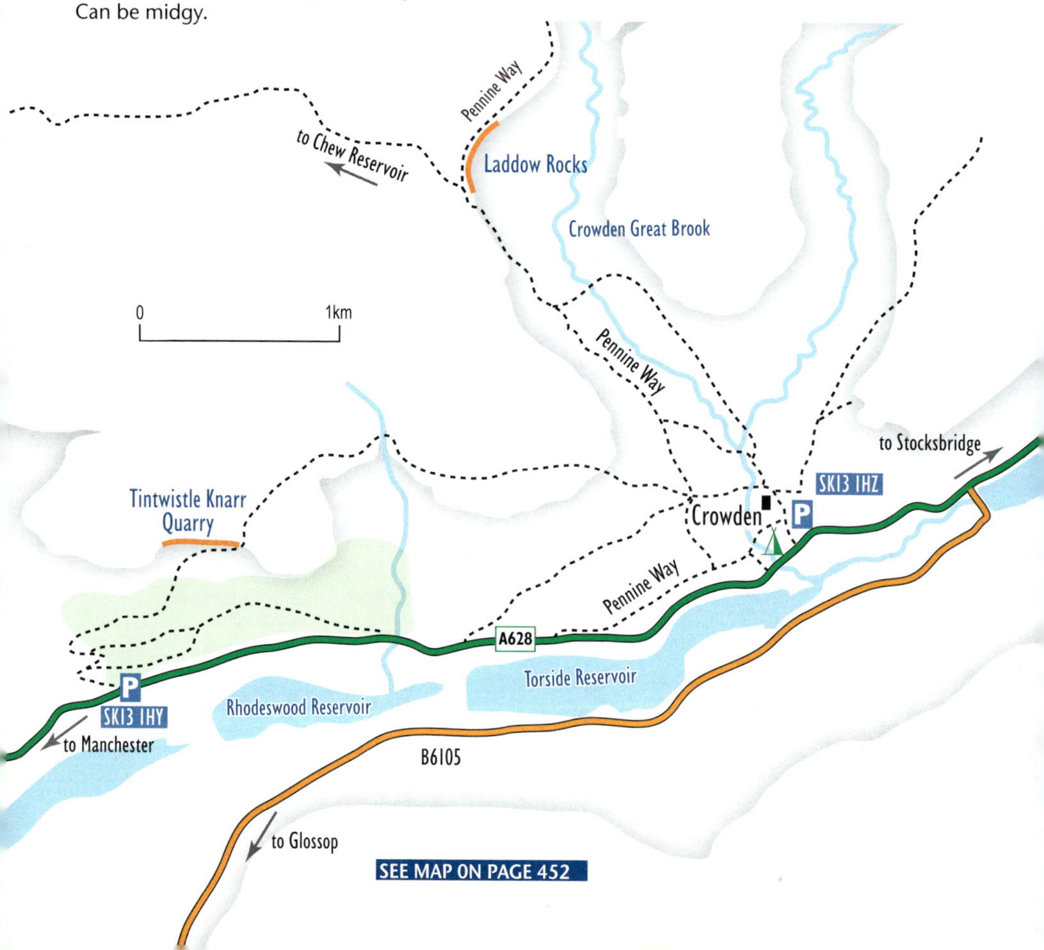

SEE MAP ON PAGE 452

Tintwistle Knarr | 455

① Scimitar 15m HVS 5b ★★
An eye-catching line. Climb a crack to the grassy ledge. Above lies technical climbing to an exposed traverse and airy finale.
Mike Simpkins, Dave Little, 1962

② Poteen 15m E1 5b ★★
Good crack climbing to an impasse beneath the roof. Stick in as much gear as you can and go for it. Once above the difficulties, the left arête of the final corner is a good finish.
R Fitton (some aid). FFA, Mike Simpkins, Eddie Birch, 1962

③ Sinn Fein 15m E3 5c ★★
The blunt rib is superb and bold. Move onto it from the left. From the overlap (wires on the right), continue to a spike on the left. Mantel onto this and continue up the slab to finish left of the overhang.
Mike Simpkins, Dave Little, 1962

④ The Old Triangle 15m HVS 5a ★★
The massive capped V-groove can suffer from seepage. At the roof the left finish is a nice 4c, the right finish a strenuous 5a. Either way, good value. May need a clean beforehand.
Joe Brown, Don Whillans, Ron Moseley, 1951

⑤ Nil Carborundum Illigitimum
15m E3 6a ★★
Tough, sustained climbing with plenty of bang for your buck. Start up the crack then use pockets to move left to a groove. Move up and then rightwards and follow a curving crack to *The Arête*.
Loz Francomb, 1979

⑥ The Arête 15m E2 5c ★★★
Balancy, technical and well protected, it's worth the price of admission alone. Start on either side of the arête and gain the flake-crack. Follow this then continue, passing a niche finishing direct.
Pete Crew, Dave Little (2pts), 1962. FFA John Allen, 1973

⑦ The Little Spillikin 15m E3 6a ★★
Make hard (crux) moves up the hairline crack to the ledge. Move rightwards and follow a groove to a dirty finish.
John Gosling, R Fitton, Mike Simpkins (aid), 1959. FFA John Regan, 1977

⑧ Kershaw's Crackers 15m E1 5c ★
Pain beyond reason; one look at the initial finger crack should tell you that. The upper cracks and corners ease off.
Barry Kershaw, 1958

⑨ Nosey Parker 15m E5 6b ★★
If you think you're having a hard time on the lower crack, you just wait until you get to the upper one: oh boy! Classic Bancroft, similar in standard to *London Wall*.
Al Parker (3pt), 1973. FFA Steve Bancroft, John Kirk, 1980

LADDOW ROCKS

OS Grid Ref: SE 057 015
Altitude: 500m

Laddow is an essential crag for lovers of moorland remoteness and climbing historians (the first E1!). The routes throughout the grades remain excellent, giving memorable climbs.

The crag gets morning sun. The routes are clean, sometimes rounded and polished, often steep, on sound rock with a mountain feel.

Approach: See map on page 454. Head up the Pennine Way from Crowden car park, just off the Woodhead Road. A steady pace will see you at the crag in about an hour.

1 Priscilla Ridge 18m HVS 5a ★★★
A fine direct line with absorbing climbing. Protection is just adequate, but the upper arête has a bold feel. A superb effort for its day.
Arthur Birtwistle, 1938

2 Priscilla 18m HVS 5a ★
From the break, pull right across the bulge, then right again into a shallow groove. Up the wall with delicate moves to the final crack. Harder than its illustrious neighbour.
Morley Wood, Fred Pigott, 1921

3 Long Climb 32m HVD 4a ★★★
Pad boldly up the centre of the slab, trending right after the break to a good stance (possible belay). Slip up the precarious scoop and follow easier grooves to a harder exposed finish up the crack on the right. ⊙ page 453

The stance half way up Long Climb is the starting point for the following two routes:

4 Leaf Buttress 18m VS 4c ★★
Traverse right, then climb the shallow groove on the left-hand side of The Leaf (the huge flake). Move right and boldly climb direct up the steep face of the flake. Finish leftwards up the pleasant top wall. Superb!
Ivar Berg, 1916

5 Leaf Crack 18m HS 4b ★
As for *Leaf Buttress*, but follow the long crack running up the right-hand side of the The Leaf. The bulge requires commitment. From the ledge continue up the wall to the right.

6 Little Crowberry 18m S ★
From the foot of the ridge move diagonally up left until an adventurous swing gains the left side of the arête. Climb this with a short diversion round the corner to avoid a blank section.
Fred Pigott, Morley Wood, pre-1919

7 Long Chimney Ridge 18m VD ★
Follow a groove up to the right. Step back left and move up to reach The Pulpit. An awkward step up left leads to parallel vertical cracks which give an exposed, and enjoyable, finish.

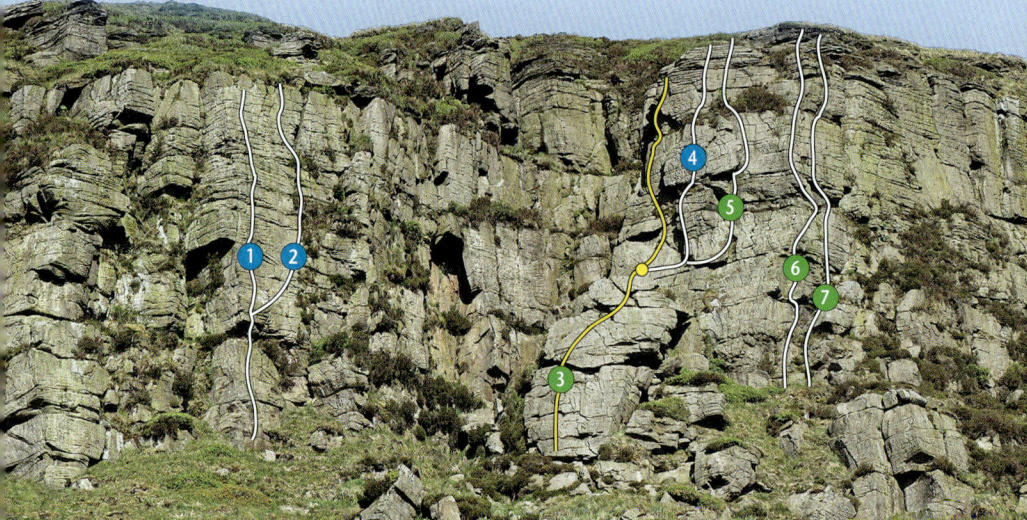

Laddow Rocks | 457

8 Tower Face 20m VS 5a ★★★
Quintessential, traditional grit. After a bold and tricky start over the initial roof, wend your way up the exposed, steep wall, following cracks to ledges and the easier finishing crack.
Harry Kelly, pre-1918

9 Modern Times 20m E3 5c ★
Move leftwards across the line of *Tower Face* to a position below the bulges. Surmount these direct to an exciting finish up the left arête.
Steve Bancroft, Mark Clarke, 1986

10 Tower Arête 20m HVS 5a ★★
The conspicuous arête is climbed on its right-hand side via a thin crack. Finish in a direct line up the arête. Superb and steep with abundant gear and an inspiring line.
Albert Hargreaves, Roy Horsman, 1927

11 North Climb 15m VD ★
Scramble up the large corner (belay). Make a delicate foot traverse out of the chimney to gain the next chimney. Finish up this.

12 North Wall 18m HS 4b ★
Absorbing climbing with the feel of a mountain wall leads to a ledge beneath a roof. This is split by an intimidating crack. Climb it!
Harry Kelly, pre-1918

THE LADDOW CAVE
The classic venue for tweed-suited sleepovers. All the routes can be split with a belay on a comfortable ledge below the upper block.

13 Cave Arête 20m VS 4c ★★★
Left of The Cave is a shallow scoop. Enter this on the left and balance awkwardly to the arête, which is followed pleasantly to the broad ledge (belay). From the ledge, climb up a wall under the overhang, hand traverse leftwards in an exposed position until a stiff pull can be made onto the final wall (4b). A thrilling finish to an enjoyable route.
Fred Pigott, Morley Wood, pre-1919

14 Cave Arête Indirect 20m E1 5b ★★
An amazing first ascent; solo and probably on-sight. The left wall of the cave has a prominent spike. Muscle up onto this, stretch leftwards to the arête and follow this to the large ledge below the overhang. The overhang is taken direct with difficult and strenuous moves (5a). All very modern.
Ivar Berg, 1916

15 Cave Crack 20m HVS 5a ★★
A century-old problem that the uninitiated will find hard. Strenuously climb the crack in the back of the cave, grappling with the rotating chockstone, to gain the easier upper crack and then the ledge. Finish as for *Cave Arête*.
Ivar Berg, 1916

SHINING CLOUGH

OS Grid Ref: SK 098 986
Altitude: 450m

A brilliant crag, sitting on the rim of the most haunted valley in Britain. An angular bastion busting at its heathery seams with quality. The crag is big and steep, one of the best crags in the Bleaklow area and has a number of routes that are essential experiences for any gritstone climber. Paradise for the VS and HVS climber.

The crag faces north at an altitude of 450m. It gets little sun other than some very early or late evening light in midsummer.

The more exposed routes can harbour lichen and vegetation. The crag is at its best in breezy midsummer when there is plenty of welcome shade.

Approach: Park where the B6105 from Glossop crosses the dam to join the Woodhead Pass (A628). Walk through double gates onto the tarmac track by the old railway cottages. Follow the track for 1300m to a cattle grid. Follow a path up the hillside, which curves round a small pond to the woods. Cross a brook and continue up its east bank for 100m before striking steeply uphill past two oak trees. A small path is found that leads to the main crag. Around 50 minutes from the car park. Please follow the described approach so as not to cause any access issues with the landowner.

EAST BUTTRESS
One of the best buttresses on moorland grit. Tall striking lines on clean, sound rock.

1 Orang Arête   12m   VS 4b   ★
Climb the constricted cleft to the break then the fine, airy left arête above.
Martin Whittaker, Chris Wright, 1986

2 Monkey Puzzle   12m   VS 4b   ★
Genius climbing for those who like to delve. Follow *Orang Arête* to the break. Traverse rightwards to a second wide crack and ape up this to finish. Strenuous for the grade.
Lowe brothers or by members of the Karabiner Club, 1940s

3 East Rib   15m   HVS 5a   ★★★
A moorland classic, the arête is as good as it looks. From a short way up *Monkey Puzzle*, traverse right and climb the arête. The situation as you pull onto the arête and climb higher is spectacularly exposed and dramatic, but with the bonus of great big holds to wrap your hands round. The direct start is E4 6a.
John Gosling, Mike Simpkins, Dave Little, T Holland, 1960s

4 Atherton Brothers   25m   S 4a   ★
The flake crack is climbed throughout until good holds on the right lead to a deep chimney. Climb outside the chockstone for maximum exposure.
Arthur Birtwistle, John Lowe, Oliver Cowpe, 1940s

Shining Clough | 459

5 Flaming Eliminate 30m HVS 5a ★
A worthwhile eliminate. Follow *Phoenix Climb* to the first ledges. Move left and climb as directly as possible, passing a ragged crack and aiming for the small triangular prow to the left of *Phoenix Climb*'s upper corner. Finish steeply up the front of this prow.

6 Phoenix Climb 30m VS 4c ★★★
The striking crack gives one of the crag's (and indeed gritstone's) best routes of the grade. Punch it out up the crack passing the unusual hole feature (large cams are useful). From ledges, sweep right and up a wide cracked groove to more ledges. Step right to the route's wonderful climax up the final arête (or, more mundanely, up the corner to the left).
⊙ page 461
Peter Harding, Norman Horsfield, Ernest Phillips, 1947

7 Via Principia 28m S 4a ★★★
A contender for the best moorland severe. The wide crack is climbed past overhanging chockstones to an earthy ledge. Move left onto the arête and climb this for a few feet. Move right into a steep crack and follow this on excellent holds and jams to a large platform. Finish up the easy wall above.
Lowe brothers or by members of the Karabiner Club, 1940s

8 Subsidiary Chimney 24m HVD
As for *Via Principia* to the earthy ledge. The deep narrow chimney above is awkward and strenuous until a platform is reached. Climb the easy wall at the back of this to finish.
Lowe brothers or by members of the Karabiner Club, 1940s

9 Ave 24m VS 4c ★
After leaving *Via Principia*, the steep flake crack succumbs to committing laybacking. The crack above is wide and tricky to enter.
Arthur Birtwistle, pre-1955

NAGGER'S BUTTRESS
The open-book to the right is a unique piece of gritstone architecture.

10 Bloodrush 14m E6 6b ★★★
The end face of the fin gives the totally uncompromising line of one of the finest hard routes on moorland grit. Start at the base of the fin and don't fall off. The first ascent used low side-runners in *Saucius* to stop the leader going all the way back down to the valley.
Andy Cave, 1996

11 Saucius Digitalis 14m E5 6a ★★★
The superb sinuous crack in the fin proves to be both hard to climb and hard work to protect. Follow the crack with difficulty to its end and make a tough move to gain the arête. A final hard move gains the top. A fine prize.
Lawrence Francomb, 1979

12 Nagger's Delight 12m HVS 5a ★
The main corner is climbed to a difficult finish.
Peter Crew, Barry Ingle, 1959

13 Naaden 12m E1 5b ★★
The fabulous crack is jammed to its end. Difficult moves up the steep wall hopefully gain the top.
Mike Simpkins and party, 1960s

14 Yerth 15m E2 5c ★
Climb through the roof and follow cracks to a large flake. Step right to a short crack. Follow this to its end then swing right onto the face and a frightening mantelshelf finish.
Mike Simpkins and party, 1960s

Peter Harding was one of the great pioneers of gritstone climbing, perhaps the best in the era immediately before the Brown and Whillans onslaught. Here, a leader is on what must be one of his finest additions, Phoenix Climb, VS 4c (page 459). It must have been an intimidating lead in 1947, because with its steepness, exposure and cams, it still is today. 📷 Pete O'Donovan

PISA BUTTRESS

This fine buttress contains some of the best and most popular climbs on the crag.

15 Pisa 20m VS 5a ★
Climb the grassy groove to a ledge. Follow cracks up the wall then right around the arête to a ledge. Finish direct up a short crack above.
Karabiner Club, 1948

16 Galileo 20m E1 5b ★★★
A brilliant route taking the clean crack system on the steep face. Climb the thin lower crack to a ledge. The overhanging upper crack is hard but well protected. Finish as for *Pisa*.
John Gosling and party, 1960s

17 Pisa Direct 25m VS 4c ★★
Not actually that direct, but a grand outing. Follow the rib and then the fine slanting crack. Traverse leftwards and finish up *Pisa*.
Arthur Birtwistle, Arthur Mullan, 1949

18 Pisa Superdirect 25m HVS 5a ★★★
One of the best gritstone routes of its grade, following the blockbuster crack system direct.
John Gosling and party, 1960s

19 Stable Cracks 18m VS 4b ★
A good straightforward introduction to the crag, following the deep cracks.
Peter Harding, Norman Horsfield, Ernest Phillips, 1947

20 The Big Wall 24m E3 6a ★★
A great route spoilt slightly by an often dirty and always reachy finish. Follow thin cracks to eventually gain a ledge on the left of the arête. Crux moves up the wall gain a cave and that reachy finish.
Mike Simpkins, T Holland (aid), 1960s. FFA John Allen, 1975

21 Cover Me In Chocolate and Feed Me to the Lesbians 24m E6 6c ★★
The direct finish to *The Big Wall*. Climb the right-hand side of the steep arête by a brilliant and committing runout. ⊙ opposite page
Dan Honeyman, 2004

22 Big Bad Wall 24m E4 6a ★
Follow *The Big Wall* to the small ledge. Step right and climb thin cracks to a bulge, which is taken directly. Finish slightly leftwards.
Mark Incles, 1994

23 Holme Moss 24m E1 5b ★
An eliminate that gives some fine and testing climbing. Climb a thin crack and the wall above to a crack through the bulge. Climb the wall above, trying to stay away from the groove on the right.
John Hart, John Stanger, 1979

24 Gremlin Groove 14m VS 4c ★★
The long groove gives a fine pitch. The crack where it bulges is tricky but soon relents.
Peter Harding, Norman Horsfield, Ernest Phillips, 1947

25 Gremlin Wall 14m VS 5a ★
Climb steep rock to a good ledge. Continue up the wall to a bulge on the right of *Gremlin Groove*. Hard moves over this gain a good ledge. Finish up the easier wall above.

26 Artifact 14m VS 4c ★
Climb a slanting crack to the arête. Follow this then finish by ducking back left under the overhang. High in the grade, but always steady.
John Gosling and party, 1960s

Yeee Haaaa! Sam Hamer enjoying one of the wildest rides on Bleaklow as he plummets from the upper moves of Cover Me in Chocolate..., E6 6c (opposite page). Dan Hamer

HOBSON MOOR

OS Grid Ref: SJ 989 967
Altitude: 300m

This convenient quick-drying roadside quarry has a lot going for it. It's a good place to push grades as well as somewhere to learn essential leading skills. Popular, with plenty of quality, well-protected routes especially in the VS to mid-E grades. It can sometimes feel a bit hollow on the back wall. Some belay stakes are dotted around the top of the crag.

It has a south to south-west aspect and gets plenty of sun. The right-hand side of the quarry is very quick to dry and as such is perfect for a quick hit. The back wall suffers from seepage. The routes here can be ferny, and may need a clean. Polished in places through its popularity, and it has a fairly urban feel (broken glass).

Approach: Turn up Hobson Moor Rd almost opposite the Waggon and Horses. Keep left and park where the road levels. Beware, break-ins have occurred here. 1 minute.

❶ Eastern Touch 16m E4 6a ★
A steep route that is usually seepage free. Use pockets to gain the break. Move up to the niche (peg) then make hard moves to a ledge. From the ledge good pockets (peg) lead to a fingery finish.
Nadim Siddiqui, Craig Hannah, Don Campbell, 1992

❷ Heatwave 18m E3 5c ★
A right pumper that requires a determined approach. Climb the shallow groove, over the overhang and slightly right to finish, pausing to clip the peg before you haul yourself over the top.
Al Evans, Andrea Evans, 1989

❸ Hanging Slab 18m E2 5b ★★
Climb the obvious and strenuous slanting flake. Finish direct if your arms can take it (peg), or rightwards.
Malc Baxter, Jim Heys (1pt), 1959. FFA Loz Francomb, 1979

Hobson Moor Quarry | 465

4 Crock's Climb 18m E2 5c ★
Boulder up on small edges then trend right to the finish of *Gable End*.
Malc Baxter, Ernie Jones, 1975

5 Gable End 18m E4 6a ★★
Fierce finger jamming that only relents when you reach the top.
Malc Baxter, Billy Graham (aid), FFA, Gabe Regan, 1976

6 Hobson's Choice 18m E5 6b ★★
A series of technical fingery moves (2 pegs). From a good hold on the right higher up launch up on fading fingers for good ledges.
Greg Rimmer, 1989

7 Great Expectations 18m E3 5c ★★
Steep, forceful climbing. Follow the slanting groove to reach the wide break (peg up and right). Swing right and follow blocky holds up to good protection. A move right onto the face leads to the finish.
Chris Hardy, Malc Baxter, 1988

8 The Scythe 18m E2 5b ★★
Follow the reachy crack to gain the curving flake that is followed carefully, to its end. Cunningly protectable.
Dave Knighton, 1977

9 Sunshine Superglue 18m E4 6a ★★
An 'interesting' start gains a glued-on hold. Crank past this to gain the break. Cross the flake of *The Scythe* leftwards to a peg and an exhilarating finish.
Nadim Siddiqui, Don Campbell, Sean Kelly, 1992

10 Bring Me Sunshine 15m E1 5b ★
A direct and boldish line up the wall via flake cracks to a ledge.
Harry Venables, Malc Baxter, Chris Hardy, 1988

11 Epitaph Corner 15m VS 4b ★
The big clean corner in the angle of the quarry.
Paul Nunn, Al Parker, 1960

12 Sunshine Superman 14m E2 5b
The flake leads to a standing position on ledges. Place gear, before moving up on small holds to reach a creaky flake. Crank up on it and make a big rockover to reach ledges.
Phil Booth, 1970s

13 Parker's Eliminate 14m HVS 5a ★★★
A classic well protected thin crackline.
Al Parker, Pete Bamfield (aid), 1957. FFA Al Parker, Paul Nunn, 1960

14 Gideon 14m HVS 5a ★★
The arête leads to a scoop and then a revealing move up a thin crack (easy if you can jam). Finish up the arête in a splendid position.
Paul Nunn, Al Parker, 1960

15 Gideonite 12m HVS 5a ★
The corner is well protected if a bit slippery.
Malc Baxter, Jim Heys (2pts), 1960. FFA Jim Campbell, 1976

16 Crew's Route 12m VS 4c ★★
A fine finger crack and a great introduction to the grade. Well protected and with a choice of left or right finishes at the top overlap.
➲ page 467
Pete Crew, 1960

17 Peak Arête 12m E1 5a ★
A committing little number with big but slightly suspect holds.
Tom Ellison, 1958

18 Steve's Dilemma 12m E2 6a
Climb the bulge on finger pockets to the overlap. A large pocket up and right is followed by a long blind reach for a pocket and the top.
Steve Bancroft (solo), 1980

19 Evening Ridge 14m S 4a
Follow the steep groove and flakes to gain a ledge and the right side of the slab. Move left via a worrying mantel. **Midnight Variation** is a direct finish at a similar grade.
Members of the Alpha M.C, 1957

20 Dragon's Route 14m E3 5c ★
A fiery number that is pumpy but adequately protected. Follow the thin crack then move left to finish via a friable crack
Loz Francomb, 1979

21 Scale the Dragon 12m E5 6a ★★
A great climb based around the high, shallow corner. Fingery moves lead up to the break. Good cams protect a strenuous sequence to reach good pockets just short of the top.
Jim Burton, 1990s

22 Drizzle 12m E3 6a ★★
Climb bravely to the break and welcome gear. A step up and right gets you established on the wall above. Keep going to the top.
Loz Francomb, 1979

23 Foghorn Groove 12m VS 4c ★
The popular slanting groove has the odd keyed in hold.
Graham West, Malc Baxter, 1959

24 The Harp 12m VS 4b ★
Good moves lead diagonally up to the overlap, which looks like it might come crashing down at any moment, but hasn't yet.
Al Parker, Pete Bamfield (aid), 1957. FFA Al Parker, 1960s

25 Pocket Wall 12m VD ★
The narrow wall via a super pocket.
Malc Baxter, 1956

26 Tighe's Arête 10m E1 5a ★★
A great little climb following the bold arête protected by an awkward small cam.
Trevor Tighe, David Holt, 1968

27 Grain of Sand 10m VS 5a
A problem start, following the seam and edges over the bulge, gains the ledge. Finish up the wall between the grooves.
Malc Baxter (solo), 1959

28 Amphitheatre Climb 8m VD
A stiff start followed by the steep groove.
Al Parker, 1957

29 Heather Corner 8m VD 4a
The corner and arête.
Malc Baxter, 1956

The Back Wall Traverse Font 6B+
The mega-classic mega-pump across the back wall is usually done right to left, and is one of the best reasons to visit the quarry.

The small quarries that inhabit the urban fringes of the Peak District may have a well-used – some might unkindly say 'scruffy' – vibe, but they serve a useful purpose in delivering quick, roadside pumps. The routes have a brutal beauty all their own and if time or weather are pressing, you could have your forearms blazing in no time. George Gilmore on the classic Crew's Route, VS 4c (page 465). 📷 Paul Evans

NEW MILLS TORRS

OS Grid Ref: SJ 000 852
Altitude: 150m

The 'Torrs' are an impressive, all-year-round, semi-urban quarry. The climbs are big, strenuous affairs where commitment is the key to success. Descent is mostly via abseil from bunches of slings. There is also some great bouldering, and bolted adventures can be found on the viaduct itself.

The crag gets afternoon sun although trees give lots of shadow and shelter from the wind. This can either be a blessing or a curse. These trees, especially when in leaf, combined with the overhanging nature of the crag, mean that the crag is surprisingly rainproof and can give sport even in a heavy downpour. The rock varies from solid and compact to quite crumbly and sandy.

Approach: The crag is directly under the Union Road viaduct in the centre of New Mills. There is plenty of signed access to the Torrs around town as it is such a popular local hangout. There is limited parking in the centre of town: Rock Mill Lane is closest but parking is more plentiful on Hyde Bank Road.

1 Alcove Crack 22m HVS 5a ★★★
A fantastic well protected crack climb.
Dennis Carr, Chris Heard, 1977

2 The Sandman 22m E1 5b ★
Climb the right corner to the ledge. The thin crack leads through a grovel hole to a crack.
Al Evans, Martin Andrew, 1977

3 Piggy's Crack 8m VS 4c ★
The punchy crack up the short sidewall.
Al Evans (solo), 1977

4 The Steeple 8m HVS 5a
Steep and pleasant moves up the arête.
Loz Francomb, Brian Cropper, 1977

5 Nutshrinker 25m E4 6a ★★
The wall left of *The Arête*, starting up the chimney. Power up the thin cracks all the way.
Paul Mitchell, Esther Horvath, 2010

6 The Arête 25m E3 5b ★★
Occasional friable rock is this diamond's flaw. Avoid the low bulge by the left then take a deep breath and head rightwards to a good rest. Frantic moves up the arête lead to some good gear in the crack and the top.
Al Evans, Gabriel Regan and Chris Heard, Paul Bolton, 1976

Another great urban quarry guaranteed to bring a smile to time-pressed pumphounds. The setting, amidst tumbledown industrial archaeology, adds to the atmosphere, but once you step on the rock forceful yarding and a soupçon of hollowness will keep your mind on the job. Dominic Oughton on Electric Circus, E2 5c (page 470). 📷 Paul Evans

7 Mather Crack 25m E2 5b ★★
Good hard crack climbing marred by the occasional suspect hold. Thankfully well protected.
Terry Wyatt, Derek Juchau (aid), 1971. FFA Dennis Carr, 1977

8 Electric Circus 30m E2 5c ★★★
The route of the crag. Climb the detached flake. From its top traverse right to a sandy scoop. Go up a short crack then move left on shakey holds to a flake (avoiding the detour is E3 5c). Climb the leaning crack to the tree.
page 469
Dennis Carr, C Heard, 1977

9 Oak Tree Wall 30m E3 5c ★
Good, challenging climbing. Traverse right from the top of the detached flake and head directly through the undercut blocks (peg) and then the roof. Another peg will see you right on the powerful upper crack.
Al Evans (1pt), 1977. FFA Nick Colton, Alex MacIntyre, 1979

10 The Grim Reaper 25m E5 6b ★
Daunting and ferocious. The lower peg almost protects the crux, and then you head for the flake and overhang. After another peg head up the slightly easier upper wall.
Nick Colton, Dougie Hall, 1979

11 Transformation 25m HVS 4c ★
Climb the crack and then up ledges at the top.
Al Evans, Martin Andrew, 1977

12 Stonewall Crack 20m HVS 5a
From the top of the stone wall, climb the narrow cracks then a wider crack from half height.

13 Confusion 20m VS 4b
The crack to a ledge and a rightwards finish.

14 Drunken Sunday 16m S 4a
The steep and enjoyable crackline.
Derek Juchau, Terry Wyatt, c1971

15 The Flake 15m VS 4b ★
Loose and rattly but very Old School. Climb as much of it as you dare then escape up the continuation crack.
Dave Holmes, 1976

16 The Foundling 15m VS 4c
Follow the crack to join The Flake.

17 The Overlooked Groove 15m S 4b
Start from the curious ochre bowl and climb the shallow right-facing groove. Good gear.
Dave Holmes, 1976

18 Original Route 15m VD ★
Climb the flakes and steps to the large sycamore. Good holds but harder than it looks.

19 Cracked Corner 15m S 4a ★
Climb directly up from the start of Original Route to a reachy crux off the upper ledge.

New Mills Torrs | 471

20 Viaduct Crack 15m HVS 5b ★
Climb the crack and exit rightwards on ledges.
Dennis Carr, 1977

21 Viaduct Wall 15m E2 5c ★
Launch up the wall directly past a large jug to a thought-provoking mantleshelf to safety.
Al Evans (solo), 1977

22 Honcho 17m E4 6b ★
Boulder up to the peg. Hard moves lead up and left to ledges and an easier finish.
Nick Colton, 1979

23 Bionic's Wall 17m E3 5c ★★★
A great route with lots of juggy yarding and friendly pegs. From the ramp, gained from left or right, or direct at hard 6b, make technical moves to gain better holds and twin pegs. Press on up the steep wall passing more pegs to the ledge.
Dave Beaver, Mike Warwick, 1979

24 Hallelujah Chorus 17m E5 6b ★
Make bold, thin moves to gain better holds and gear. Carry on steeply until near *Heavy Duty* then continue via pumpy, fingery climbing, attempting to avoid adjacent routes.
Mike Warwick, John Gosling, 1985

25 King of the Swingers 26m E1 5b ★
Big pump. Climb *Heavy Duty* to the break. Traverse this leftwards to eventually reach the gully before your arms give up. Finish up this.
Al Evans, Andrea Evans, Pete Cowgill, 1989

26 Heavy Duty 17m E2 5b ★★
A great climb – pumpy and intimidating but well protected. Follow the groove, the crack and flat holds in a fairly direct line.
Al Evans, Gabe Regan, 1977

WINDGATHER

OS Grid Ref: SJ 995 783
Altitude: 400m

This is a beginners' crag par excellence, where the number of good quality, low-grade climbs on steep, juggy rock is unmatched throughout the Peak District. Superb, juggy and friendly. Bags of routes, mainly from Diff to VS. In fact, it probably has some of the steepest easy routes anywhere on grit!

The name tells you pretty much all you need to know about the weather conditions around here! The rock is very clean, sound, and quick drying. Being west-facing, it gets the sun from the afternoon, and is a suitable venue for year-round climbing.

Approach: From Kettleshulme, take a minor road south for just over a mile and park in lay-bys by the crag. Tractors and other agricultural car-wreckers use the lane beneath the crag, so you're advised to park well into the lay-by. Approach only via the two stiles and the fenced-in alley. See access note.

Access: Please refer to the BMC's RAD. Visitors must ONLY approach the crag via the fenced alley (stile and two gates). Climbers have access to the area within the fences above and below the crag.

1 The Rib 9m VS 5a
A hard step off a block leads directly up the centre on small crimps. Tricky to protect.

2 The Rib Right-Hand 9m S 4a
From the block, climb up and right to a small flake. Use this to gain the side face and climb it until you can step round onto the front face about 3m below the top.

3 Staircase 9m M ★
The corner is a fine beginner's lead.

4 Green Slab 9m S 4b ★
Start just to the left of the wide flake-crack. Make an awkward but well-protected move off the flake and go up the wall above.

5 Black Slab 9m S 4a ★
A tricky start leads to more steep climbing. Cross the bulge, then go up a flake to finish 1m left of *Green Crack*.

6 Green Crack 9m S 4a ★★
The groove and crack give a thrilling lead, with great 3-D climbing on steep rock.

7 North Buttress Arête 9m VS 4c ★★
A Windgather classic, steep and bold, but with great holds. Surmount the undercut left side of the arête (some say 5a), then continue up the left-hand side of the arête.

Windgather | 473

North Buttress

8 **North Buttress Arête Indirect** 9m S 4a ★
Follow the exposed arête on its right side, pulling round left onto the front face near the top.

9 **Chimney and Crack** 9m HVD
Climb to the ledge. Step leftwards into the chimney crack to finish.

10 **Heather Buttress** 8m VD ★
Climb the arête and wall above the overhang.

11 **Taller Overhang** 8m VS 5b
The double overhangs as centrally as possible.

12 **Small Wall** 8m S 4b
The small wall.

13 **The Other Corner** 8m M
The obvious corner. Stepping out of it leftwards onto the platform gives an easy way up (or down).

14 **Portfolio** 8m HVS 5b ★
A steep polished testpiece. Avoiding the holds on *Wall Climb*, ascend direct to the overhang. Surmount this via a series of strenuous pulls.

15 **Wall Climb** 9m VD
The cracks into the final chimney.

16 **Central Route** 9m HVD ★
Start below a thin crack in the crag top and climb direct to it. For **Slant Start** (VD) climb diagonally to the top crack from the start of *Chockstone Chimney*.

17 **Chockstone Chimney** 9m D ★
The ragged crack gives a well-protected lead.

18 **Mississippi Crack** 9m S 4a ★
The fine bottomless crack is long and sustained, and a good first Severe lead.

19 **Mississippi Crack Variant** 9m VD ★★
An excellent, sustained combination starting up *The Medicine* then traversing left under the overlap to join the *Mississippi Crack* above its crux.

20 **The Medicine** 9m HS 4a ★
Take the poorly protected juggy bulges direct via some long pulls.

21 **M.B. Arête** 9m D
Climb up to an awkward move into a corner. This leads to the broad platform. Step left and climb the right edge of the face above.

Middle Buttress

High Buttress

22 Bulging Arête 9m S 4a
This climb takes the small overhang on its right. Demanding on the arms and with a serious feel, until you find the hidden hold.

23 The Corner 9m D
A route to consider as both an early lead and an introduction to the delights of polished holds!

24 Toe Nail 9m VD ★
Go directly through the 'toes'. Protection is a little distant above the bulge.

25 Zigzag 13m D
Start as for *Toe Nail* and climb diagonally right to a position above the nose, then finish direct. A long route on this little crag.

26 Footprint 9m VD
Climb direct through the heel of the footprint.

27 Nose Direct 9m HVD ★★
Start at the small recess just left of the arête and climb direct to the nose. Pull over it, step left, and continue direct. A problematic route, but with great protection.

28 High Buttress Arête 9m D ★★
Start at the foot of the arête and follow it almost direct. An excellent route at this grade, perhaps one of the best in the Peak.
opposite page

29 Heather Face 9m HVD
Poor gear and rounded holds and with an excellent (but protected) 'sting in the tail' at the overlap.

Windgather is a happy crag and anyone who likes bumper jugfests on steep cracks and prows will be happy here too. Gowry Sisupalan samples the massive grips on High Buttress Arête (opposite page), one of the Peak's finest Diffs. 📷 Paul Evans

30 Rib and Slab 9m M
Clean climbing just left of the gully.

31 Buttress Two Gully 9m M ★
A very traditional climb; one for your first lead.

32 Leg Stump 9m D
The easiest (but unprotected) line up the slab.

33 Middle and Leg 9m D
Good climbing and protection.

34 The Centre 9m VD
Fine climbing but unprotected until near the top.

35 Squashed Finger 9m VD ★
Good climbing; quite stiff but well-protected.

36 Struggle 9m HS 4b ★
The crack through the nose. A hard but well-protected little problem that gives 'full value' at this grade.

37 Corner Crack 9m VD ★
The crack. The one in the corner.

38 Aged Crack 9m HS 4a ★
Climb direct to the crack. Moving into the crack from *Corner Crack* makes the route VD.

39 Traditional 9m HS 4a ★
Step off the block and climb directly past the blunt flake. Small cams are useful.

40 The Broken Groove in the Arête 9m D
Steep and well-protected: a great first lead.

41 Cheek 9m VS 5a
Start from a block below the sidewall and climb up to meet the arête at the top. Short and sharp. The protection is there for those with cunning.

42 Face Route 2 9m M
Follow the broken cracks.

43 Face Route 1 9m VD
Easy climbing but gearless where it matters the most. Pull over the small overhang, then climb more easily up the face.

44 First's Arête 9m HD
Follow the right-hand side of the arête.

45 Side Face 9m S
Climb directly up the right-hand side face on sloping holds and limited gear, keeping to the left of the holly. Poor gear and rounded holds.

46 Overhanging Arête 9m VD
Hard moves lead from the gully on the left of the buttress. Move rightwards to join and follow *Leg Up*.

47 Leg Up 9m HVS 5a
From the pulpit, make a bold and strenuous pull over the nose.

48 Route 2 9m VS 4b ★
From the pulpit, step right and climb the steep crack through the overhang. Quite hard considering its shortness.

49 Route 1.5 9m HVS 4c ★
A route with adequate protection, if you have the strength and cunning to place it.

Buttress Two

Windgather | 477

Buttress One

50 Editor's Note 9m VS 5a
Pull out and up to join and follow *Route 1* on rapidly improving jugs. Small wires may help for the one and only hard move.

51 Arête Direct 9m E1 5b ★
A fun climb, usually soloed. Stretch from the ledge for good holds on the lip left of the arête and cut loose. Easier climbing remains.

52 Route 1 12m S 4a ★★
Climb part way up *South Crack*, and then traverse leftwards round the arête onto a ledge above the cave. Pull past blocks and continue to the top.

53 South Crack 9m M
Wide crack climbing in the corner.

54 Left Triplet Crack 9m D
The leftmost of the three close-together cracks. Not as easy as it looks.

55 Middle Triplet Crack 9m HVD 4a
The middle of the three twins.

56 Right Triplet Crack 9m HVD 4a
The left-hand crack. Ha ha, got you. It is actually the rightmost of the three cracks.

57 Overlapping Wall 9m HS 4b
The small bulging buttress just to the right.

58 Discontinuous Rib and Groove 9m M
Any way up the easy rock to the right.

South Buttress

CASTLE NAZE

OS Grid Ref: SK 053 784
Altitude: 400m

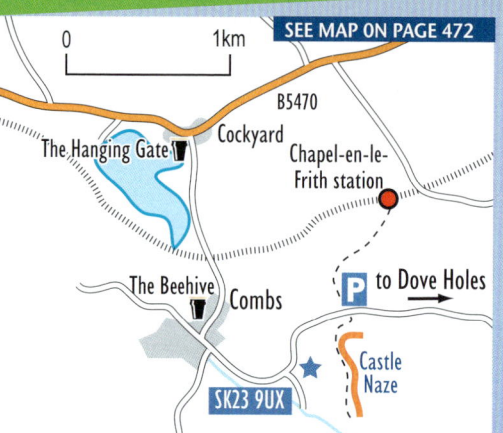

Approach: The Naze is on the moorland above the village of Combs. From the Beehive Inn follow the steep and narrow road towards the crag. On the level, two laybys will be obvious with limited spaces for about six cars.

Can also be approached from Dove Holes: from Dove Holes station, go over the railway bridge and then turn left up Cowlow Lane for a couple of miles.

A friendly crag in a great setting with a character all its own. It has a fine supply of accessible routes in the lower grades and there are enough routes in the harder categories to interest and baffle any competent leader.

It was a favourite of pioneers over a century ago and their history still hangs in the air.

The crag faces west, is fairly exposed and is clean and quick drying. An excellent evening venue with great views.

1 Double Crack 4m D
Climb the crack.

2 The Arête 4m HS 4a
The fine slabby arête.

3 Easy Corner 5m D
The wee corner in the left of the bay just right.

4 Right-Hand Crack 5m D
Another shorty up the crack and quick groove.

5 Pinnacle Crack 5m VD
Climb the wide crack and easier crack above.

6 Pinnacle Arête 5m VD
Climb the outer edge of the pinnacle to the summit. The top block is wobbly.

Castle Naze | 479

7 Sheltered Crack 5m S 4a ★
This crack is behind and right of the pinnacle.

8 Slanting Crack 5m S 4a
Climb a crack passing to the left of the jammed triangular block then finish direct.

9 Overhanging Chockstone Crack 6m VD
Climb up and over or under the chockstone.
Stanley Jeffcoat and friends, pre-1913

10 The Fifth Horseman 6m HVS 5a ★
Take the easiest line up the left-hand side of the wall. Quite bold for its size.
Jim Rubery, Dave Gregory, 1984

11 Icebreaker 6m E2 5b
A bold and reachy and enjoyable line up the slab. Head for, and use, the big pebble.
Paul Fitzsimmons, Helena Garnard, 2002

12 V-Corner 8m S 4b
A choice of starts gain the ledge via the short corner. Take the left-hand crack above.
Stanley Jeffcoat and friends, pre-1913

13 Muscle Crack 8m HVD
The blocky crack leads to the ledge. Climb the flake on the right.
Stanley Jeffcoat and friends, pre-1913

14 Block Crack Left-Hand 10m S 4a
The crack to the ledge. Take the flake above.

15 The Nose 12m HS 4b
Bridging leads up the recess, and then into the sentry box. Go back up and right from there.

16 The Nithin 12m S 4a
The steep right-hand crack of the recess leads to the ledge. Finish up the chimney crack.
Stanley Jeffcoat and friends, pre-1913

17 Main Corner 12m S 4a
A deeply traditional struggle.

18 The Fly Walk 10m S 4a
The well-worn crack just to the right.

19 The Niche 10m S 4a ★★
Steep jamming on good rough rock. Leave the niche using jams and the jammed block.
Stanley Jeffcoat and friends, pre-1913

20 Niche Arête 10m VS 4c ★★
Rounded, bold and satisfying. Climb the arête directly via long reaches.
Stanley Jeffcoat and friends, pre-1913

21 Orm and Cheep 10m E1 6a ★
The right slanting groove is climbed to a ledge. Climb the wall above directly via several shallow pockets. Side-runners at the grade.
Al Evans, 1989

22 Studio 10m HS 4a ★
Climb the major crack. page 481
Stanley Jeffcoat and friends, pre-1913

23 Nursery Arête 10m HVS 5b ★
The independent hanging arête. Step off a boulder and make tricky moves to a ledge. Climb the arête above using the breaks (but not the right-hand wall).
Paul Messenger, Rob Moran, 2003

Castle Naze

24 A.P. Chimney 10m S 4a ★★
A classic chimney that needs no description. The AP stands for absolutely perpendicular.
Stanley Jeffcoat and friends, pre-1913

25 Pod Crack 11m E1 5c ★
The thin crack with the pod halfway up it.
Jim Rubery, Dave Gregory, 1984

26 Pilgrim's Progress 11m HS 4b ★
Climb the crack and arête at the right end of the wall.
Morley Wood and Rucksack Club friends, pre-1935

27 Little Pillar 11m HS 4b
Climb the crack in the right-hand side of a rib. From the platform above, climb the continuation of the crack to the top.
Stanley Jeffcoat and friends, pre-1913

28 Ledgeway 11m HVS 5a
Climb to the ledge any way you choose, then use a flake on the back wall to reach a left slanting crack.

29 No Name 11m S 4a
Climb the awkward crack to reach the ledge. Continue directly.

30 Keep Buttress 11m HVS 5a
Climb the crack in the rib to the right and then finish up the right-hand side of the rib above.

31 Keep Corner 11m S 4a ★
A good route up the corner.
Stanley Jeffcoat and friends, pre-1913

32 Keep Arête 11m VS 4b ★★
After some good steep moves, follow the arête of the buttress as closely as you can.

33 Scoop Direct 11m HVS 5a ★★
Gain the left-hand end of the scoop (as for *Scoop Face*) and continue directly via a thin crack.

34 Scoop Face 13m HVS 5a ★★
A significant historical achievement that remains a classic problem. Start 3m right of the arête and, using polished holds and clean technique, climb into the scoop above. Traverse delicately up and right to a useful pocket and thin crack. Go up and left to finish. **The Direct Start** is E1 5c.
Stanley Jeffcoat, 1914

35 Scoop Wall 11m E1 5b
Climb boldly into the right edge of the scoop. From there, take a more or less direct line to the top. Turn the final bulge on the left.

36 Footstool Left 11m S
The corner is a bit of a struggle.
Stanley Jeffcoat and friends, pre-1913

37 Piano Stool 11m E1 5b
The arête to the right is a bold undertaking, not helped by pointy boulders beneath.
Malc Baxter, 1988

Quick access and lots of routes in the lower grades make Castle Naze the perfect place for some after-work mileage. Gareth Williams on Studio, HS 4a (page 479). 📷 Paul Evans

Castle Naze

38 Birthday Climb 16m HVS 5b ★★
Follow *The Crack* to its sentry box. Leave this by climbing up and left to the base of a flake, then follow this to the top.

39 The Crack 14m VS 4b ★★
Once one of the hardest routes in the Peak. From the sentry box, follow the alluring crack through the overhang.
Stanley Jeffcoat and friends, pre-1913

40 Nozag 14m VS 4c ★★★
The VS of the crag. Testing climbing in a superb position. Climb a crack until a step left leads onto the bold face. Climb this directly using the thin crack and a bit of bottle.
⊙ opposite page

41 Zigzag Crack 16m HS 4b ★
As for *Nozag* but follow the crack to a wider crack and an easy finish.
Stanley Jeffcoat and friends, pre-1913

42 Zig-a-Zag-a 14m D
A long easy climb. The corner and wall above.
Dave Gregory, Jim Rubery, 1984

43 Long Climb 16m VD
Take the easiest direct line to the top.
Stanley Jeffcoat and friends pre-1913

44 Central Tower 16m VD ★★
Follow the green corner to the terrace. Move back right again and climb the left-hand groove to the top.
Stanley Jeffcoat and friends, pre-1913

45 Atropine 16m HS 4b ★
A good sustained route. Climb over a projecting flake into a bay. Then climb a ramp and crack near the left end of the bay to ledges. From here, take the tough flake to the right-hand finishing crack.
Lew Hardy, 1977

46 Belladonna 17m E2 5c ★
Follow *Atropine* to the ledge and continue up the right side of the arête to the overlap. Go right beneath this and then up to the next overlap. From here, traverse back left to the upper part of the arête and an excellent finish. The arête direct is E3 5c.
Al Evans, 1977 / Malc Baxter, 1990

47 The Green Crack 14m S 4a ★
The series of corners. Care needed at the top.
Stanley Jeffcoat and friends, pre-1913

48 Chamonaze Blues 14m E4 6b ★
Desperate cracking up the leftmost of the cracks, with hard crimping and technical moves. Very small wires may be of some use.
Olly Allen, Martin Kocsis, 2003

49 Peg Crack 16m E2 5c ★
A good route up the crack in the centre of the wall.

50 Iron Age Fortitude 16m E4 6b ★
The thinner crack just right.
Neil Foster, Graham Hoey, Clare Reading, Martin Kocsis, 2003

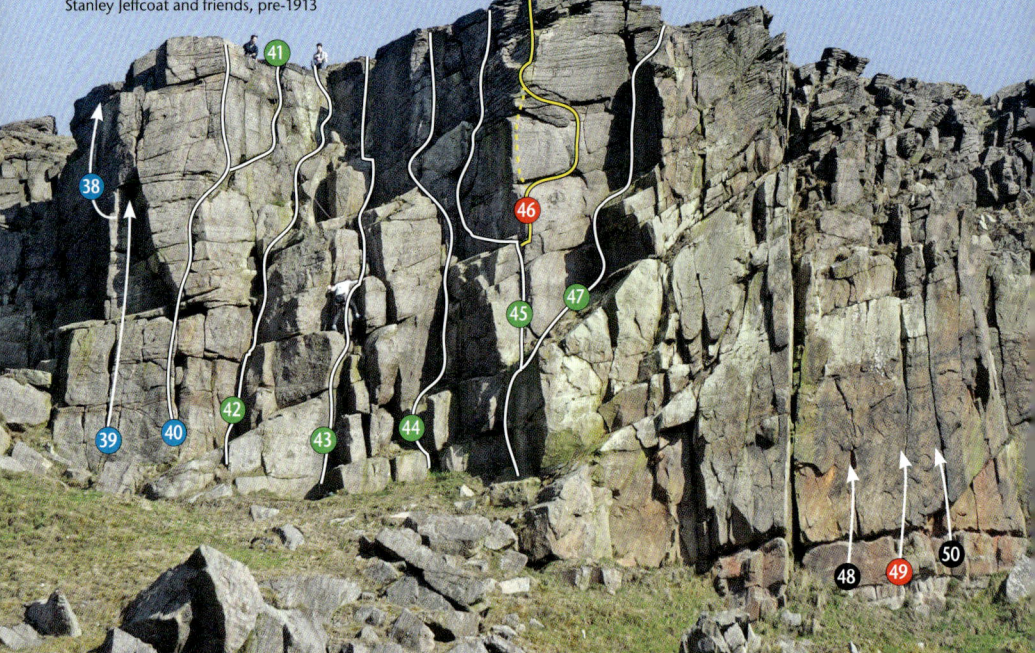

The Naze was one of the go-to crags for Manchester climbers in the early years of the 20th Century: with fairly easy access and its lofty position it's not hard to see why. Today it remains a heaven for remote-feeling climbs in the S to HVS range. Here, Roisin Joyce leads Nozag, the VS of the crag (opposite page). 📷 Paul Evans

KINDER DOWNFALL
Altitude: 525m

Approach: Park in Bowden Bridge car park (pay & display) on the outskirts of Hayfield. Continue up the road and pass Kinder Reservoir on the left. At its end, at the foot of William Clough, there are three choices: Follow the clough to Ashop Head then turn right along the crest to follow the edge (long but fairly gentle); or, from the bottom of William Clough, take the Sandy Heys path towards the edge (steep, quickest and most popular); or follow the River Kinder directly (pretty but boggy). The quickest way takes just over one hour. Approaches can also be made from Snake Summit via the Pennine Way or from the Snake Pass Inn, up Fair Brook, then questing across the trackless Kinder plateau. Drop down to the river well short of the Downfall then follow this to the crags.

Upper Western Buttress

UPPER WESTERN BUTTRESS
A nice collection of routes just below the plateau near where the Sandy Heys path reaches the Pennine Way. OS Grid Ref: SK 073 892

❶ The Dark Side of the Moon
16m   E4 5c   ★★★
A superb, bold outing. Climb to a thread. From here, reachy and technical moves gain a sloping break and then better holds out right. Move back onto the front face to finish.
Dennis Carr, Al Parker, 1976

❷ Extinguisher Chimney   14m   VS 4c   ★★★
The cleft is enjoyable and well protected.
Vin Dillon, Vin Desmond, 1949

❸ Candle Buttress   14m   HVS 5a   ★★
Step up and around the bulges. Using a small flake around to the left, make a move up the arête to a ledge. From here, the protection is sparse but the climbing easier.
R Williams, P Gentil, D Moore, 1957

❹ Candle Buttress Direct   14m   E1 5b   ★
Climb via a hole straight up the wall.
Malc. Baxter, Matthew Rhodes, Gordon Stainforth, 1995

❺ South Wall   10m   VD   ★★
Enjoyable layback moves up the large flake.
Eric Byne, Clifford Moyer, 1932

KINDER BUTTRESS
About 5 minutes walk along the Pennine Way from Upper Western Buttress, at an old dry stone wall, head straight downhill to boulders; the crag is just below.
OS Grid Ref: SK 077 889

❻ The Mermaid's Ridge
30m   HS 4b, 4c   ★★★
A superb route, in two varied and interesting pitches. From the foot of the ridge climb up past some perfect round pockets and assorted flakes. Belay on the left. Follow the right-hand side of the south facing (left) wall until a ledge traverse leads right to a wide groove to finish.
Siegfried Herford, John Laycock, Stanley Jeffcoat, 1910

❼ Left Twin Chimney   30m   HS 4b,4c   ★
An awkward corner-crack leads to a belay in the cave. Take the same start as for *The Mermaid's Ridge's* second pitch but keep traversing into the next crack along to the right.
Siegfried Herford, John Laycock, Stanley Jeffcoat, 1910

❽ Right Twin Chimney
25m   HVS 4c, 5a
Follow the rightmost groove to the ledge (belay). Enter the overhanging chimney, then climb up to a ledge. Finish up *Left Twin*.
Siegfried Herford, John Laycock, Stanley Jeffcoat, 1910

❾ Final Judgement   20m   E3 6a   ★★★
An adventure, with a hard crux low down and a wild finish up the prow. The initial arête has a taxing move leaving the prominent jug and continues up the rib. From the ledge, stretch out left to a large bird-limed jug, then keep going left with the help of a hidden pocket, to finish up either side of the prow.
Con Carey, Malc Baxter, Bob Rothwell, 1987

❿ Boulevard Traverse   14m   S 4a
Shuffle rightwards along the large curving flake, then move back out left and up a wide crack to the ledge. Finish up the short chimney.
Vin Desmond, Vin Dillon, pre-1948

Kinder Buttress

THE DOWNFALL

See map on page 484. The amphitheatre of crags that surround the Downfall is a grand place to go in high summer. The climbing is varied, and you can choose your style for the day: brutal and tough, gentle and serene, adventurous and classic. There is a great weight of history on these crags.

The amphitheater gets a fair amount of sun throughout the day. It's exposed and most is quick to dry. Some of the routes will feel grainy and gritty after rain or early in the season. Descend a gully about 200m west of the Downfall. **OS Grid Ref: SK 082 889**

1 Domino Wall 18m E1 5b ★★
Despite the occasionally friable hold, this is a really enjoyable route. Start just right of a shallow groove. Pull over a bulge to gain a good spike (runner) and move rightwards to a shelf. Continue up the shallow depression with a hard move to gain a large ledge. Finish up the easier face above and to the right.
R Williams, P Gentil, D.Moore, 1957

2 Raggald's Wall 18m E1 5b ★★
Got nerves of steel? Good. Start up *The Great Chimney Left-Hand* then traverse leftwards around the exposed arête and continue up the wall to a ledge. Finish up the easier face above.
Paul Nunn, Oliver Woolcock, 1964

3 The Great Chimney Left-Hand 18m VS 4c ★
Enter the hanging groove and continue into a niche. Awkward climbing gains the ledge. Move left and climb the blunt arête to finish.

4 The Great Chimney 18m HS 4b ★★★
Really good stuff. One of the hardest routes in the Peak when it was first done, and not all that easy now. Classic bridging and chimneying with a possible stance on the ledge. More chimneying remains.
JW Puttrell, WJ Watson, 1903

5 The Ensemble Exit 18m HVS 5a ★
Very good gear, and potentially a very good route if it were cleaner. From the small stance on *The Great Chimney*, continue up the groove then move rightwards to a ledge under a block. Make hard moves over this to finish.
Paul Nunn, Oliver Woolcock, 1964

6 Loose Control 14m E8 6c ★★
The steep blade of grit, climbed on its left, is the hardest lead on Kinder. A runner is placed in the crack just round to the right although this gives little hope on the high crux.
Pete Whittaker, 2010

7 Professor's Chimney 14m D ★★
Another classic chimney with no chance of getting lost, but with a choice of finishes.
JW Puttrell, WJ Watson, 1903

Great Chimney Buttress

Kinder Downfall | The Downfall | 487

8 Pegasus Left-Hand 14m E1 5b
Climb the short wide crack in the overhang with difficulty to gain the thin crack above. Up this with a sneaky move at the top.
R Williams, P Gentil, D Moore (1pt), 1957. FFA Con Carey, Paul Durkin, 1987

9 Pegasus Right-Hand 14m VS 4c
Right again is a thin diagonal crack. Spring up this to a hard move for the straight crack above, then follow this on hidden holds.
Al Parker, 1962

10 Left Fork Chimney 20m D
Climb easily to the fork, then take the left-hand branch on good holds to the top.
JW Puttrell, c1900s

11 Right Fork Chimney 20m S
The right-hand branch.
JW Puttrell, pre-1913

12 Crooked Arête 22m HVS 5a ★
From the toe of the buttress, climb the arête and step leftwards to gain the cave; possible belay. Climb the overhang then traverse rightwards to finish up the wall to the left of *Zigzag Climb* as for *Rodeo*.

13 Rodeo 20m VS 4c ★
A direct effort up the arête itself, with a foxing lasso manoeuvre half way up.
Rebekah Smith, Martin Kocsis, Keith Ashton, 1998

14 Zigzag Climb 16m VD ★★★
Classic, juggy climbing. Beginning at a wide crack, climb leftwards to a short crack and a flake. Move up and across rightwards to a wide crack which leads to the top. ⓘ page 489
JW Puttrell, LJ Oppenheimer, EA Baker, 1900

15 Zigzag Crack 13m HVD ★
The wide but narrowing crack, awkward.
Eric Byne, Clifford Moyer, 1929

16 Spin-Up 13m E2 5b ★
The groove feels thin, with difficult-to-place gear and steep moves. Short lived, but intense.
Con Carey, Bob Rothwell, 1987

17 Toss-Up 14m HVS 5a ★
The easier right-hand deviation is still bold.
Con Carey, Bob Rothwell, 1987

18 Chockstone Chimney 14m VD ★★
A great wrangle with cracks and chockstones.
WJ Watson, JW Puttrell, 1903

19 The Last Fling 14m E2 5b ★★
Fabulous! Steep, then delicate with just the right amount of everything. Climb the centre of the bulging wall to stand precariously on the tiny ledge of the top break. Make a delicate move up using the thin crack to gain the top.
Con Carey, Malc Baxter, 1987

20 Amphitheatre Crack 12m S
The main corner.

Zigzag Buttress

Kinder Downfall | The Downfall

21 Stuck in a Groove 14m E2 5c ★
Technical but not so frightening. A good introduction to the routes on this wall.
Steve Robinson, Emma Twyford, 2007

22 Dud Chimney 14m E1 5b ★
Reliable gear, but spooky climbing.
R Williams, P Gentil, D Moore, 1957

23 The Glorious Twelfth 20m E3 5b ★
A very strenuous route. The steep groove is followed on good, but doubtful, holds to a hard move rightwards to gain the long ledge above. Finish up the wide, bulging crack.
Richard McHardy, Arthur Robinson, 1973

24 The Hunter 22m E3 5b ★
Climb up to a long narrow flake then traverse leftwards on this to the crumbling flake. Climb up this to a niche and pass the overhang to a long ledge. Move slightly leftwards and continue boldly up the wall (crux) to an unrelenting finish. Sparse protection.
Dennis Carr, A Gledhall, Al Parker, 1976

25 The Bloody Thirteenth 22m E1 5b ★
Climb the right-hand arête following flakes on the left to a cave, then finish up a short crack.
Paul Nunn, Jim Curran, 1973

26 Shotgun Grooves 22m E1 5b ★
The shallow grooves to the Dovecote Cave then finish as for *The Bloody Thirteenth*. Tough and unrelenting.
Al Parker, M Young, 1976

27 The Gamekeeper 20m E5 6b ★
Fine climbing using increasingly smaller holds and with a sense of urgency most of the way up. Reachy, and possibly high in the grade.
Chris Reid, Helen Fawcett, Robbie Miurhead, 1999

28 Poachers Crack 18m HVS 5a ★
Solid and reliable climbing that punches a way up the crag in style.
Ted Rodgers, Al Parker, 1976

29 Downfall Groove 18m HVS 5a
The obvious groove.

30 Independence Crack 16m E2 5c ★★
The excellent technical finger crack has just the right amount of everything.
Dennis Carr, Al Parker (aid), 1976. FFA Con Carey, 1987

31 Hard Times 14m E3 6a ★
Move rightwards along easy ledges to a groove composed of two steps. A few stiff pulls will get you into a photogenic position in no time, although getting to the top might be a different matter.
Al Parker, Graham Fyffe, 1979

32 The Downfall Climb 35m M ★★
A fine scramble. Up good ledges in the right-hand corner of the waterfall, then traverse leftwards to an easy finishing corner. Best in drier conditions unless you want a drenching!

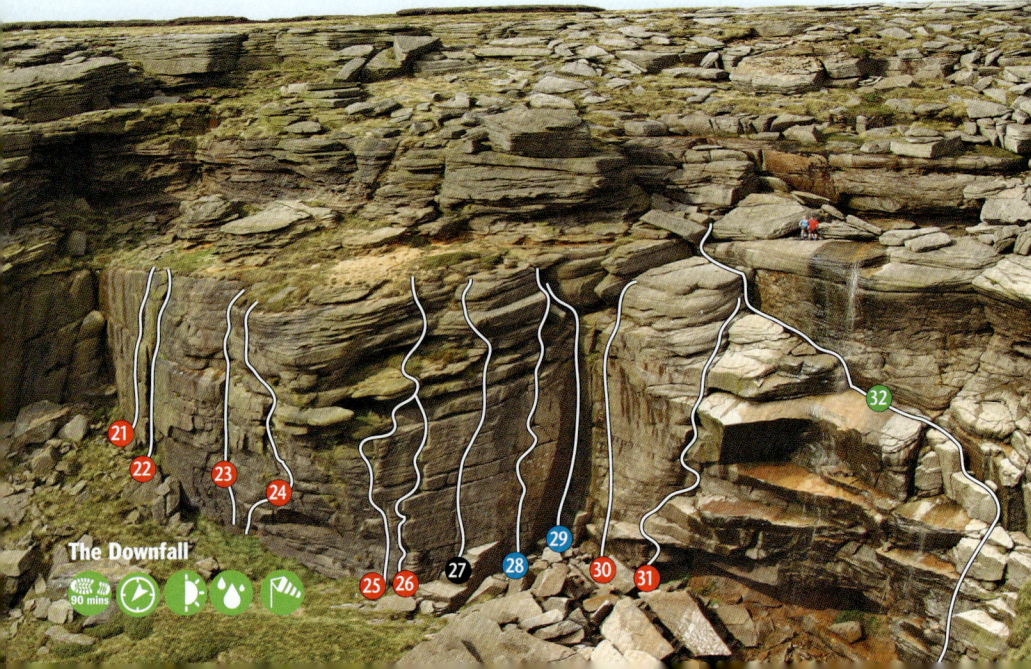

The Downfall

A fine old climb on the rocks at the doorstep of Kinder Downfall, Zigzag Climb, VD (page 487). The climbs here may be short relative to the walk-in, but on a hot summer day this is one of the great adventures of Peak District gritstone. 📷 Paul Evans

KINDER SOUTH

Altitude: 600m

SEE MAP ON PAGE 452

Kinder's southern skyline overlooking Edale. The rock here is some of the best and cleanest on Kinder and can be climbed on for much of the year. A fine selection of crags and routes are detailed in this section. These crags can be linked in either a clockwise or anticlockwise direction picking the Kinder plums as you go.

UPPER EDALE ROCKS
Diminutive yet perfectly formed, this crag has some really good routes. There is a starred route in almost every grade. The crag has a great exposed outlook, dries quickly and gets no seepage. **OS Grid Ref: SK 079 867**

Approach: Park in a layby on the road between Barber Booth and Upper Booth then walk up the road to Upper Booth. For Upper Edale Rocks, follow the Pennine Way up the main valley, passing the steepening of Jacob's Ladder, then turn right to reach the rocks after 500m. For The Pagoda, continue along the path for 1km or use the Crowden Clough approach (see page 492). Approaches take just over an hour.

Upper Edale Rocks

Kinder South | Pagoda | 491

① Pencil Slim 8m VS 5a ★
A memorable squeeze up the crack.

② Avator 9m HVS 5b ★
Pleasant climbing up the centre of the slab.
Jonny Woodward, Ian Maisey, Andy Woodward, 1980

③ Jacob's Bladder 7m E2 6a ★
From the huge block, climb up breaks. Move right and then pull onto the nose above.
Neil McAdie, 2002

④ Traverse and Crack 9m VD ★★
At the base of the crag is a huge fallen block. Gain its top and follow the corner-crack.

⑤ Well Suited 9m E3 6a ★★
Steep moves on the left side of the arête lead past a hidden pocket to a break. Easier but bolder climbing on the right side gains the top.
Steve Bancroft, Mark Clark, 1987

⑥ Bending Crack 8m VD ★★
Follow the crack up and across the wall.

⑦ Straight Crack 8m D
The groove in the corner.

⑧ Winter's Block 9m E2 5b ★
Take the obvious traverse line right out of the easy corner to finish the arête in a fine position.
Mark Clark, Steve Bancroft, 1987

⑨ Hand of the Medici 9m E4 6a ★
Climb the sharp arête on its right side.
Julian Lines (solo), 1993

⑩ Layback Crack 6m HS 4a
The left slanting crack in the back of the recess.

⑪ Our Doorstep 6m VS 4c
The short corner just to the right is a struggle.
Dave Banks (solo), 1977

⑫ Trivial Pursuits 12m VS 4c ★★
From near the top of *Our Doorstep*, descend the left arête then delicately foot-traverse the lip of the overhang (gulp!) to finish up the right-hand arête. A fantastically daft route.
Chris Hardy, 1986

⑬ Stigmata 6m E4 6b ★★
The undercut highball arête.
Andy Barker, 1994

⑭ The Mentalist Cupboard 7m E7 6c ★★
Outrageous. The hanging crack is gained by desperate bouldering.
Tom de Gay, 2001

> **THE PAGODA**
> Home to a number of rounded classics in a setting which is as perfect for picnics as it is for climbing. Exposed and fast drying.
> OS Grid Ref: SK 088 870

① Morrison's Route 15m S 4a ★
Climb the crack passing right of the projecting fin to gain the ledge. Continue up the rounded upper wall, to a poorly protected finish.
Don Morrison, John Loy, 1956

② Hartley's Route 18m E2 5c ★★
A barely believable line. It looks simple enough, but it'll kick you up the arse. Allow yourself to be led onwards and upwards to the final impossible manoeuvres that have seen more than their fair share of puzzled looks. The moves are possible, just not in the way you first imagine.
HK Hartley, VJ Desmond, VT Dillon, 1949

③ Herford's Route 17m HVS 5a ★★★
An ancient Kinder classic. A scratched wall containing a letterbox leads to a tricky landing onto a ledge. Continue more or less direct, bearing in mind that big cams make the necessary moves less brave than they were in 1910!
Siegfried Herford, John Laycock, Stanley Jeffcoat, 1910

The Pagoda

CROWDEN CLOUGH FACE

OS Grid Ref: SK 094 871
Altitude: 590m

The Clough face is slightly hidden, tucked away in a bend of the plateau. Like the approach, the routes have a tendency to sneak up on you. They seem quite benign and then, without warning, they slap you round the back of the head. Not in a brutal way, more a cheeky way that will bring a smile to your face.

Conditions and Aspect: East facing and high on the western side of Crowden Clough. The crag is cooler and shadier than the other crags in this section. Some routes can be gritty, green and in need of brushing beforehand.

> Approach: Park in a layby on the road between Barber Booth and Upper Booth then walk up the road to Upper Booth. Turn right off the road at Upper Booth using a stile just over the bridge and climb to the rim via Crowden Clough (see map on page 490). Takes about 1 hour.

1 Olympus Explorer 12m E2 5c ★
Climb the crack in the overhang then make bold moves up the shallow groove (crux).
Con Carey, Dave Banks, 1988

2 Indianapolis Slab 15m VS 4c ★
Climbs the pleasant slab firstly left of centre, then nearer the right edge to finish.
Dave Banks, Nigel Lee, 1988

3 Grassy Chimney 15m VD
The big chimney left of the main buttress has a variety of exits, subterranean or otherwise.
Arthur Birtwistle, Geoff Pigott, 1936

4 Groove Rider 15m E7 6b ★★
Audacious. Climb the arête first face-on, then on its right, to reach the *Arabia* crux with relief.
Neil Gresham, 1998

5 Arabia 18m E2 5c ★★★
A Peak classic. Right of the arête, climb the crack; hand traverse left to the arête itself, then follow this to a finish past the obvious large pocket. Bold but steady. ⊙ opposite page
Mark Clark, Steve Bancroft, Ian Holmes, 1989

6 Central Route 16m VS 4c ★★
Excellent, despite appearances.
Eric Byne, Clifford Moyer, 1933

7 Asparagus 24m E1 5b ★★
A bit of an expedition. Engage in conflict with the steep crack to the right, reaching a ledge at 6m. Move left into *Central Route* at its crux, then traverse left again all the way round the arête to finish up a diagonal crack.
Don Morrison, John Loy, 1956

8 Andromeda 15m E4 6b ★★
The curving arête is excellent, with contrasting halves. Climb the right side with a difficult crux past a good pebble to a rest. The upper arête is bold and easier on the left.
Harry Venables, Malc Baxter, 1989

9 Middle Chimney 15m S 4b ★
The clean chimney gives a good outing.
Arthur Birtwistle, Geoff Pigott, 1936

10 Liquid Skin 15m E2 6a ★
Starting 2m left of the arête, break through the bulge and climb the slab.
Olly Allen, 1999

The classic mid-Extreme of Kinder's sunny side. Arabia, E2 5c (opposite page) is a rounded ride up an exposed arête. Exciting stuff. Jim Trueman climbing. Dan Lane

UPPER TOR

OS Grid Ref: SK 114 876
Altitude: 570m

Upper Tor is obvious on the Edale skyline and always captures the gaze of those who are Kinder-bound. It is home to a number of classic routes in a moorland setting, all served up in a giant helping of rounded gritstone, breezy vistas and random brutality. The routes here are tough for the grade, often rounded and wide.

This south-facing crag overlooks Grinds Brook and receives the sun for most of the day. The well-travelled classics are clean, but the rock on the harder ones can be gritty. The crag is at its best after a couple of days of dry weather and drying breezes.

> **Approach:** See map on page 490. Start from Edale (p&d) parking and follow the path left of the Old Nags Head pub. Carry on and, at the edge of town, cross the river and follow Grinds Brook. In the river's upper reaches either strike steeply up to the crag or follow the path to the edge and go right.

1 Diamond Arête 12m E3 5c ★
The short left arête. A bold start leads to the break. Continue using a large pocket.
Chris Hardy, 1989

2 Chockstone Chimney 13m VD ★
The chimney, finishing up the right-hand crack.

3 Half a Friend 18m E2 5c ★
Boulder up the short groove to cross *Upper Tor Wall*. Boldly follow the rounded arete above.
Michael Howlett 1997

4 Upper Tor Wall 18m HS 4b ★★★
A fantastic pummel up the buttress on big features. Start in the recess and climb leftwards to a ledge. Climb the centre of the wall directly using flake holds to a ledge finishing directly.
⊙ page 496
Arthur Birtwistle, 1936

5 Hiker's Chimney 15m HS 4c ★
The glorious offwidth looks horrendous to start but saves its bite for the well-protected exit.
Arthur Birtwistle, 1936

6 Hiker's Crack 15m S 4a ★
Climb up then step left into jamming cracks which lead to easier climbing leftwards.
Geoff WS Pigott, 1936

7 Hiker's Gully Left 12m HVD
Continue direct up the cleft from *Hiker's Crack*.
Geoff WS Pigott, Arthur Birtwistle, 1936

8 Hiker's Gully Right 12m S 4a
Satisfying chimney climbing which leads to a steep exit with good holds throughout.
Geoff WS Pigott, Arthur Birtwistle, 1936

9 Hitch Hiker 14m VS 4b ★
Start as for *Hiker's Gully Right* but veer right up the awkward flake and ramp to finish.
Allan Austin, 1956

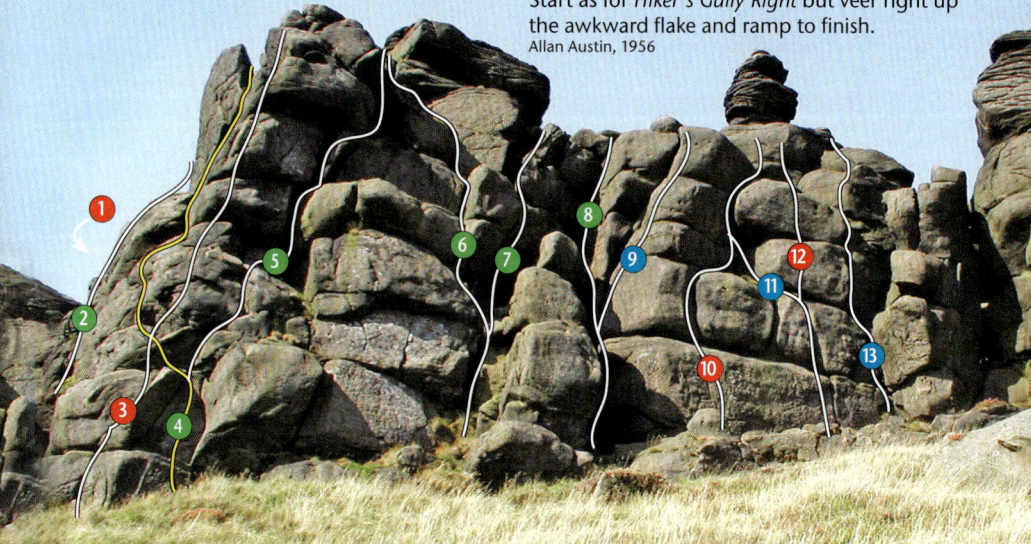

Kinder South | Upper Tor | 495

10 Three Flakes of Man 15m E1 5c ★★
Climb the wall via a finger flake to the break. Continue up the large flake to a ledge. An even larger flake crack gives a memorable finish.
Malc Baxter, Adam Longson, Keith Ashton, 1988

11 Grunter 15m VS 4c ★
Masochism. Jam up the right-hand crack before moving left and finishing up *Three Flakes*...
Don Morrison, John Loy, 1965

12 The Punter 15m E3 6a ★
From *Grunter*, climb the pocketed wall direct.
Pete Robins, 2000

13 Snorter 14m VS 4c
The left side of the pinnacle then straight up the crack in the wall above.
John Loy, Don Morrison, 1965

14 The Rock of Sir Walter 20m E1 5c ★
Traverse right along the lower break then move up to reach a conspicuous pocket. Use this to pull through the overlap to meet *The Ivory Tower*. Move left and finish up the left arête.
Keith Ashton, Dave Banks, 1991

15 The Ivory Tower 23m E1 5b ★★★
Steep moves, committing swings and a delicate wall all combine to give a great outing. Climb the bulging wall to a ledge. Follow the crack and bulge above then move left to follow a thin crack and wrinkly upper wall.
John Loy, Don Morrison, 1966

16 Artillery Chimney 14m HS 4b ★
The 'gun' goes more easily than you might expect but you're unlikely to think the same about the finishing chockstone.
Arthur Birtwistle, Geoff Pigott, 1948

17 Promontory Groove 9m HVD 4a ★
The square-cut groove is worthwhile, reachy in parts but great fun.
JW Puttrell, WJ Watson, 1890

18 Cave Rib 11m E2 5b ★
The rib succumbs via a series of thuggy moves before finishing more delicately on the right-hand side with easier moves.
Keith Ashton, Dave Banks, 1989

19 Cave Gully 14m S 4a
Start at the obvious cave and traverse out left, taking the arête to the top via a layback crack.

20 Brutality 14m E1 5b ★★
Steep climbing on good holds will lead you to the final reckoning. Climb the corner then swing rightwards onto the wall. Take the crack to the second overhang. Hand-traverse leftwards to a wide crack which provides the crux.
John Loy, Don Morrison, 1965

21 Greenfingers 9m VS 4c
A hard mantel gives access to the slab and ledge where a direct finish up a graunchy groove awaits.
Don Morrison, John Loy, 1966

22 Robert 12m E2 5c ★★★
The gushing roof-gash. Next on the list after *Brutality*. Steep, well protected and full-on.
Don Morrison, John Loy (1pt), 1966. FFA, Graham Hoey, 1976

23 Pedestal Wall 14m S 4a ★
A fun big line following the major V-groove on the right of the buttress.
Arthur Birtwistle, Geoff Pigott, 1948

Don't you just want to be there, in that sun, hands full of that great big flake of roughshod moorland grit? Amen. Sarah Clough on Upper Tor Wall, HS 4b (page 494). 📷 Martin Kocsis

NETHER TOR

OS Grid Ref: SK 121 875
Altitude: 560m

Nether Tor has a completely different nature to Upper Tor. Ancient land slippage and quarrying has given rise to some steep and unforgiving walls. The crag is steep and a little rambling. Facing south, it receives sun for most of the day. Seepage is an issue, so be prepared to stay out of the clefts if it has rained recently.

Approach: From Edale (p&d) parking, following the path to Ringing Roger then go left along the rim (see map on page 490). It can also be approached direct from the Grindsbrook path. 1 hour.

1 Loan Arranger 20m VS 4c
The steep crack and rambly finish.
Al Parker (solo), 1976

2 Beautiful Losers 18m E3 5c ★
A contrived expedition on featured rock. From *Loan Arranger*, hand traverse right to a shallow flake crack. Up this and go over an overhang onto the wall above. Mantelshelf awkwardly, continuing up a rib to finish back leftwards.
Con Carey, Dave Banks, 1978

3 The Ju Ju Tree 18m E2 5c ★
Get onto the ledge to the right by a desperate mantel. The rest of the route is insecure at best.
Martin Kocsis, Tom Brunt, Paul Fleuriot, 2004

4 Beautiful Losers Direct 18m E4 6a ★★
The direct gives a sustained outing. Follow the blunt arête to join and finish up the original.
Al Stephenson, 1994

5 Moneylender's Crack 20m VS 5a ★★
A sustained and pumpy treat following the major flaky features. Great holds and great moves are ample reward for the effort of ascent.
Arthur Birtwistle, Geoff WS Pigott, 1950

6 Mortgage Wall 22m HVS 5b ★
This is what we call beefy. First a big crack, then a big ledge to dither on and finally a pumpy wall to finish with.
John Gosling, Kenny Coyne, 1976

7 Usurer 10m HS 4b ★
The chimney.

8 Grave Crack 10m HVS 5b ★
The steep little crack.
K Taylor, D Upton, 1957

9 Coffin Chimney 10m VD ★
The chimney with a choice of ways to face.
Arthur Birtwistle, 1946

10 Shroud 10m HVS 5a ★
Climb to the roof from where wild and committing moves rightwards gain a juggy finish.
Al Parker, Peter Bamfield, 1957

CENTRAL BUTTRESS

A short way right is a concentration of routes containing the biggest and most complex routes on the crag.

11 Broken Chimney 17m VD ★
The chimney.

12 Edale Bobby 18m E4 6a ★★★
The prominent arête gives one of moorland's finest E4s. Climb to the pedestal, pausing only to fondle the strange bollards and features. The upper arête is technical and bold but fairly well protected by very small cams.
Steve Bancroft, Mark Clark, Nicky Stokes, 1987

13 Square Cut 17m HS 4b
The chimney.

14 Kelvin's Corner 17m HS 4a ★
The next corner.

15 Crimson Wall 26m E2 5c ★
Climb rightwards from the groove into a short difficult corner. From its top, traverse left then move up and hand-traverse right to a grassy ledge. Take a thin crack to a difficult landing.
Jonny Woodward, George Smith, 1980

16 Snooker Route 30m VS 5a ★
Climb the pocketed wall to the holly tree and then gain the ledge. From the perched block, traverse left and finish up a chimney. The holly is annoying but essential.
Arthur Birtwistle, Geoff Pigott, 1950

17 Flash Wall 23m VS 5a ★★★
A classic of the Peak. Start at a polished crack. Climb this to a ledge, move right and jam round the flake following good holds up the wall. Step rightwards to finish up a wide crack.
Arthur Birtwistle, Geoff Pigott, 1950

18 The Thieves' Kitchen 23m E2 5c ★★
A crimpy and technical excursion up the apparently blank wall right wall. Follow diagonal cracks and thin breaks to finish up the thin upper crack.
Keith Ashton, Dave Banks, Jonny Sonczak, Jim Moran, 1990

19 Recoil Rib 25m E3 5c ★★
Bold, committing, smeary climbing. Easily to the ledge (possible belay). The arête with side runners is climbed on both the left and right.
Al Parker, I Heys, 1974

20 The Crown 8m HVS 5b
Follow the short corner, using a crack for the right hand.
Keith Ashton, Harry Venables, 1992

21 Edale Flyer 8m VS 4c ★
Neat and enjoyable climbing up the clean corner, which is over all too soon.
Dave Banks, Keith Ashton, 1989

22 T'Big Surrey 10m E5 6b ★★
The protruding arête is a big, bold and rounded challenge. Traverse delicately right to gain the arête and follow it with sustained difficulty.
Gabe Regan, Harry Venables, Keith Ashton, 1989

Kinder South | Nether Tor | 499

EAST BUTTRESS
More tall, exciting routes.

23 Caesar Ridge 27m VS 4c ★
Start at a flake-crack in the left arête of the buttress. Follow this strenuously and finish up the arête on good holds.
Arthur Birtwistle, Geoff Pigott, 1950

24 Gallery Crack 27m VS 4c ★
Good, honest toil up the centre of the buttress via crack and flakes.
Arthur Birtwistle, Geoff Pigott, 1950

25 C.M.C. Induction Programme 27m HVS 5b ★
Start as for Gallery Crack, but traverse right to the arête, then snake your way up the front of the buttress through a variety of features; worthwhile.
Pat Cocks, Hugh Dowling, Caroline Whitehead, 1994

26 The Roman Nose 27m HVS 5b ★★
Start in the cave. Ascend the slab on the right (crux). A mantelshelf then leads into a corner which is climbed until an interesting move can be made rightwards over the nose. Enter the gallery platform and finish up the chimneys.
Arthur Birtwistle, Geoff Pigott, 1950

27 Never Say Nether Again 27m E1 5b ★★
The steep sidewall on cracks and breaks to finish up the arête.
Keith Ashton, Dave Banks, Jonny Sonczak, Jim Moran, 1990

28 Free Wall 10m VS 4c ★
Excellent climbing which is bold and exposed. Follow the wall right to a ledge then back left to finish.
K Taylor, D Upton, 1956

29 Freestyle 10m E1 5b ★
A harder, bolder line on the right of the slab requires confidence in what lies above.
Iain Johnson, Rick Adderton, Malc Baxter, 2008

30 Wee-Kinder Weekender 10m E4 6b ★
The blunt arête with a very rounded crux exit.
Adam Long, 2001

31 Atmistpheric 10m VS 4c ★
Follow the scoop features on good holds.
Iain Johnson, 2001

32 Pedestal 10m S ★
The short corner.
Arthur Birtwistle, Geoff Pigott, 1936

33 Quickstep 10m HVS 5b ★
Climb the steep, bulging left-hand edge of the wall on great good holds.
Harry Venables, Keith Ashton, 1992

34 Three Step 10m HS 4b ★
The crack splitting the buttress nose gives an enjoyable tussle.
Arthur Birtwistle, Geoff Pigott, 1936

35 Rucksack 10m HS 4b ★
A steep crack with a crux finish.
Arthur Birtwistle, Geoff Pigott, 1936

KINDER NORTH
Altitude: 600m

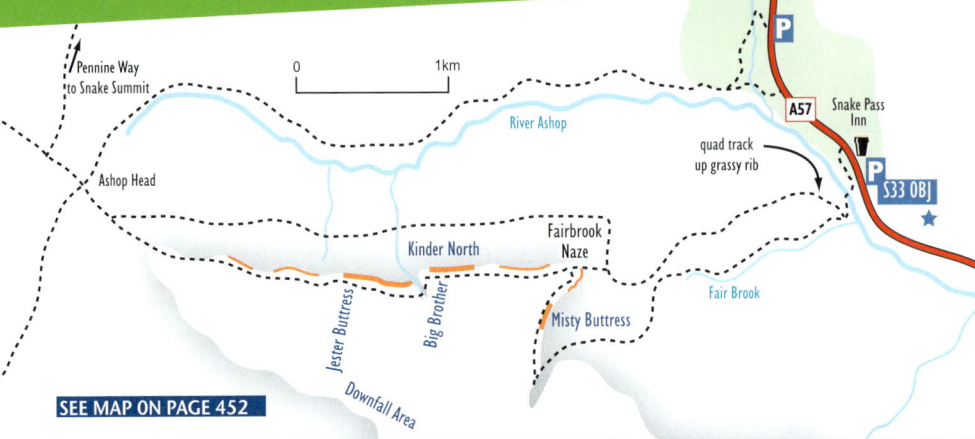

These isolated edges guard the northern rim of Kinder Scout. In the height of summer or during the glories of the high moorland spring and autumn, the Northern Edges have a peace and ambience about them that is hard to find anywhere else on grit.

It is advisable to bring some larger-than-normal cams. It's also normal practice to take a stiff brush and either clean as you go or do it on abseil, particularly on the less popular routes or early in the year.

Misty Buttress gets the morning sun. Big Brother and Jester Buttresses get a tiny bit of evening sun in the summer months.

The fact that most of the climbing will be in the shade is an obvious bonus for days when the rest of the Peak is like an oven, but it can be bitterly cold on gloomy days. The walls can retain dampness, and lack of traffic and the sunless nature means that you should always be ready for the scrittle.

Approach: Park in roadside bays near the Snake Pass Inn. Cross the River Ashop and follow the Fair Brook path to Misty Buttress or the quad track to the grassy rib aiming for Kinder North. Alternatively, park further up and take the River Ashop approach then strike up to your chosen buttress. Approaches will take an hour.

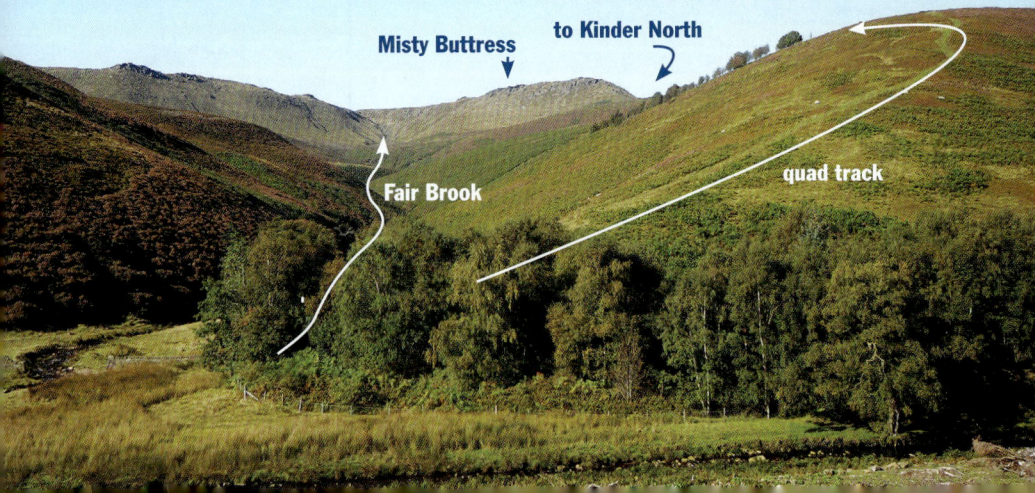

A big walk, big routes and big features: that's Kinder North. Its shadowy treasures are well kept and hard earned, but are some of the great riches of gritstone. Here, Dom Proctor zigs his way up the deep zags of Intestate, E1 5b, a true moorland classic (page 504). Pete O'Donovan

MISTY BUTTRESS

See map on page 500. Follow Fair Brook, to below the plateau. Misty Buttress is up on the right. The easiest approach is to continue up the path to the rim of the plateau and follow the path rightwards to the buttress. Morning sun. **OS Grid Ref: SK 095 896**

1 Pieces of Eight 8m S
From ledges, climb the overhang and tiny cracks on the right. Move left into a corner to finish.
Malc Baxter, Jim Heys, 1960

2 Doubloon 8m VS 4b
Climb the disjointed rib.
Malc Baxter, Jim Heys, 1960

3 Round Up 15m E1 5b ★
Reachy moves above the bulgy bits gain a short blind crack and the top.
Colin Binks, Chris Craggs, Graham Parkes, 1982

4 Misty Wall 15m VS 4c ★★★
The showpiece VS of Kinder North. Start up the right-hand arête then follow a series of cracks to the left of the arête to a position below an overhang. Finish up the wider crack above.
◉ opposite page
Alf Bridge, 1929

5 Wind Wall 15m VS 4c ★
Follow *Misty Wall* for 5m then traverse right to climb the centre of the sidewall.
Al Parker, Dennis Carr, Tony Cowcill, 1977

6 Bean Feast 20m VS 4c
A pleasant rising traverse starting up *Pieces of Eight* to finish up *Wind Wall*.

7 Deviation 12m VD
Climb the front of the buttress set back in the gully to finish up the chimney behind.
Malc Baxter, 1964

8 Fixation 15m D
The bounding right chimney of *Deviation* to the corner behind and easy finish.
Malc Baxter (solo), 1961

9 Cassandra 17m E2 5c ★
Climb up to the left-hand corner of the roof. Move out leftwards onto the rib and so gain the breaks above. Continue slightly leftwards to finish.
Nick Colton, Con Carey, 1979

10 Trojan 15m E1 5c ★★
You like beef? Climb more or less direct to the layback crack in the roof. Make hard moves up this to a huge perched block and an uncomfortable rest. Labour up the crack past two chockstones.
Pete Davis, 1961

11 Meander Arête 10m HVS 4c ★
Traverse left to the arête and follow this to an exposed and difficult finish.
Con Carey, Nick Colton, 1979

12 Dependence Wall 10m HS 4a ★
Start below a cutaway on the buttress to the right of the gully. Climb up to the overhang, trending leftwards past some 'handle with care' flakes, until it is possible to move rightwards to finish.
Malc Baxter, Jim Heys, 1960

13 Dependence Arête 10m VS 4b ★
Start as for *Dependence Wall*, but make a rising traverse out to the arête and good finishing holds.
Malc Baxter, Jim Heys, 1960

The rock architecture goes a bit west on Kinder East. Andy Birtwistle having a bit of a wrestle wth the cantankerous juts of Misty Wall, VS 4c (opposite page). ◉ Birtwistle collection

BIG BROTHER BUTTRESS
From the Snake Pass Inn, follow the quad track approach, under Kinder North, then strike up to the buttress. This is the best buttress on the Northern Edges. See map on page 500. **OS Grid Ref: SK 088 898**

14 Legacy 22m HVS 5a ★★★
The diagonal line is a fine, well-protected route: one of the moorland classics. Gain the diagonal fault from the left and follow it all the way to finish up the arête.
Paul Nunn, Al Parker, 1962

15 Intestate 20m E1 5b ★★★
Another belter, sustained and thuggy. From halfway along the *Legacy* traverse, climb the wall direct via a short crack. page 501
Paul Nunn, W Ward (1pt), 1967. FFA unknown, 1970s

16 Big Brother 20m E2 6a ★★★
A great route, but very reach dependant. Climb through the undercut to reach the vertical crack. Climb this to reach the break then an awkward move to finish.
Jonny Woodward, 1981

17 Kinsman 20m E4 6b ★★
The blunt arête is difficult, but protected with a big cam.
Al Rouse, Simon Wells, 1984

18 Brothers' Eliminate 20m E1 5b ★★
"A good old-fashioned thug route". Gain the overhang then attack the rightward-slanting crack on meaty jams to a recess. Escape up and left to finish.
Graham West, Malc Baxter, 1960

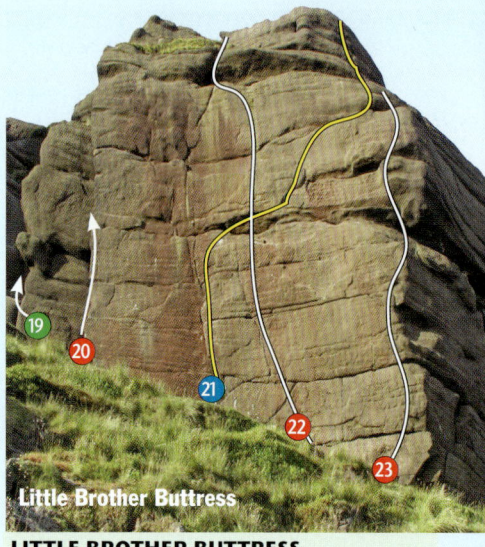

Little Brother Buttress

LITTLE BROTHER BUTTRESS
Just around the corner, a splendid sibling to the big fella on the left. Relatively clean.

19 Razor Crack 14m S 4b ★
The steep crack on the sidewall right of the chimney corner is quite steep and really good fun.
Graham West, 1960

20 The Les Dawson Show 14m E3 5c ★★
Climb the arête on the right; escapable but with fine moves.
Steve Bancroft, Mark Clark, 1989

Big Brother Buttress

21 Dunsinane 18m VS 4c ★★
A brilliant line sweeping across this fine buttress. Climb the cracky groove to the break. Move right to a flake then up to the next break. Go right and finish up the arête. ⊙ page 451
Malc Baxter, Njal Parker, Ernie Jones, 1964

22 The Savage Breast 14m E1 5b ★★
The wall to the right, climbed direct to a quick leftward finish. Excellent and safe but with a tough crux. Hard for the short.
Gary Gibson, Andy Popp, Ian Johnston, 1983

23 Motherless Children 14m E1 5c ★
The rounded arête leads to an awkward, reachy move before joining *Dunsinane*.
Chris Hardy, Harry Venables, 1988

JESTER BUTTRESS
This sits further 750m westwards along Kinder North from the Brother buttresses. An intimidating bastion, with towering arêtes and overhangs. Fabulous. See map on page 500. OS Ref: SK 081 897

24 Jester Cracks 17m HVS 5a ★★★
Classic, old school Kinder VS! Climb up a short slab to a ledge. A thin crack leads onto the arête below the Jester's beak. Move left (crux) and ascend the crack on good jams.
Richard McHardy, R Fryer, 1959

25 Grit Liars in our Midst 17m E1 5b ★
Break right out of *Jester Cracks* to finish spectacularly way out on the projecting beak.
Adam Long, Ben Tetler, James Pearson, 2004

26 Monkey Madness 20m E5 6c ★★
Outrageous, hard and bold climbing blasting straight up the front of the buttress.
Andy Barker, 1995

27 Suspension 15m VS 4c
Good old-fashioned crack climbing.
Richard McHardy, Peter Bamfield, 1959

28 Gremlin Groove 15m HVS 5b
Similar to *Suspension*, but a little bit harder.
Richard McHardy, R Fryer, 1959

29 Candle in the Wind 18m E3 5c ★★
The exposed arête. Climb rightwards to a short corner. Stretch for the horizontal break and hand-traverse left to reach the arête. Pull directly up the right-hand side of the arête (crux) to reach easier climbing above. Take big cams.
Chris Hardy, Harry Venables, 1988

30 Twisted Smile 18m HVS 5b ★★★
Everything a gritstone HVS should be. Start at a small crack and climb direct up the impressive wall via numerous breaks.
John Gosling and party, 1972

31 Count Dracula 18m E1 5b ★
Climb the green slab on the right and traverse left beneath the overhang. Pull over the roof and climb directly up the wall above. Take a large cam for the end of the traverse.
Andy Bailey, Stuart Gascoyne, 1984

32 Woe is Me 18m S
The wide crack round right of the main face.
Eric Byne, Peter Knapp, 1954

33 Harlequin 14m E3 6a ★★
A fantastic, airy route that is as good as it looks. Start up *Woe...* then traverse left above the roof and climb directly up the wall and top overhang. Commitment pays dividends.
Johnny Dawes, Al Rouse, 1985

WHERE NEXT?

A BRIEF GUIDE FOR THE BUDDING PEAK GRIT AFICIONADO

At some point in their climbing career most UK climbers, and even some from further afield, are drawn to the grit: some in fact never leave. For most visitors, this Wired guide will provide more than a lifetime of glorious days out cragging, but for those who have got a serious addiction, or who like to scope out the smaller and more esoteric venues away from the crowds which are beyond the scope of this selective guide, there are the BMC's definitive guides. These will help you explore the lesser visited quarters, discovering gems and adventures away from the hustle and bustle of Stanage Popular. They also form a definitive record of all the routes, bouldering and history.

Here is just a small sample of the thousands of other routes that are fully described in the Peak area BMC guides. This is an attempt to show you the array of grit out there in the Peak to explore. As with this Wired guide, the focus is on routes, but combine any of the BMC guides with a bouldering pad and numerous opportunities for further exploration will await.

THE ROACHES
FURTHER DETAILS PAGE 56

Away from the crowds at the main Staffordshire crags, smaller lofty tors and secluded wooded valleys are waiting for the adventurer. The combination of bouldering and a rope for a few routes will get the most out of many of these venues. The rugosities of the rock on Sly Buttress at Newstones are complemented, a short walk away at Baldstones by the bold slab of **Original Route** (E2), the superb **Baldstone Arête** (HVS) and the limb-eating **Ray's Roof** (E7). Gradbach Hill is an idyllic spot, and **The Billiard Table** (HS) will hopefully warm you up for the punchier offerings of **The Gape** (HVS), **Sense of Doubt** (E2) and the bold classic **The Phantom** (E4).

Any climber looking to have a quieter day should look no further than many of the offerings in the Upper and Lower Churnet Valleys. The spiralling **Helix** (HVS) and the fine arête of **One Chromosome's Missing** (E7) at Harston Rock point the way. Garston Rocks contains one of the best runners on grit on **The Arête** (S) and **Skull Crack** (HS) is another gem. Oldridge Pinnacle has several micro classics including **The Gateless Gate** and **Qui Vive** (both E3): scary highballs but above a perfect sunny landing or safe micro routes, you choose your style. Belmont Hall Crags sound posh, **Cave Crack** (VS) even has a gritstone seat to put your shoes on, but don't expect the butler to have sympathy if your technique is not perfect on **Kneewrecker Chimney** (HVS) and you require his assistance. Stoney Dale Quarry provides the stunning arête of **Sole Survivor** (E5). At Ina's Rock the lower hard sandy coloured rock is a complete contrast to the upper cliff's large pebble conglomerate which provides delight on **Inaccessible** (E5), whilst careful jamming is required on **Atlas** (E2) and **Ground Support** (E1).

Bosley Cloud is the probably the best outlying venue with the slabs of **Hot Tin Roof** (E1) and **Crystal Voyager** (E3) proving it is not just The Roaches that excels at this medium.

FROGGATT TO BLACK ROCKS
FURTHER DETAILS PAGE 144

This guide is jam-packed with smaller venues particularly between Beeley and Cromford, often with one or two plum routes at each crag that make a visit worthwhile. The Amber Valley is filled with gems: Eastwood Rocks contains the best, but unfortunately is "the best banned crag in the peak". However climbers with discretion may enjoy **Corpse Crack** (HVS), **Neb Traverse** (E2) and **Fat Slapper** (E7) which are all classics of their grade in the Peak. Turning Stone Edge hides in its camouflage of rhododendrons (bring some secateurs), but once on the rock **Amber Arête** (VS), **Sail Arête** (S) and **Overton Arête** (HVS) make a fine introduction to this great crag. Combine it with a visit with to Cocking Tor to tickle **Cyclops Eye** (E2) or any number of the highly adventurous routes at Ravensnest Tor, and you will start to understand differences in character of each crag. The Whatstandwell Quarries, a combination of jungle and rock, are widely known for the Duke's Quarry classics of **Great Crack** (HVS) and **Dharma** (E7). Explore further and there's no end of unloved lines that with a bit of TLC may provide a fun day, indeed **Thunderstruck** (HVS) in the Robin Hood Quarries when clean could be a match for many a celebrated classic.

Everyone loves a pinnacle: **The Original Route** (D) at Tegness Quarries can been seen from the parking at Froggatt. Its southern Peak sister, the equally fine **Easy Turnpike** (HVD) provides the easiest way to conquer The Alport Stone. The final word must go to the southern Peak suntrap Shining Cliff from the subterranean **Bat House** (S) to the more conventional offerings of **Plumber's Corner** (VS) and **Bramble Crack** (HVS). There's something for everyone when your mates are climbing indoors, having retreated from poor conditions on the more exposed crags.

BURBAGE, MILLSTONE AND BEYOND
FURTHER DETAILS PAGE 204

Surrounding Sheffield, as well as the major edges, there's a flurry of smaller crags and bouldering venues to explore. When the high moors are wind swept, and you want a change from Rivelin, a short walk will take you to the sheltered suntrap of Rivelin Quarry. Amongst the quarried bays in the trees, where owls can often be heard, are a bunch of quality routes which stay relatively clean, the best of which are in the extreme grades; **The Two Toms** (E1), **Portnoy's Complaint** (E2), **Awkward Willy** (E2), **Paddington** (E4) and **Flex** (E6) will interest any quarried grit devotee on a windy day.

Bell Hagg is an old favourite within the city limits, and a short bus ride from the city centre. Hiding in the trees are a series of small buttress containing some bouldering and short routes: a pad and a soloing head is usual, but a rope and the odd runner may be found useful for some. **Banner's Ridge** (E1), **Brown's Unmentionable** (HVS), **Hyde's Mantelshelf** (HVS) and **Leo** (HVS) are the best of the bunch.

A concerned looking Graeme Hammond, way above tiny looking mats and wearing a pointless harness soloing Rivelin Quarry's very bold Portnoy's Complaint, E2 5b (above). ◘ Mark Rankine.

Visible from Stanage End, glowing in the morning sunshine, Ladybower Quarry contains plenty of rock, much of which is friable. However, a number of routes are worth calling in for including **The Ingot** (VS) and **E.N. 24** (E1), although most will head straight for the tough jamming and layback classic **The Rat** (E1).

Occasionally locals talk in hushed tones of a place no one seems to have actually been to, and with good reason. But for those who like their grit exceptionally loose and vegetated Stannington Ruffs **1847** (HS), may provide a perfect masochistic folly.

STANAGE
FURTHER DETAILS PAGE 282

Stanage is the queen of grit with a guide all to itself. The most coveted routes are well known and have been included in this guide, however the rock is of the highest quality and stays clean, so that almost every route is worthwhile. Anyone who has explored away from the honeypot areas will have 'discovered' their own favourite. There is much variety: slabs, cracks, overhangs, offwidths, laybacks and squeeze chimneys - it's certainly not just pulling between breaks. Spend an evening blowing off steam after work, enjoying the fresh air before a perfect sunset and you will realise there is no finer place.

OVER THE MOORS
FURTHER DETAILS PAGE 416

With a lifetime of crags you've probably never heard of right on the doorstep of the climbing hubs of Sheffield and Manchester, this guide will inspire you to break from the mould on a summer's day and explore the high moorland edges. Driving through the Chew valley Upperwood Quarry stands out, with a cluster of quarried routes worth calling in for, including **Turtle** (E2), **Renaissance** (E4) and **How** (HVS). Across the valley either side of the adventuresome Main Quarry the Dovestones Lower Left and Right Quarries have some stylish offerings: **Gatepost Crack** (E1), **Ace of Spades** (HVS), **Tiny Tim** (VS) and the essential Peak splitter crack of **Bob Hope** (E4). Dotted around the Dovestone skyline, the Charnel Stone offers a number of classics including **The Wasteland** (E4) and **Broomstick** (HVS), and Wilderness Rocks provide further escapades with the expedition of **Wilderness Gully East** (M) being popular.

Surrounding Glossop small quarries and edges provide easy hits from Manchester including; John Henry Quarry's forearm-busting **Desperate Straights** (E2), Wormstones' jamming test-piece **Scrooge** (HVS), Oldpits' **Scorched Earth** (E4) and Shelf Benches' **The Muzzle** (HVS). Many of the smaller crags in Longdendale Valley, the most haunted in Britain, can be combined together with one of the major crags, to give a great day out. Alternatively take an evening walk, pack your rock shoes and take in the Windgather-esque **North Pole** (S) or **The Wall of Evening Light** (VD) at the Rollick Stones, or enjoying the views aloft The Searchtower's **Sweepsearcher** (HS). Go big; follow the majestic Crowden Great Brook under the proud line of Bareholme's **Shy Ann Arête** (E1) to Deceptive Buttress and delight in the moves and solitude of **Acorn Wall** (E1). Return via the moor top and have a mini adventure on Crowden Great Quarry's **The Shabby Tiger** (HVS) before escaping for a pint. In the northern extreme of the Peak the photogenic **Flying Buttress** (S) at Pule Hill is one of many enjoyable lower grade routes. The foreboding Shoooters Nab comes alight in summer evening sunshine with **Sweatyman** (HVS), **I See A Dark Cloud** (E1), and **Ricochet Wall** (HVS) all being enjoyable.

This list is just a taster of the lesser known, but no less worthwhile, places to climb in the Peak. For the last 12 years, the BMC's definitive guidebooks have been my almost constant companions. They've been the inspiration for countless days out exploring the Peak, and responsible for some fantastic memories. If you see some rock that isn't in this Wired guide, it's probably in one of the definitive guides. Having said that, being involved in preparing this guidebook has inspired more adventures. So, if you haven't got room on your bookshelf for all of the guidebooks, this one contains plenty to keep you occupied until you become just as obsessed as me.

Graeme Hammond

Chris Reid on the Shooter's Nab classic, Sweatyman, HVS 5a (opposite page). Shooter's Nab is one of the many, brilliant, far-flung crags covered in the Over The Moors guidebook. David Simmonite.

INDEX

17 Shades 422
1847 508
3-D Wall, The 356
5.9 Finish 312
9 O'Clock Watershed, The 348

A

A Fist Full of Crystals 47
A Flabby Crack 87
A Little Green Eyed God 380
A Problem of Coagulation 305
A.M. Anaesthetic 78
A.P. Chimney 480
Abacus 285
Above and Beyond... 248
Acarpous 444
Access Account 372
Ace 238
Ace of Spades 508
Aceldama 252
Acheron 322
Acid Drop 75
Ackit 47
Acorn Wall 508
Actress, The 336
Ad Infinitum 230
Adam Smith's Invisible Hand 219
Additive Chimney 296
Adjacent Slab 377
Admiral's Progress 185
African Herbs 322
Against the Grain 51
Aged Crack 476
Agnostic's Arête 234
Agony Crack 327
Ai No Corrida 239
Albert's Amble 343
Albert's Pillar 343
Alcatraz 99
Alcove Crack 468
All Stars' Goal 232
Allen's Slab 141
Alpha (Skyline) 74
Alpha (Curbar) 163
Alpha Arête 74
Alpha Crack 404
Altar Crack 392
Altercation 392
Amazon Crack (Burbage) 238
Amazon Crack (Stanage) 324
Amazon Gully 238
Amber Arête 506
Ami 278
Ammo 377
Amphitheatre Climb 466
Amphitheatre Crack (Curbar) 148
Amphitheatre Crack (Downfall) 487
Anarchist's Arête 193
Anatomy 352
Anchor Traverse 184
Ancient 91
Andromeda 492
Angel's Share, The 125
Angle Crack 384
Angle Rib 384
Angst 386
Angular Climb 223
Angus 280
Anji 300
Annoying Little Man, The 422
Another Game of Bowl... 319
Another Turn 260
Answer Crack 432
Ant's Arête 222
Ant's Crack 222
Ant's Wall 222
Anthrax 87
Anzio Breakout 406
Aphid's Wall 222
Apollo 149
Appaloosa Sunset 83
Apparent North 359
Apple Arête 176
Apple Crack 176
Apple Jack Crack 176
Appointment with Death 443
Appointment With Fear 443
Approach 239
April Arête 208
April Crack 340
April Fool (Burbage) 239
April Fool (Rivelin) 390
Aqua 60
Arabia 492
Archangel, The 295
Arctic Mammal 238
Arctic Nose 154
Ardua 394
Are We There Yet 397
Arête and Crack 102
Arête Direct 477
Arête Wall 103
Arête, The (Castle Naze) 478
Arête, The (Garston) 506
Arête, The (Hen Cloud) 91
Arête, The (New Mills Torrs) 468
Arête, The (Ramshaw) 97
Arête, The (Tintwistle) 455
Argosy 157
Argus 290
Ariel, The 261
Aries 274
Armageddon 142
Arrow Crack 265
Art Nouveau 72
Artifact 462
Artifax Arête 397
Artillery Chimney 495
Artillery Corner 377
Artless 141
Ascent of Man 47
Ash Tree Crack 232
Ash Tree Variation 232
Ash Tree Wall 232
Ashes 320
Asinine 430
Asp, The 330
Asparagus 492
Assegai 102
Asteris 395
Astronaut's Wall 369
Atherton Brothers 458
Atlas 506
Atmistpheric 499
Atropine 482
August Arête 308
Auricle 374
Ausfahrt 383
Austin Maxi 430
Austin's Variation 200
Authentic Boulder Climb 403
Auto da Fe 389
Autumn Gold 268
Autumn Wall 410
Avalanche 135
Avalanche Wall 157
Avator 491
Ave 460
Avenue, The 396
Avoiding the Traitors 370
Avril 264
Awkward Willy 507
Awl 330

B

B Crack 286
B.A.W.'s Crawl 314
B4XS 91
Babbacombe Lee 68
Babylon's Groove 175
Bachelor's Buttress 62
Bachelor's Climb 94

512 | Index

Bachelor's
  Left-Hand 94
Back and Foot 401
Back Wall
  Traverse, The 466
Bacteria
  Cafeteria 143
Bad and the
  Beautiful, The 214
Bad Poynt 76
Bad Sneakers 77
Badly Bitten 306
Balance 265
Balance It Is 241
Balcony Buttress 326
Balcony Climb 326
Balcony Corner 327
Balcony Cracks 326
Baldstone Arête 506
Bamford Buttress 375
Bamford Rib 374
Bamford Wall 375
Banana Finger 230
Banana Wall 408
Banner's Ridge 507
Bantam Crack 87
Bareback Rider 47
Barnacle Bulge 185
Barney Rubble 380
Baron Greenback 442
Baron's Wall 154
Barriers in Time 47
Bat House 507
Base Over Apex 229
Baseless 229
Basil Brush 286
Bat Out of Hell 255
Battery Crack 52
Battle of the
  Bulge 99
Be All, The 239
Beach Tea One 232
Beady Eye 310
Bean 330
Bean Feast 502
Beanpod 271
Beanstalk 111
Beau Geste 134
Beautiful Losers 497
Beautiful Losers
  Direct 497
Beckermet Slab 59
Bee 330
Beech Nut 142
Beer Hunter, The 149

Beer Matters 369
Beggar's Crack 352
Bel Ami 160
Belladonna 482
Bending Crack 491
Bengal Buttress 48
Benign Lives 132
Bent Crack 268
Berlin Wall 440
Bertie's Bugbear 440
Beta 141
Beta Crack 404
Better End, The 88
Big Al (Rivelin) 389
Big Al (Stanage) 268
Big Bad Wall 462
Big Ben 374
Big Black 'Un 229
Big Brother 504
Big Chimney
  Arête 236
Big Chimney,
  The 236
Big Chris 354
Big Crack, The 142
Big Dave's Wall 327
Big Flake, The 83
Big Richard 104
Big Wall, The 462
Bilberry Buttress 174
Bilberry Crack
  (Bamford) 368
Bilberry Crack
  (Burbage) 232
Bilberry Face 232
Billiard Buttress 305
Billiard Table, The 506
Billingsgate 212
Billy Whizz 200
Bionic's Wall 471
Birch 383
Birch Bark 383
Birch Buttress 383
Birch Crack 383
Birch Tree
  Variant 124
Birch Tree Wall
  (Black Rocks) 124
Birch Tree Wall
  (Stanage) 346
Birthday Climb 482
Birthday Crack 150
Birthday Groove 150
Bishop's Route 337
Bitter 176

Biven's Crack 170
Black and
  Decker 288
Black and Tans 64
Black Car
  Burning 359
Black Chimney 356
Black Crack 119
Black Eyed Dog 87
Black Finger 406
Black Hawk 350
Black Hawk
  Bastion 349
Black Hawk
  Hell Crack 350
Black Hawk
  Tower 349
Black Hawk
  Traverse Left 350
Black Hawk
  Traverse Right 350
Black Magic 340
Black Mountain
  Collage 425
Black Out 240
Black Pig, The 76
Black Slab
  (Burbage) 234
Black Slab
  (Windgather) 472
Black Slab Arête 234
Black Slab
  Centre 404
Black Slab Left 404
Black Slab Right 404
Black Slab
  Variation 234
Black Velvet 64
Blasphemy 442
Blenheim Gully 177
Blind Eye 182
Blind Man's
  Buttress 119
Blind Man's
  Crack 119
Blinkers 265
Blizzard Ridge 384
Block and
  Tackle 254
Block Crack
  Left-Hand 479
Block Wall 202
Blocked
  Chimney 438
Blockhead Direct 280

Blood and Guts on
  Botty Street 220
Bloodrush 460
Bloodshot 319
Bloodspeed 51
Bloody Thirteenth,
  The 488
Blue Lights Crack 442
Blue Velvet 381
Blunt Arête 356
Blurter, The 274
Bob Hope 508
Bobsnob 328
Boc No Buttress 330
Body Pop 97
Bodypopping 360
Boggart, The 241
Bollard Crack 137
Bolster 406
Bond Street 218
Boomerang
  (Millstone) 208
Boomerang
  (Ramshaw) 102
Boomerang
  Chimney 265
Boot Crack 334
Boot Hill 112
Boris the Bold 327
Borstal Breakout 90
Bosun's Slab 377
Boulder Climb 117
Boulevard 200
Boulevard
  Traverse 485
Bow Buttress 91
Bow, The 183
Bower Route One,
  The 113
Bowrosin 102
Boy's Own 424
Boyd's Crack 277
Boys Will Be
  Boys 306
Boysen's Delight 82
Bracken Crack
  (Bamford) 372
Bracken Crack
  (Burbage) 231
Braille Trail, The 242
Brain, The 150
Brainchild 418
Bramble Crack 507
Bramble Groove 111
Breakdance 360

Index | 513

Breakdown 446
Breakfast
 Problem 74
Bridge's
 Variation 291
Briggs' and
 Titterton's 396
Brightside 135
Brillo 252
Brimstone 206
Brindle Crack 154
Bring Me
 Sunshine 465
Broadside 187
Broken Arrow 333
Broken Buttress
 Climb 193
Broken
 Chimney 498
Broken Crack 140
Broken Groove 98
Broken Groove in the
 Arête, The 476
Broken Slab 60
Brook's Layback 238
Brooks' Crack 242
Broomstick 508
Brothers'
 Eliminate 504
Brown Crack 166
Brown's Crack
 (Bamford) 368
Brown's Crack
 (Ramshaw) 100
Brown's
 Eliminate 142
Brown's
 Unmentionable 507
Bruno Flake 78
Brush Off, The 389
Brutality 495
Buckle's Brother 149
Buckle's Crack 149
Buckle's Sister 149
Bulger, The 52
Bulging Arête 474
Bulldog Crack 146
Bulwark 86
Bum Deal 370
Bumbler's Arête 310
Bun Run 210
Burgess Buttress 230
Burgess Face 230
Burgess Street 230
Bush Off, The 390

Busker, The 231
Butcher Crack 317
Button Wall 357
Buttress Two
 Gully 476
By George 155
Byne's Crack 242
Byne's Route 318
Byne's Traverse 117

C

C.M.C. Induction
 Programme 499
C.M.C. Slab 136
Caesar Ridge 499
Caesarian 88
Cakestand 353
Calamity Crack 445
Calcutta Buttress 69
Calcutta Crack 69
Caliban's Cave 261
Calvary 308
Calver Chimney 154
Calver Wall 154
Camel Hot 122
Camelian Crack 100
Cameo 447
Camperdown
 Crawl 185
Campsite Crack 397
Campsite Crack
 Indirect Finish 397
Candle Buttress 485
Candle Buttress
 Direct 485
Candle in the
 Wind 505
Cannon, The 99
Cannonball
 Crack 48
Canoe 156
Capital Cracks 223
Capitol Climb 59
Capstone Chimney
 (Dovestones) 428
Capstone Chimney
 (Stanage Pl) 306
Capstone Chimney
 (Stanage Pop) 354
Captain Calamity 117
Captain
 Invincible 251
Captain Lethargy 55

Captain Sensible 244
Captain's Bunk 182
Carborundum 356
Cardinal's Arête 223
Cardinal's
 Backbone II 155
Cardinal's Crack 223
Cardinal's Slab 223
Caricature 94
Carpe Diem 333
Carrion 52
Cascade 434
Cascara Crack 200
Cassandra 502
Castle Chimney 349
Castle Crack 350
Castor (Agden) 396
Castor (Burbage) 244
Cataract 434
Catastrophe
 Internationale 47
Catharsis 88
Cauldron Crack 206
Cave Arête
 (Gardoms) 170
Cave Arête
 (Laddow) 457
Cave Arête
 (Stanage) 333
Cave Arête
 Indirect 457
Cave Buttress 278
Cave Climb 191
Cave Crack
 (Belmont Hall) 506
Cave Crack
 (Chatsworth) 191
Cave Crack
 (Froggatt) 135
Cave Crack
 (Laddow) 457
Cave Crack
 (Rob's Rocks) 435
Cave Crack
 (Running Hill) 446
Cave Crack
 Indirect 135
Cave Crawl 135
Cave Eliminate 333
Cave Gully
 (Birchens) 187
Cave Gully
 (Gardoms) 169
Cave Gully
 (Upper Tor) 495

Cave Gully Crack 169
Cave Gully Wall 333
Cave Innominate 333
Cave Rib 495
Cave Wall 135
Cemetery Waits 314
Censor 348
Centaur 296
Central Buttress 119
Central Buttress
 Direct 119
Central Climb
 (Dovestone) 380
Central Climb
 (Hen Cloud) 91
Central Climb
 Direct 91
Central Groove 175
Central Massif 60
Central Route
 (Pagoda) 492
Central Route
 (Roaches Upper) 66
Central Route
 (Windgather) 473
Central Tower
 (Dovestones) 429
Central Tower
 (Castle Naze) 482
Central Trinity 342
Centre Stage 326
Centre, The 476
Chain, The 184
Chalked Up 223
Chalkstorm 55
Chameleon
 (Hen Cloud) 94
Chameleon
 (Stanage) 349
Chamonaze
 Blues 482
Changeling,
 The 428
Chant, The 229
Chapman's
 Crack 138
Charlie's Crack 240
Charlotte
 Rampling 177
Charm 443
Cheek 476
Cheese Block 402
Cheese Cut 402
Cheese Cut
 Flake 402

Staffs Gritstone

Southern Gritstone

Froggatt Area

Eastern Quarries

Burbage Valley

Stanage

Northern Edges

Chew Valley

Kinder Bleaklow

514 | Index

Chequers
  Buttress 143
Chequers Climb 143
Chequers Crack 142
Chicane 78
Chicken 86
Chicken Run 58
Chiming Cracks 220
Chimney and
  Crack 473
Chimp's Corner 353
Chip Shop
  Brawl 261
Chockstone Chimney
  (Downfall) 487
Chockstone Chimney
  (Upper Tor) 494
Chockstone Chimney
  (Ramshaw) 98
Chockstone Chimney
  (Stanage) 308
Chockstone Chimney
  (Windgather) 473
Chockstone Climb
  (Burbage) 231
Chockstone Climb
  (Gardoms) 169
Chockstone Climb
  (Wharncliffe) 402
Chockstone
  Corner 82
Chockstone
  Crack 88
Choka 54
Christmas Crack 340
Cider 177
Cider Apple 176
Cinturato 296
Cioch Corner 208
Circus of
  Dinosaurs 152
Claw Climb 381
Cleft and
  Chimney 417
Cleft Wall
  Route 1 308
Cleft Wall
  Route 2 308
Cleft Wing 312
Cleft Wing
  Superdirect 312
Cleopatra 374
Clippety Clop... 100
Clive Coolhead 52
Close Shave 208

Cloud Nine 80
Cloudbusting 82
Cochybondhu 447
Cock, The 250
Cocktails 317
Coconut Ice 338
Coffin Chimney 497
Coffin Crack 440
Coign, The 294
Cold Turkey 336
Colly Wobble 100
Comedian 92
Comet 304
Commander
  Energy 55
Committed 162
Commix 207
Compost
  Corner 300
Comus 304
Concave Slab 377
Concept of
  Kinky 264
Condor Chimney 78
Condor Slab 78
Confectioner,
  The 317
Confidence
  Trick 155
Confusion 470
Congestion
  Crack 140
Congo Corner 322
Conjunctus
  Viribus 395
Connection,
  The 446
Connolley's
  Variation 332
Consolation
  Prize 443
Constipation 334
Contents 448
Contrary Mary 60
Cook's Rib 188
Cool Curl, The 285
Cool Fool 448
Cool Groove 353
Cool Moon 147
Cool Rib 435
Copenhagen
  Corner 186
Copenhagen
  Wall 186
Cordite Crack 202

Corinthian 92
Corner Crack
  (Froggatt) 138
Corner Crack
  (Gardoms) 168
Corner Crack
  (Ramshaw) 99
Corner Crack
  (Plantation) 301
Corner Crack
  (Stanage Pop) 316
Corner Crack
  (Windgather) 476
Corner Cracks 54
Corner, The
  (Curbar) 155
Corner, The
  (Windgather) 474
Cornflakes 334
Corpse Crack 506
Cosmic Crack 271
Cotter, The 252
Count Dracula 505
Count, The 286
Count's Buttress 285
Count's Buttress
  Direct 285
Count's Chimney 285
Count's Crack 286
Count's Wall 285
Counterblast 285
Counterstroke of
  Equity 71
Covent Garden 218
Coventry Street 219
Cover Me In
  Chocolate... 462
Crab Crawl
  Arête 261
Crab Crawl, The 261
Crab Walk 100
Crabbie's Crack 83
Crabbie's Crack
  Left-Hand 83
Crack and Cave 328
Crack and
  Chimney 428
Crack and Corner
  (Roaches Upper) 68
Crack and Corner
  (Stanage) 353
Crack and
  Furrow 117
Crack of Doom,
  The 400

Crack of
  Gloom 50
Crack One 388
Crack Two 388
Crack, The 482
Cracked Arête 78
Cracked Corner 470
Cracked Gully 103
Cracks, The 446
Crafty Cockney 384
Cranberry Crack 229
Crank, The 98
Crease, The 372
Crème de la
  Crème 223
Crescent 298
Crevice, The 389
Crew Cut 214
Crew Pegs Diffs 272
Crew's Route 465
Crikey 244
Crime 301
Crimson Wall 498
Cripple's Crack 262
Cripple's Way 435
Crippler, The 104
Crispy Crack 417
Crock's Climb 465
Crocodile, The 175
Crooked Arête 487
Crossover 302
Croton Oil 386
Crottle 174
Crow's Nest,
  The 180
Crown, The 498
Crucifix, The 116
Crumbling
  Crack 265
Crypt Trip, The 278
Crystal Grazer 47
Crystal Tipps 103
Crystal Voyager 506
Cue 305
Culture Shock 155
Cumberland
  Crack 403
Curfew 104
Curiosity Kitten 76
Curse, The 229
Curved Balls 402
Curved Crack 305
Curving Arête 124
Curving
  Buttress 309

Index | 515

Curving Chimney 309
Curving Crack 368
Cyclops Eye 507
Cydrax 176

D

D.I.Y. 288
Dalesman, The 278
Damascus Crack 60
Dane's Delight 186
Dane's Disgust 186
Dangermouse 442
Dangerous Crocodile Snogging 100
Dangler, The 348
Dark Continent 322
Dark Entries 149
Dark Side of the Moon, The 485
Darren Hawkins' Invisible Neck 111
David 248
David's Chimney 384
Dawn Piper 60
Daydreamer 284
Days Gone By 74
Dead Dog Crack 446
Dead Eye 182
Dead Heat 402
Dead Mouse Crack 372
Death and Night and Blood 294
Death Knell, The 54
December Arête 432
Declaration 386
Deep Chimney (Bamford) 369
Deep Chimney (Stanage) 272
Deep Cleft 375
Deepcar Named Desire 410
Definitive Gaze 74
Defying Destiny 308
Delectable Direct 202
Delectable Variation 202
Delilah 374
Delstree 88
Deluded 180

Demon Rib 124
Dennis 429
Dependence Arête 502
Dependence Wall 502
Derivatives, The 425
Derwent Groove 147
Desolation Angel 409
Desperate Straights 508
Desperation 334
Despot 193
Detour 231
Deuteronomy 270
Deviation 502
Device 188
Devil is in the Detail, The 125
Devil's Chimney 320
Devotoed 74
Dexterity 208
Dextrous Hare 208
Dharma 507
Diamond Arête 494
Diamond Crack 138
Diamond White 406
Diamond, The 420
Dieppe 311
Diet of Worms 150
Digital Orbit 435
Ding Dong 357
Direct Loss 306
Dirty Stop Out 374
Discontinuous Rib and Groove 477
Dithering Frights 332
Doctor Dolittle 157
Doctor's Chimney 262
Doctor's Saunter 262
Dog-Leg Crack 148
Dogsbody 430
Domino Wall 486
Don 295
Don's Crack 100
Don's Delight 266
Don't Bark 328
Don't Birch the Doc 383
Done Years Ago 156
Dormant in the Dormitories 434

Dorothy's Dilemma 48
Dot's Slab 288
Double Cave Climb 192
Double Crack 478
Double Take 438
Double Time Crack 432
Doubloon 502
Doug 47
Dover's Progress 236
Dover's Wall, Route 1 311
Dover's Wall, Route 2 311
Dover's Wall, Route 3 311
Dover's Wall, Route 4 311
Dovestones Edge 380
Dovestones Gully 380
Dovestones Wall 380
Dowel Crack 244
Downfall Climb, The 488
Downfall Groove 488
Downhill Racer 140
Dracula 286
Dragon's Hoard 408
Dragon's Route 466
Drainpipe, The (Burbage) 245
Drainpipe, The (Ravenstones) 425
Dream Boat 284
Dreams by the Sea 397
Dredger 422
Driven Bow, The 91
Drizzle 466
Drummond Base 163
Drunken Sunday 70
Dry Rot 352
Dud Chimney 488
Dun 330
Dunkley's Eliminate 250
Dunsinane 505
Duo Crack Climb 275
Dust Storm 430
Dynamics of Change 242

Dynamite Groove 377
Dynasty 390

E

E Route 417
E.M.F. 270
E.N. 24 508
Early Starter 308
Eartha 208
East Rib 458
Easter Rib 340
Eastern Touch 464
Easy Corner 478
Easy Gully 91
Easy Gully Wall 68
Easy Jamming 358
Easy Picking 388
Easy Turnpike 507
Easy Walling 358
Eckhard's Arête 276
Eckhard's Chimney 276
Éclair 201
Edale Bobby 498
Edale Flyer 498
Edge Lane 214
Edgehog Flavour 417
Editor's Note 477
Eight Hours! 428
Eight-Metre Corner 438
El Vino Collapso 156
Elastic Arm 82
Elastic Limit 401
Elder Crack 158
Electric Chair 86
Electric Circus 470
Electron 271
Elegy 52
Eliminator 350
Elliott's Buttress Direct 172
Elliott's Buttress Indirect 172
Elliott's Crack 177
Elliott's Eliminate 350
Elliott's Right-Hand 111
Elliott's Unconquerable 111
Ellis's Eliminate 336

Staffs Gritstone
Southern Gritstone
Froggatt Area
Eastern Quarries
Burbage Valley
Stanage
Northern Edges
Chew Valley
Kinder Bleaklow

Index

Embankment
  Route 1 216
Embankment
  Route 2 216
Embankment
  Route 3 216
Embankment
  Route 4 216
Emerald Crack 192
Emma's Delight 180
Emma's Delusion 180
Emma's Dilemma 180
Emma's Slab 180
Emma's
  Temptation 180
Emperor Crack 193
Emperor Flake
  Climb 193
Emperor's
  Struggle 193
Empress Crack 193
En Rappel 88
Encouragement 91
End All, The 239
End of the Affair 147
End Slab 125
English
  Overhang 132
Enigma Variation 75
Ensemble Exit 486
Entropy's Jaw 72
Epitaph Corner 465
Equilibrium 241
Equinox 410
Erb 212
Eric's Eliminate 276
Eros 212
Esso Extra 296
Estremo 206
Europe After
  Rain 389
Evening
  Premiere 210
Evening Ridge 466
Evening Wall 232
Excalibur 201
Exit 383
Exit Stage Left 326
Exodus 270
Extinguisher
  Chimney 485
Eye of Faith, The 172
Eyebrow 428
Eyes 314

F

F Route 417
Face Climb
  No. 1 388
Face Climb
  No. 1.5 388
Face Climb
  No. 2 388
Face Route 1 476
Face Route 2 476
Fading Star 320
Fagus Sylvatica 250
Fairy Castle
  Crack 326
Fairy Chimney 326
Fairy Nuff 419
Fairy Steps 295
Falaise de Douvre 311
Fall Pipe 223
Fall, The 158
Fallen Heroes 418
Fallen Pillar
  Chimney 324
False Prospects 419
Fantastic Edge 434
Farcical Arête 238
Fast Piping 92
Fat Man's
  Chimney 122
Fat Old Sun 422
Fat Slapper 506
Fatal Inheritance 375
Fate 275
Feathered
  Friends 268
February Crack 265
Ferdie's Folly 430
Fergus Graham's
  Direct Route 342
Fern Chimney 372
Fern Crack
  (Roaches Upper) 58
Fern Crack
  (Stanage) 290
Fern Groove 290
Fern Hill 112
Fern Hill Indirect 112
Fidget 152
Fifth Cloud
  Eliminate 80
Fifth Horseman 479
File, The 255
Fin, The 239
Fina 296

Final Crack 90
Final Judgement 485
Finale Groove 175
Finger Distance 156
Finger Licking
  Good 322
Firebird 120
First Crack 238
First Sister 267
First Triplet 433
First's Arête 476
Fish-Meal and
  Revenge 420
Fit as a Butcher's
  Dog 317
Five Finger
  Exercise 113
Fixation 502
Fizz 369
Flake Chimney
  (Stanage Pl) 302
Flake Chimney
  (Roaches) 54
Flake Chimney
  (Stanage Pop) 338
Flake Climb 406
Flake Crack 176
Flake Gully 302
Flake, The 470
Flaky Wall Direct 102
Flaky Wall Finish 83
Flaky Wall Indirect 103
Flaming Eliminate 459
Flange, The 340
Flank Crack 220
Flapjack 212
Flash Wall 498
Fledgling's Climb 52
Flex 507
Flight of Ideas 296
Flimney 54
Flipside 272
Flower Power
  Arête 83
Flue, The
  (Stanage) 326
Flue, The
  (Wharncliffe) 406
Flush Pipe 444
Flute of Hope 254
Fly Walk, The 479
Flying Buttress
  (Curbar) 155
Flying Buttress
  (Pule) 508

Flying Buttress
  (Stanage) 347
Flying Buttress
  Direct 347
Flying Buttress
  Gully 347
Fo'c'sle Arête 187
Fo'c'sle
  Chimney 187
Fo'c'sle Crack 187
Fo'c'sle Wall 186
Foghorn
  Groove 466
Folies Bergère 446
Foord's Folly 104
Footprint 474
Footstool Left 480
For Queen and
  Country 188
Forbidden
  Planet 149
Formative Years 74
Foundling, The 470
Four 330
Four Horsemen 168
Four Pebble Slab 137
Fox House Fake 250
Fox House Flake 250
Fragile Mantel 357
Freddie's Finale 438
Free Wall 499
Freebird 435
Freestyle 499
Friction
  Addiction 432
Fringe Benefit 389
Frosty 275
Full-Stop 432
Fumf 389
Funnel, The 180
Fuse 188

G

Gable End 465
Gable Route 240
Gaia 124
Galileo 462
Gallery Crack 499
Gallows 86
Gamekeeper,
  The 488
Gamma 141
Gangway 377

Index | 517

Gape, The 506
Garden Face Crack 169
Garden Face Direct 169
Garden Face Indirect 169
Garden Fence 346
Garden Wall 346
Gardener's Crack 300
Gardener's Groove 300
Gardom's Unconquerable 174
Gargantua 445
Gargoyle Buttress (Stanage) 352
Gargoyle Buttress (Dovestone Tor) 381
Gargoyle Flake 370
Gargoyle Gully 370
Gargoyle Traverse 381
Gargoyle Variant 352
Gashed Crack 357
Gateless Gate, The 506
Gatepost Crack 508
Gates of Mordor 206
Gavel Neese 409
Gemini 397
Genocide 110
Germ 265
Gettin' Kinda Squirrelly 392
Giant's Staircase (Cratcliffe Tor) 111
Giant's Staircase (Gardoms) 176
Giant's Steps 220
Gibbet, The 433
Gideon 465
Gideonite 465
Gimbals 207
Gimcrack 219
Gingerbread 201
Glass Back 82
Glorious Twelfth, The 488
Gnome's Wall 430
Goldcrest 52
Golden Days 125
Golden Wonder 417

Goliath 248
Goliath's Groove 295
Gomorrah 447
Gone to Pot 152
Good Clean Fun 264
Good Friday 336
Good Vibrations 192
Goodbye Toulouse 347
Goosey Goosey Gander 267
Grace and Danger 296
Grain of Sand 466
Grammarian's Face 411
Grammarian's Progress 410
Grassy Chimney 492
Grave Crack 497
Grazer, The 234
Greasy Chips 210
Great Arête 214
Great Buttress (Dovestone Tor) 380
Great Buttress (Wharncliffe) 404
Great Buttress Arête 404
Great Buttress Eliminate 380
Great Chimney 94
Great Chimney Left-Hand 486
Great Chimney, The (Kinder) 486
Great Chimney, The (Wharncliffe) 404
Great Crack (Burbage) 236
Great Crack (Duke's Quarry) 507
Great Expectations 465
Great Flake Route, The 250
Great Gatsby, The 417
Great Harry 198
Great North Road 214
Great Peter 198
Great Portland Street 218
Great Scene Baby 104

Great Slab Arête 417
Great Slab Chimney 417
Great Slab Right 417
Great Slab, The (Alderman) 417
Great Slab, The (Froggatt) 141
Great Slab, The (Millstone) 210
Great West Road 214
Great Zawn, The 98
Greedy Pig 135
Green Chimney (Bamford) 377
Green Chimney (Burbage) 232
Green Chimney (Stanage) 314
Green Corner 234
Green Crack (Burbage) 236
Green Crack (Curbar) 160
Green Crack (Ramshaw) 97
Green Crack (Stanage) 342
Green Crack (Windgather) 472
Green Crack, The 482
Green Death 214
Green Gut 142
Green Slab (Burbage) 231
Green Slab (Windgather) 472
Green Streak 442
Green Streak, The 261
Green Wall 354
Greenfingers 495
Greengrocer Wall 317
Greeny Crack 239
Gremlin Groove (Kinder North) 505
Gremlin Groove (Shining Clough) 462
Gremlin Wall 462
Grey Area, The 163
Grey Cliffs of ..., 312
Grey Crack 168

Grey Face 162
Grey Slab 137
Greymalkin 255
Grim Reaper, The 470
Grim Wall 429
Grime 288
Grit Liars in our Midst 505
Gritstone Megamix 184
Grogan, The 231
Groove and Chimney 443
Groove is in the Heart 359
Groove Rider 492
Groove Route 390
Groove, The 112
Grooved Arête 300
Groove-V Baby 447
Groovy Baby 104
Grotto Slab 353
Grotto Wall 354
Ground Glass 356
Ground Support 506
Grunter 495
Guano Gully 52
Guerilla Action 425
Guillotine 418
Guillotine, The 317
Gullible's Travels 356
Gull-Wing 445
Gully Arête 98
Gully Joke, The 136
Gully Wall 69
Gumshoe 99
Gun-Cotton Groove 188
Gunpowder Crack 377
Gunpowder Gully Arête 188
Gunter 276
Gutter, The 240
Gwyn 411
Gypsy Moth 280

H

Hacker, The 208
Hacklespur 206
Hades 250
Hairless Heart 141

Staffs Gritstone
Southern Gritstone
Froggatt Area
Eastern Quarries
Burbage Valley
Stanage
Northern Edges
Chew Valley
Kinder Bleaklow

Half a Friend 494
Halina 443
Hallelujah
  Chorus 471
Hallow to our
  Men 74
Hamlet's Climb 400
Hand of the
  Medici 491
Handover Arête 401
Handrail 102
Handrail
  Direct 102
Hanging Crack,
  The 433
Hanging
  Groove 440
Hanging Slab 464
Hangman's Crack 68
Hangover 344
Happy Amongst
  Friends 360
Happy
  Wanderer 374
Hard Cheese 402
Hard Times 488
Harder Faster 124
Harding's
  Superdirect 333
Hardy 448
Hargreaves' Original
  Route 340
Harlequin 505
Harp, The 466
Hartley's Route 491
Harvest 266
Harvest Moon 446
Hasta La Vista 368
Hathersage Trip,
  The 301
Hawk's Nest
  Crack 135
Hawking 52
Hazy Groove 446
Headbanger 280
Headless
  Chicken 316
Hearsay Crack 272
Hearse Arête 174
Heartless Hare 141
Heath Robinson 262
Heather Buttress 473
Heather Corner 466
Heather Crack 272
Heather Face 474

Heather Wall
  (Froggatt) 136
Heather Wall
  (Stanage) 353
Heatwave 464
Heaven Crack 320
Heavy Duty 471
Hecate 255
Hedgehog Crack 92
Helfenstein's
  Struggle 294
Helix 506
Hell Crack 320
Hell Gate 409
Hell Gate Crack 409
Hell Gate Gully 409
Hell's Bells 220
Helping Hand 406
Hen Cloud
  Eliminate 92
Hercules 163
Hercules Crack 300
Herford's Route 491
Herringbone
  Slab 443
High Buttress
  Arête 474
High Flyer
  (Burbage) 234
High Flyer
  (Stanage) 261
High Neb
  Buttress 277
High Neb Edge 278
High Neb Gully 277
High Neb
  Variation 277
High Plains
  Drifter 200
High Step 191
High Street 201
High Tensile
  Crack 87
Hiker's
  Chimney 494
Hiker's Crack 494
Hiker's Gully
  Left 494
Hiker's Gully
  Right 494
Himmelswillen 408
Hit and Run
  Driver 394
Hitch Hiker 494
Hoaxer's Crack 356

Hobson's
  Choice 465
Holly Bush Gully
  Left 295
Holly Bush Gully
  Right 295
Holly Groove 135
Hollyash Crack 236
Hollybush Crack
  (Roaches Upper) 64
Hollybush Crack
  (Stanage) 344
Hollybush Gully
  (Birchens) 184
Hollybush Gully
  (Burbage) 238
Holme Moss 462
Honcho 471
Honest Jonny 97
Horatio's Direct 188
Horatio's Horror 188
Hornblower 185
Hot Tin Roof 506
How 508
How Many
  Roads 219
Humdinger 62
Hunky Dory 54
Hunter, The 488
Hurricane 163
Hybrid 338
Hyde's
  Mantelshelf 507
Hypotenuse 377
Hypothesis 48

I

I See A Dark
  Cloud 508
I'm Back 388
Icarus Allsorts 83
Ice Boat 338
Ice Crack 435
Ice Cream Flakes 275
Icebreaker 479
Icy Crack 275
Ignis Fatuus 395
Iguanodon 446
Imaginary Boulder
  Climb 403
Impish 411
Imposition 102
Impossible Slab 276

Improbability
  Drive 306
In Earnest 354
Inaccessible 506
Inaccessible
  Crack 276
Incestuous 155
Inclusion 411
Incursion 261
Independence
  Crack 488
Indianapolis
  Slab 492
Infirmary
  Groove 168
Ingot, The 508
Initiation 369
In-Off 305
Insanity 162
Inside Route 400
Inspiration Point 71
Intermediate
  Buttress 318
Intestate 504
Intro Wall 448
Inverted V 336
Iron Age
  Fortitude 482
Iron Hand, The 244
Iron Horse
  Crack 102
Irrepressible Urge,
  The 238
Isolation 384
It Only Takes Two
  to Tango 445
It's a Cracker 278
Ivory Tower,
  The 495
Ivy Tree 232

J

Jacob's Bladder 491
Jaded 383
Jaffa 394
Jankers Crack 143
Jankers End 143
Jankers Groove 143
Janus 158
Jasmine 372
Jaygo's Pipe 318
Jeepers
  Creepers 278

Index | 519

Jeffcoat's Buttress 62
Jeffcoat's Chimney 62
Jeffcoat's Chimney Variations 62
Jelly Baby 388
Jelly Roll 68
Jermyn Street 219
Jersey Boys 354
Jester Cracks 505
Jester, The 433
Jetrunner 368
Jiggery Pokery 422
Jim Crow 268
Jitter Face 348
Jitterbug Buttress 348
John's Arête 146
Joie-de-Vivre 409
Jon's Route 314
Jonah 378
Jonathan's Chimney 384
Journey into Freedom 408
Ju Ju Tree, The 497
Juan Cur 99
Jugged Hare 141
Jumpers for Trousers 185
Jumpin' on a Beetle 125
Jumping Jack Longland 374
Jumpy Wooller 386
June Climb 430
June Ridge 430
June Wall 430
Juniper 220
Just a Minute 404

K

K Buttress Crack 372
K Buttress Slab 372
K2 91
Kaluza-Klein 117
Karabiner Chimney 75
Karabiner Cracks 75
Karabiner Slab 75
Kayak 156
Kaytoo 430
Keel, The 183
Keelhaul 212
Keep Arête 480
Keep Buttress 480
Keep Corner 480
Keep Crack 242
Keep Pedalling 316
Keeper's Crack 158
Keffer, The 236
Keith's Corner Crack 170
Kelly 369
Kelly's Corner 262
Kelly's Crack 268
Kelly's Direct 66
Kelly's Eliminate 268
Kelly's Eye 268
Kelly's Overhang 276
Kelly's Shelf 66
Kelly's Variation 277
Kelvin's Corner 498
Kershaw's Crackers 455
Kestrel Crack 52
King Kong 277
King of the Swingers 471
Kinsman 504
Kirkus Original 348
Kirkus's Corner 347
Kiss Me Hardy 180
Kiss My Arm 448
Kitten 271
Klingon 302
Knack, The 245
Kneewrecker Chimney 506
Knight's Move, The 236
Knightsbridge 214
Knock, The 242
Knockin' on Heaven's Door 158
Knutter, The 272
Kon-Tiki Korner 422
Kremlin Krack 383
Kremlin Wall 419

L

L'Horla 160
Ladder Gully 244
Laguna Sunrise 83
Lambeth Chimney 218
Lamia, The 266
Lancashire Wall 353
Lancaster Flyby 381
Landsick 169
Landsickness 169
Last Fling, The 487
Late Night Final 59
Latecomer 222
Lawrencefield Ordinary 200
Layback Crack (Dovestones) 432
Layback Crack (Gardoms) 176
Layback Crack (Pagoda) 491
Leaf Buttress (Laddow) 456
Leaf Buttress (Wharncliffe) 404
Leaf Crack 456
Lean Man's Climb 122
Lean Man's Eliminate 122
Lean Man's Superdirect 122
Leaning Block Gully 252
Leaning Buttress Crack 346
Leaning Buttress Direct 346
Leaning Buttress Gully 344
Leaning Buttress Indirect 346
Leaning Slab 376
Leaning Wall Direct 229
Ledgeway 480
Leeds Crack 97
Leeds Slab 97
Left Bannister 245
Left Block Crack 82
Left Broken 140
Left Edge 383
Left Eliminate, The 162
Left Embrasure 429
Left Flake Crack 132
Left Fork Chimney 487
Left Holly Pillar Crack 389
Left Ladder Chimney 182
Left Monolith, The 426
Left Pool Crack 305
Left Promontory Gully 120
Left Studio Climb 239
Left Triplet Crack 477
Left Twin Chimney (Downfall) 485
Left Twin Chimney (Stanage) 328
Left Twin Crack (Burbage) 238
Left Twin Crack (Chatsworth) 192
Left Twin Crack (Hen Cloud) 94
Left Twin Crack (Skyline) 77
Left Unconquerable, The 309
Left Wing 370
Left-Hand Pillar Crack 177
Left-Hand Route 69
Left-Hand Tower 267
Leftover Chimney 403
Leg Stump 476
Leg Up 476
Legacy 504
Leo 507
Leprechauner 419
Les Dawson Show, The 504
Less Bent 245
Letter Box Cracks 77
Letter Box Gully 77
Letter Route 116
Letter-Box 435
Leviticus 270
Libra (Agden) 397
Libra (Roaches Upper) 60
Licence to Run 51
Lichen 191
Lichen Slab 389
Lie Back 234

Life Assurance 240
Life During
 Wartime 377
Lighthouse 77
Lightning Crack 47
Lightning Wall 168
Limbo 277
Limpopo
 Groove 201
Lincoln Crack 411
Linden 163
Ling Crack 155
Link, The 322
Linkline 255
Lino 286
Liquid Skin 492
Little Chimney 52
Little Crowberry 456
Little Ernie 354
Little Flake Crack,
 The 338
Little Flake, The 83
Little John's
 Step 328
Little Kern
 Knots 425
Little Nasty 102
Little Pillar 480
Little Plumb 229
Little Slab 330
Little Spillikin,
 The 455
Little Tower 318
Little
 Unconquerable 309
Little White Jug 229
Little Women 359
Living in Oxford 232
Loader's Bay 377
Loaf and Cheese 97
Loan Arranger 497
Lolita 446
London Wall 218
Lone Tree
 Groove 124
Lone Tree Gully 124
Long and the Short,
 The 90
Long Chimney 411
Long Chimney
 Ridge 456
Long Climb
 (Castle Naze) 482
Long Climb
 (Laddow) 456

Long Climb (Robin
 Hood's Stride) 116
Long Distance
 Runnel 114
Long John 377
Long John's
 Eliminate 411
Long John's Slab 140
Long John's
 Super Direct 411
Long Tall Sally 238
Longships 120
Looking for
 Today 74
Lookout Arête 180
Loose Control 486
Loose End 433
Lorica 210
Lost in France 229
Lotto 216
Louie Groove 97
Louisiana Rib 322
Lucas Chimney 52
Lucky 271
Lucy's Joy 328
Lucy's Slab 274
Lung Cancer 78
Lusitania 280
Lyon's Corner
 House 212

M

M Route 327
M.B. Arête 473
Macleod's Crack 244
Mad Hatter 152
Maggie 429
Magic
 Roundabout 103
Magic Roundabout
 Direct 103
Magnetic North 359
Magnum Force 377
Mai 264
Main Corner 479
Main Crack 88
Make it Snappy 174
Mall, The 218
Mammoth Slab 430
Man of God 397
Manchester
 Buttress 352
Mandrake, The 86

Mangled Digit 447
Mangler, The 298
Manhattan
 Arête 262
Manhattan
 Chimney 262
Manhattan
 Crack 262
Mantelpiece
 Buttress 356
Mantelpiece Buttress
 Direct 357
Mantelpiece
 Crack 356
Mantelpiece
 Right 357
Mantelshelf
 Climb 278
Mantelshelf
 Pillar 401
Mantelshelf
 Route 82
Mantelshelf Slab 75
Mantelshelf,
 The 401
Mantis 74
Mantrap 104
Maquis 444
Marbellous 266
Marble Arête 266
March Hare 208
Margery Daw 301
Mark I 425
Mark II 425
Marmoset, The 268
Mars 265
Martello
 Buttress 319
Martello Cracks 319
Masochism 98
Massacre 359
Mast Gully
 Buttress 186
Mast Gully
 Crack 186
Mast Gully
 Ridge 186
Mast Gully Wall 186
Master Blaster 377
Master of
 Disguise 349
Master of Reality 86
Master of
 Thought 176
Master's Edge 214

Masters of the
 Universe 251
Mastiff Wall 146
Matchstick
 Crack 429
Mather Crack 470
Matinee 50
Mating Toads 359
Matthew's
 Crack 448
Maud's Garden 59
Maupassant 160
MAy35 370
May Crack 268
Mayday 208
Mean Streak 136
Meander 82
Meander
 Arête 502
Mechanic, The 447
Meddle
 (Burbage) 231
Meddle
 (Stanage) 274
Medicine, The 473
Meisner's
 Link-Up 266
Melaleucion 74
Mellicious 401
Mensa 150
Mental Pygmy 118
Mentalist
 Cupboard, The 491
Mercury Crack 300
Meringue 201
Mermaid's Ridge,
 The 485
Mersey Variant,
 The 324
Meshuga 120
Messiah 248
Mickey Finn 166
Mickey Thin 445
Microbe 265
Middle and Leg 476
Middle
 Chimney 492
Middle Triplet
 Crack 477
Middleton's
 Motion 77
Midnight
 Variation 466
Midrift 220
Midsummer 446

Mighty Atom,
  The 252
Mild 132
Mild Thing 72
Millsom's
  Minion 305
Millwheel Wall 250
Milton's
  Meander 304
Mimosa 445
Mincer, The 51
Mirror, Mirror 82
Miserable
  Miracle 298
Missing
  Numbers 270
Mississippi Buttress
  Direct, The 324
Mississippi
  Chimney 322
Mississippi
  Crack 473
Mississippi Crack
  Variant 473
Mississippi
  Variant 324
Mississippi
  Variant Direct 324
Mistral 69
Misty Wall 502
Modern 91
Modern Times 457
Moglichkeit 376
Moire, The 400
Monad 265
Monday Blue 309
Moneylender's
  Crack 497
Monk On 230
Monkey Corner 230
Monkey Crack 357
Monkey
  Madness 505
Monkey Puzzle 458
Monkey Wall 230
Monopoly 218
Monster Munch 395
Monument
  Chimney 183
Monument Chimney
  Crack 183
Monument
  Gully 183
Monument Gully
  Buttress 183

Moolah 392
Moon Crack 147
Moon Walk 147
Moonshine 160
Mop Up 286
Mordaunt 114
Moribund 306
Morrison's
  Redoubt 324
Morrison's
  Route 491
Mort Wall 190
Mortgage Wall 497
Mother of Pearl 266
Mother's Pride 207
Motherless
  Children 505
Motorcade 137
Mouthpiece 276
Movie Star 244
Moyer's Buttress 170
Moyer's Climb 169
Moyer's
  Variation 169
Muesli 334
Muscle Crack
  (Castle Naze) 479
Muscle Crack (Robin
  Hood's Stride) 116
Mutiny Crack 231
Muzzle, The 508
My Prune 117
Myxi 87

N

N Route 327
N.B. Corner 374
N.M.C. Crack 176
Naaden 460
Nagger's Delight 460
Nah'han 174
Nailsbane 201
Nameless One 434
Nameless Two 435
Namenlos 306
Narcissus 138
Narrow Buttress 344
Nasal Buttress 428
Nasal Buttress Right-
  Hand 428
Nathaniel 245
National Acrobat 97
Nature Trail 71

Naughty
  Nauticals 183
Nautical Crack 185
Navy Cut 78
Nays, The 314
Neb Buttress 374
Neb Corner 277
Neb Finish, The 64
Neb Traverse 506
Nectar 266
Nelson's
  Nemesis 188
Nelson's Slab 182
Nemmes Pas
  Harry 368
Nemmes Sabe 368
Neptune's Tool 440
Nettle Wine 113
Never Never
  Land 102
Never Say
  Nether Again 499
New
  Mediterranean 392
New Year
  Buttress 118
New Year's Eve 268
Newhaven 311
News at Zen 409
Nice Edge 434
Niche Arête 479
Niche Climb 262
Niche Wall 435
Niche Wall Direct 356
Niche, The 479
Nicheless Climb 356
Nick Knack
  Paddywack 245
Nicotine Stain 239
Night of Lust 104
Night Prowler 94
Nightmare Slab 284
Nightrider 284
Nil Carborundum
  Illigitimum 455
Nil
  Desperandum 424
Nithin, The 479
No More
  Excuses 272
No Name 480
No Time to Pose 425
No Zag 245
Noddy's Wall 429
Nonsuch 392

Norah Batty 448
Norse Corner
  Climb 277
North Buttress
  Arête 472
North Buttress Arête
  Indirect 473
North Climb
  (Cratcliffe Tor) 114
North Climb
  (Froggatt) 134
North Climb
  (Laddow) 457
North Pole 508
North Wall 457
North Pole 508
Northern
  Comfort 51
Nose Direct 474
Nose, The
  (Castle Naze) 479
Nose, The
  (Rob's Rocks) 435
Nose, The (Stanage
  Hollybush) 344
Nose, The (Stanage
  Martello) 318
Nose, The
  (Wharncliffe) 400
Nosepicker 78
Nosey 435
Nosey Parker 455
Nosferatu 245
Not Richard's Sister
  Direct 267
Nothing to do with
  Dover 311
Nova 201
November
  Cracks 86
Now or Never 234
Nowanda 169
Nozag 482
Nuke the
  Midges 298
Nursery Arête 479
Nursery Slab 141
Nutcracker 112
Nutshrinker 468
Nymph's Arete 172

Staffs Gritstone
Southern Gritstone
Froggatt Area
Eastern Quarries
Burbage Valley
Stanage
Northern Edges
Chew Valley
Kinder Bleaklow

O

Oak Tree Wall 470
Oarsman 185
Oblique Buttress 343
Oblique
  Chimney 111
Oblique Crack 343
Obscenity 238
Obsession
  Fatale 55
Obstinance 300
Obstructive
  Pensioner 185
Obyoyo 419
Ocean Wall 422
Ocean's Border,
  The 422
October Arête 410
October Crack
  (Curbar) 162
October Crack
  (Stanage) 268
October Slab 268
Ocydroma 395
Oedipus! Ring Your
  Mother 138
Off With His
  Head 316
Offspring 251
Ogden 76
Ogden Arête 76
Ogden Recess 76
Oh my Stars and
  Garters! 444
Old and
  Wrinkled 372
Old Dog New
  Tricks 445
Old Dragon,
  The 317
Old Friends 278
Old Salt 265
Old Triangle,
  The 455
Oliver's Twist 388
Olympus
  Explorer 492
On a Wing and
  a Prayer 312
On the Air 408
Once Pegged
  Wall 201
One Chromosome's
  Missing 506

One Step
  Beyond 157
One-Way Ticket 438
Only Just 208
Ono 275
Ontos 375
Opposite 377
Oracle 375
Orang Arête 458
Orang-Outang 266
Oread 172
Original Route
  (Baldstones) 506
Original Route (New
  Mills Torrs) 470
Original Route
  (Rivelin) 386
Original Route,
  The (Tegness) 507
Orm and Cheep 479
Ornithologist's
  Corner 438
Orpheus Wall 183
Oss Nob 132
Other Corner,
  The 473
Our Doorstep 491
Out for the
  Count 285
Outdoor Centre
  Route, The 223
Outlook Slab 294
Outside Route 400
Outsider 389
Over The
  Moors 424
Overflow 276
Overhang Buttress
  Arête 230
Overhang Buttress
  Direct 230
Overhang Buttress
  Ordinary 168
Overhang
  Chimney 438
Overhanging
  Arête 476
Overhanging Chim-
  ney (Stanage) 274
Overhanging Chim-
  ney (Wharn) 403
Overhanging Chock-
  stone Crack 479
Overhanging Crack
  (Stanage) 301

Overhanging Crack
  (Wharncliffe) 403
Overhanging
  Wall 302
Overlapping
  Wall 477
Overlooked Groove,
  The 470
Oversight
  (Rivelin) 388
Oversight (Skyline) 76
Overtaker's
  Buttress 152
Overtaker's
  Direct 152
Overtaking on the
  Outside 152
Overton Arête 506
'Owd on Arête 432
Ow't 435
Owl Gully 113
Owl's Arête 157
Oxford Street 219

P

P.M.C.1 157
Pacific Ocean
  Wall 334
Paddington 507
Paddock 255
Painted Rumour 66
Pale
  Complexion 162
Palm Charmer 389
Palpitation
  (Bamford) 369
Palpitation (Dove-
  stones Edge) 428
Pantagruel 447
Paradise Arête 304
Paradise Crack
  (Running Hill) 447
Paradise Crack
  (Stanage) 304
Paradise Wall 304
Parallel Piped 132
Paralogism 66
Paralysis 327
Parasite 304
Parker's
  Eliminate 465
Parliament 374
Parthian Shot 242

Party Animal 389
Pass By 403
Passover 302
Path of the
  Righteous Man 117
Paucity 332
Paul's Puffer 77
Pause 432
Peaches 183
Peak Arête 466
Peapod, The 162
Pearls 192
Pebble Mill 248
Pebbledash 51
Pedestal 499
Pedestal Arête 223
Pedestal
  Chimney 338
Pedestal Crack 142
Pedestal Route 64
Pedestal Wall 495
Pedlar's Arête 316
Pedlar's Rib 316
Pedlar's Slab 316
Peg Crack 482
Pegasus
  Left-Hand 487
Pegasus Rib 302
Pegasus
  Right-Hand 487
Pegasus Wall 302
Pencil Slim 491
Perched Block
  Arête 76
Percy's Prow 300
Perfect Day 170
Perforation 268
Performing Flea 140
Perplexity 207
Pete's Sake 403
Peter's Progress 236
Phaestus 446
Phallic Crack 99
Phantom, The 506
Phlegethoa 319
Phoenix Climb 459
Photo Finish 402
Physiology 352
Piano Stool 480
Piccadilly Circus 219
Piece of Mind 55
Piece of Pie 422
Pieces of Eight 502
Piety 442
Pig Head 187

Index | 523

Pig's Ear 272
Piggy's Crack 468
Pigmy Wall 417
Pigtail 187
Pile Driver 104
Pilgrim's Progress 480
Pilgrimage 406
Pinball Wizard 438
Pincer 51
Pinion, The 261
Pinnacle Arête (Castle Naze) 478
Pinnacle Arête (Wharncliffe) 403
Pinnacle Crack 478
Pinstone Street 212
Pious Flake 384
Pipe Spanner 447
Pisa 462
Pisa Direct 462
Pisa Superdirect 462
Pizza Slab 300
Plague 389
Plain Sailing Midshipman, The 182
Plastic Dream 316
Plate Glass Slab 356
Plaything 162
Pleasant Slab 275
Plexity 207
Plimsoll Line 376
Plumb Line 447
Plumber's Corner 507
Poachers Crack 488
Pocked Wall 420
Pocket Wall 466
Pod Crack 480
Polar Crack 154
Pollux (Agden Rocher) 396
Pollux (Burbage) 244
Poltergeist 438
Pool Crack 305
Pool Wall 200
Poor Pizza 300
Port Crack 103
Portfolio 473
Porthole 376
Porthole Buttress 182
Porthole Direct 182

Portnoy's Complaint 507
Portside 376
Possibility 369
Post Horn 402
Pot Black 305
Poteen 455
Potter's Wall 152
Powder Keg 188
Powder Monkey Parade 184
Prairie Dog 280
Predator 157
Prelude to Space 71
Press, The 104
Pretty Face 162
Pretzel Logic 250
Price 191
Prickly Crack 286
Primitive Chimney 369
Prince's Crack 193
Priscilla 456
Priscilla Ridge 456
Private Display 82
Private Practice 370
Problem Arête 446
Problem Corner 265
Proboscid, The 104
Professor's Chimney 486
Profit of Doom 158
Prolapse 420
Promenade Direct 184
Promenade, The 184
Promise, The 232
Promontory Groove 495
Promontory Traverse 120
Prospero's Climb 261
Prostration 100
Providence 350
Prow Corner 54
Prow Cracks 55
Prow, The 180
Pseudonym 125
Pulcherrime 231
Pulpit Groove 198
Pulpit Ridge 424
Pulsar Direct 255
Pulse 271
Punch 54

Punishment 301
Punk, The 314
Punklet 314
Punter, The 495
Pup 271
Puppet Crack, The 191
Pure Gossip 272
Puss 271
Puttrell's Progress 406
Pylon Crack 400
Pythagoras 245

Q

Q.E.2 280
Quantum Crack 271
Quebec City 368
Queen's Parlour Chimney 118
Queen's Parlour Gully 118
Queen's Parlour Slab 118
Queersville 344
Quern Crack 400
Querp 400
Question Mark 432
Qui Vive 506
Quickbrew 60
Quickstep 499
Quien Sabe? 368
Quietus 276
Quietus Right-Hand 277
Quiver 265

R

Rack, The 260
Raggald's Wall 486
Rainbow Crack 94
Ralph's Mantelshelves 77
Ramsgate 311
Ramshaw Crack 102
Randolf Cheerleader 356
Randy's Wall 377
Rapid 434
Raredos 392
Rasp Direct, The 254

Rasp, The 254   Staffs
Rat Scabies 146   Gritstone
Rat, The 508
Rat's Tail, The 252
Ratbag 136
Ratline 182
Rattus Norvegicus 202   Southern
Raven Rock Gully 50   Gritstone
Raven Rock Gully Left-Hand 50
Raven, The 255
Ravenstones Stomach Traverse, The 424   Froggatt Area
Ray's Roof 506
Razor Crack 504
Reach 375
Reagent 354
Real 20 Foot Crack, The 358   Eastern Quarries
Reamer, The 252
Recess Chimney 87
Recess Crack 368
Recess Rib 316
Recess Wall 354
Recoil Rib 498
Recurring Nightmare 244   Burbage Valley
Red Wall 202
Reef Knot 185
Regent Street 219   Stanage
Reginald 245
Regular Route 390
Remembrance Day 207
Remus 404
Renaissance 508
Renrock 402
Renshaw's Remedy 390   Northern Edges
Requiem 113
Requiem of Hamlet's Ghost 400
Reset Portion of Galley 37 60
Reticent Mass Murderer 110   Chew Valley
Retroversion 336
Reunion Crack 88
Rhodren 54
Rhythm of Cruelty 223   Kinder Bleaklow
Rhythmic Itch 172
Rib and Face (Alderman) 417

Rib and Face
  (Stanage) 326
Rib and Slab 476
Rib and Wall 430
Rib Chimney
  (Hen Cloud) 92
Rib Chimney
  (Stanage) 308
Rib Right-Hand,
  The 472
Rib Wall 69
Rib, The (Roaches
  Upper) 69
Rib, The
  (Windgather) 472
Ribbed Corner 245
Richard's
  Revenge 411
Richard's Sister 267
Ricochet Wall 508
Riddler 447
Riffler, The 252
Right Block Crack 82
Right Edge 356
Right Eliminate,
  The 163
Right Embrasure 429
Right Fin 239
Right Flake
  Crack 132
Right Fork
  Chimney 487
Right Holly Pillar
  Crack 389
Right Monolith,
  The 426
Right of Pie 422
Right On 346
Right Promontory
  Gully 120
Right Route 66
Right Route Right 66
Right Side 377
Right Triplet
  Crack 477
Right Twin Chimney
  (Downfall) 485
Right Twin Chimney
  (Stanage) 328
Right Twin Crack
  (Burbage) 238
Right Twin Crack
  (Hen Cloud) 94
Right Twin Crack
  (Stanage) 336

Right Unconquerable,
  The 309
Right Wall Route 354
Right-Hand Crack
  (Castle Naze) 478
Right-Hand Crack
  (Gardoms) 175
Right-Hand Pillar
  Crack 177
Right-Hand Route
  (Roaches Upper) 69
Right-Hand Route
  (Skyline) 74
Right-Hand
  Tower 267
Right-Hand
  Trinity 342
Right-Hand
  Twin 370
Rigid Digit 158
Rigor Mortis 327
Ring Chimney 234
Ring Climb 234
Ringo 234
Rinty 275
Rippler, The 99
Ritornel 308
Rivelin Slab 383
Rizla 425
Robert 495
Robin Hood
  Zigzag 336
Robin Hood's Balcony
  Cave Direct 333
Robin Hood's Cave
  Gully 332
Robin Hood's Chock-
  stone Chimney 332
Robin Hood's
  Crack 332
Robin Hood's Right-
  Hand Buttress 336
Robin Hood's
  Staircase 334
Robin Hood's
  Staircase Direct 334
Rock Around the
  Block 255
Rock of Sir Walter,
  The 495
Rocking Stone
  Gully 55
Rodeo 487
Rodney's
  Dilemma 384

Roll Up 425
Roman Candle 82
Roman Nose (Clouds) 82
Roman Nose
  (Nether Tor) 499
Romulus 404
Roof Climb 90
Roof Route
  (Burbage) 240
Roof Route
  (Rivelin) 390
Rook Chimney 402
Rooster 58
Root Route 390
Rope Trick 120
Roscoe's Wall 68
Rose Flake 239
Rotunda Buttress 62
Rough Shag 426
Round Table 68
Round Up 502
Route 1
  (Burbage) 228
Route 1
  (Wimberry) 443
Route 1
  (Windgather) 477
Route 1.5
  (Burbage) 228
Route 1.5
  (Windgather) 476
Route 2
  (Burbage) 228
Route 2
  (Wimberry) 443
Route 2
  (Windgather) 476
Route 2.5 228
Route 3
  (Burbage) 228
Route 3.5 228
Route 4
  (Burbage) 228
Route I 381
Route II 381
Route One 138
Rubber Band 334
Rubber Crack 102
Rubber-Faced
  Arête 432
Rubber-Faced
  Wall 432
Rubberneck 83
Ruby Tuesday 62
Rucksack 499

Rugosity Crack 356
Rugosity Wall 342
Rum Wall 185
Runner Route 60
Rusty Crack 343
Rusty Wall 343

S

S.O.S. 395
S.S.S. 212
Sacrilege 442
Sad Amongst
  Friends 360
Saddy 154
Safety Net 77
Sagittarius Flake 446
Sail Arête 506
Sail Buttress 182
Sail Chimney 182
Sailor's Crack 185
Saliva 320
Salix 163
Salmon
  Left-Hand 368
Sampson's
  Delight 374
San Melas 74
Sand Buttress 122
Sand Crack 304
Sand Gully
  (Black Rocks) 122
Sand Gully
  (Stanage) 304
Sander, The 252
Sandman, The 468
Sandy Crack 369
Satan's Slit 206
Saucius Digitalis 460
Saul 248
Saul's Arête 294
Saul's Crack 62
Savage Breast,
  The 505
Savage Messiah 114
Saville Street 207
Scale the
  Dragon 466
Scandiarête 186
Scarface 433
Scarlet Wall 69
Scarlett's
  Chimney 383
Scarlett's Climb 401

Index | 525

Scarlett's Edge 401
Scarlett's Wall Arête 401
Scarper's Triangle 132
Scary Canary 358
Scavenger 280
Sceptic 266
Schard 406
Science Friction 134
Scimitar 455
Scoop Connection 200
Scoop Crack (Millstone) 214
Scoop Crack (Stanage) 326
Scoop de Grace 446
Scoop Direct 480
Scoop Face 480
Scoop Wall 480
Scoop, The (Millstone) 214
Scoop, The (Stanage) 319
Scorched Earth 508
Scorpion Slab 300
Scouting For Boys 397
Scraped Crack 286
Scrappy Corner 346
Scratchnose Crack 418
Script for a Tear 72
Scritto's Republic 216
Scroach 163
Scrooge 508
Scrooge 508
Scruples 218
Scythe, The 465
Second Sister 267
Second Triplet 433
Second Wind 318
Second's Advance 92
Second's Retreat 92
Seconds 448
Sectioned 440
See-Saw 301
Sennapod 74
Sennapod Crack 74
Sense of Doubt 506
Sentinel Buttress 191
Sentinel Chimney 234

Sentinel Crack (Burbage) 234
Sentinel Crack (Chatsworth) 191
Sentinel Groove 191
Sentinel, The 234
Sepulchrave 114
Serrated Edge 408
Seville Flake 383
Sex Dwarves 210
Sforzando 380
Shabby Tiger 508
Shadow Wall 376
Shaftesbury Avenue 219
Shallow Chimney 162
Shape Shifter 207
Sheep Bend 185
Shelf Wall 388
Sheltered Crack 479
Shine On (Running Hill Pits) 446
Shine On (Stanage) 314
Shirley's Shining Temple 286
Shock Horror Slab 286
Short Climb 117
Short Crack 438
Short Curve 374
Shortcomings 77
Shotgun Grooves 488
Shroud 497
Shuffle 334
Shy Ann Arête 508
Shylock Finish, The 381
Sick-Bay Shuffle 442
Sickle Buttress 140
Sickle Buttress Direct 140
Side Face 476
Side Plate 275
Sidecrack 75
Sidewinder 190
Sifta's Quid 55
Sign of the Times 69
Silent Scream 251
Silent Spring 251
Silica 304
Silk 290
Silly Arête 433

Silver Crack 137
Simba's Pride 240
Sinew Stretch 280
Sinn Fein 455
Sinuous Crack 372
Sithee 288
Sithee Direct 288
Skarlati 372
Skin Grafter 288
Skinless Wonder 359
Skull Crack 506
Skyline 202
Skytrain 75
Slab and Arête 75
Slab and Corner 402
Slab and Crack (Bamford) 376
Slab and Crack (Curbar) 157
Slab and Crack (Froggatt) 134
Slab Climb 443
Slab Recess 140
Slab Recess Direct 140
Slab Route 160
Slackers 150
Slanting Crack (Burbage) 231
Slant Start 423
Slanting Crack (Castle Naze) 479
Slanting Horror, The 420
Slanting Slab 375
Slap 'n Spittle 267
Sleasy Jamming 358
Sleeping Sickness 166
Sleepwalker 284
Sleepy Hollow 54
Slimline 92
Slip Arête 190
Slip-Off Slab 432
Slippery Jim 47
Slips 75
Sloping Crack 191
Sloth, The 66
Slow Ledge 244
Slowhand 86
Small Buttress 91
Small Crack 356
Small Wall 473
Smear Test 51

Smoke ont' Watter 154
Smoked Salmon 368
Smun 82
Snail Crack 201
Sneaking Sally through the Alley 280
Sneeze 98
Sniffer Dog 426
Snip, The 394
Snivelling Shit, The 210
Snooker Route 498
Snorter 495
Snow Crack 434
Snug as a Thug on a Jug 360
Sociology 352
Sodom 447
Soft Shoe 334
Sogines 277
Soho Sally 207
Soldier Ant 222
Sole Survivor 506
Solid Geometry 91
Solitaire 384
Solo Slab 275
Solomon's Crack 143
Solstice Arête 370
Something Better Change 48
Sorb 245
Sorcerer, The 87
Sorrell's Sorrow 147
Soul Doubt 134
South Corner 125
South Crack 477
South Gully 125
South Gully Rib 125
South Wall 485
Southern Comfort 207
Soyuz 149
Space Junk 346
Space Shuffle 440
Spanish Fly 168
Spanner Wall 446
Spare Rib 76
Speak Easy 395
Spectrum 77
Spider Crack 239
Spinnaker 183
Spin-Up 487

Staffs Gritstone

Southern Gritstone

Froggatt Area

Eastern Quarries

Burbage Valley

Stanage

Northern Edges

Chew Valley

Kinder Bleaklow

Spiral Route,
    The 386
Split Chimney
    Wall 403
Splitter 403
Spring into
    Action 336
Spring Lamb
    Dopiazza 396
Square Buttress
    Arête 357
Square Buttress
    Corner 357
Square Buttress
    Direct 357
Square Buttress
    Wall 357
Square Chimney
    (Skyline) 77
Square Chimney
    (Stanage) 357
Square Chimney
    Arête 357
Square Cut 498
Squashed
    Finger 476
Squirmer's
    Chimney 443
Stable Cracks 462
Staircase 472
Staircase Rib 275
Staircase, The 245
Stairway Crack 274
Stanage Without
    Oxygen 359
Stanleyville 324
Star Trek 302
Starboard Crack 103
Starvation
    Chimney 442
Steeple, The 468
Step Buttress 192
Step Buttress
    Crack 193
Steph 390
Step-Ladder
    Crack 320
Stepped Crack
    (Gardom's) 174
Stepped Crack
    (Burbage) 234
Steptoe 229
Sterling Moss 375
Steve's
    Dilemma 466

Stiff Cheese 142
Stigmata 491
Stihl Life 114
Still Orange 236
Stoked 185
Stoker's Break 185
Stoker's Hole 185
Stoker's Wall 185
Stomach Traverse 231
Stone Loach, The 87
Stonewall Crack 470
Stoney Faced 381
Stonnis Arête 122
Stonnis Crack 122
Stonnis Wall 116
Stopper 156
Stormbringer 170
Straight and
    Narrow 344
Straight
    Chimney 343
Straight Crack
    (Curbar) 148
Straight Crack
    (High Neb) 276
Straight Crack
    (Kinder South) 491
Straight Crack
    (Roaches Lower) 54
Straight Crack
    (Robin Hood's) 116
Straight Crack
    (Stanage Pop) 336
Strain Station 77
Stranger Than
    Friction 426
Strangler, The 300
Strangler's
    Crack 191
Strangler's
    Groove 191
Strapadictomy 132
Strapiombante 132
Strapiombo 132
Street Legal 220
Stretcher Case 298
Struggle 476
Stuck in a
    Groove 488
Studio 479
Subsidiary
    Chimney 460
Substance 77
Sudoxe 270
Suicide Wall 114

Suitored 272
Sulu 223
Summary 448
Summer Climb 198
Summer
    Lightning 406
Summertime 390
Sundowner 134
Sunset 370
Sunset Crack 134
Sunset Slab 134
Sunshine
    Superglue 465
Sunshine
    Superman 465
Superstition 232
Superstitious
    Start 122
Supra Direct 208
Surform 254
Surgeon's
    Saunter 262
Surprise
    (Burbage) 245
Surprise
    (Stanage) 288
Surprise
    (Wimberry) 438
Surprise Arête 438
Suspense
    (Lawrencefield) 200
Suspense
    (Wharncliffe) 401
Suspension 505
Suzanne 357
Svelt 210
Swan Crack 429
Swan Down 429
Swan, The 51
Sweatyman 508
Sweepsearcher 508
Sweet Gene
    Vincent 154
Swimmer's
    Chimney 135
Swing Up 448
Swinger, The 104
Swings 318
Synopsis 141

T

T'Big Surrey 498
Ta Ta For Now 187

Ta Very Much 187
Taller Overhang 473
Tally Not 99
Talon 381
Tango Buttress 277
Tango Crack 277
Tar's Arête 187
Tar's Crack 187
Tar's Gully 187
Tar's Traverse 187
Tar's Wall 187
Taurus Crack 302
Tea for Two 216
Tealeaf Crack
    (Roaches) 60
Tea-Leaf Crack
    (Stanage) 332
Tears Before
    Bedtime 402
Technical
    Master 216
Technical Slab 64
Teck Crack 47
Telescope
    Tunnel 182
Telli 308
Tempest, The 384
Temple Crack 384
Tensile Test 401
Terrace Crack 136
Terrace Trog 370
Terrace Wall 370
Terrazza Crack 266
Teufelsweg 408
Tharf Cake 238
Thermometer
    Crack, The 438
Thieves' Kitchen,
    The 498
Thin Air, The 55
Thin Problem
    Crack 265
Thing on a
    Spring 51
Third Triplet 432
Thirst for
    Glory 162
Thralls' Thrutch 238
Thread
    Flintstone 380
Threatened 223
Three Blind
    Mice 239
Three Flakes of
    Man 495

Three Pebble
  Slab 137
Three Real Men
  Dancing 377
Three Step 499
Three Tree
  Climb 198
Thrombosis 327
Throttled
  Groove 191
Thrown Away 404
Thrug 76
Thunderstruck 507
Tierdrop 100
Tiger Traverse 113
Tighe's Arête 466
Tighten Up Yer
  Nuts 446
Time for Tea 216
Time for Tea
  Original 216
Time Out 103
Time to be Had 78
Tinker's Crack 352
Tinner 370
Tiny Tim 508
Tip Off
  Right 352
Tippler Direct 348
Tippler, The 348
Tiptoe 231
Titania 378
Titanic 378
Titanic Direct 280
Titanium 378
Titbit 334
Tobacco Road 78
Tody's Wall 137
Toe Nail 474
Toggle 357
Tom Thumb 111
Tom's Arete 188
Tom-Cat Slab 288
Too Cold to be
  Bold 302
Too Much 392
Top Block Rock 316
Top Secret 154
Topaz
  (Skyline) 77
Topaz (Stanage) 342
Toploader 207
Topsail 182
Torrent 434
Torture Garden 288

Toss-Up 487
Touch of Spring 420
Tower Arête
  (Dovestones) 429
Tower Arête
  (Laddow) 457
Tower Chimney
  (Burbage) 241
Tower Chimney
  (Skyline) 76
Tower Chimney
  (Stanage) 296
Tower Climb 241
Tower Crack
  (Burbage) 241
Tower Crack
  (Stanage) 296
Tower Eliminate 76
Tower Face
  (Laddow) 457
Tower Face
  (Skyline) 76
Tower Face
  (Stanage) 298
Tower Face
  (Wharncliffe) 408
Tower Face
  Direct 298
Tower Ridge 433
Townsend's
  Variation 348
Toxic 288
Toy Boy 141
Toy, The 162
Track of the Cat 71
Traditional 476
Trafalgar Crack 185
Trafalgar Wall 185
Trainer Failure 358
Trango 2 376
Tranquility 420
Transformation 470
Trapeze 141
Trapeze Direct 141
Trapezium 404
Traveller in Time 97
Traverse and
  Crack 491
Travesties 272
Tree Crack 191
Tree Groove 175
Triangle Buttress
  Arête 229
Triangle Buttress
  Direct 229

Triangle Crack 229
Tricouni Crack 102
Trident, The 440
Trimming the
  Beard 312
Trinnacle
  Chimney 426
Trinnacle East 426
Trinnacle West 426
Trio Chimney 77
Triple Point 72
Trised Crack 223
Trivial Pursuits 491
Trojan 502
Trouble with
  Lichen 375
Trouble With Women
  Is..., The 419
True Grit 426
True North 359
Turret Crack 134
Turtle 508
Twenty-Foot
  Crack 229
Twikker 212
Twin Cam 358
Twin Chimneys
  Buttress 328
Twin Crack 148
Twin Crack
  Corner 419
Twin Cracks
  (Bamford) 375
Twin Cracks (Stanage
  North) 265
Twin Cracks (Stanage
  Pop) 336
Twin Cracks
  (Wimberry) 443
Twisted Reach 193
Twisted Smile 505
Twisting Crack 276
Two Pitch Route 149
Two Toms, The 507
Two-Sided
  Triangle 137
Typhoon 274
Typical Grit 278
Tyron 201

U

U.F.O. 155
Ultimate
  Sculpture 98
Ulysses 295
Ulysses or Bust 148
Undercoat 274
Undercut Crack 370
Undertaker's
  Buttress 174
Undun Crack 425
Unfamiliar 301
Unfinished
  Arête 425
Unfinished
  Symphony 245
Uno Crack 275
Unprintable, The 348
Unreachable Star,
  The 148
Untouchable,
  The 99
Untoward 122
Up the
  Establishment 193
Upanover Crack 327
Upper Tor Wall 494
Usurer 497
Usurper 160

V

Vain 155
Valediction 265
Valhalla 302
Valkyrie
  (Froggatt) 138
Valkyrie
  (Roaches Lower) 51
Valkyrie Corner 51
Valkyrie Direct 50
Vanilla Slice 201
Vanquished 309
Vaya Con Dios 168
V-Corner 479
Velcro Arête 357
Velvet Cracks 176
Velvet Silence 125
Vena Cave-In 267
Verandah
  Buttress 317
Verandah Crack 317
Verandah Pillar 317

Verandah Wall   317
Vertigo   377
Vestry Chimney   392
V-Groove   403
Via Dexter   343
Via Dolorosa   50
Via Dolorosa
   Variations   50
Via Media   343
Via Principia   460
Via Roof Route   328
Viaduct Crack   471
Viaduct Wall   471
Vibrio   192
Vibrio Direct   192
Vice, The   261
Victory   86
Victory Crack   180
Victory Gully   180
Victory Vice   188
Virginia Calling   290
Vivien   418
Von Ryan's
   Express   200

W

Waiting for the
   Lions   98
Walking the
   Whippet   301
Wall and Groove   97
Wall Buttress   306
Wall Chimney   232
Wall Climb
   (Curbar)   154
Wall Climb
   (Windgather)   473
Wall Corner   232
Wall End Crack   294
Wall End Flake
   Crack   294
Wall End Holly
   Tree Crack   294
Wall End Slab   291
Wall End Slab
   Direct   291
Wall End Slab Super
   Duper Direct   291
Wall of China   426
Wall of Evening Light,
   The   508
Wall of Sound   338
Wallaby Wall   74

Walleroo   59
Walrus Butter   306
Warding, The   252
Warm
   Afternoon   275
Warmlove   360
Wasteland, The   508
Waterloo Sunset   175
Wazzock   248
Weaver's Crack   448
Weaver's Wall   448
Wedge Gully   347
Wedge Rib   347
Wedge, The   347
Wedgewood
   Crack   426
Wednesday
   Climb   230
Wee-Kinder
   Weekender   499
Welcome to
   Greenfield...   425
Well Suited   491
Wellingtons   98
West's Wallaby   59
Weston's Chimney   111
Whatever Happened
   to Bob?   360
Wheat Thin   396
Wheeze   78
Where did my
   Tan Go?   277
Which Doctor?   262
Whillans' Blind
   Variant   174
Whillans'
   Pendulum   340
Whilly's
   Whopper   99
White Lines   152
White Out   384
White Wall   218
White Wand   295
White Water   156
Whitehall   216
Whittler, The   396
Whore, The   219
Wild and
   Woolly   267
Wild Thing   72
Wild West Wind   346
Wilderness Gully
   East   508
Willow Farm   70
Wind Wall   502

Windblasted   378
Windblown   378
Windbreaker   446
Windjammer   236
Windrête   210
Wing Buttress   312
Wing Buttress
   Gully   312
Wing Wall   312
Wing Wing   52
Wings of
   Unreason   71
Winter's Block   491
Winter's Grip   212
Wisecrack   48
Wits' End   420
Wobbler, The   264
Wobblestone
   Crack   238
Wobbling
   Corner   422
Wobbly Wall   389
Woe is Me   505
Wolf Solent   274
Wollock   231
Womanless Wall   419
Wombat   59
Wonderful
   Copenhagen   186
Wriggler   102
Wright's Route   338
Wrinkled Wall   372
Wrong Hand
   Route   372
Wuthering   332

X

X-Ray   271

Y

Y Crack, The   348
Yarn Spinner   448
Yellow Crack   432
Yellow Peril   433
Yerth   460
Ylnosd Rib   435
Yo-Ho Crack   185
Yong   48
Yong Arête   48

Yorick's Crack   446
Yosemite Wall   344
Youth   275
Youth Meat   274

Z

Z Crack, The   349
Zacharias   434
Zagrete   337
Zapple   223
Zel   318
Zeus   250
Zig-a-Zag-a   482
Zigzag   474
Zigzag Climb
   (Downfall)   487
Zigzag Climb (Robin
   Hood's Stride)   116
Zigzag Crack
   (Castle Naze)   482
Zigzag Crack
   (Downfall)   487
Zigzag Flake
   Crack   337
Zip Crack   357
Zone, The   162